Lasst Blumen
sprechen!

Nr. 58. -

3.4. 1946.

Süsser lieber Bub!

Eine grosse Schale voll solcher blauen Veilchen steht vor mir auf meinem Tische, ich habe sie gestern im Walde gepflückt! Ihr Duft ist so süss, ihre Farbe so herrlich, ihre Gestalt so lieblich, ich kann nicht anders, ich muss Dir ein paar von meinen kleinen Lieblingen schicken, obwohl ich weiss sie werden verwelkt sein bis der Brief dich erreichen wird!

Bubelein, Du glaubst kaum

Wie sehr ich Blumen liebe
gleich welcher Art, ob das kleine
bescheidene Gänseblümchen, oder
die majestätische Rose mit ihrem
bezaubernden Duft! Ich liebe sie
alle!! Wie wunderbar ist es doch,
zu beobachten, wie sich so ein
kleines unscheinbares Samenkorn
zur Pflanze entwickelt, Knospen
treibt und diese dann an der
Sonne zu herrlichen Blüten ent-
faltet! Wie reich an Wundern ist
doch die Welt! Und wie klein,
wie nichtig ist der Mensch

For continuation of this Letter, please see
End Papers at back of the Book".

From The Embers Rising

Für Meine Anneliese
For My Anneliese
בשביל אנליזה שלי

Du bist mein Alles!

Te quiero, te adoro, mi vida!

O bell' alma innamorata,
cara sposa,
e consolatrice dei miei dolori!

אשת חיל
я тебя люблю

Acknowledgements:
Die Erkenntnisse:
הודיות:

To all my children and grandchildren
for their unstinting, loving support
לכל המשפחה , תודה רבה

A Daughter's Note

When my pragmatic mother Anneliese began to notice the ever-increasing effects of Alzheimer's on her grasp on reality, she asked me to hold a box of letters in safe-keeping for her. She said they were the correspondence between herself and my father—from 1945-1947—the years that encompassed their meeting, their separation and their reunion—all in post-war Germany. There were several hundred letters, roughly half held postmarks from Germany, some with signs of official censorship interception; the other half of the letters were sent from Brooklyn, New York to Germany with 5 and 6 cent airmail stamps. My mother said I might like to read them. Written in both German and English, I could have, but they felt far too private. They belonged to that unfathomable and sacred realm of a relationship that could really only be known by its makers.

But I saved the box as instructed and as the world my parents had constructed and lived so vibrantly with one another began to disintegrate from the chaos that Alzheimer releases upon its victims, the box of letters sat unnoticed in the corner of a closet. When my mother had all but disappeared from this world, but for her body; amid the anguish of my father's panic and denial and despair I remembered the box as if it might somehow hold, vessel like, an essence of my mother.

She had never spoken in any detail about this postwar period in her life, nor had my father. They had given us children a brief synopsis of their meeting, their instantaneous falling in love and a few quick notes about the logistics of their love before we their children, were a reality. This seemed fitting—for as children we ask for and delight in these details only for the purpose of situating ourselves into the world. "This is how my parents met: it was love at first sight (how romantic!) if they hadn't met we wouldn't be here"—end of interest. During our childhoods neither parent spoke of the war they had lived through, on opposite sides of the conflict. They like most of their surviving generation of young people had put this tumultuous and destructive episode of their lives aside to building something new and good from all the death and evil. And live they did. My parents were together for 57 years, through many twists and turns of fortune and failure, joys and losses, during which time they raised five children. Questions about the war time were routinely dismissed and remained terra incognita.

In the wake of our mother's death we children encouraged our father, Arthur, to deal with his intense level of grief and mourning by writing down some of the many stories that began to pour forth from him—as if from a font that could not be held back. It was as if our mother's passing unleashed, one might say birthed, the spirit of her eternal presence which our father caused to appear by his telling of these stories. It was then I remembered the letters in the box in the closet. What I found in them was a treasure trove. Within these letters lay the germ and first growth of a love between two individuals set against the backdrop of the destruction of the world as they had known it. And now, from behind the recent backdrop of Alzheimer's destruction, my mother emerged—unscathed, fresh, young, vibrant and courageous. Once again we could hear her "voice".

Heidi Faith Katz
6 October 2008

ii

From The Embers Rising

*How WWII and the Love
of a Courageous, Beautiful
German Girl,
Shaped Two Lives*

ARTHUR STANLEY KATZ

To order additional copies of this book, contact:
Xlibris Corporation
1-888-795-4274
www.Xlibris.com
Orders@Xlibris.com
43625

CONTENTS

TABLE OF IMAGES

Preface

TO THE CONGRESS OF THE UNITED STATES:

Yesterday, December 7, 1941—a date which will live in infamy—the United States of America was suddenly and deliberately attacked by naval and air forces of the Empire of Japan.

*   *   *

As Commander-in-Chief of the Army and Navy I have directed that all measures be taken for our defense.

*   *   *

With confidence in our armed forces—the unbounding determination of our people—we will gain the inevitable triumph—so help us God.

I ask that the Congress declare that since the unprovoked and dastardly attack by Japan on Sunday, December seventh, a state of war has existed between the United States and the Japanese Empire.

Franklin Delano Roosevelt

SUPREME HEADQUARTERS ALLIED
EXPEDITIONARY FORCE

Soldiers, Sailors and Airmen of the Allied Expeditionary Force!

You are about to embark upon the Great Crusade, toward which we have striven these many months! The eyes of liberty loving people everywhere march with you. In company with our brave Allies and brothers in arms on other Fronts, you will bring about the destruction of the German war machine, the elimination of Nazi tyranny over the oppressed peoples of Europe, and security for ourselves in a free world.

Your task will not be an easy one. Your enemy is well trained, well equipped and battle hardened. He will fight savagely.

But this is the year 1944! Much has happened since the Nazi triumphs of 1940-41. The United Nations have inflicted upon the Germans great defeats, in open battle, man to man. Our air offensive has seriously reduced their strength in the air and their capacity to wage war on the ground. Our Home Fronts have given us an overwhelming superiority in weapons and munitions of war, and placed at our disposal great reserves of trained fighting men. The tide has turned! The free men of the world are marching together to Victory!

I have full confidence in your courage and devotion to duty and skill in battle. We will accept nothing less than full Victory! Good Luck! And let us beseech the blessing of Almighty God upon this great and noble undertaking.

General Dwight D. Eisenhower
Order of the Day
June 6, 1944

Almighty God

Our sons, pride of our nation, this day have set upon a mighty endeavor.

A struggle to preserve our republic and our civilization and to set free a suffering humanity.

They will be sore tried by night and by day without rest until the victory is won.

Some will never return.

Embrace them Father and receive them, Thy heroic servants into Thy Kingdom.

Franklin Delano Roosevelt
Broadcast to the Nation
10 p.m. Washington Time
June 6, 1944

What is War? . . . we shall not begin here with a clumsy, pedantic definition of war, but confine ourselves to its essence, the duel. War is nothing but a duel on a larger scale. If we would combine into one conception the countless separate duels of which it consists, we would do well to think of two wrestlers. Each tries by physical force to compel the other to do his will; his immediate object is to overthrow his adversary and thereby make him incapable of further resistance.

War is thus an act of force to compel our adversary to do our will.

Force, to meet force, arms itself with the inventions of art and science. It is accompanied by insignificant restrictions, hardly worth mentioning, which it imposes on itself under the name of international law and usage, but which do not really weaken its power. Force, that is to say, physical force (for no moral force exists apart from the conception of a state and law) is thus the *means*; to impose our will upon the enemy is the *object*. To achieve this object with certainty we must disarm the enemy, and this disarming is by definition the proper aim of military action. It take the place of the object and in a certain sense pushes it aside as something not belonging to war itself.

General Karl Von Clausewitz. On War, Book I, Chapter I

Behold, thou art fair, my love,
behold, thou art fair, and
there is no blemish in thee.

הנך יפה דעיתי הנך יפה
ומים אין בך

Thou hast enraptured my heart,
my sister, my bride!

לבבתני אחתי כלה!

I am my belóved's, and my
belóved is mine.

אני לדודי ודודי לי

Dein ist mein ganzes Herz
für immer!

Your's is my heart alone
forever!

Foreword

In mid June 1945, in the late afternoon of what had been a lovely Spring day, in a small rural city in Southern Germany, what was meant to be came to pass. There, standing before me was the most beautiful woman I had ever seen! The sun, low in its blue, cloudless sky, enveloped her graceful form in a halo of shimmering light. She was a fairy princess come to life! As I gazed entranced upon her, an emotion I had never felt before welled up within me. I was instantly in love!

The cut of her dirndl accentuated the swell of her bosom. Her hair, shoulder length, light brown, almost blond, framed her smiling face. Her skin was clear, lightly tanned, unlined and free of makeup. Her high boned cheeks, glowed with rosy hues. Her lips were shapely, red without rouge. Her nose was straight and narrow, a pert upward tilt at its tip. Her gray-green eyes sparkled with warmth and intelligence. *She was altogether fair, and wholly without blemish!*

At a time I had not chosen. In a place I had not selected. In a way I had not imagined, something wond'rous had happened to me! At that moment I knew I had found the woman I would marry. I had found Anneliese Baur!

Who was this ephemeral being whose first appearance instantly made her the centerpiece of the rest of my life? What was there about her that so quickly captivated my body and my soul? Clearly, it was her physical beauty which immediately kindled my passions. But Anneliese's beauty was more than that of face and form. There was this aura of kindness and grace about her from which I sensed the goodness and purity of her inner self. Indeed, it was this intertwining of Anneliese's inner and outer beauty which made my first sight of her so overpowering. From the instant I saw Anneliese my life was rebuilt about her. Anneliese became my *ehven pinnah*, אבן פנה, *der Eckstein meines Lebens*, the cornerstone of my being. And for all the years we were destined to be together—and I shall relate these times to you in the telling of this tale—my first glorious impression of my beloved Anneliese was confirmed over and over and over again!

For 57 years my beautiful, belóved, wise and witty Anneliese has been the Love of my Life, and my Best Friend. For 57 years Anneliese has given me love surpassing all understanding, support in all my endeavors—whether wise or not—joy unlimited and five wonderful children. But alas, no more. The life I have known for 57 bléssed years has come to an end. On the first day of Spring, the 20th day of March, in the year 2002 of the Common Era, in the year 5762 of the Jewish Calendar, at 1:30 in the afternoon, my beautiful, wonderful Anneliese, softly and gently, *mild und leise*, slipped away from me. My daughter, Heidi, and one of the hospice ladies, opened the windows in our bedroom, and Anneliese's sweet soul slowly wafted back to God. My precious Anneliese, free of Alzheimer's cruel grasp, was now at peace, and home with her Maker. And my life, bereft of its *ehven pinnah*, of its *Eckstein*, is sorely shaken. As the bitter tears of loss course down my cheeks, I now relate my experiences as a GI in World War II (WWII), and how my service in a great war led me to a greater love, and to a life enriched by that love. *O meine Geliebte Anneliese, du bist schwer vermisst!*

Erster Verlust   *First Loss*

Poem by Johann Wolfgang von Goethe
(English Translation by Arthur Stanley Katz)

Ach, wer bringt die schönen Tage,   Oh, who can bring back those
jene Tage der ersten Liebe,   beautiful days,
ach, wer bringt nur eine Stunde   those days of first love?
jener holden Zeit zurück!   Oh, who can restore but one hour
Einsam nähr' ich meine Wunde,   of that sweet time?
und mit stets erneuter Klage   In solitude I nurse my wound,
traur' ich ums verlorne Glück.   and, with e'er renewed lament,
Ach, wer bringt die schönen Tage   I mourn my lost happiness.
jene holde Zeit zurück!   Oh, who can bring back
                                   those beautiful days,
                         and that sweet time?

How did it come about that a young, Jewish American GI, and a young, Protestant German girl—young people who would appear to be from vastly different worlds—meet, fall in love, and shape a beautiful Jewish family life together? It was the war, WWII which made it possible. It was the war, with its adventures and misadventures, which drew me, one episode after another, inexorably, to that distant place in Germany where Anneliese and I were brought together. It was predestined[1].

What Rabbi Akiva was saying is that God gives each human being free will, yet He knows which decision that person will make when faced with multiple choices. God certainly knew how I would react in different situations. As one says in Yiddish, it was *beshert*. It was meant to be. What begins as a story of war, ends as a story of love. And there can be no better ending! I start with the war.

---

[1] In the Sayings of the Fathers, Pirke Avot, פִּרְקִי אבוה, III, 19, Rabbi Akiva declares: "Everything is foreseen, yet freedom of choice is given.", הכל צפוי והדשות נתונה (יט)

Anneliese Baur, Heidenheim, Germany, June 1945

Episodes ONE through SEVENTEEN

Courage and Consequences

Let us take up the several virtues . . . And let us first speak of courage . . . Now we fear all evils, e.g., disgrace, poverty, disease, friendlessness, death, but the brave man is not thought to be concerned with all; for to fear some things is even right and noble, and it is base not to fear them e.g., disgrace; he who fears this is good and modest, and he who does not is shameless . . . With what sort of terrible things then, is the brave man concerned? Surely with the greatest, for no one is more likely than he to stand his ground against what is awe inspiring. Now death is the most terrible of all things . . . [and] the noblest. Now such deaths are those in battle; for these take place in the greatest and noblest danger. And these are correspondingly honoured in city-states, and at the courts of monarchs. Properly, then, he will be called brave who is fearless in face of a noble death; and of all emergencies that involve death; and the emergencies of war are in the highest degree of this kind.

Aristotle, *Ethica Nichomachea. Book III 6, 1115a*

THE DEAD

Blow out, you bugles, over the rich Dead!
    There's none of these so lonely and poor of old,
    But, dying, has made us rarer gifts than gold.
These laid the world away; poured out the red
Sweet wine of youth; gave up the years to be
    Of work and joy, and that hoped serene
    That men call age: and those who would have been,
Their sons, they gave, their immortality.

Blow, bugles, blow! They brought us, for our dearth,
    Holiness, lacked so long, and Love, and Pain,
Honour has come back, as a king, to earth,
    And paid his subjects with a royal wage;
And Nobleness walks in our ways again;
    And we have come into our heritage.

Rupert Brooke, 1887-1915
Born at Rigby, August 3, 1887;
Sub-Lieutenant, R.N.V.R. September, 1914;
British Mediterranean Expeditionary Force,
February 28, 1915.
Died in the Aegean, April 23, 1915.
Buried on Scyros.

Episode One

In which I give up my college student's draft deferment and enlist in the U.S. Cavalry.

In the early afternoon of Sunday, December 7, 1941, World War II entered the living room of the apartment in the East New York section of Brooklyn, N.Y. which I shared with my mother, Hilda, my father, Louis and brother, Harold. I was home alone, listening to a live broadcast of the New York Philharmonic, when an announcer interrupted the concert to state, with his excitement barely concealed, that the Japanese were bombing our Pacific Fleet in Pearl Harbor. I hadn't heard of Pearl Harbor before, but I soon learned where it was, and that my life, and that of millions of other Americans, would soon be changed materially.

I was born on March 21, 1923. On the day Pearl Harbor was attacked I was approximately four months shy of my 19th birthday, and in my Junior Year at Brooklyn College. The following day I gathered, with other students, in the College Quadrangle. There, over the public address system, I listened as President Franklin D. Roosevelt spoke to the country. There was no television then, we heard only his voice. But FDR had the gift of making you feel as if he were talking personally to each of his listeners. Thus, I still hear, ringing in my ears, as if it were yesterday, his denunciation of the Japanese attack on Pearl Harbor as "A Day that will live in Infamy!" (Considering the deplorable manner in which most schools now teach American history, I wonder how many of my fellow citizens, who were not my contemporaries in 1941, recall, or perhaps, ever heard President Roosevelt's stirring speech).

On the 16th day of November 1942, I withdrew voluntarily from the shelter of my student's draft deferment status, left the cloistered confines of Brooklyn College, and enlisted in the U.S. Cavalry, United States Army. I understood the dangers Hitler posed to my country, and to my Jewish brethren, and I was anxious to do my part in destroying him as soon as possible. I was a brash, naive, first generation Jewish American lad. On the 28th day of November 1945, I was Honorably Discharged from my military service, bearing the scars of combat wounds, and several military decorations, of which more below. Everything which has happened to me subsequent to my military service can be traced to events which took place during this span of three years. WWII was, for me, more than a military adventure, with a date certain beginning and a date certain ending. WWII was the vehicle, however it meandered, which was destined to lead me to Anneliese Baur, to that remarkable human being, whose unstinting love, courage, compassion and counsel would, forever, shape and enrich my life. But, of course, I did not know that when I enlisted.

The tale I tell is set out under the rubric: "Episodes". I believe the term "Episodes" is more appropriate than the term Chapters to set forth the independent, yet interrelated happenings which make up the story I shall relate. These Episodes will demonstrate, I believe, that my highly personal story is also one with universal appeal

Episode Two

In which I quickly learn the facts of political life.

Hitler began his war in September 1939 with his invasion of Poland and then his invasion of the Soviet Union. In November 1942 the Russians were being bested by the Nazis, with heavy losses suffered by their military forces and civilian population. Although we, Britain and the British Commonwealth, were giving substantial aid to the Russians in the form of war materiel, the Russians were pressing the Allies to open a western front in Europe. Such a front would require Hitler to divide his forces, necessitating a reduction of his forces arrayed against the Soviet Union. This would be exceedingly helpful to the Russians. However, the Allies had other military schedules and targets in mind. North Africa was then a very active theatre of war, among other military venues in which the Allies were engaged. "Open a Western Front!" became the mantra of the Communist Party, USA, and of its followers. Many of my college mates at Brooklyn College were "Lefties". I hesitate to use the term "comrades" to describe them, since I never inquired whether they were members of the Communist Party. But they were busily engaged in marching, demonstrating, banner waving—intermingling the red, white and blue of the Stars and Stripes with the Soviet Union's red Hammer and Sickle—and calling loudly for the opening of a second front to help our courageous Russian brothers-in-arms. And so, in the middle of November, 1942 I said to a number of these guys—they always went in groups of 3 to 5—"Why don't we all go down to Borough Hall [Brooklyn's administrative seat] and enlist in the military? This way, you guys, and me included, by giving up our student deferments and enlisting, will show the government that college students are so eager to accelerate the opening of a second front in Europe that they are joining up before they have to."

My lefty buddies thought my suggestion was a great one! Very patriotic for Uncle Sam, and very good for Mother Russia, too. We all agreed to meet the next day, November 16, at 8:30 a.m. on the steps of Borough Hall, and then go in, en masse, and enlist. Well, I was on those steps at 8:15 a.m. I was there at 9 a.m., at 9:30 a.m., and I was still there at 10:30 a.m. None of the Soviet faithful showed up. So at 11 a.m. I went into Borough Hall and began my enlistment procedures. The next day I saw my left wing college mates on the campus. I told them I had enlisted, and asked why they hadn't shown up. They laughed. I asked, "What's so funny?" "You are a dumb ass-hole", one of them said. "Did you really believe we would give up our student deferments and enlist?" At age 19 I had learned my first lesson in politics: people don't always practice what they preach, particularly when the preaching requires some real personal sacrifices.

Episode Three

In which I experience culture shock when Ft. Meade, South Dakota meets New York City.

The Army was so pleased that I had given up my student deferment that they said I could choose my branch of service. I chose the U.S. Cavalry for reasons which were a mix of romanticism and reality. The imagery was of stalwart men astride spirited stallions galloping to victory, bugles blaring, sabers slashing enemy foot soldiers to shreds. The reality was that I would be joining old horse cavalry units now being converted to mechanized, lightly armored, fast moving reconnaissance units, never larger in man power than regiments and squadrons. However, the basic missions performed by "old cavalry" and "new cavalry" would be the same: in the parlance of a Confederate General whose name I do not recall: "To get there the fustest with the mostest!"; to spy out the land; to draw enemy fire, if need be, to find where he is; to report this information speedily back to HQ; to stay put in a fire fight long enough until the infantry and armored vehicles came up, and our artillery fire began to fall, and then to get the hell out of there to spy again another day (or night). In short, I wanted to be in a small military unit, where our positions were never static, and where, to a great degree, I could control my freedom of movement. And you did that by knowing where you are and where you want to go.

And so, in the last days of November 1942, wearing my newly issued ODs (Olive Drab uniform), with my set of duplicate dog tags around my neck stating that my name was Arthur S. Katz, my ASN (Army Serial No.) 12185660, my blood type O and my religion H (for Hebrew), and the crossed sabers badge of the Cavalry on my Winter '42 collar, with my newly issued gear in a duffel bag beside me, I was seated on a train heading for Fort Meade, in the Black Hills of South Dakota, not too far from Rapid

City. Fort Meade was an old Cavalry Post, going back to the Indian Wars and the home of the U.S. 4th Cavalry Regiment, an old line Cavalry unit. In the Infantry, the military personnel are organized into Companies, in the Cavalry the units are called Troops, and the members are called Troopers. It was my understanding that one of the 4th Cavalry's Troops was attached to General Custer's 7th Cavalry when he and his men were wiped out by the Indians in the Battle of Little Big Horn. The 4th Cavalry had its own marching band, and when we fell out in the morning for close order drill we paraded to the 4th Cavalry March written by John Philip Sousa.

When I came to Fort Meade as a recruit I was joining an old line, regular Army unit. Its officers, and a number of enlisted personnel were professional military men. They had chosen to make military service their career choice. And then there was a very large segment for which service in the military was not wholly a voluntary act. This latter group can best be described as fuck-ups. They had experienced various brushes with the law, and the local courts, mindful of how expensive it was to maintain county and state jails, had given these men the "choice": join the Army or go to jail. And in the Black Hills joining the Army meant enlisting in the 4th Cavalry. Aside from the Officers, the bulk of the Regiment's personnel were country folks. If one chose to give them a patronizing name they would be called Hill Billies. For the most part they were taciturn, not given to small talk. If you stayed out of their way, they paid you no mind. Some of them were mean and nasty—and that was when they were sober. Booze would make some of them almost jovial. And all of them, even their women folk, peppered their conversations with liberal additions of four letter expletives. It was a military trait I soon got the hang of.

I did not travel to Fort Meade all by my lonesome. I was part of a contingent of newly inducted personnel from New York City. All draftees, other than me. We were all white, of course. At that time no blacks were sent to white units. Our ancestry was a representative sampling of the broad ethnic and religious mix which has made New York City a world unto itself. Contrast our group of recruits with the personnel of the Regiment we were now joining: The Regiment's Commanding Officer, a West Point graduate, was a full Colonel, a "chicken colonel", the one with the spread winged eagle on his epaulets (his next grade, if promoted, would be Brigadier General, a one star General). He was a Roman Catholic. However, most of the Regiment's pre-recruit personnel were mainly of various Protestant denominations, including fundamentalist Christians. The social gap between us recruits and the Troopers into which we were supposed to blend was immense. They were all locals, true blooded Amurricans! We were a bunch of foreigners from New York City. New York City! Initially, neither group related to the other. From the military point of view they were the pros, our instructors, and we were their students. Their grammar may have been poor, but they soon made it clear to us that they were going to "larn us" or kill us trying. I was the only college student in my group of recruits. When the regular Troopers learned I was a college student, and a Jew to the bargain, they began to call me "The Professor". The title was not intended as a compliment. It was used as a pejorative. The country boys among the regular Troopers tended to look down upon us recruits as a bunch of soft muscled city boys. But they also sensed that we looked upon them as a bunch of simpletons.

I will now recount one incident—still as vivid in my memory as when it happened in the last weeks of December 1942—which illustrates the attitudinal gap between the country boy Troopers and their New York City recruits. We were on our first bivouac, our first field exercise away from the Post. I had to evacuate my bowels. There was no Andy Gump facility in the meadow in which we were engaging in various military exercises. But before I would relieve myself under the cover of some trees on the meadow's edge I thought I would get some toilet paper. So I went up to the Supply Sergeant, a surly guy at best, and I said to him, quite respectfully: "Sergeant, may I please have some toilet tissue?" He looked straight at me for about 5 seconds, glowered, and with anger said: "Don't smart ass me you big city son-of-a-bitch! When you want *shit paper* you ask for it!" I never again, throughout my three years in the Army, made the mistake of improperly asking for toilet tissue.

Episode Four

In which, in a California desert war games exercise, I have my first run-in with military authority.

During the Winter of 1942 the Germans, under Field Marshal Rommel, and the Allied Forces, under General Montgomery, were heavily engaged in desert warfare in North Africa. History tells us that Montgomery ultimately defeated Rommel. However, in December 1942, and the first few months of 1943, things didn't look too hot for our side. So sometime in the dead of a very cold Black Hills winter the 4th Cavalry wended its way, in a slow convoy of vehicles, to the railroad station in Rapid City, South Dakota, where troops and gear were loaded up for the long rail trip to the deserts bordering the southeastern flank of California, and the western border of Southwestern Arizona. We were heading for desert training in order to learn how to fight in hot, sandy terrain, our ultimate intended destination being North Africa. We never did get there, the Allies defeated Rommel before we finished our desert training. But that's how it is in the military, at least how it was when I was in it: you prepare for the next battle by reliving the last one. Sometimes the exercise works, and past knowledge is effectively applied to future situations. Sometimes the past does not prepare you for the future. Learning how to cope personally with excessive dry heat and occasional flash floods, and how to handle vehicles effectively while traversing sandy, rocky terrain, and how to restore them to operational levels after sandstorms, were lessons well learned during war exercises in the desert—but of limited value, aside from the discipline such field exercises engender—when one's actual combat experiences are played out in a northern clime where rain, mud, snow, fog and sleet are really synonyms for piss poor weather. But anyway, there we were, after a long train ride, setting up camp somewhere between Yuma, Arizona on the east and Indio, California on the west, and on the morning of the first day we set up camp I went to sick call. The weather was very, very hot. But I was being treated for *frostbite* on my nose, suffered when I was sitting, in sub zero weather, jammed in the front seat of a jeep with its windshield removed (combat conditions being simulated) on the slow drive to the Rapid City train station. Such are the vagaries of life. I was now in hot weather. I was soon to be, almost, in hot water. For it was during my unit's first combat exercise in the desert that my first run-in with military authority took place. Let me set the stage, and position the players. The story unfolds in this wise:

The key function of a cavalry unit, whether on horses, or mechanized, is to seek out the enemy, find him, endeavor to learn his military make-up, and where he appears to be going, and to report this information back to higher headquarters. During World War II our armed forces did not have the high tech equipment, now in every modern army's duffel bag, to pinpoint, within meters, where an enemy is. In WWII we did it in the old fashioned way: We went out looking for him. And when we found him, or found signs of where he had been, and, hopefully, where he seemed to be going, we sent this data to our Troop's HQ which then sent it on to units higher up on the military ladder. How did we send this important data back to HQ? We didn't do it by sending smoke signals, by waving semaphore flags, by banging on drums, ringing church bells, or by releasing carrier pigeons. We did it by sending messages, sometimes coded, mostly in clear text, via Morse code tapped out on a key attached to our thigh, or affixed to a flat surface, and sent by radio, or where the distances were very short, by crank-up sound and power telephone devices. Fast, accurate communication of information was the *raison d'etre* of the Cavalry. And the single most important individual in the Cavalry, when performing its primary function: the gathering and speedy communication of information, was, you guessed it, the radio operator. And the most important radio operator in any Cavalry Regiment or Squadron was the radio operator assigned to HQ Troop. This Troop was the Intelligence Center for the entire

Regiment or Squadron. The radio operator who had demonstrated, through the training phase, that he was the fastest in accurately sending and receiving coded and plain text messages was deemed the unit's best radio operator, and he was assigned to HQ Troop. After basic training, and to my surprise, it turned out that I was the best radio operator in the Regiment, and I was assigned to HQ Troop to perform this function.

HQ Troop was small in personnel: the Colonel and his Staff Officers, the Master Sergeant and 57 enlisted men. The line Troops, the ones out in the field every day, the ones most likely to see combat, were the Reconnaissance Troops, Troops A through D, Able, Baker, Charlie, Dog. Recon vehicles were jeeps and armored cars. Then there were the two Support Troops, E and F, Easy and Fox, They were in light tanks. The Trooper strength of the line Troops was at least twice that of HQ Troop.

HQ Troop, by reason of its function, had to be a spit and polish unit. This meant it was also a chicken shit unit. HQ was the Colonel's fiefdom, and since he was being visited frequently by Army Brass (and probably thinking of getting his first star as a General) he was a stickler on form over substance—or so it seemed to me. But I didn't complain. I liked what I was doing, I was good at it, and down the road, not too far down the road, my position called for a T/5 rating, a non-commissioned officer rank of Technician 5th Grade, in short, a Corporal with a special skill. Being a non-com, even of the lowest level, would get me out of doing a lot of servile duties, such as pulling KP, Kitchen Police, working in the Mess Hall, helping to prepare food and cleaning up, afterwards. And, more, I would get more pay to be sent home to my folks and the right to go to the non-coms club. Now remember this part about my looking forward to getting my T/5 rating. It will become a vital part of my story.

All of us, from the Colonel on down, were on a learning curve in how to conduct ourselves and operate our vehicles and technical equipment in very hot and unforgiving terrain. In about a week we had gotten the hang of things, such as, when its 100° in the sun, the metal skin on our vehicles would heat up to about 140°, touch the metal skin with your finger, at that temperature, and you left the skin of your finger on that vehicle when you pulled you hand away! And we also learned that parking your vehicle on a nice flat sandy dry stream bed is not a good idea. When a heavy rainstorm came up suddenly, your dry steam bed became a fast rushing 4 to 5 foot deep river, and if you were asleep in your sleeping bag, on the nice soft sandy floor of the river bed and it rained while you were asleep, you would quickly wake up out of a dream that you were peeing in your pants! You weren't, but your privates were below water! Once you experienced this dry stream-wet stream desert phenomenon you quickly learned to sleep on the banks of dry streams. The ground was harder, but a whole lot dryer.

In a couple of weeks after arriving in the Southern California desert, the 4th Cavalry engaged in its first desert combat exercise. The military establishment refers to such exercises as war games. I was as much a novice, as were my officers, in exercising our respective skills in a war simulated environment. Such mistakes as I might make in the execution of my skills would be as obvious as their operational errors. So, at our respective levels we would all be under pressure to be as perfect as we could be

I was the best radio operator in the Regiment, which was why I had been assigned to Headquarters. But classroom experience in the sending and receiving, and in the coding and decoding of messages (which was done through the operation of an encrypting machine—make one mistake, and everything goes kablooey) is different from doing it "for real" in the field, even if the "for real" exercise in the field was only a part of war games. My Commanding Office, the Colonel, and his Staff Officers, although professional soldiers, had never been engaged in Desert War Games. And so, they and I were, as above noted, novices of a sort. But that's why we were asses and vehicle axles, deep in sand. We were there, in the middle of the desert, hot, sweaty, grimy, a tad out of humor, and training for desert warfare. In short, all of us, Officers, and garden variety GI's, were engaged in on the job training. This training exercise was intended, as one of many steps, to turn peace time regular army officers and enlisted men, and new draftees (some of whom had been dragged, kicking and screaming, into the armed services),—and the occasional volunteer, such as I was, who gave up a student deferment—into a top class fighting force. This first war game would not be an easy exercise at playing soldier under simulated battlefield conditions. As with all new endeavors, it was beset with lots of start up problems. These were compounded when one adds to general inexperience such factors as human foibles, intemperate weather and inhospitable terrain. Our unit, in company with others, was in the middle of nowhere, there, one hoped, to be shaped into superb desert fighting outfits. So let the war games begin!

My first day in the desert war games went like this: Right after sun-up I was told to climb, with my radio operator's gear, into the open back of a half track. My vehicle was part of a convoy consisting of my HQ Troop and the line troops with their armored cars, jeeps, light tanks and trucks. We drove for a considerable distance. My HQ Troop then stopped and the line troops moved on. Where to? I didn't ask, and I wasn't told. Don't ask, don't tell, was part of a GI's life in WWII long before it entered the military in another guise. As an aside, I must say that in combat, when we were fighting for real, my cavalry officers were very specific in spelling out, by map references, where we were, where we were going, and what to do to get there, and to get back. What I had been told was that the "enemy" force had aircraft together with armored ground troops. If the enemy aircraft spotted our units they would try to "bomb" us by dropping bags of flour. Groups of "Umpires" would be attached to all the fighting units. If a flour sack "bomb" fell a certain distance from us, or directly on our position, then we would be deemed "hit" or possibly "dead", and if "dead" we would be "losers" and out of the war games. I did not learn what the scoring was for the other units. Remember,

I was part of HQ. We were the Regiment's message center, its brains. I imagined this headline in the Brooklyn Eagle, our Borough paper (now defunct): "Arthur S. Katz, a resident of East New York, and a former Brooklyn College student (and a nice Jewish boy, says his Mother) was severely wounded when the half track—from whose hot, open deck he was sending and receiving coded messages as his Regiment's chief radio operator—was hit by a flour sack bomb."

My part in the war game was to send and receive, in Morse Code, coded radio messages in the following manner: The messages would be exchanged between our Regiment and the various forces on our side in the war games. The Colonel and his Staff Officers would give me plain language messages, which I would then encode and send to our allies in the games. I would receive coded messages in reply, and, after decoding them into plain English, I would give them to the Colonel. In theory, quite like my radio classroom training. But out in the field, not so. For one thing, the day was exceptionally hot. The sun shone directly down on me. When the war games started my vehicle was sitting still. But then we began to take evasive action as the planes—they were light, Piper Cub type aircraft—flew overhead, loaded with their "lethal" flour sack bombs. The half track lurched all over the place. The desert terrain was relatively flat, but it was not a paved road, either. I had the day's code and programmed it into my coding device. No sweat there. Then I was given plain language texts, and after coding them, I sent them out. That wasn't much of a problem either. However, receiving the reply, or new messages, was a different matter. Here the heat, noise, dust, and sand clouds enveloping me from my own vehicle's churning action, and from others in my vicinity, materially impaired my hearing, and my comprehension of all the Morse Code dits and dahs, despite all my concentration.

A half track is really a truck on tank treads, with a closed cab and an open metal sided box behind it. The box contained no fixed seats. I was sitting on a canvas folding chair, with my Morse Code

Key, my sending device, clamped upon my right thigh. My chair was not attached to anything. It moved about. This made sending difficult. But I was doing the best I could. I was getting hotter and grimier as the exercise wore on. Flour bombs were falling about our position. Yet not so close that the umpires would declare us hit and out of the war games. The evasive movements of the half track's driver were keeping us in the games, but wreaking havoc on my efficiency as the Regimental radio operator. I began to make mistakes, sometimes in reception of the text, sometimes in coding the text I was sending, and, in transcribing the messages I had received correctly. My printing was becoming poorer. One of the primary things you are trained to do in radio operator classes is to print quickly and clearly. The knowledge of how to print quickly and clearly, was one of the things I learned in the Service which I carried over to my civilian life. (Another, was how to hold a pair of pliers properly when cutting or connecting wire. And, best of all, in the skills department, I learned to drive motor vehicles from jeeps to 2½ ton trucks, and these were vehicles you shifted, and in the case of the trucks, I learned to double clutch).

Anyway, after about half a day into the war games, the Colonel came roaring up in his Staff car. He had a Staff Officer with him. The latter was either a Lt. Colonel, or a Major. They both have an oak leaf as their insignia of rank. The Lt. Colonel's is silver, the Major's is gold. In the dusty haze I couldn't tell the difference—even if I had wanted to. At that point I was pretty much unhappy with myself. I am my toughest judge. I was not performing as I knew I could. The Colonel called out, "Let me see what you got!" Earlier in the games he had dashed by, took the messages I handed him, glanced at them and tore off, saying nothing to me. I handed him several pages of scribbled text. He looked at them for a bit. Then he looked up at me and roared, "What the fuck is going on? I can't read this shit.!" He was pissed!

Now it was my turn to get pissed! I had had it! I was hot, dirty, thirsty, and as I said, displeased with my performance. I jumped off my canvas chair. I ripped my leg key off my thigh, threw it down, and angrily said to the Colonel, "God damn it! I'm doing the best I can! Shit, we're training! That's why we're here!" The Colonel was taken aback. He glared at me, said nothing, sat down in his Staff car and was driven away. A few minutes later the Staff Officer who had been with the Colonel drove up and sternly said to me, "Do you know who you were just speaking to?" I said, "Yes, sir, it was the Colonel." He then said to me, "Soldier, you don't speak to any officer that way, especially your commanding officer." I replied, "Yes, sir." The officer then smiled, and said, "The Colonel was annoyed. But he said you had balls." As he sat down in the Staff car he said, "Try to remember, you're in the Army." "Yes, sir", I said, and I saluted. The officer was driven off. As stated, this was my first run in with the Colonel, in particular, and with the Army, in general. There would be others—some with dire consequences to me—but ultimately everything will turn out for the better. Remember, what was happening was *beshert*, was meant to be.

As I remember it, there were several "run-in events" with the 4th Cavalry Regiment while stationed in England before the invasion of the Continent; and there was one when I was with the Military Government in Germany, after my combat days had ended. I shall detail each of them as my story unfolds. As they played out, these events were stages in the fulfillment of the divine plan designed to lead me to my belóved Anneliese. But I didn't know that as each event took place. Indeed, when coupled with other happenings, such as being wounded twice—and because of the second injury, losing the chance to go to Officers' Candidate School—these happenings appeared unconnected, and negative when they occurred. But now, as I look back, armed with the "wisdom" of hind sight, and able to connect the dots, I see that everything worked out for the best. In this regard I see parallels between my story and that of Joseph, as related in Genesis. Envied by his brothers, Joseph was sold by them into slavery in Egypt. In Egypt he rose to be Pharaoh's second in command. In this capacity, years later, he was able to save his father, Jacob, and his brothers, when famine struck Canaan, and the family sought food in Egypt. I endured various injuries and happenings in WWII, but all were part of the divine plan which led me to my belóved Anneliese. Through His wond'rous workings the Lord has blessed Anneliese, our family and me.

Episode Five

In which my 4th Cavalry Regiment moves from a hot, dry place in California, to Camp Maxie, a hot, wet place in Texas—with an interlude for a 12 hours' pass to Los Angeles.

Our desert training exercises included more than war games. We drove daily in field exercises to different parts of the desert areas in California, and on at least one occasion, we drove to the banks of the Colorado River, opposite Yuma, Arizona. We were learning how to use our vehicles and weapons effectively, and how to maintain them in a hot, hostile climate. We did not wear any heat resistant clothing for the simple reason that none was issued to us. (When, much later, I fought in Bastogne, with snow heavy on the ground, we were not issued white camouflage garments. The military establishment is a slow learner sometimes.) Yet we performed creditably. We learned the importance of keeping our heads covered during the day, that a wet kerchief around the neck cooled nicely, that it was necessary to drink a lot of water, and as I have already noted, that it was not wise to touch the overheated metal parts of your vehicle with a bare hand, lest you wanted to leave a bit of your skin behind when you pulled your hand away. Ouch! That hurt! We also learned that some of our vaunted equipment, such as our rifles, and vehicle mounted machine guns, would jam if they got exceedingly hot, especially so, if we allowed the omnipresent sand to trickle in and jam the works. Thus, with repeated exercises we learned how to maintain our vehicles, to strip down our weapons, to clean them, and to put them quickly, and properly, together again. We learned how to avoid getting our vehicles stuck in the sand, and if it sometimes happened, how to dig and pull the vehicle out quickly. In short, even though our war games were just that, games, we learned to act as a cohesive fighting force in hot, unforgiving terrain—and to do all this with no special desert gear or heat resistant protective clothing. We were becoming desert combat ready, and we were proud of that fact. *Esprit de corps* is a vital intangible for the success of any fighting unit. And the 4th Cavalry Regiment had it. Had we gone on to North Africa to fight Rommel I know we would have acquitted ourselves well. But by the time our desert training was winding down it was early Summer 1943, and by then Montgomery had defeated Rommel, And so we would leave the desert of Southern California, with its sand, dust, flash floods and solar intensity—and again by troop train—depart for another part of America, almost as parched and grimy as the California desert: the Northeastern part of Texas.

But before we arrive in Texas let me tell you that Southern California, down Mexico way, was not all war games and field exercises. We had at least one opportunity that I remember where we GIs were given leave to go "off the reservation" to visit "civilization" for some fun. Civilization was Los Angeles, La Ciudad de Nuestra Señora de Porciuncula, La Reina de Los Angeles: the City of the Queen of Angels. I remember walking down Sunset Boulevard very early on a Sunday morning. The street was almost devoid of vehicular traffic and pedestrians. Everything looked so pristine in the sunlight. The cloudless sky was an artist's dream: pure cerulean. Graceful palms, their lanceolate foliage, dark green, lined the street. When a light wind would come up their foliage would rustle ever so slightly. I saw several colorful birds—which I could not identify—flitter and twitter about. The buildings lining that part of Sunset Boulevard on which I was strolling were mostly one or two stories tall. Their stucco walls were painted white, or off white, what some call Navajo white. The sunlight seemed to bounce off these walls, and made their windows sparkle. The air smelled fresh and clean. Don't be surprised. I'm not making this up. This was early 1943 when commercial orange groves still existed in adjacent Orange County. As I gazed about me I said to myself, "Boy, this is a nice place, maybe, someday, when the war is over, I'll come here to live." Two things should be noted concerning this random observation of mine: *One:* I never thought I would die in the war. That part turned out to be true. Hitler's Wehrmacht failed to kill me, although it came close twice. *Two:* I did, indeed, settle in California in late November 1950. Anneliese and our first two children, Andrew and Heidi, both of whom were born in New York City, would shortly thereafter join me there. So that part also turned out to be true. And there in California we would live, for over 50 years, first in Pacific Palisades, and then in San Luis Obispo County, and there, in California, the Golden State, Anneliese would bless me, and the world, with three more children, Pamela, Jonathan and Benjamin, each as wonderful as the first two. This part of my story will also be more fully recounted in due course.

Before taking you with me to Northeastern Texas, and our next training site, let me get back to my visit as a GI to Los Angeles. When a GI had a pass or leave into town then the best place to go for some clean fun was to a club or canteen run by the USO (United Service Organization) or the Red Cross or other equivalent non-governmental organization. (NGO). I visited one such NGO club during my brief excursion to Los Angeles. There was pop music, pretty girls happy to dance with you, soft drinks and coffee, tea or milk and baked goodies. And there were also Hosts/Masters of Ceremony (MCs) usually prominent local performers or radio show hosts, who would "work" the audience during their allotted time on the floor.

At each venue there were tables and chairs, rather than rows of theater seats, and a band stand and lots of patriotic red, white and blue bunting. The Sunday I was in Los Angeles I visited the canteen on Sunset Boulevard. Working the room was a local Tumler (Yiddish for a comedian/stand-up comic). He moved around between tables, making light conversation, patter, with the different military personnel, and always looking for a ploy to turn a casual conversation into a comical situation—being careful not to be hurtful or offensive to anyone with ordinary sensibilities. The military was segregated at that time. And so, all the canteen's volunteers, whether the gray haired matrons or the nubile girls, and the Tumler, all were white, as were the service personnel there to be entertained. If any persons of color were present, they must have been pastel or light beige, thus making them invisible against all the white bread in the building, and against all the Navajo white painted walls. In any event, I saw no dark skin people there.

The Tumler walked around and talked to the service personnel as he passed their tables, and engaged them in conversation. "What's your name, fella?" "Where do you come from?" "Having fun yet in L.A.?" Etc. Etc. If he saw a guy with a bald head, or his hair cut very short, he might ask, "Did the Post barber cut your hair?" If the guy said "Yeah", then the Tumler would say something like this: "What did he use, a lawnmower?" And everyone would laugh, including the bald guy. Anyway, the day I was there the Tumler came to my table. He must have been attracted by my clean cut, all American appearance, my handsome, desert tanned face, setting off my twinkling blue eyes and my sparkling white teeth! Ha! Ha! "Where do you come from soldier?" "Brooklyn", I replied. "Oh? What part, Toity Toid Street?" He made a broad Brooklyn accent, which put my real one (which I then had, and some suggest I still have to a degree today) to shame. I laughed and played along. "No, I live on Toity Foist Street." He had a winner with me. I believe he was a Jewish guy, and I think he sensed I was. So he stayed with me a bit longer. "Where'd you get that accent?" "What accent? I always speak this way." This broke him up, and everybody else. "Look me up kid when you get back. We'd make a great team." Everybody laughed and he moved on. I felt great. Queen for a Day, or better said, King for a Day. Yep, the Army wasn't all bad.

After my brief, but fun filled trip to Los Angeles it was back to the desert where our Regiment was packing its gear, ready to get back on the train and move on. This time to a Post in Texas called Camp Maxie. The season was late Spring or early Summer. We were moving from the dry heat of the Southern California desert, to the sultry, clammy heat of that part of the good old US of A where Texas, Oklahoma and Arkansas come together to form the armpit of America. Which may be the reason why military installations are so plentiful there.

Camp Maxie was an encampment filled with row upon row of military barracks and training fields galore. It wasn't a real fort as was Fort Meade. But what it lacked in martial authenticity it made up in size. It appeared to stretch forever, which in a place as steppes—like as northeastern Texas didn't seem to matter. We did all kinds of regimental training exercises in Camp Maxie, none of which I recall. Indeed, about all I remember of my basic training at Fort Meade was crawling under barbed wire while real machine gun fire was whizzing over my head. At least I was told it was real fire. I never stood up to find out.

Camp Maxie was located very near the city of Paris, Texas. Paris was the city's name. But it had no resemblance to its namesake in France. It was no Paris, France, and it made no pretense to be. The first time I was given a pass from the Camp I made my way, alone, on foot, into town. As I approached the city limits my eyes lighted upon a large Chamber of Commerce billboard which proclaimed: "Welcome to Paris, Texas. The blackest earth and the whitest people." Nothing like local Sothren, that's right, Sothren pride. Good farmland and good, God fearing Christian folk are not to be sneezed at. The billboard clarified an incident which had occurred just a minute or two before while on my walk into town. I was on a narrow paved sidewalk. Narrow, but wide enough for two persons to pass each other when walking in opposite directions. A black youth, maybe fifteen or sixteen, was coming from town and walking towards me. When he was about three paces from me he stepped off the sidewalk and into the adjacent road. Thus, I had the whole sidewalk to myself when we passed each other. I on the sidewalk, he in the gutter. Strange, I thought. Then I spied the billboard. And everything fell into place. I was witnessing white, southern racial mores in action. The blackest earth and the whitest people left little room on public sidewalks for black people and white people to walk side by side.

This was the Summer of 1943, and as this black youth stepped into the gutter to avoid possibly jostling me, my beloved country, America the Beautiful, the Land of the Brave, and the Home of the Free, was gearing up to save the world from the Jap hordes, and from the evils of Hitler's Nazis, and Mussolini's Fascisti. Strange. Contrary to what Jesus taught, we see the mote in the eyes of others, but fail to see it in our own. Today, fortunately, times have changed. I doubt whether Paris, Texas still flaunts the same billboard at the city's edge. As my story unfolds I shall relate other incidents during my military service which turned on racial and religious biases. It all didn't start or end in Paris, Texas. Indeed, one of the incidents took place in Paris, France. No country, not even La Belle France is perfect.

Episode Six

In which my use of GI profanity gets me into a serious problem, from which I dance and talk my way out—evidence to me that I'd make a good lawyer.

In the military service, at least at my enlisted man's level, profanity was a basic part of speech. Four letter words, the kind referred to in polite written circles as "expletive deleted", were bandied back between the troops with the implicit understanding that the use of such language usually had no personal attribution. Thus, if a sergeant told a group of soldiers to police, *i.e.*, clean up a common area in the camp, and on inspection he noted that they had done a lousy job, he might say, and customarily did, "Hell, you guys are a bunch of shit heads! Look at all that fuckin' crap still lying around!" All the group was at fault. Sarge wasn't picking on any one individual. Profanity was so common in the military that some of it has entered the vernacular in a sanitized form. Thus, if a Line Officer, a Lieutenant had to report a botched performance by his troops to his superior, a Staff Officer, a Lt. Colonel, and the conversation was taking place at Headquarters, the Lieutenant might say to the Lt. Colonel, "Sir, a couple of the jeeps wouldn't start this morning. There was a Snafu in the motor pool." "SNAFU" is the acronym for "Situation Normal—All Fucked Up". However, some uses of profanity, if misapplied, or misunderstood, could be taken personally by the recipient or target. Then the line between banter and insult would be crossed, and the expression, "Thems fightin' words!" would come into play.

I now relate an episode in which my use of profanity almost caused me to suffer serious personal injury. The story is funny as I tell it now, because it has a happy ending. But until I hastily contrived a happy ending to my predicament, I was in deep doo-doo. Here's what happened:

It was late Summer in Camp Maxie, hot and muggy, the kind of weather that drains energy but leaves enough to permit a group of us from Headquarters Troop to sit around bull shitting and joking. At one point in this idle discourse, in which neither Plato nor politics would ever be discussed, I casually referred to one of our fellow Troopers, a guy in his mid-twenties, and a native of the Ozarks. He was a quiet fellow, not much given to conversation, and often the butt of hillbilly jokes, none, of course, told in his presence. I remember saying in a smart alecky way that he was a "dumb-ass, mother-fucker." The phrase "dumb-ass" was intended to refer to his slowness in catching on to various military procedures. The "mother-fucker" was just gratuitous profanity. Personal in description, but wholly impersonal in intent, and, as above noted, so understood by any one steeped in the use of profanity within the narrow confines of military life. My reference to this guy as a "mother fucker" was not said as an indictment of his sexual behavior. I was just being "smart-ass", which is often the flip side of "dumb-ass". When I spoke I was not aware that the object of my comments was within earshot. He was. He came racing towards me, shouting in anger, "Who you callin' a motha-fucka!?" That's how he pronounced those fateful words. He didn't mention the words "dumb-ass". It was being called a "mother-fucker" that raised his ire to white hot heat. He pulled out a knife from a scabbard on his belt. The Army didn't issue knives to us. This was his own. It looked like a Bowie knife. Shiny, sharp and very threatening! As he neared me I jumped up and tried to move away from him. The other guys who had been sitting and bull shitting with me, jumped up also. No one made an effort to stop him. You can't blame them. It takes courage and stupidity, in equal measure, for an unarmed person to try to stop a very angry man armed with a knife who comes charging in your direction. Instead, they formed a circle of spectators about us. They were watching to see whether this dumb-ass hillbilly would cut up this smart-ass New York City Jew. As my opponent lunged at me, I dodged and danced about—my footwork almost as neat as that of Gene Kelly and Fred Astaire—trying to avoid his slashing knife. Then some hitherto unknown source of wisdom (most likely sent by my compassionate God) caused me to remember that some days earlier he had proudly shown off to me, and others, a photo of a cute little girl, about three, who he said was his "darlin dotter". I shouted, as I dodged about, "Hey, you got a wife?" "Yeah", he shouted back. "Is that kid from your wife?", I called out. "Hell, yeah!", he shouted back. He's still lunging, I'm still dodging about. "Then you fucked your wife to get the kid, right?" "I sho did!", he shouted in reply. "Then you're a motherfucker!", I cried out. He stopped in his tracks, lowered his knife, looked at me a tad puzzled, and said, "I thought you was insultin' my Mama!" I quickly assured him that was not my intent. He smiled. I smiled back. We shook hands. The circle of onlookers broke up. One or two looked disappointed, there was to be no New York Jew sticking that day.

This adventure, in which I talked my way out of an incident which could have resulted in my serious injury, was an early demonstration to me that I could become a good lawyer. Before I left Brooklyn for Fort Meade, I had bought two law books which, I had been informed, would give me insight into the philosophy and workings of the Law. What better way to prepare for a legal career than by learning about the underpinnings of the Law. One book was called *The Common Law*, by Oliver Wendell Holmes, Jr., later a U.S. Supreme Court Justice; the other, *The Nature of the Judicial Process*, by Benjamin Nathan Cardozo, also later a U.S. Supreme Court Justice. Throughout the war I carried with me these two books, a pocket sized Bible containing the Hebrew Scriptures and the New Testament, together with a concise text on German grammar, and four thin paper bound booklets of British poetry, the latter five bought in England—I still have all of them, a bit beat up, but all quite readable—I would read them when we were between missions, or when we were pinned down under mortar or artillery fire, and the random pattern of the falling shells indicated to me that the Germans knew we were out there, some where, but couldn't see us. Thus, sitting still in your armored car, studying a good book, was a better way to pass the time, than jumping up and down, and running around scared in the open.

Art's Gear Ft. Meade,
South Dakota

Arthur, December 1942
Ft. Meade, South Dakota

Arthur, California Desert Training Spring 1943

Arthur and buddy, Cooling Off California
Desert Training, Spring 1943

Arthur, Camp Maxie, Texas, Summer 1943

Episode Seven

In which, in late Fall 1943, the 4th Cavalry crosses the Atlantic to England. En route I saw and heard nothing, being deep down in the hold.

Sometime in late Fall 1943 we were told that the Regiment would be leaving for a staging area from which we would go overseas. We were not informed whether we would be going to the Pacific Theater or to Europe. But when we learned we would be heading for the East Coast, we assumed, correctly, that we would be playing our combat rôle in the European Theater. Again, our Regiment's personnel and equipment were loaded on a train which chugged its way to the East. No one told me, or the other GIs, where we were headed. This was common military practice. If they told us, we would write, or telephone our loved ones, and friends, and they in turn would tell others, and the German, Italian and Japanese spies among us, if any, would overhear all this talking, and they would then transmit this information to their respective governments. At least that's what we were told, as part of the Government's self censorship campaign. "Loose Lips Sink Ships", if I remember, correctly, was one of the war time slogans found on signs posted in public places. So I only learned where the coastal staging area was when we got there. I believe they sent us to Fort Dix in New Jersey. From there I got a short leave. I went home to Brooklyn, and saw my folks, my brother, Harold and friends for the first time since enlisting in November 1942. I was surrounded by family, relatives, close and distant. and friends, the cynosure of all eyes (to quote a cliché) and told how wonderful I looked in my uniform! It was a brief and touching visit.

A number of men from my Regiment also went into New York City. Those who were accompanying me happened to be guys from the rural South. We were somewhere in the lower part of Manhattan. Before I took the Subway to Brooklyn one of these guys asked me how far it was to Times Square from where they were. They knew nothing about New York City, but somewhere along the way they had heard about Times Square. In New York, as in other large metropolitan areas, one measures distance by travel time. And so I said, thinking of the Subway route, "Oh, about 15 minutes." One of the guys looked at me, and in an annoyed voice, said, "That's a funny way to measure distance. How many *miles* is it? I said I didn't know. I told him that in New York we didn't measure distance by miles, but by the time it took to go from our starting point to our destination, As he pondered my reply I left for the Subway and home. I didn't know the mileage, or care. I knew where I was going: to the last stop on the IRT, New Lots Avenue, and the approximate time I'd get there. That's all that mattered to me.

We shipped out on a British merchant vessel. More than that I can't tell you. Not even its name. We guessed it was British because of its crew. This guess was confirmed by the kind of "food" served at mess call. I have written "food" because while it was edible, especially when ingestion was encouraged by the pangs of hunger, it was not very appetizing, and I never really knew what each constituent in our meals really was—and I was not eager to find out.

From dockside we shuffled up a long gangplank, with our duffle bags on our backs, and were led down, way, way down, into the bowels of the ship. How far down I never did learn, because, except for one rather confused drill with life vests on, I don't recall ever being allowed up on deck during the crossing of the Atlantic. Perhaps I am imagining there had been a life vest drill on deck. Many years after the war, when I allowed myself to view "war movies" on television, I saw such a drill. And this imaginary drill may have, within the interstices of my memory, taken the place of a "real one" which never really happened. Confused, dear reader? So am I.

We slept in hammocks, hung two, perhaps three high. There were portholes. They were fastened shut. Some light came through them during the day. That was one way we gauged the passage of time. Looking out we could see nothing, except the sky, unless the vessel listed sharply, giving us a scare and then we had a brief, rolling view of the sea. After a few days our air stank, but we stank, too, so after a bit we didn't notice the stink. We understood we were part of a convoy of merchant vessels, and that we were being protected by naval forces, including submarines. A lot good that would have done us were our ship struck by a torpedo from a German U-Boat, or bombed from the air, and we began to sink. We would have been stuck deep in the hold and drowned as the ship sank. Not a pleasant thought, so we dismissed it from our minds.

How long did it take our troop ship to travel from the east coast of the USA to a port on the south coast of England? Good question. I don't recall the number of days. Based upon the number of times I shaved . . . Shaved? Yes, I didn't like looking scruffy, even if I stank—and on the different chapters I read in the books I had with me, I'm guessing it was about 10 days. Remember, nobody bothered to tell us GIs in the hold anything. When someone ventured to ask one of our Sergeants what our location at sea might be, or when or where we would land, he would be told, "Why the fuck do you want to know? When we get there you'll know." No one asked any of our Officers those same questions. That's because I don't recall seeing any of our Officers during the crossing. Why descend into Dante's Inferno, when you are comfortably billeted several decks higher, in nice cabins, with an Officer's Mess, with table clothes, fine china and real cuisine? Really la, di, dah. Remember, too, this was a British vessel, and the Brits took good care of their Officers and of ours.

Aside from the shoes, socks and clothing I was wearing, my duffel bag contained all my personal gear. Our weapons were stored separately. I recall huffing and puffing up the gangplank wondering why in hell my gear suddenly weighed so much. When I got to my assigned bunk/hammock I opened my duffel bag and there, nestled on the top of my gear was a 10 pound sledge. Some smart ass had played a joke on the professor. I believe I have mentioned that by reason of the fact I was the only college level GI in my HQ Troop, and possibly, in the whole Regiment, the guys had begun to call me "professor". The term was not intended as an accolade. It was used as a pejorative. Thus, if a guy had a query about something, he might say: "What about so and so?" The subject matter could be anything. And the other guy would often say, "How the fuck should I know! Ask Katz, the professor". I was most often not better informed than they were. But as it is written: In the land of the blind, the one eyed man is king.

Episode Eight

In which I am safe ashore on the south coast of England, almost get lost in my first blackout, and learn the effects of hard cider.

We disembarked on the south coast of England. The port was either Portsmouth or Southampton. In line with Army practice, no one told us. We were immediately billeted for a short period near the beach cities of Chichester and Bognor Regis, not too distant from the ports noted. The enlisted personnel in the Regiment were housed in what we were told were temporary facilities, since we would, in short order, be relocated to another region of England where we would engage in military exercises in preparation for the invasion of continental Europe. Our quarters were tents, with canvas sides which could be furled, and wood plank floors. These tents were pitched in several rows near some railroad tracks. The tents were laid out in an area which separated the train tracks from a block of two story row houses. The space between the rear of the row houses and the line of tents measured about ten yards. This terrain had a gentle rake from the row houses down to our line of tents. Thus someone looking out a second story row house window could look into our tents if the sides were furled.

Once we got our gear stowed we were allowed to go into town to stretch our sea legs. The part of the town (whose name I do not recall) closest to our tents was maybe a 100 yards up a road which started at our line of tents. The town itself sat further up on the rake or slope I have already noted. The legal drinking age in New York State, at the time I grew up was 21. My family always drank kosher wine at a Shabbat meal, or at a Passover Seder, or when Kiddush was said over the wine after a religious service. An occasional beer was drunk at home. I don't recall anyone in our family being a drinker of hard liquor, except for downing a

Schlivovitz Cherry Brandy at a wedding or Bar-Mitzvah. During the one year period between my enlistment in November 1942 and going overseas in November 1943 I may have had a few beers. I wasn't a drinker then. (Nor am I today, although I enjoy heavy bodied beers, good wines, top of the line gins and a super Bourbon out of Kentucky, the kind so good, you sip it rather than gulp it down. I drink, but in moderation.) Thus, being in England in the Winter of 1943 put me in an environment where I could sidle up to a bar and order an alcoholic drink without having to show ID concerning my age, which, at the time, was still four months short of being 21. Naturally, the first time I went into town in England I headed for the nearest Pub. Pub is the abbreviation, I soon learned, for Public House, a licensed tavern or bar and grill in US parlance.

We GIs had been instructed that food rationing was in force in the UK. As Yanks we could not buy most food stuffs in civilian establishments, but we could buy hard and soft drinks and certain bread products. And so, at about 5 o'clock in the afternoon I was in my first pub. "Wha'tl you have Yank?" the friendly barkeep asked me. I played it safe. "What do you suggest?" "Well", he said, "We've got lots of nice beers and ales on draft. But they might not be cold enough for you Yanks. But you might fancy our cider. It's a local product and we're very proud of it. Not too sweet, and it's got a kick to it." Cider? I liked cider at home, why not try some of the local stuff? I paid no mind to the barkeep's comment concerning the cider's kick. I ordered a cider. It was served in a big mug. Nice amber color, and it tasted real good. I downed it fast. I then ordered a second and then a third, maybe even a fourth. I was the only Yank in the Pub and I was soon exchanging pleasantries with some locals standing at the bar. Perhaps one of them ordered the fourth for me and paid for it. At that point I couldn't remember. They were happy we had come over to help them get those nahrzee barstards. I looked at my watch. It was well past 6 p.m. I better head back and see if I could still get some chow at the mess tent.

Our troops had earlier been given some English currency in exchange for our US dollars. I paid for my ciders, thanked the barkeep for his advice, said goodbye to him and my new drinking buddies, parted the blackout curtain which separated the Pub's lit interior from the foyer leading to its front door, opened the door and stepped out into the street. Wow, I was in for a surprise! It was pitch black! Because of air raids there was no street lighting and all windows were blacked out with heavy cloths. I was feeling no pain. I was light headed, totally confused and stone blind! Where the fuck was I? The entry way to the Pub was paved with small stones, laid in a neat, geometric pattern which ended at the curbside of the street which became the road down to the tents where we were billeted. I had noticed this stonework when I entered the Pub. And so I gingerly moved my feet ever so slowly over this pattern of stone, not changing the direction I had been facing from the time I stepped out of the Pub. Or so I hoped. I slowly edged my way towards where I thought the street might be. I bent down, good! I felt the curbstone. It was a rectangular block of stone. And next to it there was another, I stepped off the sidewalk into the street. It was laid with cobblestones. As hazy as I was, I recalled that I had gone up hill towards the Pub. So to get back to my billet I should go down hill towards the railroad tracks. Since I couldn't see shit I got a great idea: some part of my muddled brain was still working. I walked slowly down the rake of the hill keeping one foot on the curbstones, with the other foot, the right one, set in the cobblestoned street. As long as I could guide myself downhill, one foot on the curbstones, and one on the road, I was OK. Then, having gone maybe 50 paces, I ran into a problem. A big one. I had come to the corner of the street and there my curbstone guide ended. If I turned to follow the curbstone around the corner I knew I would not be going towards the tracks. What to do? Fortunately, the town's streets were not too wide. I had noted that fact in the daylight, when I could see, and when I was more sober than now. And so I slowly inched myself forward, trying to keep the rake of the street going down.

I reached down and felt for the cobblestones. During daylight I saw that the cobblestones were, more or less, lined up in rows when laid. Moving ever so slowly, and tracing the layout of the stones as I went, I happily reached the opposite corner. I knew I was there because I felt the corner curbstone jutting up from the road bed. Great! I resumed my journey. One foot, my left, on the sidewalk's curbstones, My right, in the cobblestoned street. A herky-jerky way of walking. But I was going down hill, that's what mattered. I sensed from the passage of time that I must be near the row houses. Then I saw a glint of light, one window covering was ever so slightly askew, and I knew where I was. I stumbled into my tent. I was relieved and sweating. I didn't think of it then, but this unexpected night exercise would stand me in good stead in combat when I had to move about in darkness in hostile terrain, and doing so totally sober.

I was safe in my tent. But my cider adventure was not yet over. About six in the morning I woke up. My head ached. My belly ached. I was sick. I felt an urge to throw up. I clambered out of my cot and tottered outside the tent. I began to vomit. It flowed out of me like lava out of Mauna Loa. The sun was rising. It was getting light. There, above me, sitting at an open upstairs window, her forearms resting on the window sill, was a lady with a kindly face. She said to me, "Poor Yank! You've drunk too much of our cider." Clearly, she had seen episodes, such as mine, many times before. Once my stomach was fully purged of its high alcohol cider I was soon back to normal. After the war I would occasionally drink hard English cider. In very small quantities. I have never forgotten that first bellyache and its related upchuck.

Episode Nine

In which my regiment is relocated inland, in the Glastonbury area where kids from the big cities were sent to avoid Hitler's Buzz bombs, as were we, and my description of the regal Manor House in which our officers are billeted, and which will become center stage for my run-ins with my Colonel.

The *Luftwaffe* had been making daily forays over England from the day the war started. And these attacks were continuing when our Regiment landed in England. But the British anti-aircraft defenses, aided by the Brits' invention of radar, and their superb Spitfire aircraft and skilled pilots, were taking an ever increasing toll of *Luftwaffe* planes. To offset these losses, while continuing to punish the UK's war efforts, and its civilian population in particular, Hitler turned the benign and beautiful fireworks display of rockets bursting in air into lethal weaponry. His scientists (one of whom, Werner von Braun, Nazi though he was, became a vital part of our post WWII military armament program down in Huntsville, Alabama) developed a weaponized long range rocket capable of reaching the eastern flank of Britain. By today's military standards they were primitive rocket propelled bombs.

They were not smart guided missiles. They were launched from various parts of occupied Europe and made a buzzing sound as they flew. Hence the name Buzz Bombs. They were aimed in the general direction of major population and industrial centers. When their rocket fuel was consumed, the rockets' engines would stall, the buzz bombs would fall silent, and a short time thereafter, they would noiselessly plummet to the ground, where they exploded with great force, doing grave damage to people and structures. Thus, when you heard the buzzing sound of the rocket you knew it was flying over and away from you. But if you heard its buzz near you, and then it suddenly went silent, you knew it would be crashing down somewhere nearby. A scary feeling. Mad Hitler and his equally mad scientists had created an inexpensive weapon of terror and destruction.

The British Government instituted a safety program of evacuating children from those parts of England exposed to buzz bombs to areas further inland, such as Bristol and Bath. A parent not essential to the war effort would accompany the evacuated child or children. Otherwise, the children, properly escorted, were evacuated to safer places, and there attended to by local persons selected for that purpose. After a short time in the Chichester/ Bognor Regis area of England—where we heard buzz bombs pass overhead as they flew inland—our Cavalry Regiment was moved to the same Bristol/Bath area where the evacuated children were. We were moved there for the same reason the kids were there: our exposure to hostile fire would be materially lessened. We were billeted in Somerset County, in the environs of the medieval city of Glastonbury, noted as the site of Glastonbury Abbey, one of England's oldest religious structures.

The 4th Cavalry Regiment was billeted in various parts of the Glastonbury area. Each of the Troops was billeted separately. I never learned where the other Troops were located. The Regiment's Headquarters were set up in a large, multi-story, stone façaded English Country Manor House. The kind you see on PBS when they show dramatizations of works by such writers as Jane Austen, the Brontë sisters, and Charles Dickens. The Colonel and his Staff of Officers were billeted in the Manor House. None of the 57 Troopers making up Headquarters Troop were billeted in the Manor House. We were billeted near the Manor House in lodgings wholly dissimilar to those found in that stately edifice, as I shall shortly relate. I describe first the Manor House and its surroundings. The multistoried House was enclosed within a rustic stone wall, perhaps 8 feet high which encircled the structure on its four sides. The wall was set back from the House by about thirty feet of lawns and shrubbery, except for the entry way to the House. Here there was a large cobblestoned courtyard. One entered the courtyard through a gateway with a span of about 20 feet. There were two iron grill work swinging gates. Each of the gates was nestled behind its respective parts of the wall. I don't recall the gates ever being closed. Stout ivy vines ran up the walls. There were bush like shrubs flanking the entry. It was Winter sometime in December 1943 when the Colonel his Staff, and line officers set up their Headquarters and lodgings in the Manor House. The vines and shrubs were deciduous, and thus bare of leaves. The shrubs were pruned to be boxy in form. Perhaps they were a variety of privet. Had I been there in late Spring I would have learned what they were when they started to leaf out. Why wasn't I there? Read on, and you'll learn why.

Through the courtyard one entered the main entrance to the Manor House. There was at least one other entrance to the House. That was to the rear on one of its sides. This was the servants' entrance to the House and its kitchen facilities. The Manor House served two military functions: it was the operational center of the Regiment, its Headquarters, and it also served as the living quarters for the Regiment's officers. These consisted of the Colonel, his HQ Staff of three or four officers, including the Captain in charge of Headquarters Troop, and then the six line Lieutenants, each in charge of one of the combat troops, A through F. The Regimental HQ was visited daily by officers from British, Allied and American units in the area. To maintain security (against a Nazi parachute invasion I suppose), but primarily as an example of American spit and polish, enlisted personnel took turns, on a 24 hour schedule doing guard duty at the Manor House's gateway entrance. Enlisted personnel below the rank of sergeant were not allowed entry to the Manor House unless there on official business. Official business, as applied to us low ranking GIs did not include the use of the Manor House's numerous bathrooms/toilets. These sanitary facilities included a toilet located within the servants' side entrance area. I mention toilets now because such facilities will shortly play a vital rôle in shaping my military career.

The number of Troopers in Headquarters Troop was considerably less than in the line Troops, A through F. I never learned where, or under what conditions, the line Troopers were billeted, but our Troop's 57 Troopers, other than the Sergeant-Major and other high ranking non-coms, such as the Supply Sergeant, were billeted in free standing metal structures with wood floors, known as Nissan Huts. The sides and ceilings were made of corrugated metal, shaped as a half cylinder. The rear wall and the front entry were also made of metal, with a window on each side of the front door. Heat was provided by a wood or charcoal briquette burning stove whose long stove pipe chimney helped disperse heat before exiting through the hut's roof.

There were no toilet facilities in the hut. Such toilet facilities as we had were primitive. The "toilet facilities" were these: Some distance from our Nissan Hut a row of coal buckets had been set out. There must have been 6 to 8 of such buckets. Over these buckets the Brits had built a long, low, wooden framework upon which three or four rough hewn boards were nailed. The boards had holes cut in them. Under each hole a coal bucket had been placed. Over this contraption a shed like structure stood. I say shed like because all its sides were open, and the only covered portion was its roof, and this was a piece of corrugated metal sitting on a wooden frame supported by 6 wooden posts standing about 7 feet above grade. If these facilities were set up at a Boy Scouts' Summer Camp they might have been OK for the Scouts' roughing it for a few days. But they were clearly inappropriate as sanitary toilet facilities for grown men, especially during an English winter. Such weather was not excessively cold, certainly not like Minnesota in the wintertime. But the weather was often cold, dank, rainy and windy. If it was not Minnesota neither was it Palm Springs, California. When the buckets were almost sloshing over with urine and excrement they were taken away, emptied and returned. I don't recall that they were ever rinsed between dumpings. Such running water as we had was in the Nissan huts, and no one was about to bring these shit buckets into our quarters to wash them. The guys resented sitting bare assed over the coal buckets, exposed not only to prying eyes, but to the elements. I have gone to some length to describe these outside toilets because they become critical to the unfolding of episodes which would shape, for some time my career in the Army, and the shaping would be negative, but as things played out, a necessary step in a journey which, unbeknownst to me would ultimately lead me to my belóved Anneliese Baur. But before I get to these negative episodes let me recount some happier experiences.

Episode Ten

In which I meet some male and female British civilians and have a biking adventure to Bath.

Shortly after our Regiment was billeted in the Glastonbury area I went into town. As I have noted, food rationing was in force for the citizens of the United Kingdom. American soldiers were not permitted to buy foodstuffs in civilian shops, except for such items as bread. The bread we got in the mess hall was white bread. Soft, no hard crust. It may have been healthy, but I missed the Jewish rye, New York corn rye, and other more chewy and crusty breads I had enjoyed at home in Brooklyn. Looking in the windows of bakery shops I saw bread and rolls with real crusts. I decided to buy a couple of rolls and try them out. We had been issued English currency. At the time the Brits had farthings, as well as pence, shillings and pounds. They also had something they called a quid, a sum equal to one pound and one shilling. I found paying for something to be complicated, since the currency was not based on the decimal system. I soon solved the problem by handing over more money than called for by the purchase, and then taking the change without bothering to count it, or figure if it was correct. Since I wasn't dealing with high finance my "system" worked. Anyway, early one weekend afternoon I went into a bakery shop. It was busy. The customers were all civilian ladies. I waited my turn to be served. I then bought a couple of hard rolls. I don't recall the price. It wasn't much. Less than a shilling. Per my practice of avoiding to make change I handed over a shilling with my right hand, and with my left hand I reached out to accept the rolls from the bakery clerk. As I did so my left wrist was extended beyond the cuff of my blouse sleeve. On my left wrist I was wearing a small gold chain from which dangled a gold Magen David. I had bought it before I left Brooklyn for Fort Meade in South Dakota. A lady who had just been served was standing next to me. I'm not good at guessing ages, especially of women (I usually guess them to be younger than they are, which, if you make a mistake, is not a bad one), I thought she might be in her late thirties. She noted the Magen David on my outstretched arm. She then looked at me, but said nothing. I left the bakery shop. I held the door open as she followed me out. On the sidewalk she turned to me and asked, "Young man, what is that you are wearing on your wrist?" I told her it was a Star of David. She smiled and asked, "Are you Jewish?" I replied that I was. Her face beamed, she was quite pleased. She then told me that she, too, was Jewish, that I didn't "look Jewish", and since many young men wear charm bracelets she wasn't sure I was Jewish until I revealed that I knew that what I was wearing was a Star of David.

The lady then told me her name was Mrs. Rosenthal (throughout the book I shall not use real family names, and occasionally I shall change first names, to avoid privacy and other concerns), that she and her two small children, a girl and a boy, had been evacuated from London because of the buzz bombs, and that she was living with the children in the Glastonbury area. She said her husband worked in London, and joined the family on weekends. Mrs. Rosenthal informed me that she enjoyed having Jewish servicemen come to dinner, and she invited me to visit with her and her family. Naturally, I accepted. From this chance encounter a long friendship was established between the Rosenthals of England and the Katz family in the USA and each family visited the other. When the Rosenthal's daughter, Miriam grew up, Anneliese and I sponsored her entry into the United States. Later I helped her get her first position in the motion picture business, where she moved up rapidly on the production side of the business.

The above recital was an *Abstecher*, a side trip down memory's lane, albeit, a pleasant one. So back to England sometime in December 1943. While billeted with my Cavalry Regiment in the Glastonbury area I had sufficient time off to visit nearby civilian areas and explore their pubs. As far as I recall, there were no UK rationing regulations concerning the purchase of beer, wine and spirits, so we Yanks were able to imbibe with the Brits, to the limits of our wallets, and our physical well being. Having earlier learned my limits concerning alcoholic beverages, via my hard cider experience, I restricted my intake, each time I visited a pub, to a couple of beers or ales, maybe to three, and to an occasional gin and orange. After visiting several pubs I gravitated to a particular one on those late afternoons or early evenings when I was able to get into town. Why I picked that one I cannot now recall, other than I found it comfortable to be there, standing at the bar, sandwiched in among the locals, most of whom appeared to be family men in their forties and older. Such younger men as were present were Brits in uniform, home on leave, as I gathered from conversations overheard. Once in a while there would be a few Yanks, like me, in the crowd. After a few pints of ale, or perhaps a tad more, the urge to urinate would become overpowering, so you walked out the front door, went around back to the loo, relieved yourself and then walked back in and started the cycle again. When I related this brew buying experience years later to Jonathan, one of my sons, he laughed and said, "Dad, you don't buy beer, you just rent it." He was right.

Anyway, after frequenting the same pub for about a week, I noticed that a gentleman at the bar, perhaps in his late forties, was staring at me. I had seen him several times while visiting the pub. I had smiled and nodded at him, and he had done the same. Aside from these minimal exchanges of social niceties, neither of us had conversed. Thus, I was surprised when he approached me from his end of the bar and began to talk with me. He introduced himself, told me his name (which I do not recall) and I told him mine. He said he had been observing me, and that I appeared to be a nice chap. He then said he had a daughter. He asked me my age. I told him I was twenty. He said she was a little younger than I. He then invited me to visit his home and meet her. "You'll like her a lot. She's a very homely girl." Wow! I said to myself. Here I'm going to get a chance to meet a local girl, and she's a dog! What bad luck. I didn't want to be rude or ungrateful. I had been told in an Army orientation course that English folk, especially those in small communities, prized their privacy (they pronounced it PHRIVacy), so we shouldn't be offended if they were standoffish. And so I thanked him for his invitation and accepted it. He gave me his address and how to get there.

A few days later I was at the door of his home. I knocked. The door was opened by a very attractive young lady. She was about my height, with heels she might have been taller. She was wearing a white, button down dress which effectively showed off the excellence of her figure. Her hair was blond and bobbed. Her complexion, classic English peaches and cream. Quite a looker! "Hello", she said. "I'm Sara, my Dad said you were coming by. Please come in." She extended her hand and I shook it. Her grip was firm. Boy, what a pleasant surprise! Seeing her made it clear to me that although Americans and the British both spoke English that neither group really spoke the same language. I would reconfirm this view a bit later in this narrative. Anyway, there I was standing before a beautiful girl which her father had proudly referred to as a "homely girl". What was going on? To a big city American, like me, a "homely girl" was one lacking physical attractiveness, *i.e.*, "a dog". To an Englishman living in a rural setting, a "homely girl" was an attractive girl possessed of homemaking skills, a homebody. In short, a very desirable person. As indeed she was. We had tea and cookies. They were shortbread cookies, and very good. I asked whether she had baked them. She had, clearly a homebody. I said they were great. She was pleased. She asked how I found England. I said I found it very interesting, and then volunteered that its girls were very pretty. She smiled at my last remark and noted that she had heard that Yanks were very outspoken. It was a pleasant encounter. She asked me to come by again, and I said I would be happy to, consistent with my military duties. I saw her several times thereafter, and on one visit she lent me her bicycle. This bicycle figures prominently in "a humorous adventure" I had, which I now relate.

The Glastonbury area in England, where my Cavalry Regiment was billeted, was not too distant from the city of Bath. From ancient times Bath was noted for its hot springs with their purported medicinal properties. After the Romans expanded their empire into the British Isles they used their considerable engineering skills to develop Bath into a spa. I was told by the locals I had met in the pub, or in their shops, that Bath was a beautiful example of Roman architecture and town planning, and that I should visit it and enjoy its charm. I broached my desire to visit Bath to Sara, and I suggested that she might accompany me there. She politely declined, saying she had chores to do at home. She saw my disappointment. She owned a bicycle, and she graciously offered to lend it to me so that I could bike to Bath. She told me it was a very scenic ride, the roadway was paved, and not too hilly. I should find my ride a very pleasant experience. Neither my brother nor I owned bikes as kids. And I had not ridden one as a young adult. I didn't want to tell Sara I had no bike riding experience. I merely said I hadn't been on one for a long time. That was no problem she said. The bike had no special gears, and she showed me how to brake. "Just get started and pedal", she said. "It's easy". Her house was built on a slight rise, and its driveway sloped down towards the street. Which was a good thing. I climbed onto the bike as Sara balanced it for me. I was in my dress OD (olive drab) uniform, not in fatigues. My cap was part of my uniform. I had found that if I ran very fast, or jumped about, my cap would often fly off my head. So before I started off on the bike I took off my cap and stuck it under the epaulet on my right shoulder. Sara gave me a slight push, and with a smile intended to reassure me, she said, "Remember, just keep pedaling. You'll be all right". And off I went. With both hands gripping the bike's handlebars I left Sara without daring to wave goodbye to her. Immediately, my downhill speed seemed to be too fast. I braked. Almost too much! The bike swerved and I almost lost my balance. I braked again, this time more tentatively. I slowed down, and didn't fall off. Hey!, this could be fun! "Just keep going, Arthur, and everything will be OK", I said to myself. (Often, when I am in a stressful situation, where doing something stupid might cause me grief, I speak to myself in the third person, thus ostensibly getting the benefit of another person's counsel. Don't laugh. That's my way of doing things. As they say in German, "Jedermann hat *sein* Vogel": "Everybody has his/her bird, *i.e.* idiosyncracies").

In England, people drive on the left, not as we do in the States. I rode the bike on the right, in the direction of oncoming traffic. But that was not a big mistake. England was at war. There was gas rationing, and so there were not too many motor vehicles on the road on this weekday that I was off to see Bath. I was pedaling along, gradually feeling more comfortable in my ability to move forward and stay upright at the same time. Some of the road was in asphalt, in England it was referred to as a macadam road, after the Scotsman, MacAdam, who invented this paving material. Some sections of the road were laid in cobblestones. This made for a bumpy ride, and some white knuckle experiences. After a mile or so of peddling I felt confident enough to steer diagonally across the road to the side where I should have been at the start. Now I was going with the traffic. The day was sunny and a slight breeze blew into my face and ruffled my hair. Hey! This *was* fun! But not for long. A US Military Police Jeep came out of nowhere, and there he was along side me. The driver called out, "Put your cap on soldier, you're out of uniform!" I nodded in acknowledgment of his order. He drove off. Now this was chicken shit! How could my being on a bike, bareheaded, adversely affect the conduct of the war? How, indeed? But an order was an order, especially when it came from a military cop—a species little known for humor. My cap was securely lodged under my right epaulet. I took my left hand off the handlebars and tugged at my cap. It hardly budged. And with only one hand controlling the bike I began to swerve. Screw it, I thought, and stopped tugging at my cap. The MP jeep was about 50 yards down the road ahead of me. The driver must have seen me in his rear view mirror, He slowed down as I pedaled by. The driver bellowed at me, "Put your goddamn cap on, or pull over!" "Yes, sir", I said. I was saying "Yes, sir" to a corporal! At that point I would have even saluted, if I could, and still stay upright. Again, and in desperation, I tugged at my cap. It came free! I stuck it on my head, with the bike again beginning to weave. I remembered Sara's admonition: "Just keep pedaling". I did.

After maybe a half hour of pedaling I approached the entrance to Bath. If my memory serves me correctly you enter Bath on a cobblestoned roadway flanked on both sides by stonework columns which tied into the remnants of an ancient stone wall which must once have encircled the city. The road opened into a cobblestoned circular drive or plaza. There were sidewalks with people on them, and shops. Among the people were several groups of young girls. They looked quite attractive with their short skirts fluttering in the breeze. I pedaled around once, never stopping, for fear of falling off in front of the girls. I pedaled around a second time. I had been noticed on my first go round. As I came around the second time, the girls were laughing. I heard one of them saying, "I believe he can't stop." She was right. I should have stopped, even if it meant falling down. Then I would have met these pretty women. But my vanity was greater, unfortunately, than my desire for erotic excitement, and I pedaled around and out of Bath, never stopping until I drove up to the white picket fence alongside the garden to Sara's house where I braked to a sharp stop, jumped off the bike, and grabbed hold of the fence to keep from falling. I then knocked on Sara's front door. She was surprised to see me back so soon. I thanked her for lending me the bike, relating none of my "adventures". I said I would arrange to see her again. I never did. Other events got in the way, as the reader will soon learn. As for further bike riding? I've never ridden a bike since.

Arthur, England, Winter 1943

Episode Eleven

In which I strike up a friendship with a pretty and witty Scottish girl, a member of England's Auxiliary Territorial Service (ATS). We have fun together.

It may have been a few days after my bike ride to Bath adventure that I met Marie. She was from Scotland. She was wearing a natty blue uniform, pert hat, tunic, blouse, tie, skirt and black oxfords which identified her as a member of the British women's home military service, the Auxiliary Territorial Service, known by its acronym as ATS. Some of our Yanks, who thought ATS women were easy sexual marks, translated the ATS acronym into Army Tail Service. I never used the term, believing it to be grossly inaccurate and demeaning. Anyway, I was walking in town when I spied her approaching me. When we drew abreast I smiled. She smiled back. I said, "Hi!". "Hello", she replied. We both stopped walking. "It's a nice day", I observed. "Aye, that it is", she confirmed in a Scottish brogue. I then asked whether she was going anywhere in particular. "No, I'm just taking a walk". "Mind if I come along?" I was being bold. She looked me up and down. I was wearing my dress ODs. They were clean and neat, my boots had a spit polish shine, and, if I have to say so myself, I was a handsome chap. She must have thought so, too. Because she laughed and said, "You can if you wish. It's a free country." And so I reversed my direction and fell in beside her. I learned her name. It was Marie which she pronounced as Mah-ree with the accent on the Mah. She learned mine. Why did a Yank have the name of an English King? I said my mother had been born in England and must have liked the names of ancient English kings, naming me Arthur and my younger brother, Harold. She noted the crossed sabers symbol on my jacket and asked what branch of service that was. I told her it was the Cavalry. She wanted to know whether we still rode horses. I told her, no, that we were now mechanized. She then inquired whether we still fought the Indians. She was putting me on. I said, no, but that's why we were in England. We had to fight somebody, might as well be the Nazis. We both laughed. As we strolled along we made idle conversation, punctuated by short periods of silence. Neither of us was completely at ease. Although my mouth was not working full blast, my eyes were. What they saw they liked. In her oxfords she was a tad shorter than I. Her hair was black and curly. Her eyes dark and sparkly. Her complexion fair to ruddy, with freckles across her cheeks and the bridge of her nose. Her figure was nice, all the curves in the right proportions and all in the right places. And as our brief exchange had already indicated, Marie had a good sense of humor. I'm sure Marie was also sizing me up as we walked. We were approaching one of the many pubs in the area. I asked whether she would like to have a drink. She thought that was a good idea. So we popped into the nearest pub. I asked what she would have. Marie asked what I liked. I said I liked most everything, but that I had taken a fancy to gin and orange. She said that sounded good, and I ordered one for each of us. We talked, and each of us had a second gin and orange. Both of us were now relaxed. Although we were not yet friends, neither were we total strangers.

Marie asked where I came from in the States. From Brooklyn, a part of New York City, I said. No reason to discuss New York City's complex political geography, with its five counties which were also boroughs. Where did she come from? "Oh, I'm not a big city person the likes of you. I come from a wee town called Findochty, way up in North East Scotland." She pronounced the "ch" in Findochty in the same throat clearing way as Germans pronounce "ch" in words like "doch". I repeated the name of her town with the proper gutteral pronunciation of the "ch". "My," Marie exclaimed, "you pronounce the name so well. Most Yanks can't." I explained I spoke German so pronouncing the gutteral "ch" was easy for me. We chatted a while longer. She looked at her watch and said she had to get back to her billet. Marie told me her ATS unit was housed in a large private dwelling which the government had taken over. She asked whether I minded walking back with her. I was pleased she asked, because I wanted to spend more time with her. I said, sure, and we walked to where she was billeted. At the door to the house she turned and asked if I was free the next day. I said I thought I could work something out. "Good", she said, "why don't you then come by and knock me up at 8 in the morning." I was taken aback by her request, as I shall shortly explain, and readily agreed. "It was nice meeting you, Arthur," she said as she entered the house. "It was nice meeting you, Marie," I said as she closed the door behind her.

Boy, I was on Cloud Nine! Here I had just met this pretty woman and she already wanted me to knock her up. They have an expression in German, *"Andere Länder, andere Sitten"* "Different countries, different customs". Apparently, if a woman in the UK took a fancy to you she didn't waste any time. Alas, my erotic expectations were ill conceived. I have earlier observed that although the inhabitants of the United Kingdom and those in the United States both speak a language called English, that there are pronounced (and pronunciation) differences between UK and USA English. *Cf.* "Homely/Homebody" with "Homely/Dog", as above noted in my meeting with Sara. So, too, were there marked differences between "knocking a pretty woman up" in the UK, and "knocking a pretty woman up" in the good old US of A. I soon learned that in jolly old England the phrase meant to knock on one's door in order to wake that person, or to announce to that person that you were at his or her door, ready to meet and go out together. In the States the expression has a salacious meaning, it being the slang expression for a man and a woman having sex in which the woman becomes pregnant. When I later related to Marie my initial misunderstanding of the phrase "To knock one up" she laughed with great gusto, and said she'd now be more careful in using that phrase when talking with other Yanks.

In any case, not sure as to what erotic adventures awaited me, if any, I knocked on the door of the house wherein Marie and her ATS mates were billeted. No one came to the door. I knocked again. No response. I tried the door knob. It turned, the door opened, and I walked into a wide foyer or anteroom which opened into a large living room, nicely appointed: oriental rugs on a parquet floor, with a large table, high backed chairs, a couple of floor lamps and a sofa/divan. Before one entered the living room there, to its right was a staircase, with square white painted bannisters, which led up to the next floor. A bell had tinkled when I opened the door. Apparently it had been heard by a young, tall, attractive woman who came towards me from the living room. She was wearing a uniform similar to Marie's, except on this woman's uniform the epaulets bore what appeared to me to be several button-like objects. She looked intently at me and politely inquired, "May I help you?" "Yes", I said. "Will you please tell Marie that Arthur is here." The uniformed woman stared at me for a moment or two, then she wheeled about and quickly made her way up the stairs. Within seconds Marie came dashing down the stairs. She grabbed my arm, and without even saying "Hello" literally pulled me out of the house. Once outside she began to laugh. "What's so funny?", I was puzzled. "You just sent my Commanding Officer upstairs to get me! And she wasn't very pleased to be made into a messenger!" We both laughed. I remarked that I didn't know that the woman who inquired of me was an officer. "Didn't you see the pips on her shoulders?", Marie asked. The pips, what I took for decorative buttons, were used to indicate British Officers' military rank. One learns something every day. But I never did learn how to identify a British Officer's rank from his/her combination of pips. I guess acquiring this specialized knowledge was not worth my effort.

Marie and I went out several times after that incident. Indeed, I would, most likely, have continued to go out with her until it was time for my Cavalry Regiment to move to English Channel staging areas in preparation for the invasion of France. She was fun to be with. Ideas of love and marriage never entered my mind, although other ideas did. However, as a consequence of a series of run-ins which I had with military authority, as I shall duly relate, my opportunities to spend fun time with Marie were cut short after a few more outings with her. I believe it was our second time together when Marie remarked that I had such nice teeth. I was pleased by her observation, but a tad puzzled by it. I smiled and thanked her for her kind words. Then the reason for her comment came clear. She asked, "Are your teeth real?" "Of course they are", I replied. "Oh, sure", she said with a tone of disbelief, and, to my great surprise, she stretched out her hand, grabbed my upper teeth, and yanked down on them. I yelped. Naturally, my teeth stayed put. "Hey!, why did you do that?" "Well", answered Marie, a bit chagrined., "I thought they looked too good to be real, so if they were false, and I yanked on them the plate would come out." She apologized, and gave me a light kiss on my cheek to show she was sorry. I smiled in forgiveness, more broadly than necessary, to show off my teeth. She laughed and then, more seriously, told me that even as a child she had poor teeth, lots of cavities, and that all her family had bad teeth; that whenever she saw someone with a mouth full of nice teeth she presumed they were false. Maybe its our diet or our water, she speculated.

I think this is a good place to talk about the character and mores of the civilian British People (and under the rubric British People I include the English, Scots, Welsh, and UK resident Irish) I observed during my stay in the UK. These people had been at war since September 1939. Their troops had suffered severe defeats, and miraculous rescues, as at Dunkirk, and had won great victories, as in North Africa, but with heavy loss of life and materiel. The war was not only across the Channel, or in Africa, the Middle East or Asia. It was on their soil itself. They were exposed to Buzz Bombs and *Luftwaffe* attacks. At sea their merchant marine and Navy were frequent targets of German U Boats, with heavy losses of lives and vessels and precious cargoes. Families were separated. Food stuffs and petrol were rationed. Blackouts were obligatory when the sun set. The people were under stress, yet they bore up remarkably well under the strain. I admired them.

From what I observed, the people, viewed as a societal entity, and not as discrete individuals, demonstrated certain common traits. As a caveat, I note that I was stationed in a semi-rural part of England. Were I stationed in a large cosmopolitan community, such as London, my impressions might have been different. Hence, I write only of what I saw and experienced in my limited part of England. As a generalization the local inhabitants were restrained in expressing their feelings in public. Adults, male and female, would walk by me and rarely make eye contact. If they did, there would be a tight lipped smile, and they would be gone. Sometimes, a clipped "Good Day". The kids were more open. They would smile broadly, wave, and say such pleasantries as "Hi Yank!". Teen age boys might occasionally ask me questions about the type of unit I was in, and some might tell me of a father, brother or sister away in some branch of the British Military Services. A teen age girl, walking alone, would generally avoid eye contact. But if she were in a group of like aged girls, there would be eye contact, smiles and sometimes a wee bit of flirting. Young women walking alone, and here I am referring to those who I guessed were in their twenties and thirties (guessing a woman's age accurately was never my strong suit), whether in civvies or in a service uniform, would generally avoid eye contact. When walking in groups they would smile back when I smiled, and Hellos would be exchanged,

I was not offended by these demonstrations of public aloofness. Back in the States I was a big city boy, surrounded by millions of people, with streets, subways and buses almost always filled with bustling humanity. I don't recall making much eye contact, or exchanging pleasantries with others in the crowds about me. Further, although American troops in the UK were welcome guests, we were still strangers. In wartime England, with all its stresses, it was *de rigueur* for a Brit to be stiff upper lip and reserved in public. But among themselves, or in relaxed public gatherings, as in pubs and music halls, these same Brits would be considerably more outgoing and, indeed, very earthy. I recall a communal picnic on a sunny Sunday afternoon in a public park. People of all ages were present, among them British military personnel in uniform. Everyone was having a jolly good time, eating, drinking, singing, playing games. I noted several bottles of gin and a couple of kegs of brew which, assuredly, were contributing to the festivities. I was with Marie. As we walked by this festive group I caught some of the lyrics being sung. I can no longer recall all the words, but I do remember a couple of lines, to wit: "Roll me over, in the clover, roll me over, lay me down, and do it again!" The words "over" and "clover" were drawn out in the singing, The women at the picnic sang the song as lustily as the men. I commented to Marie, "Boy, that's a pretty sexy song to sing in mixed company". Marie, retorted, "Arthur, for a Yank you are a prude."

Marie's remark is best understood when placed in this context: (1) Although the British (and remember I use the term "British" in its broadest sense, as earlier noted) can be seen as aloof and stand-offish when they are in their "stay out of my space", personal public mode. But they are quite earthy when they are clannish, or in their intimate circles of privacy. Talking about sex was not a taboo among the British I observed in 1944-45. And had one strolled by a wooded area in the late afternoon, or at dusk, on a windless day, the sounds one heard would have have been aural evidence of either a sylvan creature scuttling through the underbrush, or of two human beings lustily engaged in concupiscent congress; (2) With so many of their menfolk away in military service, the young women of the UK found the influx of young American troops to be a pleasant invasion. Many of them enjoyed the attentions, and sometimes, the intentions of us Yanks. But these young women never did so by deprecating the virility of their absent men. Marie told me that British women joked that the only difference between us and their absent Brits at war was this: "You Yanks are over here, over paid, and over sexed.". An apt description.

Episode Twelve

In which I begin to learn the secrets of sex, but am still a virgin at the end of the episode.

I was a virgin before I went overseas and found Anneliese Baur, my first, and only love. There, I have revealed a secret previously known only to Anneliese. There was nothing in my physiology which precluded me from being sexually active in the States. My testes were working overtime producing testosterone. My hormones were humming along in top form. But I was, as Marie had sensed, a bit prudish. Brought on primarily by my Jewish religious upbringing. Sexual activity, *per se*, was not sinful. God wanted us to be fruitful and multiply. The Talmud taught us that God instilled lust into a man so that he would be physically attracted to a woman. But for a man to possess a woman, in the sense of making her a vital part of himself, and in turn, becoming a vital part of her being, lust had to transmuted into love, and this love then sanctified by holy matrimony. I enjoyed being in the company of attractive and witty women. They were fun to talk to, pleasant to look at, and they aroused me sexually. As a class, in comparison with men, I thought women were stronger, more sensitive and more intelligent. I was happy to be a man. If there were any truth in the concept of reincarnation, I would want to come back as a man. Giving birth never struck me as being fun. As a callow, pre-military service youth, I tended to put women, again, as a class, on a pedestal. I conceived of all women as being purer than men when it came to matters of sex. This, of course, was a gross misconception (which brings to mind a comment by Mark Twain, who, in the course of a lecture, was asked by a woman in the audience, what the difference was between a man and a woman. Twain thought for a moment, and then answered, "Madame, I can't conceive.") Clearly, my Jewish upbringing concerning lust, love and the sanctity of marriage, and my misconceptions concerning the sexual purity of women, inhibited my approach to sexual adventures. But inhibition did not constitute preclusion. However, as I have already declared, my beautiful and belóved Anneliese Baur was my first and only love.

Life is a learning experience. A trite, yet true observation. The lessons life offers to those eager to acquire knowledge range from the most mundane, to the most sublime. Further, the desire to learn must be coupled with the opportunity to learn. And opportunity is part choice and part chance. I was affected by all these factors, though wholly unaware of them, when, in November 1942 I enlisted in the Cavalry, U.S. Army. The Army was to be my life for three years, and during that time it would teach me many practical things, such as how to drive stick shift vehicles, how to double clutch large trucks, how to send and receive messages in Morse Code, and the proper way to hold and operate a pair of pliers when doing electrical work. This knowledge was once most useful to me in the Service, and though I remember these things still, this learning is of little use to me today. The vehicles I now drive are all automatic transmission; I have no need to communicate in Morse Code; I no longer lay wire from point A to point B, but I do have occasion to use a pair of pliers, and when I do, I hold them correctly. During the three years that my life was encapsulated within the four corners of my military service I also had the opportunity to learn other things, less tangible than the skills above enumerated, but of greater importance in helping shape my life. The Army presented me with chances to learn that wit, a way with words, and noble aims were wholly worthless when used as weapons by a Private, First Class, to fight what he saw as an abuse of military authority. Being beat about the head and shoulders—in a sense more psychological than physical—was a material part of my learning which only a military organization can teach.

My entry into the Army at age 19, sexually unschooled, also gave me the chance to couple my desire to learn about sex with the opportunity to do so. Thus the Army became the arena in which I experienced my rite of passage, tentative as that first encounter was, into the magic realm of sex. Life is a learning experience, as I have already said, and I was learning some thing about a vital life force, which, when properly applied, would become an ever flowing fountain of joy.

The episode I now relate concerns my first sexually oriented experience with a woman (I am heterosexual, thus my sexual feelings are directed solely to the opposite sex). Although I was a big city lad, and a college junior when I enlisted in the Cavalry, I was ignorant about many basic things, among them the mysterious workings of sex. Service in the military did not solely give me the opportunity to learn the arts of war, it also gave me the chance to learn the arts of life. It is in this light that the following episode should be read.

Marie and I enjoyed seeing each other. Our times together were fleeting, a few hours at most, and only several times a week. Each of us had military duties to fulfill. Thus, when together, we tried to make the most of each occasion. Marie took me to places I would otherwise not have gone to, such as a fund raising auction for hospitalized British troops. One of the items which drew a high winning bid was a large fresh lemon from the British West Indies. Quite a treat in wartime England. And then there was that unforgettable late afternoon walk, arm and arm, through a wooded area when, having observed other couples, some in uniform, some in civvies, engaging in amorous activities, some more discrete than others, I felt emboldened enough to to pause beneath a low limbed, heavily boughed oak tree. I pressed Marie up against the trunk of the tree, put my arms about her and kissed her on her mouth and cheeks. Previously I would have kissed her lightly on her cheeks or forehead upon saying good night. She did not push me away. I began to unbutton her tunic. She did not stop me. I began to unbutton her blouse. She did not resist. She had put her arms about me. Now she dropped them to her side. I gently spread apart her unbuttoned blouse. She wore no bra. I was surprised. I had thought all women wore bras. Her breasts were round and tipped with small pink nipples. I traced the contours of her breasts with my fingers. She gasped, but said nothing. I had never touched a woman's breasts, nor, other than in photos or artworks, seen a woman's breasts. As I fondled Marie's breasts there was another surprise. Her nipples became enlarged and hard to my touch. A novice in love making I was learning that when a woman is sexually or physically aroused, her nipples, engorged with blood, increase in size and harden. I was fully aroused. I pressed myself against Marie. I was sure she felt me. I lowered my face to her breasts, and cupping them in my hot hands, I kissed them repeatedly. Her arms, until now idle at her sides, rose, grasped my head and pressed me to her. I was on fire! I ran my right hand down her belly, and groped still further down. Marie gripped my arms and softly said, "Please don't". I stopped. Should I press on despite her request? I was unsure, and inexperienced. Did "Please don't" really mean stop? Or was this the way the game was played? I didn't know. I had no desire to hurt or demean Marie. I withdrew my hand. I stepped back and helped button her clothing. Her clothing in order, she took my hand, and, with nary a word being said, we walked back to her quarters. There, at the door she squeezed my hand, gave me a peck on the cheek, smiled, softly said, "Good night, Arthur", opened the door and went in.

I couldn't tell whether what had happened between Marie and me would end our relationship, or whether it would start a different one. So I waited a couple of days, and then walked over to her quarters. She was in, and seemed pleased to see me. Marie said she had a few chores to finish and then could go out for a bit. She asked me to wait in the living room. While sitting there her Commanding Officer came into the room. The one I had used as a messenger. I jumped up to show that I recognized she was an officer. "How do you do, Ma'm, I said. She nodded curtly, said nothing and left the room. Shortly thereafter Marie came downstairs and we went for a walk, and then for a drink at one of the pubs. Neither one of us spoke of what had happened, although I am sure it was as much on her mind as it was on mine. Marie had a good sense of humor, at least she always laughed at my jokes. And Marie was always telling me jokes, all quite good, and some a tad off-color. That afternoon in the pub she told me an off-color joke I still remember. Here it is:

An ATS girl came back to her billet and told the other girls that a Free French Officer (Free French were the French soldiers who had escaped from Nazi occupied France and were under the command of General Charles DeGaulle) had offered to take her for a drive into the countryside. Once out of town he made sexual advances to her. She said no, got out of the car and walked all the way back to her quarters. That was a long walk, one of her listeners noted. "Yes, it was, but my legs helped me. They were my best friends." The next day the ATS girl said, a British Air Force Officer took her for a drive in the country. When the British Officer made sexual advances to her she got out of the car and walked all the way back. "My legs helped me again. My legs were my best friends." A few days later the same ATS girl tells her roommates, that a handsome American Army Officer was going to take her for a drive into the country. Later that day her roommates see her drive back with the American Officer. They ask her, "Did the Yank Officer make sexual advances?" "Yes, indeed, "the ATS girl replied. "Then why didn't you get out of the car and walk back? You always said your legs were your best friends." "Yes", said the ATS girl. "But there comes a time when even the best of friends must part."

I laughed. It was a great joke. I got the joke. Or did I? A few days later, by reason of my various disputes with regimental brass, I was confined to quarters and couldn't go into town any more. Confinement to quarters was only the first chapter in a story filled with a sorry series of events which I shall relate in due course. I was unable to see Marie any longer. I missed her company. But I had her address, and we communicated even when I was in combat. We wrote to each other until I met Anneliese. After telling

Marie about Anneliese she stopped writing. Why she stopped is a story I shall also tell. In any event, while briefly relaxing after a combat recon mission in France I recalled Marie's joke about the ATS girl whose legs were her best friends. It suddenly came to me that Marie may have been subtly telling me that just as that girl's best friends, her legs, must part, that Marie's "Please don't" wasn't fixed in concrete. Possibly so. But it didn't matter. I liked Marie very much. She was a fine young woman, and fun to be with. But the idea of falling in love with Marie never came to mind.

It was my destiny to discover love the instant I gazed upon my beautiful Anneliese Baur. The rapture I experienced at that divinely ordained moment has never left me. My belóved Anneliese is no longer by my side. How sad, and yet, how comforting it is, that the ecstasy I felt on first seeing Anneliese Baur can still be relived.

Episode Thirteen

In which I am denied my authorized promotion to Technician Fifth Grade (T/5) a non-commissioned Officer's rating I should have received as the lead radio operator in HQ. The Colonel gave my rating to his jeep driver, not entitled to such a rating. I was left responsible to maintain my expensive radio equipment, and fulfill my duties—but without the higher rank and pay. I react swiftly and deftly, and my confrontation with arbitrary authority increases.

I turn now to a recital of a series of adventures, or better said, misadventures, which I have denominated as my "encounters/run-ins" with the Army. The encounters I now relate took place in England before I crossed the English Channel and there engaged in combat. I had several more, of lesser moment, when on the European continent than those soon to be described, but none of these affected my ability to perform fully my combat or post combat duties. However, they all figured in shaping the course of my military service, which, despite its many convolutions, was predestined to lead me to my beautiful and belóved Anneliese Baur. Thus, episodes, which, when they happened, appeared to me to be negative, were, in truth, unrecognized harbingers of wonderful things to come.

Before I recount my run-ins with the Army while in England, and the impact upon me of such encounters, I believe a dissertation upon the nature of military organizations (which I shall endeavor to set forth as succinctly as I can) will be helpful in explaining my conduct in dealing with the Army, and its reaction to this conduct. Military bodies, even those created by the most democratic states, are autocratic institutions. They are highly stratified, their composition is regulated by tables of organization, and administered through a chain of command. This chain of command consists of three basic groupings of personnel: The highest is the Officers' Corps, in the U.S. Army, from Warrant Officer through Four Star General, with the intermediate grades being, Second Lieutenant, First Lieutenant, Captain, Major, Lt. Colonel, Colonel, One, Two and Three Star Generals. The next series of rankings below that of being an Officer, consisted of Non-Commissioned Officers, or Non-Coms. In World War II the lowest ranking non-com was a Corporal, or if he was doing a technical job, such as being a radio operator, he was called a Technician 5th Grade, or T/5. Then there were a slew of Sergeants, ranging up to Sergeant Major. Finally, there is the lowest grouping, the enlisted personnel, the lowest in WWII being the Private, and then the Private First Class or PFC. In WWII non-Officer personnel (and in many instances, inclusive of Non-Coms) were referred to generically as GIs. GI was short for Government Issue, this being the designation for materiel furnished by the Government for use by its troops.

Ranking or ratings were important. The higher they were, the greater your stature and authority in the military body of which you were a member. As your rankings increased, so did your pay and privileges, and, of course, so did the duties and responsibilities which went with the higher rank. I have emphasized the issue of rank because that issue was the basis for one of my disputes with my Cavalry Regiment, as delineated below.

A military organization is a unique agency of government. It is an armed body, trained in the arts of war, for the performance of three duties: (1) to protect the State from foreign enemies, (2) to quell domestic insurrection, and (3) to act as an instrument to enforce the State's foreign policies. To achieve success in fulfilling these duties a military organization must be a disciplined body. As noted, such an organization is autocratic. It exercises absolute authority over its personnel through ever ascending layers of command, and in accordance with carefully drafted regulations. Thus, the attainment and maintenance of discipline in a military organization requires (1) that all personnel, from the highest command levels, to the lowest of enlisted ranks, must comply fully with these regulations, and (2) that these regulations must be fairly applied to all personnel. The granting of promotions and commendations, the assignment of duties, and the meting out of punishment, must, therefore, be done in strict conformity with the applicable regulations. Discipline suffers, and military authority is questioned, when personnel discover that favoritism and bias/prejudice play a rôle in the application of regulations.

In an autocratic organization, such as the military, the questioning or criticism by the lower ranks of the conduct of those over them can be an exercise fraught with danger for the questioner. "Question Authority" was a popular phrase seen on auto bumper stickers in the USA in the last three decades of the 20th century. A commendable concept, certainly one befitting our civil society, which, in the words of James Madison in "The Federalist papers", was described as a republican form of government based upon democratic principles. But we all know, particularly in times of war, or threats of war, that citizens who dissent from the government's position are often labeled by those in governing power, and their allies, as unpatriotic trouble makers. Such dissenters may even find themselves the target of criminal prosecution. And then there are the "whistle blowers", those dedicated employees of government, who reveal publicly, how their agencies, or their superiors, have failed to fulfill their duties, or have breached the public trust. A grateful public will applaud their acts of courage in coming forward. But there are those in authority in government who may make that whistle blower's continuing career in government a less than happy one. And the same result can obtain with whistle blowers in the military. If questioning authority and whistle blowing can be "frowned upon" in an open democratic society, how much more is such conduct open to official censure when directed towards an autocratic society such as the military, and in my case that part of it constituted as the 4th Cavalry Regiment? The censure imposed upon me was considerable, and uncalled for, as the reader shall discover, especially since much of it was motivated by anti-semitism. However, in retrospect, all's well that ends well, After my run-ins with the 4th Cavalry's brass, and their consequences were behind me, my subsequent career in the Army was an excellent one. I fought as a Cavalry Trooper in France, Luxembourg, Belgium and Germany, was twice hurt, was awarded The Purple Heart, The Bronze Star and Five Campaign Battle Stars. After combat ended I served in The Army's Military Government Branch, in the U.S. Zone of Occupation in Germany, and was Honorably Discharged after three years of service to my country. But the best part of my military service in WWII was that it was the vehicle which led me to discover my beautiful and belóved Anneliese Baur. Jacob worked 14 years to possess his beloved Rachel. As the reader will learn, I got the better deal. I "worked" only four years and three months to possess my heart's desire.

My first dispute with my Regiment arose on the issue of promotion. As I have noted, rank in the military is an important factor. As the Chief Radio Operator for Headquarters Troop I was the Regiment's top communications enlisted man. According to the Regiment's Table of Organization the rank of the person filling that position was supposed to be a T/5, a Technician Fifth Grade, a Corporal, a two striper. In the States I had been promoted from buck Private to PFC, Private First Class, a one striper. Shortly before the Regiment embarked for service overseas I had inquired of my Troop Commander, a First Lt., when I would receive my T/5 rating. He informed me that according to the Army's Regulations the promotion would be effective once we were stationed overseas. That sounded good to me. I would get the prestige of another stripe in recognition of the responsibilities of my position, plus the privilege of being free from KP (Kitchen Police: work in the kitchen and mess facilities, such as peeling potatoes and cleaning pots, pans, stoves, floors and mess tables). I would also receive increased compensation, the bulk of which would be sent home to my folks. However, things did not work out that way.

Soon after we arrived In the UK the new ratings/promotions were listed on the HQ Troop's Bulletin Board. I looked for my promotion. It wasn't there. I couldn't understand this. My Troop Commander had told me in the States that I would be promoted once we were overseas. We were, But I wasn't. Why not? In the States my Troop Commander had been a First Lt., now, overseas, he had been promoted to Captain. From one silver bar to two. Why didn't I get the called for promotion?

My Captain explained that the Regiment had only so many T/5 positions in its Table of Organization. Under the Table of Organization the driver assigned as the driver for the Regiment's Commanding Officer, our Colonel, was only a PFC. The driver would drive the Colonel to the British Officers' Club. While the Colonel was in the Officers' Club his driver would have to sit in his vehicle awaiting the Colonel's return. Near the Officers Club was a British NCO's Club, open only to non-commissioned officers, from the rank of corporal through the various Sergeants' rankings. The Colonel's driver, known in the Army vernacular as his dog robber, meaning he would do anything his Colonel told him to do, even to robbing food from a dog, was stuck in his parked vehicle while the Colonel was in his Club. The driver could see the NCOs' Club from his parked vehicle but his rank barred his entrance. And so there he sat, sometimes in the cold, sometimes in the rain, waiting for the Colonel to leave his Officers' Club and be driven back to the fancy Manor House I have already described. The driver must have complained that his rank prevented him from entering the NCOs' Club. The Colonel fixed that. He promoted his driver to the rank of T/5, a rating the driver was not entitled to have, according to the Table of Organization (TO) By gifting his dog robber with an unauthorized T/5 rating the Colonel exceeded the number of T/5 ratings allowed by the TO. How did the Colonel overcome this breach of the TO? Ah, the reader has guessed it. He took the T/5 rating intended for the Chief Radio Operator, that was me, and gave it to his driver. Thus, the Regimental Table of Organization did not show any excess

T/5 positions. As a consequence, despite the fact I was doing my job—and doing it well—and for which I was entitled to receive the designated T/5 rating, I did not get my promotion as called for by the Regulations. The Colonel had tossed my promotion as a bone to his dog robber, and left me with the responsibilities of my position without the requisite increased privileges and compensation. Was I upset? You betcha!

In clear, loud language, I complained to my Troop Commander, newly promoted to the rank of Captain. I was being mistreated I said. The promotion rightfully belonged to me. The TO said so. I was doing the work the rating called for, and I wanted that rating. Sorry, the Captain said, your promotion is gone. I pointed out to the Captain that I was only asking for what I was entitled to receive under the Regulations, that I could have stayed out of the Service, but, instead, gave up my student deferment and enlisted, that all I wanted was to be treated fairly, and that meant getting my promotion. Sorry, the Captain said again. He was getting annoyed with my arguing with him. So he tried to patronize me. "If you were so patriotic to give up college to serve your country, then why be so concerned about promotions. You enlisted to serve your country, and that's what you are doing, getting promotions shouldn't matter that much." Now I was getting further pissed. "Well", I said to the Captain, "If promotions don't matter that much why didn't you turn down your Captain's promotion and stay a Lieutenant?" His face reddened. "That's enough, Katz. There's nothing more to discuss. Dismissed!" I gave him a long, cold stare, turned, and left his office without saluting.

As a Radio Operator and Armored Car Commander, I had to sign various documents concerning my obligations to maintain in operating order all radio and related equipment assigned to me, and installed in the armored car in which I would be performing my duties. If I abused, destroyed or lost any of the equipment assigned to me, my monthly pay would be docked the cost of repairing or replacing the equipment concerned. I said to myself: "Shit, who needs these fucking responsibilities if I'm not getting the rank and pay which goes with the job!" And so, still steaming from the manner the Army was treating me, better said, mistreating me, I headed for the Motor Pool where the Regiment's vehicles, my armored car included, were parked.

I climbed onto the vehicle, and lowered myself down into its turret. I'll explain later how the interior of the turret looked and operated. Once inside, I disconnected all the radio equipment, and related cables, within the turret. I then placed all this gear on the hood of the vehicle's rear mounted engine, climbed out, loaded the equipment and cables into my arms—quite a heavy load—and headed back to my Captain's Office. I barged past the orderly and, unannounced, entered my Captain's Office. I plunked down all the stuff in my arms onto his desk. The Captain looked up at me in surprise. "What the hell is this?", he said annoyed and perplexed. I explained. I told him that in light of my treatment, if this was a civilian job, I'd quit. But this was the Army, and I couldn't quit, and wouldn't, in any case, but if I am still responsible for all the equipment, while not getting the proper rank and pay that go with the job and its responsibilities, then I wouldn't do the job and assume its responsibilities. That's it! I wheeled about and left his Office, without saluting. I was still pissed at the way the Army had treated me. I felt what I had done was OK. One trait of mine has always colored my behavior. I have never wanted more than I was entitled to receive. But I would fight fiercely to get what I believed was my due. That's how I looked at what I had just done.

A day after I had dumped all my radio operator's equipment onto my Captain's desk I was summoned to the Colonel's Office. The Colonel had been told what I had done, and he remembered me from the incident during our desert war games exercises in the California deserts. He said nothing about the issue of rank, where his dog robber got my T/5 rating, and which had motivated my equipment dumping action. Instead, he smiled and said I was a feisty kid, and that he liked that piss and vinegar spirit in his Troopers. He noted that I had enlisted out of college. "Why?"

I told the Colonel I had enlisted to fight fascism. "That's fine", he said, "when we cross the Channel you'll have plenty of time to fight fascism." I replied, "I'm fighting it now, sir." "Now?", the Colonel was puzzled. "Where?" "In the U.S. Army, sir". The Colonel was no longer smiling. I could see his jaws clenching. He stared at me for a couple of seconds. He then snapped, "Dismissed". I saluted and left his Office. I had taken on the Army, and it would prove to be a very uneven competition.

Nothing unusual happened between me and the Army for the next day or so. I pulled KP (Kitchen Police) and thought nothing of it. I presumed it was my turn, and PFCs such as me, not being non-coms, pulled KP. KP chores would ordinarily come around about once a week.

Episode Fourteen

In which I continue to be a gadfly to arbitrary Army authority when I object to the Colonel's refusal to let us enlisted Troopers use one of the many toilets in the Manor House, rather than evacuate our bladders and bowels in primitive open air sheds. I get the Medics to require the Colonel to give us access to a Toilet in the House, and this further raises the Colonel's ire towards me.

The reader may recall that earlier on I had gone to some pains to describe the English Manor House in which the Officers of my Regiment were quartered, and how these quarters contrasted with those provided for the enlisted ranks. As the reader may also recall, I delineated the primitive, open air toilet facilities which the enlisted ranks were required to use. Although the British Isles lie in a northern latitude in which Winter and early Spring can be very cold, the Gulf Stream makes the weather in these seasons more temperate for the inhabitants of England than that experienced by persons living at the same latitude on the American and European continents. But this is not to suggest that Winter and early Spring weather in Southwest England bears any resemblance in those seasons to the weather in Southern California or Florida. It does get cold and windy, and it rains frequently. Not a lot of fun, when you have to go out and shit into coal buckets while sitting on wooden planks in an open area where your face, your bare ass and your naked legs (pants down around your ankles) are exposed to the elements. And all the while you are being so demeaned you think of the Regiment's Officers, and non-coms comfortably evacuating their bowels while warmly concealed within the comfortable confines of their regal English Manor House just up the road a piece.

My enlisted brethren in our Headquarters Troop complained of the gross disparity between their toilet facilities and those enjoyed by their military superiors. Several said they'd rather risk being constipated than sit out there in the open freezing their balls off. "That's a stupid thing to do", I noted. "OK, professor (the title, as I have already stated, was used pejoratively), if you are so fucking smart, what would you do?" My wit and wisdom were being challenged. And I rose to the challenge—as a fish to the bait—with the same ultimate result. I came up with a neat idea. I would go on sick call and tell the doctors about our primitive toilet facilities, and how, if the enlisted men did not get some indoor toilets, there would soon be lots of constipated guys with lots of colds. I hoped the medics would then require the Colonel to give us enlisted men indoor toilet facilities. I related my scheme to my "buddies" (the reader will shortly discover why I put quotation marks around this designation of comradery), and the next morning I went on sick call and was taken to the nearest field hospital.

The Army doctor I saw that morning in the Walk-In Clinic was a Captain. He looked at me and asked, "Katz, what's wrong with you?" "Nothing", I said, "but unless certain things change I could soon be sick, along with a lot of other guys in my Troop." He looked at me as if I were crazy. So I quickly explained the situation. The Captain was intrigued. That didn't hurt in getting him to look for a way to be helpful to my "buddies" and me. He paged through some Army medical manuals. After a few minutes the Captain said, "Katz, I think I have a solution to your problem." And here he read me several portions from the Army Medical Regulations he had before him. In substance, this is what he read to me: "Our medical Regs require that all personnel of all ranks be billeted only in facilities where all can have access to adequate sanitary facilities. As I read the Regs, the phrase 'adequate sanitary facilities' means those in which their use will not be inherently dangerous or pose threats to the health of the user. The Regs further state that a military unit's commanding officer shall not billet his troops in any quarters which do not provide adequate sanitary facilities for *all* his troops, this means, inclusive of all ranks. Quarters which lack adequate sanitary facilities for all personnel must be closed and new quarters found which comply with these Regs. However, quarters need not be closed if they can be modified to provide adequate sanitary facilities for all the unit's personnel, regardless of rank." Boy, what the Captain read made me feel good!

He then asked me whether the Manor House had a number of interior toilets. I told him it did, and that there was a toilet next to the servants' entrance. The Captain said it would be hard to condemn a regimental HQ, but if he could get the Colonel to let the enlisted men use this servants' entrance toilet, he would not move to condemn the HQ. for medical reasons. He said he would inspect the Manor House that afternoon and explain the adequate sanitary facilities Regs to the Colonel. He felt that the Colonel would let us use the servants' entrance toilet. There were 57 enlisted personnel (Sergeants excluded from the count) in Headquarters Troop. But one inside toilet was better than none.

When I returned from sick call I was pretty jaunty. I told my "buddies" what I had done—that unless the Colonel gave us access to at least the servants' entrance toilet—the medics would condemn the Manor House as the Regiment's HQ, and the Colonel would have to find new quarters which met the sanitary facility Regulations. All the guys appeared pleased with what I had done, and a few even personally thanked me. So far, so good. But not for long. At about 4 a.m. the following morning—it was still dark outside—all 57 enlisted personnel were routed out of our cots and ordered to assemble in the cobblestoned courtyard of the Manor House. There, all of us were lined up in a single file. By chance, I was the last man at the left end of the line. The Regimental Master Sergeant faced us and bellowed out, "Which one of you fuck-ups turned in the Colonel!" And with the precision equal to that of a practiced ballet chorus line, the right hands of all 56 of my "buddies" simultaneously pointed to me standing at the end of the row, The Master Sergeant exploded, "I knew it was you, Katz, I knew it!" We got our indoor toilet later that day. And I got the start of "The Treatment". The Colonel and his Staff had it with me! Did they ever!

Episode Fifteen

In which the Colonel, having had it with me, and my private war against fascism in the Service, orders "Let The Treatment begin!".

    First, I was confined to quarters. That meant I couldn't leave the grounds on which our Troop was billeted. Thus, I couldn't go into town, and I never saw Marie again. However, I was able to speak with her by phone, once or twice, and later, to communicate by mail. Then I went on the KP detail, which covered all three meals, and was, therefore, an all day job. When I got off the KP work and sacked out I was awakened after a few hours and told to go on Guard Duty. This was a ceremonial operation. No one expected a *Luftwaffe* aerial assault, complete with *Fallschirmjägertruppen*, paratroopers, landing on our Headquarters. But the Manor House was the HQ. of the Regiment, and the Colonel wanted, around the clock, an armed soldier standing at the gate to the courtyard. Someone who would snap to attention and salute whenever US or Allied Officers would visit the Regimental HQ. Those standing guard at night were told they were also acting as a sentry. This meant they had the duty to challenge all personnel seeking entry into the courtyard of the Manor House after nightfall. Those standing guard at night were supposed to call out, "Who goes there?," as someone approached. If the approaching person was an officer, the guard then saluted. By the nature of the ceremonial nothingness of the position, the night time performance of guard duty soon became very informal. If the guard recognized the person approaching he would not call out, "Who goes there?" Instead he would salute if it were an officer approaching and say "Hi, sir!", or some other friendly greeting to a non-officer.
    There were two ironwork gates at the entrance to the courtyard. They were never closed. As I have earlier noted, there was a high stone wall encircling the Manor House. Each of the gates was

attached to a square masonry pillar, each pillar being about five feet wide on each of its four sides, with each pillar being about ten feet tall. The hinged open iron gates were set behind the wall. The wall itself was about two feet thick, which meant that the courtyard gate pillars projected out about a foot and a half from the front and back facings of the wall. Those standing guard did so in fair weather and foul. I believe it was OK to wear your raincoat if it was raining when you pulled your guard duty. But umbrellas were never allowed. This was war, man, and umbrellas were not government issue for guard duty. During inclement weather a guard could lessen his exposure to the elements by standing within the cove formed by the gate pillar's foot and a half outcropping from the wall. Standing there put the guard in the lee of the wall—with its limited cover from the elements—without obstructing his view of the entry to the courtyard.

"The Treatment" now being accorded me (perhaps I should write, being inflicted upon me) was so structured that I would go from KP to Guard duty *every day*, with only a few hours of sleep in between. I was getting very tired. But I didn't bitch. I wasn't about to give the Colonel and my Troop Captain that satisfaction. I don't recall how long The Treatment went on, perhaps a week or so before it evolved into the more serious phase I now recount. The season was either late Winter or early Spring. The weather had been blustery and rainy, drab and unpleasant days at a time. There I was, standing in the rain which had begun to fall after I had gone on guard duty. I was wearing no raincoat. It was the middle of the night. I was dead tired, hungry and cold and the rain was pelting down. I was getting soaked. To shield myself, if only partially, from the wind and rain, I nestled behind the cove in the wall I described above. On both sides of this cove stood tall dormant shrubs. From my new vantage point I could clearly observe all who approached the courtyard gates. But those approaching me could not easily see me standing there, sheltered within the crook of the wall and partially hidden by the dry shrubbery. Someone was approaching. It was an Officer. I recognized him when he was abreast of me, about 6 paces away. He was on the Colonel's Staff. I didn't challenge him. I was about to step out from the shelter of the cove and salute him when he saw me. I believe he was startled to see me in the crook of the wall. I was not standing out in the open where he had expected I would be. He looked at me very sternly and said, "Soldier, you're not on your post!", and he walked briskly past me.

Episode Sixteen

In which I am given a summary courtmartial, found guilty of being away from my guard post (a false charge) and sentenced to five years imprisonment.

The next morning I was awakened early and told to report to the Sergeant Major. He told me that the Colonel was fed up with me, that I had been reported as being away from my guard post, and further, that I was also asleep. I was surprised, to say the least. I tried to explain that I had taken shelter from the weather, but could still see everything, and that I was not asleep. Tired, sure, but not asleep. How could I sleep standing up? I was told to shut up. The Sergeant Major then informed me that I was going to be court-martialed, that people were shot for sleeping on guard duty during wartime. He smiled when he told me these dire things. He clearly relished seeing my discomfort. I was exhausted, emotionally drained. I heard what he said. I knew I was in trouble. In deep shit!

I must have turned off my emotional system because I remember very little of the court-martial phase. It was as if I was sleep walking through everything that was happening—as if I was draped in an invisible mantle which shielded me from the harshness of reality. I know *now* why I *then* reacted as I did, and why I suffered so little lasting emotional trauma: I was experiencing a *series* of events, negative though they seemed to be when they happened, which were part of a divine plan designed to lead me to my beautiful and belóved Anneliese Baur. I was like Joseph cast by his brothers into a pit, and sold as a slave, events he had to experience for him to fulfill his destiny. I don't recall being given any defense counsel from the Judge Advocate General's Department. I don't recall when, where or how the court-martial was held. Clearly, the proceedings were of a summary nature, and swiftly accomplished. I recall being told I was guilty of being absent from my guard post and sentenced to five years imprisonment in a military prison. Five years! I heard the words. But I could not accept their reality. (The sleeping on guard charge was not pressed, assuming there had been such a charge.) I slipped back into my sleep walking mode.

Before being sent off to military prison I was confined to quarters under 24 hours guard. Off the record, one of my guards told me that if I hadn't been a Jew this would not have happened to me. I heard what was said, but I didn't want to believe it. But as my military career evolved I began to recognize that there was latent anti-semitism at work in the Army, as well as overt hatred of the Jew, as I shall later chronicle.

The day arrived for me to be delivered to my military prison. My arms were placed behind my back and my wrists enclosed in handcuffs. I was then led to a squad car, and told to lie down on the floor behind the front seats. There I lay, on my stomach, clumped up, like a sack of potatoes. In the front seats, the Colonel's driver, the one with my T/5 rating, which began the whole string of events, the Colonel, and the Regiment's Chaplain.

No one spoke to me during the long ride to the prison. I could overhear snatches of their conversation. The Colonel and the Chaplain were laughing and telling dirty jokes. So much for the sanctity of the clergy. The prison to which I was delivered was a multi-storied gray concrete structure. I learned that it was a British prison turned over to the American military. I think it was called Blackpool Prison. It was built in the form of a rectangle, with individual cells built into the walls on each floor of the prison. My cell was on an upper floor. The cell was a small stone/concrete room, with one small barred window high up on the wall, which, I assumed, was the outer wall of the prison. Opposite the window was the cell door, with a small grated opening about two thirds of the way up the door. My bed consisted of three rough hewn wooden planks attached at each end to wooden blocks which raised the planks a few inches off the concrete floor of the cell. My bedding was an army blanket. There was no mattress. You slept on the wooden planks. I don't recall any running water or toilet fixtures in the cell. I'm a little hazy on this, but I believe you relieved yourself into a bucket which was emptied out daily.

You descended several flights of stairs, encased in high metal screens, to the ground floor where your meals, such as they were, were served. The only cutlery allowed was a soup sized spoon. No knives or forks as these could become weapons. There were no frills. The prison was clearly intended to be a place of punishment. Nevertheless, the American military conceived of the infliction of punishment as a device to foster rehabilitation. Thus, the facility in which I was confined was not called a prison. Instead, its military nomenclature was "Detention Training Center", or DTC for short.

I was led to my cell on my first day of confinement by an MP, a Military Policeman. The guy may have been a prison guard or a cop in civilian life. I could see that he held me in contempt. I was just another of those bad apples who fuck up the Army by going AWOL (absent without leave), or who murder, rape or steal, or like me, have been found guilty of leaving military posts unguarded. When I told him I hadn't done that, he said, "Sure, you're as innocent as all these other fuck-ups." Then he slammed the cell door shut and locked it.

The next morning the MP guard opened my cell door and said "Chow time." As he walked with me to the steps leading to the mess facilities below, he turned to me and said, with great sarcasm, "How did you like your bed, Katz?" "Oh", I replied. "It's OK. It's soft pine." For one moment my old cockiness had come back. It was a mistake which I recognized immediately when he said very coldly, "We don't like smart asses around here." From then on I made no more quips and avoided eye contact with him, and with everyone else in the place, guard or inmate.

I regularly wrote home to my Mom and Dad. My Dad never wrote. Nothing personal. He was not a writer. But my Mom loved writing, and she enjoyed communicating with me. And I enjoyed receiving mail from her. As any person in the military services will tell you, Mail Call was everyone's favorite military event. Although my location might change, my military address always included, as a material part, my name, rank and unit name, the unit being Headquarters Troop, 4th Cavalry Regiment. With my imprisonment my address had been changed. No longer 4th Cavalry Regiment. It was now Disciplinary Training Center. If I wrote that address, my Mother would know I was in trouble some place. How to resolve this address thing without worrying my Mom? I misrepresented where I was (after I was honorably discharged from the Army I told Mom the full story). I told her I had been transferred to a new unit called DTC, and I defined DTC as the abbreviation for Dump Truck Company. I was now in Transportation! A white lie. But better than worrying my Mom by telling her the truth.

Within a week or so of my confinement I began to feel poorly. I put it down, at first, as being a reaction to the strain I had just gone through, the physical impact of The Treatment, coupled with the suppressed emotional upset of the courtmartial and resultant imprisonment. Then I noticed my legs were beginning to swell, and that I had difficulty walking. I didn't complain to anyone. Complaining about my physical condition, and asking to go on sick call, I felt would be further evidence of the Army's power over me: not only had it taken my liberty away, it was now endeavoring to take my health, too. I wasn't about to give the Army that much power over me. And so I did not request permission to go on sick call. My physical condition worsened. I walked with ever greater difficulty. At first the prison guards, the warm and loving Military Policemen that they were, concluded that my shuffling gait was a form of malingering. "Move your ass, Katz! Move it!" But even a callous, suspicious guard can, with time, detect when an inmate is faking it, and when he is really hurting. I kept no calendar, and so my recollection of the passage of time while in prison is vague. Perhaps I was in my second or third week of confinement when one of the guards noted the labored manner in which I made my way up and down the metal stairs at mess times. I was not yet 22. I was not overweight. I looked fit. So why was I walking so funny, he wanted to know. I said it was my legs, they hurt. Let's see he said. I pulled up my pants to my knees. My legs were swollen from the arch of my feet to the knees. A solid mass, no discernible ankles or calves. They looked like the legs of an elephant. "Wow!", the guard said, "You better go on sick call." The next morning I did. Unlike the last time—when going on sick call was feigned, and a device to get better toilet facilities for the enlisted personnel—this time I was really hurting.

A medical orderly, in army jargon, a "medic", examined me in the prison's clinic. He told me to stay put, left, and a few minutes later returned with a doctor, a Captain. I don't recall the doctor's name. Nor do I recall his description of my ailment. I did not return to my cell after my medical examination was over. Instead, I was transferred to the prison's infirmary. I was hurting. I was still in prison. But my bed of rough hewn, soft pine boards had now been replaced with one which had a mattress, sheets, blankets and a soft pillow. The persons in my immediate surroundings were not prison guards. They were nurses. They had pleasant personalities. They smiled a lot and treated me as a human being. Which went a long way towards improving my medical problems. I don't recall how long I was a patient in the infirmary. More than a few days, perhaps a couple of weeks. My court-martial, imprisonment and subsequent illness were unpleasant experiences, to say the least. I am of the opinion that the human brain, working in concert with other organs of the body, endeavors to limit permanent damage to the psyche of a person experiencing a series of severely traumatic happenings by dulling the memory of such events. I was such a person, and the beneficiary of my God's protective measures going into action. Hence, I can paint a black and gray outline of my recollections. But I cannot fill in the picture with an infinite number of tiny dots of colorful detail, as Georges Seurat did so brilliantly in his canvases. The reader will recognize, as my story unfolds, that these negative happenings, as best as I can recall them, were necessary stages along that convoluted road which was leading me, ever closer, to my belóved Anneliese Baur.

I was one of a half dozen patients in the prison infirmary. They were young, some even younger than I, and I was then 21. I learned why each of them had been confined. One had struck an officer. This was a no-no. The others had been convicted for going AWOL: absent without leave. Their sentences, like mine, were also measured in years. I had learned, while chatting with some British soldiers I had met in a pub during my first weeks in England, that the Brits were less strict than Americans in meting out punishment for violations of military regulations. The average Brit sentence for going AWOL was generally measured in months. The average USA sentence for the same offense was reckoned in years. Aside from the youth and sentences we shared, the other inmates in the infirmary were wholly dissimilar from me in one major respect: they were poorly educated. None had graduated from high school. Although the infirmary had some books and magazines, none of my fellow patients was a reader. Instead, they played cards and generally horsed around, and even in the presence of the nurses they used profanity. I used four letter words, too. But never when the nurses were in earshot. And I liked to read and chat with the nurses. The nurses noted these differences. They liked me, and they would say to the other patients, "Why can't you behave like Arthur?" This would generate a chorus of raucous shouts, whistles and much laughter.

As I was getting better I turned my mind to thinking how I could get out of prison and back into active duty. I knew that as soon as I was deemed OK I would be sent back to my cell and its soft pine plank bed. I didn't want that. And I didn't want to be a jail bird. I had enlisted to serve my country, and that's what I wanted to do. I hadn't changed my approach to military justice, or better said, injustice. If I got back into active service I would be more judicious in airing my opinions. But how to get out? The prison was called a Disciplinary Training Center. This meant to me that the prison was designed not merely as a place of confinement, but also as a place where an inmate, having seen the consequences of his wrongful ways, has learned to correct them, and is thus able to be restored to active duty. In short, the former fuck-up is deemed rehabilitated, set free, and ready again to serve his country with honor. I now knew what I had to do.

Episode Seventeen

In which I write a letter of contrition and I am restored to active duty and join the 86th Cavalry.

I asked a nurse for some writing paper and a pencil. Inmates, even those in an infirmary, were not allowed pens. Pens have metal points and could become weapons if used improperly. I was given a writing tablet. The paper was off-white, almost gray, with blue lines. Not high quality stationery, war time stuff, but suitable for my purposes. I sat on my bed, and with the tablet on my lap I began my letter to the Commandant of the prison.

I kept no copy of the letter. What I am setting down is the essence of what I wrote. I told the Prison Commandant that I had given up my college student deferment to enlist in the Cavalry; that I had done so because I loved my country and wanted to serve my country in its war against Hitler and his axis partners; that I had made mistakes in the way I had performed my duties as a soldier; that the punishment I was receiving had taught me a lesson; that I hadn't enlisted to spend the war sitting in jail; that if I were given another chance and returned to active duty I would prove to the Army that I could be a good soldier. My penciled letter noted my patriotism, showed contrition for my past conduct, demonstrated my newly learned respect for military authority and begged for forgiveness.

I handed my letter to a nurse. She read it, smiled, and assured me it would be delivered to the right person. I hoped so. My letter could have easily been thrown away. I waited anxiously to learn the reaction to my letter. I didn't have to wait long. A few days after it was written I was visited in the Prison Infirmary by an officer on the prison's staff. He told me that the Commandant liked the tone of my letter and had reviewed my service record; that the invasion of France might soon take place; that my military skills were such that I could be more useful to the Army back on duty than sitting in prison; that based upon my letter my time in prison had taught me the importance of military discipline; that I was therefore, rehabilitated! The balance of my sentence would be commuted to time served! I would be released, restored to good standing and sent to a Replacement Depot for reassignment. I would not rejoin the 4th Cavalry Regiment. I was overjoyed! I thanked the officer and requested, if possible, to be reassigned to another cavalry unit. He told me that could be a possibility.

The nurses were as pleased with the Army's decision as I was. They told me I was "a nice young man", that I deserved another chance, and should stay out of fights with the Army. I assured them I would be careful. Once burned, twice shy. A Replacement Depot, known in Army jargon as a "Repple Depple", was an assembly facility, a holding station, so to speak, where newly arrived soldiers, unattached to other units, were sent to be assigned to units needing replacements, or additional troops. It was also a place where soldiers such as those newly released from confinement, as in my case, or soldiers who had been separated from their units by reason of illness or injury, and unable to be returned to their former units, were sent to be reassigned to new units. After the invasion of France on June 6th 1944, the Replacement Depots, were the centers from which soldiers were drawn and sent to units in the field as replacements for those soldiers killed, wounded in combat or injured, or as additional personnel for units whose rosters were not yet filled.

Over the years I have reflected upon the shabby, perhaps, even illegal way I was treated by the 4th Cavalry. However, I have never dwelt very long on the topic. My courtmartial, conviction and subsequent short prison confinement, were all necessary steps in that journey which led me, Thank God!, to my belóved Anneliese Baur. It was *beshert*, it was meant to be. My run-ins with the 4th Cavalry, and resultant consequences, shaped my military career. They also shaped the course of my post war life. How all this played out is delineated as my story unfolds.

On June 6th, 1944, D-Day, a massive force of Allied Troops, under the Supreme Command of General Dwight D. Eisenhower, crossed the English Channel and landed on the beaches of Normandy, France. The invasion into the heart of Europe had begun. I was in the Replacement Depot awaiting reassignment when I heard the news. The war I wanted to be part of had started, and I was still in England. I was unhappy. I had no idea how long the war might last, and I wondered when I might get to France and see some action. I even imagined that the war might end before I was in a combat unit, and then I would have missed everything! Sounds crazy. I had been cooped up, albeit briefly, in military prison, had been hospitalized and was now awaiting reassignment. Shit! I was still in England, there was a war on, and I was missing it! I shouldn't have worried. In fact, my courtmartial and resultant brief imprisonment might well have saved my life, and with my life saved, I was able to continue on that highly convoluted journey which would lead me to my belóved Anneliese Baur. I learned at the Repple Depple, a few days after the invasion, that the 4th Cavalry had been in the earliest waves of troops hitting the beaches at Normandy, and that they suffered severe losses, perhaps 40 to 60 percent of the unit being either killed or wounded. Had I still been with the 4th Cavalry I could have been one of those casualties. But it was not to be.

A few days after the invasion I was assigned to the 86th Cavalry Reconnaissance Squadron Mechanized. At the time of my release from military prison I had asked that it be noted in the appropriate file that I would prefer being assigned to another Cavalry unit, rather than go to a different service branch in the Army. My specialized military skills reinforced my desires, and the Army found it appropriate to restore me to active duty in a Cavalry unit. I told my new unit I would prefer to be placed in a line Troop, rather than go into Headquarters Troop. My experiences with the chicken shit in the 4th Cavalry Regiment's Headquarters Troop had soured me on again being in a Headquarters unit. The 86th Cavalry was only too happy to have someone with top radio operator skills, seek a berth in a line Troop. A line Troop's mission was to seek out the enemy, and when found, to report his position to HQ., and if necessary, to engage him in combat long enough to hold him in place until the infantry, artillery and air force could go to work on him, and then get the hell out of there! Headquarters Troop was the Command and Communication Center of the Squadron. Thus, while capable of engaging in combat, it was not intended that it do so in the ordinary course of events. Its mission was to receive field intelligence, analyze it and send it on to higher echelons of command. Accordingly, my new unit was pleased when I asked to be placed in a line Troop. I was assigned as a radio operator to D Troop and given the command of an armored car. This vehicle has a crew of four, inclusive of the car commander. I shall describe this vehicle more fully below.

At the beginning of this narrative I explained why, when I enlisted—and was given the opportunity to choose my branch of service—that I chose the Cavalry. Let me here restate why I made that choice: I wanted to be in a small, mobile combat unit where, to a great degree, I could control my freedom of action. I reasoned that the more independence I had in making critical decisions, the better my chances for survival. However, my reasoning was not fool proof. It did not prevent me from being twice injured as a consequence of the actions of others. I will recount these happenings as my story unfolds.

I was restored to the good graces of the Army. The swelling in my legs was gone. I was again physically and emotionally fit. I had shunted to the innermost interstices of my brain the experiences I had recently endured. I was back in service, ready and eager to do my duty. Most assuredly the Commanding Officer of the 86th Cavalry, and his Staff Officers, knew about my experiences with the 4th Cavalry. But my past was a closed book. I was just another member of D Troop, in Army parlance, Dog Troop. In WWII the Army's code words for the letters of the alphabet began with Able, Baker, Charlie, Dog. I understand that the code words are different now.

Episodes EIGHTEEN through TWENTY FIVE

Advancing Across France

We have regarded the voluntary retreat into the interior of the country as a special form of defense through which the enemy is expected to be destroyed, not so much by the sword as by exhaustion from his own efforts. In this case, therefore, a great battle is either not supposed . . . or assumed to take place so late that the enemy's forces have previously been considerably reduced.

Every assailant in advancing diminishes his military force by the advance . . . . [This] is clearly shown by military history to take place in every campaign in which there has been a considerable advance.

This weakening in the advance is increased if the enemy has not been beaten and withdraws of his own accord with his forces intact, offering a constant, steady resistance, and selling every step of ground at the cost of blood, so that the advance is a constant pushing forward and not a mere pursuit.

. . . A *regulated* daily resistance, that is, one which each time only lasts as long as the equilibrium of the combat can be kept doubtful and in which we secure ourselves from defeat by giving up at the right moment the ground which has been contested—such a combat will cost the assailant at least as many men as the defender. The loss which the latter by retreating must now and again unavoidably suffer in prisoners will be balanced by the losses of the other under fire, as the assailant must always fight against the advantages of the ground. It is true that the retreating side loses entirely all those men who are badly wounded, but the assailant likewise suffers the loss of his wounded temporarily, since they usually remain in hospital for several months.

. . . The army in retreat has the means of storing provisions everywhere, and it marches toward them, while the pursuer must have everything brought after him, which, as long as he is in motion, even with shortest lines of communication, is difficult, and on that account begets scarcity from the very beginning.

The pursuing army, therefore, from the very first day, frequently has to contend with the most pressing wants . . . .

General Karl Von Clausewitz,
On War (1831)

Episode Eighteen

In which I go to France with the 86th Cavalry and promptly on landing experience my first day under hostile fire.

Within a week of the time I joined the 86th Cavalry the Squadron was moved across the English Channel. We disembarked on the Normandy beaches in France where, weeks before, on June 6th 1944, the Allied invasion had taken place. I believe the 86th Cavalry moved onto French soil in the last week of June 1944. Once all of our units were ashore we moved in a convoy 12 to 15 kilometers inland to a staging area on the outskirts of the city of St. Lo. The terrain was flat where we dismounted, and aside from some stubble—which indicated that the last crop was some kind of grain—it was bare. We were sitting upon a piece of empty farm land, square shaped, about 100 meters in width and depth and bounded on all four sides by mounds made of earth and stones, about two meters in height, and covered with tall, unkempt bushes, one intertwined with another, into a ragged row of gray green hedges. I was seeing for the first time the French rural hedgerows which would play a material rôle in the unfolding of my combat experiences. There was no ground action near us. Overhead we could make out our fighters and bombers, and in the background we heard the rumbling sounds of artillery fire. There was a war going on, but we were not yet a formal part of it.

My fellow Troopers and I were ordered to dig slit trenches for ourselves on the edges of the field in which we had dismounted. We were told that the Germans could hit our area with artillery fire, and that *Luftwaffe* (German for Air Weapon) bombers and *Stukas* were still flying sorties. *Stuka* is the German acronym for *Sturzkampfflugzeug*: its nose diving fighter plane. The plane was designed to swoop down, at great speed, onto ground troops, with its dual machine guns blazing. This tactic was called strafing, from the German word *Strafe*, which means punishment. Some

Stukas were also equipped with light cannon and bomb racks which materially increased their fire power. They were awesome weapons. German military terms entered into the war vocabulary of the Allied forces. Thus, my introduction to the word flak came in the course of a conversation with a Brit anti-aircraft gunner in England. He related that when they shot at incoming German aircraft the sky would be filled with flak. He was referring to the shrapnel which flew from the bursting anti-aircraft shells. He was probably no more aware than I was then that the word was the German acronym for their *Flugabwehrkanone*, anti-aircraft cannon: Flak. Perhaps the most widely used German military term was *Blitzkrieg*: Lightning War. Wars are strange happenings. They twist things around, as in WWII, where the victorious Allies assimilated into their military vocabulary many German combat terms.

Back to what was taking place during that first day the 86th Cavalry was on French soil. The day we dug our first slit trenches in a hostile environment all of us Troopers were green to combat. In our basic training days we had been exposed to live fire (or at least we were told it was live). We had crawled under barbed wire while machine guns were being fired over our heads, and close by, but not too close, small explosions were going off. A tad scary. But we all knew that if we kept on crawling, and kept our heads (and asses) down, that nothing would hit us. It was just training, getting ready for the real thing. And so you wonder how you will react when faced, for the first time, with real live fire aimed directly at you with hostile intent, or aimed in your general direction, in those situations where the enemy can't see you, but knows, or senses, that you are out there in front of him. I wondered, but didn't dwell on the matter. I was busy digging my slit trench. We had been told to make it deep enough so that if a shell burst near us the shrapnel would fly over our trench or embed itself into the walls of our slit trench above our prone bodies. We were also told not to make it too wide, for that would make it easier for shrapnel to fly in.

I dug a beautiful slit trench. Straight walls on both sides and ends. Deep enough to give me at least a foot of space over my body. Wide enough for my shoulders to touch each side wall, and long enough for me to stretch out with my helmet on my head. Sounds like I was designing my coffin. But that was not my intent. The earth I dug out I shoveled neatly around the edges of my hole. This increased the safety of my slit trench. I was quite pleased with my efforts. I have referred to my carefully crafted hole in the ground as a slit trench. A proper term. However, an equally apt description for such excavations was the term fox hole. In the course of my narrative I shall use both terms interchangeably, as my fancy dictates. Shortly thereafter we had some chow. It was noontime. The day was clear with a light breeze. It we were not at war it would have been a nice day for a picnic. After chow we were told we would be moving out the next day. It was then that I learned that the 86th Cavalry Reconnaissance Squadron Mechanized (its full name) was attached to the 6th Armored Division, as its reconnaissance arm, and that the 6th Armored Division and the 4th Armored Division were the two armored divisions in General Patton's Third Army. At that point I knew very little about General Patton. But I would learn more about him, from hearsay, and from direct contact, as I shall relate as my story progresses.

Our respective slit trenches dug, my fellow Troopers and I just milled about. Overhead our planes were flying. In the distance we could hear the rumble of artillery fire. Nothing eventful was happening. Then something did. I was looking up, watching our bombers fly overhead. There were several. Height and distance? I guessed they were about 1,500 feet up, or less, and about a half mile away from our position. We had been trained to identify planes, to tell whether they were ours or theirs. And the ones I was looking at were our B19s. Suddenly one of the B19s began to emit black smoke. It began a slow spiral to the earth. It was close enough to see what was happening, but too far away to hear any sounds from the plane—and then it came apart in the air and disappeared from sight. It was unbelievable! It was like watching a silent movie. I had just seen one of our planes shot down. There were no parachutes. Those poor guys were dead! I looked around to see if any of my buddies had seen what I had. No one had noticed. American airmen had just died, and no one had noticed. Strange. Unreal. I had witnessed my first deaths in combat.

And then reality on the ground set in. It entered with a roaring whoosh, and a big bang! An incoming shell exploded beyond the hedgerow at the end of the field furthest from me. For about 20 frenetic seconds a calm afternoon became one of pandemonium. Every Trooper ran for his foxhole/slit trench. All of us were scrambling to find underground cover. I was about 10 meters from my slit trench when the shell landed. I ran to my hole, and was about to dive in, when I saw this huge guy trying to bury his bulk in my slit trench. "Hey!", I shouted, "That's my hole!" "Fuck off", he shouts back. I dart around to find an empty hole. I find one. I dive in. Not as nicely dug as mine, but I was in it. Nobody came to claim it. When that shell fell all of us, green to combat as we were, played "musical foxholes". Those not close to their own jumped into whatever was available. Only one shell fell that close to us that day. Nobody had been hit, But life had suddenly changed for all of us. *We were now in combat!* The Germans had fired on us. They couldn't observe us directly. They knew we were some where out there, but not exactly where. They were firing blind in our direction, hoping to hit something. We were lucky they hadn't. But it wouldn't always be that way.

Later that afternoon I captured my first German prisoner of war. And I did it armed only with a roll of toilet paper (or in Army parlance: shit paper). I stopped calling this necessity "toilet tissue", and adopted the basic Army term after my encounter with my 4th Cavalry supply Sergeant. You may recall the episode. It was at the beginning of this book. I was on my first field exercise, and I asked him for "toilet tissue" as I was about to evacuate my bowels. He thought I was a smart ass New Yorker making fun of his southern hill country background when I asked for "toilet tissue". And so he responded angrily, and informed me profanely, that if I wanted "shit paper" I should ask for it. And thereafter, as long as I was in the Service, that's what I asked for. The prisoner capture came about in this wise: The urge to defecate having come upon me I obtained a roll of shit paper from supplies and with the roll of paper in my right hand I entered into the shadowy confines of the nearest hedgerow. I proposed going deeply enough into this maze of intertwined branches and leaves to shield myself from my fellows. As I slowly moved forward into the thicket I heard a rustling of foliage in front of me, and, to my great surprise, suddenly there was this German soldier cowering in front of me. He was shaking, and as he shouted, *"Schiesse nicht!"*, ("Don't shoot!") he stood up and raised his arms in surrender. In the darkness of the shrubbery he had mistaken the roll of paper in my right hand as a pistol. I quickly lowered my toilet paper clasping right hand (my "weapon" hand). I called out *"Heraus!"* ("Get out!") and with my left hand directed him to walk in front of me and out of the hedgerow. Once back in the open field I marched him to our Troop HQ where I turned him over to our officers. Since I was the only one present who spoke German I interrogated the prisoner. I learned that he was not a German national, but a Slav from the Balkans, and that he had volunteered to fight in the Wehrmacht. We were to discover in the next weeks of combat that as the German Army fell back from Normandy and Brittany they left behind their Nazi supporters, from countries such as Bosnia, Hungary and Romania, to fight a holding action against our forces. The guy I "captured" said he had deserted the German Army, and was hoping to elude us as he worked his way back to his country. At least that was his story. After I related all this to my officers I rearmed myself with my roll of shit paper, entered the hedgerow again, and finally took a crap. And not a moment too soon. The story got around about my shit paper capture of a German soldier, and I was a hero for a day

Episode Nineteen

In which, in combat in Brittany, France, I receive my first wounds and the pain aside, worry whether I've lost my front teeth.

This episode relates to my Squadron's Mission in Brittany, and to the first time I was hurt in combat.

My Cavalry Squadron: the 86th Cavalry Reconnaissance Squadron Mechanized, was last all together as a unit when we arrived in St. Lo, Normandy, France in the last weeks of June 1944 where we were committed to action.

As noted, the 86th Cavalry was attached to the 6th Armored Division as its reconnaissance unit. The 6th Armored, in turn, was attached to General Patton's Third Army as one of his two armored divisions. Naturally, there was close liaison between the Headquarters of the 6th Armored and ours in the 86th Cavalry. However, in the field we operated widely separated from the 6th Armored. Like Joshua and Caleb entering the land of Canaan, we spied out the land for them, reported back what we found, and were always in the van, always on the move. In short, we were in front of the front lines, wherever those lines might be.

At St. Lo Patton divided his Third Army into two attack forces, one spearheaded by the Fourth Armored, the other by the Sixth Armored, each with its supporting units. The Fourth Armored was chosen to head directly East across France towards Germany. The Sixth Armored was given the task to head South from Normandy through Brittany towards St. Nazaire. St. Nazaire was a major Nazi *U Boot* port. By heading South, running parallel with the Brittany coast, we would cut off those German military and naval units stationed along that part of the French coastline. This would prevent these German forces from moving inland to attack Patton on his right flank as he was moving east, or prevent the Germans from moving South towards Spain where they could then turn

Northeast and join up with those German forces readying to engage Patton as he moved eastward. At the same time Allied Naval Forces were conducting a blockade designed to prevent Nazi submarines from entering or leaving their Brittany Pens.

I remember the names of several of the French cities around whose environs we had our operations. There was Brest, and Quimper and Lorient, and lots of small villages all of which appeared to be engaged in making dairy products and raising grains and vegetables. As stated, the last time the 86th Cavalry Recon was assembled as a full Squadron was at St. Lo. Until the Battle of the Bulge in December '44 and January '45, and immediately thereafter, the four line Troops, A, B, C and D: Troops Able, Baker, Charlie, Dog (I was in Dog Troop), and the support Troops, E and F, the ones with the light tanks, and Headquarters Troop, operated separately from each other. Each Troop was given daily its own mission for that day, or for the next few days. Communication was by radio, and sometimes by messenger, and always to Headquarters Troop, where the Squadron Commander, a full Colonel and his Staff officers and the 57+ or—enlisted men were stationed. My Troop D's personnel rarely moved out together as a unit. Instead, we operated in the field, mostly running patrols as individual platoons, or squads. These patrols would generally consist of one armored car and two jeeps. We were lightly armored, since our missions daily were to seek out the enemy, either by observing him, or by drawing his fire, and to report our data back to our HQ. indicating where he was, rather than sitting still or digging in and engaging in a fire fight with forces always numerically superior to us in men and fire power. Dead scouts make lousy messengers. So move out, detect the enemy or note his absence, report this info back to HQ and then get the hell out and back, either to the location from where we had started out early that a.m., or to a new location where the bulk of our Troop was now located.

As a radio operator the vehicle to which I was assigned was an armored car, since within its turret was all my communications equipment. The rounds for the vehicle's 37mm cannon lined the inner walls of the turret of my armored car, each shell/round held in place by spring clamps. This manner of storing live shells made life a bit exciting when enemy fire fell close enough to my vehicle to send shrapnel flying all about. On one occasion I remember hearing the ping, ping, tinkle of small pieces of shrapnel flying about inside the turret while bouncing off the rounds on the wall, and off their casings, the latter containing the rounds' explosive charge. Shrapnel from a bursting shell moves extremely fast and is white hot. Had a large enough piece of shrapnel penetrated any one of the shells encircling me then there would have been an explosion which, at the very least, would have blown my head off. On another occasion I recall an engagement in which mortar fire fell close to our vehicles, the shrapnel flying all about. None entered the open turret, but that evening, when I unrolled my sleeping bag, which was tied to the outside of the turret, I noted a series of tiny holes, and when the bag was fully unrolled, there inside were several small pieces of metal, not much bigger than a grain of coarse sand. I shook them out, not pleased that my bag had been air conditioned, but happy that it was the bag rather than me that had gotten hit.

In the eight plus months I was in combat, as measured from being committed at St. Lo in the latter part of June 1944, to being hurt the second time on the 20th of February, 1945, I believe I spent about 90% of my operational time in either an armored car or in a jeep. And it was as a car commander in a jeep that I suffered my first wounds. By first wounds I mean the first time in combat that I was physically hurt. I was "injured" many times in the Service when my feelings were hurt—but I'm talking now about injuries where the blood flowed and I felt physical pain. And this is how it came about the first time.

As noted, right after St. Lo the 6th Armored, to which the 86th Cavalry was attached, headed South down the coast of Brittany. Our Mission: to cut off the German U-Boot bases and naval ports from contact with German land forces stationed in Brittany, and to engage these land forces and prevent them from moving inland to join up with other German forces. After the first few days of heavy action my Troop had a few light engagements, mostly encountering pockets of German troops left behind to retard our advance by fighting rearguard actions, but who were ready to surrender if given the chance. Many were not even German, but were soldiers from fascist groups out of eastern Europe. And then there were the armed Vichy supporters, those French who went over to the German side after Germany occupied France. One of our jobs was to help the DeGaulle French forces round them up for handling by the French. And so sometime in early August 1944 I was out on patrol in an open jeep (no canvas top) with a driver, a kid younger than I was, with me sitting to his right, with a 50 caliber machine gun mounted on the vehicle's hood and directly in front of me. This lethal weapon had a two pronged trigger mechanism set atop its barrel. It was called a butterfly trigger because of its dual winged shape. The machine gun was fired by pressing on either wing of its trigger. There was no windshield of course. No doors. Nor seat belts (they hadn't been invented yet, and even had they been, they would have been a hazard in a combat vehicle.) In the rear seat there was a teenage French kid with a smattering of English, which coupled with my French, which was better then than now, enabled us to communicate quite well. He was from the Maquis, the French underground. He was suggesting where we should reconnoiter to see if we could round up the Vichy guys he was looking for. We in turn were out looking for our left behind Nazi friends. Operation mop-up you could call it.

We were in a rural, wholly farm community area. No paved roads. No sidewalks, except for occasional stretches in front of some houses where cobblestones, or some slabs of limestone, had been laid down. And the houses came up to the corners of roads. Thus, you could only see what was on the road you were approaching *after* you were past this blind corner! This meant that you could be passing this blind corner in your vehicle and then be broadside to a German vehicle, if one were there, on the other side of the corner. Surprise! And so we were very cautious, even skittish, in approaching such blind corners. If the French farm houses in the village were built to the right of a road, then there would usually be a deep ditch and a mound of earth, dug to make the ditch, on the left side of the road. And on top of this mound there would be a row of hedges which served as the boundary lines for the parcels of farm land being worked by the villagers. The layout would be reversed if the houses and farm land were to the right of the road. Remember the topography, it's a vital part of my story.

Thus, in mid-afternoon in early August 1944, in Brittany, my one jeep patrol was on this dirt road with the deep ditch and hedge rows on our left. We were approaching a blind village street corner. We were moving at maybe 25 miles an hour, not fast, but not slow for the kind of rutted dirt road we were on. I'm looking around. I see nothing. This French Maquis kid in the back seat starts to shout out and point at the corner we are approaching. Maybe he's telling us to turn there, or maybe something else. Over the sound of the jeep's engine, and the wooshing of its tires on the washboard road, I couldn't understand him. My driver looks back at the French kid, up at the fast approaching corner, and then suddenly yanks his steering wheel to the left! On a narrow dirt road he's trying to make a U-turn, and reverse our course! He told me later that he thought he'd caught a glimpse of a German armored car on the other side. We'll never know. As he jerked the wheel, and tried to reverse its course, the right side of the vehicle, my side, tilted up into the air, and on two left wheels the jeep plunged into the ditch to the left of the road. It was a deep ditch, its bottom about two meters below the surface of the road.

I remember parts of what happened thereafter very vividly. I had been thrown out of the jeep and remember standing up beside it. The jeep was on its side, and one wheel was still turning. For some reason it reminded me of a slowly revolving roulette wheel. A few weeks earlier we in the Cavalry had been issued new jackets as part of our combat uniform. They had a zipper down the front, side pockets, and a knitted collar, and, if I remember correctly, a gathered waistband. They were camel colored, a light tan. They looked like Air Force jackets. Real snazzy. We Cavalry guys were proud to wear them. They made us look special. I remember looking down on my jacket and saw blood dripping onto it. "Shit", I said, "I'm ruining my jacket!" At that moment I don't recall feeling any pain. I must then have passed out.

The next thing I remember is that I am lying on my back on a dirt road. An elderly French farmer is peering down on me. My whole face is numb. With my right hand, which hurts, and then with my left, I grope for my mouth. I feel nothing. I feel for my teeth. I feel nothing. Wow! Were my teeth knocked out? I had enlisted in the Army with a full set of teeth, and I was proud of them. When you are 21 and plan to meet a lot of good looking women, a nice set of teeth is a distinct asset. And so I remember saying to the elderly farmer, whose kindly face was now very close to me, "*Mes dents! Mes dents!*" My teeth! My teeth! He smiled, waved his hand and said, "*Sont bonnes*". "They're fine". Hearing that I conked out, and awoke only as I was placed on an operating table in a field hospital. I heard someone say, ". . . broken nose, broken right wrist, lacerations left side of face and trauma to left eye." The numbness had worn away, and I was now feeling pain, real pain. I had learned somewhere that they give you morphine when you are hurt, to dampen the pain. So I remember saying to no one in particular, there were a bunch of people looking down on me. "I'm hurting. Are you gonna give me some morphine?" Some voice said, "No. We don't give morphine to head wounds. It could kill you." This was useful information which I tucked away. And it came in handy the next time I was hurt

I remember hearing the click when my broken nose was snapped into place, and I heard someone say, "Good as new". However, I still bear the scars across the bridge of my nose, and under my left eye, where the flesh was torn away.

Now what part did the butterfly trigger on the 50 caliber machine play in my injuries? A big part. When the jeep flew into the ditch and flipped over on its side, my head smashed into the trigger mechanism of the machine gun and the damage was done. But I lived through the experience. In fact, as a direct consequence of my injury to my right hand, my ability as a radio operator to send clear text and Morse Code was improved. And that was important in the Squadron's decision to allow me to remain in my Troop after my injuries, rather than being detached and sent to a rear hospital position there to recuperate from my wounds. Further, being separated temporarily from my unit meant my mail would be held at my Troop's HQ. and might get lost or misplaced before I got back. And no GI wants his mail to get lost. I was told that with a broken hand (forget the broken nose, the facial scars and the bloody left eye) I could not perform my primary duty, which was that of being a radio operator/gunner, and accordingly would have to be sent to the rear to recuperate, since I would be useless to the Troop in combat. Now how did breaking my right hand (I understood that two bones were broken) improve my radio operator skills? And thus keep me with my unit? What I am about to relate illustrates how acts, which, when they occurred, seemed random, and unpleasant, were, in truth, parts of a chain of events designed to lead me, at some unknown time, to an unknown place, there to find my belóved Anneliese. As unpleasant an episode as it was, my injury was *beshert*, something meant to be: for it demonstrated that when faced with several choices, I had chosen the one which allowed me to continue in combat: Evidence of the workings of divine Providence.

As a radio operator I had been issued a leg key Morse code transmitter. If my memory is correct, this apparatus was designated in Army equipment listings as a "J-45". The key was attached to an expandable metal leg clamp. You clamped the key onto your thigh, and operated the key in a sitting position. This position made your thigh into a level table-like operating plane. The key was operated by pressing down on it vertically. The length of time you took to make the key go up and down created the dits and dahs of the Morse code. Pressing the key vertically required the operator to raise and lower his wrist. And if he wanted to send code fast and correctly he had to hold his forearm as rigid as possible and move his wrist as little as possible. At the field hospital my right hand was placed in a plaster cast splint which extended from my elbow up past my thumb and ended just below the knuckles on my four fingers. My hand and arm were truly immobilized. Good for recovery, bad for radio operation. I was going to be sent to the rear unless I could show I could still do my job despite my injuries. Nothing stimulates creative thinking more than when one is faced with solving immediately an oncoming negative event. So I got to work, I cut the cast where it tied my thumb down. I wiggled my thumb. No pain in my hand or wrist. The splint still held my wrist and forearm rigid. With my thumb free, and the rest of my hand and my forearm still held rigidly by the cast, I began to send dits and dahs at random. I found I was faster with my wrist immobilized than when it was free to move. And my rhythm was improved. Rhythm in sending code is very important. Morse code can easily be misread if its flow is herky jerky especially when sent in coded form and not in clear language. A dit dah sent with proper rhythm is "A", a dit dah sent with even a slight break in rhythm will be read as dit: "E" and dah: "T". I demonstrated to my superiors that I could perform my duties well, even with a broken hand. And so I stayed with my unit. Out of a negative I had created a positive. Mark up one point for Art Katz. Thank you God, for giving me freedom of choice, and the wisdom to make the right choice (which, of course, you knew all along I would).

When our jeep overturned, what happened to my driver and the French Maqui kid in the back seat? Nothing, apparently. They were thrown free, they hit nothing harder than the grassy ground. They were shaken up, but no fixed, or moving bodily parts, were injured. They were lucky. I was, too, but with more collateral damage to go with my luck. I never applied for a Purple Heart

Medal for this injury. I thought being injured while taking evasive action under the perceived threat of hostile fire did not constitute a combat injury, thus entitling the injured soldier to the award of a Purple Heart, a medal created by General Washington, and awarded to soldiers wounded in combat. And so I never reported my injury in this light. I have in my possession two Purple Heart Medals given me by the Army. One was explicitly given to me, and I will write about its basis in due course, and the second was given to me sometime before I was honorably discharged. Whether the second was intended as a fail safe copy should I have lost the first, or a valid second Purple Heart for two "qualifying wounds", I do not know. I know only that I bled twice on the fields of battle, once in France, and once in Germany. And if the ground where I bled now nurtures better crops, so much the better for France and Germany.

One last something I should mention about my first combat injury. When my jeep overturned my Troop had been in combat for about a month. I do not recall having had access to a shower during that time. And so all of the Troopers were pretty grimy. We always had enough water to drink and cook with, and to do some shaving, rudimentary washing up, mostly faces and hands, and around our private parts—a whore's bath we would call the latter—with the water poured from canteens, or from a five gallon Jerry can into our helmets. And so I remember that when I had recovered consciousness, and was lying on the operating table, I looked down at my right arm. My combat jacket had been removed and the long john underwear on my arm had been pushed back almost to my armpit. I presume this was to check my blood pressure. I noticed how white my arm looked from the wrist up, in contrast to my stained and darkened right hand and wrist. Darkened, not really dirty, but certainly, not clean. I was embarrassed. I remember saying to the medical personnel leaning over me, "I'm sorry my hands are so dirty." A dumb remark under the circumstances. One of the medics leaning over me, laughed in a kindly way and said, "Forget it, soldier, you're not on a picnic, you're in a war."

Episode Twenty

In which I explain the military mission of the 86th Cavalry Reconnaissance Squadron Mechanized in Patton's Drive across France.

From the earliest of times cavalry units were designed to be fast, highly mobile, fearsome, horse mounted vanguard fighters. Foot soldiers, no matter how well armed and armored, could rarely withstand the charge of sword wielding warriors mounted on their spirited steeds. The plunging horses, towering over the foot soldiers, were themselves instruments of terror, their sheer size, bulk and flailing hooves capable of causing severe injury and death. And then, astride them, were their riders, hacking down on their earth bound opponents. The invention of gunpowder revolutionized the manner in which wars were fought. Swords, spears, battle axes, long bows, ceased to be effective weapons. And the U.S. Cavalry in World War II no longer rode horses into battle. Over the centuries the weapons of warfare changed. Battle techniques changed. But the *raison d'etre* for going to war has never changed. The Prussian General Karl von Clausewitz, in his masterwork on the art of war, *Vom Kriege*, On War, written after the Napoleonic wars, (von Clausewitz finished his book in 1830 and died of Cholera in 1831) stated that "War is an act of force to compel our adversary to do our will". (Book I, Chap. I). In his treatise von Clausewitz set down certain principles concerning the waging of war, *inter alia*, that "The defensive is the stronger form of making war." (Book VI, Chap. I); and "A swift and vigorous transition to attack—the flashing sword of vengeance—is the most brilliant part of the defensive. He who does not bear this in mind from the first . . . will never understand the superiority of the defensive." (Book VI, Chap. V). [My English translations are from the 1943 Modern Library Edition of *On War*].

I have quoted these observations of von Clausewitz to lay a foundation for a better understanding of how the war on the European Continent was waged, and how the 86th Cavalry performed its mission in the conduct of that war. In engaging the invading Allied forces the German High Command, to the extent they could avoid the military whims and caprices of Hitler, paid strict heed to the tenets of von Clausewitz in the manner in which they opposed our forces. Thus, once the Allied invasion had breached their sea coast defenses, the German forces went into their defensive mode. They fell back in a studied retreat. There was no rout. They fought our advancing forces at long range, avoiding large pitched battles. Their favorite weapons were *Luftwaffe* bombings and strafings, heavy caliber shellings, from artillery and mortars, and anti-tank and anti-personnel mine fields. As they fell back we advanced. And as we advanced we extended our supply lines, and soon outstripped them. General Patton, in his haste to chase after the retreating enemy, and to engage them head on, began to run out of fuel for his armored units. He had to slow down—but declined to do so. German units which had faded away from him now reappeared and attacked his flanks. In faithful adherence to the teachings of von Clausewitz the Germans made a swift and vigorous transition to attack, unsheathing the flashing sword of vengeance. Fortunately for our forces, orders from Patton's military superiors, of which more below, and good weather, dulled the blade of the German's sword of vengeance. In contrast, Hitler overruled his *Wehrmachtsgeneralstab*, his military high command, and in his massive *Drang nach Osten* Drive to the East, paid no heed to von Clausewitz' teachings. He ordered his soldiers to pursue the retreating Russians. His army was soon overextended, and then the Russians unleashed their flashing sword of vengeance. The fate suffered by Napoleon was now, 130 years later, visited upon Hitler. The Russian Generals had read von Clausewitz and followed his counsel. Fortunately for General Patton, and his Third Army, and to the detriment of his overweening ego—Patton wanted to move swiftly across the undulating plains of France, take Metz in a frontal attack, and then move on to the west bank of the Rhine at Strasbourg—his superior, General Bradley, slowed him down, preventing Patton from outrunning his fuel and ammunition trains, and barring him from making a frontal attack on Metz.

All of Brittany having been secured, the Sixth Armored Division—with our 86th Cavalry Squadron leading the way as its recon arm—rejoined Patton's Third Army in the vicinity of Orleans, and there, in concert with the Fourth Armored Division, and with the other elements of his Army once again together, General Patton resumed, at an ever increasing tempo, his eastward drive across France. He was intent on catching the retreating German forces, to engage them in a major battle, and destroy them as a viable military force before they had the chance to cross the Rhine to safety, or escape to the North through Luxembourg and Belgium into the Ardennes/Eifel region of Germany.

My Cavalry Squadron was in the van of the Sixth Armored Division as it moved east as the southern flank of Patton's Third Army. Standing up in the turret of my armored car I had an unrestricted view of all that was going on about us. With our jeeps and armored cars moving at 40 miles per hour, the heavy tanks flanking us were hard put to keep up with us. Shells were exploding before us. Most were from our artillery helping to blast a path for us. I could also see and hear incoming fire from distant German artillery, and most assuredly, from dug-in *Panzerwagens* with their huge 88mm cannons. Other shells were from our Allied aircraft. I don't recall seeing any *Luftwaffe* planes. I had a 360° view of the battlefield. Such infantry units as I glimpsed were being transported in trucks. The terrain was, as I have noted, undulating, rolling countryside, spotted with small villages, groves of trees and crops still unharvested. And, coming our way, as we rolled eastward, were not German forces, but streams of French civilians, young people, old folks, kids, all on foot, some pulling handcarts loaded with whatever belongings they could grab on short order and take with them, and all terrified to find themselves in the midst of a huge military advance. Their sole concern: to get out of harm's way. Some passed so close to my vehicle that I could see the fear and anguish on their faces. They may have realized we were fighting for them. But none were keen to find themselves in the midst of that fight.

Shortly before we reached Metz our advance was halted. Not because Patton wanted it so, but because Eisenhower and Bradley did. I'm sure Patton, a Three Star General, was pissed that he was barred from trying to take Metz frontally. Patton was a student of military history. He knew that Metz lay at the summit of a relatively low mountain. But just as a one eyed man is king in the land of the blind, so a small mountain is an Alpine Peak in terrain otherwise bereft of heights. The French had built their West Point on its summit, and it was now garrisoned by Germans. But that was not the reason Patton wanted to take Metz with his forces heroically charging up the slopes in a frontal attack! As a student of military history Patton knew that Julius Caesar was the only person in the world who had attacked Metz frontally, and captured it, Patton was dying to replicate Caesar's feat. Patton could have probably taken Metz with a frontal attack. But at a great cost in dead and wounded on both sides. Instead, Patton was ordered to encircle Metz, set up a siege, and move on with his major forces. Reluctantly, he did so. In short order. Metz surrendered, and with very little loss of life on both sides.

With Metz in its fold, and the 86th Cavalry Recon in its van, Patton's Third Army, after heavy fighting, took the Alsatian cities of Nancy and Colmar and advanced to the western bank of the Rhine. There, to the extent of my knowledge as a lowly T/5, the Third Army was now clustered along the Rhine from Strasbourg to Forbach, and places north. The bulk of the German forces had escaped across the Rhine into the manly embrace of *Das Vaterland*. It is much better strategy to cross a mighty river into your own country, and use it as your front line, than to have that same river at your back while fighting in a foreign land. I am presuming that had Patton allowed his ego to guide his movements, rather than the commands of his superiors, he would have caused pontoon bridges to be built across the Rhine at Strasbourg and moved deeply into Germany. I believe then that he would have experienced von Clausewitz' flashing sword of vengeance: a severe counterattack when his lines were extended and his flanks open to *Blitzkrieg* attacks. In Belgium, in December of 1944 and January of 1945, we and our Allies would be bloodied by that flashing sword. Bloodied, but unbeaten.

Having brought my tale to the western bank of the Rhine, let me segue back to my recounting of the mission of my 86th Cavalry Reconnaissance Squadron Mechanized. In warfare—at least since the 20th century—the primary function of the Cavalry, whether soldiers on horseback, or soldiers moving in a variety of vehicles, was to obtain military intelligence (some may say, tongue in cheek, that "military intelligence" is an oxymoron). This meant, learning where the enemy was, the composition of his forces, and where he might be going next. My Cavalry Troop, D Troop (Dog Troop), was one of the four probing units in the Squadron. Then there were two support Troops, and the Headquarters Troop. The duties and make-up of each of these seven Troops which made up our 86th Cavalry Squadron will be illustrated as I delineate the mission of the 86th Cavalry. This mission, and its successful exercise, was of vital import to the Sixth Armored Division: *we were its eyes and ears.*

In common with all four probing Troops, my unit, Dog Troop, was lightly armored and lightly armed. Our vehicles were wheeled vehicles: armored cars and jeeps. The armored cars had six huge rubber tired wheels, like those found on giant farming or construction tractors. They were propelled by powerful, rear mounted engines whose broad expanse gave us the opportunity to use them to store extra gear on them—which was not their function—and which relates to a story I shall recount of our personal encounter with General Patton. The front of the armored car was slanted at about a 45° angle. This was designed to have incoming fire glance off the vehicle. The front and sides of the vehicle were covered with steel plates. I never measured their gauge, but I estimated they were at least an inch thick. Mounted atop the vehicle was a turret, open to the elements, *i.e.*, no roof. I believe the gauge of the steel turret was about two inches. Thick enough to keep shrapnel, small arms and machine gun fire from penetrating. But less than effective against a direct hit from a heavy mortar shell or a round from the 88mm cannon of a *Panzerwagen*.

Attached to the turret was a 37 mm cannon (pea shooter might be a better description as far as cannon firepower goes), a 30 caliber machine gun set beside the cannon, and designed to be sighted and fired by the gunner. Fixed to the outside of the turret was a 50 caliber machine gun. The turret, hand cranked, could be rotated 360°. Within the turret was an extensive and expensive array of radio and telephone equipment, including a key to send Morse Code. Going on a scouting mission and gathering information, and then being unable to communicate this data to Headquarters is to engage in an exercise in futility. Within the turret, and set into springlike forms encircling the turret's interior were the rounds for the 37mm cannon. Storing such rounds in this manner was neat, but not safe, as I have related in an episode illustrative of this observation. The turret contained two round seats set on posts such as one would see in an ice cream parlor. However, these seats could be raised and lowered. Raised to the highest level one could sit and peer out over the top of the turret. Of course, your view was better standing up—but also less safe in the face of enemy fire. The gunner sat on the left seat, the car commander and radio operator, that was me, sat on the right seat, and in addition to directing the operations of the vehicles and its communication functions, also operated the 50 caliber machine gun.

Sitting, stretched out on the floor of the armored car, and facing out through its sloping front were the driver and his assistant. The assistant operated a 30 caliber machine which was fixed in position near him. By reason of their recumbent positions, these two guys would have difficulty making a speedy exit from the vehicle if such a need arose.

The armored car was painted green, as were the jeeps. Emblazoned, in white paint, on the right and left sides of the vehicle's turret was a large five pointed American star. The placement of these stars also play a leading role in an Episode I shall relate anon.

Our jeeps were not armored. They had no tops, windshields, or doors. Customarily, a 50 caliber machine gun was bolted to the right side of the vehicle's hood. The jeeps were versatile, non-complaining, highly reliable vehicles (if properly maintained). I loved them.

Our personal weapons were light weight, short barreled, semi-automatic carbines, with a magazine holding 20 rounds, if memory serves. The rounds were considerably smaller than the 30mm rounds in the Springfield rifles which we used in basic training. I liked the Springfield. It had heft and accuracy. Aside from our metal helmets, we wore no body armor. That mode of protection did not exist in WWII. In the field, aside from our dress Olive Drab uniforms, we wore combat fatigues—a coverall type garment. And underneath, long john underwear. Our boots were laced well above the ankle. Under our metal helmet we wore a green, plastic helmet liner, and under that, a green knitted cap. And before going into combat our Squadron was outfitted with a snazzy Eisenhower type jacket. We liked that.

Aside from the four probing Troops, Able, Baker, Charlie, Dog, there were the two support Troops, Easy, Fox. These were armed with light tanks, hence the name support troops. If you were tied down, and needed some quick mobile fire to help you get out, theses light tanks could be helpful. I believe their guns were only 37mm. But a cluster of them helping out on your flanks, or covering your rear, were welcomed while we endeavored to move out of harm's way. The last Troop in our Squadron was Headquarters Troop. It was the reason we had six line troops in the field. It was our Squadron's Command Center, and as such, the nerve center of all our Squadron's operations. It was the liaison between our Squadron and the next higher levels of command. I had been in the Headquarters Troop in the 4th Cavalry. The reader knows my experiences in that outfit. Thus, when I joined the 86th Cavalry I requested I not be assigned to Headquarters, but to a line troop. I was pleased when my request was granted. There's only so much chicken shit that any self respecting guy can take. I didn't know whether HQ in the 86th Cavalry would be rife with chicken shit, but I didn't want to run the risk of finding out the true state of affairs. I chose the "risk" of joining a combat Troop. I felt the odds of taking care of myself in combat were better than coping with HQ politics. And I was right.

It is a cardinal principle of warfare that an advancing army not lose contact with the foe it is pursuing. As General von Clausewitz noted, *surprise* is a critical element in determining which side shall succeed in turning the fluidity of combat into the reality of victory. No military commander, whatever his brilliance as a strategist and tactician, can engage, and defeat an enemy making an orderly retreat, when he does not know, in a timely manner, the location of his opponent's forces, their composition and combat readiness. Lack of such knowledge is the breeding ground for surprise. Imagine the confusion of an army in hot pursuit of a retreating enemy—with which it has lost contact—suddenly to have that phantom fleeing force double back and attack the unsuspecting pursuer! It was a major obligation of the 86th Cavalry to help prevent such a catastrophe from befalling Patton's Third Army. Leading the Army's advance as its eyes and ears, and as its vanguard combat force, the 86th Cavalry was its initial source of contact with the enemy. Through its efforts General Patton was able to remain close enough to the retreating German forces to enable him to determine, with ever increasing accuracy, the composition of these forces, namely, the size of their infantry, artillery and armored units and their combat capabilities.

In fulfillment of the 86th Cavalry's mission its four line Troops—my Troop D being one of them—with the support of the two light tank Troops, speedily covered—well in advance of Patton's main force—vast areas of terrain of every nature on every daily patrol. Running point for Patton it was our duty to seek out the enemy, to endeavor to determine the composition of his forces, their condition, and where they appeared to be heading, and to get this information, quickly and accurately, back to Squadron HQ from whence it went to General Patton.

How did we perform our multifaceted mission? By using techniques identical with those employed by experienced Cavalry Scouts during the Indian Wars when the West was won (or more truthfully stated, stolen from the Indians). Like those Scouts we began by reading the signs on the ground. An experienced Cavalry Scout could determine, with a high degree of accuracy, the number of Braves in a war party, where they had come from, their last campsite, when they had left it, and where they were then headed. He did this by noting such small things as the direction in which blades of grass were bent, the manner in which the terrain had been disturbed, whether by moccasins, horses' hooves, or both, the quantity and type of debris left behind, and by the residual heat, if any, of the ashes of their campfire. The warmer the ashes, the more recent the departure of the Indians, and hence, the closer to the site vacated than they would be, had the ashes been cold.

Times change, weapons change, but warfare remains a constant. Horses in the Cavalry gave way to motor driven vehicles—a change for the better, not only for the horses, now spared the horrors of war—but for Cavalry Troopers, too. Our quarry was not elusive Plains Indians in a War Party, but an equally elusive German Army trying to avoid engaging with General Patton's Third Army as it sought, in orderly retreat, to reach and cross the Rhine to safety. Such a force leaves a trail behind, which, like our Cavalry Scouts of old, we soon leaned to read. Tire tracks and tread tracks were the moccasin and hoof marks of old. We learned which vehicles made which marks. These here were made by heavily laden trucks, most likely transporting troops and supplies. Those, there, were laid down by a heavy tank, possibly a Tiger Class *Panzerwagen* with its huge cannon. And these, with an extra wide tank tread, were most likely made by motorized artillery. We could determine where they had come from, and where they were likely headed, by the way their vehicles scuffed up the terrain.

The increasing number of discarded empty water and fuel cans indicated that the units before us were moving at a quickening pace. If lucky, we might find a military cap, a tattered shirt. From the insignia contained, and other indicia I had learned to read, we could identify with specificity, the units to which the former wearers belonged. And if we were especially lucky to take prisoners, we would learn much more.

All these diverse bits of information were promptly dispatched to Squadron HQ, and from there to Patton's HQ, where his Intelligence people would use this data to piece together an ever changing picture of the composition of the enemy and where it appeared to be heading. Even with the Allies' superiority in the air, which gave Patton a more far seeing eye than that of the Cavalry, it was becoming clear to him that the Germans were eluding his best efforts to engage them in the battle he was seeking.

We knew the enemy was before us, and not too far away, for daily he rained mortar rockets and artillery fire on us, all intended to slow our advance. Often he was firing blind, he knew we were out there some where, but couldn't see us. In the next Episode I shall explain how I learned to read when incoming fire was sighted or blind. I was mindful of the menace of both in running my patrols.

Cavalry patrols did not have the firepower or armor to pick a fight with the enemy—a dead Cavalry Trooper is a poor messenger—but neither would we avoid one thrust upon us— which was the case when our patrol might run into a German patrol sent out to determine how close our forward units might be to their rear. We were in the midlands of France in early August '44 when one such encounter took place. It was high noon, and we had been on patrol since five in the morning. My men—my armored car with its crew of four, and three jeeps, each with a two man team—were tired, hot, thirsty and grimy. We didn't complain. It went with the territory. But we were looking for a break. Ahead, in the rolling terrain, I spied a tree studded rise, in poetic terms: a beckoning grove of pleasant greenery. I told my driver to head for it and park within its outer line of shade. My three jeeps tagged after me.

We were perhaps fifty meters from the grove's perimeter when a German vehicle, somewhat akin to our jeep, with four soldier on board, slowly drove out. They were broad side to us as they exited, so that we were on their flank and saw them before they spotted us. There were spontaneous shouts of Germans!! from my boys. Alerted by our cries the Germans wheeled their vehicle about, and amid a shower of dust and gravel, raced back into the shelter of the grove. I signaled to my jeep crews to fan out about my vehicle and then stop. My boys knew what to do. They were soon crouching behind their vehicles, guns a'ready, with one in the chamber and the safety off, and awaiting my next orders.

I told my armored car driver and his assistant to button up and roll forward slowly about ten meters and then stop. My gunner was sighting through his 37mm gunsight, a shell in the breech. I lowered my soda fountain seat until only my eyes and my helmet were visible above the turret's rim. We had drawn no fire. A good sign. The Germans had seen the odds against them, and were, undoubtedly, weighing what to do. We held our fire. Let them stew a bit, I thought.

My German language skills, which I had previously used to interrogate prisoners brought into Squadron HQ, were now to be tested in combat conditions in the field. Nothing like on the job training to sharpen one's skills. Raising my head just a tad higher, I shouted that they were *"Umgeringt"*, surrounded, and we would not fire, *"wir schiessen nicht"*, if they came out quickly, *"Hände hoch!"* hands up! There was a rustle of shrubbery in the grove. Nothing more. I shouted again, *"Komm' 'raus!"*, come out! I then had my driver rev up his engine as if we were going to roll in. A few seconds passed, then, out from the shelter of the grove, popped one German, hands held high. Fortunately, none of my boys lost their discipline and sent off a round. Five or so seconds passed. Then the other three came out, hands held high, reassured that we were keeping our word. Whatever those German bastard SS might do, we Americans observed the Geneva Convention.

The capture of these Germans without a shot being fired demonstrated the power of the "word" over that of the gun, especially when the word is spoken in a language both sides understood. I would repeat this phenomenon several times on patrol, and on a different mode of engagement, to even greater effect, many months later.

Captured Germans were not only removed from the ranks of the *Wehrmacht*, it made them a prime source of current information concerning their military units. Every German soldier carried a *Soldbuch*, a breast sized booklet containing his military history: where and when inducted, his medical records, rank, and most important for us, it tells us to which unit he belongs, whether infantry, artillery, etc., and the name of that unit. This information was written, at Hitler's order, in an old German script called *Sütterlin*. I taught myself to read it to make sense of the data in the *Soldbuch*. Over the years I've forgotten much of it. At Patton's HQ information we obtained from captured Germans (or the dead ones sadly left behind) helped him determine what forces were before him, and to plan his campaign accordingly. Concerning the episode described where we captured those four Germans—we were congratulated by our Squadron HQ for a job well done. But no balloons, champagne or flowers. Aw, well, war is Hell!

There was another way we got information from the enemy, but in a much sadder way. As above noted, on occasion we would come across a dead German soldier left behind inadvertently by his fleeing comrades. His *Soldbuch*, his military record book, would be examined and then replaced in his tunic's pocket so that our grave registration people would keep a record of his death. One less Unknown Soldier, whether German or American.

In the earliest days of our daily reconnaissance patrols we were given maps, where available, of the areas we were to penetrate. Were we to see an enemy patrol or outpost, we were to report what we had seen and then withdraw to a prearranged position. We were not to seek a fight with the enemy. Suddenly, about a week or two after the two wings of Patton's Third Army had joined together in Orleans, with the General's desire to engage the retreating enemy in a major battle yet unfulfilled, our rules of engagement were changed materially.

The small size of our Cavalry patrols and our limited armor and fire power did not make us a formidable force for *mano a mano* combat. We were mobile, fast and had the ability and means to seek out the enemy, and if found, to report this information quickly to Squadron HQ. Now our mission was broadened. We were to seek out the enemy, and if found, to provoke him into an engagement!

Like a wolf pack attacking its quarry we were to spread out and nip at the heels of the German forces we had encountered. And we were to rev our engines and make as much clamor as possible. In the confusion of combat—von Clausewitz famously referred to it as "the fog of war"—the evanescent line between perception and imagination is easily erased. It was our mission in these engagements to create the impression, increased through the surprise of our attack, that we were in the van of larger forces. The type of fire power thrown at us: rifle, machine gun, mortar and artillery, suggested the approximate nature of the force encountered. We sent this information back to our HQ while seeking to evade the enemy's line of fire. If he advanced against us we tried, from our scattered positions to slow him up by bursts of our fire, while calling in our position for air and artillery strikes, and then we fell back, happily so, as our alerted infantry and armor sped past us as they converged on the enemy we had aroused.

Our pin prick sallies drew responses from the Germans. But they did not achieve the results intended. They never provoked the Germans to stop their orderly retreat, *turn* and engage with Patton in the major battle he sought. I enjoyed this hit, hold and run type of warfare. And I never lost a Trooper in my patrol team. My team was the same in composition and purpose as every other patrol in Dog Troop. Fighting as a Cavalry Trooper in small, self reliant units, gave me the freedom of being wholly responsible for my own well being, and that of my fellow Troopers. I liked that. I was fighting for the freedom of others, and I enjoyed that freedom on the battlefield.

The Cavalry is designed to operate as a loose aggregation of widely dispersed, highly mobile, highly communicative, small bodies of intelligent, resolute, creative soldiers. Indeed, aside from the first time we were assembled in St. Lo, France, in late June 1944, the 86th Cavalry operated as a full Squadron, to the best of my knowledge, only during the Battle of the Bulge in Bastogne, Belgium, and immediately thereafter, when because of the huge losses suffered by our infantry units, the Squadron operated, en masse, as mechanized infantry. However, aside from these three instances, all of my engagements with the enemy were wholly with small mobile units. I recall most vividly an engagement where the enemy was not more than 50 meters from us when encountered. The enemy was as surprised to see us as we were to see them. As von Clausewitz has written, surprise can be a material factor in controlling the outcome of a military contest. And this engagement came about in this wise:

The time was the late Summer of 1944. The place, somewhere east of Orleans, the birthplace of Joan of Arc.

To Cavalrymen in a line Troop, such as my Dog Troop, the front line was wherever we were. This was not a conceit. It was a military reality. Having made our determinations where the enemy lay, and having communicated this intelligence to the rear, we Troopers enjoyed pulling to the sides of roads and fields to watch the armored, infantry and artillery units pass by as they made their way up to the Front!

Back to my recital of a surprise encounter with the enemy. It had been raining, off and on for several days and nights. Since much of our scouting and patrolling was off road we were careful not to get our vehicles mired in muddy spots, especially in farmland recently tilled, or in orchards and vineyards built on a rake. Because we had earlier detected signs, such as tank treads, which indicated that a German *Panzer* unit was in the vicinity, or had recently been there, a Tank Destroyer from the Sixth Armored Division was attached to my patrol of my armored car and three jeeps, one jeep more than usual. The Tank Destroyer, as its names indicated, had but one function, to go *mano a mano* with any German *Panzerwagen* it encountered. The TD was primarily a huge, tracked artillery piece, a giant cannon, perhaps an 88mm, or higher caliber, mounted on a flatbed, so designed, that when the cannon was fired, it would safely recoil on the tracks laid down on the flat surface of the TD. The first time I saw one it reminded me of the Union Navy's Monitor of Civil War fame: "The Cheese box on a raft". The Tank Destroyer of WWII was as much an example of American military ingenuity as was its Civil War naval predecessor. The TD was much lighter in tonnage than a conventional tank, thus it moved quite rapidly, and could keep up with my patrol even when we moved at 40 miles per hour.

As our patrol moved forward the day began to wane, what had been intermittent rain showers turned into a steady rain— nothing that would ordinarily impede our forward motion. As the rain abated a light mist began to develop. The rain was warmer than the cold, muddy ground, and this combination of mixed temperatures was causing an enveloping ground fog to develop. My armored car was slowly leading the way, and it was soon becoming difficult to see more than ten meters, or so, before us. I told my driver to stop. The column of five vehicles rolled to a halt. I climbed out of the turret of my vehicle, clambered down its side and walked back to the TD to talk with its commander, a Staff Sergeant. His TD was in the rear, covering us. Although, I was in command of the patrol, the Staff Sergeant outranked me, and so I thought it wise to ask him whether he agreed that we should bed down for the night, and then move out again in the early a.m. The TD commander thought stopping now was a good idea. We had been moving along a narrow, muddy dirt road which ran parallel to equally muddy bottom land, good for agriculture, but not conducive to swift passage for either wheeled or tracked military vehicles. The terrain had been rising gently, but perceptibly, as we had advanced along this road. To avoid making a massed, straight line target of parked vehicles for any of Hitler's still flying *Stuka* bombers, I gave orders that we move off the road and spread out in the open fields surrounding it on both sides.

The terrain where my armored car slowly left the road and moved into the neighboring field was on a decidedly higher rake than the road we were leaving. Whatever waning daylight was left was being rapidly snuffed out by the ground fog, now so thick, it severely shortened our field of vision, a negative in combat conditions. However, on the good side, the fog also acted as a sound damper, thus materially muffling whatever sounds our vehicles made as they slowly moved about to find places to halt. And, as was our practice when in the field, such conversations as we had were brief in length, and muted in volume. This was one patrol where we didn't want to tell the enemy that we were out there looking for him to respond. We slowly moved at least fifteen meters, about fifty feet, up terrain whose ascending slope was becoming ever more apparent. I thought it prudent to stop, and my driver killed the engine once he got my command. I noted from the upward tilt of the armored car that we must be on at least a ten degree grade. I had been standing in the turret while the armored car was moving. I had difficulty seeing anything once we had left the road. And I saw nothing now, despite peering all about me. And my gunner could see nothing. Nor did either of us hear anything. We were in an armored car, with a crew of four, in a cocoon of fog which rendered us blind and deaf, but also made us unseen and unheard by those who might be seeking to do us harm.

Assuming there was no enemy anywhere near us, I elected to ratchet down my soda fountain seat and sleep sitting up inside the armored car. I was not about to roll out my sleeping bag on the muddy ground next to our vehicle. Before I sacked out I set the rotation for guard duty. It was 9 p.m. when I closed my eyes and snuggled within myself, with the fog as my blanket. Scattered about, in a rough circle, and blind to each other by reason of the ground fog, five American vehicles hunkered down for the night.

At about 1 a.m. I was awakened for my one hour stint of guard duty. The fog was as intrusive as ever. Von Clausewitz, in his treatise *Vom Kriege* noted that the outcomes of the best planned battles were frequently adversely affected by the vagaries of war, in his phrase, "The fog of war". Although his fog was a rhetorical one, the fog I was awakened to was the real thing. But, as the reader will soon note, it will play the same rôle as the principle expounded upon by von Clausewitz. I did my guard duty, climbed back into the vehicle's turret, lowered my soda fountain seat and quickly sacked out again.

At about 5 a.m. my full bladder awakened me. I had to take a piss. So, with my joints stiff from their cramped sleeping posture, I clambered out of the turret, down the side of my armored car, opened my fly and prepared to spray some mud off one of the vehicle's tires. The all pervading fog was now gone. It had been replaced with a sunless, early morning grayish gloom. Enough light to discern, albeit hazily, objects hidden when, the evening before, my patrol had rolled into this area. I glanced up and noted that my vehicle was sitting a few meters above the base of a hillock covered with a thicket of brush and small trees. And as my gaze moved up the face of this hillock—which had been invisible to us when we settled down for the night—almost at its foot—I saw, through the gray, early morning haze, a figure moving down the slope in our direction. He was about thirty meters, one hundred feet away. And it looked as if he was getting ready to take a piss himself. And there! Behind him, at the crest of the hillock, partially concealed by shrubbery, I saw the profile of a *Tiger Panzerwagon*, the *Wehrmacht's* largest tank, the lengthy barrel of its 88mm cannon fortunately pointing away from us. The guy getting ready to piss was a German soldier. He spotted me the instant I saw him. I shouted, "Germans!" He shouted, *Amis!* Americans! and began to run back to his tank. I turned and and clambered up the side of my armored car and into its turret. The fly of my pants was still open but the thought of taking a leak was gone. My gunner was not in the turret. My driver, who had also slept in the armored car, revved up its engine and began to make a U turn. But as he spun about he became mired in the mud. The vehicle's 37 mm cannon was not aimed at the tank. I rotated the turret around so that my 37 mm cannon was now aiming directly at the *Panzerwagen*. As was our Troop's practice, there was a round in the breach. I slammed it shut, and pressed down with my right foot on the firing pedal. Wow! The shell hit the *Panzer* dead on, right on the black and white cross on its turret! I'm certain that the projectile I fired never penetrated any part of its heavy armor. My 37mm gun was a pea shooter in comparison to the *Panzer's* 88mm gun. But when my gun's projectile hit the Panzer there was a loud explosion and a flash of red and yellow flames which almost instantaneously blossomed into a swelling red rose! It was a beautiful sight!

After the engagement was over, and I had time to reflect on the visual impact of my 37 mm shell exploding against the German tank, I recalled reading the remarks of the aviator son of Italian Fascist dictator, Benito Mussolini, who, after strafing a column of spear waving Ethiopian warriors (Italy having invaded Ethiopia) then dropped a bomb on them. Benito's son (perhaps his name was Vittorio) described the sight of the bomb exploding within the ranks of the Ethiopians as very beautiful, likening the bursting of the bomb to that of a red rose opening up its petals. How odd, I thought, that two persons at opposite ends of the political spectrum could see a bursting shell in warfare in the same way.

I don't believe that my 37mm round did any damage to any personnel within the German *Panzerwagon*. However, the shrapnel from the exploding shell could have injured or killed anyone close by. The German running back to his tank was near it when my shell exploded. Perhaps he was hit by its fragments ricocheting off the side of his tank. None of us stayed around to find out.

Instead, we scrambled to get away from the area. My driver got the armored car free of its mud pit, and followed by the three jeeps, we speedily withdrew from the area, leaving the TD to take on the German Tiger. From the distance we heard exchanges of cannon fire. Who came out ahead I never learned. We were soon off on another patrol. No one asked HQ what the outcome had been in the engagement between two giant pieces of mobile artillery. And no one volunteered to tell us. My crew and I puzzled how we managed to come so close to the German tank without seeing it, or having the Germans see or hear us. We settled on the fog as being the reason. I never raised von Clausewitz' dictum on the Fog of War to my patrol.

Episode Twenty One

In which I learn how "to read", and thus cope with incoming artillery and mortar fire. Very vital knowledge for staying alive.

    The episodes I now recount are illustrative of my experiences in combat as a Cavalry Trooper. I never kept a war diary, hence these few episodes I relate of waging war are those whose special nature have burrowed themselves deeply within the interstices of my memory. Read them as illustrative of my experiences as a GI in WWII, and as links in a chain of Episodes which were destined to lead me to my beautiful and belóved Anneliese Baur.

    The time is early Fall 1944. The 86th Cavalry Reconnaissance Squadron Mechanized, as the reconnaissance arm of the 6th Armored Division, had assisted in clearing the Brittany Peninsula of its German forces, and was now pursuing the enemy as he fell back to the east. We were somewhere between Nancy and Metz, in Alsace-Lorraine, heading towards the Rhine. My Troop, Dog Troop, divided into its usual reconnaissance units of two to three vehicles—an armored car and two jeeps, with a complement of eight Troopers—was running its daily probing actions where we tried to determine the enemy's location, and to report this intelligence back to Troop Headquarters. We in the Cavalry were not fighting as part of a more or less large, static front line. We in the Cavalry thought of ourselves as *being* the front line. We were in that amorphous combat zone which lies between the foremost, probing units of an advancing force, and the rear guard of the enemy force falling back—with the enemy not in rout—but seeking to regroup in an orderly fashion, with the intent of resuming the attack against us. It was our task, as a small, fast, mobile, lightly armed unit to find out where the enemy was, the military composition of his forces, was it infantry, armor, artillery, or if he was no longer before us, to determine where he had gone. We had several ways of accomplishing this task.

We might actually catch a glimpse of the enemy if we were occupying the high ground, and they lay before us in a lower open terrain. That happened only once. Or we saw evidence where they had been, and where they were headed, as revealed by their vehicle tracks. Or we ran into them unexpectedly, as much a surprise to them as to us. Or they saw us first and began shelling us. And then, when contact could not be made visually, we would endeavor to flush them out by revving up our vehicles' engines and moving noisily about so that the Germans, who could not see us, might think there was a large force in their vicinity. The type and amount of resulting incoming fire would reveal to us—if we survived to report our information back—the approximate strength of the German forces we had flushed out, and their possible elements. If the incoming fire were mortar shells, rounds generally smaller in explosive power than those fired by cannons, these mortar rounds would come looping in over us, whistling and then impacting with a roar. The mortar—essentially a long tube, set up on an angle, and fired by dropping a projectile down the tube—was the simplest defensive device a unit falling back could fire. It was light, quickly set up and easily moved. We soon leaned it was the favorite defensive weapon of German infantry units and supply trains. If the incoming fire came in with a roar like a railroad train bearing down on you, and impacted with a ground shaking explosion, then we were being shelled by artillery. This indicated a number of things. That there was an armored force before us, with the fire coming from *Panzerwagen* cannons, or from an artillery battery. The length of time it took for the incoming artillery fire to come in, as measured by the time you heard the boom, and then the shell impacting and exploding, gave you some indicia whether the fire came from an artillery battery or from tanks. The artillery battery would be further in the rear of the German forces before us.

I'm not talking count down from ten to one measurements. Just the difference between short and shorter. Nothing scientific. If you quickly learned how to read incoming *unobserved* fire, you took appropriate evasive action, and lived to sweat out another day of playing hide and seek with the Germans. You reacted differently with *observed* fire. In the case of the former, you knew the enemy knew that you were somewhere in his vicinity, but he couldn't see you. You had flushed him out, as above noted. You wanted to learn something about him. You wanted to draw his fire, but not get killed trying. Remember, dear reader, our recon patrol was lightly armored and armed.

Back to the difference in one's reaction to incoming fire where it is unobserved, and where it is observed. How I learned "to read" incoming artillery and mortar, and thus to cope with it, was self taught. If there was a manual on the subject, I never saw one. Here is T/5 Katz' counsel on how to avoid getting killed or wounded by incoming fire when on the move, and when, for whatever reason, your forward movement is temporarily blocked. Let's first take the situation where both sides know the other is out there, somewhere nearby, but unseen. We're advancing. They're falling back, hoping to regroup and come back into attack mode. We'll start with incoming mortar fires. An example: They are on the east side of hilly, forested terrain. We are on the west side in a bowl shaped meadow surrounded by tall trees. The first mortar round comes looping in. It clips the top of one of the tallest trees on the edge of the meadow and explodes, sending shrapnel cascading down through the tree. Had we parked for cover under the trees it could have been *auf Wiedersehen* Arthur! As car commander of the armored car I sit or stand within its turret. The turret has no cover. It is open to the elements, and to the cloud of descending, hot shrapnel. Lesson one: Never! when exposed to artillery or mortar fire, whether observed, or not, never seek cover under trees! Every golfer, whatever his or her handicap, knows never to stand under a tree during a thunder and lightening storm.

And so I tell my driver to park out in the meadow away from the trees. The next mortar round comes in with a higher arc. The Germans had corrected their trajectory. It lands at the far end of the meadow, way to my left. We sit pat. The next falls ten meters to the right of the first one, and on the same line. Closer. But no harm, no foul. The third lands on the same line with the first two, on line to hit my vehicle if the next one follows the same pattern. Ahah! The Germans are laying down a *Teppich*. A carpet. They are laying down a pattern, which if continued, will methodically blanket the area we are in. Now I instruct my driver to move out, with the jeeps following, back to our rear area. On the way we'll report to our Troop HQ the location of the German force. The Troop Commander will then call Squadron HQ and up through command to bring in aircraft to strafe the area where we flushed out the enemy. Retracing our steps was appropriate in the case I've described. Reconnaissance units are designed to locate the enemy and to report this information back. And as I have earlier noted, Dead Cavalrymen make poor messengers.

Now assume the same scenario. Except this time I quickly note that the unobserved fire is being laid down randomly. No *Teppich*. Then my patrol would be ordered to turn around and get the hell out of there! Moving around within the meadow I've described might well put us in the random spot where the next shell comes in.

Incoming artillery fire under the patrol situations we encountered was always random. But so devastating the consequences if hit, that we quickly moved out. During the Battle of the Bulge in Bastogne, Belgium, we encountered artillery fire, and it was observed fire. The response? To take secure cover. However, because of a hero complex of our new Troop commander, we did not. As a consequence we lost two men in Bastogne through observed artillery fire, of which I write more below.

Now, another example of the things I quickly taught myself concerning incoming fire. If the fire is observed fire and the confines of the area you are in precludes quick evasive movements out of the area, then the safest thing to do is to abandon your vehicle, run as fast and as far from it as you can and head for the nearest ditch and dive in! Or if there are outcroppings of stone or boulders, hunker down behind them. The *rationale* for this is that the enemy gunners are visually aiming at the vehicle I am in. I cannot, with my 37mm pea shooter fire back to protect my crew and myself. So jump out, hide, and live to fight again another day. In such situations—after my boys and I take cover—I'd call in to our HQ, the location of the incoming fire. Aerial relief will soon zero in on the source of our discomfort. The German fire quenched, we're back into our vehicles and on our way, a happy ending to a tense situation.

A final example of how I learned to live with unobserved fire. God knew I would be a quick study. He wanted me to stay alive for that glorious day I would find my beautiful, belóved Anneliese Baur! My earlier examples all turned on *when* to move and *where* when confronted with incoming fire. This last example describes when non-movement, just plain sitting *in situ*, is the best mode for survival. This last example obtains when you are in the van of a large movement of Cavalry Troops designed, not to do reconnaissance, but to cover a lot of territory quickly and hold it long enough until units with more manpower and firepower, such as an infantry division, or a tank unit would pull in and take over.

I recall one such campaign which required my Squadron—one of the few times all the Troops were together in combat—to move rapidly through hilly, heavily wooded terrain intersected with numerous fast moving streams, some wide enough and deep enough to merit being called rivers. It had rained intermittently for several days. (Rain and warfare seem to go hand in hand.) Some of the streams could be forded with our armored cars and jeeps as long as we kept moving and missed running into concealed sink holes. When this happened a lot of pushing and pulling—and profanity—freed the stuck vehicles and forward motion continued. We forded a lot of these fast moving bodies of water that day. Then we turned a corner in the primitive dirt road we were driving on, and before us was a river perhaps 25 meters wide from bank to bank. Fortunately we didn't have to concern ourselves how to get across. The French had built a wooden bridge to span this small river, now swollen with rain waters. Dog Troop, my Troop, was leading the column, and my armored car was the lead vehicle for my Troop followed by the two jeeps that made up my usual three vehicle patrol. However, sitting in our vehicles, at its entry point, the bridge looked rickety. It was made of raw sawn wooden timbers laid across three steel girders sitting on top of a series of concrete pilings. The bridge was about four meters wide. There were no railings. I hopped out of my vehicle, and with a couple of officers who came up, we carefully crossed the bridge on foot and checked it out. It had not been mined. We all concurred that the pilings and the girders looked sound, and the planking, two inches thick, looked strong enough to carry the heaviest of our vehicles, so it was agreed that we would move across it.

I climbed back into the turret of my armored car and we began to move cautiously across the bridge. It led onto a narrow dirt road which ran between the foot of the steep hills we were facing, and the bank of the river we had just crossed. Our route of march was planned as follows: Once across, my Troop and Troops A, B and E, the latter one of the two light tank support Troops, would turn left and move along that road, while the rest of the Squadron, including Headquarters Troop, would turn right. According to such map information we had, both columns would run along that river front road for about a mile in each direction, and then be able to turn in towards each other, and join up at a meadow like area, thus avoiding the steeply hilled and densely forested area before us. By splitting our forces we avoided being bunched up in close quarters which would have made moving about quite difficult were we attacked. It was a prudent plan.

When my armored car driver rolled our vehicle off the bridge onto the dirt road, he turned left, as told, and moved down that road, followed by the two jeeps in my patrol. I was standing up in the turret of my vehicle and could see the armored car which had followed my patrol's vehicles nearing the end of the bridge.

I could also see two jeeps begin to roll onto the bridge from what was now the far side of the river as related to my location. Just then I heard a mortar round come whistling overhead. It impacted smack in the middle of the bridge and exploded with sufficient force to blow a small crater into the wooden planking of the bridge. Although shrapnel went whizzing about us, none of my patrol, nor anyone in the second armored car was hit. Its driver raced his engine and roared off the bridge, and turned left as my boys had done. Within seconds another round hit the bridge, leaving a gaping hole close to the first one. Then a third mortar round tore another hole in the bridge's roadbed. The bridge was standing, but no vehicles could now safely cross it.

Somewhere, high up in the steep hillside above us, a German mortar crew could see the bridge and were accurately shelling it. But the almost straight up incline of the hill atop of which they were perched, made it impossible, I quickly sensed, for the Germans to drop a round on us as long as we hugged the toe of the hill and stayed in its lee. Their rounds could only loop over us and impact harmlessly a goodly distance away. Now the Germans knew that some of our vehicles had crossed the bridge before it was disabled. But they didn't know how many. Noting the ruggedness and steepness of the terrain I doubted the Germans would risk running headlong down to attack us. So there we were, two armored cars and two jeeps sitting on a narrow road, on one side, the steep hills, on the other, the river. Until the bridge could be repaired, or the German mortar position taken out, we were stranded, but, in my opinion, perfectly safe. And I so advised my boys, and the crew in the other armored car. I suggested we park our vehicles about ten meters apart, so that if I were wrong, and a vehicle was hit, the resultant shower of shrapnel most likely would not hit the guys in the other vehicles. I contacted HQ by radio, told them the situation, and that we were OK, and where I thought the German mortar emplacement might be, thus enabling an air strike to be set up. I arranged to have all four vehicles periodically rev their engines to make it sound as if our numbers were greater than they were, and then we worked out a schedule for guard duty and sleeping. Each crew member would sleep on a two hour cycle. I then clambered onto the rear portion of my armored car, fished through my duffel bag and took out my Bible and one of my law books. I ratcheted down my soda fountain seat within the turret of my armored car and did some solid reading. When night fell I read by a carefully sheltered flashlight. I sat and studied. When it was my turn to pull guard, I did. Otherwise, I sat and sat, and read and read. Some of my buddies were ambivalent about sitting still for any length of time, as the German would occasionally loop a mortar shell over our heads. And these guys would constantly move their vehicles about, like a cornered King trying, in a game of chess, to avoid checkmate. But I just sat and read, and absorbed a lot of book "larnin" and some good old religion. I was more rested than they when the sun came up.

Right after dawn a Piper Cub spotter plane flew over the area and spotted the German mortar position. Within an hour it was taken out by one of our fighter aircraft. The bridge was made sufficiently safe to cross, and by noon the Squadron was back on track. By that time I had placed my books, back with their mates, into my duffel bag, available for the next time I was able to get a chance to read them.

"Arthur, battle weary, Nancy, France,
Late Summer 1944".

Fruits of war, Late Summer 1944

Episode Twenty Two

In which I relate how a reconnaissance patrol should be run correctly.

Perhaps the key mission of the 86th Cavalry Reconnaissance Squadron Mechanized was identical with that of our horse borne military antecedents, and of our religious forbears, Joshua and Caleb: to go forth and spy out the land. We did this by running daily patrols, in our vehicles, and, at times, dismounted. The latter function took place when we had reached our intended goal, determined by a location found on our map, or lacking one for the area we were in, by predetermining the number of vehicular miles we would cover, then calling a halt and concealing our vehicles and ourselves as best we could, considering the nature of the terrain. We would then dig, as our outpost, a slit trench/fox hole about a 100 meters, or more, forward of where the patrol would bed down for the night. And we would take turns rotating as guard in that forward position. Sometimes, by reason of the nature of the terrain, digging a slit trench was not possible. In such cases we would pick out a natural feature, such as a copse of trees, as a landmark to identify the outer perimeter of our area, and, during nightfall, we would run periodic patrols to that landmark and back to our closely guarded base. We set the landmark about a quarter mile away from where we were bedded down. Should the man on patrol run into a problem—shouts and weapons' fire would indicate this unhappy event—the guys at our base camp would make efforts to enter the fray while calling in for help.

A patrol, sometimes one man, sometimes two—the nature of the terrain dictating the number—would move out on foot and, absent drawing fire, which would quickly indicate, as above noted, that the enemy was nearby—would note different things to report back to the patrol's base, and from there up to HQ. A well trained Trooper knew that a recon sortie in vehicles, or on foot, into territory which might yet harbor hostile elements, was not to be treated as a Sunday picnic, or as a saunter through a city park. Thus, those on patrol, particularly the first ones out, would report back on the various "things" seen in daylight. These "things" could be man made objects, such as abandoned dwellings, and farm implements, or livestock, dead or roaming about, military wreckage and even odd shaped geologic formations—and those on patrol would carefully note the location of these disparate things. Noting these items and their locations carefully was important when night fell and the patrols continued. For what might be perceived as one thing benign in daylight, could, if not recalled as previously seen, be conceived as something hostile, which could create problems for the patrol, as I delineate below.

As leader of my patrol I took it upon myself to run the first leg of every patrol. No sense being a leader if you don't lead. Thus, on more than one patrol I came upon dead horses and cattle. In combat one sees lots of dead livestock, killed in a contest of no concern to them. I had learned to estimate how long a horse or cow was dead. Gases build up within the animal's body after it has been killed. Within a week the animal's belly swells up like a balloon. The horse or cow would then roll over on its back with its legs straight up in the air, a gruesome sight! Of which more below.

And on one sad occasion, I found the body of a German soldier. He still had his helmet on. There was no smell of decay about him, so he must have been recently killed. Like us, the Germans try to take with them all their dead and wounded. Leaving him behind, and the condition of his corpse, indicated that they had moved hurriedly and recently out of the area. Thus, German forces could be just miles away. That information, and other intelligence we gathered that day, was soon sent to HQ, along with the location of this dead German soldier so that our unit which recovers our deceased could also bring his body in.

Reconnaissance scouts much prefer to capture their Germans alive. We can elicit more useful information from talkative prisoners under stress, than can be obtained from an examination of the *Soldbuch* which every German soldier carries with him. But aside from noting his unit insignia on his uniform, the only other information I could glean from him was from his *Soldbuch*. I opened the left breast pocket of his uniform and took out his *Soldbuch*, his military record, a more detailed equivalent of our dog tags. It contained a complete military record of the soldier. I noted the military information in my field notebook and replaced the *Soldbuch* in his jacket breast pocket, making sure the pocket was closed. I have seen some of our GIs remove the *Soldbücher* from dead German soldiers, and either wantonly destroy them, or keep them as souvenirs of war, not realizing, even after I tried to remonstrate with them, that they were committing those German soldiers to the ranks of the unknown, and their families to years of unhappiness as to their status. The data derived from beings as different as a dead German soldier and a dead French horse provided my Squadron HQ with the snippets of information it needed to determine where the enemy was, or had been, or might be moving to, and what units were involved. As stated, my information also included a reference to the location of the dead German soldier, so that our unit which attends to the recovery of our combat dead could also retrieve the body of this German soldier. We would have expected the German forces to treat our dead in the same manner. Except for the SS, they generally did.

Had I not reported the dead German and the dead horse, and where they lay, and nightfall came, and one of my patrol came along, and spied this dead German lying in the grass, he might well had taken a shot at him, thinking this prone German was lying in wait for him. Or seeing, vaguely, in the dark, the dead bloated horse, feet straight up, half concealed in a thicket, might have caused him to fire his weapon. And had there been Germans within sound of his gun bursts we would have given ourselves away. Hence, paying attention even to the smallest thing, is important to one on a reconnaissance patrol. And this included looking not only up and around, but down at your feet. An alert Trooper always looked carefully where he was walking.

Minefields were a cheap and very effective weapon of the retreating German forces.

This recital of reconnaissance patrol techniques leads me to my first episode with a minefield, which I now recount.

Episode Twenty Three

In which I walk numerous times unwittingly and unscathed through an anti-personnel mine field.

This Episode unfolded in early Autumn 1944 in the eastern part of France, somewhere in Alsace-Lorraine after Patton's Third Army—of which my 86th Cavalry Reconnaissance Squadron was a vital unit—had taken Metz, Nancy, Colmar and their environs. Ahead of us lay the Rhine, the west bank of which we now controlled. Across the Rhine, a wide river in this area, lay Germany. Our goal, and the goal, too, of numerous German troops in pockets which Patton had passed in his rush to reach the Rhine. Our forces were spread out from Forbach, and points further north, to Strasbourg in the South, and even lower down. Even a lowly T/5, such as I, recognized that our forces were insufficient in numbers to fully control every nook and cranny of so vast a region. Those Germans still on the loose, and these were some of Hitler's best troops, were now playing cat and mouse with us. With the help of their French Vichy supporters the mice were beginning to crawl out of their holes, and trying to sneak by us cats in an effort to reach and cross the Rhine to fight again another day. It was our job as Cavalry Troopers to find them, capture and kill them if we could, or at the very least, hold them in place until our more heavily armed units could come in and do the heavy lifting. What military strategists and tactical planners might call mop-up operations, a sort of cleaning up of tables and the dining room floor after the banquet was over, was, to us Troopers, a daily and deadly exercise in hide and seek.

Early Autumn in New England and other northern United States climes would be called Indian Summer, with the leaves of the deciduous trees turning all shades of red, orange and yellow. In our part of France the Indians and their Summer had already left us. The weather was blustery one day after another, with sleety rain mixed with flurries of snow. During the day the temperature would hover in the upper thirties Fahrenheit: two to five degrees above Celsius. During the night the temperature would fall below freezing. This weather was a key factor in the episode I now relate.

Completing our day of reconnaissance my patrol prepared to bed down for the night on the edge of what had been farmland devoted to the growing of some kind of grain crop. Here and there on the surface of the field were patches of stubble left from the harvesting. The field was about 100 meters square, flanked on its sides by rows of tall, thin, leafless trees, which, from their narrow shape, looked like Lombardy Poplars. I speculated they had been planted as much for their use as a windbreak, as to demarcate the field's boundaries. Beyond these rows of trees one could make out other fields similarly situated. Mixed in with the stubble were patches of scraggly grass which had sprung up after the field was gleaned. The field was soggy from the frequent rains, but not mushy, muddy or torn up, which would have been the case had wheeled or tracked vehicles been driven across it recently. From this I inferred that if German troops had been in the area they had pulled out before the rains set in.

We had been told we would be moving out early the next day to patrol a different sector—so no need to dig a foxhole for a point man to stay in. If such a hole were dug we would set it about 100 meters in front of our bedding down site. Instead, we would run patrols across the field to its far side and back to our position which consisted of our three vehicles, my armored car and two jeeps, parked in a circle, with each vehicle and its weapons, facing out. The guys bedded down within the circle. One would stay up for an hour, while the others slept, and one would run a patrol to the far side of the field, also on an hourly rotating basis, And this cycle would continue until dawn when we would move out to our new sector.

I was the patrol leader, and I took the first patrol. The light rain had stopped. Gray clouds lay low over us. It was late afternoon, and such light as had escaped the cloud's mantle was now waning. I started my patrol from the edge of the field closest to our circle of vehicles and headed directly across the center of the field to its far side, with a particularly tall tree being my guide post.

I did not stray about. I kept my path a straight and narrow one. A wise choice from both a military and religious point. With my carbine cradled in my arms, a round in the chamber, and the safety off, I walked slowly, very slowly, hunched over, looking carefully at the ground, and all about me. I saw nothing untoward. I reached the tall tree on the far side. I had drawn no fire. All was calm, but nothing bright. This is a play on the German Christmas Carol, "*Stille Nacht, Heilige Nacht*", "Silent Night, Holy Night, all is calm, all is bright . . ." All through my combat days I would regale myself with snatches of classical music, including operatic arias. I particularly loved to hum the stately, ethereal, soul lifting melody, carried initially by the strings, in the Third Movement of Beethoven's Ninth Symphony, *Adagio molto e cantabile*. And when I did, I would wonder how a nation that could give the world a Beethoven could also descend into the pit of depravity and spew up a Hitler and his Nazi minions of mass murderers. In the Fall of 1944 I was not fully aware of the Concentration Camps, and of the Holocaust being inflicted upon my Jewish People, and of the slaughter of millions of others. Had I known of these atrocities, my bafflement then would have been even greater.

Having reached my target tree I turned around, and began to retrace my steps back to the side of the field from whence I had started my patrol. I write "retrace my steps" because I consciously, meticulously, placed my returning footsteps directly upon those impressions I had made in first crossing the field. I had seen no evidence of mines, such as recently moved earth, or objects which seemed out of place in the landscape, but common sense dictated that if I had encountered nothing amiss on the path I had laid down, that I should be OK coming back on its now muddied surface. The whole patrol, from beginning to end, lasted about twenty minutes. Ten minutes there. Ten minutes back. A carefully paced, alert exercise. Nothing to be concerned about. And I so advised my patrol team. I cautioned them, however, to stay on the path I had made, straight across the field, straight back. My guys were no dummies. They knew the reason for my counsel, and they would follow it.

After I had returned from making the initial patrol, I telephoned our position to HQ and gave them an overview of the area. No Germans, and no signs they had been here recently. I then ate some of my canned rations and climbed into my armored car's turret. I lowered my seat, took out one of my books, read for a bit and then fell asleep. My gunner, who shared the turret with me, never liked sleeping in the vehicle. He had taken his sleeping bag and was stretched out along side the armored car. All my guys, who were as mindful of minefields as I was, stayed well within the path I had laid down. It was well past midnight when I was awakened to run my part of the patrol cycle. The weather had turned much colder as I slept. The light, cold rain which was falling when I sacked out, had changed into a snow flurry. The winds fluctuated, sometimes no more than a light breeze, then they would increase in strength. When this occurred the cloud cover would be torn open, then close, then open again, and for brief moments, the moon would shine wanly down, barely illuminating those patches of earth where its thin rays fell. The path across the field which I had made many hours before, and which my fellow Troopers had subsequently trod with extreme caution, had now become a clearly delineated narrow path of packed down mud. And when I write "narrow" I mean no more than eighteen inches wide. I stepped onto the path, staying within its narrow confines, and began my patrol across the field.

The snow flurries abated as I started my trek. I walked slowly, but securely within the path. The darkness, punctuated only by the occasional emergence of the moon's faint rays, and by short bursts from my flashlight, aimed close to the ground, precluded any rapid passage. Upon hitting the bare earth the flurry of snow flakes melted. And when they fell onto the grain stubble, or onto random blades of dried grasses, they turned into droplets of water. There was no pattern to these water droplets.

I reached the far end of the field, and began, as carefully as I had come, to retrace my steps back to the point and place of the beginning of my trek—to use language we in the Cavalry used in reading maps and charting routes of march and exit. The cloud cover had parted a bit more than it had when I started out, and through the wider openings, the moon's rays were able to shine down on me at varying intervals, and for ten to fifteen seconds at a time, before being snuffed out by the low flying clouds coming together again. It was during these brief periods of faint illumination, and about a quarter of the way back to the home side of the field, when, as I was peering down I noticed something unusual. A scant few inches from the left side of the path, and about six inches from the small toe side of my left boot I saw a Y shaped object protruding about four inches from the ground and encrusted with frost. It looked like two blades of grass of equal length coming out of a single stem. I stopped in my tracks I had not seen this type of regular shaped object before. And then I glanced to my right. And, by golly! There was the same Y shaped object, and similarly encrusted with frost. These were not natural formations. When the snow flurry flakes settled on the ground, they melted, and when they settled on the stubble or grass, vegetable matter, they melted into droplets of water. Here were objects, regular in form, on which the snow did not melt! Clearly, these Y shaped forms were not dried vegetation. They were man made! I stopped walking, and hunched over, making sure I did not shuffle my feet, and peered about me. On both sides of the path I had created during my first patrol through the field I now discerned more of these frost covered Y forms flanking both sides of the path. My God! I had walked through a mine field, and so had my men! It was in an anti-personnel, "Bouncing Betty" mine field! I was surrounded by them! Closer inspection revealed that these mines had been laid down in a pattern of straight parallel lines set about a meter apart, and running from one end of the field to the other in the direction I had taken in making my first patrol. I had been lucky to walk in a straight line through the pattern squarely laid down by our methodical German opponents. Had the mines been planted in a random pattern I might not now be recounting this tale. On reflection, however, it wasn't luck, or that the Germans were so methodical in laying their mines, it was *beshert*, it was meant to be that I not be hurt or killed in that mine field. God was not intending to leave me so short of my goal, then unknown to me, of finding my belóved Anneliese Baur. And He knew, that in my exercise of the free will He had given me that I would make those choices which would secure me to find my Anneliese Baur.

And so there I was. Standing rigidly, all nerve endings on alert and making sure I was in the very center of the well worn path, and not anywhere near any of those Y shaped, frost covered objects. Why were they frost covered? They were made either of plastic or metal, or a combination of both man made materials. When the snow flurries fell on the bare earth or on the stubble or grasses, they were colder than their host materials and soon melted into droplets of water. The man made Y shaped objects retained their cold, and when the snow fell on them it found a host as cold or colder than it was, and thus coated these Y shaped objects. Each Y shaped object protruding above the ground was the trigger mechanism for the mine to which it was attached. The mine is a canister about the size of a 1 lb. coffee can, filled with all kinds of metal scrap and buried in the ground, tied to a tether. Stepping on the Y trigger activates the mine by releasing an explosive charge which propels the mine out of the ground and when it reaches the end of its tether another mechanism explodes the mine, scattering shrapnel at about the height of a soldier's testicles, or the equivalent height of his thighs. The idea is to maim, or with luck, to kill the soldier struck by the ragged shrapnel spewed from the exploding canister.

Mines are a cheap and effective defensive weapon. If laid in large quantities and in areas which must be traversed by advancing armies, they slow the advances of such armies, as time and effort must be taken to clear these minefields, or to take circuitous routes to avoid them, all this allowing the retreating forces to fall back in a more orderly manner, thus giving them more time to regroup for their counter attacks. Further, minefield injuries, if they do not kill their targets outright, cause serious, maiming wounds. Severely wounded soldiers require long term care from large bodies of highly trained personnel, again a factor which slows the forward motion of advancing armies.

If the field was also salted with anti-tank mines I didn't know, and cared not to learn. I was safe as long as I stayed within the path I had laid down, and which my team had carefully followed. Knowing what I now knew made staying in the very center of the path the most intelligent thing I could do. It was clearly a matter of life or death or grievous injury were I to make a misstep. But it would take some doing. What had been a slow and careful walk some hours before, was now an even more suspenseful exercise. When the moon broke through the low cloud cover, I could see a few feet before me. But the moon was playing hide and seek with the clouds. There would be brief periods of faint light, lasting only for seconds, then total darkness. I was so concerned to stay right in the middle of the path, and to move ever so slowly that I had no time to be scared. If anything, I was hyper alert. Slowly, oh so slowly, hunched over, flicking my flashlight on for a second or two whenever the moon, chaste diva that she was, hid herself behind the clouds, I cautiously made my way back to my starting point, still some distance away. Place one foot down after the other Art, I told myself, just follow the footprints in the middle of the path. And so I proceeded, one slow step in front of the step completed, trying to make each footprint before me mine. As I progressed it seemed as if the field on both sides of the path was suddenly in full bloom with frost coated Y shaped objects. Probably my fevered imagination. The number of mines really didn't matter. It would take only one to do you critical, if not fatal damage. In my hunched posture I was mimicking Richard the Third or the Hunchback of Notre Dame. A foot patrol which ordinarily I would have completed at night in, at most, a half hour would now take almost an hour to complete. When I finally stepped off the path into the line of trees flanking the field, at the spot where I had started my patrol, I was physically drained, and drenched in sweat.

When I got back to where my guys were waiting for me they were relieved to see me. As the time went by, and I had not returned, they had become concerned for my safety. "Where the fuck is Katz? He should have been back by now!" They had heard no gunfire, no explosions, no shouts from me or from anyone else. They had all intelligently stayed awake and fully alert, each man with his weapon in hand, a round in the chamber and the safety off, in the event I had been captured or killed, which would mean the Germans were close by. I told them why it had taken me so long to run the patrol, and how lucky we all were. They all agreed. At daybreak we mounted our vehicles, and moved out and forward, after I had reported to HQ the existence and location of the minefield. Naturally, we avoided, like the plague, the open field before us. Instead, we cautiously moved along the outer perimeter of the trees encircling the field. The terrain here was uneven and rocky, not an easy place to mine, but equally not an easy place to traverse with wheeled vehicles. But at least we felt that the area was free of explosive devices.

Months later, I would encounter another minefield with consequences to me different from what occurred in the episode I have just related. But everything was *beshert*, meant to be. Each of my episodes, however they affected me when they happened, was bringing me ever closer to finding my beautiful, belóved Anneliese Baur. *Baruch HaShem!*

My minefield experiences have instilled within me a peculiar habit. Winters in my part of Ohio can be a series of snowfalls, followed by days of clear and warmer weather. This causes the snow to melt. Then, overnight the weather will turn cruelly cold, and the melting snow refreezes into slippery sheets of ice. Then it snows again, and these sheets of ice are covered, barely, beneath the newly fallen snow. The new snow, pristine in its silvery finery, hides its own minefield. Stepping on it, unmindful of the sheet of ice it lightly cloaks, can send you flying. I know from experience. Stepping off a train in Russian occupied Berlin in the bleak Winter of 1946, I stepped onto this concealed *Glatteis* and went sprawling on my back. (My trip to Berlin was critical in enabling Anneliese and me to marry, of which more below). Thus, during those winter days in Ohio, whenever I leave the stoop of my home to walk to my curbside mailbox—and snow has fallen, frozen and melted too frequently to make shoveling it away an easy task, and a new thin layer of snow has fallen overnight—I walk in the exact footsteps I first laid down to that letterbox, and then carefully re-step in each one as I retrace my way back to the house. And so I walk quite safely through the snow covered Ohio Winter minefields, having slipped and fallen only once when I failed to step carefully into my earlier footprints. I was not hurt. Only annoyed at myself for not following my usual WWII minefield lessons.

Episode Twenty Four

In which I relate how I got to cast my first vote and make a political statement at the same time.

While stationed in England I turned 21 on March 21, 1944. Under the law, as it then stood, an American citizen, whether native born, or naturalized, could not vote in a national election until that citizen reached the age of 21. The voting age is now 18 years. President Franklin Delano Roosevelt, a Democrat, was running for his fourth term. (The Republicans subsequently worked to amend the Constitution restricting a President to two consecutive terms in office). I was anxious to cast my first ballot, and to do so by voting for FDR. Somewhere along the way I had learned that a GI could vote via an absentee ballot. I obtained the requisite papers requesting an absentee ballot, filled them out and mailed them off to New York State, which was then my home state. This must have been sometime in late July 1944. After I gave the ballot request papers, along with other letters I had written, to my Troop's mail clerk, I gave the matter no further thought. Now, fast forward to the first or second week in October 1944. My Cavalry Troop, Dog Troop was then somewhere in the Alsace-Lorraine region in the easternmost part of north central France.

The first weeks of October 1944 were already much like the rest of 1944 would be in that part of France: rainy, damp, cold, with blustery winds, and when the weather got cold enough, the rain showers would turn into snow flurries. And the terrain was dank and muddy. Dark brown, slushy goo all over the place. When the mud dried on our vehicles, and on our boots and battle fatigues, it caked hard—like frosting on a week old slice of wedding cake—and hard to scrape off. Lucky for us guys in the Cavalry, especially those of us assigned to armored cars, as I was. For we could then pack a lot more personal gear, than the GIs in the infantry, and carry the stuff in our vehicles. Thus, we could

150

change our outer clothing, our fatigues, at least once a week, and stow the dirty stuff to be washed when and if we had the time and place to do it. I also tried to change my underwear and socks at least twice a week, and sometimes I succeeded. How's that for fighting a clean war!

We Troopers stowed our clean and dirty gear in duffel bags and sacks, which we hung on the back of our armored cars, or wherever we could find a place in our jeeps. Boots could be seen hanging down to dry from the rear ends of our vehicles. This didn't affect the vehicle's military capabilities, but it sure didn't look regulation. Our armored car sometimes looked like a laundry delivery service, or a trash pick-up truck, with a turret, 37 mm cannon and a 50 caliber machine gun going along for the ride. This mode of bedecking our armored car is the subject of another episode I shall relate in due course. It involved a one on one encounter with General Patton. Now to my absentee ballot story. My Troop had moved into a new position a day or two before the incident I now relate took place. Except for the Battle of the Bulge in Bastogne, Belgium, and the period immediately thereafter, we in the Cavalry rarely stayed more than a day or two in the same location. But however long we stayed, we always set up a perimeter defense. This meant digging at least one foxhole, or guard point, about 100 meters in front of where we had circled our vehicles. Sometimes, depending upon whether we thought the terrain on our flanks would invite easy attacks, we would dig one foxhole on each flank. And whether we had one point location, or more, we would rotate the guys sitting out there. On the day in question, I was sitting in the point foxhole. It was in an open field. Before the war came it must have been a beautiful, slightly undulating stretch of meadowland. I could imagine the sheep, goats, cattle and horses grazing in its greenery. Now the meadowland was a shit box of mud, up to your ankles. The weather that afternoon was as I have described it. If you didn't have to be in it you were the lucky one. And there I was, hunched up in my hole, trying to expose only my face to the cold wind. I heard some squishing sounds behind me. I pivoted in my hole, and there, approaching me, was my Staff Sergeant. He was wearing a fresh pair of fatigues and looked quite natty. Accompanying him was a guy new to me. It turned out he was the Squadron's mail clerk from HQ. He was dressed in a clean set of ODs, his olive drab dress uniform. When I had been in the 4th Cavalry, and attached to its Headquarters Troop, I wore, along with the other enlisted HQ personnel, my olive drab uniform.

Anyway, here they came, my Staff Sergeant in his fresh fatigues, and the HQ mail clerk in his olive drab uniform. As much as each tried to be as careful as possible in making their way through the muddy field, they were getting splattered. They arrived at my foxhole. In a voice clearly expressing his annoyance, my Staff Sergeant said, "Katz, this guy (meaning the mail clerk) has got something for you." At which point the mail clerk, in a voice echoing the annoyance of my Sergeant, asked me, "Are you T/5 Arthur S. Katz?" I avowed I was. The mail clerk then said, "Here is your New York State Absentee Ballot." Whereupon he tossed,—perhaps, threw would be a better description—a large manila envelope at me. Apparently the absentee voter law required that the person delivering the ballot to military personnel make sure that the recipient was the person named on the ballot envelope. Hence, the presence of the Sergeant to identify me as Katz, and the mail clerk's short and surly speech, reaffirming who I was before "delivering" the ballot envelope to me. These guys were really annoyed, or more bluntly put, they were really pissed off at me. They had tramped over 100 meters in gooey mud to get to me, and now they would have to slog 100 muddy meters back to drier ground. Their clean clothes and shoes they wore when they began their absentee ballot delivery service to me would be a muddy mess when they hit dry land again.

As my Staff Sergeant turned to go he said to me, "Shit, Katz, you're only one guy! How the fuck does your one vote matter?" And he and the mail clerk headed back to our bivouac area. Now it was my turn to be pissed. "Shit!", I said to myself, "I'm only one guy, what do I matter!" So I climbed out of my hole and began to follow them. I had gone only a few yards when my Sergeant heard the squishing of my boots in the mud. He turned, "Where the fuck are you going?" He was surprised and annoyed. "Well", I said, "You just told me that I'm only one guy, with one vote that don't mean shit. So I figured if one guy don't matter I might as well go in." My Sergeant stopped in his tracks, and stared at me, his face a mix of surprise and anger. He said nothing for about four or five seconds, this pause, brief as it was, was not his style. He then said, his voice steely, but with the anger gone, "OK, you made your point. Now get back into your fuckin' hole!" My point made I returned to my hole. One man, one foxhole. One man, one vote. They matter.

Episode Twenty Five

In which General Patton makes a surprise "inspection" of our field patrol when we were taking a noon break, with odd consequences.

Prussian General Karl von Clausewitz, in his seminal work on war, *Vom Kriege*, states that war—whatever else it might be to those fighting it in the field—is, from its inception, to its conclusion, an exercise in political power, in which the winner imposes its will upon the loser. Officers, and the troops they lead in combat, may not be aware of von Clausewitz' dictum. But they are all too mindful that war is a dangerous enterprise fraught with the certainty of uncertainty. Although the weaponry of warfare, and the defenses to such weaponry have changed materially over the ages, warfare has not changed. Except for those rare occasions when a carefully planned attack is carefully executed, and the results sought are fully attained, warfare, more often than not, is a hodge-podge mixture of happenings, calculated and accidental. As I experienced it in the Cavalry, war consisted of periods of intense combat activity, which kept your adrenalin levels high, interspersed with brief periods of relaxation bordering on boredom. And it was during these latter times that the pressures of combat were relieved by interludes of levity. I recount one such episode. Why do I recall this one and not others? Because its absurdity earned it a place within those convoluted interstices of that part of my brain which stored such odd memories.

The setting was that broad expanse of France best described as east of Orleans and west of Metz. The time was late September 1944. Although Summer was merging into Fall, the weather, for the most part, was still hospitable. We were constantly on the move—no boredom there—scouting and probing, doing the reconnaissance work we were trained to do. We experienced periods of intense incoming artillery and mortar fire, and ran into pockets of Germans. In brief fire fights we routed them, and captured a goodly number. Interrogating these prisoners gave me numerous opportunities to hone my German. Sometimes I found I spoke German better than they did! Those guys were eastern European Nazi Lovers who had enlisted in the *Wehrmacht*. The German High Command left them out there, along with thousands of anti-tank and anti-personnel mines, to try to slow our advance east towards Germany. The top German units were pulled back to regroup and fight again another day—which, of course, they did, and very effectively.

This episode brought my patrol in direct contact with General Patton, the Commanding General of the Third Army, in which we, in the 86th Cavalry, were a small, yet in our own minds, a vital part. In early afternoon, after a reconnaissance of a large sector revealed that our quarry had fled the area patrolled, I so notified HQ and then looked about for a spot where we could find some cover to spend the night without exposing ourselves to observation from the air from whatever was left of Goering's *Luftwaffe*, or to discovery by a rear guard group of members of the German's *Aufklärungsabteilung*, their reconnaissance forces.

We found what we were looking for in a wooded area abutting a large tract of meadowland. Close inspection revealed this wooded area was man made. It was a carefully laid out tree farm, one tree equidistant from the next, and all with similar caliper measurements—the measurement of a tree's trunk width/diameter. This meant that the trees were planted at the same time, and when the desired caliper and height were reached, each tree would be harvested at the same time. Being man made the tract had been carefully tended, with debris and undergrowth regularly removed. Now, with this part of France an active war zone, this tree farm had probably not been maintained and cleared of undergrowth for at least all of late Spring and Summer of 1944. Thus, between the straight lines of trees—they all appeared to be Birch—there were patches of knee high grasses and weeds in bloom (one man's weed is another man's flower). But still a neat place in which to bed down, concealed from aerial and ground surveillance.

So, in mid afternoon we pulled out of the meadow and parked our vehicles just within the perimeter of the tree farm. Its man made orderliness, and the uniformity of its tree saplings, with their green canopy of fully foliaged branches—through which sunlight filtered—gave all of us a feeling of comfort—the vagaries and disorders of combat replaced, if only for a brief period, by a fixed pattern of peaceful uniformity.

My men and I broke out our canned rations and mess gear, after posting the ubiquitous guard, to stand unseen at the edge of the tree farm. We then settled down for a bit of relaxation. Even when we do not encounter the quarry we are seeking, or he us, constant alertness, and the tensions it brings, are a daily part of our lives as Cavalry Troopers. And so, whenever we had the opportunity to relax long enough to dismount and lie about, I had begun the practice, wholly unofficial, to take one of my radio receivers out of its accustomed place in the turret of my armored car, and with a lengthy extension cord I had fashioned, set the radio on the ground, with my guys clustering around to listen to whatever station I could bring in. The most powerful, and thus the one most easily received, was the German propaganda station in occupied Luxembourg, "*Hier ist Radio Luxemburg*". Here is Radio Luxemburg. The announcers were mainly women, speaking an impeccable King's English. Their messages were directed to us GI Joes. To get, and keep our attention, they played a lot of contemporary American and British popular music, among them performances by Glenn Miller, Artie Shaw and Benny Goodman, not concerned that the latter two were Jewish. Once having gained our attention, these sexy voiced young women would tell us how the 4F's and the draft dodgers were, all having fun at home screwing our women while we were risking our lives fighting against the one nation, the German Nation, under its great Leader, Adolf Hitler, capable of preventing the Russian Communists, and their Jewish allies, from taking over the world! We all laughed.

We were not poly sci majors, but we all knew bullshit when we heard it, even though we couldn't smell it. And we kept on listening because we liked the music, and because the women's sexy voices created erotic fantasies. With my radio on the ground we were enjoying Radio Luxemburg when our guard came running, shouting that American officers in a squad car were approaching our camp site. Before he could catch his breath in rolls that squad car. In its front seat, the driver and a Sergeant Major, the highest ranking non-com in the Army. In the back seat, a chicken Colonel, the one with an Eagle with outstretched wings on his epaulets, and next to him, Oh my God! General Patton!.

I had never seen the General in the flesh. I had seen his photos and had heard about him. From his natty, carefully pressed uniform, to his helmet sporting his three stars, to the two pearl handled pistols in his belt, this was General Patton, our Third Army Commanding Officer! Patton's squad car rolled to a stop perilously close to my radio receiver, attached by its umbilical cord to the turret of my armored car. As Patton hopped out of his vehicle and briskly strode a few paces towards us, my men and I all jumped to attention and saluted. Patton didn't return the salutes. Instead, his aide de camp at his side, he walked about among us, a stern expression on his face, as if making an inspection. Suddenly he spotted my armored car. And what he saw was this: the large white stars—there was one painted on the right and left sides of the turret—had been muddied over to hide them from view—and on the rear engine hood was an assortment of boxes and bags of personal gear, some of it mine, and dangling from the rear end of the engine were a pair of muddy boots belonging to one of my crew, hanging there to dry, and several pairs of socks and a pair of long john underwear, all mine, drying after a recent wash. The exhaust of the engine when the armored car was running, hastened drying.

Patton was clearly taken aback by what he saw: the mud bedaubed armored car turret, the personal gear atop the engine's hood, and hanging from the engine's rear. Almost snarling, he demanded, "Whose in charge here?" I quickly affirmed I was. Coldly, he looked me up and down. "Aren't you proud to be an American soldier?" A surprising question, but I hastened to say I was. "Then why the fuck (the General knew how to speak GI) are the white stars on your armored car covered over? Ashamed to show them?" General Patton was being a tad smart ass now. I tried to explain that in our first weeks of combat our Squadron had lost several armored cars by direct hits on their turrets. A couple of captured Germans revealed that it was easy to hit our armored cars by aiming at the white stars on the turrets. So we muddied out the stars and that reduced the accuracy of German marksmanship considerably. I spoke fast, almost stuttering to get my explanation out. Patton barely waited for me to finish when he barked, "Get that shit off those stars now!" My guys immediately jumped to it. Then he added, "And get all that crap off your vehicles. They look like you're in the Chink laundry business!" Before I could begin to get my patrol out of the laundry business, he shouted at me, "Soldier, all of you are out of uniform! Why aren't you wearing your leggings?" If it wasn't the Commanding General of the Third Army chewing my ass out, I would have laughed. Leggings are canvas, button up leg coverings from ankle to knee. A carry over from WWI they had been issued to us, but except in basic training, I don't recall ever wearing them again. This sent all of us tearing through our duffel bags looking for the leggings. Some found them. I was among those who didn't. Those who had them, struggled to put them on. By now our once orderly campsite was a mess. All the crap, to use Patton's term, once on our vehicles, was now scattered on the ground, including contents of our duffel bags, emptied in search of those fucking leggings!

General Patton, having turned order into chaos, strode back to his squad car, climbed in and was driven away, as all of us saluted. Once Patton was out of sight, and assured he would not turn around and pay us a surprise return visit, we all laughed spontaneously at the absurdity of the performance in which we had become involuntary players. The leggings were removed—

reburied in their possessors' duffel bags—the "crap" removed from our vehicles returned to their former places, and the white stars on my armored car's turret restored to their muddied status, and back we went to our German Fräulein announcers on Radio Luxemburg. Yes, it was absurdity crossing the line into slapstick comedy. But upon reflection I didn't consider Patton's performance funny. I was saddened by his callous demeanor towards us Troopers—the low ranking GI Joes upon whose backs, wits and courage the best laid plans of the Brass were wholly dependent. Never once did Patton ask any of us how well we were coping in the field, how our grub was, how well our vehicles and gear were performing under combat conditions, and were there any things we guys thought might make life in combat easier for us, and harder on the enemy? The things I have enumerated were, I thought, matters of substance affecting the conduct of the war. I had been lead to believe that officers are responsible for the well being of those under their command. If this principle obtained for line officers, how much more was it applicable to Generals? Indeed. the General I encountered that late Summer's day in 1944, somewhere in France, was more the posturing martinet—than the military genius he has been made out to be,—concerned more with form than substance. How absurd, and how sad!

Episode TWENTY SIX

The Slashing Sword of Vengeance

... *[S]urprise* of the enemy ... lies more or less
at the foundation of all undertakings, for without
it superiority at the decisive point is really not
conceivable .... Secrecy and rapidity are the two
factors in this product .... [T]he weaker the forces
become which are under the command of strategy, so
much more they become adapted for stratagem, so that
to the very weak and small, for whom no prudence, no
sagacity is any longer sufficient, at the point where all
art seems to forsake them, stratagem offers itself as a
last resource. The more desperate their situation and the
more everything concentrates into one single, desperate
blow, the more readily stratagem offers itself as a last
resource. The more desperate their situation and the
more everything concentrates into one single, desperate
blow, the more readily stratagem comes to the aid of
their boldness. Relieved of all further calculations,
free from all later penalty, boldness and stratagem may
intensify each other, and thus concentrate at one point
an infinitesimal glimmering of hope into a single ray,
which may likewise serve to kindle a flame.

... First of all we must inquire into the circumstances
which lead to victory in an engagement .... There are
only three ... things which appear to us of decisive
importance, namely, *surprise, advantages of ground*
and *attack from several sides*. The surprise produces
an effect by opposing to the enemy at some particular

point a great many more troops than he expected. The superiority in numbers in this case is very different from the general superiority of numbers; it is the most powerful agent in the art of war. The way in which the advantage of ground contributes to the victory is in itself not merely a question of obstacles which obstruct the advance of an enemy, such as steep grounds, high mountains, marshy streams, hedges, etc., but that it is also an advantage of ground if it affords us the opportunity of lining up troops on it without their being seen. Indeed, we may say that even from ground which is quite without special features the person who knows it derives assistance. The attack from several sides includes all tactical turning movements, great and small, and its effects are derived partly from the doubled efficiency of fire and partly from the enemy's fear of being cut off.

Now how are the offensive and defensive related to one another with respect to these things?

... A swift and vigorous transition to attack—the flashing sword of vengeance—is the most brilliant point of the defensive. He who does not bear this in mind from the first, who does not from the first include it in his conception of defense, will never understand the superiority of the defensive . . . .

General Karl von Clausewitz,
On War, Book III, Book VI (1831)

Episode Twenty Six

In which antisemitism rears its ugly head during the Battle of the Bulge in Bastogne, Belgium, and my reaction thereto.

This episode relates to the sole clearly *overt* act of antisemitism perpetrated against me in my three years in the Army. And it took place during the Battle of the Bulge in Belgium, within the latter days of December 1944 and the first days of January 1945. I kept no diary. So that while the events are etched into my memory, the exact dates are not. There assuredly were other acts of anti-semitism committed against me, as was the treatment accorded me in England before the invasion, which ended with my being convicted in a summary courtmartial of allegedly being asleep on my ceremonial guard post—all of which I have recounted, including the happy ending. So let's move on with my story.

It was Christmas Day, 1944. We were in the vicinity of Forbach, France. We had just been served our sumptuous Christmas meal in early afternoon. I remember my mess kit was piled high with turkey, gravy, stuffing, cranberry sauce, succotash, and on the top, a slab of three flavored ice cream! I hastened to eat the ice cream first before it melted into the hot foods. I had not finished eating when, of a sudden, the order was given that we mount our vehicles immediately and move out. All we were told, at least on my T/5 level, was that the entire Squadron was moving north. And north we moved, all that afternoon and all the next day. We passed through Luxembourg and then entered, towards evening, into Belgium. We were then told that the Germans had launched a massive counterattack, and that we, along with the rest of Patton's forces were now moving into Belgium in an effort to staunch the German advance. In their onrushing drive eastward against the retreating German forces the Allies had begun to stretch their massed forces into extended, and hence, thinner lines of attack. The van began to outstrip the ability of the supply trains to keep up. As a consequence, the Allies had to slow the pace of their advance, thus exposing their extended flanks to attack. It was a military situation ripe for the German High Command to apply the teachings of General von Clausewitz which I have earlier remarked upon, namely that "The defensive is the stronger form of making war . . . . [and] A swift and vigorous transition to attack—the flashing sword of vengeance—is the most brilliant part of the defensive . . . ."

The Germans had determined, in a do or die effort, to cut through the allied forces and make it to the sea at Antwerp. Were they to succeed they would have cut our forces in two, and simultaneously obtained an Atlantic port from which their forces could be re-supplied. Quite a feather in Hitler's cap if he succeeded! The German advance had penetrated deeply in to the allied lines. On a map the penetration appeared as a wide bulge-like dent into these lines, hence the name history has given to this war shaping engagement: The Battle of the Bulge.

There was no road sign saying, "Leaving Luxembourg, Welcome to Belgium!" When and where we crossed into Belgium I know not. I learned only that the heaviest fighting was going on in and around the city of Bastogne where our forces had blunted the German drive but were threatened with being flanked and overrun. I remember seeing a battered road sign saying Marvie which I presumed was a suburb of Bastogne. There was intense fighting going on all about us. Heavy exchanges of artillery roared overhead, and our barrages and theirs shook the ground and lit the sky with flashes of red and yellow upon impact. I recall vividly how our Squadron crossed at night, slowly, single file, over a narrow wooden bridge, which swayed and creaked ominously as with stops and starts, our vehicles made their way across its worn surface with shells falling all about us. The crossing safely made, my Troop, Dog Troop, moved into our position on a high ridge overlooking a swath of snow covered meadowland. The Germans had painted much of their armor white, and had issued white coveralls to their troops, thus blending well into the snow covered terrain. Our troops did not have the benefit of such camouflage, and unless we and our vehicles were well concealed, we would stick out in this wintry landscape like the proverbial sore thumb.

Across this snow covered meadowland, approximately a quarter mile away, there was another ridge, and on this one we were told there might be Germans. The ridge on which we were encamped contained a two storey stone sided farmhouse with a deep potato cellar, now empty. The farmhouse was surrounded by numerous outbuildings, such as stables, storage and equipment sheds, all empty. Clearly, the farmer, in evacuating his farm, had taken with him whatever he felt was of value. If we parked our vehicles behind the farmhouse and the other farm structures, they and their crews would be would be unseen by any Germans on the ridge opposite us. And that was what we did. Then a point fox hole was dug on the edge of our ridge, perhaps a 100 meters in front of the farmhouse. Anyone manning this point could see, even with his naked eyes, any movement by the enemy across the meadowland towards our position. By the same token, Germans could just as easily observe us if we exposed ourselves. Thus, one could see the prudence of secreting all our vehicles and personnel behind the blind sides of the farmhouse and its outbuildings.

After moving into the position I have described, the Troop's First Sergeant called us down, one at a time, to the deep potato cellar in the farmhouse which became our field HQ. There we met, for the first time, our new Troop Commanding Officer. The one who had led us from St. Lo on had been an excellent leader and a wonderful human being. Like me, he came out of Brooklyn. He was of German ancestry and a devout Catholic. Every time we came across a church, whether empty or bombed out, he would, if combat conditions allowed, halt the Troop and go in and pray, regardless of the Church's denomination. And when he came out he would smile and say, "I prayed for all you guys, and that includes you, Katz", alluding to the fact that he knew I was Jewish and still entitled to the benefit of his prayers. On the very eve of making the long rush north from France to Bastogne we learned that our beloved Lieutenant would not be leading us. Rumor had it that he had been promoted to another command, or that he had been taken ill. I preferred to believe the former. His replacement, who had seen no combat, was a Lieutenant fresh from the ROTC, Reserve Officers' Training Corps., of Louisiana State University.

Rudyard Kipling wrote in his poem, "On The Road to Mandalay", if memory serves me, that the "The dawn rose up like thunder over China 'cross the bay." Well, Belgium was not China, nor Bastogne the bay, but the dawn did indeed rise up like thunder from the ridge across the way. The Germans were some distance away, blasting at something, fortunately, not at us. They didn't know that we were where we were. Out of sight, out of mind. The First Sergeant had called the names of several guys when he finally called mine. Apparently, he was calling us alphabetically to meet our new Troop Commander. I trudged down the stairs into the deep confines of the potato cellar. It was dimly lit by dawn's early light coming through several small ground level, glass paned, iron grated windows, and from a large, battery operated flashlight which stood on the table behind which the Lieutenant was sitting in a folding canvas chair.

The Lieutenant could have been 23 or 24, thus, a year or so older than I. He wasn't bad looking. He was thin, his face pale, his hair blond. His eyes were dark, perhaps, if the light had been better I could tell their color. But for the fact he was wearing an American Army Officer's uniform he could have been a poster boy for *Das Herrenvolk*, The Master Race, which, as I soon learned was not too far from the truth.

The Lieutenant had a Troop Roster on the table before him. The First Sergeant, who had accompanied me into the cellar, told the Lieutenant my name. The Lieutenant checked off my name on his list, and, without any small talk, and with a crooked grin on his face, looked up and said, "Katz! So you're the Jew boy! You're a white nigger Katz! If we weren't trying to save your fuckin' Jew ass, we wouldn't be fighting this fuckin' war!" At which point he laughed and waved me on my way.

Over the years I had heard, or been the target of all kinds of slurs designed to demean me and my Jewish People. But not until I was standing in a potato cellar in a farmhouse on the outskirts of Bastogne on the cusp of 1945—with a fierce war raging all about me—did I learn there was yet another derogatory way of describing who I was. White Nigger, indeed! How apt an expression from a racist and anti-Semite rolled into one. He and I were not to be friends. But having gone through a court-martial—even though a rigged one—in England before the invasion, and having experienced a brief spell of military prison time, I was going to be careful in how I reacted to his taunts. Our new Lieutenant was not only an unpleasant person, he was also, unfortunately, for our Troop, a dummy! Giving such a person a military command can be a dangerous thing. As the reader shall quickly discern.

The first morning after we had settled into our new position the Lieutenant came out of his deep potato cellar command post. He walked around our site, the First Sergeant at his side. He spoke to no one, and then descended into his deep, potato cellar haven. A few minutes later word went out through the First Sergeant that the Lieutenant wanted all of our vehicles moved away from the blind sides of the structures behind which they were parked, and moved out into the open, with their weapons aiming across the meadowland below us, and at the ridge overlooking it. I thought this was a stupid idea for a number of reasons, and I related them to the First Sergeant: 1. Moving our vehicles from their concealed positions into the open would reveal our presence to the Germans, were there any on that ridge, and expose us to their artillery and mortar fire; 2. men sitting in their vehicles would not be getting better views of that ridge, and of any German activity on it, than that afforded from the point foxhole and from any of the windows on the second floor of the farmhouse facing that ridge; 3. if there were Germans and they saw our vehicles, they might mount both an artillery and ground attack and we, with our lightly armored vehicles, and our limited firepower, would be put at a material disadvantage; 4. our primary mission as a reconnaissance unit was to be the eyes and ears of our more heavily armed and armored units, thus enabling them to do their "heavy lifting" more effectively. Once seen by the Germans our primary mission to be covert observers would be compromised; 5. it was not our "mission" as Cavalry to become a sitting target, like a bunch of ducks in a carnival shooting gallery.

The First Sergeant listened to me impatiently, "Professor", he said, using this title as a pejorative, "You're only a T/5. This is what the Lieutenant wants, and this is what we'll do. The Lieutenant wants everybody to know that we are proud Amurricans (that's how he pronounced the word), and so we ain't gonna hide ourselves behind buildings like a bunch of fuckin' fags hidin' behind their mommas' skirts." And so, within a quarter hour all our vehicles were sitting out in the open, the men manning their weapons, and these pointing across to the ridge where there might be Germans a quarter mile away.

During the night, in making our way to our present location, we had driven through snow flurries. Now, as the night faded, and a sunless, grayish day took its place, the temperature dropped markedly, and the snow flurries turned into real snow. Soon an inch or more carpeted the ground. Nothing to impede our movement on foot or by vehicle. But it made a white backdrop against our dark green vehicles and our combat fatigues. And there we were, sitting out in the open. What a target! And yes, there were Germans on that ridge! It didn't take them long to spot us. Within minutes after daylight revealed our vehicles, the first round, an artillery shell, came roaring down on us like an express train at full throttle! It smashed into our midst and exploded sending shards of shrapnel flying by, and when pieces hit something metallic and bounced off, you heard a pinging sound. That first round hit nothing but the snow covered earth. Perhaps thirty seconds later a second round roared in. This one made a direct hit on an armored car sitting in the middle of the cobblestoned courtyard in front of the farmhouse. There had been two men in the turret of the armored car. The car commander and his gunner. Neither of the two drivers had entered the armored car. Sitting stretched out in a vehicle which was going nowhere made no sense to them. They had stayed behind one of the buildings. They did the right thing, and survived.

Their second round hit exactly what the Germans had been aiming at. They could see us clearly! All bedlam broke loose! All the vehicle drivers spontaneously gunned their engines and raced back to the cover they had left barely minutes before. Fuck the Lieutenant! What a stupid bastard! A few more rounds blasted down. One hit the tip of the farmhouse's chimney and blew almost all of it away. Another hit, and destroyed, one of the empty stables. None of our men and vehicles now being exposed, nothing more was hit. After dumping at least a half dozen rounds on us—I thought one or two were heavy mortar shells because unlike rounds fired from a cannon, mortar rounds have that almost lazy whistling sound as they fall—the Germans stopped firing. Perhaps they assumed, from the racket our vehicles were making in moving to cover, and from the fact they could no longer see any vehicles or personnel in the open, that we had fled the area. They mounted no ground attack against our ridge. Perhaps they were relieved they didn't have to mount one across that broad expanse of meadowland, and then fight their way up onto our ridge.

All of our Troopers were very pissed, to put it mildly, with our new Lieutenant. All the way from St. Lo in mid-June 1944 until now, at the cusp of 1945, Dog Troop had not lost a man. We'd had a couple hurt. I was one of them, but, thank God, no serious injuries and no deaths. And we'd done our share of engaging with the enemy. But we'd never done it in the insanely stupid manner we'd just experienced.

Before the shelling commenced, and during the time it continued, our new ROTC Lieutenant was safely ensconced in his deep potato cellar HQ. He made no effort to leave it even after he received word of the terrible tragedy which had just struck our Troop. Nor did he come out to commiserate with those of us who personally felt the loss of these two Troopers, one of whom, the older of the two, and a Sergeant, had become a mentor for the younger. They had been inseparable in life, and were now inseparable in death. Nor did he find time to thank those who took upon themselves the grisly task of recovering body parts, so that the bereaved families would have something to bury or cremate. Instead, he descended, apparently unabashed about the foolishness of his order, into his *sanctum sanctorum*, his potato cellar HQ.

During the shelling the man on point in the foxhole, fled for safety behind the nearest structure. A wise decision. Now the First Sergeant approached me. Considering what had happened I began to imagine him as the Lieutenant's angel of death. I was sitting in my armored car, safely parked behind a storage shed. The First Sergeant said the Lieutenant wanted a man back out on point, and that it was my time to sit. I told him I wouldn't go. It was dumb. Whoever sat in that hole, dressed in dark fatigues against a snowy background was an easy target for a German sharpshooter. The Germans may have thought we fled the ridge. But then, they'd see this guy outlined against the snow and know we were still there, and easy targets. No, I wouldn't go. Someone carefully peering out a second storey window in the farmhouse could see as much as the guy in the hole—and do it much more safely.

The First Sergeant was tired of my lectures. He ordered me into the foxhole. I told him I'd go only after I'd talked with the Lieutenant. He was puzzled, but agreed to take me to him. In a few minutes I was standing before the Lieutenant deep down in his potato cellar HQ. The only other person in the cellar, aside from the Lieutenant, the First Sergeant and me, was the Captain's orderly, the Troop's clerk. The Sergeant explained to the Lieutenant that I wouldn't go on point until I had spoken to the Lieutenant. "OK, Katz," he said very cooly, as if nothing horrendous had happened only a short time ago, "What's the problem?" I repeated the views I had given the First Sergeant. The Lieutenant thought for a moment, then, his voice ice water, "Katz, I'm in charge here, in case you haven't noticed." He was very sarcastic. "I order you to sit out on point!"

Now it was my time at bat. "I'll sit out there, Lieutenant, if you sit with me." For a moment, everything froze in place. The orderly stopped shuffling papers. The First Sergeant moved not a muscle. The Lieutenant looked dead on at me, wordless. The time began to tick away. The Lieutenant's face reddened. His jaw tightened, "Get the fuck out of here, Katz!" I turned about, such a command didn't merit a salute, and climbed out of the cellar.

Outside the farmhouse I headed for my armored car. I hadn't gone more than a few yards when I was hailed by the First Sergeant. "Katz, I want to talk to you." I stopped and turned. He approached me, and without a word, or any sign of hostile intent, punched me hard in the stomach. As I reacted to the unexpected blow my helmet fell off and onto the ground. I made no effort to hit back. As I bent down to pick up my helmet he gave me a rabbit punch on the back of my neck. Ouch! My helmet in my hand, I backed away. He followed after me. "The Lieutenant doesn't like your attitude. And neither do I! Come on, Jew Boy, put up your dukes and fight like a man!" He was at least 185 lbs and taller than I. But that was not the reason I stayed out of his reach. Having been beat about the head and shoulders in my 4th Cavalry days I had grown "Street Smart" a city phrase referring to how one learns to cope with life's sometimes harsh realities. There were no witnesses to what was now going on. I knew, that if I hit the bastard, even in self defense, he would lie and swear I had picked a fight with a non-commissioned officer, and then hit him first. Bingo! A courtmartial offense, making an unprovoked attack upon a non-com. I told my First Sergeant I knew what his game was, but I wasn't about to play! I then slowly walked to where a couple of guys from my patrol, seeing something going on, had gathered. I was glad to see them. The son-of-a-bitch couldn't hit me now.

The Lieutenant never came out to sit with me on point. And since he didn't show, neither did I. Indeed, no one thereafter sat on point. Instead, the Lieutenant issued an order creating an observation post on the second floor of the farmhouse, on the side whose windows faced the ridge occupied by the Germans.

Playing hide and seek with the Germans we suffered no further casualties. We ran daily foot patrols (using our dark, noisy vehicles in that snow covered terrain would have revealed our patrols were there Germans in the area) as we carefully probed the terrain about us and, on foot, visually expanded the perimeter of our outpost. We looked for signs of an incursion of German troops, and for indications that the area about us had been mined. We saw none. Were mines there they lay concealed under the snow. My boys and I, mindful of our earlier nerve shattering experience with a mine field, stayed clear of all pristine stretches of snow covered ground, and walked only in the footsteps of those who had gone before them on patrol. Fortunately, that first patrol, mine, had walked unscathed. Subsequent to the incidents related, neither the Lieutenant, nor the First Sergeant ever spoke to me again. Frankly, I didn't miss their conversation.

God had given me the intelligence to choose not to lose my cool. I had completed, unbeknownst to me, another stage in my journey to find my belóved Anneliese Baur.

For two days and nights following the first time we were shelled, the Germans rained all kinds of shit down on us. All our vehicles and personnel again being out of sight, the Germans were firing blind. They hit none of us. They did manage to hit the chimney of the farmhouse again. This time toppling all of it. However, it was no fun being confined to a small area when shells were exploding randomly, with shrapnel and earth clods flying all about us. But we now knew where they were. Now it was our turn. I was the number one radio operator for the Troop, and when the Lieutenant, through the First Sergeant, told me to inform HQ that there was a nest of German artillery on that ridge, I told him I had already done so. Instead of showing any appreciation for my actions, he grunted some expletive I couldn't catch, and turned away. Within a day of the time I had called in my information to my Squadron's HQ one of our spotter planes flew over the ridge occupied by the Germans. Then, within hours, one of our bombers appeared and blasted the German's position. A column of black smoke rose, accompanied with sounds of munitions exploding. I don't know how many Germans were killed or wounded. But all our guys felt we had avenged the loss of our two buddies. With the German position destroyed we experienced no further shelling.

About two weeks later, our daily foot patrols finding no evidence of any German movement in our direction, our Troop, Dog Troop, was ordered to move to the rear to join the Squadron's other Troops. The 86th Cavalry was together again, as once we were in St. Lo in June 1944. The German's flashing sword of vengeance had bloodied our Allied Forces. But now that sword lay broken. The Nazi forces did not get to Antwerp. And we, the 86th Cavalry Reconnaissance Squadron Mechanized, again in the van, were moving east to resume the Allies' attack on *Das Vaterland*. But now we were advancing, as a unit, more as mechanized infantry, than as individual Troops, each fighting on its own. We were acting in this rôle because of the heavy losses suffered by our infantry during the Battle of the Bulge.

Episodes TWENTY SEVEN and TWENTY EIGHT

Daring Strategy and Tactics Succeed!

As danger is the general element in which everything moves in war, it is chiefly courage, the feeling of our own strength, that influences our judgment in different ways. It is, so to speak, the crystal lens through which all images pass before reaching the intelligence . . . .

. . . [C]ombat gives birth to the element of danger, in which all the activities of war must live and move, like the bird in the air or the fish in the water. The effects of danger, however, all pass on to the emotions, either directly, and thus instinctively, or through the intelligence. The effect, in the first case, would be a desire to escape from the danger, and, if that cannot be done, fear and anxiety. If this effect does not take place, then it is courage which acts as a counterpoise to that instinct. Courage, however, is by no means [only] an act of intelligence, but likewise a feeling like fear; the latter is directed to physical preservation, courage to moral preservation. Courage is a nobler instinct . . . .

. . . [I]t is certain and must be regarded as a truth of the first importance that *to attack a war seasoned enemy in a good position is a dangerous thing* . . . .

It was for a time the fashion to speak slightingly of entrenchments and their effects . . . . What would be the point of having entrenchments at all if they were useless for strengthening the defense? No, not only reason but experience . . . shows that a well-designed, well-manned and well-defended entrenchment is *as a rule* to be regarded as *an impregnable point*, and is also so regarded by the assailant. Starting from this point of the efficiency of a single entrenchment, we argue that there can be no doubt as to the attack of an entrenched camp being a most difficult operation, and one in which in most cases it will be impossible for the assailant to succeed.

It is natural that an entrenched camp should be weakly manned; but with good natural obstacles and well-made entrenchments, it can be defended against a great numerical superiority . . . .

If the front of a position through entrenchments and obstacles to approach is so strong that an attack becomes impossible, the enemy is compelled to turn it, in order to make his attack from a flank or from the rear . . . .

General Karl von Clausewitz,
On War, Book II, Book VII (1831)

Episode Twenty Seven

In which events occur on February 20, 1945, a fateful day and night, which will materially change the course of my life.

In the late afternoon of February 20, 1945 (I remember this date for a number of reasons, one of them, that it was literally burned into me) I was awakened by my communications sergeant and told that he and I were to lay telephone lines between two of several German concrete bunkers, situated about 50 meters apart, and which were among several taken earlier that day. How they were taken, and by whom I shall shortly relate. When awakened I was wearing my dress uniform of olive drab (ODs) trousers, shirt and my Eisenhower jacket. Before taking my nap I had changed into this uniform from the combat fatigues I had been wearing earlier that day. The next morning, at 5 a.m. I was scheduled to leave for Paris and enrollment into the OCS: Officer Candidates School. I had been selected to be trained to become an Infantry officer, a Second Lieutenant, (a "90 Days Wonder"). As I noted in writing about the Battle of the Bulge, fought in December 1944 and January 1945 in the vicinity of Bastogne, and in which battle my Cavalry Squadron was a participant, the Germans mounted heavy infantry, armored and artillery attacks on our forces. Our infantry units bore the brunt of these attacks, and, in fighting them off suffered heavy losses of personnel and materiel. We, in the Cavalry, by the nature of our mobile mode of fighting, sustained much lighter losses. Thus, it came about after the Battle of the Bulge was over—and the Allied Forces had gone back on the attack and were again moving east towards Germany—that the Army looked to its other branches for rapid replacement of its lost line infantry officers, and for these other branches to operate more like infantry units. As a consequence of this change of strategy the various Troops of our 86th Cavalry were now acting much more closely together than they had since

175

they were assembled in St. Lo in Normandy, in late June 1944. Ordinarily, we would have been operating as independent Troops, performing various reconnaissance functions with units as small as eight to twelve man patrols. Now, post Bastogne, we were operating more like mechanized infantry. We would move in our vehicles to a predetermined point. There we would dismount, move out on foot, with armored, air and artillery support, to seek out and engage whatever enemy was still about. On the 20th of February 1945 the entire 86th Cavalry Squadron was operating in the vicinity of the city of Prüm, just inside Germany, across the Belgian border, northeast of Bastogne, and near the northern tip of Luxembourg. Prüm is located in a steeply sloped, hilly, mostly forested region which the Germans call the Eiffel, and the French the Ardennes. (This region was also the site of fierce World War I battles.) A couple of days earlier I had been called to Squadron HQ. Based upon my experiences on being called to meet the Brass in the 4th Cavalry, my first reaction on being summoned was negative. "Now, what the fuck did I do wrong?" But I was not being called to HQ for any negative reasons. I was being called to be complimented.

I was told that on the basis of the manner I had been performing my combat duties I had demonstrated courage and leadership skills which indicated I could make a good infantry officer. If I said, "yes", I would be recommended by the Squadron's Commander to attend Officers' Candidates School (OCS) in Paris, to be trained to be an infantry officer. I had been shot at in the Cavalry, so being shot at in the Infantry wouldn't be much different. Besides, I had always wanted to be an officer in the Army. Simply put, being a lowly Second Lieutenant in the Infantry, was *mucho mas mejor* than being a T/5 in the Cavalry. It took me only seconds to say "Yes!". Unknowingly, I was adding another link to the chain of happenings which would lead me ever closer to my beautiful, belóved Anneliese Baur!

It was approximately 7:30 p.m. on February 20, 1945 when my communications sergeant shook me awake. It was dark, there was no moon, a leaden sky during the day was now dropping a light rain. Noting the rain I reached into my duffel bag and pulled out my GI issue raincoat and put it on. I didn't want to dirty my ODs before leaving for Paris. Now, why had I been sleeping so early in the day? Because I was exhausted. Not physically. I was elated. I had been on an emotional high, and this had drained my battery. How come? Earlier that day I had successfully completed a mission which was intended to test my leadership abilities under fire. An officer had been sent the day before from Division HQ to see how I would perform that mission.

My mission was to plan, and execute a successful attack against one of a series of concrete bunkers, surrounded by mine fields. These bunkers were doing what the Germans intended them to do: they were slowing, and in some cases, barring our advances into Germany, necessitating time expenditures and fuel consuming detours. Although I had been in combat since late June 1944, and had led numerous reconnaissance missions into and across German lines, and had been the target of incoming mortar and artillery fire, and had engaged in fire fights while probing the enemy's flanks, I had never been asked to attack a fixed, highly fortified target head on, and to do so essentially on foot. New targets called for new tactics. So let's first examine these new targets before determining the new strategies and tactics needed to confront them.

Our Squadron was encamped at the base of a rapidly ascending range of hills running north and south. The heartland of Germany lay east. To avoid making circuitous runs north or south, and thus exposing our flanks to attack, the best way forward was to move forward. Namely, to move east. Simple enough. Our Squadron officers had found the best way to advance rapidly was up this steep valley which lay before us. The grade was between 30° and 45°. The valley can best be pictured as an alpine meadow, about 500 meters in width, flanked on its southern and northern sides by densely wooded, boulder strewn terrain. It was a broad, natural pathway to the east. The Germans had noted that fact.

They took steps to make this opening in the woods as inaccessible as possible to invading forces. First, they denuded the meadow of its trees and shrubs. Then they salted the bare terrain with anti-tank and anti-personnel mines. This done, they built—better put—buried into the hillside, a series of squat concrete bunkers, huge emplacements, with heavy machine guns and bazooka type weapons being the armaments of choice. Long snouted cannon would have been ineffective weapons for reasons I shall soon recite. From the distance of 100 meters an attacking force would see only the curved concrete roof and part of the curved concrete face of the bunker. An attacking force would have to get within range of the bunkers' weaponry before one could open fire on it. This was because of the clever way the bunkers had been constructed. If you approached the bunkers on foot, or in a tank or armored car, you first went over a rise or lip of mounded earth, and then were heading downhill as you neared the bunker. Imagine the bunker as an upside down teacup in a saucer. As you slide down the slope of the saucer you are a super target for fire coming from the bunker. Not good if you are advancing dismounted. If you are in a tank it must come to the edge of the rise or lip, and move partially over it in order to lower its cannon to fire at the bunker. When it does this it exposes the belly of the tank. Not a good place to be hit.

The bunkers were so located that each covered about a 180° field of vision, with these fields overlapping on their edges. In short, no blind spots. Good for them. Not good for us. And then between the more distant bunkers the Germans had dug connecting trenches. Really well designed. They were not built with one straight line extending from point A to point B. Instead, their line of direction was straight, but the trench itself consisted of a series of zig zags. The reason was simple. If a shell landed in a trench which was a straight line from end to end, then the shrapnel from the bursting shell would fly unimpeded down the length of the trench and kill or maim just about everyone in the trench, much as a strike in bowling knocks down all the pins. But if the trench is made with zig zags, then the exploding shell is confined to the zig zag area into which it has fallen. Casualties are confined to that area. Of course, the total consumed distance of the zig zag trench would measure longer than a straight line trench. But that was not an issue with the Germans.

The bunkers and related mine fields I have described were part of Germany's Siegfried line. The Germans invented the *Blitzkrieg*, the Lightening War, where fast, heavily armored forces with powerful cannons, and supported by mobile infantry, and related air and artillery support, could smash through fixed objects, or go around them, as the Germans did with the Maginot line built by the French. So why did the Germans build their line of bunkers? They built them as a delaying device, giving them more time to regroup as they fell back. They knew they could be overrun in time. But for our forces to get past them we would have to go around them, which takes time and exposes our flanks to attack. Or we could take them on frontally, as I would shortly be asked to do. Such a frontal attack would expose us to fire from the bunkers, but before we even reached the bunkers we would be exposed to injury, or death, by the setting off of the anti-tank and anti-personnel mines which the Germans had planted on all the approaches to their bunkers. An exploding anti-tank mine could destroy, and seriously wound or even kill the crew of the small tanks assigned to our E and F Troops. Our substantially larger, and more heavily armored tanks (none of which were part of my Cavalry Squadron's armament) could be disabled by an anti-tank mine, with injuries to its crew, and, unless the tank caught fire and ignited its ammunition before the crew could abandon it, there would be injuries, but less likelihood of death resulting to its personnel. But the greatest losses in attacking the bunkers frontally would be suffered by those dismounted troops setting off anti-personnel mines. These mines, whether they were a shoe box mine, or a Teller mine: a dinner plate shaped device, or a "Bouncing Betty" type (I explain below what these terms mean), were all designed to injure grievously the soldier struck by them. Sometimes they could kill their target. But doing injury of a non-lethal serious nature was their primary purpose. Why? Because a retreating force wants to slow down its pursuer as it falls back to more secure positions where it hopes to be able to regroup and counterattack. Such a force knows that if it kills one soldier of the invading force that such a loss will require its pursuer to engage but two to four of its forces in collecting the body of the dead soldier, putting him into a body bag, making sure his personal records (such as dog tags) are preserved, and through them, his identity properly recorded, and his remains sent back to the morgue in the rear.

But what happens when an anti-personnel mine wounds a soldier? The shoe box and Teller mines are designed to blow the unlucky soldier's foot off to just above the ankle. The wounded soldier might bleed to death if not promptly and properly treated by medics in the field. He would also be in shock, and in great pain. How many personnel must now care for him? There are the medics, maybe two or more. Then the stretcher bearers and the ambulance driver, and the field hospital and a staff of doctors and nurses to attend the wounded soldier, then transportation to a military hospital in the rear, followed by long term care. A retreating enemy knows this arithmetic of delay. Thus the Siegfried line served its purpose, if by wounding as grievously as possible as many of us as it could, it slowed, even slightly, our advance into Germany.

I've described the shoe box and Teller mines. I now describe an even more diabolical anti-personnel device: the "Bouncing Betty". A cute name for an inexpensive but effective weapon. Imagine a coffee can shaped metal canister. Fill it with metal sweepings from your munitions factory floors, *Schrott* in German: nuts, bolts, ball bearings, glass shards, nails, screws, anything rigid and ragged which, if they penetrate a soldier's body can do him great harm. Place the canister into a half a meter deep hole. Attach a thin chain, or strand of wire, about a meter in length, to the bottom of the canister, tie the other end to an explosive charge fitted with a detonating device, Rig the top with thin Y shaped stiff wires which will protrude from the top of the canister, and when soil is lightly tamped about the canister, these wires will look, to the unsuspecting eye, like blades of grass. (You may recall my earlier, and happier experience with such a device.) When stepped upon, the device is activated. The canister flies out of the ground to the length of its chain or tethering wire. It then explodes and sends its shrapnel of nuts and bolts, etc. into its target at about the height of the target's testes. If the testes are not hit, then hitting the thigh at the same height *ist auch gut.* In either case the Germans have got an *Ami* down with a serious, dirty, painful, deep penetrating wound—and one which can also kill—if an artery in the thigh is severed and the flow of blood not quickly stemmed. If death, does not result, the wounded soldier will still require surgery and hospitalization for many weeks, perhaps, months, with lots of personnel attending him. I should also point out that one need not step on a Bouncing Betty mine to activate it. If the mine was booby trapped, that is, if its firing mechanism was tied to a wire stretched some distance from the mine, then a soldier could trip the mine into action by catching his foot on the wire. This would activate the mine to the same effect as if it were stepped upon.

My mission,—if successfully completed would send me on to Paris and a 90 days' OCS Course—was to plan and lead an attack on one of those German bunkers dug in to the steeply ascending, heavily mined terrain which barred my Squadron's forward progress. To test my leadership abilities I was given *carte blanche* to plan my attack, to pick my team and to select the equipment I would need. As previously noted, I would be doing something I had not done before as a cavalryman. I would be making a frontal attack on a dug in, fortified position from which the enemy could see me approaching, and I would be doing so over a wide, heavily mined expanse of bare terrain.

As I have observed, new targets require new tactics. One did not have to be too swift to recognize that advancing on foot under the facts related would have been stupid and extremely hazardous to my team's health, and to mine. I recalled seeing photos of Russian troops going into battle riding on the upper surfaces of their tanks. Riding that high off the ground protected these soldiers from being hurt by the explosion of anti-personnel mines tripped by the tank they were riding on. These mines would explode harmlessly against the lower sides and treads of the tank. Good idea. I would mount my team onto a tank. But what kind of a tank? My Squadron had light tanks in its E and F support troops. These were light, small, and thinly armored vehicles, easily destroyed by an anti-tank mine, with death or serious injury resulting to the crew. And as for carrying my team, uh, uh, they were way too small. My team would consist of a patrol sized unit, seven men and me, making eight in all. Well, I'd ask my officers to "borrow" the largest tank used by the Sixth Armored Division to which my Squadron was attached as its recon unit. And then I'd mount my team, Russki style on this tank. This, as I have explained, would remove the risk of any of my team being hurt from exploding anti-personnel mines. The large borrowed tank would not only serve as safe passage for my men and me, it would also provide me the fire power, or the appearance of fire power, I would need in approaching and attacking my fixed target. In formulating my thinking on how to select my team personnel, and its weaponry, and how to shape my method of attack, I relied upon my own combat experiences, and on my recollections of the writings of military geniuses such as that of the Napoleonic era Prussian General Karl von Clausewitz. Sometime in 1943—I was already in the service then—Random House published in its Modern Library series a translation of von Clausewitz' primer on the art of war, *Vom Kriege*, On War. I read a good part of it, but did not take the book overseas with me. It was too bulky, and it gave way to my Bible and two law books. Now, six decades later, I have the luxury of returning to my copy of von Clausewitz' work and quoting verbatim those portions which had given me the principles upon which I relied in planning and executing my mission. Thus, in Chapter IX of his Book VII, "Attack of Defensive Position", von Clausewitz wrote:

> "[I]t must be regarded as a truth of first importance that to *attack a war seasoned enemy in a good position is a dangerous thing.*" [emphasis von Clausewitz].

The target of my mission would be a massive concrete bunker dug, with excellent defensive design, into steeply rising, heavily mined terrain. Such a position falls under the rubric "entrenchment" and ". . . A well-designed, well-manned and well-defended entrenchment is *as a rule* to be regarded as an *impregnable* point." [emphasis von Clausewitz]. The entrenchment I would be attacking was one of many which lay clustered on the heights before me. I have already described the intricate, interlocking manner in which these entrenched bunkers were constructed. A group of entrenchments is referred to by von Clausewitz as an entrenched camp, of which military formation he had this to say:

> "It is natural that an entrenched camp should be weakly manned; but with good natural obstacles, and well-made entrenchments, it can be defended against a great numerical superiority."

Further, on the issue of attacking an entrenched camp von Clausewitz opined,

> ". . . there can be no doubt as to the attack of an entrenched camp being a most difficult operation, and one in which in most cases it will be impossible for the assailant to succeed."

I had a vague recollection of this passage at the time I was planning my mission. I agreed with the first part, but my self confidence was such (or was it my ego?) which caused me to discount the second part of his statement.

I was undertaking my mission to succeed, and I would not contemplate any other result. How to achieve success? Even had I not recalled von Clausewitz' observation that a bunker of the type we would be attacking would be "weakly manned", *i.e.*, with a small contingent of defenders, I had already figured that out. I estimated the bunker would hold a crew of four to six men. The Germans didn't need more than that number inside a well fortified, dug in position, surrounded by mine fields, to hold off an attack, even if the attackers were more numerous than they. We, the attackers, would be better targets for their fire, than they from ours, ensconced as they would be behind thick walls within a well-made and well-planned entrenchment, and we out in the open. How to overcome this advantage of situs which the Germans enjoyed?

In discussing my mission my officers had informed me that prior to the time I began my attack, and continuing as I moved forward, the artillery would be laying down a barrage of fire at the cluster of bunkers before me, directed by low flying spotter planes which were supposed to watch our progress, and as we moved ahead, I was to call to the artillery to raise its sights and to drop fire ahead of us, rather than on us. To this end I was given a rolled up red plastic tarpaulin, about as long and wide as a household hallway runner. When we got close to the bunker I was attacking I was instructed to unfurl the tarp and lay it on the ground. The spotter planes would see it and call the artillery to move its fire further ahead of us. Sounded simple enough. But as I shall relate it didn't quite work out that way. I liked the idea of an artillery barrage leading our way on the ground. If any Germans had the heroic idea of jumping out of their bunker and facing us, *mano a mano*, falling shells would act as a deterrent. I felt, however, that the Germans would stay snug inside their bunker and play the "come and get us" game. I however, didn't intend to play that game.

But then, how to get Jerry into surrendering, without involving my team, and my tank crew, in a fire fight in the open which we could not win? I had to work up a stratagem to make them come out and surrender as promptly as possible after we had made our presence known to them. So promptly, in fact, that we drew little, or no hostile fire. My stratagem had to be one based upon surprise. Early on in combat I learned that the vagaries of war were frequently multiplied by the unanticipated, by the unexpected, in short, by accidents of surprise. However, the surprise I was considering was the surprise which an adversary *creates* to gain an advantage over his opponent. In Chapter IX of On War von Clausewitz noted:

> ". . . the *surprise* of the enemy . . . lies more or less at the foundation of all undertakings, for without it superiority at the decisive point is really not conceivable." [emphasis von Clausewitz]

In Chapter X of his treatise von Clausewitz observes that "Stratagem presupposes a concealed intention . . . ." He then states;

> ". . . There is a degree of stratagem, be it ever so small, which lies at the foundation of every attempt to surprise."

Perhaps these principles of stratagem and surprise were lodged deep within the interstices of my brain, and I drew upon them in formulating my surprise mode of attack. But I was not consciously thinking of von Clausewitz when I worked up my "surprise" for my bunker opponents. This is where I thought the borrowed heavy tank could play a major role in an attack mode, in addition to being the vehicle carrying my team safely through the mine fields and to our target. I would ask my officers to have the tank equipped with armor piercing/concrete penetrating shells. These shells do not immediately explode upon contact with the target. They penetrate a short way, in the manner of a drill bit boring into a piece of wood, then they explode. The degree of penetration is dependent upon the thickness of the target they hit. I had no familiarity with the penetrating power of such a shell shot from the muzzle of a 75mm or 88 mm cannon. I knew that our heaviest tanks were outfitted with one or the other of such cannons, if not of larger caliber. Whatever the cannon's millimeter ratio, I was sure that a lucky hit of one of the bunker's observation or firing slits might penetrate and its shrapnel might do much damage to the bunker's interior—or at least to the crew inside, or the force of the concussion on the exterior wall, with its attendant explosive noise, would reverberate within the bunker—and with some "encouragement" from me, as I shall explain, cause them to surrender without engaging in a fire fight with us. My stratagem was to stage an attack which, if properly executed, would avoid a one on one fire fight with them (such a fight would be to our great disadvantage) but which would surprise the Germans into believing we had them surrounded and would not go away until we had reduced their position to rubble, to avoid such a result, they surrendered.

How to stage an attack which would quickly destroy the equanimity of Germans who felt secure behind the massive walls of a bunker set within a masterfully designed entrenchment? How? Scare them fast, make them feel they were *trapped* within their bunker, *rather than secure* within its confines, make them feel that the *Amis* before them were vastly superior in numbers and firepower—and most important of all—that unless they surrendered immediately, they would never come out alive. Again, quoting von Clausewitz: "When it [surprise] is successful to a high degree, confusion and broken courage in the enemy's ranks are the consequences." And the German language would be the key element in my plan of surprise. If I were right, words would trump weapons, God willing!

With a careful mix of fire power with word power—this odd combination being the surprise factor—I proposed to talk the bunker's crew into surrendering bloodlessly by communicating with them in German! I spoke German, My ability *deutsch zu sprechen* had stood me in good stead in my reconnaissance operations, and in the capture of German combatants, (it is easier, and more humane, to talk a surrounded German, hunkered down behind a boulder, into surrendering, than to throw a grenade at him and blow him to pieces). Further, my knowledge of German enabled me to interrogate a prisoner more effectively concerning his unit and related German forces before us, than just leafing through his *Soldbuch* which, as I have noted, primarily contained his name, rank, serial number, pay and medical data.

The mission was mine to organize and execute—and to do so successfully. My ticket to Paris and my future as an officer candidate were on the line. And to the extent any leader of an assault team can be responsible for the safety of his men, I had that responsibility. I did not take it lightly. I had that odd combination of being keyed up, yet confident. Not cocky, confident. I was in charge of my future, and I liked that. In my previous eight months of combat I was at my best as a soldier when left to my own devices. The primary reason I had chosen the Cavalry as my branch of service when I enlisted was because I knew that the Cavalry worked in small formations which gave individual Troopers greater freedom to think for themselves, and to react accordingly on the field of battle.

The only time I had been injured in combat was back in August 1944 in Brittany. We were on patrol when my jeep driver, in taking evasive action to avoid what he thought was a concealed German Panzer up ahead, lost control and ended us upside down in a ditch at the foot of a hedgerow. I suffered a smashed left eye, broken nose, broken right hand and facial scars. Although bandaged and splinted, I never lost a day of line duty. Other than that experience, I'd gotten through so far unscathed. Shrapnel which went whizzing by, or embedded itself in your sleeping bag, or bounced off the turret of your armored car, went with the territory, and a miss was as good as a mile, as the saying went. And I had avoided setting off anti-personnel mines.

But now I was facing a different adventure. The primary difference was that now I would not be fighting as a mobile force. Once through the mine fields—a ticklish enterprise—I would be leading a dismounted attack against a highly fortified, entrenched enemy. Something I had never engaged in as a Cavalry Trooper. But I would have total control. No errant jeep driver to fault. If I fucked up there would be no one to blame but me. But I didn't intend to fuck up. As I explained my surprise plan of attack to my officers on the morning of February 19th I felt confident. I had worked it out in my mind. All that was left was to execute the plan. That sound cocky? Even crazy? Thinking back now, six decades later, it was cocky and crazy. But that was 1945. I was 22 and being given a chance to show my stuff. There were three or four officers listening to me outline my surprise plan of attack. One of them was the observer from Division HQ. I told them how I would mount my team of eight, including me, on the borrowed tank, Russki style, to avoid anti-personnel mine injuries, how the tank would mount the lip of the earthen mound long enough to fire its first round, then it would quickly back down and move a few feet to its side. Such a move would not give the Germans enough time to shoot at the underbelly of the tank. And when the tank popped up again it would be in a new location, leading the defenders to think there was more than one tank. My men would quickly dismount from the tank after it fired, and stay low. A few seconds after the tank fired off its armor piercing round, which I assumed would rock up those inside the bunker—even if it didn't penetrate all the way in—I would crawl up to the edge of the lip, peer over it and shout, in German, that they were surrounded, that unless they surrendered, the next round would go right into them. I would then slide back from the lip, count to ten, then crawl up again to the edge of the lip—but from a different spot—this would not give them a chance to draw a bead on me—peer over and shout that they had ten seconds to come out with their hands in the air, or the next round would be coming in.

If nothing happened I would then tell the tank commander to fire again. The second armor piercing round should do the trick. I remember how the officers looked at each other after I had finished my spiel. None of them said anything for a bit. Then one of them asked whether I could really speak German. I assured them I could, and had used it to advantage in the field. It never occurred to me to ask them if they had any suggestions, and none were proffered. The officers huddled together for a minute or so. Then the observer officer said, "Katz, its your mission. You'll have your tank. Get your team together. Be ready to take off at 6 a.m. tomorrow morning. Oh, this tank doesn't have any armor piercing rounds, only anti-personnel. Get a good night's rest. I'll see you in the morning." No armor piercing rounds. Now he tells me. Anti-personnel rounds are designed to be used on soft targets, such as soldiers, and thin skinned vehicles. They shatter on contact, releasing a lot of shrapnel, very effective against personnel; they don't make big holes in thick concrete, but the force of their concussion can reverberate inside the structure hit. I hoped this would be enough to contribute to the surprise of the Germans. We'd soon find out.

With my plan approved I met with the tank commander and crew of the borrowed tank and explained my plan to them. They offered neither advice nor objections. Their only concern was not to run into any anti-tank mines. I then selected the seven men to go with me. Six of them would be armed with infantry rifles, not the pea shooter carbines we carried in the Cavalry. The seventh man would carry a BAR, a Browning Automatic Rifle, a hand-held machine gun like weapon, very effective at close range. I would carry an infantry rifle, and be mindful for the red signal tarp. I felt comfortable with these guys. I had been on field operations with them. The seventh man was a guy I had not had any field experience with. He was transferred to our Troop after we lost those two men in the Battle of the Bulge. He was a tall, strapping guy, about my age, from one of the Dakota states. I assigned the carrying of the BAR to him. After Bastogne, when our mode of combat was changed to conform more closely to the style of the infantry, lots of the guys bitched about having to campaign dismounted. But this guy said he liked fighting on foot. It gave him a better chance to kill Germans. As of the time I picked him for my mission he had neither killed, wounded nor captured any of the enemy.

At 5 a.m. on February 20th 1945 I was dressed and ready to go. In the dark I roused those members of my team still in the sack. I don't recall what I had that morning, most likely nothing but coffee. Food was the last thing on my mind. At about 6 a.m. the starless darkness of night slowly yielded to the drabness of a gray, cold, late winter day. I rounded up my team and we headed for the heavy borrowed tank. The observer officer and an officer from my Squadron were waiting by the tank. They asked if I were set. I said I was. They wished me, my team and the tank crew, good luck. We all nodded our thanks. My guys then clambered atop the heavy tank and I followed them, lugging my rifle and the red tarp. As I was about to rap on the turret of the tank to get it moving the first rounds from our artillery flew overhead. You could hear them exploding up the slope. It was good to know we were not going to be totally alone out there. I had told the tank commander to head up the slope on its left flank. We would be heading east and this flank would be the northernmost part of the meadowland in which the entrenched bunkers lay. As I stated earlier, this field of bunkers lay in steeply rising terrain, a swath of mined, denuded earth about three hundred plus meters wide, bounded by dense forest on the north and south, My mission was to capture a bunker. If my team went down the center of the field we would be in the middle of the entrenchments' full field of fire. However, the first bunker we would encounter on the left flank would be up against the woods on its north side. No fire on us from that side. Such fire we might encounter would come from the bunker itself, and possibly from the bunker, further up the slope, to its right. So we would move out paralleling the woods on our left.

I rapped on the tank's turret. And we were underway! The tank was fully buttoned up. Draped around its turret, crouching as low as we could, were my seven men and me. Everyone was tense. No one talked. And even had we wanted to, the roar of the tank's engine, and the crunching sound of its treads biting into the denuded slope's hard terrain, would have drowned out our voices. The tank slowly lumbered forward and upward, occasionally lurching from side to side as it adjusted to the undulations of the terrain. And we, crouching on top of the tank—for my men and me this was our first ride on the exterior of a tank—held tight to whatever we could grasp.

We hadn't gone more than fifty meters up the slope when the tank set off the first anti-personnel mine. It flew out of the ground and exploded harmlessly against the side of the tank, its shrapnel pinging off the tank's treads and wheels. The shrapnel never flew higher than four feet from the ground. Selecting a large tank as my attack vehicle, and mounting my team on it was a good idea. I was pleased. And as we ascended more anti-personnel mines went off, all exploding harmlessly beneath us. Our first concern had been licked. We had one less thing to occupy our thoughts. But there were anti-tank mines out there. And if we got through unscathed we would then be facing our primary target. Well, one thing at a time. *Una la volta, per carità!* All of us had been tense. Now we were showing some signs of relief. Here and there, an exchange of furtive smiles. Except for one man. My BAR carrier. The big, "I'm gonna kill me some Germans" guy from the Dakotas. He was next to me, clinging to the side of the tank's turret. I heard him say, "I'm not feelin' OK." I looked at him. Even with the early morning sky barely lit I could see his face was pale. "I gotta get off!", he said. "We haven't gone too far. Can't we turn around and get me back?" "Turn around?" I was pissed. "You must be out of your fucking mind! You want off, then get the fuck off!" I banged on the tank's turret, and shouted it to stop. The tank stopped. I took the BAR from the big, frightened guy, and ordered him to get off the tank. He did so very slowly. "Stay here until we

get back, or start walking down in the tracks made by the tank."
By following the tank's tracks he would be walking in a narrow
path cleared of anti-personnel mines set off when the tank ran
over them. I banged on the turret and shouted, "Let's go!" The
tank started up. I was now loaded down with the BAR, my rifle
and the tarp. A load I didn't relish. None of the other guys said
anything during the entire episode. But as we moved up the steep
slope we all looked back and saw the big guy from the Dakotas
still standing where we had left him. He was clearly too scared
to move. "Tough shit!", I thought, and then I turned to peer for
the sight of the bunker we were out to attack.

The artillery's fire was heavy, screaming overhead and
exploding with a roar in front of us. We could see bursts of light
against the light gray sky, followed seconds later, by the booming
thunder. We noted a spotter plane slowly circling overhead. As we
slowly made our way up the steep slope the shells seemed to be
falling safely away from us. We knew the fire was friendly, and
we assumed—or at least we were hoping—that the spotter plane
had seen us. A misguided round of friendly fire can kill you as
easily as one fired by your enemy.

We moved slowly forward and upward, one hundred meters,
two hundred meters, the tank rocking as it adapted to the
terrain's undulations. Overhead our artillery's fire flew, and as
we progressed anti-personnel mines activated by the movement
of our tank popped up, exploded and sent showers of shrapnel
pinging harmlessly off its treads and wheels. The Dakotas guy left
standing in the field was now out of sight. Then, there! slightly to
our left, not more than 50 meters away, I saw the earthen mound
encircling our target. And behind the mound I could make out
the roof of the bunker. Shit!, that mother looked huge! And I
was seeing only a small part of it. I crawled past several of my
guys clustered around the tank's turret. I rapped hard on it. The
tank stopped. The turret hatch opened slightly, enough for me
to rehearse quickly with the tank commander the routine I had
worked out with him, namely, that he would maneuver his tank

so that he rolled up onto the earthen mound only far enough so that the front portions of the tank's treads would be at highest edge of the lip. If he moved any further he would expose the soft underbelly of his tank to fire, and possibly even tip into the saucer portion of the entrenchment where he could be trapped for lack of space to move about. Once he reached the mound's lip his gunner would lower his cannon so that it pointed down at the bunker's face. If he had the time to aim at one of the bunker's firing or viewing slots, wonderful! I knew he didn't have armor piercing shells, but that first round, wherever it hit, and no matter how shallow it penetrated into the bunker's concrete hide, would shake up the Germans. Immediately after firing his round, he would back down off the earthen mound, and move to his right. He would then be out of the bunker's line of sight. When he came up for his second shot he would be in a different position, and the Germans could believe that several tanks surrounded them. And that's what I wanted them to think. My men and I would be holding on for dear life to whatever parts of the tank we could grab while the tank commander was performing his maneuver. I had carefully explained my surprise attack plan to my men. They knew that immediately after the tank had fired and backed down, made its side movement, and stopped, that they were to slide off the tank and remain clustered next to it. They knew I would then go into my "surprise routine", and they knew what to do thereafter. A neat plan, now to see it executed successfully.

My refresher conversation with the tank commander completed he battened down his hatch. I rapped on it, and slowly, ever so slowly, the tank moved forward. The concave top of the bunker was now in full view. All of us on top of the tank were tense. And I'm sure so were those buttoned up within the tank. The tank, its engine roaring in low gear, inched up the earthen mound. The German defenders may have heard us coming. Now for the first time they saw us. How were they reacting? At the crest of the mound the tank lowered its cannon. "Fire!", I shouted, and the tank's cannon blazed, and almost instantaneously—the distance between tank and target being so short—there was an orange, red, yellow burst of flame, like a rose exploding—the same sight I saw when many months earlier, I had fired upon that partially concealed Panzer in France—the sound of the detonating shell was deafening, with pieces of its shrapnel, and rock sized chunks of concrete blasted from the bunker's face whizzing by overhead. As planned, the tank then reversed immediately and swerved down the mound to its right. It was no longer visible from the bunker.

Now it became time for me to go into my "routine". I told my men to dismount from the tank, and to hunker down on the ground, below the earthen mound, and to spread out on that part of the terrain churned up by the tank when it made its position changing maneuver. Clearly, had there been any mines there, of whatever type, the tank's movements would have set them off. The terrain was safe for them. My men knew that I would now crawl up to the lip of the mound, peer cautiously over, only my face and helmet would be above grade, and that I would shout for the Germans to surrender. None of my men understood German, but they knew the gist of my message. Gray smoke was wafting off the face of the bunker, and drifting slowly skyward, mixed with the acrid stench given off by the exploding shell. I had slid off the tank clutching the heavy BAR that our absent friend from the Dakotas should have been lugging. I was crawling in one of the tracks gouged out by the tank as it mounted the earthen mound, fired and backed down. Concern about a Bouncing Betty hitting me was not on my radar. I eased my way up to the lip of the mound. Poked my BAR over it, as much for a show of firepower—ineffectual though it would have been—as to keep from lugging it further. Only seconds had passed from the time the tank had fired. I slowly raised my helmeted head, my eyes and nose barely above the mound's edge and shouted as loud as I have ever shouted, *"Ergebet euch! Ergebet euch! Der nächste Schuss geht durch!"* "Surrender! Surrender! The next shot goes through!" And I ducked below the mound's lip. I knew we had no armor piercing rounds. But they didn't. I counted to ten. No reaction from those inside the bunker. *Nichts*. Nothing. I crawled a few feet to my right, in the direction of the tank. I wasn't about to raise my head a second time in the same spot where I had been should someone in the bunker have drawn a bead on me and was waiting for me to pop up like a target in a shooting gallery. At the lip of the mound I again shouted for them to surrender, *"Ergebet euch! Eure letzte Gelegenheit!"* "Surrender, your last chance!" I ducked down and again counted to ten. No reaction from the bunker. I was about to retrace my way back to the tank to tell the tank commander to fire a second round when I saw something stuck on a rod like object start to come up from what must have been the chimney or air vent pipe of the bunker. What I saw was a dirty white piece of cloth, maybe a towel, maybe someone's underwear. The stick waved slowly. Hey! The Germans were waving the white flag of surrender! They were giving up! Wow! Yeah, but this could be a trick. So I called out to my guys to fan out, some to my right, and some to my left and to poke their rifles over the edge of the mound's lip. The Germans would then see evidence of more men, but not be sure of how many. I shouted to the tank commander to move up on the mound just enough to show the snout of his lowered cannon, but to hold his fire until I called out. I then told my guys that I would order the Germans out with their hands up. Each of the men's rifles had a round in the chamber, with the safety on. I told them to release the safety, that if the Germans opened their bunker door and came rushing out with weapons, to shoot to kill, otherwise to hold their fire. All this whispered talk took only about 20 seconds. Again peering over the top of the mound I shouted at the Germans, *"Heraus! Heraus! Hände hoch! Wir schiessen nicht!"* "Come out! Come out! Hands up! We won't shoot!" I had called out to the Germans using the *du* form, the familiar form of address one used in speaking with family members, intimate friends and, conversely, in giving commands to animals, or inferiors. The *Sie* form was the formal or polite form used in addressing strangers, or persons of higher rank or stature than the speaker, such as an enlisted man addressing an officer. The Germans understood my use of the *du* form. We had the upper hand. We were their superiors. And that's the way it would be.

A door on the left side of the bunker slowly opened. It opened onto a small concrete deck, or landing which led to six concrete steps, the uppermost being even with the lip of the earthen mound surrounding the bunker. A German soldier, his arms raised in the air, hesitantly stepped through the doorway onto the landing. He looked apprehensive. In his position I most likely would have looked the same. Upon later reflection I gave him credit for trusting me not to shoot him in cold blood. His ten fingers were outstretched and poked straight up. Clearly he was carrying neither a pistol nor a grenade. I stood up, telling my guys to get up to a crouching position and cover me. I was standing about three meters from the foot of the steps. *"Herunter, schnell, schnell!* Come down, quick, quick! The German hurried down the steps and stood at their base. I waved my BAR at him. Although he was ten feet away I could see him blanch. *"Halt dort!"*, Stay there!, I ordered him. I yelled again for all those inside the bunker to come out. I imagined they were hesitant to come out until they knew what would happen to the first guy who surrendered. In short order, three more came out, empty hands held high. They huddled together, their furtive glances showed their anxiety. I had one of my men frisk them. He found no weapons or grenades concealed on them. In answer to my sharp queries: yes, they were *die ganze Mannschaft*, the bunker's complete complement, yes, no one was hiding inside, yes, the bunker's interior had not been booby trapped. I told them to walk down the slope, hands held high, so that none of our guys would shoot at them, and that they should walk in the tank's tracks to avoid the mines. I think the last advice was surplusage, they knew the drill better than we did. The activities described took less than a minute, during which time our artillery fire was ongoing overhead and falling safely ahead of us. My guys and I watched as the captured Germans, *Hände hoch*, slowly wended their way down the slope to its foot where our MPs would take them in tow.

Hey! We had taken our objective! Now to call Squadron HQ report the good news and get the fuck out of here! In recounting this adventure I neglected to mention that we had a small radio/telephone unit with us. I had rolled it into the red tarp. In the Cavalry, where our primary *raison d'etre* as a reconnaissance arm was communicating information, I had taken for granted we carried such ubiquitous devices with us all the time. An alert reader (hopefully, every reader of this tome) would have noted that I earlier pointedly referred to the fact that I had armed my men on this mission with infantry rifles, in lieu of our Cavalry issued carbines which I had condescendingly referred to as "pea shooters". In short, what we took for granted, we took for granted.

I had been instructed to lay down the red tarp when we were near our target, to alert the spotter plane we were closing in. They would then instruct the artillery to advance its line of fire away from us. That was the principle. It did not work that way in practice. Stretching out an eight foot long tarp in what might be mined ground and before I had started my surprise stratagem didn't make sense. So the tarp and the radio/telephone were still on the tank. Just as the upraised hands of the last of the four Germans disappeared from sight as he descended the deep slope there was a screeching whistle and a roar as one of our artillery's rounds slammed into the ground about fifteen meters to the right of us, sending clods of earth flying overhead! Had the round fallen fifteen meters to the left of where it fell we would all have been bits of skin and bones and tattered clothing fluttering through the air. The spotter plane was clearly not aware that we had outstripped the artillery in our advance. It had seen no red tarp. I told my guys to run into the bunker. Bad guys out! Good guys in! I then rushed over terrain now familiar to me—no anti-personnel mines to fear—grabbed the rolled up tarp where it was nestled against the tank's turret, ran to the steps of the bunker and unrolled the tarp across them and clutching my radio/telephone I scrunched down in the corner made where the landing of the steps joined the wall of the bunker. As I did so another shell came screaming and roaring in, and impacted less than ten meters from me, so close that I felt the ground shake, and heard the sounds of debris whirring about me! Hey! That was too close for comfort! I yelled into my phone, "We've taken the bunker, and we're all OK! Lift your fire! Lift your fire!" The voice at the other end, whose I never learned, nor did I care to know at the moment, shouted back, "Can't hear you Katz, speak up!" Shit! Can't hear me? Just then another shell impacted. Thank God, not any closer than the last one! I shouted back, as loud as I could, "Lift your fucking fire! We took the bunker and your shit is falling on us!" There was a moment of silence on the other end, then the voice, now quite excited, said "Great! We'll lift the fire!" Very welcome words. I then scurried into the bunker to join my men. Safe inside I peered into the sky. There was the spotter plane. I saw him slowly turn, and fly towards us. He must have gotten words from HQ and went looking for that red tarp. He must have seen it. Another round whistled in and dropped ever so close, and then about thirty seconds later, maybe a tad longer, the next shell I heard exploding landed higher up the slope and away from our newly captured bunker. My radio/telephone didn't work too well from inside the bunker, too much concrete and steel I guessed. I ventured out onto the landing and called down to HQ. With no bombs bursting nearby communication was easier. I repeated my information that we had taken the bunker, that none of my men were hurt, nor was I, that the tank and its crew were OK, and that I'd sent four German prisoners down the slope, none of them wounded. I then said I'd mount my team up onto the tank and retrace its tracks down to our base. Wow! My mission was over! I'd won my trip to Paris and to OCS! Right? Wrong! As I soon found out.

I went into the bunker and sat down with my men. The tank crew felt secure in their tank and didn't join us. We were all elated! Mission accomplished! Nobody hurt on either side. Let's go home. Then the phone in the bunker rang. It was the German phone connected to the other bunkers. I picked it up. An excited voice at the other end called out, *"Helmut, hier. Wo sind die Amis?"* "Helmut here, Where are the Americans?" I replied in German, *"Wir sind hier!"* "We're here!" Helmut was clearly surprised. He hung up on me. I said to the guys, "The son-of-a-bitch hung up on me!" And we all laughed. Then a phone rang again. This time it was ours. My Troop Commander was on the line. I recognized his voice. I walked with the phone to the bunker's doorway to hear better. The shells were still falling, but further off. My Troop Commander sounded pleased, he told me I had done a great job! And then he said, "You're doing great! So go on and take the next one!" Hey! Wait a minute! The deal was I'd lead a mission to take a bunker, *singular, a bunker* as in *one* bunker! If I succeeded that was it. I'd have proved my organizational and leadership abilities. Well, I'd kept my part of the deal and proved that sometimes its easier to talk an enemy into surrendering than engaging in a costly fire fight to make him do so. Sometimes, even in war, the tongue was sharper than the sword. Right! Except I was only a T/5 and I had just been ordered to move on and do it again, or at least try to do again, what I had just done. What I had understood—and I am even better in English than I am in German—was that if I succeeded in capturing a bunker I'd have earned my spurs, so to speak, and would soon be on my way to Paris and OCS. But now it looked as if I was embarked on an open ended military exercise. I was pissed. But looking back I recognize that what was then happening to me was *beshert*, that it was meant to be, that it was a vital part of the divine plan which was leading me unknowingly, but steadily, along a path of adventures and misadventures which, ultimately, would lead me to my beautiful, belóved Anneliese Baur!

My telephone conversation with HQ over I told my team we still had work to do. I wasn't sure from the short conversation I had just completed with HQ whether taking another bunker would complete my mission—or were we to try to sweep the slope clean of all the bunkers? Well, as we progressed, we'd find out. My surprise mode of attack, coupled with my use of

German, had worked with the *Mannschaft* who had manned
the bunker we were now occupying. Would it work the second
time? In a few more minutes we'd find out. Nobody on my team
complained when I said we had to move against another bunker.
But neither did anyone shout with glee. Their first exercise had
gone well. Traversing the mine fields had caused no injuries,
nor had the attack on the bunker. So far so good. The barrage of
our artillery shells flying overhead, and impacting safely in front
of us, indicated to them that although we were just one team of
seven guys atop one tank we were not wholly without support.
Before leaving the captured bunker I rolled up the red tarp, and
loaded down with it and the BAR I clambered aboard the tank
with a number of hands helping me up.

I informed the tank commander of our new orders. He was as
surprised as I had been that our mission had been extended. He
shook his head and said, "Shit!" An appropriate comment under
the circumstances. The tank commander told his driver to start up.
With a roar the tank became alive, and with a shudder throughout
its body it slowly backed away from the captured bunker, turned
and moved forward, onward and upward towards the next bunker.
Referring to my Boy Scout training in compass work I believe
we had headed NNE to encounter the captured bunker we were
leaving behind. We were now headed NE where, approximately
seventy five meters in front of us, we could see the base of an
earthen mound as it rose from the terrain. Behind it we knew
our second target lay entrenched. The shelling barrage which
had begun in the morning had alerted the German bunker crews
that they were under attack. How the attack would be mounted
they had to guess at. Would it be only artillery? Or artillery and
aircraft bombing? Or a ground assault? And if so, what kind?
Or a combination of all these attack elements. Fortunately,
these Germans didn't know the strengths, or lack thereof, of our
forces. But they had heard the sounds of our tank moving up the
steep slope. They had heard the sounds of anti-personnel mines
detonating. They had heard the fire from our tank, and, I am sure,

that Helmut, the guy whose call I answered, had quickly informed all the other bunker crews that the *Amis* had already overrun a bunker. How big was the *Ami* force, and where would it strike next? Exposed as we were to mines, we still had the psychological advantage over the Germans. We were out in the open. We were moving. We knew where they were. We were calling the shots. *They were cooped up in a concrete box*. They knew we were out there, somewhere. They didn't know our numbers or armament. And based upon knowledge I had acquired over my previous months of combat, the crews manning these entrenched positions were not from the top tier of Hitler's *Wehrmacht*. These were second team players. Many were not even native born Germans. Instead, they were mainly Nazi sympathizers from occupied countries. When push came to shove the German High Command did not expect such personnel to fight to the death. They were not the *SS*, Hitler's fanatic top killers. The function of such bunker bound personnel—in concert with the mine fields laid about them—was to slow down our advance into Germany, as I have already discussed. My stratagem of coupling a surprise mode of attack with a German language command to surrender was based upon this knowledge. Its first application worked. We would soon see whether it would work again.

As we moved forward the tank tripped anti-personnel mines. These Bouncing Betty mines exploded harmlessly against the tanks's treads and wheels. On top of the tank, high above the shrapnel blasts, we were safe from injury. Safe, but never wholly at ease. The bunker we had captured lay about fifty yards behind us (in WWII we still measured distance in feet and yards). The military now uses the metric system of measurement. A much easier way to figure. I have tried to use meters in my story. Should I regress, let it go. Suddenly I spied the earthen lip of the mound surrounding another entrenched bunker, about 45° to our right. The tank commander saw it at the same time. His tank changed direction and headed for our second target. My guys and I scrunched down behind the tank's turret as the tank slowly edged itself up the face of the earthen mound. He lowered his cannon. I yelled fire! He did. The noise, the smoke, the imagery, were as before. As he backed down, my men and I quickly descended into the area the tank had vacated. Again, thank God! no exploding mines. I went into my "routine". Still clutching that damn BAR I crawled to the lip of the earthen mound surrounding the bunker. I loudly recited my catechism of surrender. No response. Neither word nor shot. I did my counting. I cautiously peered over the mound's lip and warned them that the next round was going all the way in. Counted again. I was about to signal the tank to fire a second round when the Germans threw in the towel. Actually, they raised *their* version of a white flag, a pair of grayish long johns. Whatever the color of the cloth they were waving, they wanted out. We were happy to accommodate them. The bunkers were mirror copies of each other. After assuring the Germans that we would not shoot them if they came out with their hands up, the bunker's door opened and five Germans slowly walked down the six steps to ground level, hands held high. My men frisked them. One of the Germans was an *Unteroffizier*, a sergeant. He was wearing a holster with a pistol in it. I took the pistol. It was a beautiful P45. This weapon and a *Dolch*, a dagger like knife were the only things I ever took from any German, soldier or civilian. I declared these two weapons to my unit. I was told I could keep them. I took them home with me. And when in the States I gave them away. My kids say I should have kept them as *souvenirs de guerre*. Perhaps. Oh, yes. I took one other thing. From a German military library. A copy of Hitler's *Mein Kampf*, his antisemitic tome, *My Battle*, which he wrote in prison before rising to power in 1933. I have this book on a bookshelf next to Karl Marx' *Das Kapital, Capital, the bible of Communism*. If ever I should forget the evils wrought on society by these two opposite poles of totalitarianism, I shall need but glance at these two books as they sit next to Adam Smith's 1776 masterpiece *A Wealth of Nations*. Next to—but a million light years away in thought and deed.

But back to my narrative. We had taken our second bunker. We had now captured nine Germans. No one hurt on either side. And only two tank rounds had been fired. From the point of view of expenditure of ordnance, what a bargain! All of us were keyed up. But always cautious. Our artillery was still firing, close enough to be helpful, but not too close for comfort. Mines were a constant concern. But our experiences with them had been good. None of us had stepped on any, or set any off, nor had the tank run over any anti-tank mines. I telephoned down to HQ. I told them we had taken our second bunker, no one hurt on either side, and five prisoners coming down. The response, as I feared, was highly laudatory. Keep up the good work, Katz! Take the next one you see. I thanked my Commanding Officer for his confidence in my team and me. Silently I cussed him out. He was taking advantage of us. We'd been lucky so far. But luck, by its very nature, tends, at some point, to run out. I told my Commanding Officer that I'd look for a third target. Before starting off on my mission I had learned there were five or six bunkers barring our Squadron's way. Apparently the Squadron, buoyed by our early success, was now intending we try to take all of them! Shit! Getting to Paris and OCS was looking less and less attractive. To make a long story short (to coin a phrase, ha! ha!) that's what seven cavalrymen astride one tank did. We captured *every* bunker on the slope, opening the way for our forces to advance further east into Germany. We did it with only one round of tank fire per bunker and with my now practiced German language surrender routine—and without hurting any of our guys or theirs. If my memory is correct we took twenty four German prisoners. Not too bad for what had started out as a one bunker mission. In the course of our mission we worked our way up the steep slope until it crested overlooking some gently rolling, lightly wooded countryside which, even in winter, gave a hint of the greener, flower bedecked meadowland it would be in the summertime. The topmost bunker we took was positioned just at the slopes's crest. An ideal location for an artillery observation point. This latter point figures into my story a bit further on.

My knowledge of German, and its use as a battle field tool, enabled seven Cavalrymen, mounted on a tank, *bloodlessly* to clear away an entire cordon of entrenchments which had been barring my Cavalry Squadrons' deeper entry into Germany. I have emphasized the word "bloodlessly" because that was, to me, the crowning achievement of my successful mission. In the Introduction to his masterful treatise *Vom Kriege, On War*, Karl von Clausewitz succinctly defines what war is all about:

War is . . . an act of force to compel our adversary to do our will. [Emphasis Von Clausewitz]

> . . . Force, that is to say, physical force . . . is thus the *means*; to impose our will upon the enemy is the *object*. To achieve this object with certainty we must disarm the enemy, and this disarming is by definition the proper aim of military action . . . ." [Emphasis von Clausewitz]

In my own small way I had accomplished that object on the 20th of February 1945 by devising a stratagem of surprise—in which the tactical use of the German language was an essential element. I harbored no illusions that we could easily shoot our way into our entrenched bunker target. But I strongly believed we could talk our way in. And that we did. Several times over. By their nature and aims, wars are cruel and destructive undertakings. Karl von Clausewitz makes that observation numerous times. But he also noted that successful strategies, tactics, stratagems and surprises can make imposing one's will upon one's enemy less costly in blood and treasure. I have never kept a diary. However I had a pocket sized spiral notebook which listed the Jewish Holidays (as if I would have had time to celebrate any of them) and in which

I would jot down poetry. That evening, before I changed into my dress Olive Drab uniform, I remember jotting down the statement: "I was a soldier's soldier today." That said it all. I was pleased with my performance. And I'm a tough critic of myself. If I can yet find that notebook squirreled away somewhere among my effects I will photocopy the page and insert it into this book.

Back down from the slope my men and I, and the tank crew, were congratulated by our officers and fellow Troopers. Nothing fancy. Just words of appreciation for a task well done. I don't recall any formal celebration. I do recall, however, a singular event. Maybe that's why I remember it. At the base of the slope I was approached by an MP sergeant who now had custody of the German prisoners we had earlier captured. He understood I had led the mission. He asked whether I had taken anything from the prisoners. I said the Germans had been frisked for weapons when captured, that my men found none, and took nothing, that I had taken a P45 pistol from a German sergeant, and that this was allowed under the Geneva Convention. The MP sergeant laughed and rolled up the sleeve on his left arm. From his wrist to his armpit the arm was filled with wristwatches. Laughing, he said, "Man, you didn't frisk so good. You missed twenty four watches!" And that's how I know I captured at least 24 Germans that day.

When I related the story of this mission to Anneliese, and later to our kids, no one asked me whether I was scared at any time. A good question—but one which they may have thought impolite to ask. I had been in many engagements prior to this one—although, as noted, never against a cordon of entrenched bunkers—and I don't recall ever being scared, if being scared one means feeling fearful, alone and helpless. No. Never. I was always mindful of my surroundings, always very alert, always apprehensive. But never fearful. But neither was I cocky. I am of the opinion that people become scared or fearful when they find themselves in—or imagine themselves to be in—an environment or situation where they feel they have no control over what is happening, around them. As long as I could control my actions and reactions under fire, I felt OK. As I have earlier related, once I learned "how to read the pattern" of incoming artillery or mortar fire, whether the fire was observed or blind—blind meaning where the Germans knew we were there but couldn't see us—and whether blind or observed fire—to recognize early on that it was falling in a fixed measured manner, as a *Teppich* or carpet bombing—once I had acquired this skill I controlled my destiny. I knew when it was safer to stay with my armored car, and when not to, and when dismounted, where to find the best cover from hostile fire. In short, being fearful means being unable (i) to cope, (ii) to adapt, and (iii) to act with independence. Being a loner by nature, my wits served me well in combat. The two times I was injured (the reader knows of my first injury, and will shortly be apprised of my second) I was hurt through actions instituted by others.

Back to my narrative. The tensions of the mission just completed were beginning to take their toll. I was elated, but very tired. I stayed awake long enough to wash my hands and face, give myself a quick whore's bath, and then don my Olive Drab uniform, ready to leave at 5 a.m. the next morning for Paris and OCS. I looked forward to getting a good night's sleep. Instead, a few hours later I was awakened by my communications sergeant. As the reader knows, the sergeant got me up to help him lay some telephone wire between two of the bunkers my team had taken earlier in the day.

I was told by my sergeant that the artillery unit which had been raining shells over my team as we made our way up towards the bunkers was now itself moving up to occupy the heights—and that the Squadron would now resume its Eastward Drive into Germany—which move had been made possible by my team's removal of the bunkers as military obstacles. He further informed me that the artillery had already established an observation/command post in the last bunker we had taken. This was the one positioned at the crest of the slope, near the right flank of the cordon of entrenchments. I was told the artillery wanted to link their observation/command post with another artillery position to be set up in a bunker situated on the left flank of the entrenched area. It was his job and mine, to run a telephone line between these two widely separated bunkers.

As I got ready to go up the slope again—this would be the sergeant's first time—it began to drizzle. It was late afternoon. There was still daylight, but the sky was overcast, turning our surroundings gray, and, as if there were need to add to the drabness of the weather, it had begun to drizzle. I fished out my raincoat from the bottom of my duffel bag. Normally, rain would not bother me. Certainly not a drizzle. But I was wearing my dress olive drab uniform, and didn't want to get it wet or muddy before I left for Paris at 5 a.m. And so I donned the raincoat, but left it unbuttoned, to have more freedom of movement in carrying several sound and power telephone units and several coils of wire.

Before we started our way up the slope I reminded my sergeant that the slope was heavily seeded with anti-personnel and anti-tank mines. Thus, we should walk only in the tracks made by our tank during our assault, since such mines as were there had been tripped and exploded. "OK, professor", he said, "I've heard the story. Let's move out, it's getting dark." He had called me "professor". He was using the title as a pejorative. He was a high school graduate. I was a third year college student. I might be smarter, but he outranked me, and in his thought processes he clearly was a devotee of the dictum: "When ignorance is bliss, 'tis folly to be wise." (I believe Longfellow wrote that.) And so, each of us heavily laden, slowly made our way up the slope. I led the way, being careful to follow the tracks made by the tank.

We got to the lip of the earthen mound surrounding the highest bunker on the slope. We were standing where our tank had sat when it fired its first round at the bunker—and its last—in the course of our mission. To the left of the bunker, and just behind a line of barbed wire, the Germans had dug a trench which ran to the outermost bunker on the left flank. Our job, the sergeant said, was to run our telephone wires from the bunker outside of which we were now standing to that other bunker. There was an opening in the barbed wire through which one entered the trench. I said, "OK. Let's get into the trench and pay out the wire in it." I told my sergeant that when I interrogated the prisoners taken from this bunker that they had informed me that the trench had not been mined or booby trapped. Why would it have been? They were using it routinely, and when they realized that a large American force faced them below, they had neither the time, nor the inclination, to do anything but stay put in the safety of their bunker. Now this German trench had been built most cleverly from a military point of view. Instead of being laid out in a straight line from Point A to Point B, it had been dug so that it consisted of a series of zig zags made by alternating a right side up V shape with an inverted V shape. As I have noted, the beauty of this design was that if a shell or grenade fell into one of the V shaped portions the resulting explosion would be confined within that portion. The German zig zag design trench was militarily better than a straight line one. Its only "negative aspect" was that it was twice as long as a straight line trench covering the same area. Thus, were we to pay out our wire in this zig zag trench we would be walking more and laying out more wire, than if we went straight over and across the terrain between the two bunkers.

As soon as I had made my observation concerning using the German trench to lay our wire my sergeant said to me, with a smirk on his face, "Professor, What's the shortest distance between two points?" "A straight line", I said. "Right! So that's why we're going to lay our wire straight across the field to that other bunker. It'll soon be dark. Why waste time and wire going through that fuckin' twistin' trench while there's still enough light to see where we're going." I was stunned! I always thought the guy was an ass hole. But I never thought he was so stupid! "OK, if that's what you want." I said reluctantly. Rather than going through the opening in the barbed wire which led to the trench, I climbed over the perimeter barbed wire which encircled the left side of the bunker. He followed me. I moved slowly, very slowly, very cautiously, peering at the ground for any signs of bouncing betty mines. I was hoping the dummy would change his mind and we could lay the wire in the trench. I had moved about two meters from the point where I had climbed over the barbed wire when he clambered over it. Apparently he had snagged a pant leg in getting over. I was carrying a sound and power telephone and holding one end of the telephone wire. And I was beginning to pay it out by slowly pulling it from the spool he was carrying. He was about a foot or so inside the barbed wire when he called out to me, his voice betraying some apprehension, "Yeah, maybe you're right, let's use the trench." "OK", I said, quite relieved, "Now let's go back just the way we came." I began to turn about in place, that is, I had begun to pivot my body towards the barbed wire fence, but had not yet moved my feet, when I heard a shout. At that exact moment there was a deafening explosion! Although my back was turned to it, a bright burst of light enveloped me and simultaneously I felt a blunt, hard hitting, searing pain in the small of my back, as if I had been hit by a baseball bat and a red hot poker. My sergeant had tripped a booby trapped Bouncing Betty mine! He shouted when his foot caught the mine's trip wire. The mine exploded next to me. Its full force struck me. My body shielded him from any harm.

I was now lying face down on the ground. My sergeant was still rooted to the spot where he had tripped it. "Are you hurt?" he called. His query wasn't funny. I laugh now. It reminds me of those slapstick comedies I saw as a kid when a guy would tumble down a flight of stairs and be prostrate at its base and a bystander would come running up and ask "Are you hurt?" "Yeah, I'm hurt," I said. "Can I help?" However, he made no effort to approach me. Which, as far as I was concerned, was all to the good. At that moment I believed I had been hit in the lower back. I remembered from my Boy Scout First Aid training that if a person appeared to be suffering from a back or spinal injury, that one without medical knowledge should not move him, because an improper movement could permanently damage the injured person's back. "No, no, not now," I gasped. Then I felt a new sensation. The bolt of pain in my back was gone. Pain has, clearly, different ways of communicating its message of injury. Now I felt extreme pain in my right thigh. And I felt something wet and warm running down my right thigh and leg. I was bleeding from a wound somewhere in my upper right thigh. I tried to get up. I was feeling a little dizzy, light headed. I called to my sergeant, "Yeah, give me a hand." He approached me cautiously, fortunately no more anti-personnel mines were tripped. He helped me up and together we went through the opening in the barbed wire perimeter and slowly made our way to the bunker. Painfully, I made my way up the same six stairs into the bunker over which earlier that day I had stretched out that red tarp as a signal to lift our artillery fire. Inside, there were four artillery officers sitting at a table and playing cards. My right side was now throbbing, and I was beginning to feel very queasy. I remember approaching the table, leaning over and plunking my elbows on it, upsetting their card game. Had I not done that I would have fallen down. "Excuse me, sirs, but I've just been hit." I was an enlisted man, and I'd just fucked up their game. The least I could do was say "Excuse me." I don't recall any of them showing any emotion. One of them said, "Oh, was that the noise we heard?" Imagine, an explosion almost on their doorstep, and none of them bothered to look outside! Such are the vagaries of war.

I was fading fast. I gather they lay me down someplace and called the medics. The next I remember there was a medic leaning over me. I was still in the bunker. He took out a pair of scissors and cut my beautiful OD pants down past my ankle. "Hey, those were my best ODs!", I mumbled stupidly. His laconic reply, "You won't need them where you're going". With my pant leg cut open, my long john underwear on my right thigh and leg were exposed. In getting dressed to go to Paris I had put on a clean pair of long johns. They were British Army issue, part of the exchange program between our forces and theirs. We gave them 50 destroyers when they needed them, and they now gave us Cadbury chocolate bars and gray colored underwear, a fair exchange. By now the medic had unbuckled my belt and gently pulled my pants off, and he began to do his scissors number on the right leg of my long johns. It was soaked red with my blood. The left leg was still a pristine gray. The medic placed a compress over the wound, or maybe he applied a tourniquet around my thigh to stanch the blood flow. I was floating in and out of awareness of my surroundings. The medic may have had an assistant, at that point I wasn't sure of anything. Funny how the mind works. Despite my pain the following image jumped into my mind: I remembered that in the 8th grade, upon graduation from P.S. 173 in Brooklyn, in June 1936, I played the Court Jester in the graduation play. My costume consisted of a jester's belled cap, a multi-colored shirt, and a pair of tights in which the left leg was gray and the right leg was red. There I was, painfully wounded, lying on my back, on a stretcher on the floor of a German bunker I had bloodlessly captured earlier that day. It was February 20, 1945, we were on the outskirts of Prüm, Germany—but my mind had brought me back, if only for a moment, to that happier time—almost nine years earlier—when having a gray leg and a red leg was fun. Oh, the mysteries of the mind!

Knowledge acquired in the course of my first injury—when, the reader will recall, I suffered a broken right hand, a broken nose, injury to my left eye and facial scars—now came into play. When first picked up by the medics I asked them for morphine to lessen my pain. No, I was told, my beat up face suggested I might also have a head wound, if so, a dose of morphine might do me more harm than good, it could kill me. So no morphine. But my wound now was nowhere near my head. So, in one of my lucid moments I said to the medic, "I don't have a head wound, how about some morphine?" He laughed, "You learned that somewhere?" "Back in Brittany, last August." He gave me a shot of morphine. In a few moments I was asleep. Aside from being briefly awakened when my stretcher was jostled in getting me off the slope, my mind was thereafter a total blank. For how long? I don't know. When you are in a drugged state—or dead—time does not exist.

When I awoke, that is, when I could open my eyes and see, albeit blurry eyed—where was I? I remember finding myself lying on my stomach, on some kind of thin mattress like material. The mattress appeared to be resting on a floor made of well worn wood planks. I raised my head slowly, much like a turtle lifting its head out of its carapace. There, facing me, appeared to be a bare, flat, white surface—a plastered wall. As I slowly raised my head—mind you, I was on my stomach, and my neck was stiff—I suddenly saw a large crucifix on the wall! "My God!", I thought, "I'm dead. I'm in Heaven—and they put me in the wrong place!" The idea of being dead didn't bother me. Being dead—and not with my fellow Jews—and for eternity—that bothered me!

As my mind cleared I soon recognized that I was not dead. I was in a small church in Luxembourg which had been turned into a US military medical evacuation way station by the removal of all the church's furnishings, from pews to altar, leaving only the crucifix on the wall. It was left there to calm those passing through. However, its initial impact upon me was to the contrary. At the time I was on this church's wooden plank floor I was the only GI patient. In a few hours an ambulance came to take me to a medical evacuation train which would deliver me to a military hospital to Paris. Yep! I was going to Paris! But neither the way I had wanted, nor to the place I had there expected to find. What shitty luck! Instead of attending OCS, and becoming an officer, I was going to spend an unknown amount of painful time in a military hospital. Clearly, that was no way to advance my military career. To put it mildly, I was pissed off at this turn of events. Little did I then know that this episode of being grievously wounded—an episode I deemed to be wholly negative when it happened—was but another link in that chain of episodes which was leading me ever closer to my belóved Anneliese Baur.

Episode Twenty Eight

In which I relate my experiences on the way to a military hospital in Paris, and while there.

On the morning of the 21st of February 1945 I had expected to be on my way to Paris, there to spend 90 days in OCS, training to be an infantry officer. From the events just related the reader knows I never got to Paris as an OCS candidate. I did get to Paris. Not sitting up proudly as a passenger in a jeep, but as a wounded soldier lying partially on my side in a military hospital train. My recollections are hazy for that period of time immediately after I was wounded. I don't recall being placed aboard a hospital train en route to a military hospital in Paris. Clearly, I was being given pain killers which were performing as such sedatives should. So I'd be awake for a bit, then out, then in, then out again. Time at this point was as meaningless for me as it would be were I really in Heaven. Heaven is for eternity, and time is meaningless in eternity. But at one point I awoke, and was alert long enough to gaze languidly about me. I was in a long railway car. I knew I was on a train because I could hear the rhythmic clickety clack of its wheels on the tracks.

There was a smell in the air, not unpleasant, just different, a bit pungent. I learned during the many hospital days that lay before me, that I was smelling a mixture of antiseptics, pain killing drugs, and the sweet scent of blood oozing from bandages, with a bit of urine added for good measure. The railway car was configured like a Pullman sleeping car. I was lying, strapped down, on a comfortable mattress, my head resting on a firm pillow, with the bed linens all crisp and clean, and a warm blanket over me. Quite a difference from my beat up (but still serviceable) sleeping bag out in the field. Aside from being strapped down—and to further assure I didn't fall out from my bunk style bed—a railing, which could be raised and lowered, ran along its outer edge. This outer

213

edge faced the aisle running down the middle of the car. I was lying on the top bunk of a two bunk arrangement, much like the bunk beds kids have when they are growing up together. But there were no kids on the train that day, certainly none in the five to ten years range. Yet, on reflection, there was a kid on that hospital train. Across the aisle from where I lay there was the same double bunk bed arrangement, which ran the full length of the car on both sides. Directly across the aisle from me—and I could see him when I stiffly turned my head to the left—was a soldier younger than I. In February '45 I was 22, and I thought I looked young for my age. But that guy, that kid across the aisle, really looked young. I guessed he was 18, maybe 19. And he was a talker! He kept jabbering away. To no one in particular. He just kept on talking. There was no other conversation in the car. You could hear some guys softly moaning, some snoring, or coughing, but aside from these random sounds, and that of the clickety clack of the train's wheels, the only other thing that I heard was this kid talking up a storm. He was not talking sad stuff. He was not bitching. At one point he got very animated, and he began to laugh. It was not a ha! ha! belly laugh. It was a sort of nervous laugh. And when he laughed his voice became louder. I wasn't trying to listen to him, or to hear what he said. In fact, I wished he would fuckin' shut up so that I could get some shut eye! But after hearing one loud, enthusiastic "Yeah!", I turned my face to him again. "Yeah", he repeated, "this shit is all over for me now! I got it made! This fuckin' Army ain't gonna see me again! I'm goin' home for good! Yeah! No shit! I got it made!"

The kid sounded happy, but he also sounded near his breaking point. Half asleep as I was, I was still alert enough, curious enough, to wonder what was making this kid act so high. And so I peered more closely at him. The railway car was not brightly lit. Wounded soldiers stacked in bunks in a military hospital train don't need lights to read by. But there was enough light to see him stretched out in his bunk bed. In his agitated talking he had partially kicked loose the blanket over him. And as I ran my eyes down his figure I saw—and it was a shock for me—that his right leg ended as a stump just below his knee! His right foot and ankle were gone! His injury showed every sign that an exploding anti-personnel mine, either a shoe or Teller mine, had blown away much of his right leg. The surgeons had amputated his limb to just below the knee. This would give him the chance, when he was later fitted with his prosthetic device, to walk with a more measured gait. But right now this kid was in pain, emotional and physical. Perhaps he had been a top high school football or baseball player, or a track star, a great dancer, and thus a hit with the girls. And now all this was gone, and he knew it. And so, by his non-stop bull-shitting, to no one I particular, he was endeavoring to compensate for his physical loss, he was trying to turn a negative into a positive. I felt very sad for him. And a tad guilty. I too, had been wounded by an anti-personnel mine. I was badly hurt, but I hadn't lost a limb. When, with some effort, I wiggled the toes on my right foot, I confirmed I still had my leg. I was lucky.

I didn't learn how lucky I had been until I was told in the hospital, in Paris, that the shrapnel from the exploding Bouncing Betty mine had penetrated deeply into my right thigh, and that one piece of jagged metal—some German tool and die factory floor sweeping, I suppose—had come within a couple of centimeters of severing the femoral artery in my right thigh. Had that happened, I most likely would have bled to death before the medics could have gotten me off the slope. But it was not my time to die. It was not meant to be. I was on yet another stage of a long, meandering journey, which, unbeknownst to me was drawing me, inexorably, through all kinds of adventures, nearer to that unknown distant place where I would discover my beautiful, belóved Anneliese Baur!

As previously noted, I was heavily sedated on my journey from the battlefield near Prüm, Germany, to the military hospital in the Bois de Boulogne district on the outskirts of Paris. Thus, except for episodic awakenings, as when I noticed my distraught

comrade—worse off than I—across the aisle in the hospital train,
I slept my way almost to the portals of the building in the Bois de
Boulogne, an ornate structure which had housed a school before
the USA converted it into a military hospital. I remember being
aroused from my drug induced slumber by the feeling that my
bed, actually the stretcher onto which I was securely strapped, was
undulating. And it was. I was being carried by two civilians, one
at the foot of my stretcher, the other, behind me. Tied down as I
was, my field of vision was limited to what I could see directly
overhead, and to the right and left to the limited extent I could
turn my head from side to side. Thus, I noted I was being carried
through a wide and high portal into a large open area, a rotunda
of sorts. Directly overhead I could see a curved ceiling, perhaps
a hundred feet above me, with what appeared to be a circular
skylight in its center. I caught a glimpse, as I was carried in, of
a curved staircase attached to one side of this huge area. I could
not see the floor. My stretcher bearers must have been wearing
metal studded, or heavily soled shoes, for as they walked I heard
the sharp sounds one hard object makes when striking against
another hard object. So I surmised I was on some kind of a stone
floor. Later, when I became an ambulatory patient, I saw that the
floor was marble interlaced with tiles. I couldn't see the full width
of the area I was in. But even in my medicated state I recognized
I was not in an ordinary dwelling. However, my attention soon
turned from architectural speculations, to concern for my own
well being. I noted that my stretcher was now on a slant, my head
higher than my feet, and that I was being carried, head first, up
a winding staircase. My stretcher was being turned from side
to side by my stretcher bearers as they adjusted to the changing
configurations of the staircase they were ascending. The wall of
the building was to my left. To my right was a beautiful stone
balustrade. Later examination established that it too was marble.
In making their way upstairs the curvature of the staircase required
the man carrying the front end of my stretcher, the end where my
head was, to project the stretcher out over the balustrade so that

the bearer at the foot of my stretcher could navigate the turns. In so doing, the head end of my stretcher was tilted out over the balustrade. This tilting meant nothing to me until I turned my head to the right, and from my slightly tilted position I could see almost straight down! At that point I was about ten meters above the floor below. Suddenly, I was frightened! All through combat I had never felt fright. I had felt concern. Incoming fire was never a welcome sight or sound. You learned to live with it, if you wanted to cope. As long as I was free to move about, able to make choices, to be in charge as to where I wanted to go, or what I wanted to do, I was never frightened. But looking down ten meters to a hard stone floor, while tied to a tilting stretcher being carried by two strangers, laughing and chattering away in French, as they carried me up this winding staircase, hell, that scared me! I suddenly feared I would fall! I had no freedom of movement. I had no ability to make choices! I had come this far through the war, a bit the worse for wear and tear, but still very much alive. And here, these two French clowns were scaring the shit out of me!

Oh!, Oh!, I cried out, Oh!, Oh!. By reason of the anxiety expressed in my voice, and the fear clearly etched on my face, my two stretcher bearers, for the first time, paid attention to me. Before, I was just another sedated, wounded American soldier. They had probably carried a couple of hundred sleepy guys like me. I was, to them, therefore, as alert to the surroundings as any couch or sofa they would move about. But now they noted I was awake and very uneasy. The one at my head, the one who lifted and tilted my stretcher out over the balustrade, as required in following the curvature of the staircase, laughed and said, *"Ne pas de souci"*—"Don't worry". And not sure I understood his French, he said, "Relax", in English. Where, or from whom he had learned that word I never found out. But clearly he knew what the word meant. To the extent I could, I relaxed, But I was not fully at ease until my stretcher bearers brought me to the bed which was to be my abode for the next seven weeks, and carefully laid me onto it. A nurse standing nearby smiled at me, said, "Hi, soldier!", covered me with a sheet and blanket, adjusted my pillow, took my temperature, pulse and blood pressure, wrote something down on a card, placed the card in a holder at the foot of my bed, smiled again, and left. I lapsed quickly back into a dreamless sleep. I had completed another step on my journey towards Anneliese Baur.

During my seven weeks as a patient in the military hospital in the Bois de Boulogne area of Paris I have very little memory of what went on about me except for those few events which I shall shortly recount. I was most likely operated on soon after I was admitted. I remember nothing of the procedure itself, being sedated before, during and after the surgeons had done their work. I believe I was bedridden for at least ten days after the operation. The pain was localized in my right thigh, there was bleeding, and my surgical dressings were changed frequently. Relieving oneself into the receptacles designed for such singular activities, while lying recumbent, were awkward, and initially, embarrassing physical exercises. The idea was to evacuate your bowels and empty your bladder without making a mess on yourself and on your bed linens. Aside from an initial mishap, and with the help of a nurse or orderly, I soon got the hang of it—if that's an apt way to describe the experience.

Only after a couple of weeks when I was allowed to become a bit ambulatory did I look at my medical chart at the foot of my bed. To the extent I could decipher the notations on the chart my condition was described as: "Deep pen wound debridement.". "Crazy," I thought, "I wasn't stuck by a pen! And what the fuck was debridement?" I queried one of the nurses. She explained that "pen" was an abbreviation for "penetrating", and that "debridement" was the medical term used to describe the surgical removal of foreign matter and dead tissue from a wound. This surgical cleansing would prevent the deep wound from becoming infected. Thus, my surgery, *inter alia*, had consisted of the surgeons' cleaning out the wound made in my right thigh when the shrapnel from the exploding Bouncing Betty mine tore deeply into it. As I have earlier noted, the shrapnel in a Bouncing Betty mine was made up of the factory floor sweepings, or tailings from metal working machinery, including nuts and bolts, *Schrott* being the German word for this metallic garbage—all of it sharp edged and dirty. A deep incision had to be made into my flesh, and a goodly amount cut away to remove all the shrapnel and to insure that enough tissue was also removed to preclude the possibility that infection might result were even a bit of tainted flesh left intact. The incision the surgeons made was deep. For many years after my return to civilian life I could put the four fingers of my right hand, to the depth of the first knuckle on each finger, into the cavity in my thigh. Over the years the depression in my thigh has become less obvious. But on close inspection it is still there, visible to eye and touch.

My wounding, at the time it happened, was perceived by me to be an event adversely affecting the furtherance of my career in the Army. My entry into Officers' Candidate School (OCS) had been delayed, perhaps completely thwarted, and I was hurting, and hurting badly. But as I have pointed out repeatedly (perhaps too frequently) in this saga, these negative happenings were links in that chain of events which were designed to shape my life for the better. Thus, unwittingly, I was being advanced on a path, however circuitous, which was leading me ever closer to my belóved Anneliese Baur. Nor, of course, could I be aware of the fact that on returning home, as a wounded, honorably discharged veteran, I would be eligible to receive disability compensation (which at one point in my civilian life was the only income I received), and able to receive the funding which allowed me, under the GI Bill, to enter one of the leading law schools in the United States, to become a lawyer, and, as I grew older to receive, at no cost, medical treatment of the finest kind. But none of these future events, each of which would help shape my life for the better, were known to me as I lay painfully on my hospital bed recovering, ever so slowly, from my "deep pen wound".

Recuperating from a deep flesh wound I learned, was a slow process. The body had to regenerate new tissue, blood circulation restored, muscles strengthened. Frequent inspection of the wound had to be made to assure that it was free of infection. For the first few weeks of my hospitalization I was confined to my bed. Then the day came when I didn't have to use a bed pan to relieve myself. I never liked that aspect of being bed ridden. I found it unseemly. But it didn't faze the nurses. The first time I was allowed to walk the short distance down the hall to the bathroom, with a nurse at my elbow, I felt pretty good, quite manly, even though she stood outside the door and asked me several times, "Are you OK?"

Time passed slowly. I began to have the same feelings as I had experienced in England when, because of my "difficulties" with my officers in the Fourth Cavalry, I missed landing in France with the first wave on D-Day. I began to feel that there was a war going on, and I was missing my chance to be in it. Becoming ambulatory, even with slow, measured steps to the toilet and back, only increased my sense that there was a war going on, and I was not taking part. I mentioned this concern early on to one of the doctors who came to check on my condition. The doctor laughed and told me I was in no condition to do any fighting right then, but even if the war against Germany was soon to be over, I shouldn't worry, there was still a big war going on against Japan, and once I got out of the hospital, I might well be sent to the Far East. This didn't happen to me. But it did to my brother Harold. When the war ended in Europe his Engineers unit was shipped off to the Far East. Fortunately, when he got to Japan the war had ended.

For the most part, being a hospital patient was a boring experience. Thus, very few things have registered in my memory. I do recall five episodes because of their singularity. Three took place within the confines of the hospital. Two occurred in Paris itself when, in the last weeks as a patient I was allowed to go into town to acclimate myself to walking about in a civilian environment to exercise my right leg, and to do so without the need for crutches or a cane. I shall recount them in chronological order, although the last would become the most important in drawing me ever closer to Anneliese.

The first concerns a Spanish gentleman, an employee in the hospital. He was a cleaner of the windows in the ward where my bed was located. Before the building had been converted into a military hospital it had been a school of higher education. I had noted the structure's architectural beauty while being carried in on my stretcher—and dangerously so I then feared—up its spiral staircase. This same beauty was evidenced in the large amount of glass, from floor to ceiling, which made up much of the building's outer wall. The glass panes were huge and set within metal frames. It took time to clean them, and this Spanish gentleman, perhaps in his forties, was one of the crew of window cleaners who came into my ward on their weekly cleaning rounds. I learned later that he was a refugee from Franco's fascist Spain.

As a prelude to telling my tale concerning the Spanish window cleaner I am going to take you back to an episode which occurred in the Alsace-Lorraine region of France in the Fall of 1944. As part of General Patton's Third Army the 86th Cavalry was now operating in an area bounded by Forbach on the north, Metz and Nancy on the west, Colmar on the south and Strasbourg and the Rhine river on the east. We were in this rectangle of rolling terrain flushing out pockets of Germans and in participating in a build-up of forces which, at some point, would contrive to cross the Rhine into Germany. However, we never made that crossing. Instead, as I have related, we made that dash north—commencing on Christmas Day—through Luxembourg, and into Belgium, to participate in the war tide turning Battle of the Bulge at Bastogne.

The U.S. Army, in common, I am sure with all military forces, whatever the country, is a learning laboratory. In the course of my soldiering I learned many prosaic, yet useful things, such as how to drive a variety of motor vehicles, and how *not* to buck authority. I also learned a lot about myself, and that was good. As Polonius counseled his son, Laertes in Hamlet (I'm quoting from memory) "Above all else, to thine own self be true, and it shall follow, as the night the day, that thou canst be false to no man". But I also learned a lot of gross, coarse, vulgar, common things, all neatly contained within the German word: *Gemeinesachen*. Which is why I refer to a learning episode which took place in the area just described. The lesson of that episode ties in with what I learned from the Spanish refugee window cleaner. And the lesson I learned was that appearances can be deceiving, and that beauty, particularly female beauty, does not equate with purity. The reader can surmise how naive I was at age 22, even after almost two years in the military, that I was still learning basic social truths. During the time period noted my Troop, in concert with other Troops in my Squadron, would make daily patrols, in ever widening arcs, of the areas surrounding our positions.

The German forces in our portion of occupied Alsace-Lorraine had fled across the Rhine. And many had previously surrendered. But remnants remained in hiding, and these were associated with local French Nazi sympathizers. The two groups needed each other to stay alive, and to plan for the day that the *Führer* would return triumphantly at the head of his Nazi hordes. It was our job to hunt them down and round them up, and to make sure that anti-tank and anti-personnel mines had not been laid clandestinely, and if they had, to make sure they were neutralized before they caused damage to us or the civilian population. Thus, in the course of these widening patrols I, and the two other members of my team, drove our jeep into the center of a town we were seeing for the first time. The town was new to us. But the layout of its center contained all the elements we had seen many times before. The French town centers I observed were the hubs of their communities. Generally laid out in the form of a square, there was the local church, the City Hall, and the ubiquitous ornate fountain, water gushing, flanked by monuments, of all sizes and shapes, honoring the local fallen in previous wars, a tavern or restaurant, and small shops. Pavements were laid in granite blocks, their austereness set off by the greenery of tall, wide limbed, aged trees, and the splashes of color in carefully tended plots of bedding plants. And most welcoming of all were the benches fixed firmly to the ground, lest they vanish over night. (As I get older I measure the humanity of a country, and its cities, by the number of benches set out for the perambulating public.) There were three very attractive young ladies, sitting on a bench, chatting animatedly, when we drove up to the edge of the square, and parked our jeep. Looking at their well formed figures I guessed they were at least 17. They saw us and walked over to our vehicle. We made our usual perfunctory inquiries: were there any Vichy regime supporters hiding out, any reports of German soldiers lurking in the area. We had learned not to expect any affirmative answers—and we were not disappointed—we got none. The conversation then turned to matters more interesting to them and to us. My French was pretty good then, and their English, obviously acquired through dealings with other American soldiers, was perhaps, better than my French. We communicated well. We talked and joked. They seemed so sweet, so small townish, so ingenuous, until the conversation turned to matters amorous, as it was wont to do, when sexy, small town girls spoke with lonely, oversexed GIs. The most forward of the three had curly black hair, sparkling dark eyes, a saucy smile and a great face and body to match. Quite a package! Clearly, I was looking at Bizet's Carmen come to this little French *ville*. One of my buddies made a play for her. She knew where he was coming from, and where he wanted to go. "No way, buster", she said, using American slang. "I once had one of you Yanks as a boy friend, and I don't want another one. He became a pain in the ass, and I told him to get lost." She had clearly learned to speak basic American 101. She rattled on, mixing French and English, "But he kept showing up, trying to make it with me. He was a *peste*". French for a nuisance. Her unsolicited recital intrigued us. We were all curious, how did she get rid of the guy? "Well", she said, "He taught me a lot of American *merde*, shit. And so, the last time he was here, he put his arms around me, after I said no, and he grabbed my tits. I then said low in his ear what I learned from him: Kiss me quick, I'm coming! Kiss my ass, I'm going!—and I yank hard on his balls and run away! I never see him again." She laughed heartily, as did her two friends. My buddies and I were taken aback by what we had heard. The lesson I learned that day (and perhaps they did, too) was that sweet, innocent looking small town girls ain't necessarily what they first appear to be.

This saga of Alsace-Lorraine sexy stuff is by way of a prologue to my experience at the hospital with the Spanish refugee window washer. In Spain, before Franco, he had been *"Un profesor de literatura contemporanea en una escuela superior"*, a professor of contemporary literature in a school in Spain equivalent in academic stature to a German *Gymnasium*. Now he was a window washer, and, once a week, unnoticed, he went about his chores near us. The focus of attention of wounded, bedridden soldiers is inner directed. And I was no exception. As my days in the service grew, so did my knowledge of things good and evil. As I have noted, the Army is a laboratory of learning. And so along the way I had learned a Spanish ditty whose filthy lyrics were set to a catchy melody. Really, quite coarse. No one around me knew Spanish I thought, and so, from time to time, I would sing it aloud, sitting up in bed, to amuse myself. Looking back I see this was a stupid thing to do. Over the years I have learned to limit my stupidity. Notice, I said limit, not eliminate. Anyway, one afternoon, stupid Arthur is singing this awful, filthy song when a voice behind me softly says in Spanish, *"Joven, aquella canción es muy mala."* "Young man, that song is very bad." It was the refugee Spanish window washer. He assumed I knew Spanish from the song I was singing. I immediately felt ashamed. I replied, *"Si, señor, Ud. tiene razón."* "Yes, sir, you are right." I did not continue with the song, and I have never sung it again, Thereafter, when he came by on his weekly window cleaning chore he would ask, *"¿Joven, siente se mejor?"* "Young man, are you feeling better?" And I would smile and reassure him that I was *'más mejor"*, much better, and we would exchange pleasantries and small talk, which is how I learned of his pre-Franco background.

My second recollection concerns a common place experience for a recuperating patient in a military hospital. It was boredom, and in my case, coupled with the knowledge that the war was winding down—there was a clear scent of victory in the air—that I was missing being a part of the closing action. But boredom was the prevailing mood, which was not aided by the slow pace of the healing of my wound. One day that boredom was punctuated by the visit to my bedside of the Red Cross Lady. Always smiling, always eager to make our pains seem less obvious—even for a brief period—and to help to make our long days and nights less dreary. So this cheery messenger would ask each of us, were we awake when she came by, "How're you doing, soldier? Anything I can do for you?" I remember a guy two beds down from me taking her up on her offer, but not in the manner she had anticipated, "Yeah", he said, "How about fixing me up with that blond nurse at the end of the hall. The tall one with a nice smile and big boobs!" There were several nurses at that station, and so he was being very specific in his physical description. He knew that this Red Cross worker was not in the sexual fixing up business, but why not give it a try. She had asked what she could do for him, and he had told her. The Red Cross worker, herself a comely lass, with a keen sense of humor, told him that the filling of such requests was not within the scope of her authority. The first few weeks I was in the hospital I was either asleep when the Red Cross Lady made her rounds, or not alert, or away having my wound cleaned and dressed. But sometime in the first or second week of March 1945 I was awake when she came by. She looked at the chart at the foot of my bed to learn the nature of my condition. She began with her usual throw away line: "Is there anything I can do for you, soldier?"

She asked me, I told her. "Yes", I said, "My brother, Harold Katz, is with the Construction Engineers, somewhere around Rheims (the last time I had heard from Harold, by letter, a few days before I was wounded on February 20th, he was in that area), I'd sure like to see him." The Red Cross Lady didn't seem fazed by my request. She took down whatever information I could give her, and told me she would see what she could do. I didn't put too much stock in our conversation. I should have. For a week later, to my great surprise, and exceeding joy, there was Harold, standing at my bedside! We embraced, our tears of happiness mingling on our faces! The hospital administration did a slight bit of furniture re-arrangement. A space was opened next to me, and a bed made up for Harold. His visit was a brief one. Harold had been given a seventy two hours pass. He spent one night, and one and a half days with me before leaving to return to his unit. During his welcome visit he and I jointly penned a letter to our parents. When I returned home I learned they were thrilled that we had seen each other, and that I was well enough to write. The folks back home, with loved one's in combat, always dread that unwelcome telegram, or officer's visit. Conversely, any evidence that all is well with a loved one is eagerly received.

A word or two about my brother, Harold. He is 23 months my junior. I was born on March 21, 1923, Harold on February 20, 1925. That's the only thing I have over him. He and I graduated from Thomas Jefferson High School in the East New York section of Brooklyn. In the 1940s it was one of the best high schools in New York City. Harold graduated as the top male student in his graduating class. His name, and that of the female leader are emblazoned upon the walls of the School. He went on to the University of Chicago where his scholarship earned him a Phi Beta Kappa Key. The only other person in our family circle to be awarded a Phi Beta Kappa Key is our daughter, Heidi. My claim to academic fame was being the class clown, a position which earned me many visits, with my Mom, to the Principal's Office. Only in my Senior Year, when my writing skills as a staffer on the Class Yearbook for June 1940 made me a winner of both the Prose and Poetry competitions, did I garner any awards. I was the first student to win both competitions. I enlisted in the Cavalry in 1942. Harold tried to enlist. By reason of his poor eyesight he wasn't accepted. However, when his draft number came up, Uncle

Sam was happy to take him, thick glass lenses and all. Without proper glasses Harold could not see too well. Yet, to this day, Harold without glasses is more perceptive than I. I remember my Mother recounting that when Harold was in the first or second grade his teachers told her that Harold was retarded, so poorly was he doing in school. My Mother disagreed. My Mother said Harold was doing poorly because he couldn't see the blackboard. She was right! He was fitted with glasses, put in the front row, and "miraculously" Harold's academic status changed from "retarded" to "brilliant". Imagine what may have happened to other kids so afflicted who did not have a wonderful, intelligent Mama, as did Harold and I.

My third military hospital recollection is not of a person, or of a happening, rather it concerns an inanimate object. This object would immediately banish from my consciousness any thought of going to Officer' Candidate School. Instead, it would lead me on the last leg of my long, meandering journey to find my beautiful, belóved Anneliese Baur. The object was an Army placard. Sometime in April 1945 I had begun to walk the hospital's lengthy corridors. I was told to do so to toughen up my leg muscles before I'd be allowed to stroll the streets of Paris for further exercise. I must have walked down that particular corridor a dozen times before I noticed that placard one afternoon. It was one sign among many. Perhaps it had just been posted. In any event, there it was. I don't recall its exact text. But I clearly remember its gist. It caught my eye because I believe it was captioned: *Sprechen Sie deutsch?* It then went on to say that if you were competent in the German language the Army would like you to join one of their military government teams which were being set up to administer occupied Germany once the war was over. Even me, a lowly T/5, shambling about within the confines of a military hospital, knew that the war was quickly coming to an end, which it formally did on May 8, 1945.

The "Invitation" in the placard intrigued me. As General von Clausewitz had noted in his treatise *Vom Kriege*, wars were not ends in themselves. They were a means to a political end. What better way to end this war than to use it to restore democracy to Germany? I liked that idea. Indeed, wasn't that principle subsumed within the reasons I had voluntarily given up my student's draft deferment, left the safe, cloistered confines of college, and enlisted in the Cavalry? I was still eligible, once discharged from the hospital, and restored to active duty, to enter Officers' Candidate School. And even though the war in Europe was ending, we were still actively at war with Japan. I could still get into combat once I graduated from my 90 days of training in OCS. Yet once I saw the military government placard my thinking changed. Becoming an Infantry officer suddenly seemed less important than going into Military Government, even though I would be doing so as a lowly T/5. How odd for one who always wanted to be an officer to make such a choice. But it was *beshert*, it was meant to be that I choose not to become an officer candidate. Instead, I chose to continue on my then unknown journey to find my beautiful, belóved Anneliese Baur!

Around the latter part of April 1945 I was told by the doctors that my "pen" wound had sufficiently healed, internally and externally, so that I could be discharged from the hospital ready to return to duty within my Cavalry Troop. I learned that my Troop, together with the rest of the 86th Cavalry, was in the vicinity of the German city of Plauen near the Czech border. I called my Squadron Commander, told him I was going to be discharged from the hospital, and that I was interested in transferring to the Military Government unit of the Army, unless he needed me. My Squadron Commander knew I spoke German. He had seen the benefit of its use when I used it to capture those six German bunkers on February 20th. "Hell no, Katz. We don't need you. We're up to our asses in mud, and there's no fighting here. We'll get the paper work done to transfer you to the Military Government guys." We then chatted briefly. He asked how I was feeling. I told him I was almost as good as new. And he wished me well in my new assignment. I hadn't got the assignment yet. I had to take a German language examination. So some days before I was discharged from the hospital I was given a written and oral examination to test my German language knowledge. The exam took place somewhere in Paris. At the exam I was competing against some refugees from the Nazis. They were mostly Jews. Their knowledge of German was better than mine. But from the way they spoke English I gathered I would grade considerably better than they would on the English comprehension part of the examination. In any case, I was accepted for service in the Army's Military Government Program.

Sometime in April 1945, I can't recall whether it was before or after I took and passed the above noted exam, the hospital gave me daily passes to go into Paris to walk around and exercise my leg. I had gotten a new uniform while in the hospital, and I looked pretty natty. During the time my Cavalry Squadron was in the Alsace-Lorraine region it held drawings for three day passes to Paris, the City of Lights. Neither I, nor any of the lower ranks ever "won" any of the drawings. The "winners" seemed always to be upper rank "non-coms. A lot of the guys griped that the drawings were rigged. But as I had learned in my 4ᵗʰ Cavalry experiences in England, it was the better part of valor to let the issue lie. The prize wasn't worth the possible collateral damage. But now, courtesy of the mine laying activities of the *Wehrmacht* I was finally in Paris, and free to look around. This freedom to look around resulted in the two episodes which illustrate, sadly, the less pleasant side of *les peuple de Paris*. Paris, indeed, all of France should have been appreciative of the fact that we Americans, and our allies, liberated *la belle France* from her Nazi occupiers. And if they were reluctant to show such appreciation, then they should have been appreciative of the fact we didn't rub their noses in it to show how poorly they had fought against Hitler's hordes, and how quickly they set up a Vichy "government" which sucked the Nazis' asses, while sending its own Jewish citizens to the Nazi gas chambers. Instead, we allowed De Gaulle, with his Free French Forces to march into Paris as conquering heroes, after we had done all the combat work, with our casualties, dead and wounded in the thousands. But why bear resentment to the French? After all, for their own political reasons, they enabled us to win our Revolutionary War against the British in 1783. So *Vive la France!* But all too often the French are a narrow and venal people. My two episodes during my walking exercise periods illustrate this last point.

I have never been addicted to smoking cigarettes. As a youngster I tried a puff or two—and I did not inhale! I knew there were dangers in smoking, but in the 1940s hardly anyone spoke of them. In any event I never acquired the habit. The Army issued cigarettes to us. I would take my ration. But I would later trade them off for chocolate and other things I needed. Indeed, the gold wedding bands which Anneliese and I wore were purchased by me in Germany, with the "currency" being cigarettes. A carton of ten packs of American cigarettes, known in Germany as a *Stange*, or bar, was worth its weight in gold. The post war Occupation Powers issued new notes in lieu of German Marks. Most Germans distrusted this "funny money", hence the growth of a barter system. The water color painting (of which more below) which has graced the walls of every residence Anneliese and I have lived in as husband and wife, was purchased in 1945 from the artist for *"eine Stange Zigaretten"*. The artist wouldn't accept any other form of payment. Later Anneliese told me I had "overpaid" by two packs, that the artist would have accepted 8 packs in full payment!

Although I was not a cigarette smoker, I had acquired a taste in the Army for pipe smoking. And it came about in this manner: Somewhere in my Stateside training I met a Jewish soldier a few years older than I. I believe he was from Michigan. He smoked a pipe. He was well spoken, had a good sense of humor, and was dignified, without being stuffy. I admired him very much. And so I bought a pipe in emulation of him. He was in another Troop, and even were I to remember his name, consistent with my policy, I wouldn't mention it. I enjoyed pipe smoking. Experimenting with different tobaccos, packing the pipe, cleaning the pipe, inhaling the pleasurable scents of burning pipe tobacco swirling about my nostrils, and the appearance of manliness which I thought a pipe clenched in my mouth added to my persona. I gave up the pleasures of pipe smoking in the 1960s for health reasons, although I am still doubtful whether the amount of pipe smoking I did could have been detrimental to my health. Anyway, back to Paris in late April or early May 1945. And here is where my pipe smoking becomes relevant to my tale.

On one of my daily walking exercises I saw this tobacco shop. A middle aged woman was behind the counter. I had come in to buy a pipe and tobacco. I was in my dress Olive Drab uniform. I walked with a limp. If she noticed it, she made no comment. In one of the cases I saw a pipe I thought I might like. I pointed to it and asked, *"Combien?"* "How much is it?" She told me. The price was clearly outrageous, gouging might be a better term. Very politely, I said, *"Madame, c'est trop cher."* "Madame, that's too expensive." She looked straight at me. The lips on her unsmiling face tightened, and coldly she said, *"Vous marchande comme un Juif!"* "You bargain like a Jew!" Now, I looked straight in her face, and in a firm voice, said, *"Madame, je suis un Juif!"* "Madame, I am a Jew!", and as I stalked out of her shop I saw the surprise on her face. Clearly, even after five years of Nazi occupation the average French *citoyen* had learned nothing, and sadly, was still as antisemitic as ever.

I have just related one of the two episodes I remember which happened on my sorties from the hospital through the environs of Paris and into its heart. I now relate the second. There, in its heart, the city of Paris had created an elaborate and efficient subway system known as the *Metro*. As with every visitor to Paris, even one who had not come there as a tourist, I wanted to experience a ride on the *Metro*. So at a station closest to the hospital I climbed aboard the next train which rolled in. As usual when I rambled about in Paris I was wearing my dress Olive Drab uniform. The car I entered was crowded. Standing room only. No empty seats, except at one end of the car I saw several. My leg was beginning to pulsate and ache. I wended my way through the standing passengers to the corner of the car where I had seen the empty seats. Above these seats was a metal sign: *"Reservé pour les blessé"* "Reserved for the wounded." A nice gesture. And so I sat down. The moment I did, it seemed as if all the passengers in the car turned their heads towards me and glowered. I was perplexed. Then I heard a voice hiss, *"Reservé seulement pour les blessé!"* "Reserved solely for the wounded". I was wounded. I was hurting, and I saw no sign saying "Reserved only for the French wounded." And so I said, with as stern a voice as I could command, *"Je suis blessé"*, and I remained seated. There was some muttering. But none of the passengers thereafter said anything to me, good, bad, or indifferent. I was tempted to get off at the next stop. But I felt this would look to these Frenchies that I was cutting and running. So I stayed on for two more stations, and then got off. I made my way back to the hospital on foot. My sentiment as I entered the hospital was, "Fuck those fuckin' frog eaters!" When push comes to shove, I could be as narrow minded as they were. Fortunately for me, that was the only time I ever felt that intensely about any group of people.

Arthur with medics, Military Hospital Paris, Spring 1945   *233*

Episodes TWENTY NINE and THIRTY:

Discovering Love!   *Restoring Democracy!*

PANTHEA

Nay, let us walk from fire unto fire,
   From passionate pain to deadlier delight,—
I am too young to live without desire,
   Too young art thou to waste this summer night
Asking those idle questions which of old
Man sought of seer and oracle, and no reply was told.

For, sweet, to feel is better than to know,
   And wisdom is a childless heritage,
One pulse of passion—youth's first fiery glow,—
   Are worth the hoarded proverbs of the sage:
Vex not thy soul with dead philosophy,
      Have we not the lips to kiss with, hearts to love and
         eyes to see!

*   *   *

This hot hard flame with which our bodies burn
   Will make some meadow blaze with daffodil,
Ay! And those argent breasts of thine will turn
   To water-lilies; the brown fields men till
Will be more fruitful for our love to-night,
Nothing is lost in nature, all things live in Death's despite.

*   *   *

So when men bury us beneath the yew
    Thy crimson stained mouth a rose will be,
And thy soft eyes lush bluebells dimmed with dew,
    And when the white narcissus wantonly
Kisses the wind its playmate some faint joy
Will thrill our dust, and we will be again fond maid and boy.

*   *   *

Ay! Had we never loved at all, who knows
    If yonder daffodil had lured the bee
Into its gilded womb, or any rose
    Had hung with crimson lamps its little tree!
Methinks no leaf would ever bud in spring,
But for the lovers' lips that kiss, the poets' lips that sing.

*   *   *

And we two lovers shall not sit afar,
    Critics of nature, but the joyous sea
Shall be our raiment, and the bearded star
    Shoot arrows at our pleasure! We shall be
Part of the mighty universal whole,
And through all aeons mix and mingle with the Kosmic
      Soul!

*   *   *

We shall be notes in that great Symphony
    Whose cadence circles through the rhythmic spheres,
And all the live World's throbbing heart shall be
    One with our heart, the stealthy creeping years
Have lost their terrors now, we shall not die,
The Universe itself shall be our Immortality!

Oscar Wilde

In May 1944 the U.S. Military Government in Germany issued a Directive to the American Forces declaring that as Germany wa a defeated enemy State all fraternization with its German population was forbidden.

Episode Twenty Nine

In which, after my release from hospital, I join our Military Government and am sent to a rural county in Southern Germany, and there what was *beshert*, comes to pass: **I find Anneliese Baur and instantly fall in love with her!** We discuss and resolve religious issues.

Sometime in the last week of May 1945, or perhaps, in the first week of June, I was informed that I had passed the Army's German language exams and had been transferred from my Cavalry Squadron to the Army's Military Government branch. And so I sallied forth from Paris to my new posting in the Headquarters of the Military Government in the resort city of Bad Homburg. Bad Homburg is located west of Frankfurt in the Taunus area of Land Hessen. (This was the German state from which the Hessian mercenaries were sent to fight with the British against the nascent American Army in our Revolutionary War.) In all my Army experiences, whether stateside, in the UK or in Europe, Bad Homburg had to be the cushiest yet. Bad Homburg was a world renowned spa, noted for its mineral baths. When Hitler began World War II he turned Bad Homburg, with its regal hotels, pensions, medical facilities and curative waters into an Open City under the Geneva Convention. Red Crosses were painted on the roofs of the buildings, offensive military activities prohibited, and the city became a medical facility for wounded German military personnel. The Allies respected the Convention. The city was never bombed. At war's end Bad Homburg was as picture perfect a resort as it had been before Hitler invaded Poland in September 1939. Thus it was the logical venue in which to house the Headquarters of the Army's Military Government operations. Certainly, the Army wouldn't want Political Science experts who had sat out the war earning their graduate and post graduate degrees within the ivy covered walls of such eminent institutions of higher learning as Princeton, Harvard, Yale and Stanford—and now sporting their spanking new tailor made uniforms as Officers of the Army of the United States—and ready to bring the blessings of democracy back to Germany—surely the Army would not want to house these laurel leaved representatives of a conquering army to be housed in a bombed out facility. Would it? Of course not! The Army, in its wisdom, and with keen insight into its own creature comfort requirements, was happy to turn Bad Homburg into its Military Government HQ. And who was I, a lowly T/5 to complain?

And so, it was to Bad Homburg, with its pre-war beauties unblemished, to which I was sent. Things were looking up for me. Remember this phrase "looking up" dear reader, as it plays a prominent part in the story I shall shortly relate. I was assigned a very nice room all to myself in one of the top hotels in town. In peace time the hotel would have been rated four to five stars. As unreal as my new surroundings were, in contrast to my grimy months in combat, and my recent hospital experiences, the realities of military life were all about me. For example, there was roll call in the morning., All personnel, officers and enlisted men, were required to spill out of their hotel billets and then line up in the streets fronting our hotels, there to answer when their names were called. My attendance at my first roll call, the morning after I had reported for duty was an eye opener. The uniforms, with their unit designations, of those clustered about me, and the physical appearance of those filling these uniforms, indicated to me that I was perhaps the only GI there who had not only been in a combat unit, but had also been in combat. I was not faulting these guys, most were fresh from the States, and were doing what they were assigned to do. But they were a motley crew! When we lined up on the street before our hotel, with German civilians passing by on the sidewalk, and gawking at us, we looked awful! Our ranks weren't straight. Some of the guys were slouching rather than standing straight and tall. Some were disheveled, hair uncombed, military caps askew, jackets improperly buttoned, shoes unlaced and unshined. And there we were, the victorious American Army on public view at 7:30 a.m., in full view of the conquered *Herrenvolk*, who, as they hurried by, in their pre-war clothing, looked a lot neater than did we. I was embarrassed for my country! What a lousy impression we were making.

And so, there I stood, for my first roll call as a Military Government soldier, in the third rank of a mass of soldiers, when a Sergeant, some ten meters or more away from me began to call out names from his roster. Each time he called out a name someone in the pack of bodies around me would recognize his name and shout "Here!" or "Yo!". The names were being called in alphabetical order. The Sergeant was going through the J's. The K's would be next. I waited to respond to my name being called. The Sergeant called out a name which I thought sounded like Katz. I hesitated to respond, not being sure he was calling my name. To my surprise, someone to my right shouted "Here!" Either there were two Katzes, or some guy mistook my name for his and answered for me. The next name was a also a K name, but no where near Katz, Kotz or Kurtz. Then the Sergeant was into the "L's", and on through the balance of the alphabet. Attendance being taken, we were ordered to fall out and go about our assigned duties. No duties having yet been assigned to me, I went to my room, lay down, and "fatigued" by my morning experiences I fell asleep awaking in time to go to the Chow Hall for lunch. *Yom Echad*. Day One.

The next morning I fell out again with my Military Government complement. Again there was roll call. This time I waited until that guy called "Here!" to what was clearly my name. "Hell!", I thought, no need to fall out again. As long as that guy is here, I'm here. And so as long as I was stationed at the Military Government Headquarters in Bad Homburg I never again reported for roll call! Indeed, for the next two weeks I was there, but I wasn't there. I was like the description of the California city of Oakland given by an expatriate author, who, when asked why she remained in Paris and didn't return to Oakland, replied, "There's no there, there."

On May 8, 1945 the German *Wehrmacht, Marine* and what was left of the *Luftwaffe*, surrendered, and the war in Europe was over. I believe my tour of duty in Bad Homburg began about that time and ended near the last days of May. And the end came about in this wise: I was in my room, resting from an earlier bout of resting—one must experience multiple episodes of resting to appreciate how tiring such repetitions of resting can be, especially to one who had always been an active doer type—when I was summoned from my room and told to report to a Major, waiting for me in HQ. Oh, Oh, they've caught me. They've figured out I was not reporting in at roll call. Well, what could they do to me, that hasn't already been done. So I went into Military Government HQ, on the ground floor of the hotel in which I was billeted. I told the guard who I was looking for and he pointed the Major out to me.

The Major was in his late 20's or early 30's. His insignia indicated he was in the Engineers. He had a folder in his hand. He said nothing to me about missing roll calls. Instead, he told me to walk with him to the courtyard in the rear of the hotel. The courtyard was neatly paved with cobblestones, and from it one looked up at eight floors of suites of rooms, each suite having double French glazed doors opening onto wrought iron railed balconies which ran the width of the French doors. Very attractive. The railings were painted black and stood about a meter high. The side railing of one balcony was separated from the side railing of the balcony in the adjoining suite by about one and a third meters, maybe four feet in USA/UK measurements. In short, there was about 4 feet of space, empty air, between the adjacent side balcony railings from one suite to another.

The Major said to me that according to my military records file, which he apparently had in his hands, I was trained as a radio operator. Did that mean I knew how to lay telephone wire and connect up portable phone systems? I told the Major that this was one of my jobs in the Cavalry. "Good", he said, "then you are the right man for the job we have to do." "What is that?", I asked. The

Major explained that the Commanding General for our Military Government Headquarters was going to be billeted in a suite on the 8th floor of the hotel, and his aide-de camp, a Colonel, was going to have the abutting suite, and the General wanted phone service to be set up between the two suites. "No problem", I said. I explained that I'd get the necessary materials and equipment and run the telephone wire from the baseboard of the Colonel's suite out onto the hotel corridor and and run the wire along the corridor's baseboard into the General's suite and do the same in his suite as I would have done in the Colonel's. I told the Major the work would be done neatly, there would be no loose wires to trip over. My installation explained, I asked the Major, "Sir, from whom do I get the keys to the suites of the General and the Colonel?" A simple enough question. The answer stunned me. The Major informed me that I could have the key to the Colonel's suite, but that the General wanted no one in his suite before he got there. "Then how can I string the wire from the Colonel's suite to the General's?" "Well", the Major says, looking up at the 8th floor line of suites, "You can run the telephone line from the Colonel's suite out onto his balcony, and from there you could toss the General's phone and its wire [these were sound and power crank-up phones securely encased in steel, and they could take a degree of banging about] over onto the General's balcony, and you could then jump from the Colonel's balcony to the General's, and when you are done, you can jump back onto the Colonel's balcony, and leave through his suite."

What kind of madness was this? I was not quite a month out of the hospital after spending seven weeks recovering from a deep penetrating wound in my right thigh. I was still hurting. But to jump from one balcony to another when these were about 4 feet apart and 8 stories up, this was madness, even were I wholly restored to my former strength. Trying to keep my cool I said to the Major, "Sir, you have my MOS records. Where do they say I'm a paratrooper? If I wanted to jump from high places I would have joined the paratroopers. Look, I've been through a lot in this war, hurt twice, but still alive, and I'm not about to kill myself trying to jump from one balcony to another 8 stories up because some General wants his privacy!" As I spoke I could hear my voice rising. I was really pissed.

The Major was taken aback by my reaction. But very cooly he says to me, "Are you refusing to do this job?" "I sure am, Major. What you want me to do is stupid!" At that point, without being dismissed by him, I turned, left him standing in the courtyard with my file under his arm, and went back to my room.

I anticipated hearing shortly from Headquarters, but nothing happened the next day. But the second day after my experience with the Major I was summoned down to HQ. There I was told that the attitude I had displayed to the Major demonstrated that I was not the type of soldier who belonged in a Headquarters unit. (Remember the trouble I had in England in another Headquarters unit?) And so I was being sent out to join a Military Government Team being set up in a rural part of Germany, southeast of Bad Homburg, and on the easternmost edge of Wuerttemberg, one of the German *Länder*, a region politically equivalent to one of our States. I was being sent to *Kreis Heidenheim* (*Kreis* in German means both circle and county) far out to a cow county in the boonies, Heidenheim bordering on the western part of Bavaria. The county seat was the semi-rural city *Heidenheim an der Brenz*.: Heidenheim on the River Brenz. The last link in a crazy chain of events had been forged, and what was *beshert* what was meant to be, was about to be. But, of course, I was not aware of this as I left the metropolitan spa of Bad Homburg for the modest community of Heidenheim an der Brenz.

The jeep ride from Bad Homburg to Heidenheim, with the German roads in the beat up condition they were in 1945, took about five hours, with a pit stop on the way to water some wispy roadside blooms. I was being driven to Heidenheim, so I had time enough to concentrate on my thoughts rather than on the road. I thought back to my "problems" with the 4th Cavalry command in England before the invasion, and to my run-in with our replacement troop commander during the Battle of the Bulge in Belgium—both examples, already recounted, of the evils of anti-semitism at work in a military purportedly designed to safeguard our democracy at home and to spread its blessings abroad. I remember saying to myself, "Arthur, you're going to another HQ type unit. As long as you watch your mouth, you won't have to worry about covering your ass." I remember saying that. And I remember hearing myself reply, "Yeah, sure!" So much for self counselling.

I had been assigned to Detachment G-27, Co. A, 2nd Military Government Regiment, U.S. Army. In all my military government activities I had no dealings with a Co. A or a 2nd Military Government Regiment. My military government duties all fell within those performed by Detachment G-27. This Detachment, if memory serves me well was a team of five officers and seven enlisted personnel, vested with the responsibility, as an agency of the American Government, the Occupying Power, to govern the County of Heidenheim, and its various cities and towns, while participating in the search for, and capture of, hardline Nazis, in the housing and rehabilitation,—and ultimately—the repatriation of refugees, mostly Jewish concentration camp survivors, and surviving Russian prisoners of war, and in the billeting of U. S. Troops passing through on their way back to the States. In addition to maintaining hands on control of daily civil government operations, our Military Government Team, in common with all the others, had the duty to start the rebuilding of the German economy. Heidenheim was primarily a rural county. The Army had done its homework well. The Detachment's commander was a Captain in the Cavalry, a line officer comfortable in working with small units. The other four officers filled different slots, from police work to administering the banking system. The tasks assigned to me were supervising public sanitation, that is, street cleaning and trash removal, and in housing and repatriating refugees and American troops, and in doing such tasks where communication in German was of importance.

When I joined the Military Government Detachment in Heidenheim I became the last member of its roster of seven enlisted personnel. I found, to my great surprise, and pleasure, that I was finally in a military unit where I was not the only Jew. In fact, I was the fourth Jew in a team of seven! I was the only member of the Detachment who had been in combat. My combat status became a plus factor in the performance of my military government duties, as I shall shortly relate. The Detachment had begun its operations in Heidenheim about a week before I arrived. The Detachment set up its Headquarters, and billeted its officers and enlisted men, in what was perhaps the most beautiful villa in Heidenheim. The villa had many bedrooms, and I was assigned one which even had an adjoining bathroom! My sleeping bag, and slit trench latrine days were clearly ancient history. The villa was owned by one of the wealthiest families in Heidenheim, one with close ties to the Nazi Party. The Army took over the property and magnanimously allowed the family, a mother in her forties and two teen age girls, to move into the servants' quarters of the villa. I never saw the father, perhaps he was dead, or in the Army's custody. The villa, a well designed multi-story building, was located in an upscale part of the city of Heidenheim, and nestled within a a park like setting which I estimated to be about two and a half hectares (about five acres) in size. The villa was encircled on three sides by a cobblestoned courtyard. The villa's kitchen—which I later learned was as large, and as well equipped as one would find in a German country inn—was located on the left side of the building.

Officers and enlisted men ate at the same time in the villa's dining room. Thus we enlisted men were enjoying the same cuisine being served the officers. I use the word "cuisine" advisedly because the meals were the best I had ever had in the military! But then, I'd never been in a twelve person military unit being served out of its own kitchen with its own German chef and culinary staff. Our meals were served to us by some of the women who also cleaned our rooms. The Detachment was enjoying excellent meals in a dining room with a decor, table settings and furnishings which would have been envied by a five star restaurant. But our mess, fancy as it was, was a military mess, and so the chef never came out of the kitchen to chat with any of his clientele, as he would have done, in a commercial setting. As I have noted, I joined the Detachment about a week after it had begun its operations in Heidenheim. Thus, I took no part in the vetting and hiring of any of the Detachment's German civilian staff.

Within a few days I had meshed into the Detachment's daily routine. Aside from one of the Officers—a naturalized citizen from one of the Nordic countries—I was the only team member who was fluent in German. Hence, I was immediately busy acting as the Detachment's interpreter and translator in its dealings with the local population, and with those refugees who spoke German or Yiddish. Thus, a few days after I joined the Detachment I was called in by its Finance/Business Officer. He informed me that I was to visit the various banking entities in the county to distribute to them the new occupation currency in exchange for the German Marks which no longer had any value. And so, early in the morning, on what would have been just another day in mid-June 1945, I set out in a half ton truck loaded with the appropriate banking records and with what the Germans would soon call "funny money". Since I didn't know my way around the County at that time I had a German, who had been "cleared" by our intelligence people, to drive me to where we had to go. The German officials at each location were ready for us. They gave me their supply of German Marks, currency and coin, and their supporting financial data. I gave them our occupation money, with supporting documentation. Signed documents were exchanged and I was on my way.

Much like the time we were in England before the invasion, when we American troops were not allowed to buy British foodstuffs, because of the rationing of civilian foodstuffs—except for bread and rolls—so, too, did the same system now prevail in Germany, for the same reasons. So during the day I never stopped to buy any foodstuffs. Instead, I made do with a bread and butter and cheese sandwich I had made for myself at the breakfast table. It was well past 5 p.m. when we drove onto the cobblestoned courtyard facing the entrance to the villa. Barely had my driver parked the truck when I hopped out, my account books still in my hands, and headed, not for the front entrance to the villa, but for the side of the building where I knew the kitchen lay. I was too late for dinner but felt I could wrassle up something to eat in the kitchen. I turned the building's corner—AND ENTERED A NEW WORLD!

There, in mid June 1945, in the late afternoon of what had been a lovely Spring day, in a small rural city in Southern Germany, what was *beshert*, what was meant to be, had finally come to pass! Standing before me was the most beautiful woman I had ever seen! The sun, low in its blue, cloudless sky, enveloped her graceful form in a halo of shimmering light. She was a fairy princess come to life! As I gazed entranced upon her, an emotion I had never felt before welled up within me. I was instantly in love!

The cut of her dirndl accentuated the swell of her bosom. Her hair, shoulder length, light brown, almost blond, framed her smiling face. Her skin was clear, lightly tanned, unlined, and free of makeup. Her high boned cheeks, glowed with rosy hues. Her lips were shapely, red without rouge. Her nose was straight and narrow, a pert upward tilt at its tip. Her gray-green eyes sparkled with warmth and intelligence. *She was altogether fair, and wholly without blemish!*

At a time I had not chosen. In a place I had not selected. In a way I had not imagined, something wond'rous had happened to me! At that moment I knew I had found the woman I would marry. I HAD FOUND ANNELIESE BAUR!

Who was this ephemeral being whose first appearance instantly made her the centerpiece of the rest of my life? What was there about her that so quickly captivated my body and my soul? Clearly, it was her physical beauty which immediately kindled my passions. But Anneliese's beauty was more than that of face and form. There was this aura of kindness and grace about her from which I sensed the goodness and purity of her inner self. Indeed, it was this intertwining of Anneliese's inner and outer beauty which made my first sight of her so overpowering. From the instant I saw Anneliese, my life was rebuilt about her. Anneliese became my *ehven pinnah*, אבן פנה, *der Eckstein meines Lebens*, the cornerstone of my being. And for all the years we were destined to be together my first glorious impression of my belóved Anneliese was confirmed over and over and over again!

Although I knew the instant I saw Anneliese that I would marry her, I waited three days to tell her so. I wanted to chat a bit with her so that she could get to know me enough to see that I was not using my declaration of marriage as a GI's ploy to get her into the sack. The American Army had issued regulations against troops fraternizing with our former enemies, the Germans. Thus, the idea of an American soldier marrying a German girl was crazy! Anneliese was mindful of these regulations. When I told Anneliese I was going to marry her, she smiled, and her eyes twinkled. "*Wir werden sehen*", she said. "We'll see." She let me put my arm around her waist, and I kissed her on her forehead. She blushed, pulled away from me, and said, "*Ich muss arbeiten.*" "I have to work." And she went back to her job of administering the operations of our Detachment's kitchen.

The manner in which Anneliese obtained her position with our Detachment, and the adventures, for good and ill, which led me ultimately to become a part of a Military Government Detachment in a remote part of Germany, demonstrate how the disparate events of her life and mine were meant to be meshed together into an harmonious union of two bodies and two souls.

The reader knows how I became a member of the Military Government Detachment in Heidenheim. How did Anneliese become the Head Chef administering its kitchen? I was not a member of the Detachment which did the hiring of German personnel. I learned later that Anneliese was among the first group of eligible candidates sent by the German *Arbeitsamt*, the

German Employment Agency, to the Detachment for selection as its Head Chef. The *Arbeitsamt*, the German Employment Office, in good Nazi style, kept two personnel lists. One of Nazi Party members, *"Parteimitglieder"*, and the other, of non-party members. During Hitler's *"Tausendjährige Reich"*, his "Thousand Years Empire," Party members got the good jobs, and the shit jobs went to non-party members. Neither Anneliese, nor any members of her family, had ever been Party members, so she was on the *Arbeitsamt* Shit list. The Detachment used the Party-member list as a tool to track down Nazis wanted for various offenses, and the shit list to find its Staff. Anneliese's maiden name was Baur. Candidates with appropriate skills were sent in alphabetical order to the Detachment for interviewing. Thus Anneliese was in the first group of Chef candidates. Whoever interviewed her hired her immediately!

Anneliese was not a native of Kreis Heidenheim, or of its county seat, Heidenheim an der Brenz. Anneliese was a native of Schwenningen am Neckar, Schwenningen on the river Neckar, a small city on the edge of the Black Forest, near the Swiss border to the South, and an hour's drive to the border of France in the West. The Neckar is a fabled German river, and its *Ursprung*, its source, is in Schwenningen. When the war ended, Anneliese's hometown fell within the French Zone of Occupation. Anneliese had been working in Heidenheim as the Housekeeper for a wealthy family. The husband was a businessman with "appropriate" connections to Party members, which enabled him to conduct a profitable manufacturing business during the war. His wife, however, was fervently anti-Hitler, which, of course, was kept secret. Anneliese related to me that the wife, let's call her Frau Rapp, not her real name, would take Anneliese into her bedroom,—after the rest of the household staff had gone home—close its doors and windows, and then tune into the Allied radio channels to hear the news from a point of view diametrically opposed to the propaganda broadcasts of the Nazis. Anneliese told me she enjoyed working with Frau Rapp, a highly cultured person. Then, sometime in late

January 1945, when the war began to turn badly for the Nazis, Hitler decreed that all household help, even those employed by the wealthy classes,—who were ostensibly benefiting from the war,— had to be removed from private employment and made available to the State for use in the war effort. So Frau Rapp had to let Anneliese go. Anneliese then had to register with the *Arbeitsamt*, which put her on its non-party shit list, and then ordered her to a job at a local hospital where she cleaned up the operating rooms after the surgical procedures were done. A bloody, dirty job.

After the war ended on May 8, 1945, Anneliese wanted to go home to Schwenningen. But she could not. The Allies imposed travel restrictions on all Germans to facilitate their search for, and roundup, of Nazis suspected of war crimes. The Allies were not looking for people such as Anneliese. But it was simpler for them to issue blanket restrictions on travel than to start to screen, so soon after the war's end, for those Germans who could travel, and those who should not. And so Anneliese was stuck in Heidenheim, at a time, and in a place she did not want to be. For over a month, she had not heard from her parents, or her younger brother and sister, and she was concerned for their safety. But it was meant that each of us be there in Heidenheim to find each other. It was *beshert*!

I was led to Anneliese in the second week of June 1945, and left her reluctantly, in the first week of November 1945, to return to the States to receive my Honorable Discharge from the Army, and to resolve the reasonable concerns my Mother and Dad had raised when they learned I had fallen in love with a German girl, non-Jewish, to boot, and that I intended to marry her. This period of five months, measured from the time I first saw my belóved Anneliese, to the day I left her to return home, was the most wonderful period of my life! And, so too, for Anneliese, as she confided to me. It was a time of bliss! No pressures of any kind.

The war was over. At least it was over for me. The war with Japan would go on for a while longer. My service could have ended in May 1945. The Army had a Points System to determine when a GI was eligible to leave the Service. The points were based on such criteria as the number of engagements/campaigns you had been in. This was denominated by Battle Stars. I had earned 5 Battle Stars. Points were also awarded for military decorations earned. I had won the Bronze Star, and had been wounded twice in combat, giving me two Purple Hearts. Thus I was told early in June 1945 that I had at least 80 points, which meant I could go home immediately, and be Honorably Discharged. But having found Anneliese, I had no desire to go home any time soon. To use a cliché, which sometimes is the best way to describe something basic: I was head over heels in love! To use another cliché: I'd have been nuts to leave Anneliese so soon after finding her! And so I extended my enlistment on 30 days intervals. My folks soon noted that other neighborhood boys were coming home and wondered why I wasn't. I told them about Anneliese. This raised family issues, which had to be resolved harmoniously.

I discussed everything with Anneliese. She recognized the depth of the problem. For one thing, she was non-Jewish, for another she was a German, and then there was the Holocaust, that evil engine of Nazi mass murder, with its gas chambers and crematoria, and the killing of millions of innocent men, women, and children, including the genocide of six million Jews. Although she was totally blameless, Anneliese understood that in the post war world then evolving, she could easily be tarred, merely by being a German, with the bloody brush of Naziism. She did not wish to suffer this experience, or visit its consequences on me. And so we sat and talked things out. I was teaching Anneliese English. She was a quick study. I was desirous of improving my German, so I would shift into that language as often as possible, these possibilities becoming limited as Anneliese's English improved. She soon learned to write an excellent English, as correct in grammar, syntax, and word choice, as that of any well educated native speaker. However, she never lost her soft southern German accent. With time, I never noticed that she had an accent. This recalls two humorous events, which occurred years after

Anneliese and I were married and raising a family. They both turn on Anneliese's pleasant accent, and how our family ceased to notice it. Our oldest, Andy, was about seven, and the age when kids begin to call each other on the telephone. A boy, Andy's age, called. Anneliese answered the phone and then told Andy the call was for him. Andy picked up the phone, listened briefly, then laughed. Anneliese asked him later what was so funny. "Nothing, Mother", Andy said, "The kid asked me who answered the phone. I told him it was my Mother. He said, she talks funny, I said, no she doesn't. She always talks that way." And then, some years later, when Pamela, our third child, was about thirteen—and moving in a circle with girls from lah-dih-dah families—one of these girls called Pam. Anneliese answered and then called Pam to the phone. When Pam picked up the phone, the girl at the other end said, as related to Anneliese by Pam, "Gee, Pam, I didn't know you had a Swedish maid!" Nothing more lah-dih-dah than that.

However, back to the issue of my going home. I told Anneliese that if I left, I would be coming back for her. She assured me she had no qualms on that score. She did not want to be a source of friction in my family. That was her sole concern. Such friction as might arise would primarily turn on religion. I had been raised an Orthodox Jew. I would go to Cheder, a Jewish religious studies school on my way home from public school. I had been a Bar Mitzvah in the Shul, the Synagogue my Zaydeh, my Grandpa Katz built into the basement of his house in East New York, Brooklyn. My Mother kept a kosher kitchen until my brother Harold and I were in our late teens. I enjoyed studying the Hebrew Scriptures. We were proud Jews, but didn't make a big thing out of it.

And so, Anneliese and I addressed the religious issue. I began by noting I didn't want a household where there was no religion, or two in competition. Anneliese agreed. So which religion should it be? We both recognized that religion could be a creative force, setting down principles of morality,—distinguishing between good values and bad acts,—which would guide our conduct, and that of our children. But religion, if Husband and Wife could not agree, could be, indeed, would be, a source of friction and division. Neither of us wanted that. And so I compared Christian concepts, with those of Judaism. In form, but not in substance, Judaism is an archaic religion. Had the Temple in Jerusalem not been destroyed in 70 CE, one might speculate whether Jews, in seeking expiation for their sins, might yet be offering animal sacrifices to honor God, and to ask for His blessings, and for the forgiveness of their sins. But Judaism should not be measured by those parts of its ritual, which some may believe are outmoded. Judaism must be measured not merely by the forms of its rituals, but by the substance of its Message. The Message is that there is but one God, that He/She (for God is both male and female) created the universe and all that is in it; that God gave humankind free will, and thus the ability to choose between good and evil, between life and death, and God said, choose life because I, your God, love life; and He chose the People of Israel to be His Messenger to the world; and God made clear that he chose the Jews as His Messenger, not because they were better than any other people, but on the contrary, as evidence of His Power that he could take a stubborn and stiffnecked people, and, by His Teachings, make them a Light unto the Nations. And the Jewish People, through the millennia, have borne the burden of being God's Chosen Messenger.—I say "burden" rather than "blessing" because history has demonstrated that the proposed beneficiary of the message would often rather kill the messenger than accept the message. Judaism, with its universal message of monotheism, and its moral teachings, was the progenitor of Christianity and Islam, and Judaism's teachings, as practiced and expounded by its prophets and sages, has, for over 3,500 years, helped shape the world for the better.

Judaism is a live and loving religion, and the right one for me. But I would not foist my religion on Anneliese, nor would she impose her's on me. Anneliese was *Evangelisch*. In Germany, that meant she was a Protestant Christian. In the United States, she would be denominated a Lutheran. At 14, she had her

Confirmation (as did her younger sister and brother). Anneliese told me that she was not a churchgoer, but her mother, Christine, and her maternal grandmother did attend Sunday Services regularly. Her father, Wilhelm, Anneliese said, was not a believer in organized religion. She quoted him as saying, "If you want to find God, walk in the woods, admire the beauties of nature, the trees, the flowers, the birds, enjoy the wild strawberries." And he had contempt for the *Prediger*, the Preacher, who would preach a wonderful sermon on Godliness on Sunday, and then short change you in his shop on Monday.

Now it might strike the reader as strange that two young persons, in the throes of the passions and ecstasies of first love (for both of us were virgins when we were brought together), should take the time to discourse on matters spiritual which might affect their future life together, when the sexual pleasures of the moment were so consuming. But as my narrative has demonstrated, it was *beshert* that Arthur would find Anneliese Baur, and that she,—with her beauty, courage, grace, and wisdom—would guide me in the fashioning of a fruitful family life. Thus conversations on the issue of religion in the family arose quite naturally. In every society, family life is built about the mother. She bears the children, nurtures them, counsels them, and, by example, teaches them the difference between right and wrong. Her rôle in a Jewish household is of even greater importance. Under Jewish religious law, if the mother is Jewish, her children are Jewish, whatever the religion of the father. Further, Anneliese and I recognized that too often, families with mixed marriages result in children reared in no religion, or in an atmosphere of rancor. Neither of us wanted such a union. Choices had to be made.

I told Anneliese I would be very uncomfortable converting to Christianity, whatever the denomination. The issue was not Jesus Christ. He was born a Jew, and he died a Jew. The issue was Christianity itself. I perceived Christianity,—whatever its representations of being a universal religion of love and eternal redemption,—as having demonized the Jew and his Faith, from the first Gospels, through the Crusades, through the Inquisition, through burnings at the stake, through mass deportations, through pogroms, through ghettos, through forced conversions, through Martin Luther's hatred for the Jews (how sad that he who so masterfully translated the Hebrew Scriptures into German failed to see the beauty of its teachings), through the latent and patent anti-semitism of masses of *Das Deutsche Volk*, which Hitler unleashed to organize and operate his program for "*Die Endlösung der Jüdischen Frage*": "The Final Solution of the Jewish Question," which culminated in the Holocaust. I recognized that not every German was an anti-semitic Nazi. Neither Anneliese nor any member of her family joined the Nazi Party to the family's great economic distress, of which I shall relate more below. But I could not see myself converting to a faith, which, for two millennia, had demonstrated a constant hostility to mine.

I made my sentiments clear to Anneliese. I loved her! I adored her! I was overwhelmed with passion when I was with her! She had become the cornerstone of the new life I had begun upon finding her. She was the Sun, and I the Earth circling about her, and drawn into her. I could not conceive of living happily without her sweet presence at my side and in my bed. What to do? In her quite way Anneliese resolved everything. "Arthur", she said, after one of our conversations on the issue where I was on the verge of tears, fearful she might decline to be converted to Judaism, "*Arthur, ich liebe dich sehr, und ich weiss genau, dass du mich auch liebst*, and that is enough for me." As Anneliese's knowledge of English increased both of us shifted from one language into the other, even in mid-sentence. And then she set all my fears to rest, "I understand how you feel. *Ich werde froh sein eine Bekehrte an deinen Glaube zu werden.*": "I shall be happy to become a convert to your belief." I was overjoyed! I clasped her to me, and began to cry. She did, too. As we kissed, our tears of joy mingled on our lips. Never did salt taste so sweet.

The religious issue resolved, the talks turned on my going home. Despite the concerns of my Mom and Dad, I did not want to leave, at least not right away. I thought of getting my discharge in Germany, and then taking a civilian job in Military Government. I made inquiries. I was told that I could not be hired as a civilian in Germany, that I had to go back to the States, there to be hired as a civilian working for the Military Government in Germany. This information was wholly erroneous, as I learned when I got home. It would take me ten agonizing months to get back to Germany, and to my belóved Anneliese, as more fully related below. As I have noted, the five months' period from the middle of June 1945 to the first week of November 1945, when I left for the States, was the most wonderful period of our lives. Anneliese and I had been brought together, as God had meant it to be. And I liked the work I was doing in Military Government. I was part of a team running the County of Heidenheim. It was quite an administrative feat: attending to the restoration of the well being of concentration camp survivors and refugees, and to their repatriation, billeting American troops passing through on their way to ports of embarkation, working to round-up key Nazis, and to do all these things while supervising the daily administration of county government.

Yes, the middle of June 1945 started a new life for me. Combat was over. There were still dangers out there, but no one was shooting at me, and there were no mine fields to be wary of. My face and my right thigh bore the scars of war wounds, the pain was still there, but nothing I couldn't handle. I was eating three excellent meals daily. And I was proud to know who was responsible for them. I had no financial concerns. I was quartered in a warm, sunny room in a beautiful villa. The weather, for the most part, was super. And, best of all, I was passionately in love! My reborn life revolved about Anneliese. I was with her every day. Hand in hand, like the young lovers we were, we strolled in the nearby fields, meadows, and wooded glens. Nothing could be more tranquil and exciting at the same time. We would pick wild flowers—Anneliese seemed to know the names of all of them—and wild strawberries, and currants and blackberries. We would sit on a grassy knoll, or under some trees and watch the birds flitter by, and exchange hugs and kisses as we enjoyed their songs.

Anneliese knew all kinds of German folk songs, some primarily intended for children. She taught me a number of them. One concerned the birds, *Die Vögele*, which flew all about us on those beautiful Summer days. I recognized some as being of the same species I knew in Brooklyn. These were blackbirds, thrushes, finches and starlings. Anneliese taught me the children's verse which referred to these birds: "*Amsel, Drossel, Fink und Star, und die Ganze Vogelschar, wünschen euch ein gutes Jahr und alle Segen.*" Amsel, Drossel, Fink and Star translate into English as Blackbird, Thrush, Finch and Starling. The balance of the verse says: "The whole flock wishes you a good year and all blessings." A delightful, little song.

During those five wonderful months with Anneliese she taught me other childrens' songs, all of which Anneliese and I put to good use when we had our own kids and grand kids. There was this one: "*Kuckuck, Kuckuck, ruft aus dem Wald, lasset uns singen, tanzen und springen, Kuckuck, Kuckuck ruft aus dem Wald.*" 'Cuckoo, Cuckoo calls from the woods. Let's sing, dance and jump about. Cuckoo, cuckoo calls from the woods." And then there was this one, especially designed for kids under three that we could sing and act out as they sat on our knees: "*Huppi, huppi, Reiter, wann er fällt, dann schreit er. Fällt er in den Sumpf, macht der Reiter plumps! Fällt er in den Graben, fressen ihn die Raben!*" "Hoppi, Hoppi, the rider [on a horse], when he falls off he cries. When he falls into a swamp the rider goes plop! When he falls into a ditch the ravens will eat him!" This is funny/scary language for a very young child, particularly when it is accompanied by the appropriate movements of the parent or grandparent holding the child. Thus, on the *Huppi, Huppi* part, Anneliese or I would create a riding motion for the child by pumping our thighs up and down, and then, on the falling part, we would drop our knees, while holding tightly to the child. He or she would experience the sensation of falling down. Shouts of anxiety would mix with laughter when the "rider" recognizes that Mother or Dad, (or Oma or Opa) were not about to let the rider fall. The children laughed at the *"plumps"* part, but some were sometimes scared at the part where they are eaten by the ravens.

Anneliese also taught me the way Germans closed most of their fairy tales. Thus, in the tale "Sleeping Beauty", in German *"Dornröschen"*, where the prince awakens the spellbound princess with his kiss, the story ends—or does it?—as follows: *"Und wenn sie nicht gestorben sind, so leben sie noch heute."* "And if they haven't died, they are living today." Our Anglo ending to the same fairy tale reads: "And they lived happily ever after." I liked Anneliese's German ending better. Its cryptic language carried the magic of the tale to its very last words—and beyond—leaving the reader/listener to ponder the uncertainties of life, real or imagined.

I recount with joy, mingled with sadness, those special times with Anneliese, and the special things I learned from her. They rekindle for me wonderful memories when, for five glorious months I, a prince clad in military olive drab, lived a fairy tale with Anneliese Baur, my beautiful, belóved, dirndl clad, fairy princess. Each day was bathed in light and warmth as the sun moved across a bright blue cloudless sky. Or so I remember it. And there was no gloom in the darkness of the night. Instead, the moon, whether full, waxing or waning, and riding in a sea of scintillating stars, cast its light through the open window upon a prince and his fairy princess enveloped in each others arms. For fifty seven years I was blessed with the loving, living presence of my beautiful, courageous, wise and witty Anneliese Baur. We had joyous times together. Some matched, in their glorious, delirious delight, those five months in Germany, in 1945, which Prince Arthur and Anneliese Baur, his Fairy Princess, then shared. But none has surpassed the magic of that time. My consolation as I write, is that I can still recall the magic.

I have described the most idyllic period of my life. But at the same time I was living in a state of rapture with my belóved

Anneliese, I was also performing my Military Government duties. And so, during these five months of all consuming love, when my soul would soar whenever I was in Anneliese's presence, or dreamed of her, when I was not—I worked in a broken, sordid, post war world—and keenly felt its negative impact upon me. In the immortal words of John Donne: "No man is an island entire to itself." In the next episode I delineate this unique phase of my military career. Were it not for the redeeming presence of Anneliese I would have found some of my Military Government experiences more damaging to my emotional well being than those which impacted me during my pre-combat and combat service periods.

Anneliese and Arthur
Heidenheim, Germany June 1945

Anneliese and Arthur
Heidenheim, Germany June 1945

Anneliese and Arthur
Heidenheim, Germany
June through October 1945

Anneliese and Arthur
Heidenheim, Germany
June through October 1945

Anneliese and Arthur
Heidenheim, Germany
June through October 1945

Anneliese and Arthur
Heidenheim, Germany
June through October 1945

Anneliese with Arthur's Uncle Sid Mencher

Anneliese and Arthur
Heidenheim, Germany
June through October 1945

Anneliese, Arthur and his Uncle Sid
Heidenheim, Germany
June through October 1945

Anneliese and Michelle Grossi, Heidenheim,
Germany, Late Summer 1945

Anneliese and Arthur, Heidenheim,
Germany, Late Summer 1945

Anneliese, Arthur, Dom and
Michelle Grossi and Zeiners
Heidenheim, Germany
September—October 1945

Anneliese Baur
Heidenheim, Germany
June—October 1945

Anneliese Baur
Heidenheim, Germany
June—October 1945

Anneliese Baur
Heidenheim, Germany
June—October 1945

Anneliese Baur
Heidenheim, Germany
June—October 1945

Anneliese Baur
Heidenheim, Germany
June—October 1945

Anneliese Baur
Heidenheim, Germany
June—October 1945

Episode Thirty

In which I recount some of the situations encountered in performing my military government duties; how the Government's ban against fraternization with Germans threatened my relationship with Anneliese; and to my surprise, being awarded the Bronze Star Medal for my combat leadership on February 20, 1945.

In November 1945, on my way home to be discharged from the Service, I was euphoric one moment, and forlorn the next. I was ecstatic that I had found Anneliese, and my reborn life—like the Earth circling the Sun—revolved about her. I was saddened (distressed might be a more apt word) by the need to leave her, and concerned when I'd be able to return to her, and whether my folks would understand that the love we bore for each other was more than the passion of young lovers, which, of course it was—but a love which would last forever—whether the erotic passion flamed or slowly turned to embers. And then, if the thought of leaving Anneliese behind in a hostile post-war environment was not enough to dampen my spirits, there were my recollections of things I had seen, or experienced, during my Military Government tenure which weighed upon me, some more heavily than others. As I have noted, the sweet, gentle presence of Anneliese, the comfort of her arms, and her courage in coping with adversity, were the vital factors which secured me from despair and prevented those gross, banal cruelties I observed, from irreparably damaging my psyche.

I begin by recounting two examples, one which pitted German against German. The other, wherein civilians who themselves had just been released from the shackles of Naziism, vented their anger against another set of unfortunates: Jews just released from their concentration camps, and now wending their way back to their *shtetls* (if they still existed) in Poland, Hungary and Romania. These will serve as an introduction to the unfolding of distressing examples of the manner in which war, with its vagaries, often exacts a greater toll on non-combatant civilians, than it does on those who shouldered arms.

First, my German against German recollection. The war ended in May 1945. Even had the German farmers possessed the seeds and fertilizers, the fuel for their trucks and tractors, the feed for their horses, cattle and fowl—assuming some of these had survived the bombing and strafing inflicted upon them and their masters—it was too late to plant anything of sufficient volume to feed large numbers of the population. Further, many hectares of once arable land were now unworkable until they were cleared of the unexploded shells, and untripped mines still embedded in the soil. Further, German weather, except for such fortunate areas as the *Bodenseegebiet* in Southern Germany, is often cruel from late Fall to late Spring. As Anneliese humorously reminded me, the weather in her Black Forest region of Germany was *"Drei Monaten Winter, neun Monaten kalt"*, three months Winter, nine months cold. And the Fall to Spring weather in Germany in 1945 and 1946 would turn out to be particularly cruel. Mass starvation, and the civil unrest and criminal activity which would inevitably flow from the hordes of hungry peoples seeking food stuffs, of whatever kind, from whatever source, were problems which we, the Military Government arm of the U. S. Occupation Forces, now faced, and which we had to solve, to fulfill our Geneva Convention obligations as occupiers of a beaten nation, to do all we could to assure the general welfare of the civilian population.

Thus, one morning, in early July 1945 in a two and a half ton truck, with a German driver and two burly helpers, we drove the short distance across the border from Heidenheim in *Wuerttemberg* into neighboring *Bayern*, Bavaria. The only weapon on board was my carbine. I had occasion to use it only once in my nearly six months in Military Government, a brief story I shall later tell. But it was comforting to have it with me. There were still a lot of crazies out there. My mission, to bring back at least twenty *Zentners* of potatoes. In U. S. measurement, at least 2,205 lbs. of potatoes. We had learned that Bavarian farmers had squirreled away in their deep cellars tons of storable crops such as potatoes. These Bavarian farmers refused to sell their potatoes, or any other foodstuffs they had, except for an occasional carton of cigarettes, or a piece of jewelry or a silver table setting, all barters items. We had called in all the German Marks and had issued our own Occupation Scrip. It was legal tender, but tell that to the average German, particularly a Bavarian. It was in the beer halls of Bavaria that Hitler got his start, and it was in Nuremberg, in Bavaria, where the edicts which began the Holocaust were promulgated. And so I knew it would be a difficult task to buy potatoes from Bavarian farmers. I made my way to a farm a short run inside Bavaria, where our intelligence had told us that a farmer had stashed away tons of potatoes and other goodies. We drove up to one of many barn like structures he had on his property. Clearly, he was well off. We had been told this barn contained the potatoes. The farmer came out of his house when he saw me, in my military gear, Eisenhower jacket neatly pressed and all beribboned, and my cap jauntily on my head, jump out of the truck's cab. We exchanged cool, but polite greetings.

I informed the farmer that I was there to buy some potatoes from him. I must have come to the wrong place, he said. He didn't have any potatoes to sell. In fact, he was lucky enough to still have a couple of *kilos*, abut five lbs, for his family. And he smiled, with as much congeniality as shown by the Cheshire Cat. He turned to enter his house. At that moment one of my helpers had entered the barn where we had been told the farmer had his potato cellar. He called out excitedly, in dialect, *"Mensch, er hut a huffa Kartoffel!"* "Wow, he's got a lot of potatoes!" The farmer turned to face me. No more pretense of being friendly.

Coldly, he asked, why are we confiscating potatoes from him? Doesn't the mighty American Army have enough of its own food to have to take it from us poor Germans? Got to give him credit for balls. There I'm standing, an American soldier, a carbine slung over my shoulder, and he's reading me the riot act! This was not a *Beschlagnahme*, a confiscation, I told him. We would pay a fair price for what we took. He interrupted me. He wouldn't take the American funny money. Well, I told him, we'll take whatever potatoes we could load onto the truck and I'd leave him the fair value in our Occupation money. That was it! Let's put an end to this conversation. As I turned to signal my men to start loading up the truck with potatoes I told the farmer that the potatoes were not for our American troops, they were for Germans. They were for *Wuerttemberger*. The farmer became even more agitated than he had been. *"Wuerttemberger sind nicht deutsche!. Wir Bayern sind die echten deutsche!"* Wuerttemberger are not Germans! We Bavarians are the real Germans! So much for *Brüderschaft*, brotherhood among defeated Germans.

The truck loaded with its important cargo, I walked to the farmer's front door and knocked. He didn't come out. I knocked again. The same result. So I placed the occupation money, which I had calculated was a fair payment, on a small wooden table near the front door, picked up a rock, placed it on the money to keep it from blowing away, turned, climbed into the cab of the heavily laden truck, and drove back across the border into Wuerttemberg, the home of the *fake* Germans, if the Bavarians are to be believed. My truck driver, who had witnessed my exchange with the Bavarian farmer, said to me, as we drove into the warehouse where the potatoes were to be unloaded, *"Diesen Bayern sind dumme Vieh!"* These Bavarians are stupid cattle! He laughed. He had got his lick in.

Before I move on and tell you about the Jews and their post-war experiences, I'll tell you a little story about potatoes and my sister-in-law, Hilde, Anneliese's younger sister by eight years.

Hilde had been accepted as a student in a highly accredited school. The year was 1947. But the shortage of food was still a reality in Germany, as witnessed by the weekly packages I had earlier sent to Anneliese in 1945 and 1946 (and of which I relate more below). Thus, in addition to the tuition my in-laws had to pay, Hilde had to bring with her a *Zentner*, 110 lbs. of potatoes! These were to be used to help feed her on campus! Without the potatoes, no matter the level of her scholarship, *"kein Eingang"*, no entrance into school. The lowly potato, that once exotic import from the Western Hemisphere, became the source of life for many Europeans. Look at the faces of the peasants in Van Gogh's painting the "The Potato Eaters", and think of the famine among the Irish in the 1840s when a blight killed their potatoes.

Back to the Jews who survived the Concentration Camps. They were now, several months after their rescue, freshened up in body, if not wholly in spirit, and properly housed in apartment blocks cleared of their German tenants, now quartered in other, more cramped quarters. But be assured no one was put out onto the streets.

Summer, short lived as it might be in Germany, was, in July and August, as good as it would get. Thus, it was time to start moving the refugee Jews, and such Russian soldiers who had survived execution after their capture, to their home countries. In the case of the Jews, mainly to Poland, and to Hungary and other central European countries. In addition to being brought back to a level of health where they were fully ambulatory, these former concentration inmates had to be clothed and provided with provisions to sustain them as they made their way home.

Civilian clothing, as with everything civilian at that time, was in short supply. And the ability of the German clothing industry to supply the necessary garments ranged from zero to next to nothing. Even had the German textile industry—pre-war a formidable one—the necessary fabrics, thread and buttons, its factories lay in rubble after repeated allied bombings.

So Military Government had to find another solution, and with American ingenuity, it did. Why not dye the olive drab uniforms of our enlisted personnel, sans all indicia of rank, another color, say blue, and thus outfit the refugees returning home with serviceable clothing they could wear on their trek, with an additional set for good measure, and put this clothing, including underwear, and a week's supply of basic foods, such as bread and hard cheese and powdered milk, into a knapsack, also dyed blue. We had plenty of OD uniforms, and more were easily obtainable.

A great plan! And it worked. In short order, the first batch of blue clad Jews, and others, ready and eager to return home, were placed on trains and moved from Wuerttemberg through Bavaria eastward towards Czechoslovakia, and northward into the Russian Zone of Occupation which had to be crossed to enter into Poland, Hungary and Romania. Once these refugees left the American Zone of Occupation, they were no longer under our protection, and their continued well being would now be the obligation of the Russians, and of the countries through which they would be traveling.

Those returning home were in a festive mood. They had, for the most part, shed their slave mentality, and were learning to think of themselves again as free human beings, entitled to share in the bounty of God's world. The war was over. Naziism was dead. A life of peaceful regeneration lay before them. So they thought, and so did we in Military Government. We saw the first group off with great pride, for we had done a wonderful job of rehabilitation! Had people at home in America known of the work of our Detachment, they would have been proud of us for the considered manner in which U.S. taxpayer money was effectively being spent in turning a war torn Europe into a reborn, peaceful society. As much as I might have been considered a "decorated, wounded, combat hero" (and this cachet was used by my Military Government Detachment to its advantage, as I shall explain), I felt equally proud that I was Part of a team which was helping Germans, in particular, and other Europeans, in general, to hasten their post-war recovery.

I had left the cloistered confines of my college, and given up the protection of a draft deferment to enlist to protect my nation, and my Jewish brethren. I was pleased I could demonstrate that a soldier could be both an agent of war and an agent for peace. My pleasure, and that of my Detachment, on an important job well done, was, unhappily, short lived.

Within a week from the time the first group of repatriates in their blue garb were moved by rail out of the American Zone, what began as a trickle soon turned into a torrent. They began to return, some walking, some crawling. They had been beaten, robbed, and, in the case of some women, raped. They were in rags again, having been stripped of their blue dyed U.S. Army clothing. In the Russian Zone they were set upon by the local German population who could not brook the idea that these Jews were faring better than they. And the Russian troops, equally infected with the virus of antisemitism, gave the Jews no assistance, indeed, at times they participated in the attacks. Those Jews who managed to make their way unscathed through the Russian Zone were not so lucky when they crossed into Poland. Here the same evil of antisemitism took its toll. The local Polish Catholic population, in great numbers, in perhaps Christendom's most pious nation, could not stomach the sight of well fed, well dressed, well provisioned Jews coming back to Poland. They were surprised to see that their Auschwitz and other German controlled *Kazetts*, had not given Hitler his desired Solution of the Jewish Question. And so, they endeavored to do to these returning Jews what Hitler had failed to do. Some they murdered, the others, "the more fortunate ones", they despoiled, and sent stumbling back to us

How horrific it was to witness their return! As a human being, as a combat soldier, as a Jew—all three in my consciousness being aspects of the same identity—I was sorely depressed by what I saw and heard recounted by the beset upon returnees.

Anneliese noted my depression that evening when we were together in her lodging. I had always tried to be upbeat, even bubbly, whenever I was with her. And if I wasn't, she soon had me relaxed and totally happy to be with her. But that night was different. I told her what I had experienced that day. All our Military Government efforts seemed to have gone for naught. We had just fought a world war in which millions of soldiers had been killed, and many more wounded and maimed, and all supposedly to stop the mass killing of civilians because of their race, religion or ethnicity. And with actual hostilities hardly over, the civilians we had fought to save from Hitler were now off on their own rampages. All seemed to be a waste of time, money, effort and, yes, blood. I was so drained that I could not muster up tears.

Anneliese enfolded me in her arms. She kissed me lightly on my forehead, cheeks and lips, and with my head on her breast she quietly said:

"*Bub*, (the term of endearment she had given me) *sei nicht traurig. Du, und deine Kameraden, tuen wunderbaren Sachen für die Entstehung Friedens! Aber man kann nicht eine Welt die total kaputt ist, in einer kurzen Zeit verbessern. Ich weiss wie mutig du bist, aber auch wie empfindlich. Es tut dir weh wenn du siehst wie hässlich manche Menschen sind. Bleib' tapfer, Bub! Ich bin stolz über dich! Ich liebe dich so! Und ich wünsche nur ein langes, liebes Leben mit dir zu verbringen. OK, Bub?*"

"Bub, don't be sad. You and your comrades are doing wonderful things for the establishment of Peace! But one cannot, in a short time, improve a totally broken world. I know how courageous you are, but also, how sensitive. It hurts you when you see how hateful many people are. Stay brave, Bub! I'm very proud of you! I love you so! And I wish only to share a long and loving life with you. OK, Bub?" She then kissed me fully on my mouth, and I began to cry. Anneliese had brought me peace! And she did so with her warmth, her empathy and her words of wisdom. God was great! He had led me to Anneliese, and was giving me a helpmate who would forever be the Cornerstone of my life! ברוך השמ! Blesséd is the Name!

Now I turn to a matter which affected me personally more than the episodes just related. Its affect upon me was paramount because it concerned, indeed, it threatened my relationship with my beautiful, belóved Anneliese Baur. With the war over the American Military instituted a Policy of Non-Fraternization. The term is derived from the Latin word, *fraternitas*, meaning brotherhood, which word, in turn, is derived from *frater*, brother. At war's end the U.S. Military intended that there be no societal or fraternal contacts between the victors and the vanquished enemy, *das deutsche Volk*. (The reason why Anneliese and I could not be married in Germany.) Harsh as it was to us, one can understand why. The victorious Allies were intent early on in bringing to justice those Germans who had participated in the Nazi program of genocide, and who had committed other war crimes. The simplest way of doing this was to isolate the German population from any societal contact with the Allied troops until the process was completed of (a) weeding out the Nazis from the mass of German citizens, and (b) the subsequent classification of these Nazis according to their degree of guilt. I discuss the Allies' policy of Non-Fraternization more fully further on in this story. A mass intermixing of Allied troops with Germans would inevitably have diluted the effectiveness of the Allies' efforts to round up the war criminals and their abettors. The intent behind the World War II slogan displayed in private work places and in public areas, and addressed to the population, military and civilian alike, that "Loose lips sink ships", was behind the Allies' Non-Fraternization Policy in Germany. Indeed, the stern message against fraternization was clearly enunciated in materials distributed to the American occupying troops. The photocopy of the cover of the Army's Pocket Guide To Germany issued in 1945, and here inserted at page page 236.

Although the Non-Fraternization Policy remained in force until July 1947, its provisions were heeded less and less as the redevelopment of Germany began to take shape, and as our Government needed access to such Nazi scientists as Werner von Braun, for our space and military research programs. However, the Policy was in full force when I met, and instantly fell in love with Anneliese, and she, happily, fell in love with me. Notwithstanding that Anneliese and I were as discrete as we could be in the public manifestation of our mutual love, it soon became obvious to my Detachment's Commanding Officer, the Captain from the Cavalry, and even to the most non-discerning enlisted members of our team, that Anneliese and I were more than just co-workers in our Military Government Detachment G-27, U. S. Armed Forces. Anneliese had become my Sun, and everything I did, every thought I had (aside from those affecting the execution of my military duties) revolved about her. I was continually extolling her grace and beauty and intelligence to all about me. But I was careful never to go into her kitchen, the work domain she ruled, except on one or two occasions when I came in for a snack, having missed a meal while on the road. Whatever young lovers do, or dream of doing, we did, but off camera, so to speak.

Perhaps two weeks had gone by, as measured from that glorious day when first I gazed with awe upon Anneliese, and was instantly consumed with love, that one of my Detachment buddies told me the Captain wanted to see me in his Office, which served as the Detachment's HQ. I entered with some concern, being called into a commander's HQ—with one exception—had always been a sign that I was in some kind of trouble. The Captain remarked, in a pleasant manner that he, and others in the Detachment, had observed that I was clearly very fond of Frl. Baur, the Detachment's Chef, and he could understand why. She was a very beautiful, soft spoken, intelligent and amicable person. But she was also a German employee. Clearly not a Nazi, nor even a Party member, for had she been one she would not have been hired. He went on, was I not aware that the Army had instituted a Policy barring its troops from fraternizing with the enemy. I bristled. "She is not an enemy, sir", I said quietly, trying to stay cool. The Captain quickly acknowledged that Frl. Baur was not an enemy in any real sense, but she was a German citizen of a defeated enemy nation, so within the purview of the Policy she was an enemy national, and the policy prohibited American troops from fraternizing with the enemy.

"Well sir", I said, "if you are telling me not to see her any more, I'm telling you now that I won't stop seeing her. I've told Frl. Baur I'm in love with her, and will marry her in the States once she and I leave Germany. And seeing that I do love her, she has said she loves me too, and will be happy to marry me when the law allows." I was at that point speaking animatedly, and I'm sure my face was flushed, because I sensed moisture on my upper lip.

The Captain noted my concern and recognized my sincerity. So instead of reprimanding me for openly stating I would flout the ban against fraternization, he informed me that the Army Brass understood the difficulty of enforcing a ban against fraternization when there were young American soldiers on one hand, and attractive German women on the other, and both seeking what young people generally seek. He was careful not to say what they were seeking. And so the Army was instituting a program of social clubs, much like the USO clubs for GI's in the States (I've described visiting one of them during my desert training times in California in 1942-1943). There would be no objection if I took Frl. Baur to one of these authorized social clubs. But in order for her to be able to enter such a club with me she would first have to be examined by our military doctors to determine whether she was free of any sexually transmitted diseases, and free of other communicable disorders. If she tested clean, and he hastened to say he had no doubt Frl. Baur would, she would get a card with her photo, and then I could be seen more freely in public with her. In short, if the German woman were a healthy slut, or a whore, she could be seen in public with a GI—as long as she was a card carrying slut or whore!

The Captain thought the social club proposal had solved his fraternization problem with me. He was wrong. I was offended by the very thought of having Anneliese demeaned by going through such an intimate examination. I told him I would not subject Anneliese (referring to her as Frl. Baur) to such an invasive medical procedure. I would not attend those clubs, so there was no need for Anneliese to be medically examined. Frl. Baur had her own lodgings in the home of a family friend in Heidenheim. And it was there, in the evenings, that I would spend time with her, and, weather permitting, after my daily tour of duty was over, and her work day done, and on our days off, we would be found walking in the woods and meadows which ringed Heidenheim. Thus, I made clear to the Captain that Anneliese and I would continue to see each other, but to do so in a discrete manner. I then saluted smartly, turned, and left the Captain's office.

A week passed. I went about my duties. The fraternization issue was not raised. Of course I told Anneliese of the fraternization episode. She listened intently and admonished me not to enter the Villa's kitchen, her domain, except when I had truly missed a meal and came in for a snack. And she suggested, smiling as she did, that I not try to embrace her, and steal a kiss while she was still on the grounds of the Villa. That was a difficult request to heed. I was crazy in love and couldn't get enough of her physical and spiritual presence to satisfy my longing for her! But I followed her counsel, albeit reluctantly. I might have had more book learning than she, but she was always more intelligent than I in understanding how life works.

Shortly thereafter, one of the Detachment's enlisted men entered my office to tell me that the Captain wanted to see me in HQ. "Oh, Oh!, I'm in deep shit again!" Clearly this fraternization business was not over. And so, with trepidation I fought to conceal, I entered the Captain's Office. At my last visit he was all alone. Now he was there with the full complement of our Military Government Detachment, G-27: five officers, and six enlisted me, and with me, seven. And they were all lined up in front of his desk. Now I was in for it! The Captain crisply told me to fall in with the enlisted men. I did so at the end of the line. The last time I fell in, and was at the end of the line, was in that English courtyard at 4 in the morning in January 1944 when my stupid, one man fight against fascism in the American Army, as demonstrated by its operation in the 4th Cavalry, ended with my courtmartial and short term confinement. This was clearly not a good sign. And everyone stood there unsmiling. "Fuck!", here we go again! And all I could think of was, am I going to be separated from Anneliese?

The Captain stood in front of this line of officers and enlisted personnel. He held a one page document, and what appeared to be a small, oblong, dark leather covered box. He began to speak He had brought the entire Detachment together to perform a special duty—oh!, oh! I'm gonna get it now!—but a pleasant one, he said. "I proudly hold in my hand a Citation awarding Technician Fifth Grade Arthur S. Katz the Bronze Star medal for demonstrating outstanding leadership in the assault on fortified pill boxes near Dahlen Germany on February 20, 1945, and for volunteering to lay wire through mine infested country during which he was wounded by an anti-personnel mine." I had already received the Purple Heart Medal in the hospital in Paris. But I was not aware, until that moment, that I had been awarded the Bronze Star Medal.

Smiling, the Captain stepped forward, opened the leather bound case, took out the Medal—I was not wearing my Eisenhower jacket—and proceeded to pin the Bronze Star over the left breast pocket of my shirt. He may have never decorated anyone before, and in attaching the Medal its pin penetrated not only my shirt, my underwear, but me, as well. I reacted slightly to the prick of the pin. I could feel blood begin to trickle. But so what! I was a hero, and back in the Captain's good graces!

And all assembled heartily congratulated me. My momentary concerns about being separated from my belóved Anneliese Baur dissipated. That was perhaps the best part of the pinning ceremony.

That evening I showed Anneliese my Citation and Bronze Star Medal. I said I would translate the Citation. Previously I had only talked in passing about some of my combat experiences. They seemed to have no relevance when you are deeply in love. I had begun to aid Anneliese in learning English. No, she said, let me practice by trying to translate your Award. It was a daunting task for one just beginning to study English—and doing so informally—since I was as anxious to improve my German, as she was to learn English. And so we ended up jointly translating the citation, with frequent reference to our dictionaries. The translation completed Anneliese threw her arms about me, kissed me and kissed me and said with a hearty laugh, *"Ich wusste vom Anfang an, dass du mein Held warst. Jetzt habe ich den Orden als Beweis!"* I knew from the beginning that you were my hero. Now I have the Medal as proof! Anneliese had a great sense of humor. She needed it over the long haul in living with me.

I remarked to Anneliese how surprised I was to be awarded the Bronze Star Medal. It had never entered my mind that I would be decorated for doing what I had set out to do: Namely, to complete a successful combat mission and earn the right to go to Officers' Candidate School in Paris. The mission worked well in every respect. It, and being wounded that evening by an anti-personnel mine, got me to Paris, not to OCS, but to a military hospital, which, as God had intended, set me on the last stage of my convoluted journey to find my beautiful and belóved Anneliese Baur!

I have not endeavored to recount all, or even most of my Military Government experiences in Heidenheim, Germany. My daily experiences in military government are for the most part long since forgotten, or buried so deeply within the convoluted interstices of my brain as to be almost impossible to bring up. Despite the fact that I enjoyed my duties in Military Government, and understood their importance when they were being performed, these duties, and the experiences resulting from them, were offset by my concurrent experience of finding Anneliese, and falling instantly under her sway. Anneliese never made demands of me. She didn't have to, even had she been so inclined, for I was so desirous of pleasing her. And, as I have already written, the most vivid memories of my life are those five months I spent with Anneliese in Heidenheim. And these therefore, in most cases, obliterated from my memory military government events occurring during the same period. But I do recall one in particular. It concerns the only time I fired my weapon in anger since the end of my combat days. And it came about in this fashion.

From time to time I had to deliver supplies, or pick up materiel, or visit with local German civilian officials. Depending upon the nature of the chore this was usually done by driving a jeep or a half ton truck. In basic training I had learned to drive all kinds of vehicles, including two and a half ton trucks which required double clutching to run correctly. In fact, until I joined the Army I didn't know how to drive. Tell that to a nineteen year old today! Well, after breakfast on the day this story takes place I went to our motor pool on one side of the Villa, picked out a jeep and selected one of the German guys hanging around, all waiting for a chance to drive to make a few funny money occupation scrip, or for someone to give them some cigarettes in lieu thereof. As I already explained cigarettes at that time in 1945 were more valuable than any forms of legal tender.

I was heading south to Ulm, a city much larger than Heidenheim, on the Danube River. Across the river, on its Bavarian shore, was Neu Ulm. Before I left I went around the corner to the kitchen. The door was open. I poked my head in. Anneliese had told me not to come in unless it was to get a snack after a missed meal. That was a result of this fraternization flare-up, which had by now almost sputtered out. But I was following her orders. I wasn't entering her Kitchen, just poking my head in. She was at the far end, supervising the clean-up work of one of her kitchen staff. *"Grüss Gott, Fräulein Baur!"* I shouted. Good morning Miss Baur! Literally Greet God! The Schwäbisch form of greeting. Anneliese looked up, smiled broadly and waved naughty, naughty with her right hand. I had left her lodgings very early in the morning. The memories were still vibrant, yet I had to see her before I took off.

The distance between Heidenheim and Ulm is not great, about 30 kilometers or 20 miles. In 1945 the road between the two cities was paved, one lane in either direction, and no shoulders of any material width on either side of the road. The road was built above grade, so if you went off it you went down some distance into some farmer's field. And, of course, there were no overtake lanes. This particular road was paved in asphalt, but showed spots where the asphalt had been chewed away. It was a short distance to drive, but not a fun one. Fortunately there was very little traffic. I had completed my business in Ulm and now we were retracing our way back to Heidenheim. When we left the Villa we were required to take a weapon with us. Primarily, as a sign of who was boss, since Germans were forbidden to have weapons. But also for our personal defense. There were still Nazi remnants floating about trying to find ways to leave for such safe havens as Argentina and Paraguay. And there were black marketers and other criminal elements always lurking about. And some of these might be stupid enough to try to rob an American soldier, or steal his vehicle. And so I had my carbine with me. The Jeep was topless and the windshield had been removed. No need to have it up this time of the year and subject to being broken by debris kicked up from the roads. My carbine lay across my lap, the muzzle pointing away from the driver, even though there was no round in the chamber, and the safety was on.

About half way back to Heidenheim we encountered our first vehicle. It was a large flat bed type of truck, with wooden slats running around its bed. It had four huge rubber tired wheels, the kind one sees on large farm tractors. It was moving slowly, perhaps twenty miles an hour. Chugging along. It was not burning either gasoline or diesel. It had one of those Stanley Steamer like stoves which was burning wood and generating steam which powered the truck. There were two or three people in the truck's cab. The cab projected above the top of the slats on the truck's bed. There were about half a dozen people sitting or standing in the bed. They all appeared to be having a fun time, laughing and passing a bottle about. The truck was driving straight down the center of the road. My driver came up close to the truck and signaled that it move over so that we could pass. Nothing happened. The truck did not change its course. I stood up in the Jeep, shouted and waved for the truck to move over. Nothing, except the truck driver looked over his shoulder and laughed. And then the people in the truck bed began to laugh, and wave. Their hand movements suggested *"Vick dich!"* Fuck you! in German. We were approaching a straight stretch of the road where the shoulder on the left side would be wide enough to pass safely. My driver moved to the left side of the road. And the son-of-a-bitch in the truck slid over almost forcing us off the road. I jumped up, this time with the carbine in my hand. I waved it at them. The truck driver just turned his head and laughed, as did the people in the bed of the truck. They were having a ball. They were mocking the Amis, and getting away with it! Bullshit, they were! I released the safety, pulled back the bolt and now there was a round in the chamber. I stood up, bracing myself as best I could. I aimed at the left rear tire and fired. The carbine is not a noisy weapon, but it can be heard. I then turned to fire at the right rear tire. I didn't have to get the shot off. The truck suddenly veered to the right, almost off the road, and we drove past, with me standing there with my carbine cradled in my arms. I didn't say anything as we drove by. I didn't have to. My carbine had done the talking. And it was the last time I fired any Army ordnance.

One of my Military Government duties, as I have noted, was to handle the housing of refugees, and of Germans displaced by the former being moved into their residences. And on the military side I was responsible for the quartering of American troops who would bed down for short periods of time in Heidenheim until they could move on to the port staging areas in France where they would board transport to take them home, or on to the Pacific Theatre, where the Allies were still at war with Japan. As the enlisted man responsible for civilian and military housing in Kreis Heidenheim—I was graced with the fancy title of Billeting Officer—I had set up a tent city on the outskirts of the city of Heidenheim where I would direct incoming troops to bed down. These troops came in as intact units. We couldn't accommodate a full armored division, for instance, but we could billet some of their elements in our tent city, and direct the rest to our neighboring communities in the Kreis where I'd set up similar tent communities. Nothing fancy in these tent communities, but they offered better accommodations than getting shut eye in a sleeping bag spread out on the turf, with washing and shaving done out of a helmet full of water. And the latrines, while rudimentary, were all under canvas, and a million light years better than those open air "facilities" in England. The reader may recall that my complaints about our not so sanitary latrines started me on that downward spiral in the 4th Cavalry. All of which became ancient history once I crossed into France in mid June 1944 with my new outfit, the 86th Cavalry Reconnaissance Squadron Mechanized in which I spent all my months of combat in France, Luxembourg, Belgium and Germany.

My Detachment generally had no problems in billeting troops passing through. Their stay in our Kreis was generally only for a few days. And for a few days, living in a tent community was probably more relaxing than either sleeping in your tank or other vehicle, or sacked out on the ground. Those troops seeking billeting accommodations went first to the Captain's Office. He, or any other duty officer then in charge, would meet with the Officer sent by that unit, find out its requirements, give me a phone call, tell me who would be coming by, and detail their billeting needs. In the few minutes that it took for that officer to come to my office, I already knew where I would billet his troops. On rare occasions the system wouldn't work that smoothly. I recall one such incident which occurred about two weeks after I had been presented with my Bronze Star Medal. An Armored Division had rolled into our *Kreis*. The Armored Division to which my 86th Cavalry Squadron was attached, was the 6th Armored. It was one of two Armored Divisions in General Patton's Third Army. The other was the 4th Armored.

These two low numbered armored units saw heavy fighting throughout the war. The Armored Division which had just rolled in had a double digit number, which I won't reveal, since the story I relate reflects negatively on the unit. This high Division number coupled with the knowledge I had inquired of combat operations while in the hospital in Paris, indicated to me that this Armored Division had seen some fighting, primarily mop up stuff. But it certainly didn't have the combat records earned by the 4th and 6th Armored Divisions. I cite all this by way of background because the Lt. Col. who came to the Captain from this Division became irate when informed that his troops, including the Officers, would be billeted in tents, and that T/5 Katz would handle the billeting. His Division, including Officers, in tents, and being told where to go by an enlisted man? Hey, there were several housing blocks he had seen coming into Heidenheim. Roust the Germans out of them! He assumed the occupants were Germans, when, of course they were recuperating Concentration Camp survivors. My Captain informed the Lt. Col. what the facts were, and repeated that he should talk with me concerning billeting his troops. The Captain said the Lt. Col. then really blew his cork! He then proceeded to lambast the Captain, and the entire Military Government operation, for baby sitting a bunch of foreigners, and suck-assing the German population while housing his American fighting men in tents! What kind of shit is that? My Captain was no dummy. He politely suggested to the Lt. Col. that he go into the Villa's living room where one of the household staff would get him a coffee while he, our Captain, called his HQ to see whether something satisfactory to the Lt. Colonel could be worked out. The Lt. Colonel grumbled but went into the Living Room where one of the housekeepers got him his coffee. My Captain then got on the phone to me.

"Katz, are you in shirt sleeves?" It was a warm day for Germany, and I answered in the affirmative. "Well, go to your room, put on your jacket, and get back to your office. I'm sending over a very angry Lt. Col. from that armored division that rolled in this morning. He doesn't like the idea of being put up in tents when he sees our refugee charges, and the local Germans in houses. I'm sure you'll know what to do when you meet him" And he hangs up. I scoot to my room, one flight up in the Villa, and not too far from my office. Not only did I put the jacket on. I put on a tie. And I dug up my cap. I was dressed to kill military style! Very spit and polish.

I wasn't in my office more than maybe a minute when a very agitated Lt. Col. walks in. The door to my office was always open. I hop out of my chair, salute, and ask him how can I help. He doesn't return my salute. He begins to rattle off the same line he tried to lay on the Captain. His boys had been fighting long and hard and deserved better accommodations than being lodged in tents while foreigners (I guess foreigners is as good a word to describe Jews, as any) and Germans were being housed in real structures. I leaned across my desk, making sure that the ribbons on my chest were highly visible, and I spread my arms before me. This highlighted my 6th Armored Division patch, and those little strips of yellow/gold cloth, low on your left sleeve which tell how long you've been in the Service. With each medal won you are given a matching ribbon. I was wearing my Purple Heart ribbons, my Bronze Star ribbon, and my European Theatre ribbon with five campaign stars. It had taken me a long time to earn my Good Conduct ribbon, and I might have been wearing it too. And my cap bore the yellow piping of the Cavalry, and my jacket's lapels bore the crossed sabers insignia of the Cavalry.

I could see that the Lt. Col. was observing my tent show. He said nothing. I began my spiel. I told him I knew his unit had been in combat. But too bad they came in so late as to miss most of the action. Ha! I guess I've had more fun than most of your guys, and I rattled off, in general terms, where we had been: across France, Luxembourg, Belgium and the Battle of the Bulge, and then into Germany. I would have still been with my Cavalry Squadron, except the second time I was wounded I didn't get out of the hospital until about the same time you guys got into it. Stick it to him! I enlisted out of college to beat Hitler, and I joined the Military Government when the war ended to help restore democracy to Germany. Isn't that why we fight wars, to do good? And then I put in the clincher. "Colonel, our Military Government operations are underfunded and understaffed. I'm working my butt off doing the best I can to help rehabilitate refugees so we can then send them on their way home. I'd like to put your men up in real houses, but it's not possible. Won't you help me make my job a little easier?" And I handed across my desk the paper work which showed where his Division would be billeted in *Kreis Heidenheim*.

I realized I was talking to a Lt. Col., and talking down to him. But what could he do to me—that hadn't already been laid upon me? Nothing! Exactly! The Lt. Col. stared at me for a moment. He had been taken aback by my decorations, and blunt language. He stood up. "I'll relay your request to my HQ." Unsmiling, he picked up the papers. I stood up and saluted. He didn't return my salute, and left. Neither the Captain nor I heard from him again. I believe I was called upon one more time to go into my combat jacket routine. With similar results.

Schloss Hellenstein, Heidenheim

Combat Damage, Heidenheim

Military Government Prisoners
Kreis Heidenheim

Military Government Court
Kreis Heidenheim

Military Government Staff: American GI's and
Germans, and one Russian Officer,
with Arthur in background, below
Kreis Heidenheim

Arthur and Grossi with Russian Major
and German Staff Member,
Kreis Heidenheim

Art and Buddy, Mil. Gov't Fun

Arthur and his assigned Fiat,
Kreis Heidenheim

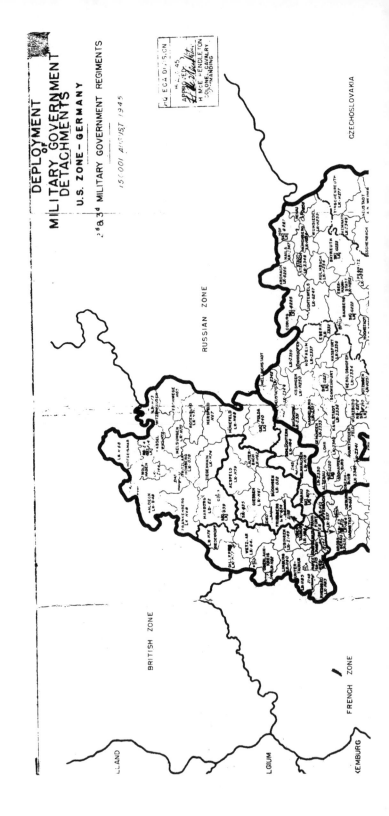

302

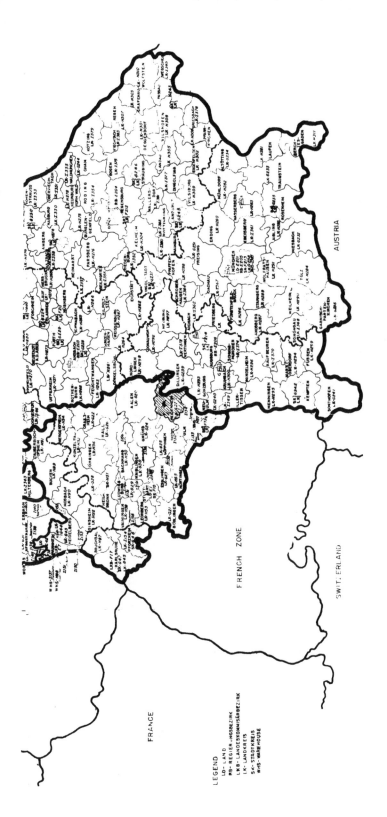

Location of Kreis Heidenheim shown in shaded area.

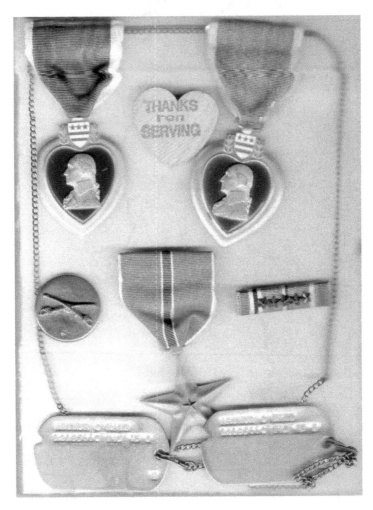

Arthur's Military Decorations

HEADQUARTERS SIXTH ARMORED DIVISION
OFFICE OF THE COMMANDING GENERAL

Award of the Bronze Star Medal
Citation

TECHNICIAN FIFTH GRADE ARTHUR S KATZ, (Army Serial Number 12185660), Cavalry, Troop "D", 86th Cavalry Reconnaissance Squadron Mechanized, United States Army. For meritorious achievement in connection with military operations against an enemy of the United States in the vicinity of Dahnen, Germany on 20 February 1945. He demonstrated outstanding leadership in the assault on fortified pill boxes and volunteered to lay wire through mine-infested country. While laying wire, he was wounded by an anti-personnel mine. Entered the military service from New York.

Arthur's Bronze Star Citation

305

MILITARY GOVERNMENT · GERMANY

Detachment I 14 G3

Company G, 3d ECA Regt

APO 658
4 AUGUST 1945

TO: All Military Personnel.

This is to certify that

ARTHUR S. KATZ, Tec 5, ASN 12 185 660 is a member of Mil Govt Detachment G 27 operating in Landkreis Heidenheim/Brenz (Germany) and as such is authorized to carry out the instructions of the Commanding Officer.

He is also authorized to carry civilian personnel in US Army vehicles.

By Order of MILITARY GOVERNMENT:

F. R. Edwards jr.
FRANCIS R. EDWARDS
Captain, Cav
Military Govt O
Commanding

UNITED STATES FORCES
EUROPEAN THEATRE
MILITARY GOVERNMENT
DETACHMENT G 27

Episodes Thirty One through Thirty Three

Taking Care, Taking Leave

Good night, good night! parting is such
sweet sorrow,
That I shall say good night till it
be morrow.

Romeo and Juliet, **Act 2, Scene 2**
William Shakespeare

Episode Thirty One

In which I take Anneliese from Heidenheim, our Military Government location, to her home in Schwenningen am Neckar in the Black Forest region, where I meet her mother, younger sister and brother, a German soldier, two years my junior, who'd lost a leg in the war and initially was not keen on meeting me, assuming, perhaps, I was just having fun and games with his sister. Her father's absence is explained.

In the latter part of October 1945 I informed the Army that I was ready to exercise my right, frequently deferred,—as I have noted—to go home, and there to be honorably discharged from the Service. I packed my gear and wrote to my folks that I'd be home probably within a month. Was I eager to go home? Why should I be? I was leaving my belóved Anneliese behind. Was I ready to go home? Not by a long shot! Before I left Heidenheim for the States I had to make provision for Anneliese's well being until I could return to Germany, rejoin her, and start the governmental procedures to bring her back with me to America. Anneliese lived in Heidenheim with a family she had gotten to know while working for Frau Rapp. They were nice people. But she didn't wish to stay in Heidenheim, nor continue to work with my Military Government Team were I not there. Mail service was now functioning between the four Military Zones of Occupation. Thus Anneliese had learned some good news and some bad news concerning her family.

The good news: her Mother, Christine, her younger sister, Hilda, her younger brother, Kurt, her maternal grandparents, (her paternal grandparents were deceased) and all her aunts and uncles and cousins were OK, actually Kurt was not doing too well. I shall shortly explain this last cryptic statement.

The bad news: A day or two after the war formally ended on May 8, 1945, the French, the Occupying Power in Anneliese's part of Southern Germany, rounded up all the able bodied men they found on the streets of Schwenningen, and marched them off to internment camps approximately 100 kilometers away in France. Her father, Wilhelm, was on his bicycle returning home from a short shopping trip into town when the French dragnet pulled him, bike and all into its net. Her father was then in his late forties. The French were making a broad sweep of German males in their search for Nazi war criminals. The French never told the German population where the men had been taken, or how they were faring, or what was being done with them. As of the first week in May 1945, her father was missing, his location and condition unknown, (he would return home, the way he left, on foot, none the worse for wear, in the third week of February 1946). Anneliese also learned that in the last days of the war Schwenningen had been bombed by the American Air Force, that the target was apparently the railroad station in Schwenningen, that some bombs missed their target, and that one of these fell on her grandparents' house, destroying a large part of it, but sparing her grandparents from injury.

Anneliese wanted to go home to her family. She said the warmth of family and familiar surroundings would make it easier to await my return. I understood. But there was a problem: a matter of obtaining military clearances for Anneliese to travel from one Occupation Zone to another.

The authority of each occupying power was restricted to its own Zone. Thus, I could ask my Team Commander in Heidenheim to issue me a document permitting Anneliese to leave the American Zone for the purpose of returning home. Whether the French would honor this U.S. travel document and permit Anneliese to enter the French Zone was not clear. The indiscriminate hostility of the French against anything German at war's end was manifestly unfair to innocent Germans, such as Anneliese. However, in the context of the time, the French attitude could be understood. Although the Quisling style Vichy regime installed by the Nazis made their occupation of La Belle France less onerous than, let's say, the Nazi occupation of Poland, still the Nazis had militarily devastated France. Thus, from the war's end in May 1945, until at least the end of 1947, the French, in concert with all the other Nazi occupied countries, lumped all Germans under the rubric "Nazi". If you were a German national you were on that former occupied country's "hate list". Further in this narrative I shall relate an episode in which Anneliese was subjected to such blanket discrimination. In light of the foregoing realities, how to insure that Anneliese would be permitted to enter the French Zone of Occupation, and allowed to stay there? Ay, there's the rub—to poach from Shakespeare.

What, I said to myself, do the French particularly prize about themselves? What was this ethos? It was their special understanding of Love, Romance, L'Amour that, in the French psyche, set them apart from all other nations. OK, I said, I will use the special relationship which the concept of romantic love had to the French people as a ploy to get Anneliese back home. (I would later use this same ploy to get Anneliese out of Germany, and on her way with me to the States, except the second time around I would have to hassle with the French *and* the Russians.) And so, to complement the U.S. travel papers that I knew I would obtain, I worked up a travel document directed at the French. I wrote it in French and in English. In 1945 my French was a lot better than it is today. The old saying is correct: use it or lose it.

On the official letterhead of our Heidenheim Military Government Team I wrote, *inter alia*, that Frl. Anneliese Baur was a trusted employee of our U. S. Military Government Team; that I was a member of that Team, having joined it following my recovery from wounds suffered in combat (nothing like a little truthful flag waving to indicate I had fought and bled for French freedom); that Frl Baur and I had fallen in love; that before we would became engaged to marry, Frl. Baur and I wished to discuss this important matter directly with her family, so that they could meet me and, hopefully, approve our engagement; that Frl. Baur's family resided in the French Zone of Occupation, thus I was respectfully requesting the assistance of my fellow French comrades in arms in making Frl. Baur's trip to her home a pleasant one. I did not formally ask for permission, and said nothing to indicate Anneliese would not be returning to the American Zone.

It was either in the last days of October, or the first days of November 1945 when, after Anneliese had said her goodbyes to our military government personnel, and to her host family in Heidenheim, that we set out, in a military government jeep for Anneliese's hometown: Schwenningen am Neckar, Schwenningen on the Neckar. Schwenningen is the Allemanisch word for town of Swans. A swan is the main feature of the city's Stadtwappe or City Emblem. The Neckar is a fabled South German river. Its source (in German, its *Ursprung*) is in Schwenningen, and from there it flows north, ultimately to become part of the Rhine. Schwenningen lies on the eastern edge of the beautiful Black Forest (*Schwarzwald*), and astride the European Watershed (*Europaische Wasserscheide*). From that area rivers flow north and east. The source of the Danube (*Die Donau*) lies a few miles from Schwenningen and flows east to empty as a mighty river into the Black Sea. I'm repeating information I learned from Anneliese. She was interested in everything, but especially keen on geography (*Erdkunde*).

The weather in southern Wuerttemberg, (later to become the land or State of Baden-Wuerttemberg, Baden lying to the west of Wuerttemberg, and between it and France), was chilly when we set out. I had put the windshield up and snapped the Jeep's canvas roof into place before we left Heidenheim. The sides were open. It was drafty. Both of us were warmly dressed. But the wind swirled in and nipped at our cheeks and noses. We drove southwest. Anneliese was pensive. She would look over at me and smile her beautiful, warm, radiant smile. It always made my heart leap! And occasionally she would reach out a gloved hand and place it over mine when it rested on the knob of the stick shift.

Approximately an hour after we had left Heidenheim we approached the easternmost edge of the French Zone of Occupation. There was a wooden lift gate up ahead, and before you reached it there was a large sign, in English, French and German, indicating we were leaving the American Sector and entering the French Sector. We rolled past the sign and to the lift gate. There was a French soldier standing there. I could see that Anneliese was apprehensive. *"Hab' kein'Sorgen,* don't be concerned", I told her, and squeezed her hand reassuringly. She said nothing, gave me a quick smile, and sat bolt upright. I hopped out of the jeep and walked briskly to the French guard. I smiled broadly, greeted him in French, told him I was taking my fiancée home, and handed over my two travel documents, the one issued by my Team Leader, and the one I had drafted. He glanced at them, told me to wait and, with my papers in his hand, entered a one story structure which stood a few meters away, and must have been the guard house. Perhaps thirty seconds passed. No one came out of the building. I turned and blew a kiss to Anneliese. Still sitting upright she smiled back, Another ten seconds passed. It seemed as if I had been standing there forever. The guard emerged with an officer. I knew he was an officer by his natty uniform and epaulets. As I have noted, I never learned to recognize the *indicia* of rank worn by foreign military officers. I guessed by his age, he was not much older than I, that he must have been at least a Lieutenant. To play it safe, I saluted him. He returned my salute. He had my papers in his hand. He glanced down at them, and then he looked over at Anneliese. He gazed at her for a bit, then turned to me and said, *"Votre fiancée est tres belle. Vous a de la chance."* "Your fiancee is very beautiful. You are a lucky man." He then turned to Anneliese, smiled, and said, with a slight bow, *"Bonjour, mademoiselle."* Anneliese smiled back, much relieved at the reception being accorded us. The Lieutenant handed my papers back to me. I thanked him, saluted, he returned my salute, told the guard to lift the gate and went back into the guard house.

The guard lifted the gate and I drove past it, then stopped a short distance away. I was relieved, as was Anneliese. But now I needed some other relief. I had to take a leak. I figured Anneliese would also welcome a pit stop. I asked the guard whether there was a toilet we could use. He said there was one in the guard house. I helped Anneliese out of the jeep and we both went into the guard house. There was only one toilet. I waited until Anneliese came out, and then I went in. Having done what I had to do, Anneliese and I walked out to the jeep. Wow! There was no jeep! Concerned with showing my papers, I had hopped out of the jeep, but left the key in the ignition. Stupid of me. "*Où est mon jeep?*", I anxiously asked the guard. He laughed. Don't worry, he told me. His unit had a bunch of newly enlisted personnel. They had seen lots of jeeps, but never one close-up, and they couldn't resist giving it a spin. Fifteen fretful minutes later my jeep roared into the guard facility. It was dusty, but undamaged, and loaded with 5 young French soldiers. With peals of laughter they told me that *le jeep Américain* was fun to drive. It was, and Anneliese and I were happy to have it back, and on the road to Schwenningen.

We had left Heidenheim at about 7:30 a.m. It was now about 10:30 a.m. We were averaging 35 to 40 miles an hour, and were on the last leg of our journey to Schwenningen. We were on the typical German rural road. Paved, but barely wide enough for two vehicles to pass safely abreast of each other. No shoulders. Just a deep ditch on each side for drainage, with trees lining the side of the ditch furthest from the road. The weather was living up to Anneliese's humorous description of it: 3 months winter, nine months cold. There was one row of trees on each side of the road. They were tall deciduous trees, now bare of their leaves. Beyond the trees lay fields now bare of whatever crop they had grown. The road wound its way, conforming to the vagaries of the terrain. Aside from two or three French military vehicles, and one slow moving German *Lastwagen* (truck) running on energy obtained from burning wood—much like an old Stanley Steamer vehicle—the roadway was empty and we made good time. At about noon we rolled to a stop in front of Anneliese's home, a rented house at Bürkstrasse 68. It was a narrow, stucco faced 2 storey house on a treeless street. Not too far away was the Hotel Ochsen, a small country hotel, much favored by traveling merchants, where Anneliese, as an apprentice, had learned the craft of running a commercial kitchen, and had honed her skills as a chef.

Anneliese had written her mother, Christine, giving her the approximate time of our arrival. Her mother, and her sister, Hilde, then 16 years of age, were sitting at a front window, awaiting our arrival. They saw us. They rushed out of the house. There was a lot of hugging and kissing and joyous crying. I stood there, as happy as the three of them, and on the verge of tears. Anneliese was home at last. I was about to leave her, for how long I did not know, and that saddened me, but my sadness was tempered by the fact that I knew Anneliese was now safe at home. Anneliese took my arm, she was brimming with joy, and laughing, and in German, she said, let's go inside, the neighbors are beginning to look out their windows. Once inside, all attention was now focused on me. Her mother and sister clasped my hands in theirs and thanked me for taking such good care of Anneliese, and now bringing her home. Anneliese had sent them photos of me. Both said I looked even handsomer than in the pictures. I laughed, and thanked them. All discourse was in German. Anneliese had written her mother and told her that our relationship had ripened into a deeply intimate one, in short, we were lovers. I presumed her sister knew that too. If first impressions matter, I made a good one. They saw before them two young people very much in love, clinging to each other, she, dazzling in her dirndl, he, in his olive drab, dress uniform, clearly under her spell. Consistent with German custom I immediately began to address Anneliese's mother as *Mutter*, and when I finally met her Dad, I called him *Vater*. Anneliese always addressed me, aside from terms of endearment, as Arthur, until our first child, Andrew Elliott, was born. From then on she almost always called me Dad, the English equivalent of Vater. *Mutter* asked whether I would like some *Tee und Kuchen*, tea and cake. I said I would. She went into the kitchen with Hilde. There was a third person in the house when Anneliese and I drove up. Her younger brother, Kurt. He did not run out to greet us. Let me tell you why.

At the time I took Anneliese home Kurt, the youngest of the three Baur siblings, was not quite 20. As I have mentioned, none of the Baur Family members belonged to any Nazi party organization. For that reason Anneliese could not get permission to leave Germany for Switzerland, just across the border, where she hoped to continue her culinary studies. Nor could her father, Wilhelm, a German Army World War I veteran, and a winner of the Iron Cross, get any government contracts for his machine tools business. However, as the war began to turn against Hitler and his minions—and the body count kept rising—Kurt was drafted into the Army, and at age 18 was assigned to a *Panzerabteilung*, a tank unit. Sometime in November 1944, near Aachen in Germany, Kurt's tank column was strafed and bombed by allied aircraft. The planes were aiming at the tanks in dropping their bombs. In such an attack the tank's cannon is useless as a defense mechanism, and machine gun fire not very effective against a target moving at several hundred miles an hour. Hence, the best thing a tank crew can then do is to bail out of the tank and run for the cover of the nearest ditch or depression in the ground. That's what Kurt did. He jumped out of the tank and into a ditch. The attacking planes dropped their clutch of bombs. One missed its intended target. It exploded in the ditch in which Kurt was lying and blew his right leg off up to the knee. Anneliese told me she had visited Kurt in his military hospital, when civilian rail travel, though hazardous, was still possible. She was then working at Frau Rapp's house in Heidenheim. She found Kurt disconsolate. He had been an excellent *Turner*, a gymnast, and skier, and now he saw himself going through life as a cripple. Anneliese left him feeling as unhappy as he was. As she walked to the railroad station to return to Heidenheim, allied planes suddenly appeared and dropped bombs on the station. Anneliese recalls lying between the rails of the train tracks and praying that what had happened to her brother would not happen to her. Thank God it didn't.

I relate all this about Kurt to explain why he did not come out to greet his sister and me. He couldn't do so easily. He had been fitted by the German military doctors with a false limb. It was intended to be a temporary one, ill fitting and painful. With the war now lost, the prospect of Kurt getting a more comfortable false limb appeared to him to be light years away. Anneliese had informed me that Kurt, even in the best of times was not much of a talker. Over the years I have gotten to know Kurt very well. He is an even tempered, good natured, intelligent man and a skilled artisan in the designing and construction of complex machinery. But he is still not much of a talker. But back to the time when we first met.

Kurt was sitting in the living room when Anneliese and I entered. She quickly went to him, put her arms about him, kissed him on his cheek, told him he looked well, that she was so happy to be home again, that she was sure *Vater* would soon be home, safe and sound. Anneliese was in high spirits. Kurt said nothing, although he did squeeze her hand. Kurt knew who I was. The letters Anneliese had written home about us had been shared by *Mutter*, Hilde and Kurt. The family pleasantries over, Anneliese then introduced me to Kurt. I extended my hand to him, smiled, and said, *"Grüss Gott, Kurt, es freut mich sehr, dich endlich kennen zu lernen."* *"Grüss Gott"* is the Swabian / South German form of greeting, which I followed up by saying I was very pleased finally to meet him. Kurt did not take my hand. He acknowledged my greeting with a nod, nothing more. I knew how painful combat wounds can be. I'd had my share. But I had not lost a limb. I could not feel *his* pain, but I could sense his bottled up anger. The loss of a limb by this young athlete was an injury which exceeded mine. I was ambulatory. He was not. Anneliese noted immediately the tension between us. I could see she was distressed. I told her in English not to be concerned, to join her mother and sister in the kitchen, and that I'd sit with Kurt for a bit. Dispirited, she said OK and left the room.

Kurt didn't invite me to sit down. So I pulled up a chair and sat down opposite him. What was he thinking? Here he is, a cripple, sorry for himself, and concerned for the safety of his missing father. And here was this *Ami*, this American soldier, two years his senior, also combat wounded, as he had learned from Anneliese's letters, but there was a difference, a big one, I was able to walk about and he couldn't. And this *Ami* was sleeping with his sister. Did he really love her, as Anneliese had written to the family? Did he really want to marry her? Or was he just having his fun with a beautiful *Fräulein*? He knew I was Jewish. But I didn't think that colored his thinking about me. Right now I could walk, run, climb steps with ease, drive a car, dance, make love to his sister, and not worry about the future. And there he was: restricted in his movements, still suffering the phantom pain one often experiences after an amputation, very little food in the house, not many briquettes for cooking, none at all for heating, his father missing, his country a total mess. He was a loser, living in a land of losers. *Scheisse*! What reason did he have to be happy?

My conjecture of what Kurt might be thinking circulated within seconds through the interstices of my brain, there to register an indelible picture of a bitter and unhappy young man. Kurt sat, silent as the Sphinx. (A cliché, but it makes my point). My efforts at small talk generated no responses. Further silence would become awkward. Shit!, I said to myself, this is putting a damper on the joy Anneliese should be having on being home at last. Seeing Anneliese distressed bothered me. What the fuck should I do, could I do, to break the ice? (Another cliché—as I have noted words or phrases become clichés because they are the only words or combination of words which aptly express the desired thought). For want of anything else to do I looked about the room. There, on a wall shelf I thought I saw a box marked *Schachspiel*, Chess Set. I got up, walked to the shelf. Yep, it was a chess set. I turned to Kurt who was still sitting as impassively as when I entered the room. *"Spielst du Schach?"* "Do you play chess?" He nodded affirmatively. *"Willst du spielen?"* "Do you want to play?" He said nothing—a long ten seconds of nothing. Then, surprise! *"Ja"*, "Yes", he said. With some effort Kurt swiveled his chair about so that it faced the table in the middle of the room. I did not offer to help him. I knew from my own recuperation experiences that a well meaning offer to help a disabled soldier move or turn, or sit up, is seen by him as further evidence of his own failings, and not as a generous offer of assistance.

I set up the board. I didn't offer to toss a coin to see who got white or black. White opens. Instead I said I would pick black. It was my favorite color because all other colors are in it. At least that's what I understood, and what I told Kurt. He had white, he would open. I'm a competitive person. I enjoyed being a trial lawyer for a half century. It was an arduous way to make a living—but never a dull one. And so every contest I go into, whether a trial, arguing an appeal, playing Scrabble or chess, I go in to win. I'm not a good chess player, never studied it enough to learn its intricacies. I know it's a war game, the purpose being to win by killing your opponent's king. The game ends when your opponent is "checkmate". Checkmate in English is *Schachmat* in German. The game originated in the Middle East. In Hebrew the word *"met"* means dead. I believe *"mat"* means dead in Arabic. *Schach* is the German equivalent for Sheik, the Arabic word for leader or king. So *Schachmat* means the king is dead. This happens when the king cannot escape his opponent's attack, no matter what moves he makes. Check Mate/*Schachmat*, you're dead. Game Over. Would that real wars could be fought that bloodlessly.

The game begins. It soon became apparent that Kurt knew how to play, and that he would beat me. I didn't try to throw the game. I really tried to win. But in less than 20 minutes it was *Schachmat*, my king was dead. I lost. While contemplating our moves, and making them, neither of us had uttered more than a few spontaneous ohs and ahs or a *"shit!"* from me or a *"Scheisse!"*

from Kurt. Both of us were free with this expletive. The game over, I sensed a relaxation in Kurt's stoic demeanor. He grinned briefly while saying "*Schachmat!*". Hey! How about another game? I suggested. I'm just warming up. Sure. Really. I was full of shit—and I believe Kurt knew that.

We had a second game. Kurt beat me again, and within a tighter time frame than in the first encounter. By now Kurt was almost convivial. He began to speak in full sentences. We spoke in German. Kurt knew no English. Perhaps winning at chess, and against an *Ami* was helping to restore his self confidence. Perhaps he began to recognize that although the loss of a limb affected adversely his ability to move about, or to engage in sports, it had no impact upon his mental skills. Perhaps he now saw that despite his severe injury he would be able to cope with life (which he did). I am postulating all this based only upon what I observed after Kurt won the second game of chess. Then, again, it might have been nothing more than his getting even with some one who had trespassed the close of his family. Nothing like beating the guy who is laying your sister. One way of getting even for the family's honor. I am not sure that at that time Kurt believed I loved Anneliese and couldn't wait to marry her. Kurt knew soldiers. He knew that as human beings, they were basically the same, regardless of the uniform they wore, or the politics they followed. If that is what he thought, I couldn't fault him. He was not there to observe me at that first precious moment I saw Anneliese, and fell instantly in love with her. Had he been, he would have had no qualms about his family entrusting his sister to me.

Episode Thirty Two

In which I arrange with some of my Military Government buddies for the well being of Anneliese and her family while I'm in the States, by setting up a program to have mail and food parcels delivered to her.

Anneliese was now safely home with her mother and two siblings, all praying for the safe and early return of Vater from whatever place he had been taken by the French. The Winter of 1945 and the Spring of 1946 were to be bad times. For one thing, the weather, never very good in those seasons, would be unusually bad. Extremely cold. The last stages of the war having been fought on German soil the planting of crops, and the harvesting of whatever was there, was very limited. As a consequence, at war's end, everything edible, and cooking/heating supplies, such as coal, charcoal and wood, were in short supply. The United States and Great Britain were not yet geared up to help the German populace. The Russians and the French showed no intention to aid their conquered enemy. Black marketeering was rampant. The four Allied occupying powers had declared the German Mark non-legal tender, and each issued its own occupation scrip, which few merchants or farmers would willingly accept. Instead, in 1945 and 1946, and even into 1947, the average German engaged in commerce through barter. Modern wars bring back ancient ways to do business. This is illustrated in the manner in which I "purchased" a painting. The place was Heidenheim.

The focal point in Heidenheim, in the center of the city, on a low hill, is Schloss Hellenstein, a small but picturesque castle, several hundred years old. Visiting an outdoor art show in Heidenheim, Anneliese and I saw a watercolor of the castle to which both of us took a fancy. Thinking of the home we would one day have, we wanted that painting to grace our walls as a pictorial reminder of the place we had met. I asked the artist how much he wanted for his work. He said he wanted no money, *"Nur eine Stange Zigaretten"*, only a stick/carton of 10 packs of cigarettes. I've already related that the painting, which hangs to this day in our dining room, was bought for the carton of cigarettes that the artist wanted.

Now, would the *Maler*, the painter, a smoker, smoke the cigarettes? The cigarettes were money. How often, if ever, does a person want to see his money go up in smoke? Infrequently, at best. I would guess the painter might smoke a pack or two, but trade the rest away for food, clothing, painting supplies, and shelter. An unopened pack would go from hand to hand, in a barter system, until it ended up in the hands of a black marketeer who could "afford" to put the contents of the pack to their intended purpose, *i.e.*, to smoke them.

The house on Bürkstrasse, in which the Baur family lived, had neither central heating nor cooling. But it did have a deep cellar, with much storage space cut into the thick white plastered walls, and cold all year round. An excellent place to store foodstuffs, both fresh and canned. The day I was there Anneliese gave me a "tour" of the house, from *der Keller*, the cellar, to the bedroom on the second floor. In Germany this level is called *Der Erster Stock*, the first floor. What we generally call the First floor, the Germans call *Das Erdgeschoss*, the Ground floor. I have put quotation marks around the word tour, since the word is much grander than the house. Size may be a factor in making a house valuable. But size is not a factor in turning a house into a loving home. And that's what the Baur Family had done. I was pleased to see the cellar. It fit into my plan to communicate with Anneliese, and to provide food stuffs and other necessities to Anneliese and her family during my absence in the States, and before I could return to take her home with me to America.

Both of us assumed that this plan would be short lived. Based upon information I had been given, we expected that it would be easy for me to sign up in the States for a job which would return me quickly to Germany as a civilian employee in Military

Government. In short, go home, get your Honorable Discharge, get your civilian job and return to Germany and Anneliese. So simple. Unfortunately, that information proved erroneous. When I got to the States I was told I should have been hired in Germany as a civilian employee in Military Government! It would take me 10 months to get a government job, which would permit me, as a civilian, to return to Occupied Germany. Neither Anneliese nor I had anticipated I would be away that long. Thus, this plan, which she and I had set up as a "bridging of the gap" type of thing, became a vital factor in keeping her and her family well fed, and both of us in reasonably good spirits considering that our separation grew longer than anticipated.

Why would it be necessary to set up an elaborate program in order to engage in correspondence, and to ship gift parcels from the USA to Germany? Simply because Germany, at war's end ceased to exist as a sovereign state. The four victorious Allied powers were now engaged in the early stages of their four zoned occupation of Germany. Thus, the customary mail and parcel services between sovereign states did not then exist between Germany and other countries. From the end of the war in Europe in May 1945 until at least mid 1947, mail and parcel services in Germany were administered through the four military zones of occupation. Military censorship of mail and parcels was in force. After the first year or so of the Occupation German civilians were able to send and receive mail and parcels from abroad. Even were the bulk of censored letters ultimately received by the addressees, the same could not be said for parcels, particularly when the mass of Germans were short of such basic foodstuffs as flour, cooking oil, and sugar, and when such simple items as yarn and thread for mending threadbare clothes were in short supply. Parcels sometimes seemed to be "misaddressed, and hence undeliverable", or some so poorly packed, as "to fall apart in transit." The plan I set up with Anneliese was designed to preclude the loss of letters and the disappearance of parcels. And it worked this way:

I had a buddy in the Military Government Team in Heidenheim who would be staying on there for a considerable period. For one thing, he had no combat points for an early discharge from the service, and for another, he had met a girl in Heidenheim, and he had no desire to leave Heidenheim any time soon. I arranged to send parcels and letters addressed to him. Aside from the addressee on the outer letter envelopes and parcel packaging, the contents were all for Anneliese. These were numbered. Until German civilian travel between Occupation Zones was permitted, and Anneliese could travel to Heidenheim to pick up the parcels and letters, my friend agreed to deliver them, on a weekly basis to Anneliese. He never breached his promise to me. The parcels and our respective Love letters were all subject to military censorship.

I was at home away from Anneliese from the beginning of November 1945 until I got back to Germany in the first week of September 1946—a long 10 months! During my stateside absence Anneliese and I wrote to each other several times a week. Each of us eagerly awaited word (and photos) from the other. Each of us recounted the numbers on the letters we received. Sometimes there would be time gaps of a week or more, and both of us would fret, and imagine all kinds of unpleasant happenings, and then I would receive a letter from Anneliese in which she would say she had just gotten letters 21, 22, 23 and 24, etc. Previously, she may have gotten No. 25. And I would recount the same turn of events. The letters we exchanged were old fashioned love letters. Initially, we wrote to each other in German. But as Anneliese's fluency in English grew, we wrote in English, or in a mix of both languages. Anneliese wrote, not only to me, but to my Mom and Dad. The only knowledge they had then of how wonderful Anneliese was had come from my lips. One could not fault them if they discounted much of my description of her many virtues. But once she began to write to them, in her warm, slightly stilted English—she had found an American born English language tutor who, before the war had married a German and was there throughout the war—they were quick to discover that she was indeed, a remarkable human being. I remember saying to my folks soon after returning home in November 1945 that if I was old enough to fight wars, I was old enough to know what was good for me, and Anneliese was not only good for me, finding her was the best thing that had ever happened to me! A week or so after bringing Anneliese to America in the first week of February 1947, and my folks had gotten to know her, one on one, they both came to me, separately, and said, "Arthur, Anneliese is too good for you." They were right. She was.

But back to the letters and parcels. Each of us, on our respective sides of the Atlantic, saved every letter received. Together they number more than 500. They were collected and placed in a box, and put away in a closet. During our wonderful 57 years together neither of us thought to get out that box and recall those 10 months of absence. We had each other, and all the love in those letters was paltry stuff to the love we were sharing each day and night. Times have changed. My beloved Anneliese has been taken from me. I am all alone in a physical sense. Emotionally, she is with me every minute of the day. Anneliese wished to be cremated, and I have her ashes at home. And every day, when the garden is blooming—and I call the garden, Anneliese's Garden—I pick fresh flowers to grace her photo and ashes, and when the garden flowers are gone in the late Fall and Winter, I buy fresh blooms for her. Anneliese loved to garden. And on Friday nights, before the Sabbath begins, I light the Sabbath candles and recite with her the blessing over the candles that she, as Mistress of the House, used to make, Now these love letters are the most vibrant link I have to Anneliese. But I could not get myself to look at them right after losing Anneliese.

Heidi is a very orderly person. She has assembled all the letters in numerical sequence, placed each one in a plastic envelope and made copies. I lost Anneliese on March 20, 2002.

In the late Summer of 2005 I felt strong enough to try to read some of these letters. I discussed this with Heidi. She agreed I could cope emotionally with reading them. For starters, she sent me six. Three written by Anneliese, two to me, one to my Mom and Dad, and three by me to Anneliese. When I read Anneliese's letters, two in German to me, and one in English to my folks, I was transported back to that ten months period between November 1945 and September 1946 when I was in the States and trying feverishly to get back to Germany and Anneliese. I cried when I read the letters, tears of joy and sadness ran down my cheeks. There she was, alive and vibrant on each handwritten page! In one of the letters her salutation was *"Geliebtes Herz!"* Beloved Heart! I cried to find myself so addressed! In another letter, this one also in German, she sets out examples of the English lessons she is getting from her American born tutor. She then contrasts these orderly lessons with those I held with her in my room in the villa my Military Government unit occupied. She says I must now be thinking of those lessons, and laughing in remembrance of them, since most were filled with kissing, caressing and joking, with English vocabulary and grammar banned to the background. Oh, how I remembered those sweet times when I read her observations. In another of the letters Anneliese describes the joy in her household when her father returns, uninjured, from his military imprisonment in France. That one was dated in February 1946. And so the exchange of these letters helped fill the void of ten months of separation. These letters sustained our spirits, but Anneliese and her family needed more than my words to survive. Sending parcels of food and other necessities was a chore I happily undertook. And although we in the States were a million times better off than most of the German civilian population, certain foodstuffs in the good old US of A were not easy to come by in 1946. In particular, "luxury items" such as olives stuffed with pimientos. I liked them, and thought Anneliese and her family would also enjoy them. And so, in almost each package I sent I enclosed a jar of pimiento filled olives. I must have sent about two dozen jars. I laugh as I write these lines. For when I returned to Germany in September 1946 I promptly traveled from Offenbach, the situs of my civilian job with Military Government (a city near Frankfurt/Main in Land Hessen) and went to Anneliese's home in Schwenningen. After the tears of a joyful reunion were quelled, I met Anneliese's father, Wilhelm. He had been a civilian prisoner in France when I was in Germany. I was warmly greeted by him. Then Anneliese took me down to the cellar to show me where she had stored the foodstuffs I had sent her. I recognized the contents of the last two parcels I sent. And I saw something else. There, in one of the storage areas built into the cellar wall, were bottles of olives stuffed with pimientos, all neatly lined up, three rows deep! What's this? I asked. Anneliese laughed. She told me no one in her family had a fondness for olives. They had never had them before the war, and Anneliese then recited the German saying, *"Was der Bauer nicht kennt, frisst er nicht."* What the farmer doesn't know he doesn't eat. I asked why she didn't tell me to stop sending them. She said she recognized they were a specialty thing, and surmised I had gone to some effort to buy them. So she didn't want to hurt my feelings by telling me not to send any more olives. Besides, she had tried to barter them away with neighbors, but no one was having any. We all laughed at her story. I took some back with me to Offenbach.

One more tale must be told to fill out this saga on how I provided for the well being of Anneliese and her family during my 10 months absence. Times in Germany were at their lowest ebb for the German population when I left for the States in early November 1945. Black marketing was an unpleasant fact of life then. And envy is a sin which becomes particularly prevalent in bad times when one person appears to have more, much more than another. I recognized that Anneliese would be receiving parcels of foodstuffs through my military buddy, arriving at her door in a US Army jeep. And the neighbors would see this. And I speculated that when German civilian travel restrictions were lifted, and Anneliese could travel to Heidenheim to pick up some parcels herself, that the neighbors would also see her coming home laden with packages. And so before I left for the States I had the sense to draft a letter, in French and in English, on my Heidenheim Military Government Letterhead, in which I stated that Frl. Anneliese Baur was my Fiancée, and that I would be sending her food and clothing parcels from the United States. My French was pretty good then. It is rusty now. Sure enough, the letter came into play. Sometime in the first weeks of February 1946, when the German Winter was most severe, and the hour close to midnight, a French officer, accompanied by two soldiers, knocked loudly on the front door of the Baur home, waking everyone. He demanded to search the house, and immediately headed for the cellar. What he saw there were numerous cans and jars of foodstuffs, all bearing USA brand labels. When Anneliese saw the French soldiers go down into the cellar she ran up to her room, found the letter I had drafted, and ran down and showed it to the French officer. Anneliese told me later that the officer read the letter several times, handed it back to her, smiled, and in German said to her, "*Sie sind kein Schwarzhändler.*" You are are no black marketeer. He wished everybody good night and left with his soldiers. That was a stressful incident for Anneliese and her family. Clearly, one or more of the neighbors, envious of the packages being received by the Baur family, had reported the Baurs to the French occupation forces as being engaged in black market activities. Fortunately, I had the foresight to anticipate the happening of such an event. I'm not always that swift.

I relate two more events which reflect the meanness in Germany of the Winter of 1945/46. And, as I have already noted, winters in Southern Germany consume the Spring. That's a long period of bitter cold. Hungry people, cold people, people without much hope to see their lives soon made better, tended to be short fused people, given to what we today would call trash talk, and to doing rash things. Thus, as the months rolled by, and I did not return, some of the women neighbors bluntly told Anneliese: Your *Ami* had his fun with you, but he's never coming back. Anneliese ignored them. She knew better. And then Anneliese told me of her father's experience concerning my relationship with her. Somehow the neighbors learned I was Jewish, and a woman neighbor, one who claimed to be a highly pious Lutheran, said to her father one day, *Herr Baur* how can you allow your daughter to marry not only an *Ami* but one who is also a Jew? Her father replied that he was pleased she was marrying a Jew. He hoped that his son, Kurt would marry a Catholic, and that Hilde would marry a Moslem! The lady never spoke to her father again. Which he did not mind. Kurt in fact married a Catholic. Hilde has never married.

And then in late Summer, something terrible happened which impacted upon Anneliese and me. At that time the mail situation between the USA and the American Zone of Occupation had begun to normalize. Letters and parcels from the States could be delivered directly into the American Zone. This lessened the need for my friend to maintain his steady courier service. Anneliese could travel by train to Heidenheim and come back with whatever was there, and then shortly after, US mail could be delivered into the French Zone.

I've been writing about the mundane matter of mail delivery to keep from writing what I must now relate. My friend had this German girl friend. I knew her. She was no Anneliese Baur. Indeed, light years away. But then, who could compare to Anneliese? My friend (I decline to name him) and she became lovers. When she inquired, quite properly, about the future of their relationship, he told her that he intended to marry her, that he couldn't do so in Germany because of the fraternization regulations then in force, that he would go home, get discharged and then come back and take her to the States for their wedding. She was happy. Then a few days before he was set to leave he told her he really didn't love her enough to marry her, and so he wouldn't be coming back for her. He told her he had enjoyed her company, that she was a nice person, but that was that. And it was for him. Somehow she got possession of an Army 45 caliber revolver and shot him dead the day after he had told her they had no future together. I do not know what thereafter happened to her, and I do not wish to know. A sorry end to a relationship which was never meant to be. The relationship between Anneliese and me was *beshert*, it was meant to be. Thank God!

Episode Thirty Three

In which I spend a heavenly, last night with Anneliese before leaving for the States.

    With two chess victories to his credit Kurt now recognized that the handicap of a lost limb did not lessen his ability to compete successfully in those contests where his mental agility was brought into play. His self esteem restored, so too, was harmony returned to the Baur household. Anneliese noted Kurt's improved demeanor. What had I done to bring this about? "Nothing, we just played two games of chess". "*Kurt war der Sieger. Er ist ein begabter Spieler.*" "Kurt was the winner. He's a gifted player." Anneliese was pleased I had helped to change Kurt's negative mood. The *Mittagsessen* (the midday meal), was on the table, Anneliese said, so let's sit down and enjoy with me my homecoming meal. Anneliese took my arm and we walked into the kitchen. She called out, "*Kurt, kommst du?*" "Kurt, are you coming?" He called back, "*Ja*". We could hear the rasping sounds of his artificial limb and his crutches as he made his way across the hardwood floors. *Mutter* sat at one end of the table. The rest of us sat around the table. Vater's place at the head of the table was left open for him. We all prayed silently that he might come home soon and safely. I enjoyed being in a family setting. It reminded me of home in Brooklyn.

    As the day waned, so did my spirits. I would be leaving tomorrow to return to Heidenheim, and from there to be shipped back to the States. I would be leaving my belóved Anneliese without knowing when I'd be rejoining her. I knew that Anneliese was having the same somber thoughts. We literally hung on to each other. *Mutter*, Hilde and Kurt could see our shared sadness. They left us to ourselves. Anneliese's bedroom was on the second floor. Actually, it was the attic which had been converted into a bedroom. It had grown colder outside. It was not much warmer inside. Anneliese, her Mother and her siblings were wearing sweaters. I had my long johns on, and never removed any part of my uniform until I got to bed. Where would I bed down? We were not in Heidenheim where Anneliese and I slept together. We were now in her home. What was the situation here? I did not want to leave without sharing my bed one more time with Anneliese. I needn't have worried. After sunset, the house was quite cold. Anneliese came to me and said, with a smile, *"Bubelein, lass' uns ins Bett gehen."* "Bubelein (My little boy, one of Anneliese's terms of endearment for me) let's go to bed." She had talked to *Mutter*—who knew from Anneliese's letters that we slept together in Heidenheim as if we were already husband and wife—and asked whether it would be all right with *Mutter* that we slept together in Anneliese's bedroom. *Mutter* respected Anneliese's judgment, and she had now met me, and liked what she saw. She recognized we were not having a transitory affair. Most patently her daughter loved me, and I loved her daughter. *Mutter* gave her permission. Like the two excited lovers that we were, we hurried up the stairs to the second floor to Anneliese's bedroom. I remember running my hand along the wall leading to her room. It was a plaster wall, and coated with frost! That's how cold it was. Once in bed the cold didn't matter anymore. We lay snug under the feather filled comforter. With lips ablaze, with arms and limbs entwined, we were two passionate beings lost in our own mad, wonderful world! We were storing up memories which would have to keep us warm through many months of absence. Sated, we slept, dreaming dreams of delight. The sun rose too soon and roused us. We lay, side by side, hands clasped, knowing that the time to say goodbye was drawing nigh. True it is, as the Bard proclaimed, parting *is* such sweet sorrow. That blissful period of five magical months together was coming to an end. Anneliese and I would share more than a half century of happiness. But nothing would ever equal the splendors of those first five months.

The moment which I had postponed so long had come. I was leaving Anneliese to go home. I was leaving that perfect being who, from the magical moment I first saw her, had become the cornerstone of my life. I was leaving her safely restored to her family, an island of decency within the whirling vortex of a broken country, no longer at war, but not yet at peace. This troubled me. Anneliese knew I would return. She had no qualms about that. But when? The absence of a date certain was a concern to both of us. But my primary concern before I left Anneliese was to make provision for her material well being, and that of her family, until I returned. And that, as noted, I had accomplished.

Anneliese and I came down stairs and found the family waiting for us to join them for *Frühstück*, breakfast. "Good-Mornings" were said. No one asked whether we had slept well. An innocent query ordinarily. However, under the present circumstances it could have been perceived as prying into an intimate relationship.

After breakfast, when *Mutter*, Hilde and Kurt had exchanged *Auf Wiedersehens* with me and had wished me "*Eine gute Reise nach Hause*", a good trip home, Anneliese walked with me to my jeep. We had kissed and hugged and cried inside the house. There would be no farewell scenes outside to titillate those curious neighbors. I climbed into my jeep, made a U turn in the street to head back to Heidenheim, waved, and called out to Anneliese, "*Ich liebe dich!*" I love you! The last image I would have of Anneliese, until I returned to her 10 months later, was seeing her dirndl clad figure grow ever smaller in the side view mirror of my jeep. The first phase of my new life with Anneliese had ended.

Sadness, last week October '45
Arthur is leaving for the States

Hier hast Du mich
in meinem
„Teddy - Bär"
Mantel!
Nun, wie
gefällt er Dir?

[Anneliese had made the coat from camel hair fabric
I had bought for her in Germany in 1945 before I left
for the States.]

"Here you have me in my Teddy Bear
Coat! Well, how do you like it?"
Anneliese, Schwenningen, Germany, January 1946

334

Anneliese, Schwenningen, Germany, January 1946

Episode Thirty Four

Home is the Trooper

God Bless America
God Bless America,
Land that I love.
Stand beside her, and guide her
Through the night with a light from above.
From the mountains, to the prairies,
To the oceans, white with foam
God Bless America, my home sweet home.

Irving Berlin

Episode Thirty Four

In which I come home, receive my Honorable Discharge, and despite contrary advice, tell Zaydeh, Grandpa the family patriarch, about Anneliese and our plans to marry, and that she would convert before marriage. Zaydeh listens intently, asks only whether we are really in love. Upon my affirmative emphatic answer Zaydeh says, "Git! We lost six million, now we get one back." Once Zaydeh spoke the issue was never raised again.

I cannot recall a thing about my journey from Germany to the States. Not even blurry images, the kind one sees when sitting at the window of an express train as it whizzes by a local station: *Rien. Nichts.* Nothing. My whole being was filled with visions of Anneliese—smiling and radiantly beautiful in a dirndl—and with longings for her burning in my groin. I just wanted to get home as quickly, and as uneventfully as possible, get my Honorable Discharge, say hello to my family and relatives, and promptly be on my way back to Germany and my Anneliese. As I have noted, it did not work out that way. I arrived home in Brooklyn, N.Y. in late November 1945. I did not get back to Germany until the first week of September 1946. Again, on the face of it, a negative happening, but in retrospect it was *beshert*, a passage of time during which events took place which made it so much easier for Anneliese to be welcomed warmly into our family circle when I brought her to her new homeland in February 1947.

I enlisted in the Cavalry, U.S. Army, November 16, 1942 and was Honorably Discharged on November 28, 1945. As I have earlier stated, this period was the most important in my life: everything which thereafter happened to me had its genesis in its three years' span. In June of '45 I had just turned 22. But my life began anew from that blessèd moment on the sixteenth of

June, '45 in Heidenheim, Germany, when I found Anneliese, my fairy princess!

I was welcomed home as a Hero! There was a sign at the entrance to the apartment house on New Lots Avenue, in East New York, Brooklyn, where my Mom and Dad, and my brother, Harold lived, and where I had been listening to a Sunday broadcast on December 7, 1942 of the New York Philharmonic when an excited announcer interrupted the broadcast to report that the Japanese had bombed Pearl Harbor in Hawaii, a place I did not know existed until then. The sign said: "Welcome Home Arthur! We are proud of you!

World War II was a "good war". It was fought for a purpose which we, the people, understood. And so the warm treatment accorded veterans of that war was wholly different from that given to veterans of the war in Vietnam. The people saw that war as being a needless war, and hence, a "bad war". Thus, the boys fighting in it bore the brunt of the public's displeasure, plus the trauma of guilt which haunted some because of their participation in the slaughter. We, the boys of WWII, that so-called "Greatest Generation", got love and kisses. *C'est la guerre. C'est la vie.*

That part of East New York in which my family lived was a neighborhood made up almost solely of Jews and Italians living harmoniously side by side. Indeed, until I was 12 or so, when my Dad decided to move the family to the Fort Hamilton area in the westernmost part of Brooklyn, an upscale, almost 100% Anglo neighborhood—bordering on The Narrows, the entrance to Upper New York Bay, and the gateway to Manhattan Island, the heart of New York City—I thought all the world was mostly Jews and Italians, with a few Poles and an occasional Negro wandering through. And so it was a great shock to hear people call me nasty names I had never heard before, and to chase me home from school amid shouts of Christ Killer! This reminds me of an episode which occurred in the high rise apartment house in which we lived on E. 96th Street. The structure was built as a quadrangle with an open courtyard in the center. Aside from us there were two other Jewish families in what must have been a 50 family apartment building. The wife of one of the Jewish tenants always meticulously prepared for the Friday night start of the Sabbath by cleaning her windows. Although she lived on an upper floor she would raise her windows, sit partially on the window sill, a dangerous feat I thought, and clean her windows, inside and out. One Friday afternoon when she was doing her window cleaning I heard a raucous woman's voice call out from a lower floor, "How come you're always cleaning your windows, you dirty Jew!" Not long after this event my Dad moved us back to East New York. Back home with Jews and Italians who never called each other nasty names.

Before I got home I had written my Mom and Dad quite a bit about Anneliese. I extolled her inner and outer beauty, and the photos I sent home confirmed the latter, knowing her personally would affirm the former. They knew she and I were deeply in love, that we would marry as soon as I could get her to the States, and that she would convert to Judaism before the marriage. They knew all this, but whether they were fully in accord with my views I was not sure. As was the custom when I grew up in Brooklyn, Jewish family groups tended to live in close proximity. Thus, living on New Lots Avenue we were but a few blocks removed from Ashford Street where my Zaydeh and Baba Katz, my father's, Mother and Father, lived with a number of their married daughters, and their families, in a two story row house—the house next door being occupied by a large Italian family. My maternal Grandfather and Grandmother Glicenstein, lived in their 2 story row house on Vermont Street, about a mile away from our New Lots Avenue apartment house. My father was one of six. My mother was the oldest of seven, five girls, two boys. The Glicenstein children, all of whom were married when I enlisted, lived with their families in the surrounding neighborhoods. On Shabbat, and special occasions such as Jewish Holidays and birthdays, we would visit Grandma's house, or Baba's house, (Baba being the Yiddish for Grandma). No one ever visited Grandpa's house or Zaydeh's house

(Zaydeh being Yiddish for Grandpa). Nor, as I later learned, do any other ethnic groups visit anywhere but Grandma's house. Clearly, it's the women who make a house a home. Indeed, in Jewish mysticism, the Kabbalah, it is noted that the wife is the foundation of a man's house, in that it is by virtue of her presence that the Divine Presence does not leave the house. Thus, when I came home I was surrounded by *Mishpacha*, immediate family and *Machatunim*, relatives, close and distant. They had learned from my Mother about Anneliese and me. They all said to me, "Don't tell Zaydeh." (My Grandpa Glicenstein had passed away a few months before I came home). Both sets of Grandparents were Orthodox Jews, they kept kosher homes and observed the Sabbath and all the Jewish Holidays. Indeed, my Grandpa Katz built his own *Beit Knesseth*, his own Synagogue in the basement of his house. Orthodox Jews, (as do the Muslims), segregate the men from the women in prayer. The men prayed in the front portion of Zaydeh Katz's Shul (Yiddish for Synagogue). The women, concealed from the men by a curtain, prayed in the back. Orthodox Jews did not mix the sexes in prayer, lest the mens' attention to prayers would be distracted by their physical proximity to women whose beauty would turn their thoughts from matters spiritual to matters carnal. In this same vein, Orthodox women never allowed men, other than their husbands, to see their flowing tresses. These were concealed beneath wigs, called *shetels* in Yiddish. However, some of these wigs were so stylishly coiffed as to defeat the purpose for which they were purportedly intended—not to look attractive to another man.

My aunts, uncles and cousins had all counseled me not to tell Zaydeh because they felt his response would be negative, and I would be hurt by his reaction. After all, I was going to tell him that I was going with a non-Jewish girl, that I proposed to marry her, and worse yet, she was a German! My Mom and Dad did not press me to tell or not to tell. I was a big boy. I'd do what I had to do. So I said to my well meaning *Machatunim*, my relatives. "I will not live a lie. I will tell Zaydeh." And I did. I went to him and told him about Anneliese, how I met her, that she was not Jewish, that she was a German, but not a Nazi, that she had worked for the American Army, I showed him her picture, that she would convert to Judaism before we married, and—I was becoming quite animated—Zaydeh cut me short. In his Russian accented English he said to me, "*Alter*", my Yiddish name, "Do you love her?" "Of course", I answered. "Does she love you?" "Of course, she does, Zaydeh". "Git", he said, Yiddish for good, and he smiled. He took my two hands and cupped them in his and said, in English, "We lost six million. Now we will get one back." I threw my arms around him. I had never done that before. I thanked him profusely. He waved his hand indicating the matter was finished. He was a small man, about 5'4". But he was a big hearted man, a wise man. He knew the power of Love. I was elated! Once all circles in the family knew what Zaydeh had said no one ever raised the issue again in my presence, or said anything more to me. Zaydeh had spoken, there was nothing more to say. Speech was out, but other avenues were still open, perhaps, to make me change my mind. And that's when a strange series of events began to unfold—although when they were taking place they did not seem unusual.

I had been home about a week, and had talked with Zaydeh, I had begun to write my letters to Anneliese, and to put together the first food parcels to her, each letter and parcel numbered in conformity with the program we had set up. I told Anneliese of the arrangements I had made to return to Brooklyn College to take the few courses needed to graduate with a Bachelor of Arts degree, that I required such a degree to be eligible to enter a first class law school, that I had begun to visit the various governmental employment agencies to see what job I could find which would get me speedily back to her. So my days were spent scurrying about doing different chores, but always with *das selbe Ziel*, the same goal: to return quickly to Anneliese. Side by side with her, or away from her, my life now revolved about her.

Suddenly, my routine began to be interrupted by different young ladies, who always seemed to be casually passing through the neighborhood, and, having heard I was home, thought they'd drop in to say hello and inquire how civilian life was treating me. Each of these women was Jewish. Some I knew when they were in High School with me, some were College classmates, others were neighborhood girls. I had considered them friends, young, bright, pretty women to banter with. I had never thought of any of them as "girl friends" in the amorous sense. There was a whole slew of them. They all told me how great I looked. They all asked what they could do to make me feel at home again and forget the war. One or two almost fawned on me. I got the impression they would welcome any advances I might make. I was tempted. With Anneliese I had discovered the elixir of love, and how intoxicating it was, and now, home, alone, I thirsted for it. These young women, so available, aroused my libido. I was being tested. What I felt with each of them was lust. There was not a spark of love. I was being tested, and I passed the test. I told each one that I admired her, that had I not already found the woman I would marry, I would have liked getting to know her better. I told them about Anneliese. Showed them her photos. So, please, girls, don't make my absence from Anneliese more painful than it already is! They understood, and went their separate ways.

I then pondered, how did all these women descend upon me en masse? I thought I knew the answer. I said to my Mother, "Mom, how come just about every Jewish girl I ever knew has visited me these past few days?" My Mom laughed and acknowledged she had "arranged" for each of them to come by and say hello. My Mom was pretty sure from what I had told her, that Anneliese loved me, and that my love for her was real, but what's the harm in finding out if it was? What's the harm? Surely, that's the least a Jewish Mother should do, isn't it?

Episode Thirty Five:

Two Hearts Apart—Too Long

Languir per una bella
e star lontan da quella,
è il piu crudel tormento,
che provar possa un cor.
Forse verrà il momento:
ma non spero ancor.

Longing for a beautiful woman
and being far from her,
is the cruelest torment
a heart can bear.
Perhaps the time will come:
but I have no hope as yet.

Giachino Rossini, L'Italiana in Algeri, Atto. I,
Scena 3 (Lindoro's Aria)
(English translation, Arthur Stanley Katz)

Episode Thirty Five

In which I find I cannot return promptly to Germany. Instead it takes ten months during which two love sick people exchange hundreds of love letters.

In November 1945 when I left Germany for the States I had every expectation that I would speedily find a job which would send me back to Germany, at U.S. Government expense, to work as a civilian employee in the U.S. Military Government. And once back in Germany I presumed it would not take me long to prepare the governmental documents needed to obtain approval from the four occupying powers for Anneliese to leave Germany—and in the case of the United States—for her to receive a visa to enter the States, especially when I intended to cut the red tape by "walking" these documents through the appropriate governmental agencies. I figured that within six months, at the most, I would have accomplished everything, and Anneliese and I would be in Brooklyn in time for a big Jewish wedding in June 1946. But it was not to be, as I, in my mind's eye, and in my heart, had projected. As Robert Burns noted in his poem, "To a Mouse, On Turning Her Up In Her Nest with the Plough.":

> But, Mousie, thou art no thy lane,
> In proving foresight may be vain;
> The best-laid schemes o' mice an' men
>> Gang aft agley,
> An' lea'e us nought but grief an' pain,
>> For promis'd joy!

Our promis'd joy was postponed, but ultimately, all worked out, as the reader shall learn—except that Anneliese and I never had that big Jewish wedding in June 1946. A small Jewish wedding in February 1947 had to do, and well it did.

After ten agonizing months of separation I had the job which sent me back to Germany and Anneliese the first week of September 1946. Day after disappointing day I would visit the governmental employment agencies looking for an offer of civilian employment in Germany. It never occurred to me to contact my Congressman, or my Senators, to solicit their help in my job quest. Perhaps they could have gotten me back to Germany sooner. I used this futile quest period to engage in some rewarding activities. I returned to Brooklyn College to complete the Senior year of schooling I needed to earn my B.A. Degree, and I shopped for food and other necessities to be shipped to Anneliese, and engaged with zeal in an exchange of letters with her. Each of our letters was numbered so that we could tell whether what each of us sent was received. Anneliese and I exchanged several hundred letters in the course of our ten months separation. Reading them now, through teary eyes, past recollections recorded spring to life. These letters, all handwritten, some in German, some in English, some a mixture of both, were letters of Love. They mirrored the emotions, the mutual longings, the desires unfulfilled, which separation—with no time certain of reunion—imposed upon the distant lovers. But these letters were always chronicles of hope. During our separation we exchanged hundreds of them. Each contained *die Hoffnung, HaTikvah*, The Hope that we'd soon be together again. Love letters by reason of their intimacy, are perhaps, the most revealing expression of the writer's persona. A small portion of this exchange is set out in chronological order, and in two sections, one containing the exchange between Anneliese and me, the other, letters between Anneliese and my parents. Love letters between Anneliese and my Mom and Dad? Indeed! When one reads the few enclosed, one will see the growth of the loving bond which quickly developed between them. Anneliese's grace and warmth, and need for their love and understanding, are quickly recognized by my Mom and Dad—and sweetly given. Long before they met her, Anneliese had captured their hearts, as she had captured mine. God has blessed me with a loving wife and loving parents. I have translated into English those letters written in German. It is one thing, however, to see the reproduction of a letter, expecially one in translation. It is quite another experience, and a moving one, to see the handwritten text of the same letter in its original tongue. Hence, at the end of this Episode the reader will find photographs of the complete texts of selected letters as written in their original language. Some, especially those penned by Anneliese, contain delightful drawings. One of her many gifts. I begin with a selection of those written between Anneliese and my Mom and Dad, for these address the issue which most distressed my parents: that their son had fallen in love with a non-Jewish girl, and a German, to boot, and intended to marry her.

The letter which follows was written in Heidenheim by Anneliese to my folks about two months before I left for home to get my Honorable Discharge, and then, as expected, to return promptly to Germany and Anneliese. It was the first she would write to them.

16 Sept. 1945

Dear Mr. and Mrs. Katz!

Arthur has asked me to write you a few words in English. Arthur has told me how unhappy you have been over the news that we are to marry. I am sorry if I have made you unhappy. But you must believe me, when I say that everything will be all right! And I love Arthur so so very much, please, love you me a little!

Anneliese wrote the balance of her letter in German.

Before I translate the German language portions from Anneliese's letter, and from others I shall set down, including those from letters of mine, let me say something about translations. Translation is both a skill and an art. The skill turns on knowing such things as the grammar, vocabulary and syntax of the language of the original work, and of the language into which it is being recast. Translation is an art when it captures, in the translation, the intangible qualities of the original work—its essence, its flavor, its "specialness"—so that the translation fairly represents what the author of the original writing said, and his/her special way of saying it. A difficult thing to do successfully. Anneliese's letters to me, and mine to her, were not intended to be literary works, or indeed, to be read by anyone other than the two of us. They were Love Letters! Spontaneous writings, written in the heat of emotion—where the heart, rather than the head—controlled the pen. Letters of Lovers separated too soon, and already far too long. Letter of Lovers longing to be swiftly reunited. Letters which kept hope burning in our breasts through ten long months of uncertainty and separation. These letters are not literary works, but they deserve to be translated faithfully, so that the sparkle one finds in the original—more so in Anneliese's letters than in mine—is not lost in translation. I trust I shall succeed.

Herewith, the English translation of the German portions of Anneliese's 16 September 1945 letter to my parents:

I know that what the world says about us Germans is very bad; but isn't it enough, that in all these past years we suffered under the Nazi regime? Does this hatred go on and on? Surely there are good and evil persons in every People, please believe this too about us Germans. And soon, when Arthur comes home, he will tell you so much about me, I hope you will be pleased with me.

My love for Arthur is something holy, the entire substance of my life. And we are both so happy with each other. Please, please, do not destroy our happiness, and when I later come to you, please have just a little bit of love for me, so that it will not be too hard for me at the very beginning.

I am diligently studying English, my Bubelein helps me nicely with my studies.

I understand quite well that Arthur's resolve to marry a German girl is strange to you in that the Nazis were so horrible to the Jews. But please believe me, most of us did not know, or even suspect the happening of such horrible things.

And when two people really love each other and are happy, religion ought not be a wall. All of us believe in one God, we are his creatures, and we all have the same right to live.

> *Love, affectionate Greetings from your Anneliese*

Anneliese's warm, yet forthright letter immediately endeared her to my Mom and Dad, as it confirmed, in her words, what I had written to them about her goodness and intelligence. My Mom, a highly literate person, fond of reading and creative writing, and for the most part self taught—as the oldest in a Jewish family of seven, she was put to work at age fourteen, and thus never able to attend high school (although later in life she secured her Equivalency Diploma)—was soon engaged in exchanging letters with Anneliese. Here are excerpts from one written to Anneliese just a few weeks before I left Germany for the States.

Sat Oct 27,/45

Dearest Anneliese,

It was a pleasure to receive another one of your sweet sincere letters, in fine German and good English considering that you are a beginner. You certainly can be proud.

I am enclosing a gift handkerchief for you. Some friend gave me a few, and I wish you to have one. It came from Switzerland and I know you will like it. I do also hope you received the earrings in a letter I sent to Arthur, and in due time you will also get the other stockings and hankies.

Let me thank you, for the understanding you have about Arthur coming home first . . . I know if one loves, this will be a trying time and a lonesome one, but there will be a pot of gold at the end of the rainbow.

His father has much in the way of business waiting for him which will help you both to live in comfort and in America, the land I know you will love. Germany has been and will be again a land of culture and harmony, too. I regret that I can't write German to you, although I can speak it sufficiently to be understood, when you get here.

Herr Katz and I "Kusse die Handt" [Yiddish for "Kiss your hand"] *and we say affectionately good night to you and to your warm heart.*

Love
Mother Katz

In a letter dated Saturday, December 8, 1945, my Mother explains to Anneliese why she hasn't sooner answered those letters earlier received from her. The reason is set forth in the first sentence of my Mom's letter:

My dearest Anneliese,

Forgive me, if I haven't written any sooner, but I was expecting Arthur to come home, and now that he did, the time just flies.

[My Mom then explains that I didn't come in as expected, and that she and Dad ate the big turkey she had prepared "all week"]. I now set forth further excerpts from her letter to Anneliese:

Then, when I knew to the day that he was coming, I stayed home, so when the telephone rang, I would be there. Well, it did on Sat, Nov 24 at 7 o'clock.

"Hello, Mom, this is Arthur", he said. You can imagine my joy at hearing him after 2 years. It seems he was gone 3 years, because I only saw him a few times the first year, while in training.

He called me again the next day, then said he will let me know, next when he'll come home after being discharged.

Wednesday, I baked pies, & cakes, & in fact I've been busy for days, getting in the food he likes, in cans, jars and bottles.

While I was stuffing a chicken about 6 o'clock, at night, the phone rang again, and Arthur says "Hello, Mom, I'm at Grandpa Katz's house, come and take me home because it is raining & I can't see the way by night, with my heavy pack on my back, in the dark."

You see we had moved, while he was away, so he didn't remember the vicinity, although it is near enough our old house & near to his grandparents. I dropped everything and ran & he seemed so tall and handsome, when I opened the door, & looked so good with the pipe in his mouth.

His grandparents were overjoyed, as they are very aged and always prayed God, to live to see him and all of their grandchildren home from the wars. Then his father, who was called from the office came in too, and more hugging and kissing was going on. We drove him in our car, to see my parents, his other grandparents, too. Again, the same happiness in reunion.

Since then, a few times each week in the evening, I'm having a few friends and family to meet Arthur quietly. He doesn't like too much crowds and noise, you should know that.

Of course, you know his Uncle Sid, well that made Arthur's home coming easier and pleasanter, because they both have memories of you.

Arthur is not very happy, because he has left you behind, in that upset world and that you have been ill in the hospital and lonesome, too.

I try to do the little things for him, he goes to shop for clothes & things for himself & also for you. He is making many packages, and I do hope they reach you.

Please God, a way be found, wherein he can go to you or get to you, to fetch you over and be married, real soon.

I thank you very much for allowing him to come home to see us. It was a fine and noble thing to do; because you loved him so much and wanted to make him happy.

I'm sure by doing that, only good will come and must come from it . . . .

I do hope all the letters reach you.

Do write me a letter as I am anxious to hear from you and I hope you will enjoy this letter to you of Arthur's home coming.

Give my husband's and my regards to your mother, father, sister and brother.

I love you, because Arthur does, and because you will someday be his, God willing, and mine.

Love,
Mother Katz Hilda

The letters between Anneliese and my folks flowed back and forth, not as great in number as those between Anneliese and me, but filled with the same love and warmth which suffused her letters to me. Here is a letter from my Mom to Anneliese and her family dated January 5, 1946:

It pleased me very much, that you sent me a lovely letter in answer to the one, I wrote you about New Year's time. You express yourself very well in English for the short time you have learned the language and when Arthur reads me your letters in the German language, you write like a story and your words are like a picture scene. You do speak "Hoch Deutsch!"

Arthur is sometimes hard to live with. He misses you very much, and although I am his mother and do all I can to make him comfortable, he is not always happy because you are not with him.

Only God and the healing of time can make this come sooner, for you both to be together. I will say as it is written in the Bible, "If it is of God, it will stand; if it is of man, it will fall."

Thank you for your sweet letter to Harold, who is expected home soon, this month, we hope, and also for your fine compliment to me and Arthur, in the pictures he sent to you. I am glad you think I look young. I try to feel and look well for my new daughter-in-laws, some day; America still is kinder to her people. The war did indeed add troubles to your mother and other mothers. May they now have peace forever.

Give my kindest respects to your dear parents, sister and brother. I hope God keeps him in a right way with his new problem. He is a fine looking young man. [My Mother is referring to Kurt, Anneliese's younger brother who lost a leg in the war]. *In fact all of your family is nice. I close with love to you.*

Mom

The letters kept flowing, from Anneliese, from my Mother, from me, sometimes with heart wrenching irregularity. Here is one, dated February 22, 1946 from Anneliese to my Mother illustrating the last point:

My dear Mom!

I have not got a letter from my Arthur for three weeks, his last letter was written 19th January.

Is Arthur ill or are some things not good? Please, please tell me! I am very sorry and unhappy, because I do not know is my sweet heart well, for he writes me very often to another time. What can I think?

I hope a new letter will come from him in the next days or perhaps, Arthur will come back very soon!

O, this would be the most beautiful day for me and for him too!!

Dear Mom, how are you and Dad? I wish I could be with you and with my sweet Bubelein, but I must wait!

All the many food which you have send is very useful and pleasant for me and my dear family we are always very thankful to you! I like the blue nice sweater and all the other things very much!

Yesterday and today winter is coming once more with a lot of snow 40-50 centimeters, but it will stay here only a short time.

My, dear Mom, please answer as soon as you can! I look forward to your letter!

A sweet kiss to you, and Dad and to my Bub!

Behüt Euch Gott! [God Protect You!]

Your Anne

26.2. 1946

*Today, I have received your dear letter, written at 30ᵗʰ January!
Very very much thank!! And with your letter it came four letters
from my Arthur with very nice pictures from him and his family!
O, I am so very happy now!!!*

*And our dear father is at home now! You can think how many
joy we do have now. Father is well, happy and glad!! And we
with him!!*

My love!
Your Anne

Letters cross each other, as did my Mom's of February 22 to
Anneliese:

My Dearest Anna and dear Family,

*It was a pleasure to receive your sweet, honest letter of January
17ᵗʰ. I shall try to write simple English to you, but as I am so
experienced in English* [my Mother was born in England] *I forget
and write hard words.*

*We, too, are having snow this week, but it may not be so cold as
in the Black Forest. I do hope, by now, you have more coal and
wood to keep your stove warm. Arthur and I pray that you do not
have too many hardships (trouble).*

[In a letter to me dated March 27, 1946, of which more below,
Anneliese tells me that the day before she and her Mother spent *den
ganzen Tag*, the whole day, in the forest gathering firewood, since
their supply of combustible materials was running out, with no new
allotment from the government in sight. She states the work made
her very tired, but in her customary upbeat manner states, "*Gott sei*

dank, wohnen wir ja in einer waldreichen Gegend!" Thank God
we live in a forest rich region! [That's my Anneliese!]

Back to my Mom's letter to Anneliese of February 22, 1946:

*We are looking forward to our Harold's coming home, any day
now, and I can imagine, how you all must feel about your "Vatti".*
[Mom had not yet received Anneliese's letter telling of her Father's
return home on February 25].

. . . *He* [Arthur] *goes to school and studies very hard,* [I was
finishing my Senior year at Brooklyn College which I had left
to enlist in the Cavalry] *but always has time to write to you and
your family. He wishes you were here. God will solve that problem
soon, too.*

*He looks better now, and is more quiet in temper since he goes
to school. He is always anxious to join you.*

We are all happy, you are well and learning English so quickly.

Give my dearest love to your brother sister and parents. [My Mother
then asks Anneliese for her recipes for *Kalbschnitzel* veal cutlets
and *Griess Pudding*, semolina pudding, which my Mom says I liked
the way Anneliese made them. In a letter dated the 17th of March,
1946, of which more below, Anneliese encloses these recipes].

"Eich Kusse die Handt." Yiddish for "I kiss your hands."

Love
Mom

Dad is always busy, so I write for him, too.

Der Briefwechsel, the exchange of letters between my
Mother and Anneliese continued apace. I shall set forth a few

more to demonstrate the ever closer ties being woven between my Mother and Dad and Anneliese before my belóved ever set foot on American soil. Anneliese's skill, already noted by my Mom—who knew good writing when she saw it—to delineate the beauties of nature in a few words, is evident in Anneliese's letter of March 28th 1946:

My dear parents!

Today it was a very very nice spring day, the sun so warm and the air so mild! I was out for a walk with my youngest cousin Ingrid who is nineteen months old. Yes, the nature [in German *die Natur*, hence Anneliese's use of the article "the" with the word "nature"] *is wonderful now!! The grass is nice green and on the meadows there are the first flowers and enjoy us with their beautiful shining colors! But it would be more beautiful if I could be with my dearest sweetest Arthur!! O, I miss him so very much!!*

Dear parents, how are you? And how is your Harold and my Bubelein? I hope you are well and I think you are glad and happy because your family is again together. We know it from ourselves since our dear father is again at home. He still is so merry and so full of humour as he was before he came at imprisonment. [Anneliese is referring to when he was rounded up off the street with other male civilians by the French at war's end in their search for "war criminals"]. *He works every day and my brother also will begin to work at his earlier business next week. Since he has his new foot the life* [in German *das Leben*] *is much easier for him and he has more pleasure than before. I could feel with him how hard it is for a young man.—*

Dear Mom, I thank you for your sweet letter which you sent me with Arthur's letter! I am so happy, that I can read and understand the most part of your letters! O yes, I also must learn very much, my teacher is exact because she wishes to teach me as much as possible! But this pronunciation!!! O it is very hard for me, sometimes I think I shall never be able to speak such komische [strange] words!!! Yet my teacher says I speak pretty well but I am not satisfied with myself! . . . .

If I have made too much mistakes please excuse me, in German I should be able to write a much better letter! Yet I hope my English letters will be better each time!!

I wish you merry Easter! Dear Mom and Dad a very sweet kiss and all my love!

> *Your thankful Anne.*
> *My family send its love!*

On May 1, 1946, while visiting Heidenheim, Anneliese wrote:

My dear Mother and Father!

Yesterday I recieved [Anneliese wrote the word correctly the first time then changed it] *two letters one from my Arthur and the other from you which you wrote in Ellenville!*

Indeed it is a pleasure to get a such nice letter and every time I can read and understand better what you wrote.

Arthur also told me, that you are in the country for some days that he and Harold are alone at home. He told too, that he is the cook now and the Griess-Pudding which he cooked was very fine! O, I know my Bubelein likes to eat good dishes! Yes, yes, "Die Liebe dess Mannes geht durch den Magen!" Perhaps translate: "The love of the man goes about the stomach!" Please don't laugh if I did not translate it well!! [My Mother had asked Anneliese

whether she was working. Anneliese replied she was working
at home helping her Mother] *Our mother is not more so young,
the care about my father and brother while of the war made her
much older than in a normal time. Yet we are so happy that our
family is perfect now. And so it is very fine when I can work at
home and my English lessons, my hand-works need very much
time too . . . .*

*You told me about your Passover—holidays and your Religious
custom. Of course I don't know so much about this, but I possess
my own bible, that was a gift to my confirmation and in the old
testament of the bible I can read very much about the Jewish
Religions. But I know that you will tell me very much when I
shall be with you!!*

*I will close this letter with many wishes and many (or much?)
Happieness (sic) for you and your dear family!*

*And a sweet kiss to my Bubelein! A sweet kiss to you Mom and
to Dad too!*

Your Anne

In a letter dated May 14, 1946 my Mother wrote to Anneliese:

*It was indeed a pleasure to get your latest letter of May with the "Sprig
of Lily of the Valley". It is my favorite flower. When Dad and I got
married, the flower girls and I, carried them to the "ceremony".*

*I also received your letters in answer to my Passover ones. As I had
been away to Boston, and when I came back, I found the house in
need of cleaning again. Three men are not too capable of doing
that as one woman; so time sped and no letters to you.* [My Mom
mentions that she flew, for the first time, in coming back from
Boston] . . . . *I was a bit frightened, but it was some experience and*

something to remember . . . . [Mom then predicts correctly, *Some day, soon, all will fly, as easily as riding on trains.* She became a great air traveler].

It is understood that you do have much work to do at home, and all together again, and if you have no need to work, outside for others, you do not have to . . . .

I suppose Arthur has told you, about returning to Germany, as a civilian employee of the U.S. Gov't. With all my heart, I hope all his desires are granted by God, and that you see him. I hope his plans in going there do not fail. [My Mother then writes that the United States had just celebrated Mother's Day, and explains the holiday, stating she was not sure whether Mother's Day was celebrated in Germany—which, of course, it is. She then writes:

I have tried out your "Calfs cutlets", and they are delicious, but Art says it is still not like yours. After all, I just follow directions & never saw it made or ate it. Your Farina Pudding is good too, but we are not used to it, yet.

I shall close now with lots of love to all.

Mom.

Herewith, in her letter of June 16, 1946 Anneliese clearly enunciates to my Mom and Dad her familial obligations to them and to me.

My dear Mom and Dad!

It is Sunday afternoon but the weather is too bad to go out for a walk. Sometimes rain, sometimes sunshine but nevertheless the wind is cool and so I prefer to stay at home any more.

I am in thoughts with my Bubelein and if I peruse his sweet letters I get much near with him. [Her English syntax is taken directly from the German].

A fortnight ago I received his latest letter, he wrote that he will be with me very soon! Of course you can imagine my very big joy! And now I am waiting with impatient heart and with all my warm love for my sweet darling!

No mail from him, no mail through my friend Kitty, what can I think? Perhaps Arthur will surprise me with his own person very soon!! O, this would be very fine!

Dear Mom and Dad I know how you will feel, if Arthur will leave you once again. Yes I feel how very sad you are, and therefore I have a big obligation for you and I will promise you only to bring happieness and joy for your Arthur.

Please Mom write me once again I look forward to your dear letter!

How is your Harold? Has he many school lessons? Give my warmest regard to him and tell him that I should be very happy if he would write to me once.

Behüt Euch Gott u. tausend liebe Grüsse! God protect you and a thousand loving greetings!

Your Anne

In this letter of July 19, 1946, the next to the last in this cross section of letters exchanged between Anneliese and my Mother, the reader will see why my Anneliese and my Mother related so well to each other: both were endowed by God with wisdom and compassion, and thus, the bond between them was much more than that of Mother-in-Law and Daughter-in-Law, it was more closely akin to Mother and Daughter in love with each other. God blessed me when he placed me within the embrace of these two beautiful women!

My Dearest Anne,

I have received a few of your letters recently, and had so many things to do, that the time just flew, to answer you.

My father became very sick last week [my Grandpa Glicenstein passed away shortly before Anneliese and I came to the States in February 1947. I loved him dearly]. *And Dad and I went on a trip to the Capital City of the U.S. Washington, D.C. You know that the Jewish People are fighting to get into Palestine, the Promised Land, and promised by England to be ours. Now we are having trouble again, so many Jewish people marched in the Capital Streets and came from all over the country to appeal to our Congressmen to get help from England. God help us to win as we need a home for those who want to go there.*

The time is drawing near when Arthur will come back to you.

I know you love him sincerely and I hope all of your family will too. He is my most cherished possession, (his brother too) and is gentle and delicate. Marriage is forever, and knowing that he is a Jew and an American and an Idealist, and you will have to live with him forever, and seeing all of these things and believing in him, may be very hard in your land but I have faith and trust in you and yours, to protect him from all harm.

Yes, we will miss him, but we know as soon as he can come back with you, you will.

See that he keeps the laws of the Army, and does not get into trouble when he wants to see you. He loves you so and is so impetuous (hot lover). [My Mother knew of the problems I had encountered in fighting arbitrary authority in the Service, and wanted Anneliese to watch over me, and counsel me in dealing with authority when back in Germany with her].

He has many a good plan for the future and may God Bless you both.

Harold is continuing with his school and hopes to go to a college in the middle of the U.S. about 1,500 miles from New York City. [University of Chicago]. *Again my house will be empty, but this time there is Peace, and we hope for long.*

Do not mind if I wrote this letter so long, and what I have said is from the bottom of my heart and Dad's. I know you will understand, as you both want, to be happy.

I shall close now with Love to you all from

Mother and Dad

The last letter in this section of communications between my Mother and Anneliese is out of sequence chronologically. It is dated April 19. 1946 and is from Anneliese. In it she notes that the American soldier that she and I were using to receive mail from both of us, at that time when international mail flow was restricted, was being restationed, and thus could no longer be a "mail agent" for us. This greatly disturbed me, particularly where parcels to Anneliese were concerned. Anneliese suggests several substitute ways the problem might be resolved. But her primary concern was the negative effect the matter was having on me. Thus, she writes:

Dear Mom, I know Arthur is very sad now, please give your motherly consolation and assistance to him! . . . . As much as I liked to read books, my thoughts are with my Arthur, my head aches when I go to bed in the night! But Mom, don't tell him what I write you because I will not [want] that he still is more sad!

This letter excerpt demonstrates the strength of the bond that their letter writing had created between them. It is one woman writing to another to ask her discrete help in comforting a man they both love very much. Oh! How I love them both!

I turn now to the letters exchanged between Anneliese and me. *"I am my beloved's, my beloved is mine . . . ."* לדודי ודודי לי אני (שיר השירים) 6:3, The Song of Songs). In the ten months we were apart, Anneliese and I wrote hundreds of letters to each other. They were intended as much to show our undying love, as to keep our spirits from flagging as the days of separation turned into weeks, and the weeks into months. Each letter (and each of the numerous food and clothing parcels I sent to Anneliese) was numbered, so that we could keep track on what arrived, and what might have gone astray—but hopefully, could yet arrive. All traveled a circuitous route to arrive at their destination—as related in the letters. Were this book sold as a collection of love letters, it would be a simple task to set the hundreds out in chronological order. I am faced however, with a different situation.[2]

Choosing which letters to include was not easy. This was not a case of gleaning the wheat from the chaff. There is no chaff. I was blessed with a multiplicity of riches—each of Anneliese's letters is a Jewel! How to share this treasure with my readers, knowing that her love letters—forget mine for the moment—are

---

2   This is a story of war becoming a story of love. Hence, a selection of letters is called for. The task of choosing was not easy.

a component, albeit perhaps the most compelling component in this book on War and the healing power of Love? Since this book is essentially an *hommagée a* Anneliese I thought it best to begin with letters, and excerpts, of letters written to me in February 1946, a month when almost four months of separation were taking their toll, when the embers of desire, too long unfulfilled, glowed red and then burst into flames which could sear even the strongest of hearts. These letters demonstrate that Anneliese's faith, hope, patience, goodness of soul and spirit, were sorely tested by my absence from her, with no assurance then of a date certain when I would be able to return to her, in light of U.S. policies which frowned upon fraternization with Germans, and barred marriage to them in Germany, and, were I able to return to Germany, made extremely difficult the obtaining of a visa for a German fiancée to enter the United States to marry her American fiancé. The reader will delight, perhaps with tear filled eyes, to see how my courageous Anneliese met and bested all these tests. In sustaining her spirits she helped sustain mine.

Dear reader, to better understand the import of these letters, let me put them in context. Arthur and Anneliese were not merely young virgin lovers who, together, had discovered the mystery of love, that miraculous merging of body and soul into an ecstasy defying fair description. They were not only lovers of diverse backgrounds drawn together because their coming together was *beshert*, was meant to be, they were now lovers widely separated in space, affected by, and for a time too long for them, kept apart by a war just ended which had left the world spinning erratically, with armed hostilities over, but hatreds not. Anneliese's letters, and others of hers beyond February 1946 (and mine), should be read in that light.

No. 33
2 February 1946

Schwenningen

Darling, Bub! [Anneliese's term of endearment for me]

*Greetings, my Love, here I am again!! Does that make you glad?
Yes? Good!*

Hale and hearty I arrived home this afternoon [from Heidenheim where God had led me to find Anneliese, in the American Occupation Zone, where our letters were sent and received, and my parcels for Anneliese, too. Schwenningen was in the French Zone, and at that time, there was no postal service directly from the USA] *heavily laden like dear Father Christmas! Hilde* [her younger sister] *had fortunately awaited me at the train station and was curious as to what would appear out of the large, heavy box.*

My loved ones were all very enthusiastic over all the grand things you sent me. Hilde couldn't admire enough the exquisite purse, the linens, and all the other things. Mother wishes with affection, to thank you and your parents for their love and kindness and yours.

My father was unfortunately not here as I had hoped, but to make up for that—there was a letter from him. He is now in an American camp, probably in the Marseilles area for some relaxation before he is released and can come home. Dad wrote that everything is going first rate for him, finest care, and when he is finally released he will be well fed. Isn't this joyful news?! Oh Bub, we will all be so very happy when our father is again with us!!

Two of your letters, Nos. 16 and 17 awaited me at home.

Your pictures Bubelein are very, very handsome, even if they are not especially clear, but I can easily recognize you, your loving face, oh Bubelein, you look as a civilian exactly as I thought you would! Oh Bub, when I see you in those pictures I have such great longing for you that I believe I simply can't bear it any longer without you! And yet, so must it be, I belong to you only in my thoughts, but later, oh sweetheart, when we shall be together again, I shall bestow upon you all the love I am able to give.

Only come soon, let our joint life begin shortly!!! I greatly hope that you will succeed in getting a position in the Military Government!

Oh, I pray to God that He will quickly send you to me!!!

Bub, your language exercises are very interesting and I follow them with great zeal! One can never learn enough. I find your German really very good, I thought you would lose it, now that you are where you hear only English, but wholly to the contrary, it becomes better in every letter, to my great astonishment! If I could only master the English language as you do the German! Still, what is nothing can yet become something! Tomorrow, straight away, I shall again study hard so that I can make up for last week's neglect . . .

Today, for the first time, I tried on the new pullover, it fits as if poured on me! Wholly first class!!! It's a shame you can't see me!

Love, next week I begin to sew the new white dress, what do you think if I embroidered it with red and blue yarn? Do you think it will be pretty? And would it please you? Do you like embroidered clothing? I also have thread and buttons to go with it, it should really be very pretty.

Bubelein, my good, loving darling, a thousand kisses for a good night!

Your Anne

I now set out a letter I wrote on the Ninth of February 1946 to Anneliese, a week after her letter to me of February 2 (which I had not yet received). Remember, dear reader, I'm setting out only a very few letters—or excerpts thereof—of the hundreds we exchanged during our ten month separation. Making the selection was difficult.

No. 30
9-2-46 Brooklyn

My sweet, dear Anne!

Do you know, Angel, what I like to do best when I am so very lonely? Yes, you've guessed it! When I am totally lonely, I must write you something, so that I can always be closer to you! Thank God! we are able to write to one another. This time of separation is bad enough, how would it be without our letters? I become fearful thinking of such things! Really!

It's a rainy afternoon—and I don't like a wet climate. My upper thigh hurts me a little, [as the reader will recall, I was wounded in the upper right thigh during the war] *and I begin to become a bit melancholy. I need you so very much!*

Let us both pray and hope we will quickly be together again!!

This morning I sent you a book of fairy tales by Oscar Wilde. The book contains the tale "The Happy Prince". You have asked

for *"The Valiant Prince"*. But the only *"Prince Tale"* that Wilde
has written is *"The Happy Prince"*. And so I believe that it is
what you want. It was difficult to find the book. But I found it
finally, and you will have it to read and enjoy, and that alone is
important!

And last week, I sent you a copy of our favorite song, *"Why do
I love you?"* Think of me when you read the beautiful words!
OK?

I hope you are beginning to receive some of the packages my
mother and I have sent to you. If you have received none, or
only one or two, by the time you receive this letter, then, Anne,
write to Capt. * * * and ask him whether it would be possible
for * * * to bring the packages to you. Or perhaps your Uncle
Arthur can go to Heidenheim for them?—in case the packages
are not left at Stuttgart as you had arranged. Or you can write
again to * * *. He is in love with a girl, too. And he knows what
it is for someone to worry about the health and welfare of his
sweetheart. I am sure, that if he can, he will help us as much
as possible.

What do you hear concerning your father's release? Does he
know about us, or have you withheld this news from him? I am
curious to hear his opinion concerning us!

I am listening to the opera, *"Tosca"* by Puccini, as I am writing
to you. I love to listen to music as I write or study. That is an
old habit that I have. The only time I do not particularly care to
listen to music, is when I am with you. Just looking at you puts
music into my heart and makes my whole being sing with joy!
Of course, when I write letters to you, I'm constantly thinking of
you—and then the music fades into the background as something
soft and pleasant, as soft as your white skin, and as pleasant
as your happy laughter! And as the music fades you begin to

live again for me! And before I know it—I'm back in our own, special world! A world that today is only a dream world—but a world that will someday live again for both of us—as we begin to live in it!

—Now don't forget "Luft Post Briefe sind am besten": Air mail letters are the best."

Deiner Bub,
Arthur

Ich liebe Dich!: I love you!

Excerpts from Anneliese's Letter No. 34, much of it written in English and dated 5 February 1946, are here set forth:

My darling!

Good evening my sweet Bubelein, how are you? I hope you are so well, as I am!

I think of you every day, in the morning, in the afternoon and in the night I dream from you! I can't think another thing, you live in my warm heart. I know you think so too!

Oh, I wish you were here so very much, but I must wait of that day which will bring you to me!!!

Darling, my Arthur, come back, come back soon, let us begin a new beautiful life, to be happy and glad!! Do you can work in the Mil. Government? Oh, this would be very fine! . . . .

This afternoon, while I have learnt my English, Hilde was reading a book, Mother was knitting and the radio have played a very good concert music.

Your new English-German Dictionary, which you have send me, is my best friend and help, but of course, you are my best, nearest friend too!!

Now I will show you what I have learnt today! Here a translation of the twelfth lesson of my English language—book: [In her letter Anneliese sets out two pages of her lessons, here are two examples]:

What will you buy from the draper?
Was willst du beim Tuchhändler kaufen?

I will buy ten yards of cloth and four yards of linen.
Ich will zehn Yards Tuch und vier Yards Leinen kaufen . . . .

Enough for today!

You see, I have much work to do, and I often wish you were close by and could help me . . . .

Darling, sweet Bub, I love you so very much and you know, I shall be always faithful to you!!! . . . .

Your happy Anne!

My love to your dear parents!

On the 8th of February 1946 Anneliese sent Letter No. 35 to me: Anneliese acknowledges that the mail would go faster were she back in Heidenheim, in the American Zone of Occupation, rather than in the French Zone. She is reluctant to leave her Mother alone until her Father returns, but: *if you absolutely require me to return to the American Zone I will do it!*

[Anneliese then says her English teacher is very satisfied with her progress, but she, Anneliese, see lots of difficulties ahead, she continues]

Dear good Darling!

Do you still have trouble with my letters? I hope that they all arrive very soon, and in good condition. You see, today I am sending the 35th since we began, thus I am wholly and completely not the guilty one if you get only a little mail!

Now, how is everything with you? Yes, I know you feel well and healthy, but so very alone!! Oh yes my Bubelein, I know, my heart cries for you, I would therefore give everything, sacrifice everything, if I could only be with you!!! Bub, your Anne is homesick, longing for your kisses, your hot, sweet untiring love. Hopefully I shall not have to wait much longer. "May be!"

. . . . Bub, darling, sweet Bubelein I am waiting for you, I am ready to bestow upon you everything which a loving wife is able to bestow!!! . . . .

[Then, writing of her English studies, Anneliese observes]: *See, Bub, you complain about the German language with its difficult complicated grammar, and I find the sentence structure in your language to be so peculiar! To say nothing of the pronunciation!!! I believe one day I will tear my tongue apart with the many "th, u, on, e", and so forth. These sounds are still unfamiliar to my speech organs which thus produce them imperfectly. Yet I hope, in time, this will improve.*

Later, when you are with me again, you must speak a lot of English with me, since one learns best through practical exercises!

After completion of this letter I shall again read your book "One God", each time I can understand more and more. And if strange words make difficulties for me, then your dictionary, my friend, is at hand.

I know Bub I must learn very much until I am what I want to be!! To be a wife to you who is not only loving and supportive in daily domestic concerns, but also a helper and comrade in intellectual matters, a wife who can share everything with you, your own personal interests, your attitude as it relates to people and the world! Yes Bub, now and again you will need to have some patience, but I know you love me very much, as I love you!!

Darling, come soon and everything will be fine!

Goodbye, sweet Bub, I love you so very much!

Your angel Anne

On the 17th of February 1946 Anneliese wrote letter 37 to me. She asked that I excuse her for not writing to me the week before, explaining she had visited for two days a cousin of her Mother's in Baden who had invited her, her sister Hilde and her aunt Martha, to an Hawaii Night party. (Baden borders Wuerttemberg on the west and is now joined with it as Land Wuerttemberg-Baden in the current German Federal Republic.) Anneliese writes it was a fun party. She describes in great detail her colorful Hawaiian costume, and that she wore earrings and even put on lipstick! However, she was greatly disappointed to find no mail from me upon her return, indeed 14 days having gone by without a letter. She continues, expressing great concern:

I am now quite anxious about you! Bub, has something happened to you, are you sick?? Tell me Bubelein, please please always write everything openly and honestly, I can bear the truth even when it often hurts, but such uncertainty, all this doubt and anxiety make me sick! I hope that a letter arrives from you shortly and everything will then be good again.

Bubelein, are you now going to school or do you have a prospect for a position in Germany? Always again the same worrisome question, how long must I wait for you?? Bub, please don't be angry with your impatient Anne, but sometimes it is so difficult to be without you, without your love, without your kisses, your loving truthful eyes! What is a picture, a thought for wonderful, sweet reality!! No! No!! Only a small poor substitute!

Oh, why then is the world so strange, so peculiar? Everything is wrongly arranged, what one has, is not the right thing, or good enough, and what one wishes for, what one desires is far, far away!! In an almost unreachable distance! Why, Why?! I believe the people themselves bear the greatest blame with their excessive desires, with their avarice!

Bubelein, sweet Love, I have always told you that to you alone do I belong, and the longer I am away from you, the more I know how very much I love you, how great my wish, my passionate longing to belong only to you!! If I can be with you now only in my thoughts, that day must yet come for both of us when we shall be united forever!!! And I believe in you, Bubelein, I believe in your trust, your honesty, in your great, great Love!!

Tell me Bubelein, are your dear parents satisfied with me? Oh, they will certainly love me, when they see for themselves, how happy I am making you!!

Write me soon, write often Bubelein, you know how much your Anne awaits your letters!

*I am sad, and yet so happy whenever I think of you, for I love you
so so much!! A thousand kisses!!*

Your Anne

On the 19th of February 1946 I wrote my Letter No. 36 to
Anneliese. It was a three page letter of which the first two thirds
were in German. And I begin by saying how unhappy I was because
three days had gone by without a letter from her. Her beautiful, loving
letters had become the mainstay of my existence! I had become
spoilt, Anneliese wrote with such Teutonic orderliness, that when
postal difficulties interfered with the timely arrival of her letters I
was much aggrieved. I knew it was not her fault, but whenever the
regularity of receipt of her letters was broken, so too was my heart,
as the reader will note when my German is translated.

Again I remind my dear readers that I am reproducing in this
book only a very, very small number of the hundreds of letters
Anneliese and I wrote to each other during our separation of ten
months. Herewith my Letter No. 36:

No. 36 My sweet, loving, dear Anne!

*A very unhappy man is writing this letter. Every evening I am a
little melancholy, but this evening I am definitely sad! It's been
only three days since I've received no mail from you. But the days
are so irksome without your loving letters! It makes no difference
how busy I may be, I can't really be happy. What I need so very
much I do not have!*

*Anne, I am working very hard in the University! It's not easy after
three and a half years to begin again. As a former soldier I attend
school "for free". The Government pays for everything, and I also
receive $65 support money per month (almost 650 Reichsmark).
Yes, I am clearly not in need concerning money. I have already
made clear my sole need!*

But I know, sweetheart, that when we are finally together, that these hours of separation, which appear to be filled with so much sadness and unhappy reality, will quickly vanish when we shall embrace each other, and the past will seem to have been only a bad dream!!! And the future will be a new life for us!!

Don't you believe that? YES □ NO □ (Like Hitler, I made the NO box very small!)

There are six or seven times more female students than male students here in my school. But do not be concerned! The more girls I see, the more do I heartily wish to have you again beside me.! I am working, and living, and studying so much until my head aches, and for only one thing: that I may return more quickly to you.

I know, too, Anne, that in winter it is always more difficult to bear the time of separation, than, for example, in summer. During the winter everything is so gray and cold and dark with deep shadows. But in summer the sun shines more, the grayness of the earth vanishes, and everywhere one sees only new life; trees show their fresh green leaves to the world, flowers blossom, older people find new strength, and those who are sad and lonesome find new Hope! I am anxiously awaiting the spring, and for the time when I can again embrace you, love you and kiss you.

Around my neck I am wearing your little heart, and in my heart, in my mind [Sinn] (or is it better to say in my thoughts) [Gedanken]?, I hold you fast! Wherever I go you go with me! You are always with me. And so must it be!

In the balance of the letter I shift to English and tell Anneliese about my German, Spanish and French language courses, and that my German professor told me: "For a man who hasn't been in school for 3½ years you have a remarkable

German vocabulary!" (For which I can thank my combat days and then the instruction from Anneliese.)

My Letter No. 37 was written over a two day span: February 20-21, '46. In it I mentioned, in the English portion, of returning to the Boy Scouts as an Assistant Scoutmaster, and I outline Scouting's program to Anneliese. I then tell her I had received her Letter 25 that morning and was . . . *especially happy because in it you said what I'd hoped you would say: "O ja, ich will Dir versprechen . . . ganz so zu leben, wie Du mich alles nach Deiner Art, nach Deinem Sinn lehren wirst!"* [Trans.]: *"Oh yes, I promise you . . . to live as you do, according to your ways, and what you will teach me!"* [Trans. End] I then tell Anneliese that my folks were very pleased to hear her words. I also tell Anneliese that theology means nothing to me, that there are numerous paths to the one God's Heaven. I then write:

. . . *Anne, I know it is very hard to be a Jew. But my People are truly an ancient People, and our history a long and full history. Yes, I am proud to be a Jew. And the man who hates a Jew just because he is a Jew is really sick! If we both could live happily without religion that would be wonderful! But if I have to choose, I take what I now have! I shall never change.*

I then tell Anneliese of a suit I bought, primarily for school, and what I paid for it. I tell her of the different parcels my Mom and I are sending her and her family. In an earlier letter Anneliese had written, worried that my folks might think she was *"ein armes würmchen"* a poor little worm. To which I replied:

You are my Bride, may I not send gifts to my Bride? Naturally, I am right! So say no more.

I then tell Anneliese that the U.S. Government had made it easier to send larger quantities of food parcels to Germany, and that the Postal service to Germany might improve in the next months. And I continue:

Oh, Angel, I miss you so much! My vocabulary will never be large enough for me to be able to really describe my love for you. But I know when I am with you again, that you shall read and understand the love in my eyes and burning face! And I can still see your wondrously beautiful eyes, they were like two brilliant, green, bottomless pools! . . . . Anne, Darling, I am always with you in spirit! "one with my Love"—always!!!—Anne, don't forget to take the vitamin tablets. That's very important! They will help you and your family to remain healthy! I love you so much!!

Give my regards to your parents.

Your Bub
Arthur

In the few letters set forth to this point the reader may have noted that Anneliese and I expressed more than the sensual longings of lovers too long separated. We also addressed issues less amorous, such as our religious, intellectual and artistic compatibilities, issues perhaps, too many lovers overlook in their heated passion. The reader may recall that in the summer of 1945, in Heidenheim, Germany, shortly after I had been led by providence to Anneliese, that consumed as we both were with love, issues of religion and the commonality of interests were discussed. We were, indeed, virginal young lovers, but we were also intellectually mature young adults. I have never asked myself how our relationship may have developed—if it developed at all—had Anneliese chosen not to convert to Judaism. But she chose freely to do so. Thank God! And without ever yielding up any part of her own considerable intellectual and artistic personality—or being asked to—she learned how to mesh hers with mine, and I, in turn, tried to emulate hers. And our letters—love letters though they be—reflect this beginning of a process, a magical process, in which our own unique bodies, souls and minds began, imperceptibly, to be woven into one greater united being. Thus, it was quite natural for Anneliese and me to write about these matters, even as dreams of ecstasies past, and of ecstasies yet to be, occupied much of our sleeping and waking hours. And, in so doing, Anneliese and I attained a rare commonality without losing our individuality.

My Letter No. 38, dated February 23, 1946 and Anneliese's No. 38 dated February 25, passed each other in the mail. I quote from Anneliese's first because it contained momentous *news.*

No. 38
25.2.1946

Schwenningen

Beloved Heart!

Today is a really big Holiday for us! Father has come back! Oh what joy for all of us! I'm sure you can imagine why. And Father is still as merry, as cheerful as he was before. He is also very healthy and looks well!

Father arrived here this morning at 6:30 a.m., since the whole house was still closed, he knocked on Mother's bedroom window and what joy for Mother to see Father outside!! Oh what happiness for all of us to be together again!

And today's work day became a Sunday.

And Father said nothing, as I told him my, that is, "our" story. He thought we were both old enough and smart enough to know what it means to build a life together! And Bub, Father is very pleased to get to know you personally! And hopefully soon!

And as a perfect ending to my Holiday, the Postman brought me three more letters from you!! Am I not an envy worthy, happy person? Yes, that I am, and so shall I always remain, since everyone who knows you has to envy me that I possess such a splendid, loving, manly fellow, such as you are!!! Yes, I am wholly earnest when I write to you, since everything I can wish for, everything I need, you bestow upon me, Happiness, Love and Trust!! Everything that makes a life worth living!

And you write so lovingly in your letters, including your English ones, these are naturally, still somewhat difficult to read. But then when I have read through each letter, sentence by sentence, I can understand everything, and I am pleased that I am always learning more and more of your mother tongue. But Bub, you must have some patience with me when I still make so many errors in my English letters. But you have always said to me, that one cannot learn without making mistakes. And I also agree with this point of view!

A thousand thanks for the photos, oh how dear you look in all of them! And so far out of reach! So far away! I am beginning to get jealous of all those people around you! No, how wicked of me! Forgive me, Bub!

. . . It's all the same to me where I live, as long as you are with me, my home is where you are, and even should you have selected the North Pole!! I follow you wherever you go!

I know, you will come back to me as soon as possible, I pray to God, that you shall soon succeed in finding an opportunity to return. Oh, I yearn for this day, for I love you so very, very much! And I shall be very happy with you!! Always and always!!

. . . . Your letters which came today bear Numbers 26+25+29. Some are always missing in between, but these can always still arrive. In the next few days I shall again make a visit to Heidenheim!

A thousand Greetings and kisses also from my "whole" family!

Your sweetheart

Anne

I believe this letter, and others I shall quote from, reveal a warm, loving, beautiful human being, wholly without guile. These intangible traits enveloped her with a grace, invisible to me, but which I sensed, the first moment I saw her. Clearly, the reason why I fell instantly in love with Anneliese!

That portion of Anneliese's letter in which she states she would follow me wherever I chose to go was preceded by her reference to the times I had suggested to her that since I was a risk taker we might consider living in places other than the States, such as in South America, Colombia or Chile, specifically. Her letter gives her resolute answer to my suggestion. But even more important to me was the way Anneliese's response mirrored that of Ruth, one of Israel's matriarchs (out of whose womb sprang the House of King David, and then Jesus).

The Book of Ruth in the Hebrew Bible recounts that Naomi, and her husband, Elimelech, with their two sons, left Bethlehem in Judah for Moab. There was famine in Judah, but not in Moab. In Moab each of Naomi's sons married a Moabite woman. One of the wives was called Orpah, the other, Ruth. Elimelech dies, as do the two sons. Naomi, bereft of family, other than her two widowed daughters-in-law, and having learned that the famine in Judah was over, decides to return home. Naomi counsels her daughters-in-law to go back to the house of their respective mothers, hopefully there to find new husbands, and not to follow Naomi as she returned to Judah. Orpah and Naomi decline to leave Naomi. Naomi persists in her counsel. Orpah then leaves, reluctantly. But Ruth refused to leave Naomi, and said to her:

"Entreat me not to leave thee; and to return from following after thee; for wither thou goest, I will go; and where thou lodgest, I will lodge; thy people shall be my people, and thy God, my God; where thou diest, will I die, and there will I be buried; the Lord do so to me, and more also, if aught but death part thee and me." Ruth 1:14-1:17

My belóved Anneliese was, and remains, my Ruth. Anneliese's love, like Ruth's, was unselfish and devoted. Where I ventured, Anneliese went; where I lived, she made our house a home of grace; my people became her people; and my God became her God. From this Earth did death part Anneliese from me. Yet her Love envelopes me daily, and sustains my body and my soul, as I await that bléssed day when Anneliese and I shall again be together, walking hand in hand, and rejoicing in each other through eternity.

On February 23, 1946 I wrote Letter No. 38 to Anneliese, again a mix of German and English. Incidentally, at that time my German syntax was quite poor:

My sweet love, dearest, exquisite Anne, etc!

It is Saturday afternoon, and I have just this moment finished my French and Spanish studies. And now I have time to write to you again!

Yesterday was a holiday, and naturally, the Post Office was closed. But today the Postman came again and brought two wonderful letters from my Darling! (Numbers 33 and 34, your first since your return from "the beautiful city of Heidenheim, which lies in the green Brenz Valley, with pretty girls and little Plum gardens everywhere"). Am I not really crazy? YES □ NO □ (Here is a bit of good advice for you, before you vote—a rumor is going about that your Bub is not really crazy, only that he is totally drunk [using two words to say the same thing] *from happiness and your sweet Love—and thus it would be better to vote "Yes".*

Yes, Darling, I am very happy today! I am happy that you are home again, that your Dad is again under American authority, and that what I sent pleases you and your family.

Anne, how much did you give away? I ask, because I can scarcely believe, that you put everything into one box. I trust you kept enough for your own use.

Today I bought more foodstuffs for you. I know how much you like grapefruit juice, and so I've bought another can—with other things. And today I also sent you six different newspapers together with a small package of rubber garters, among other things.—Yes, I was busy today, but I like doing many things for you. (I'm really a lazy Bub, now, to my regret, I have no time to be lazy!!) Am I not a poor thing?

I then tell Anneliese that I would be getting a military disability pension from the government, which was now low in amount, but which the government said would be increased once they had all my records. I also point out that as an honorably discharged veteran I get extra points when I take a government job test, which increases my chances of getting the job. Isn't that nice of the government! And then, with dark humor: And I must also be a bit thankful to the Wehrmacht they made it possible that I now get this disability pension. (But I'm making a joke now, war is dumb and terrible—as your own brother, for example, has experienced—but enough of such thoughts! Let's speak of nicer things.)

Yes, Anne, I find a white dress with beautiful embroidery very attractive. I am pleased you come to me for advice. Thank you.

And I am sending film to you so that I can see my Angel in her new Pullover. I hope it doesn't shrink too much when it is washed, and you know why! A man sees only one thing, or should I say, two things? when he see a pretty girl in a pullover. Isn't that right? And I am very jealous concerning my Anne! . . . When are you going [to Heidenheim] *for the other packages? I wish you to have enough in your cellar to open a grocery store! And excuse me when everything is almost the same. You know, I can't send any fresh things.*

My letter continues:

So you are surprised my German is getting better? Well, you shouldn't be, look at how much German I learn just from reading your letters! And then, I promised you that when I came back, I'd speak better than when I left. I intend to keep my promise. That is why I am studying so hard.

Your command of English is, of course, surprising and gratifying. I am very proud of you, as I've already said a million times. Why don't you also study French with Hilde? I think you can handle both languages at one time.

Ask Hilde whether she wants me to send anything special to her—and ask Kurt too, has he enough cigarettes, and does Mom need anything? Please let me know.

I send you all my happy thoughts, and all my desires for a quick reunion.

Your loving, devoted Bub,
Arthur

Sometime in early 1946 I began to incorporate the numbers of my letters into little drawings. Anneliese noted this and began to do the same thing, but with more artistry than I could command. Anneliese was gifted in drawing—among her many other abilities, which included being a professional chef and a skilled gardener—and her letter of February 24, 1946 (written one day before her letter announcing the return of her father, which letter I have already set out) demonstrates her talent. Anneliese's letter, written wholly in German, is unusual for several reasons, one, that it begins with a touching couplet by Schiller, and for others which I will discuss after the reader has read Anneliese's letter. All of Anneliese's letters touched me deeply, this one thrust its way deep into my heart—and soul. I cried when first I read it. I cry now, six decades later. Herewith Anneliese's letter:

Früchte reifen an die Sonne,
Menschen durch die Liebe!
(Schiller)

Fruits ripen in the Sun,
People through Love!

24. 2. 46

Dear good heart!

If I am not near you, I am, nevertheless, very close, in your heart, in your thoughts! And for your birthday this year, I wish you all love and good things, may this year bring only happiness and contentment, and a joyous reunion with your Anne who longingly waits for you!!!

Bubelein, yesterday three letters arrived from you and after three long yearning weeks of waiting your letters were a gift from Heaven for me! I was so concerned for you, I already thought you were ill, perhaps, and I so far away from you!! Oh, Bub, I know it is often very hard to be separated so long, and it is not easy for me, either. I feel I am no longer myself, my own being is melted together with yours, united, wholly your possession! If I have joy, so are you joyful with me; am I sad, so do you also share this with me!

Oh, it is a glorious feeling of blessed happiness to belong to such a loving person, with everything that a wife can give! And I belong to you! Bub, Love, do you hear? I am yours, and nothing in the world can rob me of this Love, come what may!! Always, always I will stand at your side, even when life exacts from us struggle and hardship! I will be your true comrade in the sunny days and dark days of life!! Bub, please believe in me, as I believe in you!! Don't cast me away, don't let go of me!!

Yes, Bub, I promise you to live wholly in accord with your religion, to become as you are in your heart! But you must help me, help me and have patience with your Anne! Do you hear?!

And come back to me soon, let us soon begin a life together!

I know it is not so simple for you to return to Germany, but perhaps you will succeed in obtaining a position in the Military Government, or has your application already come back unsuccessfully?

Bub, please don't trouble yourself so much about me, I am well, I am now working at home, and I am waiting for you, however long it may last! You ought not always have such crazy thoughts, seek some kind of diversion, I grant you some pleasure, I know for certain that you will nevertheless remain strong and brave, and true to both of us!! I have your heart, you cannot lose it to anyone else!!

I love you Bubelein, as only a loving wife is able to love!!

Deep, sweet kisses from
Your Anne!

Your letters are
Nos. 22, 23, 24
20+21 are still missing!

I believe the reader can sense in this letter Anneliese's strength, her sensitivity, her courage, her qualms—briefly expressed—her loyalty and her sense of humor: granting me the right to go out and have a good time, but to remain true to her and myself while doing so. My Anneliese was a remarkable human being, God's personal gift to me, and a blessing to me, our children and our families! *O Anneliese, Du bist schwer vermisst!!*

On February 28, 1946 Anneliese wrote her letter No. 39 from Heidenheim where she was visiting the Zeiner family with whom she had lodgings when working in Heidenheim, and where Anneliese and I spent many a glorious evening together. As the reader has learned, because of mail delivery problems in the French Zone of Occupation I was sending letters and packages to Anneliese via the good offices of my fellow soldier who was still in the Service in Heidenheim, and who, upon their receipt, would deliver them to the Zeiners, and there Anneliese would travel to fetch them. This system of delivery obtained until, many months later, U.S. mail could be delivered directly into the French Zone.

Anneliese's letter was a seven pager! written in her highly literate German, with words and idiomatic expressions which sent me frequently to my German dictionary. She was exceedingly happy for the letters and packages awaiting her, and for my good mood, as expressed in my letters. The excerpts which follow illustrate Anneliese's ebullience:

Nr. 39
Heidenheim 28. 2. 1946

My beloved Bubelein!
Here I am again for a few days as the guest of the Zeiner family!!

And what kinds of expensive things did I again find here from you!! Bub, you are spoiling me much too much!! Don't you agree?

Five loving sweet letters, Nos. 27, 28, 31, 32 + 33 welcomed me. And packages Nos. 15 through 19!! A thousand thousand thanks!!

And then those pretty pictures! Darling how dear and sweet you and your Mother look!! Your camel hair coat has turned out to be quite handsome! I hope that my coat will likewise please you. (I had obtained some camel hair fabric. I gave some of the cloth to Anneliese. We both made coats from the material. She made her own, I had mine tailored). Do you know which picture pleased me the most? The one on which you wrote on the back: "And here I'm studying the grounds for your use of different words. You know how curious I am."

Yes, I know how curious you are, and desirous of acquiring knowledge, you go directly to the basis of every thing. And I can perceive exactly from your mien and facial expression what you are thinking!

And Bub, your letters now sound so happy and joyful, I clearly sense that your heart is lighter, now that you are getting more mail from me. And I am very very happy about that!! You see, Bub, I'm writing to you often, are you now satisfied with your Anne?!! Yes, yes, I know . . . you think only the best of me.

And now to your packages! Bub you sent me such charming things!! Oh, beloved heart how can I thank you for them! With the

*wonderful wool you have made me especially joyful! You know
how much I like knitting. I'm going to knit a very pretty jacket
for myself, I have already selected the style from the Handwork
Book you enclosed!*

One of the packages contained cosmetics, lipstick, powder,
etc. Anneliese thanked me for my thoughtfulness but wrote: *You
surely know I don't like powder and make-up in daily life!* (As the
reader recalls, my description of Anneliese at that glorious moment
when I first I saw her, was that she had a radiant complexion
free of make-up. Sending her cosmetics, with that knowledge,
demonstrated my stupidity, like gilding the lily. Anneliese made
her views clearly known. And then, with her gift for resolving
differences, without there being winner or loser, suggested there
might be that exceptional occasion when a little bit of powder and
paint might not be too bad: *Aber es gibt auch mal ungewöhnliche
Tage, u. ein klein bisschen Puder oder Lippenrot ist ja dann nicht
so schlimm. Nicht wahr Bub?* Anneliese then asked whether I
had yet made a thorough inspection: *Generalbesichtigung* of my
Mother's sewing box to see if I could find things she needed, such
as colorful ribbons. Clearly, she didn't want me to buy sewing
materials, such as ribbons when there might be some at hand.

*The grand box of cream filled chocolates was an especially
enrapturing sight! It seemed almost wrong to eat them!!*

Anneliese then says she is sure I will not be angry with her
when, from time to time, she makes small gifts to others from what
she has received from me. She continues: *". . . from childhood
on I was raised to share fairly and make others joyful.* Anneliese
then tells me not to be concerned, they won't run short, that almost
everyday at home they eat something I had sent them, and that
they saved up a good portion of what I had sent them so that
Father, when he returned, could enjoy the delicious things I had
sent. She then says if I could only see Ingrid, her 19 months old

cousin, how she enjoyed getting a little chocolate or a cookie! Anneliese notes that for years children couldn't get good sweets. *Ingrid says in amusing childish speech: "Please, please, Annis, goodies—goodies" and I know exactly what the dear little person wishes!!*

Anneliese says that with the cigarettes and pipe tobacco I sent she will definitely please Father and Kurt. She closes with:

Well, until tomorrow my Love, when I shall write again!!! May God Protect You! A thousand ardent thanks, also to your loving parents.

In a P.S. Anneliese notes that a bra I had sent her was a tad too large, but that she was going to adjust it to fit. She hopes that packages 12 and 13 would yet arrive, and that they were not lying on the bottom of the ocean!

I trust the reader remembers that I am only setting out certain of the hundreds of letters Anneliese and I sent each other, and in some instances, only excerpts. Anneliese was my jewel, my precious possession, and just as the facets of a carefully cut flawless diamond reveal different beauties of the stone as light scintillates from their surfaces, so too, do Anneliese's letters—written without pretense, without guile, solely from the heart—disclose the many sparkling facets of her being. A trio of letters Anneliese wrote me in March 1946, just a few of many that month, should confirm to the reader the truthfulness of my statement.

Nr. 46
8 März 1946

Darling,

Please excuse me for not having written to you for two days, but despite that, I did think of you. And you surely know that!

But here I am again! Isn't that very pleasing? Really, truly,
positively, surely, clearly!!!! I know you are laughing when you
read these words, and think, as I do, of how much fun we had, and
how we were richly amused whenever we discovered new words!

Oh! How glorious that time was, sweet and precious! Didn't we
exploit it fully and well? I believe we shall now make more out of it, as
it is with everything, one first perceives the value of things when one
has lost them, or has been separated from them!! Don't you agree?

In referring to that glorious, sweet and precious time Anneliese
was recalling those five wonderful, heavenly months we spent
together after I was led to Heidenheim to find her there in June
1945.

But we will quickly make up for everything we missed as soon as
we are together again. And we'll laugh about the unnecessary
troubles we now have, and soon forget everything! Oh, it will be
wondrously beautiful!!!

But until that day we must be very patient, waiting and praying
for our happiness!

Anneliese then says her parents are pleased she is staying home
with them, and not returning to Heidenheim to facilitate receipt
of my letters and parcels—but she reaffirms her willingness
to return to Heidenheim if I insisted upon it—which I did not.
Anneliese then writes of her emotional ups and downs, the same
kind I experienced:

I also forget sometimes for a moment, and I am unburdened,
serene and merry, then in the next instant, upon thinking of you,

a little sadness, melancholy and longing mixes in. Everything would be so much grander and so much more satisfactory were I able to share this or that joy with you personally, and not only in letters!!

Anneliese then says I shouldn't worry about her well being, or that of her family. No one is going hungry. What I send her is a great help. And she notes that almost every morning she eats a bowl of hot oatmeal! And she is also faithfully taking the vitamins and mineral supplements I had sent her. *You can see for yourself from the photos that I am still the same Anne, your Anne!!!*

Anneliese then writes she went to the movies with Hilde. But the picture was not good, and had she known that beforehand, she would have stayed at home and worked on the knitting of her jacket. *You will scarcely believe what great joy you have given me with your wonderful wool!*

I'm so tired now and shall go directly to bed, alone, always alone, without my dear sweet Bub!! For how much longer?? Bubelein, your Anne caresses and kisses you. I love you!!!!

The second of the trio of March 1946 letters selected for the reader's perusal was Anneliese's No. 49, a two part missive dated 15. 3. and 16. 3, 1946. (Incidentally, the periods after the numbers 15, 16 and 3 are intended to be read in German as the *funfzehnten, sechszehnten, dritter*: fifteenth, sixteenth, third). I treasure all of Anneliese's letters. But this one is an especial favorite, for it shows Anneliese at her happiest, her love of nature, coupled with her ability to make this evident in a few well written sentences, and her keen sense of humor, with accompanying drawings:

Nr. 49
Schwenningen 15. 3. 1946

My Beloved Bubelein!

Darling here I am! Greetings! It is so nice this evening in my warm room while outside a fine drizzling rain is falling, and, thank God, is taking away the last remnants of the dirty snow! Yes, thank God, cold Winter is finally over, Spring must then surely be coming, and with it, sun, warm breezes, fragrant flowers, fresh greenery, and the glorious warbling of lively flocks of birds!! And if it is Spring, Summer will come to the land afterwards and perhaps my good sweet Bubelein too!

But now back to the present, since the chirping of the birds and the flowers are not yet here, but just thinking of fresh life makes the spirit freer, happier, and gives new courage and new hope!

Radio Station Voralberg is playing lovely merry folk music and I am so happy when I now think of you, thankful and happy that I have you, if now only in my thoughts and in my sweet dreams!!!

Und gell Bub Du machst Dir nun gar keine so grossen Sorgen mehr um mich, so lange ich gesund u. zufrieden zu hause bin, hast Du auch keinerlei Gründe dazu! Hörst!!

And Bub, its right that you don't worry so much about me now as long as I am healthy and content at home you have no reasons at all to do so! Do you hear!!

Yes, Darling, you are really a poor thing, doing so much work with my packages, and having so much to do for school! Really a poor Bubelein! (Anneliese is mimicking my description of myself in an earlier letter—she is not making fun of me!). *I am frequently sad, that I can't send you or your parents anything, but once I*

have you with me, everything will be made right, I will then make
a present of myself, and will you then really be wholly happy?

Bubelein, the radio is now playing a merry little Tiroler song:

"Geh' mach Dei Fensterl auf
i' wart' schon so lang drauf!
a einzigs Busserl möcht' i' nur
vielleicht lass i' Dir dann Dei Ruh!"
Verstascht!!!

"a Busserl" ist bayrisch-tiroler
Diälekt u. heisst auf gut deutsch
"Einen Kuss!" Und was das ist,—
brauche ich wohl kaum näher beschreiben!!!

"Go, open your window
I've been waiting a long time outside!
I would like just a single kiss
perhaps I'll then let you alone!"
Understand!!! [Schwäbisch for 'understand', directed by
Anneliese to me].

"a Busserl" is Bavarian-Tirolean dialect,
and in good German means "A Kiss!"
And what that is,—I need hardly to describe further!!!

Anneliese then asks whether I've heard of the romantic
"Fensterln" custom in Bavaria and the Tirol: *Hast Du schon mal*
vom romantischen "Fensterln" in Bayern u. Tirol gehört? Assuming
I hadn't, which was true, she then describes the custom:

This song [the one being played on the radio] *refers directly to this*
Fensterln! And this is the way it works: When a young lad is fond
of a girl but is not allowed to go into her little room, the brave

suitor places a ladder under the bedroom window of his beloved and during the night, when all is quiet and asleep, climbs up, taps lightly on the window and asks whether he might come in, only to get a kiss, or perhaps more, depending upon how far love had developed between the two young people!! However, if the window is not opened, the suitor knows its all over with love! So that's how the romantic regional custom of "Fensterln" works in Bavaria and Tirol!!! And the young lads and girls have their fun with it!!! Were you to knock on my window, I'd gladly let you in! Thus does every land have its own beautiful and idyllic customs and ways!

Gut Nacht Bubelein, tausend so süsse "Busserl" von Deine Anne: Now enough with these Swäbisch—Bavarian—Tirolean stories! More tomorrow! In the meantime it's become ten thirty, and high time for little girls to go to bed! Good night Bubelein, a thousand very sweet "Busserl" from Your Anne.

As I have noted Anneliese's Letter No. 49 was written over two days, March 15 and 16 of 1946. That of the 16th was a card, both enclosed in the same envelope. The card of the 16th was artwork drawn by Anneliese which shows her sitting at the open window (an actual photograph of Anneliese shows her seated at the window sill) of her upstairs room with a ladder on the wall leading to her. The text under her drawing is that that of the Busserl song she had set out for me in her letter of the 15th of March. Then, on the reverse side of the drawing she wrote the following:

Beloved Bubelein!

See Darling, when you go to your little bed in the evening, knock quickly on my window, first take off your shoes, climb up the ladder, I shall then quickly open the window, you give me a sweet Busserl and then you will be able to sleep much, much better!!!

Deeply your Anne

To fully understand the card's drawing, and its text, one must see the card. Its key element being the fact that Anneliese cut out the card on three sides over the window space, thus making a "flap" window covering which could be opened and closed. When the flap was opened Anneliese's photo would be seen. Arthur was instructed to climb up the ladder, open the window covering—designed as wood planking, with a heart cut in the center—kiss the image of Anneliese so revealed, and, thus relieved of his tensions, Arthur could then sleep much, much better! And it worked!!! God Bless My Anneliese!

On March 21, 1946 Anneliese sent me her Letter No. 51, the third of the March trio I have referred to. March 21 is my birthday, (in 1946 it was my 23rd) and Anneliese's letter was, *inter alia*, a birthday greeting to me. She decorated the first page of her letter with a drawing of *Das Blumenkind*, The Flower Child, a sign, as she wrote, of the beginning of Spring. Her drawing was accompanied by two dried flowers. Anneliese was in high spirits when she wrote her six page letter to me, wholly in German. In her letter she answers all my then pending queries, displays her considerable sense of humor, and discusses the intricacies of English and German grammar. But woven within the fabric of her otherwise joyful letter is a single poignant paragraph in which Anneliese describes her struggle to overcome the bouts of sadness which suddenly engulf her when she contemplates our separation. Herewith, Anneliese's letter of March 21, 1946:

21.3.46.
Thou my everything!

Now, my dear Birthday Child, how are you? I hope you received my letters and photos promptly, and that they pleased you!

Today became a holiday for me too, because 4 loving letters from you, and one from your Mom, fluttered into the house. And your words sounded so loving, so glorious and good!! I hear you speaking from each line, your loving blue pupils looking at me, oh, you live in my thoughts, so real, so near and lively! And I know how lovingly and frequently you think of me.

Your small sketches with which you decorate the numbers of your letters are really quite lovely, and I will make an effort to think up something nice for my letters. Today The Flower Child greets you as a sign of the beginning of Spring.

In the last few days I was sadder than usual, there were no letters from you, the weather was glorious, and you so far away, I had to fight hard to swallow my tears! Sometimes I simply have such sad hours that I am barely brave enough to resist them, nothing helps, they are suddenly there.

But today I am happy and joyful again, I know you are getting mail from me, and I from you, and I rejoice with your family that Harold is again home. Isn't that reason enough to be happy? Of course!

Bubelein, I hereby commission you to give your brother a kiss as a greeting from me, but only on his forehead or cheeks, since one kisses only 'his darling" on the mouth. Understand!!! Yes! [Anneliese wrote the German word for "understand" in the Schwäbisch dialect].

Anneliese then writes that her brother, Kurt, is now walking about with his new artificial leg, that yesterday he tried riding his bike and was pleased with his performance, and that he would soon start to work again, which would be good for him, . . . *Since at work one forgets unpleasant things more rapidly.*

Anneliese then tells me what use she had made of the wool I had sent her, a jacket, with the rose colored wool, which had turned out to be quite pretty, the green for a pullover with short sleeves, and some of the red wool to repair a wool dress, emphasizing to me that everything I sent her was put to good use and Anneliese adds: *. . . and many an envious look falls on this or that pretty thing you have given me! . . .*

She reiterates, as she does in other letters, that her family is grateful for everything my family and I send to them. It must be noted that food supplies, of any kind, as well as items of clothing, were in short supply in the post-war Germany of 1945 and 1946. The foodstuffs I sent to Anneliese enabled her and her family to maintain themselves in good health, but also put some variety in their diet, thus Anneliese writes: *what you are sending is very helpful to us, and allows us to prepare meals with greater variety.*

Bub, it's really very nice of you to correct my English letter. Thank you! I know I still mix up some things, especially sentence structure. And your parents should please excuse me when my letters to them are sometimes written with many errors!

Little Darling I had to laugh heartily at your conjugation of the German word "verliebt" [in love with someone] *!!! Genuine Bubelein!! Yes, yes, in love, engaged, married. In reality, however, the word "verliebt" is not a verb, but what is called an adjective in English, yes, "lieben" to love, that is what one does, thus a verb, but "verliebt", one is in love (or not) and therefore, an adjective!!! But we here also use the word sequence in love, engaged, married!! . . . .*

I knew Anneliese had an English tutor and I was concerned whether Anneliese ever showed her English letters to her tutor for correction before sending them on to me. Anneliese assured me that she had never done that, nor would she: . . . . *Since these are purely personal matters, and I would rather send letters to you with errors, and you are then so good to correct everything for me. Right!!*

Anneliese then thanks me for sending her a fresh batch of airmail stamps and regrets she didn't have them when she mailed her last two letters which went by regular mail. She closes by saying, enough for today, and sending me a sweet, glorious kiss.

I cannot leave Anneliese's 21. 3. 46 letter without making these observations:

Like Anneliese I was often engulfed by sudden onslaughts of sadness when a current happy event recalled happy times with Anneliese, and she now so unattainable, and I, too, had to fight hard to swallow my tears, and often, I was not as successful as Anneliese.

Although Anneliese was never the beneficiary of a formal education beyond the eight years of public schooling—where she had excellent grades, I've seen her school records—her family could not afford to send her to a Gymnasium, and then onto a university. Since neither she, nor any family member, was a Nazi Party member—she received no government scholarship. Instead, at age 14 she was apprenticed to a small local hotel, *Das Schlössle* (Little Castle) close to her home, there to learn the arts and crafts of running a commercial kitchen and becoming a chef. What she learned at the hotel stood her, and ultimately me, in good stead, for it was her hotel training which gave her the Chef's position in, and administration of, the kitchen facilities for my Military Government Unit in Heidenheim. At the Schlössle, a favorite stopping place for traveling businessmen, Anneliese also learned how to cope gracefully with roving eyes, and attempts at roving hands, from both management and guests. As the reader has surely seen from Anneliese's letters, she wrote (as my Mom noted in one of her letters), *"Hoch deutsch"* High German, in an engagingly literate manner, that she had an extensive vocabulary, a great sense of humor, and was an avid reader. Yes, Anneliese's formal schooling was far less than mine, but she more than compensated for her ostensible "lack" of formal academic training by being essentially self taught. And when it came down to the nuts and bolts of daily living Anneliese stood heads and shoulders way above me! Anneliese had more *sechel yashar* שֵׂכֶל יָשָׁר, Hebrew for common sense, more people skills than I ever had. And she was more disciplined and more practical than I. In short, I got the better part of the bargain when Anneliese and I joined our lives together. And my courageous Anneliese never complained, regardless of the situation. Never!

Numerous letters were exchanged between Anneliese and me in March 1946. I've set forth only a few. Here is one from me to Anneliese dated 27-3-46. The No. 48 is set into a drawing of children's play blocks. On the face of one block I have affixed the photo I took in applying for my passport which I would need in order to return to Germany. The letter is written wholly in German. Before the body of the letter, and next to my passport photo I wrote: *The picture is the photograph I had made for my Passport. The picture is strange, isn't it? I look so serious—too serious, I believe!* (Frankly, looking at it six decades later I think I looked pretty good!).

Sweet Darling!

Greetings, Angel! I am completely happy this evening, since I've received your Letter (No. 46), and also a very loving letter from your dear Dad. And then my parents were very, very pleased with your last letter which you wrote in English. My Dad was particularly astonished, that you can write so exquisitely in English!

It was a nice surprise to hear so quickly and lovingly from your Father! But do you know, it was very hard for me to read his handwriting? But I finally got it done. What an exercise! But as the saying goes—"Practice makes the Master", right? Certainly!

Yes, Anne, my love for you is a true and pure Love. I love you not only for your sweet lips, or for your deep eyes—I love you for your warm heart and for your honest Soul. I love the way you speak, the way you laugh and how you understand a joke! I love your prudence, your faithfulness, your humanity. I love you because I need you, especially when the tears come. I love you because I know for a certainty that you love me too! Is that not so, my Darling?

I'll know in 8 weeks whether I can go to Europe this Summer. Oh! Anne, I am hoping so very much that it will be possible!! But should I not succeed in coming to you in the last part of this year, don't be too sad, Anne! It is also difficult for me to bear this time of separation.

Yes, as you have written—when we are together again, we'll quickly forget the grief and tears and sorrow of this time of separation, as we love, laugh and live!

Everything is going great with me in the University. All my teachers are satisfied with me! Especially my German teacher. He is now an American, but he comes from Berlin (or Brandenburg), He enjoys speaking with me, and about a happier Germany. And next week my brother also starts in the University!

In the last paragraph of my letter I suggest to Anneliese that she must have made an error in giving me her bra size, because the one I sent was much too large according to the size, which she had transposed from the German measurement to the American. So I wrote: *So, take your bust measurement again. (You have enough, Anne, I certainly know that, but you don't have that much!!)*

I love you! Warm greetings to your family!

In Anneliese's letter No.58, penned to me on the third of April, 1946, one discovers that she was passionately in love with flowers, and, yes, with me. Anneliese's love for flowers was an expression of her sensitivity to the beauty of all things, great and small, which she, as a country girl growing up in the bosom of fertile fields and verdant wooden slopes, found in the beauty of flowers, wild and cultivated, surrounding her. They were a vital part of her Being.

her love for flowers and for the God who created them—and her regret that so much beauty is passed by, unnoted by many who saw only within their own unhappy selves—is set forth succinctly in language as beautiful and as exquisite as the flowers she loved. My translation, over which I labored, does not fairly recreate the beauty of Anneliese's simple, yet elegant German.

Text of Letter:

Let flowers speak!
[In original letter three pressed violets were attached here]
3.4.1946

No. 58

Sweet belóved Bub!

A large bowl filled with such blue violets sits before me on my table, I picked them yesterday in the woods! Their scent is so sweet, their color so magnificent, their form so lovely, I can't resist, I must send you several of my small favorites, although I know they will be wilted by the time this letter will reach you!

Bubelein, you can scarcely believe how much I love flowers, what ever the variety, whether the small, unassuming goose blossom, or the majestic rose with its bewitching scent! I love them all! how wonderful it is to observe how a simple grain of seed develops into a plant, brings forth buds and these then unfold in the sun as magnificent blossoms! yes, how rich in wonders is the world! And how small, how vain is Man in contrast to Nature's perfect creation. Sadly, so many people pass by all this beauty and have no love or eye for it, knowing only their own "I", their personal interests and thus never becoming happy, remaining dissatisfied unconcerned people!

Oh Bub, I am so happy that you, too, share the joy which I feel in such things. I know for certain how deeply you love what God, through His Creation, has given us!

Oh Bub, belóved, dear darling, I love you so much, more than I can express!!

How I long for you, for your love which you have bestowed upon me in such abundant measure!

Oh, I look forward with joy for your next letter, I hope I need not wait too long. And I hope it will have a happy and contented ring, not as sad as was the last one.

Be well my Love, may God protect you and your dear family.

Your Anne

P.S. Today a letter is going through the civil postal service. I am curious to see how long it will be enroute.

When I left Germany for the States in early November 1945 I had six goals in mind: To get my Honorable Discharge from the Service; To remove all familial objections to my marrying Anneliese; To get my college degree—interrupted when I enlisted in the Cavalry in November 1942—by completing my Senior Year at Brooklyn College; To get a U.S. Government job which would send me back to Germany; Once back in Germany to get all the documentation necessary for me to get Anneliese out of Germany, and into the States; To get married *so schnell als möglich*, as quickly as possible!

With my Honorable Discharge I would be eligible as a veteran to get the benefits our grateful country was then extending to those who had served honorably in the war. With full hearted, loving acceptance of Anneliese by my immediate family, and close relatives, her happiness—and hence mine, which was wholly dependent upon hers—would be assured. With a full four years undergraduate degree from a respected academic institution in hand my chances of getting into a prestigious law school were materially enhanced. With a U.S. Government job assured I would, during this post-war period of acute security concerns, be able to reenter Germany, and to travel there at Government expense. With me back in Germany, and reunited with my belóved Anneliese, my anxieties for her well being would be stilled, my passions fulfilled—and the process of getting the necessary clearances from the Four Occupying Powers allowing Anneliese to leave Germany, and a visa from our State Department allowing Anneliese to enter the States—would, I believed, be a brief, easy, matter of my hand carrying papers from one governmental agency to another for their approvals. (It turned out to be a much more difficult task as the reader shall learn). Finally, with Anneliese safely at my side in the States, the *ratio decidendi* for all the foregoing would be accomplished when a Union, ordained and sanctified by God, would now have the additional imprimatur of secular and religious authorities! That was my "game plan". It took ten months of agonizing separation, and five more trying—but happier—months in Germany, before the final stage in what was *beshert*, what was meant to be, came to pass!!

The struggle to accomplish all these goals—the hopes dashed, the hopes realized, the joys of attainment are expressed, more eloquently in our Letters of Love, penned in the heat of the moment, than I could now express simply by recalling a plethora of names, places and dates. And so, it is back to a selection of these Letters that I go to use as the vehicle to take you, dear reader—and me—to that joyous reunion of Anneliese and Arthur in Germany, early in September 1946!! You've come this far, stay with me! The best is yet to come!

Let me start in what is often called The Merry Month of May! And this letter from Anneliese, her No. 74, dated May 1, 1946, is in fact a merry one, as the following excerpts demonstrate: She starts by making a sketch of a number of balloons, one bearing the number 74, with Anneliese waving them off and saying, in English: *My dear air-balloons fly out to Brooklyn and bring my sweet Bubelein! many sweet kisses from me!* She then tells me that my Mom had written a very fine letter to her . . . *and she told me about the Passover holiday and the religious customs!* And then she tells me that . . . *the jeep with the Post fell into the Brenz* [the little river on whose banks Heidenheim stands] . . . . *And of course, the most part of the letters was swimming in the water!!* . . . some were . . . *quite wet* . . . . *But thank heaven your letter was* [only] *damp! Do you see how quick a such misfortune is here??* And then Anneliese shifts into German: *Es ist alles komisch, kommt die Post gut über den grossen Teich u. in der kleinen Brenz wird sie doch nass! Gott sei dank, dieses passiert ja nicht alle Tage! It's very strange, the mail crosses the great pond safely and still gets wet in the little Brenz. Thank God, this doesn't happen all the time!*

Anneliese then writes its 11 p.m., she is really tired, and has to go to bed. She then asks *Willst Du nicht mit mir schlafen gehen? Wie kann ich nur so dumm fragen! O Deine Annis ist wirklich ein dummes Gänzlein!!! Don't you want to sleep with me! How can I ask such a dumb question! Oh Your Annis* [childish rendering of Anneliese] *is really a silly little goose!!!* Anneliese then engages in some really humorous mathematics:

Verstaschst!!! I weuss, I weuss, mei Bua versterit me guad!!!*

Anne

One kiss on your dear eyes
One kiss on your dear nose
One kiss in your right ear
One kiss in your left ear
One kiss (especially sweet) on your mouth
Total: Five kisses from your Anne
Each kiss 10 RM! An expensive matter!! Now would you have so much money available?!! However with larger quantities, delivery costs would be reduced! [Now, here Anneliese shifted into the Schwäbisch dialect script]: *Do you understand!!! I know, I know, my Bub understands me well!!!*

Anne

This letter is an endearing example of my Anneliese's sweetness and wit!

I now turn back to the month of April 1946 to reproduce excerpts from, several letters I wrote, as these tie in with certain of Anneliese's already reproduced, in whole, or in part—and illustrate how this flow of intimate correspondence, with its mix of sorrow and humor, helped sustain her spirits, and mine—during our separation, and as I sought to find a Government position which would send me speedily back to Germany for a reunion devoutly wished for by both of us.

In my letter No. 53, written on the 9th and 10th of April 1946, I drew a pile of phonograph records, and sheet music, flying off into space, with No. 53 on the label of the leading record, followed by a second with the label "Ich Liebe Dich". The letter, written wholly in German, illustrates the way Anneliese and I used humor to salve the wounds which separation had inflicted upon our souls.

---

*   This last sentence is written in Schwäbisch dialect.

My sweet, beautiful Anne! I had wished to sketch a beautiful sketch—but you can see what came to be! (Now look [I used a Schwäbisch expression] *I'm also a poet!—Oh "for God's sake!") This fountain pen does only one thing well, it can make a lot of ink spots! Positively, clearly, of course, really, probably, self evident, truly and really? Well, Anne, what's missing? My sweetheart, young woman, girl laughs, I know fully, with certainty, exactly—Oh, enough of these crazy and so forth sentences!*

Anne, tell me, in ernest why do you love such a crazy fellow? I'm like the weather, one time I'm as cool as the wind in "The Lorelei". And then I'm hot like a night in Summer—or happy as a little brook, or wild as a thunderstorm. But despite everything, you love me! Is it then strange that I love you so much and do so much for you?—and with all my heart! No, it's not something extraordinary! Certainly not! You need me—and I need you—there you have the whole story! There you have the reasons for our great Love. And so, our Love is not only for today or for tomorrow—our Love is forever! Right? [I used the Schwäbisch word *gell*, which I had learned from Anneliese, and which translates *as "right? or 'Isn't that so?*]

I close the April 9th portion of my letter by saying I'm tired and going into my dear little bed. I then write, ... *Liebes bettchen habe ich gesagt? Nein, nicht ganz—es ist leider zu, zu leer! Gute Nacht, Anne!* [Trans.]: *Did I say dear little bed? No, not really—it is sadly too, too empty! Good night, Anne!*

The portion written on the 10th concerned itself with details of a package I had just sent off which included a small amount of sweets which Hilde, Anneliese's sister could have some *zum essen, nicht zum fressen.* A play on words. Essen is the verb "to eat", and is applied only to human beings. Fressen, which also means "to eat" is applied only to animals. When a person eats too much, one says he or she fresses, eats like an animal / over eats. And then I told Anneliese that per her order to give my brother, Harold, a "welcome home from the Service kiss from her", but only on his forehead or cheeks—my kisses being reserved only for her lips—that I had done so, which surprised him: "Why was I so loving?" When I explained Anneliese's order he said, "Oh, you are a happy pair, and you both will soon be even happier!"

Our Letters of Love were windows into our grieving hearts and souls, and into the *ways* each of us endeavored to cope—some days more successfully than others—with the ebb and flow of conflicting tides of hope and despair. In the end, we did more than survive—we conquered, we overcame every obstacle, our shield, and our sword, were the love and trust we reposed in each other, and in ourselves. No matter the post-war hostility to Germany and things German, no matter the depth and width of the chasm between Jews and Germans, Anneliese and I were two decent young people, from loving families, who wanted naught from life but to be reunited, to become husband and wife, to merge two bodies, two souls into one Being which death itself could n'er tear asunder! And death has not succeeded!

How did Anneliese and I make our daily rounds during those bitter months of separation? Our letters tell the tale. Anneliese loved to read, to learn a new language and new ways, to garden, to write, to draw, to knit and sew, to cook, to walk the meadows and wooded ways of her countryside, to know the birds and their chatter, to know the flowers, to pick and press them, and send them on to me. Her letters recite all these activities, and more, and all the while she longed for me, cried out for me, dreamed of me! And I, how did I fare? I, too, felt the burning pangs of longing, of desire unfilled. I, too, tasted the salty tears coursing down my cheeks, and dreamed of enfolding her again in my embrace, feeling her heart pulsate against my breast, in time with mine! You, dear reader, have been privy to a glimpse, or two, into Anneliese' daily life, and the means she employed to live with our separation. Let me now give you a peek or two into mine, as expressed in excerpts from several letters.

In my Letter No. 56, written in mid-April 1946, and almost wholly in German, I write of my great love for classical music, and tell Anneliese, by composition name, of my most recent purchases of recordings of Schubert and Schumann Lieder, and of a book I had just read describing the life of Beethoven between the time he wrote his Eroica Symphony and his Waldstein Piano Sonata, and that I owned recordings of both works. And I continue:

While I wait for you, I live with my music. And as beautiful as the music is, it's only a poor substitute for my sweet, loving Anne. Oh, how I long for you! With music being the centerpiece of this letter I go on in this vein:

Were I a good poet, I would write you a love song. But my brain and my heart are not good co-workers now. My brain works, day and night on plans and dreams, and my heart cries often from pain. If I only say—I love you—it is because I can't better express my great love for you.

Do you know Angel, when I hear such a song as "Remembrances" (I Think of You) by Beethoven from his Song Cycle—"To The Distant Beloved", I'm again living with you and when I also hear "The Poet's Love" songs I don't only hear Heine's words or Schumann's music. I also hear your sweet voice and I again experience those glorious days, when we were so close. I can never forget such days, especially when I always hear such songs as: "When a Youth Loves a Maiden", "I Cried In My Dream", "When I Gaze Into Your Eyes" and "All Through The Night I See You In My Dreams". Yes, through my music

I'm always brought closer to you! (But, sorry to say, not close enough!!!)

—

It is now 1:05 AM—I'm the only one up—all the rest are asleep—including 2 of my cousins who have come to visit for the Passover Holidays. I have just finished listening to the haunting, passionate strains of Beethoven's "Appassionata" Sonata. And as the last note died away, my desire for you was reborn more strongly than ever. Oh, Anne, I need you and your loving warmth so very, very much! Ja, ich brauche Dich u. Deine süsse Wärme! Yes, I need you and your sweet warmth! When shall I once more sleep with you nestled in my arms! Life is so very short—and I ache/long so to begin living it again. How I envy the joy of all those in love that I see around me. Our happy days lie behind us, Anne—but our happiest days still lie before us. But as sure as the sun will rise tomorrow—so will our love someday flower in all its splendor! We need but to hope and to wait—and to have patience that we might continue to hope and to wait! Geduld, das ist unser Sprichwort! Patience, that is our Motto!

I need you—I'm thinking of you—always—always—always! Our Day will also come. God will not forget us. We are not praying for money or such things, we are praying only that we shall quickly have each other! He will hear us. I love you!!

May God protect you!

> *Your poor Bub,*
> *Arthur*

On the 24th of April, 1946 I sent Anneliese my Letter No. 59. In it I finally poured out to Anneliese all my pent-up frustration, sorrow and anger. Prior thereto I had always laid bare my love for her and my desires for that time to come speedily when we

would be together again, and joined forever as husband and
wife. And I wrote about my family, my schooling, my occasional
recreational activities and about the things I was sending to her.
But I never dwelt on the repeated, and fruitless efforts I had made
to get a government job that would send me back to Germany. I
kept repeating the same refrain, the same mantra: *"Hab' Geduld!*
Alles wird bald besser sein!" Have patience, everything will
soon be better! I held back telling "all" to Anneliese as I felt she
shouldn't have to bear my sorrows together with her own. Not a
smart decision! But in this letter I finally pulled the stopper, and
it all poured out!

Mein Liebchen!

Heute war wirklich ein komischer Tag. Ich begann den Tag
mit Freude, aber zwei Stunde später war ich im tiefsten Tal
der Traurigkeit—ich ging nicht in die Universität—ich war
melankolisch. Aber, allmählich, als ich mich an Dich erinnerte, fang
ich wieder an, glücklich zu werden. Und jetzt bin ich ganz glücklich!
Jetzt kann ich sagen: Ruhe, meine Seele, alles ist wieder wohl!

My Little Darling!

Today was really a strange day. I began the day with joy, but two
hours later I was in the deepest valley of sadness—I didn't go to
the University—I was melancholy. But gradually, as I thought
about you, I began to be happy again. And now I am completely
happy! Now I can say: Peace, my soul, all is well again!

I know you are confused. So let me explain everything . . . . I begin
by explaining I had learned that the Government was looking for
Civil Mail Censors for Germany, just the job I was looking for;
that I immediately went to the Labor Department, only to learn
that the hiring deadline was last week!

Sorry? Oh God! All at once I was angry, mad, heartsick and Oh sooo sad! Again too late! I leave the Government Office. "The devil is playing with me", I complained. But then I thought, "if you don't believe in angels—when you always say there is no angel (Anne is the only angel)—how then can there be a devil?!" And thus did I speak with my "inner Self".

And while in the subway on the way home (I didn't go to the University, it was already too late (always too late!), besides, I couldn't bear a school day), I thought of you—"I have to remain completely well for Anneliese, I must not aggravate myself so much!" And I thought further—it's not too late, everything is not lost. With Life, Hope and Belief/Faith everything is possible! Go home, write a letter to the Authorities, perhaps they will make an exception for you—perhaps (Thank God for the word "perhaps"!) .... I write the letter; I mail it. Then I say—"Now, that's how a man works—Activity, not Tears!"

I then thank Anneliese for three letters from her, one from her sister, Hilde, and one from Frau Zeiner, at whose home Anneliese had lived while in Heidenheim, and where many of my letters and packages for Anneliese were going. I then begin to explain to Anneliese why, until now, I had not told her of all my cares:

Oh, Angel, I'm always very honest with you. But until now I have never told you of the many ways and means I have tried so that I might be with you quickly. I thought—why must Anne also bear my sorrow? But I could not keep my secret any longer. Why does one have a wife—only for lovemaking?, no—he has a wife, and she, a husband, so that both can make something glorious from a shared life. Joy is two times more enjoyable, when shared by husband and wife, and the grief only half as much, when both can share it. And for these reasons am I writing such a letter to you. One can become satiated with fun making, caressing, laughing and kissing—but never with a wise and understanding wife!

I then interrupt the letter to tell Anneliese that I have to make dinner for my brother, my house guests and me, in the absence of my folks. The mealtime over, I then practice writing some sentences in the old German script, and, in English, chat with Anneliese concerning the excellent school grades of Hilde, and joke with her by suggesting that Hilde is ". . . *the clever one in the family*". I ask her to send me a menu of the average daily fare she and her family are eating, so that I might check on the food variety and calories she was getting. I enclose two local newspaper clippings concerning Heidenheim which I thought she might enjoy translating. I write *Incidentally, your English is getting visibly better every day. Oh, I'm so very proud of you! . . . .* I proceed to correct the English in her last letters, and ask her to thank Hilde for her Passover greetings, and I send greetings to her family, and in German, ask that she quickly send me photos of herself—for I'm hungry to see her sweet face!!!

Per her letter No. 76, dated May 3, 1946, Anneliese responded to mine of April 24th. She wrote that my letter, with its emotional highs and lows, caused her much concern. She wryly noted that had she been with me she would have comforted me—but then, had she been with me, I would not have had the sorrows I related! Attached to her letter was a freshly pressed *Maiglöckchen*, Mayflower, the first of the season, which, she wrote, with its pretty little flowers and enchanting scent, was bringing her heartfelt greetings to me. It made her happy that I was honestly telling her my feelings and entrusting all my secrets with her. Then, referring to my disappointing experience at the U.S. Labor Office, she writes:

I can see your disappointed face when you were told at the Labor Office that your application was too late! Yes, Bub, too late or too early, sometimes things appear bewitched! But don't let your head hang! You are truly a strong self willed man!! You know, too, how much I would have liked to be with you, but our time will come, we must remain strong and brave, we must have patience, lots of patience, hope and belief in our great Love! And all will work out!

Now listen to me, Bub, please tell me of all your troubles, everything that oppresses your heart! Even when you believe that you would thereby make me sad. Why indeed, do you have me? Only to share your bed at night, or to be loved and kissed in your arms? Naturally, these things also belong to life, but exactly in those hours of sorrow, of grief, of real need, must one hold together! See my Bub, when something weighs upon your heart, when you are plagued by innermost discord and uncertainty, tell everything to your Anne, she understands you, she helps you bear everything, is ready to help you!! You must always come to me and pour out your sorrow laden heart to me!

Oh Bub, I love you so much, and how immensely do I miss you! I pray that we shall soon find a way to be together again!

How little did Anneliese then know that her prayer was on the verge of being answered.

In my Letter No. 62 of 2 May 1946 I had great news for Anneliese. I told her that my letter to the government (as noted in my Letter No. 59) had been successful. I was granted an interview and given the job as a Civilian Censor with the US Military Government in Germany! But I wrote I wouldn't be sure of anything until I was back in Germany.

Anne, I've gotten a position in the Military Government!!! Yes! It is almost totally sure—I'm only waiting for my passport before I can go to Germany! But I believe that by the end of June or the beginning of July I will be in Germany—if everything is in order!!

I then write that receiving all of her letters at one time had made me "so nervous" I could scarcely write, so I would write her more tomorrow.

The next day, May 4, 1946 I wrote to Anneliese at her home in Schwenningen, not sure how long the Heidenheim connection would continue. The Letter bore the No. 2, this being the new Schwenningen series. In it I told Anneliese that the letter I had written in desperation after learning I had applied too late for the positions offered in Germany—and requesting that an exception be made in my case—had been answered promptly. I was given an Interview Appointment for the following Monday. At the interview everything went well and I was given a job with the Civil Censorship Section of the Military Government in Germany. Not the level job I wanted, but certainly better than none. (Shortly after starting to work in Germany I was promoted higher up in the job level, and hence, received more responsibilities and pay).

In the same letter I write:

I enjoyed your illustrated card containing a stanza in the Bavarian-Tyrolean dialects. It was a very clever idea to make such a card! Imagine my surprise and pleasure when I opened the shutter and found a sweet picture of you on the inside!!

And of course I enjoyed your letter containing the beautiful pressed violets—they arrived looking as fresh as they must have looked the day you picked them. Thanks—Bitte sehr! . . . . Well, I hope everything will soon be straightened out—that we needn't have to resort to letters as a means of contact. Yes it will be truly wonderful to be together again. And all these bitter past months will fade away into nothingness!

Auf Wiedersehn!

Dein Bub.
Arthur

The day before, the third of May, I had written my Letter No. 63 in the Heidenheim series. By reason of the uncertainty then existing as to which address letters should be sent I was doubling up my mailings. Thus there was some repetition. Having had so many disappointments, I was reluctant to accept at face value that I did indeed have a job in Germany—even after the Labor Office assured me that the position was secure. Thus, in this regard I wrote to Anneliese, ... *I believe it's better to be restrained now rather than optimistic today and disappointed tomorrow.*

In her letter No. 86, dated May 26, 1946 Anneliese acknowledges receipt of the foregoing letters from me concerning my obtaining a job in Germany, and my doubts until I was actually on the job in Germany. She writes that by reason of my letters . . . *ich wirklich ganz närrisch im Kopf u. so so so glücklich im Herzen bin!!! I am really wholly crazy in my head and so, so, so, happy in my heart!!!* Anneliese has never "lectured" me. But she had a way of getting her point across. Thus, in this letter she writes concerning my doubts about the job:

Bubelein, why are you still doubtful that you will succeed in being with me soon?? Bub, really believe it, oh it must surely be true, our sweet Dream will yet become a glorious reality! Naturally, both of us have been frequently disappointed, but there shall come a time when the Goddess of Luck must fully favor us! Don't you think so, too? Yes, yes, I know, I know!

Oh if I could have you here now Bubelein, so much joy and rapture are cherished in my thoughts, and the big, important things contained in your letters have made my head spin!

Anneliese then relates that she went to the U.S. Consulate in Stuttgart to see if she could start the procedure to get a visa to come to the States, but was unsuccessful, and she hastens to say:

But that's not so bad, much more important is that you will
soon be with me! Oh Bubelein, my heart is filled with sunshine
and my thoughts of you so dear, so honest and filled with great
longing!!!

Anneliese then says her parents will be very happy when she
tells them the good news about me. She then expresses concern
for my parents, knowing how sad they will be that I would be
leaving them so soon after returning from the war—but then,
perhaps, within a year, I would be bringing her home with me.
She then advises me that the mail system is back in order, and
thanks me profusely for all the packages I've been sending her
and her family (the word "profusely" doesn't adequately reflect
her frequently stated deep appreciation for these packages).
And she closes, writing in English, that within . . . *a few*
weeks . . . you will come to me, for ever time, for our happiest
days, which still lie before us!! You know how I long for you,
how I miss you and need you! As our letters will reveal, our
reunion would take more than a few weeks, but, fortunately,
not much more.

Neither Anneliese, nor I, ever adapted to being separated
for ten months—twice as long as the five months we were
together when first we met in Heidenheim. The glory of those
five passionate months, in our *own* Garden of Eden, has never
faded from our memories! It was the talisman which buoyed
our spirits when they flagged, and enticed us with visions
of pleasures restored. Necessity required that we leave Our
Garden and separate, so that the world outside might make
its peace with us—and that done—that Anneliese and I would
return to Our Garden, there to love, frolic and laugh, now, and
throughout eternity! Anneliese and Arthur yearned to go back
to that magical place where she had been his Fairy Princess,
and he her Prince Charming! They prayed for that time to
come speedily!

My letters, beginning in May 1946, gave the first tangible sign that our prayers might soon be answered, that the End of our Separation was in the offing—if not this month, then perhaps the next month, but certainly, in the very near future! What boundless joy did that Prospect bring to Anneliese and me! The letters, or excerpts, which next I set forth, delineate our fevered anticipation of the speedy fulfillment of that Prospect! So, dear reader, come with Anneliese and me, as we travel steadily, if not as speedily as we desired, to that glorious day when once again I will cradle my beautiful, belóved, precious Anneliese Baur in my arms, press her to my breast, feel the warmth of her body suffuse mine, hear and feel the frenetic pounding of her heart, as she senses mine, and drink the salty sweetness of her kisses as our tears of joy mingle, and her hands lightly trace the contours of my face, as if to confirm that they are the same she had last seen ten months before, and thereafter, only in her dreams! Oh what ecstasy! What a wonderful day, and glorious night, that would be!!! *O nuit divine!* And Anneliese's letters, and mine, will take you, dear reader, with us—but only to the door!

But until I had been issued my passport and was on the boat headed for Germany would I allow myself to believe 100% that I was on my way back to Anneliese. I checked frequently with the Government. Everything was proceeding apace, relax. Easy for them to say, but I tried. And our letters flowed, our lifeline remained intact. We would ask questions of each other, or make observations, and two weeks later, sometimes much sooner, as the international mail service improved, we would get the responses. Each of us hung on every word! We laughed and cried, chatted, joked, discussed life's meanings, explored the intricacies of English and German grammar, talked, talked, talked about our Love for each other, about the life we would build together, and fervently wished we were speedily reunited so that no longer need we be content only with protestations of Love!! Excerpts from

several letters written in May 1946 are illustrative. In my Letter
No. 64 written on May 6th, I write:

*I'm . . . a bit jealous of you when I read your English sentences.
You write so well and so lovely—and if, perhaps, you make an
error I correct it as quickly as possible. But you, my Treasure,
what are doing for your poor Bub? He makes many mistakes
and you don't write even one word. Is that proper of you?
Is that kindness, loving humanity, being good natured, and
so forth? I believe not! For example, how many times have I
so written? . . . . "I here enclose three letters . . ."—And you
know, much, much better than I that this is not correct!—Now
I know, that one must write the sentence this way: "I enclose
three letters here . . . . I learned that from my/through my
studies—after "many difficult hours". But was it necessary,
that I had to learn so much grammar—especially, when my
Anne is so intelligent? Is it nice and proper of you that you
hide your wisdom? Absolutely not! I know you are laughing,
but I'm serious* [ernst, is also a man's name in German, so I
make a play on names] *I'm ernst (I'm Arthur, but I can also
be Ernst—Oh!!!) You must help me. I have so much to learn, I
certainly can't do it all alone!! . . . .*

I then discuss the nature of life with Anneliese, and how she
and I relate in the scheme of things. I close by writing: . . . .

*I know what kind of a girl you are, Anne. You are brave and
honest—"complex" yet simple. You know what the word Life really
means. You will be my true mate!! Yes, we will have a glorious
Life together!! Never again shall we let our heads hang! I love
you! I love you! Do you hear? I love you! Your crazy Bub! Arthur*

Our interchange of letters sustained our hopes. We bathed
emotionally in their flow, and we learned from each other. With
each letter from Anneliese I broadened my German vocabulary,

or honed my modes of expression in German. She in turn learned from me. We were separated, our emotions were jangled. We needed each other, and both of us used our correspondence as a support mechanism as well as a learning tool. In our five months of intimacy in Heidenheim we each probably discovered as much about the "other" as we did about the "self". Love is a learning experience. And during our ten months of separation we continued to learn more about each other, and about ourselves. We learned how to cope with the travails of separation. Both of us used the time to lay a proper foundation for Anneliese's arrival in America, and for her seamless incorporation into the fabric of my family. Such qualms as Anneliese had about her acceptance into my family were allayed through the loving correspondence she had with my Mom and Dad, and put to rest by my Zaydeh's unconditional acceptance of her. Her concerns about being able to communicate effectively in English, quite a factor when our separation began, were materially lessened by her increasing ability to master the English language. She never lost her soft south German accent, but that only added to her charm. I've already set out examples where Anneliese and I used our letters to enhance our respective language capabilities.

While openly, both of us were cautious in measuring when I'd get back to Germany, in our hearts we knew it would happen, sooner, rather than later. And our letters, in late Spring and into Summer reflected this change in our beliefs. We both continued to express our great love and longing for each other, but in addition to matters grammatical, Anneliese and I addressed other issues, of concern to Anneliese, of which more below. On matters grammatical, I give several examples.

In my Letter No. 3 dated 8-5-46 and sent to Schwenningen—this being a duplicate of the higher numbered one sent to Heidenheim—I was not sure then whether my friend was still in Heidenheim to receive and forward my letters—I devoted my letter to matters grammatical. The letter is written in German and English:

Dearest Darling Anne!

. . . . Anne, I'm going to use this letter to correct some of your minor mistakes in English. (You never make major ones any more, since you have learned too much already). [I set out eight corrections in my letter. I cite three here].

2. It is better, when we go together, then Kitty speaks . . . .

It would be better if we went together since (oder / or) because Kitty speaks . . . .

5. We understand us very well—ist viel besser, wenn Du schreibst—[it is much better if you write] We understand each other very well. (Reflexive)

6. Vergess nicht, dass die dritte Person einzahl in der Gegenwart immer mit einem "s" geschrieben ist. [Don't forget, the third person singular in the Present is always written with an s] He hopes, she cries, it rings, etc.

. . . . But let's put an end to this school hour—let's talk now a little about ourselves.

I then quote from a letter from Ernst, one of the sons in the Zeiner family in Heidenheim. He was about my age. Ernst tell me that Anneliese had visited them at Easter, and that it was a shame that I couldn't see her. She was tanned and looked so fresh and sweet, that I would have been totally enraptured had I seen her! He says he was sending me photos of Anneliese which would be a poor substitute for how she really looked. He than added, *Sie lebt nur für Dich u. trägt eine gute Eigenshaft—die Treue . . . . She lives for you alone, and has a good quality—faithfulness . . .*

Oh, Anne, how I long for you!! When we are finally together how beautiful life will be, how glorious every hour, how indescribable every sweet night!!

I have everything a modern man believes necessary—money, health, parents, a brother, etc. But I'm lacking something quite important—my wife! But I know she is waiting for me (and with excitement, I hope). Have patience, Anne, the time is coming! Greetings to your parents, and your sister and brother, and May God Protect! Your Bub, Arthur

In my Letter No. 4 in the Schwenningen series, and dated 11-5-46 I wrote to Anneliese that: . . . . *All your last letters were written with so much love and with so much ability, that even were I to write 10 pages, I couldn't adequately praise them! If ever I were in doubt about your love for me—or about your intellectual abilities (of which I am not) your excellent letters would quickly dispell* [my misspelling] *any doubts lingering in my mind. (This English passage might sound confused to you—but you'll have to excuse me—when I write to you, "mein Kopf ist ganz wirr!")* The last words, in German: "my head is totally confused!"

In the same letter: . . . . *As much as I cherish your letters, I wish the time would soon come when I would no longer need to receive them. That would mean, of course, that I would again be with you—and therefore in no need of a "schriftliche Verbindung!"* ["written connection"] *And something tells me, that that time is coming very soon!!*

[I then sketched in some musical notes] . . . . *I'm peculiar. (You've noted that for a long time you say?—I can certainly believe that). But let me proceed: As you are, I, too, am spoiled. When, for example, more than two days go by without letters flowing from you, I am very disappointed. But when your letters come to me, especially when they arrive in a great quantity—oh, then I forget the past, the present, and everything! And I live only with you—and in a glorious future. But, sadly, after some hours the magic of your letters is dispelled. And I am again alone in the rawness of reality—so lonely and so sad! Our connection by mail is a wonderful thing—but it can never be more than a small substitute! But nevertheless, we must be very thankful, that the little that we have, brings us so much joy! But you understand what I'm trying to say: namely, we are all poor children, we can look into the window of a fancy bakery. We may enjoy everything, but only from a distance, but we are free to create fantastic visions in our minds. But we can't get a crumb. We can't touch anything!— Neither money nor a window stands between us. Only an ocean. Only—that's all! End of the song!* [Musical notes followed]

. . . . You asked whether I can cook a meal without a cook book. Aber natürlich! [but of course]. I believe I'm more of a fancier of fine foods. And so I learned a long time ago to test everything by myself.

I'm a good businessman, therefore, please send me "a large quantity" of your kisses, each of which costs 10 RM. But you have promised, that a larger quantity would be more cheaply delivered. Well then? What's the selling price now? I can quickly use a gross!

Greetings to your parents, siblings, relatives, acquaintances, and so forth

Always your Bub
Arthur

In my Letter No. 5 to Schwenningen, dated 13-5-46 I told Anneliese, *inter alia*, that my Mom had made *Kalbschnitzel*, Calf's cutlets, from the recipe she had sent my Mom, and that the *Schnitzel* was wonderful! In that letter I then went to our *"Verbesserung Stunde"*: *Improvement Hour*. I was always trying to be humorous. The letter continues: *Bist Du schon bereit? Gut!*

Are you ready? Good! Anne, Angel! When I read a sentence in one of your last letters, I really had to laugh! You made the same mistake in English, which the students in the University make in German. You wrote: "Kitty and I are sitting on the table writing . . . etc." Perhaps it suits you to sit on the table while you're writing!! But, sorry, it doesn't suit me! I'm more comfortable when I write sitting at the table. But as I've said, perhaps you are also comfortable on the table. (I know you are very good with your bodily exercises, perhaps you are doing two necessary things while you're writing—who knows?) Oh, excuse me, I'm making a dumb little goose out of you, when, in reality, you are sweet, intelligent and exquisite!!! Are you angry with me? Remember, however, people usually write at the table, and sit on chairs. But in English, as in German, people can place things on the table. School is out!

Do you know, Angel? When I write to you, it appears as if you are very close to me, so close, that I can almost embrace you—almost—a-l-m-o-s-t, but, sorry to say—not quite! (But I am happy, nevertheless, almost is much better than nothing. Don't you agree?)

My love to every body!!

Dein Bub
Arthur

But patience, patience! The time is coming, perhaps a little too slowly for two impatient souls (such as we are)—but—one can already perceive the changing circumstances. We can surely say: Tomorrow will be better—and the day after tomorrow even better, and so on!!!

I've already written that if I had to describe Anneliese in one word, that this word would be "courageous"! For that she was: a small town German girl, at the end of a bitter war, in which her nation had committed horrendous evils (in which she was not involved—but nonetheless, included under its rubric—for that girl to allow herself to fall in love with an American soldier, a Jewish one, no less, and then, to keep his love, to agree to adopt his religion, learn his ways, learn his language, leave her family, travel to his distant country—the victor in the war—and there, in a milieu wholly dissimilar to her own, to adjust, live and raise a family, and to further increase the pressure on her psyche—to encounter the slings and arrows of those in her German community who resented her alliance with me, an American and a Jew, and who were jealous of the numerous food and clothing parcels she was receiving at a terrible time in Germany, when food and clothing were scarce commodities.

In her letters to me Anneliese rarely wrote of these concerns. But when she did, and mostly, in passing, I attempted to allay her fears by writing what, too often, were convoluted dissertations on certain people in particular, and on life in general. My Letter No. 6 to Schwenningen, dated 14-5-46 is such a letter. An essay on morality in a love letter? Unusual! Perhaps, but so was our Love!

. . . . *Yesterday I received your Letter No. 76—and my Mom received one, too. The lily-of-the valley's were still as fresh as the days you plucked them for our pleasure. My Mother was particularly pleased, since they are her favorite flower. I'v just written Lily-of-the-valley's as the plural form of these flowers. But now that I think of it—I think that the plural is really Lilies of the Valley. The more I study languages, the more I see how little I actually know—especially about my own language! N'est pas? Nicht wahr? Verdad? Right?*

Time is dragging now. I feel as if I'm hanging in mid-air. I want to start to do things—and I shall—but at the present I can only prepare and plan. I don't know where I'd be if I didn't possess the little patience I do!!

Anne, please don't care what other people do or say. I've come to the rather sad conclusion that most people are mean and evil-minded—to say nothing of begrudging a neighbor his good fortune. What do you care what people say? Sure! I know it hurts to be talked about. But as long as you know—deep down inside—that you are right in doing what you are—then their talk can't harm you. And neither can it harm me. In a world as small as ours is today, people cannot successfully isolate themselves physically from the rest of the world. We can't—and shouldn't build walls around ourselves, real walls, that is. But by believing in ourselves—and by having faith in our future—we can build invisible "walls" of self-assurance behind which we can retire to live in happiness—even in the midst of a raging sea of hate, coarseness and mass cruelty. Reality is relative. The "realness" of these days of separation will quickly disappear under the "realness" of our love, when once we are together again. And so, we can see that the world around us is only as "real" as we make it. As far as we are concerned, the only "real things" in the world today are you and I—and our measureless love for each other. Nothing else matters. As I've mentioned before, it is both wrong and well nigh impossible for us to erect isolating walls about us. But by seeing—and judging the world in the light of the statement that all reality is relative—we can do much to mitigate the forces and effects of the unpleasantness that appears to surround us. Among the Spaniards there is a phrase that "La Vida es Sueño" Life is a dream. And in many ways it is. Let us make our dream a happy one. Let us, while living in the happy memories of the past, plan and work in the present—that our future may be a golden and glorious one!!

Let those people who love to gossip talk—let them! Life is not a fairy tale of gay adventure—but life isn't as bad as it sometimes appears to be. Singly we are not much of a match for a seemingly bitter world. But together, sharing our love, joys and burdens, we can make "a go of it". We can—and we shall!

My sweet Anne! Perhaps this letter will be a bit difficult to translate. The ideas are complicated, even when one reads them in English. But you will surely understand everything, because you and I always think in the same way. Life is only what we shall make of it. As long as we remain brave and patient, daily life will become ever more beautiful!

I love you! I love you! This time of separation is bad! (But as a soldier I saw worse times—and you did, too—I believe). Remain happy and hale! Our time is coming! Heartfelt Greetings!

Always, your Bub

[And then as a joke, and in Old German script I write: Arthur *Published by Arthur. All rights reserved.*

On 30.5.46 *Himmelfahrtstag (Asencion Day)*, Anneliese so noted the day and date of her Letter No. 88 from Schwenningen. She states at the outset that *Heute ist Feiertag, Today is a holiday* thus she has no English lessons. She states she came back safely from Stuttgart, and that the train connection from Stuttgart to Schwenningen is almost as good as before the war. Now that mail is going via Stuttgart it's so beautiful that she hears much faster from me, especially *when my letters contain such wonderful, wonderful news!!!*

Oh Bub, I can't describe my joy when I think about it, that you will shortly be with me!! But later, in every kiss, in every embrace, and caress will I then be able to show you my joy, my great happiness, how much I love you, how good, honest, and true I shall always be to you!! I know for a certainty how glorious our life together will be, all our holy sweet dreams will be realized and we shall never be alone again!

Bub, my parents and my sister and brother are very joyful to see you soon again, especially my Father, he is excited to meet his future son-in-law!! I am sure that both of you will relate well.

See Bub, it's the same with me, as with you, first as I read your news, I cried out loud with joy, but then I thought to myself, Anne, remain objective and curb your joy as long as the matter is not yet one hundred percent sure.

Anneliese then writes that she then tries to remain cool and quiet, but can't help thinking how wonderful everything would be were we to see each other shortly . . .

Then my heart begins to beat in anxious expectation, my desire and my longing grow so strong, that I make myself believe that in a few weeks I shall have you with me forever! Yes Bub, your Anne is sometimes a little, dumb girl, but also your sweet little Angel who loves you so so so much!!

Anneliese encloses a clipping from a local German newspaper which states that France will now recognize marriages entered into in Germany between German women and French men where the marriage is valid under German law. She writes that she hopes the American Government will take note of what France has done and allow Americans to marry Germans in Germany—which by reason of its non-fraternization policy it would not allow—the reason why I had to get Anneliese out of Germany so we could get married in the States. Anneliese closes by stating as I had done earlier, that she wanted to get married as soon as possible . . . *since I do not like living and loving out of wedlock, I feel the same as you do . . .*

In a five page letter, No. 96, dated 3 June 1946, to which she added a postscript dated 4 June, Anneliese covers three pages with detailed examples of the English lessons she is now taking with a private tutor (an American woman married to a German). Having just completed numerous German-English, English-German translations she notes:

". . . mein Kopf ist jetzt ganz brummig . . ." *". . . My head is now all a 'buzz . . ."*

Before I translate into English excerpts from Anneliese's letter of June 3/4, 1946, I believe it appropriate to explain why Anneliese signed her letters during our ten months' separation as Anne and not as Anneliese. It was all based on my idea, and her desire, as usual, to please me. Stupid me!

Anneliese is a beautiful name, a melodious name, and not a common one in Germany. In English it translates as Anna Louise. When I met Anneliese I thought her name would be unusual to Americans, and thus add another factor to her being "different". In German, the first part of her name is correctly pronounced "A'hneh", and the balance as "leezeh". I, in my misguided way, thought pronouncing her name would be difficult for us tongue tied Amurricans. And so, early on, I suggested to Anneliese that I call her Anne, not Anna, Anne, plain old, vanilla Anne. Nothing more white bread than that. She was puzzled when I broached the idea, but readily agreed to be called Anne. All that mattered to her was that it pleased me. By the time we both were in the States I realized my error, and she became Anneliese again—except that I mispronounced her name as Anneliese, putting the accent on the third syllable, when the correct emphasis is on the first part of her name: Áhneh. Anneliese never complained. Then, one evening, a few months after we had joyfully celebrated, with our children and grandchildren, our 50th Wedding Anniversary, we were relaxing in our living room after an afternoon picking fruit in our orchards (which Anneliese had turned into a line of handmade preserves and jelly for her specialty foods business) when she turned to me, and out of the blue, and in an off hand manner, said, "You know, Dad, you've been mispronouncing my name, its ÁHnehliese! She smiled as she spoke, and her eyes twinkled. Wow, what a surprise! I remember jumping out of my chair and calling my daughter Heidi, and my son-in-law Carl, in Rochester, NY to recount this disclosure to them. I had been mispronouncing Anneliese's name for half a century, and she had never, until now, said a word of correction. They both laughed and said, "Well, that's Mom, nothing seems to bother her." And every time for the next year or so when they called, and I answered the phone, they would pointedly ask, "And how is ÁHneliese?" She was something extra special, and she was mine. I turn now to my translation, into English, of excerpts from Anneliese's letter of June 3/4, 1946.

. . . How nice it would be when, side by side, we could help each other with our schoolwork! But you know, Bub, when we are together again, we will learn a lot, isn't that right? I know you are thinking of those hours at Voith's, [name of the villa our Military Government Team took over as our billet] *and laughing at the same time, since those hours of instruction were mostly filled with kissing, caressing and having fun; grammar and English words were banned far into the background. But Bub, I speak with "Ernestness" when I say that I wish to learn a lot with you, so that both of us can understand each other in German and English. Yes, Bub?*

. . . Now, Bub, Love, will you be coming to me soon? Forgive me when I am sometimes so impatient. But you know well how much I long for you! And how deeply I love you!

A thousand loving greetings and sweet little kisses from your Anne. I also send affectionate greetings to your family!

4. 6. 1946

My Love!

Glorious weather today, don't you want to take a walk through the blooming meadows and the verdant fields? I heartily invite you to do so! Perhaps Ingrid [a first cousin] *will visit us, then I'll go walking with her!* [Here Anneliese was sweetly reminding me of those glorious days during our idyllic five months in 1945 when we wandered, hand in hand, through the meadows and fields of Heidenheim, stopping to kiss and caress whenever we found a secluded, shady knoll.]

Good-bye my boy, my sweet sweet Darling!!

Your Anne

In folklore, June is a special month for lovers. It certainly was for Anneliese and me. For it was in June 1945 that what was *beshert*, what was meant to be, came to pass: Arthur and Anneliese were brought together in Heidenheim, Germany! I am setting forth, almost *in toto*, two letters which address this life changing occasion for both Anneliese and me. Mine was written on the 10th of June 1946, Anneliese's on the 16th, so I begin with mine, but for reasons of chronology only—Anneliese's plumbs the depths of Life and Love much more than I could ever do!

Nummer 70
10-6-46
Brooklyn

"An meine ferne Geliebte" Anne!

Mit der Hilfe Beethovens habe ich diesen Brief angefangen. Ich bin sehr, sehr glücklich! Jetzt, mein ganzes Dasein brennt mit ein heiliges Feuer, das Deine warmen, lieben Briefe erregen haben! Heute habe ich das Lied, "Ich hab' mein Herz in Heidelberg verloren" gehört. Aber wenn ich das Lied singen könnte, würde ich is so singen: "Ich hab' mein Herz in Heidenheim verloren— bei dem Brenzenstrom!" Ja, diese Monat vor ein Jahr war der Arfang eines neuen Lebens für uns beide!! Vielleicht das Leben war nicht ganz süss—und sogar ein bisschen zu "scharf" für unseren "Geschmack"—aber wir müssen nicht vergessen—die Hauptsache ist—wir haben das Leben!—und die Zeit kommt, wenn wir es zusammen für eine herrliche Ewigkeit geniessen werden!!

"To my distant beloved" Anne!

I have begun this letter with the help of Beethoven. I am very, very happy! Now, my entire Being burns with a holy fire which your loving letters have stirred up! Today I heard the song, "I Lost My Heart in Heidelberg". But if I could sing the song I would sing it this way: "I Lost My Heart in Heidenheim—Beside the Flowing Brenz!" Yes, a year ago this month a new life began for both of us!! Perhaps Life was not wholly sweet—and even a little too "sharp" for our tastes—but we must not forget—the main thing is—we are alive!—and the time is coming when we shall enjoy a glorious Eternity together!!

I was so alone without your beautiful, sensitive letters. Yes, you were always with me—in spirit—but do I have to tell you how difficult it is to make love with a "spirit"? Clearly, your letters are only a substitute for you. But when I read them, over and over, I create before my eyes, almost as Pygmalion did, my "Dream Girl"—You!! Your sentences reveal the true nature of my Anne's soul. I sense everything! And my enraptured mind creates for my pleasure an Anne who is almost real! But sadly, I cannot hold in my arms, press to my heart and kiss my creation! How sad!—but my heart is filled, and while I sit and dream, I'm almost "drunk" with Love! That's the way it goes with your loving letters. Am I a child to play this way? If yes, then let me remain a dumb child forever!

(This letter discussed matters already recounted in this tale, as. for example, my reluctance to believe 100% I had a job that was taking me back to Germany, until I had all the necessary papers in hand, and was on the boat.) My letter continued, in English:

.... *Your English is really wonderful!! I particularly like the way you are grasping the principles of English syntax. I wish my German word order were better!—We are all wondering what you are making for my mother! She was very pleased with your last gift. Anne, dear, I have written you many letters via the regular Postal system—and I hope all of them will soon arrive. Tell me too, if they are censored* [all our mail was, with a few exceptions] .... *I hope too, that I need not write you further from America! Oh, God! How I want to be with you again!! I have made many sets of plans for our future—but to begin to properly put them into effect I must be with you—I need you so much!! (And I imagine you need me too, eh? Anne?)*

.... *Do you know, Anne—you do things just as I do? When you wrote the words: "Für neugierige Menschen" on a piece of paper slipped into an envelope to keep people from reading its contents—you did what I did . . . except that I wrote in "slangy" English—"For nosey People"—"Für Menschen, die ihre Nase in alles stecken" . . . "For people who stick their nose in everything".*

.... *I'm glad that my food packages are helping to maintain a fairly decent caloric rate for you and your family. In case you don't know it yet—I've just sent a skirt and blouse set to [name deleted] for you. Wear it well!*

All my burning love,
Dein Bub
Arthur

On the 16th of June, 1946, per her Letter No. 93, Anneliese wrote recalling when first we met, and a new, and exciting life, began for both of us. Her letter was written on the exact date, one year earlier, when first I saw my Fairy Princess, and she her Prince Charming, and when I instantly fell in love with her, and knew I had found the woman I would marry! When what was *beshert*, came to pass! It took Anneliese a tad longer to fall in love with me. A sentence in her letter reveals her reason for hesitation. She was concerned by what to her seemed to be apparent disparities. There were none! All I saw before me was a beautiful young woman, warm, gracious, intelligent, and exceedingly desirable! I wanted to possess her, body and soul! I wanted to be part of her, body and soul! I ached to have her, to have her want me, as much as I wanted her! That I succeeded is something I have never understood. Whatever the reasons, I am grateful she became mine, as I became hers! Here is Anneliese's letter:

Nr. 93 [Anneliese wrote this, and other letters, on Heidenheim Military Government stationery I had given her. It was nigh impossible for Germans to buy stationery at that time at any price.]

16.6.1946

Mein geliebtes Herzchen!/My Beloved Darling!

In an unaccustomed late hour I am writing this letter, in a few minutes it will be midnight, and I have been lying in bed for two hours and can simply not fall asleep.

My thoughts are always with you, my longing for you is so great, so unspeakably painful, that sometimes I can scarcely believe that I have lived so long without you, without your love.

And now, where the mail is so irregular in delivery I often become impatient, and I have promised you to remain strong and brave. Oh, Bubelein, how easy it is to speak all these big words, but how can a hot longing heart cope with them? You know too well how difficult it sometimes is! And when I think, that all this loneliness, this anxiety, will soon be a thing of the past, that you shall again be with me, and this time for ever! Oh Bub, it's really a wonderful destiny that life, in its ever changing game, has given us as our share!

Do you know that today is an anniversary for me, indeed, for both of us? Today is exactly one year that I entered into my service at the Villa Voith! [I remind the reader that the U.S. Army took over the Villa Voith, from its German owners, and used it as its Military Government HQ in Heidenheim, and as its billeting and mess quarters for our Unit.]. *The day I saw you for the first time. Can you still remember that?* [Remember? How can I forget that glorious moment!!] *Oh, yes, never would I have then dreamed, that I, a simple girl from the kitchen,* [a simple kitchen girl?—Ha!] *would one day become your wife?* . . . . *How glorious were all the secret hours of love with you, and how holy, and paradise-like those heavenly nights!! And it shall again become so, God means well for us, and our pure, honest Love is no sin, have we both something to regret, have we done something wrong? No, no, let people say what ever they desire, from their ugly talk envy and jealousy are speaking, let them talk, one day they'll tire of it.*

Our "secret hours of love" were not required because of any qualms on my part, or on Anneliese's, that our love was wrong— but because it was barred by the Army's Regulations prohibiting fraternization between us victorious Americans and the beaten Germans. The reader will recall how I faced this issue when it was raised directly with me. Still, one did not have to wave red flags in front of bulls.

And wasn't this time of separation actually a good, if also a hard test for our Love for our beliefs in each other? Whatever else life will bring, we will hold together, we will not perish, and our life will be a life of readiness.

Oh Bubelein, if you were only already here beside me!!! . . . .
Bubelein, sweet Love, your Anne is full of expectation her heart
beats violently, thinking always of you, of our early reunion!

Today I wrote to your parents, they are surely sad when you
leave them again, but isn't this the way the world runs? A Mother
carries her children under her heart, brings them into the world,
sees them develop under her care and rearing, grow up, Father
and Mother teach them to be good people with healthy minds and
understanding. And then the day comes, on which the big child,
who, with time has grown into an adult, then goes on its own way,
into the open arms of the world, and into the arms of another for
whom the child leaves its parents and drawn to different people.
Yes, I can feel how much this leaving hurts, but, yet, aren't the
parents also happy, when they know their child has found what gives
substance and meaning to life, what brings happiness and joy?

See, my Bub, sometimes I appear like a thief who has stolen you
away from your loving parents! Foolish thought!! But I hope that
once your parents get to know me personally, that they will then
be pleased with me! Don't you think so, too?

Always Your Angel
Anne

Darling, good night now, dream sweetly, and I will pray that we
are soon together. Excuse my shaky handwriting, but in bed one
does not write better.

Anneliese always wrote beautiful, insightful letters. This one is
special for several reasons. It was written when her pounding heart
kept sleep at bay. "O sleep, why dost thou leave me?" (Handel,
Semele, Act II). And it is at such emotional times that the heart
speaks forth, unfettered. And so did my beloved Anneliese. She
recalls that glorious day when first we met—and both of our

lives started anew! She sees herself as a Cinderella, when, in truth she was a Fairy Princess! Oh, how clearly did she, in this letter, face harsh realities, meet them head on, and with her trust in God, in me, and in herself, sweep them aside. In discussing our separation she turned a "negative" into a "positive". Anneliese acutely observed that this period of separation was a good, if hard test of our love and faith in each other. Her view accorded with mine. This testing of our mutual resolve, and of our individual reactions to negative stimuli was critical in determining the nature of our future relationship as wedded man and wife. That each of us came out of this agonizing ten months of separation with our love and faith in each other unimpaired—indeed, strengthened—demonstrated, yet again, that we had been meant for each other, meant by God to live harmoniously together in this life, and thereafter, in eternity!

Anneliese's prayer in her letter for our speedy reunion—together with others each of us had repeatedly made—were beginning to bear fruit, as evidenced by my Letter No. 77 dated 29-6-46.

Mein süsses Herzchen! My Sweet Darling!

Here is Radio Katz—Bubelein's Station: Attention! Attention! Here is the Time: "Bong!" The exact time is 9 hours and 22 minutes (p.m.) And now we bring a bit of good news: Angel, yesterday your Bub finally received his "Pass" for Germany! But that is only half the story. He has to wait until the American Secret. Police have examined him. And when they say he is no criminal (and believe me—I'm not-) then he can return to Germany! Isn't that glorious? But, of course—clearly, it goes without saying—(and who knows what else) But, listen—here is more news; Yesterday your Bub found a store which carries fresh butter in tins—fat and so forth (for example, powdered milk containing sugar and 4 vitamins), And naturally, I bought quite a bit for you. And I also got two more pounds of sugar. Now I have 7 pounds for you (not to speak of quite a bit of honey). Yes, I clearly know what a sweet tooth my Anne is, and I'm putting together a lot for you. (But "don't be annoyed", I'm also bringing a lot of love with me—enough for several centuries!)

I then went on to say I had been to Yorkville, where I had bought the above noted items, and had discussed importing products for the owner, and had also bought 4 German language recordings of songs such as *"Die Lorelei"* and *Heidenröslein*. I also wrote that I thought Anneliese would be comfortable visiting Yorkville. I noted the names of cafes such as Café Mozart, and shops such as Würst Geschäft *(Sausage Business)*, that there were lots of newspapers and magazines in German, and war relief agencies: *"Deutsche Nothilfe"*: *Help for the German needy*, with the slogan: "Children don't make war—they only pay for it": *Kinder machen keinen Kriege—aber sie bezahlen (sie tragen die Kosten) für ihn."* I told Anneliese that visiting Yorkville would help acclimate her to America, the transition from one language to another would be made easier.

Continuing in English:

I have only one sad note to relate in this letter. This morning, I rose to find that the chain holding your little heart had broken while I slept. And while it is being repaired I am unable to wear it—for the first time since I left you, Angel—your heart is not about my neck! But your loving thoughts are safe within my own longing heart!—Behüt Dich Gott! [God protect you!] Dein Bub, Arthur

The three months Winter and nine months cold which Anneliese had jokingly used to describe her native Black Forest weather, were all too real in the Fall and Winter of 1945, and in the Spring of 1946. And this pattern would repeat itself in the Fall and Winter of 1946. The most basic foodstuffs and commonplace things one ordinarily gives little thought to, such as cooking oil, needles and thread, yarn for darning, wool for knitting, were then either non-existent, or so scarce, as to be beyond the purchasing power of most of the inhabitants of Occupied Germany, including the Baur Family. Being well aware of all this, I was profoundly concerned for the well being of Anneliese and her family. Thus, accompanying the expressions of hope, love, longing, and desires unfulfilled, which these letters recited, fare one might expect to find in letters of Lovers apart, there were also detailed references to "packages" with contents fully described and each carefully numbered. These packages contained basic food stuffs, sweets and other treats, and household supplies. Examples of this intertwining of spiritual sustenance for the heart, with material for daily survival, are set forth in excerpts from two of my letters to Anneliese, These follow excerpts from Anneliese's letters of July 4, and July 12, 1946. These two letters reveal that special grace and beauty which enveloped her being, and which I sensed that glorious first moment I was in her presence!

Her letter of July 4th was written wholly in English (with the exception of a few phrases), and well written, too. Anneliese was quickly mastering the language which would be her major vehicle for communication for the rest of her life. She wrote her letter before she learned I had received my Pass to travel to Germany and start my job there—with my leaving for Germany dependent only upon a security clearance—which posed no problem. She missed me greatly—as I missed her—but her inner strength, and her ability to see beauty in even the simplest things, sustained her morale.

My dearest Darling!

How is my little Bub today? Well? O, I hope very much; your Anne feels well too! Yes, and I arrived at Schwen. punctually last Sunday, as I wrote you in the letter via the regular mail.

I hope you are receiving all my letters written in Schwenn. and Heidenh. and I look forward for sweet letters. The day is so long without them, although my thoughts are always with you!

When will you be able to return to Germany? Please excuse me when I always grow so impatient, but you know very well how I long for you!!

The sun shines so warm and the nature is so beautiful now, but my sweet heart is so far away, I am sorry to say!! And what are all the beautifulness and joys without you? Only the half part of them.

Today I was with my mother in our field we had to hoe the potatoes and vegetables and to water everything, so that they grow much better. Your seeds came too late, but it is not so bad, we can keep them for the next spring.

Bubelein, you should see my flowers at the window of my room! O, they look very nice!! Their blossoms are so beautiful and their smells so sweet, and the colors are so pleasant for my eyes.

And beside your pictures, which are standing on a small table near my bed, there is always a vase with flowers. Now there are red roses, I know you like these flowers very much, don't you?

I cried when I read these lines the first time in 1946. I cry again, six decades later when I read them. They recall the words of Mimi, in her first aria in Act I of La Boheme, where she recounts who she is, that she lives in a small room in the attic (Anneliese's small room was created out of the attic in her house!), that she loves flowers, and that a rose blooms in a vase in her room, and that she breathes in its scent, petal by petal, oh, how beautiful is the perfume of a flower: *Germoglia in un vaso una rosa, foglia a foglia la spio. Così gentil è il profumo d'un fior*. Anneliese was always my heroine. She placed me on a pedestal. Actually, I was her footstool.

This evening I have to learn a little more for the tomorrow's lesson. Forty new words and a few of them are so "komisch",

wirklich sehr komisch!! [are so strange, really very strange!!]
Don't laugh!!! . . . . Bub, please come back very soon, for I love
you and need you, as you love and need me too!

Eight days following Anneliese's penning in her July 4th letter
she received mine of June 29 telling her I had received my Pass
to travel to Germany. She now knew that my return to her, was
a reality, and that my actual arrival could not be too far off. Her
Letter No. 102, dated 12. 7. 46, from Schwenningen, leaves no
doubt concerning her reaction to the news.

My beloved Darling,

Oh, how shall I begin!? My joy is indescribable, because our good
Mother Zeiner sent a package containing three of your letters.
And the letters contained such wonderful news that I'm really
completely, completely happy!!

You now have your Pass for your trip to Germany! Oh, the
thought that you will soon be with me is wondrously beautiful
and glorious! And then for our glorious happy life forever! Now
I know that one day, suddenly, you will appear before me, you
are finally underway as I write you this letter!

I was quite saddened as I read the first half of your letter No. 75.
All your grief, all your painful loneliness spoke from it. I know how
difficult it is to be separated so distantly, and for so long, from one's
most beloved and dearest possessions on earth. But Darling, soon
soon all this sorrow shall be taken from our hearts, together we
shall enjoy all the beauties and wonders of nature, we shall delight
in the happy chirping of the birds, of the manifold blooming of the
trees and flowers, the Sun, with its rays will warm our hearts our
minds, oh my dear Bubelein, our future will be wonderful! And
when life demands struggle and sacrifice from us, we will struggle
together, we are both young and strong enough for that!

Und ich bin auch glücklich dass Du nun endlich meine Briefe, die ich direckt aus Schwenningen schicke, erreichen u. bis dieser Brief in Deinen Händen ist, hast Du sicher schon vieler meiner Briefe von hier u. von Heidenheim erhalten. Deine Briefe durch die reguläre Post erreichen mich erfreulicherweise schnell u. in geordneter Reihenfolge. Vor zwei Tagen kam Brief Nr. 12 u. auch ein von Deiner lieben Mutti. Ach Herzchen, sie schreibt immer so lieb u. gut u. ich werde ihr u. Deinem Vater immer ein dankbare liebe Tochter sein!—

And I am also happy that now, finally, my letters that I'm sending directly from Schwenningen are reaching you, and by the time this letter is in your hands, you should have received many more letters from here and from Heidenheim. Your letters via the regular mails reach me fast enough to satisfy me and in proper sequence. Two days ago your Letter No. 12, and also one from your Mom arrived. Oh Darling she always writes so lovingly and well and I shall always be a grateful and loving daughter to her and your Father!

I'm astonished by your zealous business abilities, and how quickly you move all these matters along. Yes yes, "Detestable one, where are you hurrying to?"

[Anneliese is making fun here. She is quoting the opening line of the Act I aria by the heroine Leonore in Beethoven's opera, Fidelio, upon seeing Don Pizarro, the opera's villain,—and the man who had falsely imprisoned her husband, Florestan—go rushing by. Fidelio is one of my favorite operas. Its theme: how a courageous and faithful wife saves her husband's life and secures his freedom. In the opera's final scene Florestan sings to Leonore: *Deine Treu' erhielt mein Leben, Tugend schreckt den Bösewicht.—Your faithfulness sustained my life, Virtue terrifies the scoundrel.* And Leonore replies: *Liebe führte mein Bestreben, wahre Liebe fürchtet nicht: Love guided my efforts, true love fears nothing.* The Chorus then sings: *Preist mit hoher*

Freude Glut Leonorens edeln Mut: Praise with joy most ardent, Leonore's noble courage. [My translations]. Anneliese loved classical music and opera as much as I did. And the theme of Beethoven's only opera resonated with both of us. Relieved that I would soon be back with her, but knowing that after our marriage business matters might require me to travel from time to time, and leave her behind, Anneliese expresses her concerns on this issue obliquely and with humor. Thus, after our marriage whenever my law practice required me to make extended business trips abroad on behalf of clients, I made it a practice to take Anneliese with me as frequently as possible. As Anneliese has noted, our long separation tested our virtues, but it also dissuaded us from being apart too often. I continue with my translation: *No Bub, I would definitely never say that, I would clothe everything with nice, loving words: something like this, "Oh, my Bub, do you have to go away again so soon? It's quite sad that you are again letting me sit alone. But go then, I know that everything is all right, come back soon to your Anne!" Satisfied my Master?*

Your business card looks very good, simple yet very distinguished! Really, I'm very proud of your abilities.

Anneliese then writes of my report to her of my visit to the Yorkville German District in New York City. She found it very interesting, and believes that in such a neighborhood she would soon feel right at home. I had told Anneliese that when in Yorkville I had bought recordings of German folk songs. She continues, writing in her customary High German, except, for the last portion where, being in a fun mood, she lapses into south German dialect:

Wie nett dass Du so liebe gute Heimatlieder auf Schallplatten hast! Ich liebe diese alten guten u. doch immer jungen Volkslieder sehr, findest Du wirklich "dass Küssen keine Sünde ist?" [dialect]

I glaub' net! Und überhaupt, wenn moi' anander gern hot! Moinscht net An? Ha jo Ha Ja!!!

How nice that you have recordings of such dear good Homeland songs! I love very much these good old, yet ever young folks songs, do you really find "that kissing is no sin"? [A folk song] *I don't believe it's a sin. And definitely not, when one likes the other! Don't you think so? Ha jo, Ha yes!!!*

Writing solely in English, Anneliese concludes her letter with:

And now a little English. Well I learn more and more every day, but I also know, that I have to learn much more till I am able to speak, write and read a good English. Bub, will you help me?

This morning my dear teacher invited me to spend a few hours with her tomorrow evening. Of course, I will go to her, then the conversations with her are always very nice and interesting! She is indeed a very dear lady! Now I have to close because I must still write very much for the lesson. Good-bye my dearest, God bless you and your dear Family! I love you and hope to have you with me soon. Your Anne

When we met in June 1945 Anneliese knew no English! Her grasp of the language, in one year, much of it self taught, is clear indicia of her drive and intellectual prowess! In these last two letters Anneliese was clearly heartened by the news that I was about to embark on another crossing of the Atlantic—this time to bring me back to her. I, too, was upbeat, but still very much concerned to maintain her, not only in good spirits, but in good health. My concerns, and the means I used to abate them—if not wholly to allay them—are set forth in my letter No. 16 to Schwenningen, dated 8-7-46 which crossed her's of the 12th of July.

Nummer 16
8-7-46
Brooklyn

My Darling!

See, I was right—today is Monday—and as I had previously said, some of your letters have arrived! Number 96 and 97 from Heidenheim. I hope, when you receive this letter, that you are home, quite hale and hearty . . . .

And today your "Coffee Cozy" also arrived. My Mother was very, very pleased with it. Your handiwork is exquisite! And the Card with the pressed flowers was charming! The flowers look so "real"—and "fresh! The pattern was also very pretty! My Anne is clearly clever!

Today I made arrangements whereby the Zeiners will receive a package of food weighing 49 lbs—when packed. This food was brought by a non-profit organization here in America from the US Arrmy—for distribution among various European peoples, Since no packages can as yet be sent to the French Zone—I had the package sent to the Zeiners. But nevertheless—the package is for you—and it is an expensive package ($15) but an excellent one! I know—I ate the identical food during the war. Please notify Frau Zeiner to hold the package for you—and when it comes divide everything on a ¾ to ¼ basis. 3 for you—one for her. Most of the food will be packed in 10's—since the food was meant to feed 10 soldiers. But the butter—sugar and jam will be found in 2's or 4's. The total caloric value of the package—(which is really 4 packages in one) is over 40,000 calories! Isn't that wonderful! I am writing a letter tonight to [name deleted] in which I shall enclose illustrated information in regard to this package. It should arrive within 2-3 months at the latest. And I hope to be with you when it arrives. If you like the contents I can always order more. I then return to German:

Aber die Zeit kommt—und mit ihr komme ich auch zurück! Doch! Doch! Habe ich das nicht versprochen?

But the time is coming, and with it I am also coming back! Definitely! Definitely! Have I not promised that I would?

> *I love you!*
> *Always your Bub,*
> *Arthur*

Two days later I sent Anneliese the following letter:

Number 16 [The Number was incorrect]
10-7-46
Brooklyn

My Darling!

The last few days have been wonderful ones for me—from the point of view of receiving mail from you! Yesterday my folks received your letter from Heidenheim. And since they are not here—I opened it—gosh! You are writing excellent English—keep up the good work! And then I received Nr. 98 from Heidenheim and Nr. 5 from Schwenningen—written on the fifth of June. And this letter wasn't even censored—at least the envelope had no censorship marks!

I hope you returned all right from Heidenheim. I worry so about you! I'll miss your letters again—but I'll just have to be patient.

Yesterday I wrote to Frau Zeiner explaining my arrangements in regard to the sending of packages. Now all that remains is for them to arrive!

And this morning I mailed out Pkg. 53 to you. This one contans Sugar, Coffee, Canned Milk, Candy, Nuts, Tobacco [for Vater's pipe and cigarettes for Kurt], *Soap, Pudding Powder, 12 spools of white thread and other things you can see. When you open the package, turn it upside down—for the Post Office put the stamp on the bottom side. I hope I'm with you—by the time this package arrives! The chances are really good!!*

You have written that the word "inquisitive" fits me. Yes, yes, you are right. I am "inquisitive"—but not like an old virgin—but like a scientist. As with you, everything interests me. And it's for that reason that I love you so very much! Your thoughts are always like mine!!

Regards to your Family—especially to Hilde!

May God protect you!

Your Bub,
Arthur

Enclosed with this letter was a pen and ink drawing of me sitting on an ocean dock, surrounded by my luggage, with me seated on a steamer trunk and looking at my watch. The drawing contains four lines of verse, two in English, two in German, to wit:

> I hope I don't have to wait much longer
> —I'm getting very tired—and so very lonesome!
> Ich hoffe, ich brauche nicht viel länger zu warten
> —Ich werde sehr müde—und so sehr einsam!

My letter No. 20 in the Schwenningen series was dated 19-7-46, It contained exciting news, and as I had done with other news of similar import, "I sent it by radio"!

Because of its unique content I set forth the opening portion of my letter in its original German text.

Hier ist Radio Katz, ein Sender des Bubeleins: Wie haben lieben Hörer ein unterhaltendes Programm von Heimat Klängen und lustige Tanzmusik. Wir fangen unsere Sendung an, mit dem Lied . . . Achtung! Achtung!—wir unterbrechen dieses Programm ein sehr wichtiges Stück Nachricht zu berichten! "Aus New York kommt die frohe Botschaft, dass Arthur nur für ein "freies" Schiff wartet! Alles ist in Ordnung! Hab' Geduld Anne, sagt er, ich komme!" Wir fahren das Programm fort "Ich hab'-"

Nun "Annis" hast Du diese Nachricht "Wohl behalten"?

Sweet Darling! Here is Radio Katz, Bubelein's radio station: Good Day! We are bringing our dear listeners an entertaining program of Homeland sounds and merry dance music. We begin our broadcast with the song—"I lost my heart in Heidelberg—Enjoy! [music, with song lyrics] *Attention! Attention!—we interrupt this Program to report an important piece of information! "Joyful news from New York: Arthur is waiting only for an available ship! Everything arranged! Have patience, Anne, he says, I'm coming!" We continue with our program* [music, etc].

Well, "Annis" did you keep your composure after hearing this news?

Well, today I was again in the Government Office. And before I could ask my perpetual question, the girl in the office said to me—"I requested your travel orders on Tuesday (today is Friday), and as soon as they come in you are on your way!"

Naturally, I was a little bit happy! And when I could again form words in my mouth I asked when this glorious time would be here. "Soon", she answered, "maybe in a week-or perhaps not for another three—but soon enough." "Soon enough?", I said to myself—"no", and I shook my head—"no it can never be 'soon enough'". *Right? But as long as the time is coming I shall be happy and grateful!*

Tell me—are you happy too? How much? For Heaven's Sake! So much? Girl! Is that possible? It is? Wonderful!!

O Anne, I can hardly wait! I wish I were on the boat already— better yet—I wish I were already in Germany! But let's not forget our motto—"Be Patient" Our time will come—our time is coming—our time will soon be here!

Keep happy—and healthy!

Dein Bub
Arthur

Regards to the family!

On July 21st Anneliese wrote me a four page letter. With the exception of a few sentences in German, she expressed her thoughts eloquently in well written English. She knew I had received my Pass to enter Germany, and was thus moving forward on the path which would return me to her. It would be some weeks before she received my "radio letter" of July 19th, and thus was not aware I had completed all the steps necessary to return to Germany as a civilian employee of the Military Government in Germany—and that I was waiting *only* to be assigned to a government vessel which would carry me across the Atlantic back to Germany and to her! The dreaded uncertainty of whether—at some vague time—I would return to Germany had been replaced with the knowledge that I *was* returning in the very near future— but the exact time was still unknown to Anneliese. Until we were once finally together again, embracing, kissing, crying for joy, there lurked a smidgin of concern within the deepest recesses of her mind. This is reflected in her letter.

My sweet little heart!

Sunday—afternoon and I am home quite alone and lonely, only my thoughts are with you!

The sun shines brightly and warm, my aunt was here to fetch me for a walk, but I have preferred to stay at home and I told her, that I have much to learn. Of course I have had to write a little, but to say the truth I want rather to stay here than to go out. My heart is so sad today, because I love you so very much and miss you and you are so far away, so far far away! And I receive so little mail from you now, that is also a thing that me make so sad. O I know Bub that you always write, but the letters are in Heidenheim and I am in Schwenningen!

But what can I do? It is very difficult to go by train without a pass but never the less I will try to go at the end of this month or at the beginning of the next. I hope very much that perhaps (in?) the meantime will bring/come? very good happy news from you, that you will write the best news, your arrival in Germany!!

Do you hear my knocking heart if I think of you and of the time, when we are together again??

O Bub, your Anne is some times like a little impatient child, please excuse when I have so stupid thoughts.

Today, my aunt Elsa told me, that Dieter [Elsa's son, and about 5 years old] *asked her, when you will come once again. He (alway) still remember you. Aunts Els told him, that you are in America now, but that you will come very soon, and that you have to cross a large sea! Do you know what he said, "Ja Mutter, hat dann Arthur keine Angst, dass das Schiff mit ihm untergehen könnte?" "But Mother, isn't Arthur afraid the boat might sink with him on it?"*

Nun Bubelein, hast Du wirklich keine Angst? Aber natürlich "nein"!! Warum auch! So tapfer u. mutig wie Du bist!!!! Now Bubelein, are you really unafraid? Of course you aren't! Afraid for what reason? You are too brave and courageous to worry!!!!

Dearest Love, May God Protect you! Your Angel Anne awaits you with great longing.

I enclose four pictures, I hope you will like them! Am I slender enough for you? Yes! □ No! □? I learned this from you!!

Mail received brought joy! Lack of mail brought sadness.! Thus, Anneliese's moods and mine, were materially affected by this phenomenon. Our letter writing was a constant—unfortunately, mail delivery was not. My Letter No. 24 dated 30-7-46 deals with this issue:

Number 24
30-7-46

Oh my dearest, sweetest possession!

Your Bub is a happy man today! Why, simply because he received some mail from you! Did I say "simply"? Yes, the action of receiving mail from you is a simple one—but such simple things make me so very happy!

In the morning mail I received 2 uncensored letters direct from you—they are numbered 8 and 10. [from Schwenningen] And in the afternoon, I received a letter from P which contained your letter number 103, written on the 15th of July. The envelope also contained a brief note from Frau Zeiner stating that a number of packages had been received. That last news was very good. But the best news was just hearing from you! That's all—just hearing from you—again a simple act—but still a powerful one!

Whenever I find mail from you waiting for me in the letter box a wonderful metamorphosis takes place within me. All the old fears fade away, all my sorrows dissolve into nothingness, and my soul gives birth to a new being—to a happier Arthur!

As I read your letter, drinking in each wonderful word with hot, searching eyes, the vision I continually carry with me—my vision of you, grows larger in form, and bolder in outline—it grows until I am almost sure it is real! And it almost is—as real anyway, as my desires can make it. And then you are again beside me, laughing and talking and loving me and living for me—as I do for you. And I am happy and you are happy! And all the world is good and all our problems are simple! And your lips are sweet and my caresses are tender—we are loving again and living again! And living is a pleasant dream! And I read and read—I hang onto each word—and I do more than read your words, I try to delve into the thoughts behind your words—I seek the true Anne in her letters to me—and I find that which I search for. But I no longer search for proof of my Anne's goodness; I have long long proved that point to myself! Instead, I search for my Anne's soul—I search for it that I might enter into its protecting, comforting folds! And in every letter I find your soul—and I enter into it. And I am then a happier, calmer and more hopeful man. Oh Anne, how grateful I am for your letters; they bring the happy past to life, they help conjure up visions of a still happier future, and they help so much to make the dull present brighter and encouraging!! Your letters more than repay me for anything I might have done for you, your family and friends. And when I return you shall make me still happier. I know!

Now do you know why I am a happy man today? It is just a simple matter of receiving mail from you, that's all (but that is enough!)

Now to answer a few questions:

The word "campus" comes from the Latin word field and it is used in America to designate the grounds about the college and university buildings. Clear?

"Now let me tell you how my trip back was". is a perfectly good English sentence. Good for you!

Anne, darling—check your spelling of especially and teacher, otherwise your last letters were very good—and I'm very, very, very proud of you, Ja, sehr!

I hope you will be enjoying the shoes I sent, by the time this "missive" arrives.

I then write about the situation where Anneliese, without obtaining a U.S. travel pass went by train to Heidenheim, and on the way back to Schwenningen, in the French Zone, was stopped by a U.S. soldier guard who asked for her pass. Having none, she showed him the letters from me which she had picked up in Heidenheim. The soldier looked at them, and let her proceed. I caution her not to travel again without a pass:

Before I close, I must give you a "warning". Please don't go to Heidenheim without a Travel Pass. Please! You were certainly clever to talk to the soldier as you did. But perhaps the next one will not be so nice. Frau Zeiner says that she can ship small packages to you. And so—wait for permission. I'm coming shortly—believe me! "Be good"!

Your happy Bub!
Arthur

Heartfelt Greetings to the whole world! (Nobody excluded!)

Things now began to move quickly—my love and longing to be with Anneliese was greater than ever—absence does in truth make the heart grow fonder, and a long absence especially so. But when the date for my departure for Germany was finally set for the latter part of August 1946, and I began assiduously to prepare for that long awaited day, my letters to Anneliese filled with details, cautions and concerns, to the extent some took on an almost perfunctory tone. As excerpts from our letters in July and August 1946 note, Anneliese and I were last together on the 27th of October 1945, and were not again to see each other until the 7th of September 1946. We had survived more than ten months of a heart and soul rending separation. When I would return to Germany was no longer an issue. But my arrival in the American Occupation Zone in Germany would not, of itself, resolve the issue of separation. Anneliese and I would no longer be separated by thousands of kilometers of sea and land. I was to be stationed in Offenbach, a small city near Frankfurt, in Land Hessen. Separated from Anneliese by only a few hundred kilometers! Closer to my beautiful, belóved Anneliese Baur, but not close enough! She lived in the French Zone of Occupation, and I would be working and living in the American zone. In the post-war world of 1946, travel between the two zones, particularly for German nationals, was heaped about with onerous restrictions. Further, any overt signs of our relationship as lovers would fly in the face of U.S. Military Government strictures against fraternization with Germans. These were slowly being honored in the breach in late 1946. But they were still the law, and neither Anneliese, nor I, wished to do anything to prejudice my Government employment, or to interfere with my efforts—which I would shortly undertake—to obtain the necessary clearances from the Four Occupying Powers allowing Anneliese to leave Germany, and the visa from our State

Department, permitting Anneliese to enter the United States for the sole purpose of marrying me.

Aware of all these realities I wrote cautionary letters to Anneliese as to how she and I were to comport ourselves until I could figure out the lay of the land. Having come this far I didn't want either of us to do anything which could cause us grief. Further, I wanted the contents of our letters in Germany to be circumspect—as devoid of emotion as our long contained desires might allow. I did not know whether our letters in Germany would be opened by censors, American or French. Almost all our letters, and my packages, when I was Stateside, had been censored, with no ill effects to either of us. But now, in Germany, the situation might be different. Further, I didn't want a fellow censor across the table from me, to read aloud a love letter from Anneliese to me—and snicker as he did so! Grr!! These observations having been made, I return to our Love Letters, or their excerpts, which shall bring our tale to that glorious stage where Anneliese and I are brought together again!! What happened afterwards? Dear reader, stay yet a little while with me, and the remaining Episodes shall tell you!

In my Letter No. 27 to Schwenningen, dated 15-8-46, I wrote to tell Anneliese that I was just days away from leaving for Germany:

Mein süsses Herzchen!

The writing of this letter can only be an anticlimax! Hopefully you already know the good news: "namely": Your Bub departs on the 20th of August for Germany!! A Chapter has ended—a new one—and surely, a better one is now beginning!

Yesterday I received the sweet news. And it was really sweet— wholly delightful! Oh Angel—I can't write—I only want to dream! May I?

I went shopping again for you today—and I bought 2 more pairs of hose for you. And I've finally been able to buy some canned bacon—4-1½ lb. cans—and good canned beef—and more fat! I'm bring these things along with me.

I've been waiting so long—and you have too, that my pending departure has lost most of its aura of joy—but still, I'm happy that I shall finally be on my way—and I know you are happy too!

Today I received Letter 102 via Frau Z. it was a wonderful letter! But I shall save discussing it—until we can do it together. OK?

Dein glücklicher Bub!

Arthur

A few days earlier I sent a letter to Anneliese which contained a letter, written in English and French, to the French Military Government authorities, requesting that they permit Anneliese to travel to the American Consulate in Stuttgart to seek a visa to travel to America for the purpose of marrying me. The French gave her a pass to travel to Stuttgart. But the U.S. Consulate would do nothing for her (or me). I ultimately got Anneliese's visa, as I shall relate.

On the 17th of August, in an unnumbered letter, Anneliese writes from Schwenningen, that she had received from Frau Zeiner two of my Express packages and that she was really enraptured by their wonderful contents! The brown shoes I had bought her were very nice, a tad too large, but worn with socks they fit well. She said I had made her Dad and Kurt very happy with the different tobacco products I had sent them. *Nun haben unsere Männer wieder die beste Laune!!: Now our men are again in the best of moods!!* And the many food products I sent were *wie ein Geschenk dess Himmels!: like a gift from Heaven!* And she thanked me a thousand times for my caring help. Especially dear was my birthday card—her birthday was the 23rd of August—with some verses I had written. Anneliese continues:

Doch ich hoffe immer noch, dass Du mir persönlich Deine Glückwünsche zu meinem Wiegenfest überreichen kannst! Und Bub, das wäre wirklich herrlich u. das Allerschönste für mich! Noch kann ich ja hoffen u. ich will auch gar nicht mehr ungeduldig werden, ich verspreche es Dir, wirklich Bubelein!!—

Yet I am always hoping that you can personally deliver to me your congratulations on my birthday! And Bub, that would really be glorious and the most beautiful thing for me! Still I can hope and I also promise you I will no longer be impatient!!

Anneliese then describes an enjoyable day trip she took down to the *Bodensee*, a large lake bordering on Switzerland, and a unique agricultural area, where she bought fruit and vegetables for home canning. When we are together again we should visit it, she writes. She is sure I would like *dieses nette Fleckchen Erde,: this pretty little piece of earth*. On returning home she found three of my letters awaiting her, July 12, 15 and 22. She said I wrote so lovingly and that she was happy that she could read and understand my English so well. The thing that pleased her most was the news I was ready for my trip back to Germany. It might even be possible that I'm already on the way [The ship left port on the afternoon of August 23, Anneliese's birthday, a gift to her *in absentia*] . . . *herrlich der Gedanke, dass Du bald bei mir sein kannst!: glorious is the thought that you may soon be with me!*

Then, referring to one of the matters we had previously discussed, Anneliese writes:

You're right, Bub, we both have really no reason to complain. We hear much from each other, even if we sometimes have to wait for the letters, but finally they do come; both of us are healthy and I'm feeling well and happy to be at home with my parents and my sister and brother, how rich am I in contrast to all those millions of people without homes and relatives. And one day you shall return to me, and remain with me forever! Yes Darling, we certainly ought not complain, and should thank God for each happy healthy day He bestows upon us. Isn't that right, my Bub!

Anneliese then says she has some bad news to relate. She's losing her English teacher who is going to Munich to work with the U.S. Military Government. But who would now give her lessons? Me, perhaps? She would happily agree to such a substitution! It's time for her to go to bed. Tomorrow is Sunday, and she'll write me again!

. . . . Mein Gott, da gibt es einmal sehr viel für Dich zu lesen! Hab keine Angst, ich werde Dir dabei helfen! Gute Nacht, träume süss, u. Gott möge Dich behüten!

Deine Anne

My God, you have a lot to read at one time! Don't worry, I'll help you with it! Good night, sweet dreams and may God protect you!

Your Anne

My Letter No. 28 to Schwenningen was written on 19-8-46. It was wholly in English, and, as noted in the opening sentence, dealt "with dry things" concerning my employment in Germany, and cautionary counsel to Anneliese.

My Darling!

This will be a letter dealing with dry things—dates and names etc. But still, I believe you will find its contents interesting.

For one thing: tomorrow my baggage will be loaded onto the ship. No—I don't know the name of the vessel. I thought I'd be leaving tomorrow—but it appears as if loading will take some time—and therefore I shall not leave 'til Thursday or Friday. I'll write you again—just before I leave.

I shall be working for the Civilian Censorship division of the Army. My hours are 40 hours per week = 5 days x 8 hours per day. And so I shall have quite a bit of free time—especially on weekends. Naturally, I'll try to come to you the very first chance I can get. I won't say when, since I do not know what travel restrictions, if any, apply to civilian employees. And until I tell you otherwise, do not try to come to Frankfurt. I do not want you near any American Army installations—I don't think I need explain why—I say this for your benefit. Do not misunderstand me, Anne!

As soon as I arrive at Frankfurt I shall call or telegraph— whichever is more convenient.

The last time I saw you was on the 27th of October, of last year. Right? I certainly believe we both shall be with each other again—before that date rolls around again!

For once I hesitate to plan ahead—I know what it is to work for the government. And, of course, I want to do nothing to jeopardize my stay in Germany.

I shall keep my eyes and ears open for better job opportunities— by better I mean those jobs which give me more freedom of movement—and even better pay.

But our road ahead is a long one, Anne. We must be grateful for what we have—we must make the best of our lot—and we must continuously hope, and plan for a better and freer future for the both of us! Am I not right?

The next few days will be the hardest for me, as if the past months weren't difficult enough! I'm happy I shall be nearer to you. But somehow, all this waiting has taken the edge off of the real happiness this trip would normally have had. And worst of all. I'm tired—mentally and physically, before I have even started!

Oh Engel, how I need you!

GEDULD! [PATIENCE!]

Dein Bub,
Arthur

My APO number will be 757. I'll give my complete address later.

That this nuts and blots letter *was* a love letter is reflected in but six words: *Oh Engel, how I need you!*

Per my Letter No. 29 to Schwenningen, dated 22-8-46, and written wholly in German—but for the last paragraph—I kept Anneliese apprised of my progress towards her.

My Darling!

Tomorrow at 2 in the afternoon your Bubelein will be traveling to Germany. Finally!

But is he happy? no, sadly, not entirely! For so long a time no sweet letters of yours have arrived. I know that Frau Z. Is getting my packages, but you? Are you also getting them? And the shoes? And—

I still have so much more to ask, and yet you are so far away. And when I am in Frankfurt, or perhaps, in Offenbach, I shall also be far from you. Closer than now, but far enough!

I don't know now how easy it will be for me to travel to you, or to write.

Naturally, I shall try everything to be with you shortly. And I shall see if I can transfer to Stuttgart or Heidenheim.

If only you were not in the French Zone! But I cannot demand that you leave your parents. But don't worry yourself, Angel, everything will work out for the best!

A large food parcel is now on its way to Heidenheim—it's for you. This one is also a 10-1 parcel.

Be patient, Anne!—I love you so very much! Remain well!

Please write to [name deleted] and ask him how the procedure is in regard to German civilians writing to American civilians stationed in Germany. OK? I have already done the same.

Dein Bub
Arthur

In these last days before sailing I wrote at a dizzying pace to Anneliese. I wanted her to know so much—and I knew that any letters written on board would most likely not be posted until we docked in Germany—and that I might even be with Anneliese—oh, a blessed thought!—before she received these. Thus, my Letter No. 30 to Anneliese in Schwenningen was written on 23-8-46 in the morning. If my vessel actually sailed as scheduled that afternoon, this letter, all in English, was mailed in the morning of that day.

My dearest beloved!

I have a few hours remaining before leaving for Germany. And in this, my last letter to you from this side, I wish to bring a number of points of interest to your attention.

For one thing, Anne, my letters to you written from Frankfurt, etc will not ring as clearly as those I write from here. I do not know the censorship regulations abroad. And if our letters are read, I do not wish that your heart be exposed to the licentious gaze of shallow and callous government employees.

I do not wish them to consider you just another poor German girl looking for favors from an American.

I do not want them to think of you as a prostitute! And that is why I do not wish you to come to Frankfurt—and why my letters might sound noncommital and almost cold.

But do not fear this apparent coldness. Beneath the austere lines of my letters you will sense the hot, pulsating desires I have for you.

I do not like this damned "concealment"! But we must do nothing to jeopardize our common future. Remember but one thing Anne—when everything else appears in doubt—remember that I love you dearly!

Regards to your family.

Dein Bub
Arthur

On the 23rd of August, 1946, the same day I began my Atlantic crossing journey to Germany, Anneliese wrote me an unnumbered four page letter, all in English, except for a small paragraph at its end.

My dearest, sweetest Darling!

The latest few days were wonderful days for me, for the mail man brought so many mail from you and from your mother. And all your letters contain so good news that I am very satisfied now and very happy!

Your Mom's letter was dear and full of love for you and for me and of course she will be sad when you leave the home and as she wrote, Harold will leave the home too, to study at another town, far away from Brooklyn! Poor Mom and Dad, then your home will be very empty, but soon, we all will be with them again, to begin/start? our happy common life. Time flies so quickly, a year is so short, and who can know, what the future will bring for us! [Anneliese's reference to a "year" was based on her understanding that my contract with the government was for a year, and in the interim all paper work necessary to secure her departure from Germany, and entry into the States, having been successful, I would then return, with my beautiful, belóved Anneliese Baur at my side. My idea, which I later explained to Anneliese, was to proceed immediately to round up all the necessary paper work, and this done, to leave promptly for the States. Leaving before my contract term was up would mean that I would have to pay my own way home, via a non-governmental carrier, in addition to paying for Anneliese. Getting home as soon as possible, I thought, was well worth this extra cost.]

Today is my birthday, a warm sunny day, but I am sorry to say, I am still alone. Of course I am a little disappoint that you are not with me now, for I have always hoped that your own person will surprise me by that time. But what can I do? Shall I cry? No, no your Anne is not so stupid, because she knows, that you will come as soon as possible and maybe you are already in Europe in this moment.

Although you are not with me today nevertheless I have had my little joys, for all my little cousins have come to congratulate me and each of them brought me very nice flowers. My teacher's daughter was here too and also brought flowers and kindest regards from her and her mother. My room looks like a flower— store now, and you know my Bub, how much I like flowers with its beautiful colors and sweet scent!

And then I received very dear letters from mother Zeiner and Heiner. [one of the Zeiner boys] *And one of the letter enclosed the wonderful news, that you wrote to Heidenheim you would soon be able to begin your long journey to me! Oh my sweet heart, can you imagine my joy and happiness? And one letter enclosed three nice pictures too you took at the beach with your brother and his friend. You look so sweet and well, so fresh and nice, that my longing for you grows more and more, but a gentle voice in my loving heart tells me, that you will be with me very soon, perhaps sooner than I think! I want to follow our Motto: "Be patient, be patient!" All the time will be much easier with patience.*

[Anneliese then relates, in some detail that the Zeiners had told her that Kitty, a local girl who had befriended Anneliese, had jilted her American soldier boy friend who had returned to the States, and that she then immediately became engaged to another American soldier! She, in common with the Zeiners, was shocked by such callous and shallow conduct on Kitty's part. And, in German, she sets forth what Heiner wrote to her]: *"Wenn er wüsste dass ich auch so etwas machen würde, dürfte ich gar nie mehr zu ihnen in die Reute kommen!"* Were he to learn that I had also done something like that, I could never again visit them in The Reute!

[their neighborhood]. Aber hab keine Angst Bub, Deine Anne wird die immer treu bleiben u. nur Dich lieben solange ich lebe, mag kommen was u. wer da will. But don't worry Bub, your Anne shall always remain true to you, and love only you as long as I live, come what may.

Auf Wiedersehn mein Bubelein!: See you soon, my Bubelein!

Einen süssen Kuss von Deiner Anne: A sweet kiss from your Anne

Here the reader has yet another example of how blessed I was that God had led me to my beautiful, belóved Anneliese Baur!!

At sea, over the course of four days, I write a letter to Anneliese. In the upper right hand corner is this notation: 26-8-46 U.S.A.T. Alexander at sea. I believe the initials U.S.A.T. mean United States Army Transport, or maybe the T means Trawler. In any event, it was a military vessel. The letter, except for the salutation, is written wholly in German over a four days' period from the 26th of August through the 29th. Indeed, the text for the last two days is written in the Old German script used by Anneliese's mother and father, and revived by Hitler for use in all official German documents. I had begun to learn how to read and write it while in combat, since the military documents carried by the German soldiers we captured were written in this script. Some six decades later I had difficulty in reading my own letters written in this script as I endeavored to translate them into English. Anneliese had offered to help me translate German to English. If she were only here now!!! My letter, written at sea:

My Darling,

I believe you can surely imagine how lonely your Bubelein is. But do you know how sad he is? Yes, sad! In a week I shall again be in Germany. But the closer I come, the more my anxiety. Strange?

Not wholly. Let me explain: For example, I do not yet know how civilians working in Germany can write letters to Germans. I'm writing tonight—because I must, because I am so lonely, because I long so much for you—but I don't know whether I can send this letter to you!

Yes, and this week the Governmental authorities have made more, and stricter laws concerning marriage between Americans and Germans. The English, the French, and the Russians also, see things completely differently—but that's the way it is,

Our common path is long, steep and clearly not planted with roses!

I should be crying now. But crying doesn't make Life a little lighter. No, I shall not cry!!

I've already come so far—and you have waited so long, that we both must remain brave!

You know, Darling, as I write this letter, I become happy! It's something "magical", something I can't describe—but—I need only to think of you—and Life is again bright and glorious!

Oh Angel—only a little more patience! As soon as possible I shall again be at your side. Perhaps for only a day—for some hours. But we must always be grateful for all the joy that Life gives us. Really, it makes no difference how small our "Portion" of joy. Isn't it true, as the saying goes: "Shared joy is doubled joy"? And I shall always share my portion with you. And when you are "hungry" I shall "feed" you—and so shall you do with me! And in this way both of us shall always be filled with Joy and Love—filled, yes, but never satiated!

I have often thought—but enough for one night! My head is now spinning! I'm going to bed hoping that perhaps I shall dream of you. If I do not possess you, I have to live with your images. Am I satisfied? Yes—you know how it is: Images and dreams are lovely—But heavenly reality is so much better!!

I'm back, Darling, the sun is shining this morning so wonderfully warm!—but I have no desire for sunshine, I must absolutely write to you again! Life is so empty without a connection to you!

I'm beginning again: Darling, I've often thought that perhaps our lives would have been "easier", had we never met each other! Yes, am I not being nasty? Am I not really talking like a stupid child? Of course, of course! But haven't you had the same thought? Oh Life is difficult, almost too difficult. Anne, should I lose my patience, please give me yours. Please? Oh, thank you so much!

Now I'm going back on deck; a little sunshine before I eat Lunch. God Protect you!

That I am not quite "all there", and have lost track of time is evidenced by the dating I gave to my next two days' additions to my letter commenced on board on the 26th of August. Portions written on the 28th and 29th of August, month eight, are noted as written in month seven: July. Clearly, while physically at sea, I was also mentally *at sea!* I noted, in reviewing the letters I wrote to Anneliese during my first week in Germany—which was the first week of September 1946—that I numerically noted the month as 8, when, of course, it should have been 9 for September. Most assuredly, I must have fallen and hurt my head alighting from Cloud Nine onto which I had clambered once my voyage to Germany began! My entries on the 28th and 29th were written in German, but in its now antique *Sütterlin Schrift*. I had last used it in combat, and would now have a chance to use it again in performance of my duties as a censor of German language communications since many elderly Germans and some Nazi Party members still used this script. Although I had sent Anneliese a birthday card, I assured her that her birthday had not been forgotten—the date was imprinted within my memory. I hoped that she and her family were well, and that she had received my last shipment of packages.

I have no recollection where my vessel docked in Germany, or when. (I suppose if I researched it I could find out). Upon leaving the States I had sent a telegram to Heiner Zeiner in Heidenheim, told him I had left Brooklyn on the 23rd August for Germany, and to tell Anneliese. He sent her a garbled text telegram which indicated I was leaving on the 28th. An 8 and a 3 can be mixed up. My ocean transport letter quoted above began by noting that on the 26th of August I was "at sea". Whatever. My first letter when I was back in Germany was dated, "4-8-46 Offenbach a. Main". Clearly, I was still "out of synch" between July and August. The letter, a short one, read:

Sweet Anne!

I believe you have already received my telegram. The news was good, right?

I'm now in Offenbach. And I believe I shall remain here. How long? I don't know that yet.

Write me often—but—you know!

As soon as possible, I'll try to come to Schwenningen

Write Frau Zeiner, that I'm now back in Germany. And Ernst too.

The journey was very nice and enjoyable. Now I'm brown as a nut! And naturally, I'm more than a little happy.

Heartfelt greetings to your parents and to Kurt and Hilde.

Your Bub

As the reader can see, I was very circumspect in my letter writing, and even reminded Anneliese: write, but you know . . . meaning "be reserved".

However, once I checked out the censorship regulations as they pertained to communications within Germany between U.S. Government civilian employees and German nationals—and found no monitoring—I relaxed my self imposed strictures. Anneliese tried hard to comply with my "edict", but never quite succeeded during the short time my "caution light" was on. It was irrational for me to expect anyone so filled with love and longing to keep her emotions under wraps—especially when the object of her desires was finally so close!

In an unnumbered, joyous letter, dated 7.9.46, Anneliese wrote in German:

My beloved Bubelein!

Again in Germany! This news makes me so happy! Inexpressibly happy, I can show you my happiness only through letting you experience and feel my great heavenly blissfulness!

And when will you be coming to me? Must your Anne with her impatient heart wait much longer? Two days ago you were in Frankfurt perhaps you will be able to come to me in the next few days! Oh how glorious! I'm almost giddy at the thought that I shall soon have you with me, to be able to see your loving face and your good true eyes, to hear your voice which always sounds so pleasant and soft in my ears!

Oh my Love, how endlessly grateful I am for your abundant great Love! Day and night my heart thinks only of you, and it shall make you happy and bring you joy!

Come soon Bub, I can hardly await 'til you are standing before me! Tomorrow is Sunday, how beautiful if you could spend it with me. May I hope? Oh, yes, I can and I may, and I also know that all my patience, all my passionate waiting, will be rewarded with the highest Prize: your sweet presence!

Please Bub, don't let me wait too much longer!

Always Your Anne

I didn't! I didn't! As she was writing her letter I was dispatching a telegram telling her I was traveling down to Schwenningen the next day, Sunday. I was as madly desirous of seeing her as she was of seeing me. As a civilian employee of the U.S. Military Government I had no access to a vehicle for non-governmental activities. Rejoining your belóved was a non-governmental activity. Hence, I took the train. To get to Schwenningen from Frankfurt you took a train south to Stuttgart, the Capital city of Wuerttemberg, and then another down to Schwenningen. I recall nothing of the journey other than that the weather was dry and cold. Along the way visions of Anneliese danced in my head to the rhythm of train wheels clacking on their tracks. At Stuttgart I changed trains for one headed to Schwenningen. Anneliese and I had been separated for ten month, and now, in Stuttgart, I was approximately 100 kilometers away from the Center of My Universe!! In 1946 Schwenningen was not a big railroad station. I believe it then had four sets of rails, *Gleise*, and two platforms. Anneliese knew when I would arrive, and on which platform,

As the train slowed on its approach to the station I could see Anneliese!! She was dressed in a dirndl, and as beautiful as the day I last saw her slowly fade from my sight in the side view mirror of my jeep, as I left Schwenningen for Heidenheim. But now her beautiful image was becoming larger the closer the train came to the platform. Oh the joy! Oh the glory! I opened the door of my compartment before the train barely ground to a stop—and with my traveling bag in hand—I literally leaped out, and there, oblivious to all about us, Anneliese and I embraced, laughter mixing with tears. This was Schwenningen, not Brooklyn. But in an instant I was home again! I held my beautiful, belóved Anneliese Baur once more in my arms! Enraptured, neither of us noted the cold, nor our breaths turning to steam, nor the people about us, as we hugged and kissed! *Folle amore! Folle ebbrezza!* Mad Love! Mad Rapture! Thank you God for bringing me safely back to the one you helped me find, back to my Anneliese Baur!!

After ten long, lonely months, two heart sick young lovers are reunited!! And for both it was as each had imagined: a time of utter, absolute, total Joy!!! Words are useless to describe an episode so devoutly wished for, and so long denied. And even were words at the ready, what need to describe Heaven, once one had been there! At this reunion Anneliese and I were together for less than a full day. We savored each minute of each hour. We dared not leave *each other* too long out of sight, lest the other would disappear! True Love is more than the enjoyment of sexual acts, as vital as these are. True Love transmutes the sensuousness of the carnal, of the physical, into the sublime, the ethereal. The effect of the latter lasts forever, unlike the fleeting impact of the former. Of course, Anneliese and I were creatures of desire. We were young, virile, and throughout our separation had remained true to *each other*. In the few intimate hours of our reunion the fevered figments of our desires deferred became realities! And then? Then there was this overwhelming, all consuming feeling of peace, a sense of belonging one to the other, of two hearts beating as one, of two souls entwined, as moments before our arms and limbs had been, *Oh Mad Love! Oh Mad Rapture! Oh Glorious Peace!*

Anneliese and I would have a long, winding, bumpy road to traverse in Germany before we could be joined as Man and Wife in America. But today, at our reunion in Schwenningen, after only a few hours together, the longings and sorrows of our ten months' separation were already fading fast away. And the dream of reunion turned into reality with our first kiss on that windswept railroad platform in Schwenningen!

Dear reader, in light of what I have just stated, when you read Anneliese's letter, written over two days on the 9th and 10th of September 1946, I believe you will sense the depth of her emotions concealed beneath the cloak of her restrained language. She was, faithful Darling, trying to comport with my instructions (which early on, proved needless).

My Dear! 9th Sept. 1946

Only a very short but loving greeting to you my Darling! I'm so tired, and I'm going to bed immediately. I hope you arrived well in Frankfurt, and not too late.

10th Sept.

Good morning my Bub, are you fresh and well? I slept until 9 a.m. and so deeply and solidly, that I didn't dream even once. But upon awakening I imagined you were still with me, I could feel your nearness, the last hours with you were so beautiful, as in a fairy tale and Dreamland.

I hope you didn't have any difficulties because you came back a little late. Now I look forward to our next reunion, if it's not next weekend, I hope then the following one. If only it wasn't so far to you, or if I could at least get a Pass. Bub, my heart is now so light, so happy, I again saw you, and quite healthy, I am so enriched by your great glorious Love! Have I really earned so much happiness?

Bub I shall write to you every day, even if only a few lines. And please do the same. You know how hungry I am for your letters!!

Anneliese then says she has written to my parents and to Frau Zeiner and Ernst, and that she feels they all will be happy to have heard from her about us.

Remain well Bub, come again soon and dream of our glorious happy hours.

Always your Anne

In a footnote she refers to a sketch she made on page one of her letter which shows where we might meet in Stuttgart.

Per an unnumbered letter, wholly in English, and dated 11-9-46 Offenbach a. Main (with the name of the city written in Sütterlin script), I wrote to Anneliese:

Dearest Anne,

Well, here is the letter in English which I promised to send. Were it not for your sweet and sensitive letters which I carried away from our last visit, I would be very lonely for news from you. I read your letters over and over while on the train. And as I read them I laughed with you—and I cried with you. And all the time I was so very near to you.

Now that I am back in Offenbach, I'm more than a bit lonely. No letters yet. Perhaps tomorrow—always "perhaps". But always hope!

I'm a bit angry with you for your refusing to take some of the sandwiches which your mother made up for me. And I'm angry with myself for not requiring you to take some. As it was I had too much—and gave some of them away to the German policeman who guards our billet. And I know you must have gone hungry while waiting for your train—and riding back. Please eat as much as you can, Engel, grow strong—strong in body, for I know you are strong in heart!

I have just about decided to attempt a trip to Heidenheim. If I go I shall take along more food, etc. for you—and have Frau Zeiner ship it to you.—I can't afford to be late—because I believe they are already promoting me one grade higher—and that means more money for our future!

Now don't forget—eat as much as you can—study your English—and try to get a pass! Remember! "Um meines Willen!": "For my sake!"

Thank your family for their hospitality!

Love, Dein Bub,
Arthur

This letter is interesting in that it is the first time—and I think, the only time—that I express a bit of anger concerning Anneliese's actions, and anger against myself, for not requiring her to take some of her mother's sandwiches with her as she waited for the train to take her back to Schwenningen. Anneliese had taken the train with me to the edge of the French Zone to be with me as long as possible—and then she returned to Schwenningen. In her letter dated 17.9.46 the reader will note the inoffensive, humorous manner by which she responds to—and disposes of—my expressions of anger. Another example of why I was so enamored of my Anneliese!

On 11.9.1946, in her Letter Number 2 (new series now that I was back in Germany) Anneliese wrote:

Mein lieber Arthur! [I believe this was the first time she so addressed me].

As promised, you will receive a small Greeting every day, so that you are not so lonely.

My thoughts are still completely filled with the fabulous beautiful hours of our reunion, my heart is now so light and filled with Love and Happiness! Can it be otherwise? No, we two are happy and destined for each other, and no power in the world shall ever be able to separate us! And I now live again in joyful expectation of our next time together!

And how are you my dear? I hope you are feeling good, as good anyway as you can be without me. Do you have a lot of work? . . . . I wrote to your parents yesterday and I definitely did not spare the praises and thanks, how handsome you looked, and how loving and honest you were with me, and how both of us enjoyed, unburdened, our restored happiness.

I have likewise informed Frau Zeiner that we will be coming most likely over the Sept. 21-22 weekend.

Your letter which you apparently had mailed last week in Frankfurt has not yet arrived, I fear that the mail may always be a long time in transit.

Last night I began to knit my new Jacket, and I'd like to show you in the enclosed sketch how I wish to make it, and whether you would like it if made that way. (See page 541 for Anneliese's sketch). Bub, could you provide me with some stationery? I would be very grateful to you to have some.

A Nice Greeting from little Ingrid, she was here yesterday, and has always asked about you. See, the Little One has already locked you into her heart. Clearly no wonder, since you are so loving to everyone.

But isn't it true Bubelein, that the one you love the most is your Anne?

A sweet kiss from your Anne

I loved Anneliese's up beat ending to her letter, in fact I adored everything about Anneliese! I had succeeded in returning to Germany. We had quickly had a rapturous day together! Naturally, that had only whetted our appetites for more. We were finally together again in the same country—no, not quite—Anneliese and I were in the same general geographic area where a "Germany" once existed. Now it was a "non-country" carved into four Allied Zones of Occupation, each with its own rules and regulations. German civilians, such as Anneliese, and even American civilian employees of the American Military Government, such as I, could not travel unhindered from one Zone into another. Passes were required, much like visas in peace time travel between countries. Hence, our letters were speckled with repeated references to "Passes". Until I could determine how I could bring Anneliese lawfully into Offenbach, my distant beloved, *meine ferne Geliebte*, would be tantalizingly near, but not close enough. We could be weekend lovers. But we wanted more than that. We deserved more than that. We were hungry for each others company. Making love was wonderful! But so, too, was walking hand in hand through a beautiful sylvan setting, reading prose and poetry aloud to each other, making a meal and eating it together, making jokes, just sitting there, side by side, saying nothing and wondering what the other might be thinking. Knowing, when we gazed at each other, that the whole world was mirrored in our eyes. To live as *if* we were Husband and Wife, despite the Government's ban against a union such as ours in Germany. Our next letters lead Anneliese and me closer to that goal.

My Letter Nr. 1—New Series is dated 13-9-46. Although we were separated by Zone boundaries the mails were beginning to move more rapidly, so much so that if either of us wrote a letter on Monday and posted it on that day, it would be delivered on Wednesday, and if a reply was penned and posted that day, it would be delivered on Friday. And if that wasn't fast enough, we could send a telegram. Anneliese's family had no telephone.

My Darling,

It was so very wonderful to receive your letter written on the tenth! It was waiting for me when I returned to my quarters during today's lunch hour. Since the letter came so quickly I'd prefer your writing all your letters to this address. And disregard the other addresses I gave you.

No, even though I returned late I had no difficulty. I probably won't get paid for the day I missed, but being with you was certainly worth a day's pay!

I am so very happy that "Dein Herz ist jetzt so leicht, so glücklich—usw. And why need you even ask me: "Habe ich wirklich so viel Glück verdient?" You have, you have! Merely by remaining "tapfer" ["brave"] have you earned that right to so much happiness. And you have been more than brave; you have been patient, helpful and true! All the joy that I shall try to provide for you in the future which lies before us, shall be only an insufficient expression of my love for you!

Anne, when you get your pass to enter the American Zone, I shall meet you at the spot you indicated in your little sketch. I know the place you mean. And then, if you wish, I will take you to Offenbach. I believe you might be able to get a job with my organization. That would be nice, wouldn't it? I inquired today on this very subject, and after 1 October you could be interviewed for a position in censorship, etc. I suggest you tell the French officials that you need the pass to apply for a position. And then too, there are some papers that I sent you from home. They should have since arrived and perhaps they will be useful in obtaining a pass.

Tomorrow I shall try to make it to Heidenheim with food for you—which Frau Z. will express to you. And Monday I shall try sending a 1 lb. pkg via the Reichspost. Anne, wenn Du wieder schreibst, benütze nicht die Worte—"US Civ" Gell? [Anne, when you write again do not use the words "US Civ". Right?] Nun—bleibe gesund und munter! [Now—remain healthy and merry!]

Dein Bub, Arthur

In this letter's margin, in Sütterlin script, I sent greetings to her family and brother and sister.

As I told Anneliese in the above letter, I would try to go to Heidenheim the next day—and I did! My Letter No. 2 dated 15-9-46, was written with particular relish, as a reading of the letter will reveal.

My Darling,

I arrived home but half an hour ago. I've just had time to wash my dirty face. And though I have lots more yet to do—I'm letting everything hang in mid-air until this letter has been written.

I've just spent a pleasant weekend in my "old home town"— Heidenheim!

Mother Zeiner, Heiner and father were naturally surprised to see me so soon! Nevertheless they were very pleased. And they made everything comfortable and cozy for me.

I also spent several hours with Ernst and his assistant. And I went upstairs to his new apartment to see his parents and sister. And I visited Frau Voith so that she could see that Mr. Katz had really returned!!

She was very nice to me and said she always knew that I would return! And when I gave her a funny look, she quickly said again, "Yes! Mr. Katz, that's true!"(?) And she asked whether you were well, etc.

The reader may recall that my Military Government unit had taken over the Voith Villa for our offices and living quarters, and it was there, outside its kitchen, that my eyes first alighted upon my beautiful, belóved Anneliese Baur! Frau Voith believed, I'm sure, that I was just another over sexed American soldier taking advantage of yet another lonely German Mädchen. And when I returned to the States I know that too many about me believed "the flip-side", that Anneliese was just another lonely German girl taking advantage of one of America's war heroes! Fortunately, Anneliese and I had, from the outset of our relationship, agreed to let *"them"* think what they will—hurtful as it was—*we knew the Truth!* But it *was* hurtful! Now, in my encounter with Frau Voith I was facing an obvious doubter, and able to put the lie to her face, and to do it without impairing my dignity, or Anneliese's. Quite an achievement for a guy with a short fuse, and a lot on his mind!

I then tell of a pleasant meeting with our friend and our vital mail conduit, and his girl friend Katie, who I noted *"war wie immer 'wortlos'"*: *"was as always, 'totally silent'"*. (Sadly, she shot him to death when he told her he was going home and would not marry her!)

I relate that the visit was beautiful, only the travel back was difficult. I even had to have Heiner ride me on his motorbike to a different railroad station in order to make a connection which would get me back to Offenbach on time. The ride was a "hairy one". I still remember it!! I inform Anneliese that *Mutter* Zeiner is sending off to her by express the packages she had received from me, together with a postal check for Anneliese's use. I remark that at the Zeiner's *ich war sehr "zu Hause": I was very much "at home".* And I continue: . . . . *Aber doch so sehr einsam! Ich schlief am Sofa. Und ich glaube Du kannst vorstellen, die Gedanken ich hatte! Kannst Du? [But I was also so very lonely! I slept on the sofa. And I believe you can imagine the thoughts I had! Can you?]*

I then tell Anneliese I'm trying to see if I could get transferred to another location closer to her, and then, concerning our getting together, I write:

Saturday at 1 o'clock (1300 in German time) I shall again travel to Stuttgart—to meet you. If you've gotten a Pass send me a telegram immediately—and also, if not, so that I can know whether it's worthwhile to go to Stuttgart. Understand? [Written in dialect for humorous effect]. *And if you are going, tell me when your train will be in Stuttgart. I'll be wearing civilian clothes!*

Your "Greeting Letter" to me was very nice. Many thanks for it!

Now, I have to go to bed—I'm very tired. God protect you! I love you!

Your Bub,
Arthur

Excuse me if my handwriting is more peculiar than it usually is. I'm definitely very tired! Really! Really!

On 16-9-46 I wrote my Letter Nr. 3 to Anneliese. In it I ran the gamut of my emotions from the lowest level of unhappiness to the heights experienced when I am fully at peace with Anneliese at my side.

Süsses Herzchen!: [Sweet Darling!]

Today I was a happy man again! Why? The reason is very simple: namely, I was greeted by two of your wonderful letters1 Numbers 2 and 3 arrived at 2 o'clock!

I believe it will be certainly be difficult to travel to Heidenheim again. But nevertheless I shall undertake this journey on Saturday. As you have said, I shall travel directly to Heidenheim. Hopefully I shall arrive without trouble. And hopefully you will also be there!

Write me immediately whether you are successful, or not, in obtaining a Pass. Even better—send me a Telegram!

But enough with this talk! Everything will certainly work out! Don't you believe so? Of course, etc.!

I'm pleased with your sketch. (See page 541 for Anneliese's sketch). I know that the sweater will look great. Knitting is very easy for you, right?

I am pleased that you write so nicely to my parents. Do you know, Angel you are more loving than I—certainly. It's like this with me: I get angry very, very slowly, but when I'm finally angry, then I remain so. Not for Eternity, naturally not. With time one changes everything. But at home, unwittingly (perhaps) many people tore my heart apart, and with their feet stomped all over the tatters! They made fun of us—and I can never forget that! Perhaps when I was with you, you sensed that I was not wholly "free". I wasn't Anne. No, it was not your fault. You were never sweeter! It was only that my thoughts "were not yet pure". My Soul was not yet healthy. Now it is!! And I have you to thank for that. With you I can battle against everything. Without you I am dejected, lonely and always sad. Thank God that I have you! I love you! And how!

Your Bub
Arthur

Our Love Letters were not merely vehicles of communication. They were vessels into which, unashamedly, we poured our innermost feelings. We emboldened each other by sharing our concerns, our desires, our hopes. Our spiritual intimacy, honed by our Letters, made our physical intimacy ever so sublime!

In these pages I have set forth a selection of Love Letters, or excerpts therefrom, which have chronicled a tumultuous year of separation and reunion—although the latter event was celebrated, at best, on weekends. I now set forth the last two letters in this cycle. They are the last because they demonstrate the efforts Anneliese and I expended in traveling from Point A to Point B, or sometimes to Point C, in order to see each other, if only for brief, but heavenly hours together. And they set the stage for Anneliese to seek that job in my Civil Censorship Group in Offenbach I had told her about in my Letter No. 1 New Series. Anneliese applies. She gets the job! I find her an apartment in Offenbach. I still have my own military billet. We are footsteps apart, but finally together! Need I say more, dear reader? Now to these last two letters, and then some observations from me to close this Episode in my tale.

My Letter Nummer 4, dated 17-9-46, aside from its opening phrases, and its closing words, is in English:

Du, mein schönes Kind!: You, my beautiful child!

Ich habe ein bisschen gute Nachricht Dir zu erzählen, aber ich werde alles auf englisch schreiben, weil so geht es schneller.: I have some good news to relate to you, but I will write everything in English, because it goes faster that way.

For one thing it is now possible for persons in the States to send 11 lb. Packages to the French Zone! And so I have already ordered an 11 lb. Package sent directly to you from a food house in New York. This package will contain 4-1½ lb cans of bacon—of the type I brought you—2 lb can of beef and about a a pound of fat. I imagine it ought to arrive in 6-7 weeks.

And now for the other news. On the 26th and 27th of September we have a very important Jewish Holiday—the beginning of the Jewish New Year. And the government permits Jewish personnel to have those two days off. And since those two days fall on Thursday and Friday—I can be off till Monday morning—since I do not have to work Saturday or Sunday! Just think, 4 days mit Dir! I have also applied for a pass to enter the French Zone, so should you not be able to get a pass for the American Zone, I will travel down to you—otherwise I shall spend a happy 4 days with you in Heidenheim.

"Meantime" I hope to see you in Heidenheim this weekend.

One more thing: I tried mailing you a 1 lb package—but I was a few grams over—and I couldn't, Well I'll bring the package with me "wenn i komm".

Now be patient—and eat as much as you can. I like a woman with a "little meat on her bones"!

Regards to your family—and to you—all my love!

Dein Bub!
Arthur

As I was writing my Letter Nr. 4 on 17-9-46, Anneliese was trascribing in German her Nr. 5 of even date.

Nr. 5 Schwenningen 17. 9. 46

Mein liebes Bubelein!

Today is again a happy bright day for your Anne, and why not? Because of the simple reason that the postman brought three dear letters from you. You are again the only author of my joy. One letter, No. 28 came from Brooklyn, the two others from Offenbach of the 11th and 13th Sept. A thousand loving thanks! Praise God that you returned safely to Offenbach and had no further difficulties. I have to laugh that you trouble yourself so much about my daily bread, don't worry Bub, I eat as much as I can and as much as I have, and at the moment I'm not lacking in appetite. And I certainly didn't suffer from hunger on the trip home from Tübingen!

Your Letter No. 1 of the New Series contained more very gratifying news. Do you really think it will be possible to find a position in Offenbach? Oh Bub, that would really be wonderful!! Then this wish that I could always be with you would be fulfilled. You have surely received my last letters, (mail goes blessed fast now) and that you are in accord with my proposal to travel next weekend to Heidenheim. Uncle Arthur spoke again today with the Official in charge of issuing Passes, and he promised to do as much as he could so that I could get my Pass by Friday. You know Bub, all requests for approval must first be sent to Tübingen, and that takes, naturally, a few more days. In any case, on Saturday the 21st of Sept., I'm traveling to Heidenheim, leaving here at 5:32 and arriving there in the evening, a bit before 6 p.m. I really hope that I can meet you there, if not, inform me immediately, the best way by writing to Heidenheim. (I shall not wait in Stuttgart).

I'm very busy every day, writing, studying and sewing and sewing and some housework. And during all this work I think of you, especially when, in the evenings, I sit alone in my little room, and would much rather be with you. But do I have reason to complain? Oh no, Life has meant it well for me, it has bestowed so much happiness and joy upon me. Therefore I should not be ungrateful, we shall soon be together again . . .. every day a new fresh day and every night an adventure!! Remember?

God protect you! And remain well!

Your Anne

That was the last of the Love Letters I have placed in this book. It is fitting that the first and the last were written by Anneliese. This Episode is hers! This book is hers! From the God given moment I first saw Anneliese on the 16th of June 1945 in Heidenheim, Germany, the life I had known ceased, and a wonderful new life began! Anneliese became my Everything!, *Mein Alles*! I was reborn. In every aspect of my being I was a better man, a better human being! Once under Anneliese's spell how could it have been otherwise?

How could I knowing her—in ways both physical and spiritual—not wish to emulate her myriad virtues? This "simple girl from the kitchen", her self effacing description in her June 16, 1946 letter—and one wholly, wholly inappropriate—shaped my life for the better. And Anneliese performed this feat without one word of censure! She did it solely by example! I endeavored to follow her ways. I stumbled along the way. I strove throughout our blesséd life together to be what she saw in me. Sometimes I succeeded. Too often, I did not. The fault was always mine. I have earlier noted that Anneliese put me on a pedestal—when, in fact, I was her footstool.

In the last weeks of writing this book I penned a poem, in German, to my beautiful, belóved Anneliese Baur. Poetry, even poor poetry, is more perceptive than prose, in plumbing the depths of one's emotions. I wrote the poem spontaneously in German because that tongue was the primary language of our Love Letters. Our Love Letters were messengers which brought Anneliese and me longingly, yet happily, ever closer together. This poem, written in but moments, with tears streaming down my cheeks, and quickly translated into English, says all that I can really say about my Anneliese! Here, where I have ceased quoting from those Letters of Love—written six decades ago, and which sustained us until Anneliese and I were gloriously reunited—is a fitting place to set down this poem, and to close this Episode. It is written in the present tense: *in der Gegenwart*. My beautiful, belóved, courageous, wise and witty Anneliese Baur lives!, and blesses me, every day!!

AN ANNELIESE

Du bist mein Alles
alles alles dreht sich
um Dich!

Du bist die Sonne
die Morgens mich aufweckt,

Du bist der Mond
der Abends mich bedeckt,

Du bist die Sterne
die flimmern nur für mich,

Du bist mein Alles
alles, alles
alles dreht sich
um Dich!

TO ANNELIESE

Thou art my Everything
everything turns about thee!

Thou art the sun
which in the morn awakes me,

Thou art the moon
which in the eve protects me,

Thou art the stars
which glimmer just for me,

Thou art my Everything
everything, everything,
everything
turns
about
Thee

16. Sept. 1945.

Dear Mr. and. Mrs. Katz!

Arthur has asked me to write
you a few words in English. Arthur
has told me how unhappy you have
been over the news that we are to
marry. I am sorry if I have made
you unhappy. But you must believe
me, when I say that everything will
be all right! And I love Arthur so so
very much, please, love you me a little!

Ich weiss es ist sehr schlimm,
was die Welt über uns Deutsche sagt;
aber ist es nicht genug, dass wir all die
vergangenen Jahre schon unter der
Naziregierung zu leiden hatten? Geht der
Hass immer immer weiter! Es gibt wohl
in jedem Volk gute und böse Menschen,

16 September 1945 Anneliese to
Arthur's Mom and Dad

Bitte glauben Sie dieses auch von uns
Deutschen. — Und wenn Arthur bald
nach hause kommt, wird er Ihnen
so viel von mir erzählen, ich hoffe,
Sie werden mit mir zufrieden sein.

Meine Liebe zu Arthur ist
für mich etwas Heiliges, der ganze
Inhalt meines Lebens. Und wir
beide sind doch so glücklich mitein-
ander! Bitte, bitte, zerstören Sie
unser Glück nicht, und wenn ich
später zu Ihnen komme, haben Sie
mich bitte nur ein klein bisschen
lieb, dass es anfangs nicht all zu
schwer für mich sein wird.

Ich studiere jetzt fleissig
Englisch, mein Bubelein hilft mir
so schön dabei.

Ich verstehe Sie sehr gut,
dass Sie Arthur's Entschluss, ein

deutscher Mädchen zu heiraten,
fremd gegenüber stehen, wie die
Nazis gegen die Juden so grausam
waren. Aber bitte glauben Sie mir,
der grösste Teil von uns hat von
so viel Grausamkeit nichts ge-
wusst, ja nicht mal geahnt.

Und wenn zwei Menschen
sich wirklich lieben und glücklich sind, darf die Religion keine
Mauer sein. Wir glauben doch alle
an einen Gott, wir sind seine
Geschöpfe und haben alle das
gleiche Recht zu leben!

Liebe, herzliche Grüsse

von Ihrer Anneliese.

Sat Oct 27/45

Dearest Annalisa,

It was a pleasure to
receive another one, of your
sweet sincere letters, in fine
German and good English
Considering that you are a
beginner. You certainly can be
proud.

I am enclosing a gift
handkerchief for you. Some
friend gave me a few, and I
wish you to have one. It came
from Switzerland and I know
you will like it. I do also hope
you received the earings in
a letter I sent to arthur

October 27, 1945 Arthur's Mom to Anneliese

And in due time will also get the & the stockings and hankies.

Let me thank you, for the understanding you have about Arthur coming home first, in order in that way, to enable to have you come after him, perhaps, that much sooner. In doing so, you will have bettered his position and thereby yours. I know if one loves, this will be a ~~long~~ trying time and a lonesome one, but there will be the ~~pot~~ gold at the end of the rainbow.

His father has much

in the way of business waiting for him which will help you both to live in comfort and in America, the land I know you will love. Germany has been and will be again a land of culture and harmony, too. I'm sorry that I can't write German to you, although, I can speak it sufficiently to be understood, when you get here.

Herr Katz and I "Kusse die Hand" and we say affectionately good night to you and to your warm heart,

Love

Mother Katz.

My dearest Annalisa,

Forgive me, if I haven't written any sooner, but as soon as I was expecting Arthur to come home, and now that he did, the time just flies.

The first week, I was told by the ship's office, he may be in, I roasted a big Turkey. You know "'em Kendrick" Its bigger than a large chicken & says "Gobble Gobble." As he didn't come in, we ate it all week.

Then, when I knew to the day that he was coming, I stayed home, so when the telephone rang, I would be there. Well, it did on Sat, Nov 24, at 7 o'clock.

"Hellow, Mom," this is Arthur, "he said. You can imagine my joy at hearing him, after 3 years. It seems he was gone 3 years, because I only saw him a few times the first year, while in training.

He called me again the next day, then said he will let me know, next when he'll

December 8, 1945 Arthur's Mom to Anneliese

come home, after being discharged.

Wednesday, I baked pies, & cakes, & in fact, I've been busy for days, getting in the food he likes, in _cans_, jars & bottles.

While I was stuffing a chicken about 6 o'clock, at night, the phone rang again, & Arthur says "Hello, mom, I'm at grandpa Katz's house, come and take me home because it is raining & I can't see the way by night, with my heavy pack on my back; in the dark." You see we had moved, while he was away, so he didn't remember the vicinity, although it is near enough our old house & near to his grandparents. I dropped everything and ran & he seemed so tall & handsome, when I opened the door, & looked so good with the pipe in his mouth.

His grandparents were overjoyed, as they are very _aged_ and always prayed God to live to see him and all of their other grandchildren home from the wars. Then his father, who was called from the office came in too and more hugging and kissing was going on. We drove him in our car, to see my parents, his other grand parents, too. Again the same happiness, in reunion.

Since then a few times each week in the evening, I'm having a few friends & family to meet Arthur quietly. He doesn't like too much crowds and noise, you should know that.

Of course, you know his Uncle Sid, well, that made Arthur's home coming easier and pleasanter, because, they both have memories of you.

Arthur is not very happy, because he has left you behind, in that myself would only that you have been ill in the hospital and lonesome too.

I try to do the little things for him. he goes to shop for clothes & things for himself & also for you. He is making many packages, and I do hope they reach you.

Please God, a way be found, where in he can go to you or get to you, to fetch you over and be married, real soon.

I thank you very much for allowing him to come home to see us. It was a fine and noble thing to do, because you loved him so much and wanted to make him happy.

I'm sure by doing that, only good will come and must come from it.

He cannot decide about any college entrance, or work until he hears from the state dept. or Government for civilian work back in Europe.

He took some pictures, while I was cooking, of him and me, and he will send you them.

I do hope all the letters reach you. He sent the capt. & Perlow some money, for themselves, for Christmas presents, (because they are kind)

Also write me a letter as I am anxious to hear from you and I hope you will enjoy this letter to you of Arthur's home coming.

Give my husband's and my regards to your mother, father, sister and brother.

I love you, because, Arthur does, and because you will someday be his, God willing, and mine.

Love,

Mother Katz
Hilda

496

1.)   Heidenheim 1st of May 1946.

My dear Mother and Father!

Yesterday I recieved two letters one from my Arthur and the other from you which you wrote in Ellenville!

Indeed it is a pleasure to get a such nice letter and every time I can read and understand better what you wrote!

Arthur also told me, that you are in the country for some days that he and Harold are alone at home. He told too he is the cook now and that the Gries-Pudding which he cooked was very fine! O, I know my Bubelein likes to eat good dishes! Yes, yes, "Die Liebe dess Mannes geht durch den Magen!" This is an old German saying! Perhaps translate: "The love of the man goes about the stomach!" Please don't laugh if I did not translate it well!!

Dear Mam you asked me,

1 May 1946 Anneliese to Arthur's Mom and Dad

2! whether I work out or whether I stay at home! Till now I stay at home and I have to work very much! Our mother is not more so young, the care about my father and brother while of the war made her much older than in a normal time. Yet we are so happy that our family is perfect now. And so it is very fine when I can work at home and my English lessons, my hand-works need very much time too.

If the Mil. Gov. will still stay at Heidenheim for longer time I will try to get a fit business here, but it is very bad to get it.

You told me about your Passover - holidays and your Religious custom. Of course I don't know so much about this but I possess a own bible, that

3.) was a gift to my confirmation.
And in the old testament of the
bible I can read very much about
the Jewish Religions. But I know
that you will tell me very much
when I shall be with you!!

I will close this letter with
many wishes and *(a much!)* many happie
ness for you and your dear family!

And a sweet kiss to my
Bubelein! A sweet kiss to your
Mam and to Dad too!

your Anne.

July 19, 46

My dearest Anne,

I have received a few of your letters recently, and had so many things to do, that the time just flew, to answer you.

My father became very sick last week and Dad and I went on a trip to the Capital City of the U.S. "Washington." D.C. You know that the Jewish people are fighting to get into Palestine, the Promised land, promised by England, to be ours. Now we are having trouble again, so many Jewish people marched in the Capital streets and came from all over the Country to appeal to our Congressmen to get help from England. God help us to win as we need a _home_ for _those_ who want to go there.

The time is drawing nearer when Arthur will come back to you.

July 19, 1946 Arthur's Mom to Anneliese

500

I know you love him sincerely and I hope all of your family will too. He is my most Cherished possession, (his brother too) and is gentle and delicate.

Marriage is forever, and knowing that he is a Jew and an American and an Idealist, and you will have to live with him forever, and seeing all of these things and believing in him, may be very hard in your land but I have faith and trust in you and yours, to protect him from all harm.

Yes, we will miss him, but we know as soon as he can come back with you, you will.

See that he keeps the laws of the army, and does not get into trouble when he wants to see you. He loves you so and he is so impetuous. (hot lover)

3

He has many a good plan for the future and may God Bless you both.

Harold is continuing with his school and hopes to go to a College in the middle of the U.S. about 1500 miles from New York City. Again my house will be empty, but this time there is _Peace_, and we hope for long.

Do not mind if I made this letter so long, and what I have said is from the bottom of my heart and Dad's. I know you will understand as you both want to be happy.

I shall close now with love to you all from

Mother and Dad.

Früchte reifen an der Sonne,
Menschen durch die Liebe!
(Schiller)

24. 2. 1946.

Liebes, gutes Herz!

Bin ich auch nicht bei Dir
ich bin Dir trotzdem ganz nahe,
in Deinem Herzen, in Deinen
Gedanken! Und alles Liebe, alles
Gute wünsche ich Dir zu Deinem

24.2.46 Anneliese to Arthur

503

diesjährigen Geburtstage, nur Glück u.
Zufriedenheit möge Dir dieses Jahr bringen
u. ein frohes Wiedersehn mit Deiner
Anne, die so sehnlichst auf Dich
wartet!!!

Bubelein, gestern sind drei
Briefe von Dir eingetroffen u. nach den
drei langen sehnsüchtigen Wochen des
Wartens waren mir Deine Briefe ein
Geschenk des Himmels! Ich habe mir
schon so viel Sorgen um Dich gemacht,
ich dachte schon, Du seist vielleicht
krank u. ich dann so weit weg von Dir!!
O, Bub, ich weiss, es ist oft sehr schwer,
so lange getrennt zu sein, es ist auch
für mich nicht so einfach. Ich fühle,
ich bin nicht mehr ich selber, mein
eigenes Ich ist verschmolzen mit Dir,
vereinigt, ganz Dein Besitz! Habe ich
Freude, so freust Du Dich mit mir; bin
ich traurig, teilst Du auch dies mit mir!

O, es ist ein herrliches glückseliges Ge-
fühl, einem so lieben Menschen zu gehören, mit allem was eine Frau geben
kann! Und ich gehöre Dir! Bub, Lieb
hörst Du? Ich bin Dein, u. nicht's in
der Welt kann mir diese Liebe rauben,
mag kommen was will!! Immer, immer
will ich Dir zur Seite stehen, auch wenn
das Leben Kampf u. Härte von uns fordert!
Ich will Deine treue Kameradin sein in
sonnigen u. dunklen Tagen des Lebens!!
Bub, bitte glaube an mich, bitte bitte,
wie auch ich an Dich glaube!! Wirf
mich nicht weg, lass mich nicht los!!!
Ja Bub, ich verspreche Dir ganz nach
der Art Deiner Religion zu leben, so zu
werden wie Du im Herzen bist!! Nur
helfen musst Du mir, helfen u. Geduld
haben mit Deiner Anne! Hörst Du?!

Und komme bald zu mir zurück,

lass uns bald ein gemeinsames Leben
beginnen!

Ich weiss, es ist nicht so einfach
für Dich nach Deutschland zurück zu kommen,
aber vielleicht gelingt es Dir doch noch, eine
Stelle in der Mil. Gov. zu bekommen,
oder ist Dein Gesuch schon ergebnislos
zurück gekommen?

Bub, bitte mach Dir keine so
grossen Sorgen um mich, ich bin gesund,
arbeite bis jetzt nur zu hause, u. warte
auf Dich, mag es auch noch lange
dauern! Du darfst nicht immer so
verrückte Gedanken haben, suche irgend-
welche Zerstreuung, gönne Dir ein
Vergnügen, ich weiss ja, Du wirst
trotzdem stark u. tapfer bleiben, u.
Dir u. mir treu!! Ich habe ja Dein herz,
Du kannst es zu gar niemand anderes
verlieren!!

Ich liebe Dich Bubelein, wie
nur eine liebende Frau zu lieben vermag!!
Innige süsse Küsse von
Deiner Anne!

Deine Briefe
sind N. 22.23.24.
20.u. 21. fehlen noch!

506

MILITARY GOVERNMENT
HEIDENHEIM

Schwenningen 25. 2. 1946.

Geliebtes Herz!

Heute ist ein ganz grosser Feiertag für uns! „Vater ist gekommen!!!" Ach welche Freude für uns alle!! Das kanst Du Dir ja denken! Und Vater ist genau noch so lustig, so vergnügt wie zuvor! Er ist auch kerngesund u. sieht gut aus!

Vater ist heute morgen um ½7 Uhr hier angekommen, da das ganze Haus aber noch verschlossen war hat er bei Mutter's Schlafzimmerfenster geklopft u. diese Freude für Mutter Vater draussen zu sehen!!! Ach welch ein Glück für uns alle mal wieder bei einander zu sein!

Und der heutige Werktag ist zu einem Sonntag geworden.

25.2.46 Anneliese to Arthur

Und Vater hat gar nichts gesagt,
als ich ihm meine, das heisst
unsere „Geschichte erzählte." Er
meint, wir seien ja beide alt u. klug
genug zu wissen, was es heisst ein
gemeinsames Leben aufzubauen!
Und Bub, Vater freut sich sehr, Dich
persönlich kennen zu lernen! Und
hoffentlich bald!!!

Und zur Vollendung meines
Festtages brachte mir der Postbote
noch drei Briefe von Dir!! Bin ich
nicht ein beneidenswerter, glücklicher
Mensch?! Ja ich bin es, u. ich
werde es immer bleiben, denn jeder-
man der Dich kennt, muss mich
doch beneiden, so ein prächtiger,
tüchtiger u. so lieber Kerl zu
besitzen wie Du einer bist!!!
Ja, ich bin ganz ernst wenn ich
Dir das schreibe, denn alles was
ich mir wünsche, was ich brauche

schenkst Du mir, Glück, Liebe u. Ver-
trauen!! Alles was ein Leben lebens-
wert macht!

Und Du hast so lieb geschrieben in Deinen Briefen, selbst Deine
englischen, die für mich natürlich
noch etwas schwer zu lesen sind.
Aber wenn ich dann Satz für Satz
durchstudiert habe, kann ich gut
verstehen u. ich freue mich, dass
ich immer mehr u. mehr von Deiner
Muttersprache lerne. Nur Bub, Du
musst halt etwas Geduld mit mir
haben, wenn ich in meinen englischen
Briefen noch so viele Fehler mache!
Aber Du hast ja immer zu mir
gesagt, dass man ohne Fehler nicht
lernen kann!! Und auf diesen Stand-
punkt stelle ich mich nun eben
auch!!

tausend Dank auch für die Bildchen, ach wie lieb siehst Du über all
darauf aus! Und so unerreichbar
weit!! So weit!! Da fange ich an auf
alle die Menschen, bei denen Du jetzt
bist eifersüchtig zu werden! Nein,
wie hässlich von mir! Verzeih Bub!!

Und von Grussi hast Du also
auch gehört! Fein! Grüsse ihn herzlich von mir! Oder meinst Du, ich
könnte ihm mal schreiben? An
Marcelle habe ich schon 2 mal
geschrieben, aber leider noch keine
Antwort von ihr, obwohl sie doch
sicher durch einen franz. Soldaten
mir Nachricht geben könnte. Die
franz. Militärangestellte im Hotel
Ochsen, im Rang eines Oberleutnant
geht morgen wieder nach Frank-
reich, ich werde sie bitten, ob sie
mir noch einmal einen Brief an
Marcelle mit nimmt! Sollte ich dann
Post von ihr bekommen, werde ich es
Dir oder Grussi mitteilen. Jajo, armer
Don!! Verheiratet u. doch getrennt!

510

Bubelein Liebes, Deine Idee, später
einmal in Südamerica zu leben, ist
mir nicht ganz neu. Du hast mir
schon in Heidenheim viel davon erzählt. „Weisst Anne" hast Du damals immer gesagt, „Südamerica, besonders Chile oder Columbien ist
fast noch demokratischer als Nord-
america u. ein Leben dort wäre sehr
schön. Ich kann spanisch u. Du
könntest es gut auch lernen!" Ja
Bub, so hast Du zu mir gesprochen,
ich entsinne mich noch gut daran!
Für mich ist es ganz gleich, wo ich
lebe, nur Du musst bei mir sein,
wo Du bist ist meine Heimat u.
Wenn Du gar den Nordpol dazu
auserlesen hast!.! Ich folge Dir
überall hin!
Ich weiss, Du wirst so bald
als möglich zu mir zurück kommen,

ich bete zu Gott, dass es Dir bald gelingen wird, irgend eine Gelegenheit zu finden! O, ich sehne mich nach diesem Tag, then I love you so very very much!! and I shall be very happy with you!! always and always!!

Du Bub, ich benutze immer Dein Briefpapier, nur schneide ich den Briefkopf mit der Anschrift weg, denn sollte einmal kontrolliert werden, so kann doch niemand daran auszusetzen haben.

Bitte Bubelein, schreibe mir auch immer die Nummern meiner erhaltenen Briefe!

Deine heutigen Briefe tragen die Nummern 26 + 25 + 29. Es fehlen immer wieder einige dazwischen, aber diese können ja immer noch eintreffen! Ich werde in den nächsten Tagen wieder einen Besuch in Heidenheim machen!

Tausend Grüsse u. Küsse auch von meiner „ganzen" Familie!

Deine geliebte Anne

Schwenningen 15.3.1946.

Mein geliebtes Bubelein!

Herzchen hier bin ich! Grüss
Gott! Es ist so nett heute abend in der
warmen Stube, während draussen
ein feiner Regen nieder rieselt u. Gott
sei dank die letzten Reste dess schmutzigen
Schnee's weg nimmt! Ja Gott sei dank,
denn ist endlich mal der kalte Winter
vorbei, muss doch das Frühjahr kommen,
u. mit ihm, Sonne, laue Lüfte,
duftende Blumen, frisches Grün,
u. der herrliche Gesang der munteren
Vogelschar!! Und ist es Frühling,
kommt darnach der Sommer in's
Land u. auch vielleicht mein liebes
gutes süsses Bubelein!

Aber nun zurück zur Gegenwart, denn Vogelgezwitscher u. Blumen sind noch nicht da; aber

15.3.'46 Anneliese to Arthur

allein schon der Gedanke an das frische Leben macht das Gemüt freier froher, giebt neuen Mut u. neue Hoffnung!

Sender Vorarlberg bringt wunderhübsche lustige Volks-musik u. ich bin so glücklich, wenn ich jetzt an Dich denke, dankbar u. glücklich, dass ich Dich habe, wenn auch jetzt nur in Gedanken u. in meinen süssen Träumen!!!

Und gell Bub, Du machst Dir nun gar keine so grossen Sorgen mehr um mich, so lange ich gesund u. zufrieden zu hause bin, hast Du auch keinerlei Gründe dazu! Hörst!!

Ja Herzchen, Du bist wirklich ein armes Ding, machst Dir so viel

Arbeit mit meinen Paketen u. hast doch
so viel für die Schule zu tun! Wirklich
ein armes Bubelein! Es tut mir oft so
leid, dass ich Dir oder Deinen Eltern so
gar nicht's schicken kann, aber habe
ich Dich erst wieder bei mir, soll alles
Gut gemacht werden, ich werde mich
dann selbst zum Geschenk machen u.
wirst Du dann auch wirklich ganz glücklich sein?

    Bubelein, eben bringt der Radio
das lustige Tirolerliedchen:
 „Geh' mach Dei Fensterl auf
  i' wart' schon so lang drauf!
  A einzig's Busserl möcht' i nur „
  vielleicht lass i' Dir dann Dei Ruh!
Verstascht!!!"
  A Busserl' ist bayrisch-tiroler
Dialekt u. heisst auf gut deutsch
  „Einen Kuss!" Und was das ist, —

brauche ich wohl kaum näher beschreiben!!!

    Hast Du schon mal vom
romantischen „Fensterln" in Bayern
u. Tirol gehört? Gerade auf dieses
Fensterln bezieht sich dieses Liedchen!
Das ist nei hinach so: Hat da so
ein junger Bub ein Mädel, das er
gerne hat u. darf aber nicht zu ihr
ins Stübchen, so stellt der tapfre
Bursche des Nacht's, wenn alles
ruhig ist u. schläft, eine Leiter
unter das Kammerfenster
seiner Geliebten, steigt hinauf,
klopft leise ans Fenster u. fragt
ob er zu ihr rein kommen darf.
Ob dann nur um ein „Busserl"
zu bekommen oder vielleicht auch
mehr, je nach dem, wie weit
die Liebe geht zwischen den beiden
jungen Leutchen!! Wird aber das

516

Fenster nicht geöffnet, so weiss wohl
der Bursche, dass es aus ist mit der Liebe!
So geht also das romantische ländlich-
übliche Fensteren "in Bayern u.
Tirol!!! "Und die jungen Buben u.
Mädel haben ihren Spass damit!!!
Wenn Du also an meinem Fenster
klopfen würdest, ich liesse Dich gerne
herein'! So hat eben jedes Land seine
Sitten u. jedes ist in seiner Art
schön u. idyllisch!
        Nun aber Schluss mit den
schwäbisch-bayrisch-tiroler Geschichten!
Morgen dann wieder!
        Es ist nun inzwischen ½ 11 Uhr
geworden, u. daher höchste Zeit für
kleine Mädchen, ins Bett zu gehen!
        Gut Nacht Bubelein, tausend
so süsse "Busserl' von
                Deiner Anne

517

...stes Bubelein!

Siehst Du Herzchen, wenn Du abends ins Bettchen gehst, klopfst noch schnell an mein Fenster, nimmst Deine Schuhe ab, damit ja alles leise geht, steigst die Leiter hinauf, ich werde Dir dann ganz geschwind aufmachen. Du gibst mir a süßes Busserl u. dann kannst Du viel viel besser schlafen!!!

Innigst Deine
Anne

16.3. '46 Anneliese to Arthur

Geh' mach dei Fensterl auf
i wart' schon solang drauf.
U einzig Busserl möcht' i nur
vielleicht Lass' i dir dann dei Ruh'!

Geh' mach dei Fensterl auf
i wart' schon so lang drauf.
A einzig Busserl möcht' i nur
vielleicht Lass' i dir dann dei Ruh'!

Du mein Alles!

Nun mein liebes Geburtstagskind, wie geht es Dir? Ich hoffe. Du hast meinen Brief u. die Bildchen noch rechtzeitig bekommen u. auch Dich darüber gefreut!

Für mich ist der heutige Tag auch zu einem Festtag geworden, denn 4 liebe Briefe von Dir u. ein von Deiner Mutti sind heute morgen ins Haus geflattert!! Und wie lieb klingen Deine Worte, wie ehrlich u. gut!! Ich höre Dich aus den Zeilen sprechen, Deine lieben blauen Augensterne schauen mich an, ach, Du lebst in meinen Gedanken so wirklich, so nah u. lebendig! Und ich weiß, wie lieb u. oft auch Du an mich

21.3. '46 Anneliese to Arthur

denkst.

Deine kleinen Skizzen durch die Du
die Nummern Deiner Briefe ankündigst, finde
ich wirklich wunderhübsch, u. ich will mir
Mühe geben, auch für meine Briefe etwas
hübsches auszudenken. Heute grüsst Dich das
Blumenkind, als Zeichen des Frühlings-
anfangs!

In den vergangenen Tagen
war ich mehr traurig als jemals es
gab keine Post von Dir, das Wetter
war so herrlich u. du so weit weg,
ich musste krampfhaft meine
Tränen hinunterschlucken! Manchmal kommen einfach so traurige
Stunden für mich u. ich kann mich
noch so tapfer dagegen zur Wehr
setzen, es hilft alles nichts, sie sind
ganz plötzlich da.

Aber heute bin ich wieder glücklich u. froh, ich weiss Du bekommst
Post von mir u. ich von Dir, ich
freue mich mit Euch, dass Euer
Harold wieder bei Euch ist! Ist das

522

nicht Grund genug um froh zu sein? Doch!

Bubelin, bitte gib deinem Bruder in meinem Auftrag einen herzlichen Kuss als Gruss von mir, aber nur auf die Stirne oder auf die Wange, denn nur "sein Liebchen" küsst man auf den Mund!! Verstascht!!! Ja!

Kurt marschiert jetzt wieder ganz gut auf beiden Beinen, natürlich jetzt im Anfang ist das Gehen mit dem Kunstbein noch etwas beschwerlich, aber mit der Zeit gewöhnt sich Kurt auch daran. Er hat gestern sogar schon das Radfahren versucht u. ist ganz zufrieden mit seinen Leistungen. Er will in der nächsten Zeit auch wieder seine Arbeit aufnehmen, u. das wird sehr gut für ihn sein. Denn gerade in der Arbeit vergisst man am schnellsten alles Unangenehme!

Herzchen Du willst wissen, was ich alles aus Deiner Wolle stricke? Ja, ich will es Dir mal erzählen. Also aus der dicken erika farbigen Wolle habe ich mir bereits schon eine Jacke gestrickt u. sie ist ganz wunder hübsch geworden. Die grüne gibt ein Pullover mit kurzen Ärmeln, u. die rote Wolle verwende ich zur Umänderung meines dunkelblauen Wollkleides, das etwas beschädigt ist, um so wieder ein brauchbares Stück zu gewinnen. Mein Kleid kann ich natürlich nicht mit Deiner Wolle besticken, dazu brauche ich Stickgarn, u. dazu genügt mein alter Bestand.

Du siehst also mein Herzchen, alles was Du mir schickst wird gut verwendet u. manch neidvoller Blick fällt auf dieses oder jenes hübsche Ding, das Du mir schenkst! Neulich hast du mal bei mir angefragt ob meine Angehörigen etwa einen extra Wunsch hätten. Bubelin,

meine Eltern sind Dir ja so sehr dankbar für alles was Du uns sendest, es
hilft uns so viel u. ermöglicht, viel
Abwechslung in den Mahlzeiten zu be-
reiten. Natürlich Vater u. Kurt sind
Dir besonders dankbar für Rauchwaren,
u. kannst Du vielleicht mal ein paar
Feuersteine schicken? —

Bub, wirklich sehr nett von
Dir, dass Du mir meine englischen
Brief korrigierst! Danke schön!! Ich
weiss, ich bringe noch manches durch-
einander, besonders die Satzstell-
ung. Und Deine liebe Eltern möchten
doch bitte entschuldigen, wenn ihre
Briefe manchmal mit vielen Fehlern
geschrieben sind!

Herzle über die Konjugation
dess deutschen Wortes "verliebt"
musste ich herzlich lachen!!! Echt
Bubelein!! Ja ja, verliebt, verlobt,
verheiratet! In Wirklichkeit ist

aber das Wort „verliebt" gar kein
Zeitwort, sondern ein Eigenschafts-
wort (ich glaube man nennt es im
Englisch Adjective) Ja „lieben" das
tut man, daher ein Verb, aber
„verliebt" ist man (oder nicht) u. dess-
halb ein Adjective!!! Aber man ge-
braucht auch bei uns die Wortfolge
verliebt, verlobt, verheiratet!! Bubelein,
hab keine Sorge, ich habe meiner
Lehrerin noch nie einen Brief zur
Verbesserung gebracht, nein, das werde
ich auch nie tun! Denn das sind doch
nur persönliche Angelegenheiten u.
lieber schicke ich die Briefe mit
Fehlern weg, u. du bist dann so
gut u. verbesserst alles für mich! Ja!!
    Ich bin froh, dass ich wieder
„Air-Mail-Stamps" besitze, die
letzten zwei Briefe musste ich leider
als gewöhnliche Post wegschicken.
Hast Du die Briefmarken von der franz.
u. amerik. Zone erhalten? Soll ich noch
welche schicken?
    Für heute nun Schluss!!
Einen süssen herzlichen Kuss von deiner Anni

Meine süsse, schöne Anne!

Ich habe gewünscht, eine wunderbaren Skizze zu skizzen— aber du kannst sehen was ist geschehen!

(Siehe mal! ich bin auch ein Dichter! — ach— „um Gottes Willen!")

dieser Füllfederhalter tut nur eine Sache (Dinge ganz gut — er kann viele Tintenflecke machen! Bestimmt, klar, freilich, tatsächlich, (wahrscheinlich) selbstverständlich, wahrhaftig u. wirklich? Hm, Anne, was fehlt noch? Mein Mädchen, Fräulein, Mädel lacht, ich weiss Bescheid, gewiss, genau — ach, Schluss mit diesen verrückten, verflixten usw. Sätzen!!

Anne, sag mir im ernst, warum liebst du solch ein' verrückten Kerl? Ich bin wie das Wetter, einmal bin ich so kühl wie die Luft in der Lorelei. U. dann bin ich heiss wie eine Nacht im Sommer — oder glücklich wie ein Bächlein, oder wild wie ein Gewitter. Aber trotz alles, liebst du mich! Ist es dann fremd, dass ich dich so viel liebe, u. für dich so viel tue? — u. mit ganzem Herzen! Nein, es ist nicht etwas ausserordentlich! Bestimmt nicht! Du brauchst mich — u. ich brauche dich — da hast du die ganze Geschichte! Da hast du die Gründe für unsere grosse Liebe. U. so, unsere Liebe ist nicht nur für heute oder für morgen — sie wird für immer sein! Gell?

Jetzt muss ich den Brief hier schliessen, es ist spät, u. ich schaue so gerne mein liebes Bettchen an (liebes Bettchen habe ich gesagt? nein, nicht ganz — es ist leider — zu, zu leer!). Gute Nacht, Anne!

10-4-46 - 4:20 PM

Süsses Herzchen! Ich habe bis jetzt gewartet, diesen Brief zu fertigen.

9./10.4. '46 Arthur to Anneliese

527

in der Hoffnung einen neuen Brief zu bekommen. Der Postmann kam u. ging - aber leider hat er gar nichts für mich von dir gebracht! Besser Erfolg morgen - ich hoffe!

Morgen schicke ich weg ein kleines Päckchen, es enthält zwei Märchen Bücher, (auch englisch), Tabak u. ein bischen Süssigkeiten. Ich hoffe, dass alles dich u. deine Familie gefallen wird (oder werden - ist alles unten einzahl oder unten mehrzahl?) Ich glaube, dass Hilde sicher die Bücher ganz gerne lesen wird - u. natürlich, die Süssigkeiten auch gerne abessen - nicht fressen, Anne. Ich habe nicht genug geschickt, dass man sie fressen kann. (Das Päckchen war zu klein - oder vielleicht es war nicht gross genug - Ach, wieder mit meinen Spässen! (u. ich habe fast all die "M-en" vergessen.)

Ich beschliesse zwei Päckchen Feuer Steine. Wenn sie nicht genügend sind, bitte, sag es mir, u. ich werde mehr kaufen u. schicken.

In meinem nächsten Päckchen werde ich auch verschiedene Sämereien schicken. Dann können sie alle eure eigenen Gemüse wachsen. (Passt das dir Anne?)

Vorgestern habe ich meinen lt. Bruder ein Küsschen auf die Stirne gegeben. Er war sehr erstaunt - "warum so lieb?" hat er gefragt. U. dann habe ich ihm dein Schild erzählt. "Ach ihr seid ein glücklich Paar "P"! "

Ja, u. wir werden bald noch glücklicher werden.

Behüt dich Gott!
Give my love to your family.
Dein Bub,
Arthur

Heidenheim 1st of May 1946.

My dearest Darling Bub!

Just now I have finished the letter for your dear parents and so, I will write you a little letter too!! I don't know how many letters I can send you after wards, and as often as I can write you now I shall do it!

my dear air-balloons
my dear air-balloons
fly out to Brooklyn
and bring my sweet Bubchin!
many sweet kisses from me.

How are you my dear boy? Well? Of course!!! Are your Parents here again? O, your Mam wrote very fine and she told me about the Passover holiday and the religious customs!

Bub in your last letter you told me the plan perhaps to go into South-America. Why should we not be able to live there? I should go to America, to Afrika or to stay in Europe, but only with you, then where you are, there is my home!!

1.5. '46 Anneliese to Arthur

529

Many people think that I will only marry that I can go to America! O, many people think so!! But you know my Bubelein, that doesn't this is so! I can live in another country too! The people are bad and so full of envy.

1. This afternoon I was with Kitty out for a walk and afterwards she drank tea with me. It's so fine, when we can spoke to each other from the past year and from our happy future! Indeed, Kitty is a very very nice girl!! Tomorrow I will go to her and then we shall go to the office to look for letters from our darlings!! I hope a long dear letters will enjoy my! (of course your letters are always sweet!)!! Did you get Ernst's packet with his pictures? I hope! And did you get my packet with the photos of myself too? I hope too? In the last few days father Zeiner sent you a packet with Feuerzeugen!! Wir hoffen, dass alles gut übers grosse Wasser kommt!! (fach nicht) Don't laugh, then for two days the jeep

530

with the post fell into the "Brenz" near by Königsbronn!!! And of course, the must part of the letters was swimming in the water!! Kitty's letter from Smitty was quite wet too! But thank heaven, your letter was still damp! So you see how quick a such misfortune is here!?

Es ist alles komisch, kommt die Post gut über den grossen Teich u. in der kleinen Brenz wird sie doch noch nass! Gottsei dank, dieses passiert ja nicht alle Tage!

So mein Bubelein, nun muss ich aber wirklich zu Bette gehen, es ist 11 Uhr, u. Deine Anne ist reichlich müde! Willst Du nicht mit mir schlafen gehen? Wie kann ich nur so <u>dumm</u> fragen! Gell! O, Deine Anni's ist wirklich ein dummes Gänslein!!!

Einen Kuss auf Deine lieben Augen
Einen Kuss auf Deine liebe Nase!
Einen Kuss ins rechte Ohr
Einen Kuss ins linke Ohr
Einen Kuss (besonders süss) auf den Mund

Zusammen: <u>fünf Küsse</u> von Deiner Anne.

(wenden

Pur Kuss 10 Rll: Eine seltne Sache!!
Oder hättest Du noch so viel Geld
übrig?!!!   Anne
Doch bei Abnahme grösseren Quantums
wird billiger geliefert!! Verstascht!!!
I weiss, i weiss, mei Bua ver-
stoht me quad!!!

N. 76.

3. Mai 1946.

Geliebtes Bubelein!

Die ersten Maiglöckchen
mit ihrem bezaubernden Duft
bringen Dir herzliche Grüsse von Deiner Anne. Ich
habe die beiden Blümchen heute abend während
eines kleinen Spazierganges gepflückt.

Und heute mittag hat mich Dein langer
Brief N. 59. beglückt! Mit ihm kamen auch
zwei Päckchen N. 32 u. N. 2 für Ernst! Tausend
lieben Dank! Ach Bub, wie kann ich all Deine
Güte u. Deine Hilfe vergelten!! Ich bin oft so
traurig, dass ich Dir u. Deinen lieben Eltern so
gar nichts schicken kann!

Ja lieb, Dein heutiger Brief hat mich
anfangs ganz verwirrt, erst die zum
Hitrel jauchzende Freude u. nachher dein zu
Tode betrübt sein! Armes Bubelein, ach
wäre ich doch bei Dir u. könnte Dich trösten!
Aber natürlich, wenn ich ja bei Dir wäre,
hätten Deine gegenwärtigen Sorgen alle
ein Ende!

Ach es macht mich so glücklich,
dass Du mir alles so ehrlich erzählst,
dass Du mir Deine Geheimnisse alle anver-
traust!! Wie lieb, dass ich Dir durch ein gutes

3.5. '46 Anneliese to Arthur

533

Wort, durch einen lieben Brief helfen, Dir Mut zusprechen kann! Ich kann gut verstehen, wie enttäuschend u. entmutigend es für dich ist, dass all deine Pläne, so bald als möglich nach Deutschland, zu Deiner Anne, zurückzukehren noch nicht in die Tat umgesetzt werden konnten. Ich kann Dein enttäuschtes Gesicht sehen als man Dir auf dem Arbeitsamt die Mitteilung machte, dass Deine Meldung zu spät kam! Ja Bub, zu spät oder zu früh, manchmal sind die Dinge wie verhext! Aber lass den Kopf nicht hängen!! Du bist doch ein Mann mit starkem eigenen Willen!! Du weisst, wie gerne auch ich bei Dir wäre, aber einmal wird auch unsere Zeit kommen, wir müssen stark u. tapfer bleiben, Geduld haben, viel viel Geduld, hoffen u. an unsere grosse Liebe glauben! Und alles wird gut werden, muss gut werden!!

Und hörst Du Bub, bitte erzähle mir alle Deine Sorgen, alles was Dein Herz bedrückt! Auch wenn Du glaubst, Du würdest mich dadurch traurig machen!! Wozu hast Du mich denn? Nur um Dein Nachtlager mit Dir zu teilen, oder in Deinen Armen geherzt

3.1 u. geküsst zu werden? Natürlich, auch diese
Dinge gehören zum Leben, aber gerade
in den Stunden der Sorge, dess Kummers
u. der seelischen Not muss man zusammen halten! Siehst Du mein Bub,
wenn Dich etwas im Herzen drückt,
wenn Du von innerem Zwiespalt u.
Ungewissheit geplagt wirst, erzähle
alles Deiner Anne, sie versteht Dich,
sie hilft Dir tragen ist bereit Dir
zu helfen!! Immer musst Du zu mir
kommen u. Dein kummervolles Herz bei
mir ausschütten!

    Ach Bub, wie sehr ich dich
liebe, u. wie unsagbar vermisse
ich Dich!! Ich bete, dass wir bald einen
Weg finden werden, wieder bei einander zu sein!!

    Gute Nacht mein Lieb, morgen
schreibe ich wieder u. will Dir einige
Deiner Fragen dess letzten Briefes beant-
worten!   Grüsse Deine Eltern u.
Deinen Bruder!   Und Dir einen lieben, süssen
Kuss als Gute-Nacht-Gruss!
    Deine Anne.

MILITARY GOVERNMENT
HEIDENHEIM

16.6.1946.

Mein geliebtes Herzchen!

In ungewohnt später
Stunde schreibe ich diesen Brief, es
ist in wenigen Minuten Mitter-
nacht u. ich liege schon zwei Stunden
im Bett u. kann einfach nicht
einschlafen!

Immer sind meine Gedanken
bei Dir, meine Sehnsucht nach
Dir ist so gross, so unsagbar
schmerzlich, dass ich manchmal
kaum glauben kann, so lange
ohne Dich, ohne Deine Liebe gelebt
zu haben.

Und jetzt, wo die Post
so unregelmässig kommt, werde ich
gar oft so ungeduldig, u. ich

habe Dir doch versprochen stark u.
tapfer zu bleiben! Ach ja Bubelein,
wie leicht sprechen sich all diese
grossen Worte, aber wie soll ein
heisses sehnsüchtiges Herz damit
fertig werden? Du weisst es ja
zu gut, wie schwer es manchmal
ist! Und wenn ich denke, dass
all diese Einsamkeit, diese
Unruhe bald vorbei ist, dass Du
wieder bei mir sein wirst u.
dieses Mal für immer! Ach Rut,
es ist wirklich ein wunderbares
Geschick, das uns das Leben in
seinem wechselvollen Spiel zuge-
teilt hat!

Weisst Du auch was
heute für ein Gedenktag für mich,
ja für uns beide ist? Heute ist es
genau ein Jahr, dass ich meinen
Dienst in der Villa Voith angetreten

537

habe! Als ich dich zum ersten
Mal gesehen habe. Kannst du
dich noch daran erinnern? O ja
wie hätte ich damals geträumt
dass ich, das wunderbare Mädel
aus der Küche, jemals deine Frau
werden würde? Anfangs war
ich ja nur um dein leibliches
Wohl besorgt; aber später,
je später ist alles ganz anders
geworden! Wie herrlich waren
all die heimlich verliebten Stunden
mit dir, u. wie heilig u. paradie-
sisch schön jene himmlischen
Nächte!! Und es wird wieder so
werden, Gott hat es gut mit un

gemeint u. unsere reine, ehrliche
Liebe ist keine Sünde, haben
wir beide etwas zu bereuen,
haben wir etwas falsch gemacht?
Nein, nein, mögen die Menschen
reden so viel sie Lust dazu haben,
aus ihren hässlichen Reden
spricht Neid u. Missgunst,
lassen wir sie reden, sie werden ja
eines Tages doch müde werden.

Und war nicht gerade diese
Trennungszeit eine gute, wenn
auch die harte Probe für unsere
Liebe für unseren Glauben an
einander? Was nun er auch,
das Leben bringen wird, wir
beide halten zusammen, wir werden
nicht untergehen, und unser
Leben wird ein Leben der Liebe
der Bereitschaft sein.

Ach Bubelein, wenn Du nur
erst wieder bei uns bist!!!
          Kitty schrieb mir ver-
gangene Woche, dass keine Briefe
für mich gekommen sind. Darf
ich das als gutes Zeichen annehmen?
Bist Du am Ende schon unterwegs?
          Bubelein, ach was Liebe,
deine Anna ist voll Erwartung
ihr Herz klopft in stürmischen
Schlägen, immer denke ich an Dich
an unser baldiges Wiedersehen
          Heute habe ich Deinen
Eltern geschrieben, sie sind sicher
traurig, wenn Du sie nun
wieder verlässt, aber ist dies

nicht der Welt Lauf? Eine
Mutter trägt ihre Kinder unter
ihren Herzen, bringt sie zur Welt
sieht sie unter ihrer Fürsorge
u. Pflege gedeihen, heranwachsen
Vater u. Mutter erziehen sie
zu guten Menschen mit gesundem
Geist u. Verstand. Und dann
kommt der Tag, an dem das
grosse Kind, ihr Kind, inzwischen
zum reifen Menschen erwachsen,
davon geht auf eigenen Wegen,
in die offenen Arme der Welt
u. in die offenen Arme eines,
für die verlassen Eltern, fremden
Menschen zieht. Ja, ich kann
fühlen wie sehr dieses Verlassen
schmerzt u. doch sind die Eltern
nicht auch glücklich, wenn
sie wissen, ihr Kind hat das

gefunden, was dem Leben den
Inhalt, den Sinn gibt, was
Glück u. Freude bringt?
Siehst Du mein Bub,
komme i.de mir manchmal
wie eine Diebin vor, die dich
Deinen lieben Eltern gestohlen
hat! Närrischer Gedanke!, Aber
ich hoffe, wenn mich Deine
Eltern einmal persönlich kennen
lernen, dass sie dann zufrieden
mit mir sein werden! Meinst
Du nicht auch?
Herzchen, nun aber
gute Nacht, träume süss
u. ich will beten, dass wir

bald wieder beieinander sind!

Immer Dein Engel

Anne,

Entschuldige meine wacklige
Schrift, aber im Bette schreibt
sich nicht besser.

Mein Herzchen!...

Siehst du, ich habe Recht gehabt – Heute ist Montag – und wie ich vorhergesagt habe – sind einige Briefe von dir angekommen! Nummer 96 und 97 aus Heilbronn. Ich hoffe, dass wenn du diesen bekommst, dass du wohl und recht munter zuHause bist. Ja – "wer nicht wagt – der nicht gewinnt" – aber bitte, Engel – hab' ich nicht "Sorgen genug". Ende vom Lied;

Und Heute ist dein "Coffee-Log" auch angekommen. Meine Mutter war sehr – sehr zufrieden mit ihm. Deine Handarbeit ist wunderschön! Und die Karte mit den gedruckten Blumen war entzückend! die Blumen sehen so "echt" – und frisch aus! das Muster war auch sehr nett! Meine Anne ist bestimmt klug!

Today I made arrangements whereby the Ziners will receive a package of food weighing 49 lbs – when packed. This food was bought by a non-profit organization here in America from the US Army – for distribution among various European peoples. Since no package can as yet be sent to the French Zone – I had the package sent to the Ziners. But nevertheless the package is for you – and it is an expensive package (15) but an excellent one) I know – I ate the identical food during the war. Please notify Frau Ziner to hold the package for you – and when it comes divide everything on a 3/4 to 1/4 basis: 3 for you – one for her. Most of the food will be packed in 10's – since the food was meant to feed 10 Soldiers. But the butter – sugar and jam will be found in 2's or 4's. The total caloric value of the package – (which is really 4 packages in one) is over 40,000 calories! Isn't that wonderful! I am writing a letter tonight

8.7. '46 Arthur to Anneliese

②

to Armed in which I shall enclose illustrated information in regue to this package. It should arrive within 2-3 months at the latest. And I hope to be with you when it arrives. If you like the contents I can always order more. ——

Ja, ich weiss ich mache viel Sorgen für mich selbe – aber ich kann nicht mehr leiden weg von dir ... Weibem! Lieb Gott helf mir (wenn es gibt einen Gott) – lass mich schnell bei meiner Anne sein. Ich bin so sehr einsam hier!

Aber die Zeit kommt – und ... ihn komme ich auch zurück! Bald! Bald! Habe ich das nicht versprochen?

Ich liebe dich!
Immer dein Bub.
Arthur

Vergiss nicht an Frau Zimer zu schreiben.

My darling!

The last few days have been wonderful ones for me from the point of view of receiving mail from you! Yesterday my folks received your letter from Heidenheim. And since they are not here – I opened it – gosh! you are writing excellent English – keep up the good work! And then I received Nr. 98 from Heidenheim and Nr. 5 from Schwenningen – written on the fifth of June. And this letter wasn't even censored – at least the envelope had no censorship marks!

I hope you returned all right from Heidenheim. I worry so about you! I'll miss your letters again – but I'll just have to be patient.

Yesterday I wrote to Frau Zeiner explaining my arrangements in regard to the sending of packages. Now all that remains is for them to arrive!

And this morning I mailed out Pkg. 53 to you. This one contains Sugar, Coffee, Canned milk, Candy, Nuts, Tobacco, Soap, Pudding Powder, 12 spools of white thread and other things you can use. When you open the package, turn it upside down – for the post office put the stamps on the bottom side. I hope I'm with you – by the time this package arrives! The chances are really good!!

Du hast goldrichtig, dass das Wort "inquisitive" passt mir. Ja, ja, du hast Recht! Ich bin "inquisitive" – Aber nicht wie eine alte Jungfrau – aber wie einen Wissenschaftler. Wie mit dir – alles interessiert mich. Und deshalb liebe ich dich so sehr viel! Deine Gedanken sind immer gleich meine!!

Grüsse an Deine Familie – besonders an Hilde!
Behüt' dich Gott!   Dein Bub.
                                        Arthur

10.7. '46 Arthur to Anneliese

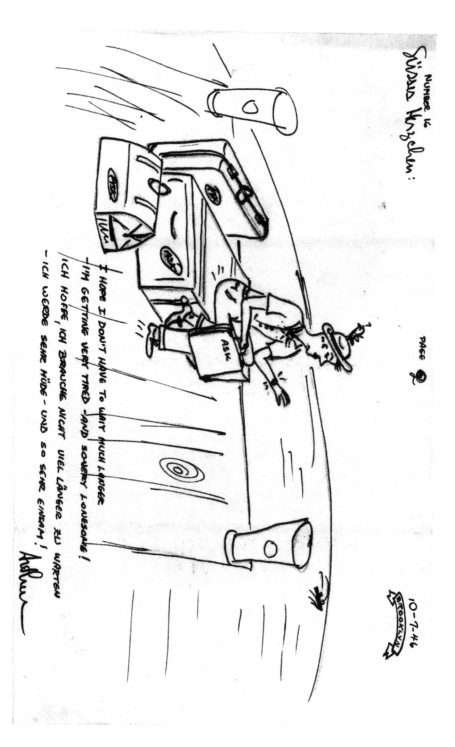

547

Examples of censorship of mail
between Anneliese and Arthur
1945-1946

Eine Jacke, hochgeschlossen,
die ich gleichzeitig auch als
Pullover benützen kann.
Rücken, Ärmel u. Kragen
ganz Blau, nur für
Vorderteil ein Muster mit
weisser Wolle eingestrickt.
Dieses Muster nennt man
bei uns Norweger Strickart
u. ist sehr "sportlich u. modern.
Die Muster sind in Wirklichkeit viel schöner als sie hier
aufgezeichnet sind. Nun wie
würde es Dir gefallen. Sei ehrlich
u. wenn es Dir nicht gefällt,
werde ich es anders stricken. Nur musst du es mir rechtzeitig mitteilen! Habe ich nicht grosse Sorgen?

Anne.

Sketch by Anneliese of a wool jacket she proposes
to knit, and asking Arthur whether he likes the
design—and to be honest in his response—if he
doesn't like it, she'd make another design, but he
must be prompt in advising her.
Schwenningen, Germany, December 1945

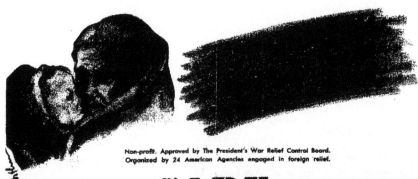

Non-profit. Approved by The President's War Relief Control Board.
Organized by 24 American Agencies engaged in foreign relief.

COOPERATIVE FOR AMERICAN REMITTANCES TO EUROPE

CARE

CARE is a non-profit organization through which individuals, groups and organizations may order "standard food packages" for delivery to designated relatives, friends, groups and organizations* in certain European countries.

THE STANDARD FOOD PACKAGE is called the "10-in-1" because it was originally designed by the U. S. Army to feed American soldiers in groups of ten. To provide variety in diet, government specifications called for five different assortments. Occasional substitutions were also authorized.

CONTENTS. Standard specifications provide for an average of over 40,000 calories, and for approximately 30 pounds net weight as follows: solid meat, stews and hashes 9.8; cereal and biscuits 6.5; fruit jam and pudding 3.6; vegetables 2.3; sugar and candy 3.9; cocoa, coffee and beverage powders 1.1; evaporated milk 0.8; preserved butter 0.5; cheese (included in one assortment) 0.4; and miscellaneous other supplies including soap, chewing gum, matches, etc., 1.2 lbs. Gross weight — in heavy-duty, waterproof container — 49 lbs.

*If you wish to send a food package without designating a beneficiary, write "general charitable contribution" on the application blank. In consultation with local authorities, CARE will select a needy individual to receive the package.

A typical "10-IN-1" Package

COST OF PACKAGE $15, covering everything — contents, shipping and delivery. *If a package cannot be delivered within a reasonable length of time, full purchase price will be refunded.*

Arthur sent such CARE Food Parcels to Anneliese

Episodes THIRTY SIX and THIRTY SEVEN

Wieder in Deutschland!

Now faith is the substance of things hoped for, the evidence of things not seen.

Hebrews 11:1

Bei dir allein

Bei dir allein
empfind' ich, dass ich lebe,
dass Jugendmut mich schwellt,
dass eine heitre Welt
der Liebe mich durchbebe;
mich freut mein Sein
bei dir allein!

With you alone

With you alone
I feel alive,
filled with youthful courage,
a happy world of Love
coursing through me;
my whole Being joyful
with you alone!

Bei dir allein [First Stanza]
Johann Gabriel Seidl (1804-1875;
used by Franz Schubert as a Lied text
[D866] in his song cycle,
Schwanengesang [D 957]. English
translation, Arthur Stanley Katz

Episode Thirty Six

In which, after a ten months' effort I return to Germany, and undertake the arduous task of obtaining the approval of each of the four Occupying Powers to allow Anneliese to leave Germany. Should one decline, exit is prohibited. I obtain US and UK approval. I resort to "creative efforts" to obtain the Russian and French clearances.

Bringing Anneliese back with me to the States under the post war conditions then prevailing in Occupied Germany would require Anneliese and me to overcome numerous governmental hurdles. Despite the fact that neither Anneliese, nor any of her family, had been Nazi Party Members—as duly noted in the Party's own carefully maintained records—and that Anneliese had been cleared to work for our Military Government Team in Heidenheim, and cleared again to work for the American Occupation Forces in Offenbach when she joined me there, she still had to obtain the formal written permission of the four occupying Powers in order for her to leave Germany. This permission or clearance would require each Power to determine whether Anneliese had been a Nazi Party member, and, if so, the nature of her actions as a Party member. The Four Powers were looking for evidence of such conduct as would fall under the rubric: crimes against humanity. Any suspicion that a person seeking to leave Germany might have participated in such crimes would bar such person from exiting Germany until such suspicions were resolved in that person's favor. And even were clearances obtained from the four Powers—and I had no qualms that such clearance would readily be obtained for Anneliese—Anneliese still had to obtain a Visa from the Consular Section of our State Department in Frankfurt which would allow her entry into the United States. And I didn't think that would be a problem either. Having learned to wend my way through the maze of Military Government Procedures, I presumed I could speedily "walk" Anneliese's papers through the Headquarters of the four Occupying Powers, and through our own consular service. I was wrong. It took me approximately five months, and a lot of running around, and a lot of talking, to get all the documentation I needed to permit Anneliese to leave Germany and to enter the United States.

Before I relate the difficulties I encountered in obtaining the necessary clearances for Anneliese from the four Occupying Powers which would allow her to exit from Germany, and those I confronted in getting an Entry Visa for Anneliese from our own State Department, I believe it would help the reader better understand the problems Anneliese and I faced in bringing Anneliese to the States if I outlined the Denazification Program set up at war's end by the victorious Allies to determine (a) on a case by case basis, whether a German national had been a Nazi party Member; (b) if non-Party Membership was established (which would be the case with Anneliese), that person would ordinarily be cleared, and no further examination pursued, but human frailties and preconceptions being what they are, the clearance of such a person might still encounter difficulties, requiring the expenditure of much time and effort to overcome such simple things as clerical errors (as happened, unfortunately to Anneliese, of which more below); (c) if Nazi Party membership was established, then the investigation proceeded to determine whether that person had participated in the commission of one or more crimes against established international norms, such as a violation of the Geneva Convention on the treatment of captured military personnel and of civilians in occupied territories, and more broadly, whether such participation as a Nazi Party member involved the commission of crimes against humanity such as playing a role, however small, in the genocide of 6 million Jews, and in the murder of millions more, in Nazi Concentration camps.

To accomplish this screening the Allies created, under the rubric "Denazification Program", in German *Das Entnazifizirungsprogramm* (an example of German word building) three classes or degrees of individual liability. The class with the highest degree of liability was labeled in German *Schwerbelastet*, literally, Heavily Burdened; a tad lower on the scale of liability was the *Minderbelastet*, the Less Burdened; and then there was the *Mitläufer*, the Follower, someone who runs with the pack but does not actively participate in any wrongful acts, a person who joined (or had to join) the Nazi Party in order to get, or keep, a job with the government, such as an office clerk. The Follower was part of the huge crowds one saw in the early Nazi newsreels, right arm stiffly raised, giving the Nazi salute and shouting "Heil Hitler!" As Anneliese explained, these were the *"Ja, den Führer! Volk"*, "Yes, The Leader! People". The masses who were the asses. Had enough of them—and their churches—had the courage of their professed religious beliefs, perhaps Hitler would never have risen to power. And juxtaposed to these three classes of Nazis was that small group of non-Party members to which Anneliese and her family belonged. Nevertheless, Anneliese had to go through the Denazification Program to establish that she was never a Party member, or involved in the commission of any atrocities. In short, she had to prove a negative. Ordinarily not easy proving a negative. However, with her record of service in our Military Government in Heidenheim, and later of her work with the U.S. Occupation Authorities in Offenbach, and with my running around with her papers to the various Occupying Powers, and to our State Department, that particular mission was accomplished. It took much time and effort. And then there were other approvals I had to obtain for Anneliese, so that she could leave with me for the States, as I shall relate. But before I do, let me write a bit about the mechanical workings of our Denazification Program. I was involved in its execution in my small way as Translator/Interpreter/Censor.

Middle rank Nazi Party officials were generally placed in the *Minderbelastet* class. These officials might include a Railroad Station Master. He was responsible for maintaining his Station and related tracks in good operational order so that troop and war materiel trains, as well as cattle cars loaded with death camp victims, were sent on their way. Unless it was established that this Station Master regularly beat or killed any of these *"Kazet"* (German abbreviation for *Konzentrationslager,* Concentration Camp) bound victims, he would be deemed Less Burdened, and dealt with accordingly.

The top Nazi officials, civilian and military, were placed in the *Schwerbelastet* class. Hitler would have been in this list had he been captured alive. Goering was, as was Adolph Eichmann, the Administrator of *Das Programm für die Endlösung der Jüdischen Frage,* The Program for the Final Solution of the Jewish Question. The Allies never brought any of these three to justice. Hitler committed suicide, as did Goering, even though he was in Allied custody when he died by swallowing a cyanide tablet secreted on his person (who patted him down?). And it was the Israelis who tracked Eichmann to Argentine, carried him back to Israel, rolled in a rug, where he was tried and executed. The only exception Israel has made to its no death penalty policy.

The *Schwerbelastet* class also included rocket scientists, such as Werner von Braun. His *V-Eins* and *V-Zwei,* V-1 and V-2 rockets were the Buzz Bombs which created so much fear, death and destruction when launched against the civilian population of England's cities and towns. Werner von Braun was never tried as a war criminal at Nuremberg. Instead, the good old U.S. of A brought him to America and gave him a top scientific position in our Space and Missile Program. Why hang a top Nazi war criminal, or put him in the can, when you can put him in your Lab, working for you? Why, indeed?

I believe the way the Allies created and conducted their Denazification Program in WWII was more intelligent than the Program set up by the United States—with good poodle Blair trotting along—to purge members of the Baath regime in Iraq. As I have endeavored to demonstrate, the Allies did not lump all card carrying Nazi Party members, nor all members of the

German *Wehrmacht, Luftwaffe* and *Marine* into a homogeneous mass. Liability was assessed on the basis of personal conduct. Did the individual do—or fail to do—acts in violation of the rules of war, or of the prevailing norms of human conduct? By fairly applying an intelligently designed program to assess individual guilt the Allies avoided the hostility within a defeated population, which would have arisen, had guilt been assessed heavily across the board, with no effort made to distinguish degrees of liability, or total freedom from any liability. In Iraq, *all* the Baathists were dismissed from public service, and *all* the Iraqi armed forces disbanded. Dumb, dumb. dumb! The United States and its rag tag "coalition of the willing" are daily eating the bitter fruits of their stupidity.

As earlier noted, Anneliese was never a member of the Nazi Party, nor was any member of her family. Yet she was caught up in the net of rules and regulations set up by the Allies' Denazification Program. This meant I would have to shepherd her papers to the appropriate officials in each of the four Zones of Occupation, there to get the necessary clearances allowing Anneliese to leave Germany, and then to our State Department's Consular Service, to obtain the visa allowing Anneliese to enter the United States. I returned to Germany in the first week of September 1946. On the last day of January 1947 I left for the States, triumphant, with my beautiful Anneliese safe at my side! During that period of almost five months I was leading a hectic life. I was busily engaged in fully performing my duties as Translator/Interpreter/ Censor (much of which required me to frequent public places, of which more below), and in running around with Anneliese's papers from one governmental entity to another.

All this frenetic activity took place in the Fall and Winter of 1946/1947, a period of beastly cold weather, lots of snow and freezing rain pouring down in blustery sheets, which, overnight, froze into translucent panes of ice, slick and slippery and not easily seen. *Glatteis* the Germans called it. And it was dangerous! I slipped on a patch of *Glatteis* on alighting from the train in Berlin where I had gone, at the height of winter, seeking the approval of the Russians for Anneliese's exit from Germany. I arrived at night, and had barely gotten both feet on the ground when the frozen terrain seemed to slide away from me. I was sent sliding like a hockey puck, banging my head and shoulders as I went. What a way to enter the Russian Zone! I was not sure of the reception my visit and related request would receive. And this mode of entry was not a good omen.

My sole purpose in returning to Occupied Germany in the Fall of 1946 was to do whatever was necessary to be able to take Anneliese home with me to America. The vehicle which allowed me to do this was my employment by the U.S. Government to work as a civilian employee in the Military Government operations of the U.S. Occupation Forces. Thus, I had the duty to my employer, the U.S. Government, to perform fully those tasks it assigned to me. And I faithfully performed this duty. But every spare moment that I had, or could create, consistent with Government employment policies, I used to assist Anneliese in filling out each *Fragebogen*, Questionnaire, she was given concerning her political background, and those in support of her application for a Visa to enter the United States for the sole purpose of marrying an American citizen—the so-called "War Bride Visa". And when this multi-paged paper work was completed, I hand carried the documents to the appropriate agency within each of the four occupying Powers—and their various headquarters were widely separated—and concerning Anneliese's Visa application, my dealings were with our State Department in Frankfurt/Main in Hessen. Time was always of the essence. I wanted so very much to gather up Anneliese in my arms, never let her go, and swiftly carry her with me to the States! And so, from the moment I returned to Germany I was constantly on the go, working for the government and working for her—actually working for both of us—for Anneliese had long since become the cornerstone upon which I was rebuilding my life.

Many of the governmental tasks I was called upon to do required me to work on the "outside", in contrast to working "inside" at a table or desk. Thus, I was called upon to travel about in trains, and to frequent train stations. I was out there to mix with the German populace, for the purpose of gathering "intelligence", as I shall more fully explain below. My job on the "outside" necessitated that I dress in civilian clothes. When working in house I wore a uniform. This consisted of an Army Officers' tunic, trousers and hat, with no indicia of rank. Very snazzy looking. Working on the outside I wore my pre-WWII civies. In the States such clothing, although clean and wholly in good shape, was now out of style, passé. However, in Germany in the Fall and Winter of 1946/47, my suits, which I had not worn for the three years I was in the Army, looked very upscale when compared to the garb worn by the average German male. My civilian attire was a pin striped, doubled breasted suit, black oxfords—with a spit polish shine—a clean shirt, and bright tie, and topped off with a felt slouch hat, with brim deftly shaped, the kind worn by Humphrey Bogart in his films. This outfit made me look very dapper indeed, the very image of a guy who was making out OK despite the hard times then engulfing most of the German population. On trains and in railroad stations, people quickly noticed some one as "flashily" dressed as I was. That was the idea. Such a guy, could mean only one of two things. I was either a black marketeer looking for deals, or a former Nazi Party bigwig awaiting his like dressed contact who would spirit him along to the next contact and then, hopefully out of Germany to a safe haven abroad. The "gentlemen" would approach me, and cautiously begin a conversation. Although my German was very good, my accent was not that of the local population. After the exchange of a few pleasantries I would usually be asked where I came from, Poland?, Hungary?, Romania? No one took me for an American. My job was to casually ferret out information. Whether the information I brought back to our Intelligence people was useful, I never learned. I brought the stuff in. They analyzed it and followed up as they saw fit. That was there job, not mine to ask or to know.

The cars on all the trains running out of Frankfurt were always packed. I picked up snatches of conversation very easily when standing cheek to jowl with a bunch of the locals. You quickly got the feel of what the average German was complaining about. Again useful information for an occupying power to learn. If a program was going well, keep it up. If the people are bitter about something, try to rectify the condition before it festers into nasty expressions of discontent.

The railroad cars were not heated, or if they were, I never noticed the heat. The weather was very cold outside, the widows were therefore closed, and the mass of human beings sandwiched against each other, each dressed in worn, thick clothing, and breathing, coughing and sneezing in your face, soon created a dank, stinking, unhealthy environment. It was part of my job to be there, but it was the part I liked the least. Then there was the day that I couldn't find even a smidgin of room in any car. I had arrived at the station just as the train was about to pull out. I ran alongside it, looking to see where I could squeeze myself in. No one volunteered to help me get on board. Then I remembered that at the end of each train was a car with this notice painted on its side: *"Nur für Kriegsbeschädigt"*, in a literal English translation: only for those damaged in the war, *i.e.,* the car was reserved for war wounded German veterans. I had previously observed that this car was never packed; always plenty of seats. I had not sat there before because if I'm out to absorb information from the masses, I have to be where the masses are, and the war wounded car was not such a place. But I was going to miss this train if I didn't get on board immediately. So as the train slowly pulled out I climbed the steps of the car reserved for German wounded veterans. I made my way down the center aisle of the car. On each side there was three across seating. In the middle of the car I sat down on an aisle seat. The other two seats being occupied by men in their mid-thirties, I guessed. Some of them were still wearing parts of their old uniforms, with the swastika insignias removed.

I'm dressed, as above described, quite a contrast to these two guys, and to the rest of the men aboard. I noticed one or two had a leg amputated, and one had an arm missing from the elbow on down. As I sat down I said cheerily, in my best Hessian dialect, *"Morjeh!"* *Morjeh* being the Hessian way to say *Morgen!* Morning/ Good Morning. Nobody responded. The train had now picked up speed and was click clacking briskly. I sensed I was being eyed by all aboard. I just sat there. I made no attempt at further conversation. My former military persona came to the fore. "Fuck 'em!", I said to myself. "If they don't want to be sociable, so be it." Perhaps a minute passed in total silence, then the German veteran next to me said, rasped out of the corner of his mouth—not looking at me—*Der wagen ist nur für Kriegsbeschädigt."* *"Ich weiss"*, I know, I replied. *"Ich bin Kriegsbeschädigt".* I am war wounded. Every head in earshot pivoted towards me. My seat mate turned to face me and asked, *"In welcher Abteilung waren Sie?"* In which Unit were you? In German, I told him I had been in the 86th Cavalry Reconnaissance Squadron Mechanized. He thought for a moment and a tad puzzled, said that he had never heard of such a unit in the German Army. I replied—our conversation always being in German—that my *Abteilung*, was not in the German Army, it was in the American Army! I then observed that the car was marked *"Nur für Kriegsbeschädigt"*, and that it didn't say *"Nur für Deutsche Kriegsbeschädigt"*. Only for *German* War Wounded! My German War Veteran seat mate thought for a moment, laughed, clapped me lightly on my back, and said *"Ja, Sie haben recht!"* "Yes, you're right!" And all the others in earshot laughed, too. Until he got off a few stations down the road, we had a spirited conversation. I learned, that for a brief period, when my Squadron and General Patton's Third Army were near Colmar, in France, that his infantry unit was opposing our forces. *C'est la guerre. C'est la vie.*

About a week or so after I got settled in my job, and knew the drill, I arranged for Anneliese to be interviewed for a job in my Military Government Unit. Anneliese's English was now quite good, ten long months of exchanging love letters had honed her English skills, as it had sharpened mine in German. Her ever expanding English abilities, when coupled with those of being a native German speaker, made her an asset to our Government. She was hired right after her first, and only interview.

I was billeted with the American personnel. It would have set too many tongues wagging were she to have moved in with me. Although there was much promiscuity going on about me, I had no intention of exposing her to any embarrassment as being perceived as a beautiful *Mädchen* I had been lucky to latch onto for fun and games. And so I found a small flat for her in Offenbach, in a tenement building which had survived our wartime bombings. And it was there, when I was not away from Offenbach on official business, or on the road, hand carrying her papers about, that we spent many wonderful hours together, we were young lovers clinging to each other, fearful lest we should again be separated. And then there were evenings when, for warmth, we huddled together, as close as we could get to the small pot bellied stove, the only source of heat in Anneliese's flat, with its warmth coming from glowing charcoal briquettes. I would regularly supply Anneliese with these briquettes. One evening I noted Anneliese had placed only six or seven briquettes in the stove. She would never light the stove until I got there. The day before I had brought her a goodly sized sack of briquettes, perhaps two dozen pieces. I asked Anneliese why she didn't put more in to burn. Someone had broken into her flat when she was away, she said, but had stolen nothing but the bar of soap on the sink and almost all of the briquettes I had given her.

I was pissed! Not at her, of course, but at the idea of having her place broken into. My voice agitated I inquired, why had she not told me about the break-in, why did I have to learn about it indirectly! I believe this was the first time she saw me at less than on my best behavior. The moment the words were out of my mouth I regretted them. I saw the surprise and hurt on her face. She flushed, but immediately recovered her composure. I didn't want to tell you, she said, because you always worry so much about me. Why bring you more troubles? Her softly spoken words instantly brought me to tears. Her concern for my peace of mind had vastly overshadowed that for her own well being! Anneliese was an Angel! a *Mensch*! a much better person than I could ever hope to be. That same magical feeling welled up within me as it had the first time I gazed upon my Fairy Princess! I rushed to her, embraced her, kissed her on her lips, her cheeks, her forehead, and begged her to forgive me for my outburst. My darling, there is nothing to forgive, she said, and then, in German, *"Ich schätze sehr deine Besorgnis für mich."* I treasure greatly your concern for me. And she, too, began to cry. There, in her cold flat, the pot bellied stove not yet lit for warmth, the blustery rain beating against the windows—as if seeking a haven from itself—there we stood, two young lovers, holding tight to each other, our tears mingling, And neither of us felt the cold.

September 1946 gave way to October, to be succeeded by November, and then December yielded to January and the start of a new year, 1947. The boughs of the evergreens, *Die Immergrün*, the Pine, the Spruce, the Hemlock, sagged under the weight of snow and rain congealed into ice. The leaves of the deciduous trees, the Oak, the Ash, the Maple, the Apple, Cherry, Pear, Peach and Plum, had long since fluttered to the dank earth. *Die Amsel, Drossel, Fink und Star*, the Blackbird, Thrush, Finch and Starling had flown to warmer climes. And as the days melded into weeks, and the weeks into months, I wended my way, from one governmental agency to another, with Anneliese's papers stowed in my briefcase which I shifted from hand to hand, as I alternated them for warmth in my coat pockets, for even felt lined leather gloves were not impervious to the cold.

I started my rounds of the four Occupying Powers by going first to our own HQ, in Frankfurt. As anticipated, approval for Anneliese's departure from Germany was soon secured from the U.S. Occupation Authorities. "Soon", in the context of the times, meant approximately three weeks. My combat service was an asset in accelerating review and approval of Anneliese's papers, in that many of those examining the papers had been in the Service, or still were; they were cognizant of my military record, they saw from my demeanor that I was very much in love with a beautiful German girl and that I wanted to take her home with me and get married. If I recall correctly, the Non-Fraternization Regulations of the U.S. Occupation Forces in force in 1946/47 did not permit American military personnel, and civilian U.S. citizens to marry German nationals within any part of Occupied Germany. Hence, the need to get Anneliese from Germany into the States.

Approval from the American military authorities having been secured, I now turned my attention to the British Occupation authorities. I had no trouble with the Brits. I recounted how pleasant I had found the UK's towns and countryside, while stationed there before the invasion, and how I admired the courage of its citizens, and I made passing reference to my combat experiences, including being wounded. My observations on Britain were well received, and my military record noted with approval, by the officials with whom I met. In short order I got the necessary British Clearance, and as I left, with the precious signed document tucked into my briefcase, the officer who had handed me the papers smiled, shook my hand and said, "Good Luck Yank to you and your fiancée!" How nice of him! Two down, and two to go.

After several weeks of intensive, no time off work on my job, including inside and outside work, as above described, I accumulated enough free time to set off to meet with the authorities in the French Zone of Occupation. Although Anneliese was then residing and working in Offenbach, in the U.S. Zone, she was still, formally, a resident of Schwenningen, and this city was in the heart of the French Zone. Negative action by any of the four Occupying Powers could prevent Anneliese from leaving Germany, subject to possible reversal through cumbersome appeals procedures. However, the position the French took, if negative, would effectively slam shut any door marked "Exit From

Germany". She was a German national within their exclusive control as the Occupying Power. Scary thought. Thus, I pondered on the approach I should take in seeking French clearance for Anneliese. Patriotism, a people's love for their country, is the glue which binds disparate individuals into a nation, with the State often seen as a Father or Mother protecting their children. To Germans their country is *Das Vaterland*, The Father's Land. Russians, whatever their economic status, lovingly refer to their vast country as Mother Russia, and the French embody their love of country in the image of a beautiful warrior woman protecting the liberties of her subjects. And the French have taken their love of country and transmuted it into the conviction that they alone, of all the world's other peoples, understand best the meaning of romantic love, wild, unrestrained sensual love. To the French *L'Amour est un oiseau rebelle* Love is a rebellious bird, as noted by Carmen in the Habanera aria she sings in Bizet's opera.

I mused on the relationship in the French national psyche of love of country with romantic love, and how to make that relationship work for Anneliese and for me. I knew that the French were not proud of their lack of military prowess against the invading Nazis, and that they were further demeaned by the Vichy regime which the Nazis set up to administer the French nation they had conquered. The French also recognized that their freedom had been restored by the combined efforts of the United States, Great Britain and the Soviet Union. Whatever assistance given by De Gaulle and his Free French Troops was of minimal military value. Through its own conduct the honor of the French State had been besmirched. That rankled. But France was free again, and insofar as its treatment of Germans was concerned, back in the saddle. France did not hesitate to get even. Its indiscriminate round-up and jailing of German civilian males, including Anneliese's father, an episode I have chronicled, is an example of France's immediate post war attitude to the German people. I recognized that the French Government would not be inclined to be helpful to German nationals who needed something from them, such as permission for Anneliese to leave the French Zone and Germany.

I decided to tone down the brothers in arms approach which I had used in dealing with the U.S. and British Authorities. Instead, I would play on the special French relationship with *L'Amour*. No true Frenchman could resist that approach. Right? I was wrong. The French official congratulated me on my military record which I had raised in passing. However, he saw no reason to grant a clearance for Anneliese to leave the French Zone for the purpose of going to America to be married. "Nothing personal", he said, "but we French suffered very much under the Nazis, and even if you say your fiancée is not a Nazi, she is a German, and we do not make distinctions between the two." I played my love card, the special French national understanding of *L'Amour*. The guy wasn't buying. "Look", he tells me "you're here in Germany, she's here. Make love. Maybe in a year or two your government might let you get married here. Maybe we'll change our views, too." I was crestfallen. He could see my disappointment. He inquired whether I had the other three Allied clearances. I told him I had the U.S. and UK clearances and would soon be traveling to Berlin to get the Russian clearance. "Don't bother", he tells me. "The Russians suffered more from the Germans (he didn't distinguish between Nazis and Germans) than we did. They'll never give you any favors such as a clearance for your German fiancée." I was grasping at straws. "What if I got the Russians to give my Fiancée a clearance, would you then give her one?" He laughed, "Yes, I would. But I don't think I'll ever have to." And he laughed again. I was miserable.

When I got back to Offenbach Anneliese asked how everything had gone. I couldn't see myself hurting her. No sense both of us feeling bad. So I told her the French were working on her papers, and they don't work too fast, I reminded her. If she didn't believe me she didn't let on. That was the way she was.

Concurrent with seeking the four Power clearances for Anneliese I had obtained from our State Department in Frankfurt the consular papers which had to be filled out for her to apply for a visa to enter the USA for the purpose of marriage to an American citizen. Anneliese and I had filled them out and I had returned them to the Embassy. Several weeks had passed and I had heard nothing. I wasn't concerned since I had not yet obtained all the four Allied clearances. But I would go to the Embassy as soon as I had all clearances in hand.

Again, by dint of working long hours, I built up some free time. This time had to be used during a work week. Weekends would find none of the Allied Governmental offices open. Still smarting from my rebuff at the hands of the French I took the train for Berlin in the Russian Zone. I was wearing my civilian employee military officer's uniform, as earlier described. It made me look like an American soldier. This made me feel more comfortable than traveling into the Russian Zone in civilian clothes. I had heard tales that the Russian soldiers on board these trains would often rob the passengers. I had also heard that these soldiers were poorly trained, ill educated, poorly disciplined, and heavily armed. Not a comforting picture for one traveling at night into the heart of the Russian Zone. Nothing untoward happened coming and going on the train, other than the episode of slipping on the *Glatteis* on alighting from the train in Berlin, an episode I have already related. However, on the way there—the only passenger in the car—a Russian soldier came into my poorly lit compartment. An automatic weapon, maybe a submachine gun, was slung over his shoulder. He was a young kid. He stared at me for a couple of seconds. Said nothing, and left. I was relieved.

If the train had been a plane, the flight would have been referred to as a red eye flight It arrived in Berlin around 5 a.m. before the sun came up, such sun as one would see that time of the year, with the sky then almost always overcast. The trip had taken about 8 hours, lots of stops on the way. I had not slept. But I didn't feel sleepy. I was all hyped up for my meeting with the Russian official. The meeting had been carefully arranged, and I was there, in his office, waiting for him. I was early. He came in at the scheduled time, 8 a.m. He was in uniform. In my Military Government days in 1945 I had worked with a Russian officer in arranging for the repatriation of such Russian soldiers which the Germans captured, and did not summarily execute, in violation of the Geneva Convention, and in handling the repatriation of Russian Jews capable of walking on their own power after recuperation from their concentration camp experiences. He had told me he was a Major, and from the identical pips on this officer's shoulders I gathered he, too, was a Major. I had learned some Russian in the course of my soldiering, such phrases as "How are you?" "Do you speak Russian/English?", "Yes", "No", "Thank you", "Please", etc. I tried these out on the officer. He smiled, acknowledged, in Russian, my greeting, and then, politely suggested we converse in English, which he spoke quite well. I asked, whether he spoke German, he said he did, but preferred not to. I understood.

I was off to a bad start. I began with my military service ploy. He listened politely and thanked me for helping his people defeat the Nazis. I then told him about Anneliese and me. He knew about Anneliese, he had a copy of her papers, most likely received from the U.S. and French authorities. I told him I needed his government's clearance so that Anneliese could leave Germany and accompany me back to the States to get married. Would my fiancée get his government's clearance? I held my breath. I didn't have to hold it long. He said, "Nyet", and then, in English, "No". Here we go again, I thought. "Why not?", I queried. "My fiancée had done nothing wrong to anyone, let alone to his countrymen, she had never been a Party Member. She . . ." He interrupted me, "She's a German. Germans have killed twenty million of my people." He couldn't tell which Germans were guilty of what crimes, and which were innocent, assuming any German was innocent. I tried to interject that Anneliese had never been a Nazi, had never hurt anyone. To no avail. He didn't distinguish between Nazis and ordinary Germans. On this issue his approach was identical to the Frenchman's. I tried my last ploy: LOVE. I said the war was over, the killing was over. Wasn't it time for those of us who had fought, suffered, and survived to start making new lives for ourselves? Wasn't this the time for Love to overcome Hate. I was becoming emotional! I had just bet my last chip on black and the roulette wheel was slowing to a stop. "Love has nothing to do with clearances. This is a political issue. Germans are Germans, they slaughtered us, we hate them! I am sorry for you that you fell in love with a German girl. You showed me her picture, she is very beautiful. But she is a German and love has nothing to do with it. I will issue no clearance". He began to rise from his chair. The meeting was over. Desperate, I jumped out of my chair and cried out, "I knew it!, I knew it!" Intrigued, he sat down. "What do you know?" "The French officer assured me that you Russians wouldn't give my fiancée the clearance. Why? Because Russians don't care about love, they know nothing about love, they don't know the excitement of romance!" I was almost shouting. The Major's face reddened. "That French fart said that about us Russians? Well, he's wrong! Wrong! Has he ever read Pushkin or Tolstoy! I can see you are very much in love! We Russians care about love!" He paused. "I'll give your beautiful German girl her clearance! It's my present to both of you! Make love all day and night! Make babies! We Russians know what love is! Tell that to that French piece of shit when you see him!" Whereupon the Major opened a desk drawer took out the clearance document, signed, stamped and dated it, and handed it to me. I could have kissed him!

The train trip from Berlin back to Frankfurt took the usual eight hours. But the run was now all in the daytime. And although the skies were still leaden, with a hint of oncoming rain, I imagined I was surrounded by a brilliant light. I was all aglow, inside and out! I could scarcely wait to tell Anneliese the good news, and then dash off to the French Zone to tell that French Fart, that French piece of shit, that he had lost his bet and owed Anneliese her clearance! Except I wouldn't call him a fart or a piece of shit, at least not to his face.

Within days of my return from the Russian Zone I was again with the French officer who had refused to issue a clearance allowing Anneliese to leave the French Zone of Occupation. He was surprised to see me. Very surprised! I told him that the Russians had cleared Anneliese, and I showed him the document I had obtained in Berlin from the Russian Major. He asked if he could examine the document. For a moment I hesitated to hand it to him. What if he refused to give it back, or in a moment of pique, tore it up? These were crazy thoughts. But I had no choice. Unless he satisfied himself that the document was genuine he would certainly not proceed with our meeting. I handed him the document, a piece of paper, a fragile object, but oh so precious to Anneliese and me! The French officer examined the document carefully, paying close attention to the Russian seal stamped on its face. He handed it back to me. Relieved, I put the Russian Clearance back into my briefcase. Smiling I politely reminded him that he had said that if I got the Russians to give my fiancée their clearance—that the French Occupation authorities would do the same. "Yes", he replied, "and France keeps its word." At this moment, so important to Anneliese and me, *he* was France. He was Louis XIV. *Je suis L'Etat*, I am the State. He got up from his desk, walked to a file cabinet, retrieved a document, inquired as to the spelling of Anneliese's name, confirmed her address in Schwenningen, signed and sealed the document, and handed it to me. I accepted it with profuse thanks, and placed it carefully— lovingly might be a better description—into my briefcase.

As I turned to leave, the French officer asked, "How did you get the Russians to sign off? "I told the Russian official that I had just come from the French Zone, where I had told you that I was now going to see the Russians for the same reason I had seen you—to get Russian approval for my fiancée to leave Germany so that she could accompany me to America to get married; that the French officer remarked I was wasting my time, the Russians would never give me such approval because they hated the Germans more than the French did, and even though the war was over they would continue to hate the Germans, including my fiancée, because, unlike the French, Russians did not care about love, or understand the meaning of love and romance. When the Russian official heard what you had said, he became angry, declared that you French were wrong about them, that the Russian people cared about love and romance more than anyone else, and, to show that Russians cared about love, he signed my fianceé's clearance, told us to make love all the time and have many babies."

The French officer stared at me, a puzzled look on his face. "I don't recall saying that about the Russians." "Well", I replied, "I must have misunderstood, I smiled, and left the Frenchman's office. I never told him that the Russian had called him a fart and a piece of shit—and all without reason. I had tricked the Russian and the Frenchman. But all is fair in love and war, *n'est pas*?

When I had returned from the Russian Zone to Anneliese in Offenbach, and had shown her the Russian approval document, she was thrilled, clapping her hands, hugging and kissing me. She then asked when I might be going down to the French Zone to pick up the French clearance. I had, by design, left her with the impression that the French were working on the clearance. I had not told her that she had been turned down. Why cause her grief? But now that all the clearances were obtained I showed Anneliese the French clearance and gave her a full account of what had happened, and how I got the Russians and French to give her their clearances. Anneliese laughed, hugged me, kissed me and kissed me, and jubilantly exclaimed, "My Bub is so clever!", and then we danced an awkward waltz, humming The Blue Danube!

Now, all that remained to do, before we could say Goodbye Germany!, Hello America!, was to take the Four Power Clearances to the United States Embassy and pick up Anneliese's Visa. Sounds simple. Unfortunately, it wasn't. Which gives me an opportunity—one I would rather have desired to avoid—to relate another episode in the saga: Arthur and Anneliese wend their way to America.

My darling,

Ich glaube du kannst sicher vorstellen, wie einsam dein Bübelein ist. Aber weisst du auch wie traurig er ist? Ja, traurig! Ich werde in einer Woche wieder in Deutschland sein. Aber je näher ich komme, desto mehr Angst habe ich! Komisch? Nicht ganz. Lass mich erklären. Zum Beispiel, ich weiss noch nicht — wie Zivilisten, die in Deutschland arbeiten, an deutsche Bräute schreiben können. Ich schreibe heute abend — weil ich muss, weil ich so sehr einsam bin, weil ich sehne so nach dir! — aber ich weiss nicht, ob ich diesen Brief an dich schicken kann!

Ja — und diese Woche haben die Behörden mehr — und strenge Gesetze in betreff Eheschliessungen zwischen Amerikanern und Deutschen gemacht. Die Engländer, Franzosen und die Russen auch sehen alles gar anders — aber so geht es.

Unser gemeinsame Weg ist lang, steil und sicher nicht mit Rosen gepflastert.

Ich würde jetzt weinen. Aber das Weinen macht das Leben nicht ein bisschen leichter. Nein, ich werde nicht weinen!!

Ich habe schon so weit gekommen — und du hast schon so lang gewartet, dass wir beide noch tapfer bleiben müssen!

Weisst, Herzchen, während ich diesen Briefes schreibe, werde ich glücklich! Es ist etwas „zauberisch", etwas das ich nicht leicht beschreiben kann — aber — aber ich brauche nur an dich zu denken — und das Leben ist wieder hell und herrlich!

Ach Engel — nur ein bisschen mehr Geduld! So schnell wie möglich werde ich wieder bei deiner Seite sein. Vielleicht nur für einen Tag — für ähnliche Stunde. Aber wir müssen immer dankbar sein, für all die Freude das das Leben uns gibt. In der Wirklichkeit es macht nicht wie klein unser „Portion" der Freude ist. Ist es nicht wahr, dass ein Sprichwort sagt: Geteilte Freude ist doppelte Freude? Und ich werde immer mein „Portion" mit dir teilen. Und wenn du „hungrig bist", werde ich dir „Essen" geben — und so wirst du mit mir tun! Und in dieser Art werden wir beide immer voll mit Freude und Liebe sein — voll, ja — aber

26.8. '46 Arthur to Anneliese
written crossing the
Atlantic on his return to Germany

immer Gott!

Ich werde sehr schwer arbeiten, viel Geld zu verdienen – und viel zu sparen. Ich werde unsre gemeinsamen Pläne machen. Und ein Tag unsre Zeit wird kommen!

Oft habe ich gedacht – aber genug für eine Nacht! Mein Kopf ist ganz wirr jetzt! Ich gehe ins Bett in der Hoffnung, dass vielleicht ich an dich träumen werde. Wenn ich kann dich noch nicht haben, muss ich mit deinen Gesichten leben. Bin ich doch zufrieden? Ja – aber, du weisst wie es ist: Gesichte und Träume sind schön – aber die himmlische Wirklichkeit ist immer so viel besser!!

27-8-46 — Ich bin zurück, Herzchen. Heute morgen scheint die Sonne so wunderbar warm! – aber ich habe keine Lust für die Sonnenschein, ich muss unbedingt wieder an dich schreiben! Das Leben ist so leer ohne Verbindung mit dir!

Ich fange wieder an: Liebling, oft dachte ich, dass vielleicht unsre Leben „leichter" gewesen wären, wenn wir einander niemals getroffen hätten! Ja! Bin ich nicht hässlich? Spreche ich wirklich wie ein dummes Kind? Doch, doch! aber hast du nicht das selbe denken gehabt? Ach das Leben ist schwer, fast zu schwer. Anne, wenn ich meine Geduld verlieren soll, bitte gebst du mir deine? Bitte? O danke sehr!

Nun gehe ich wieder auf deck; ein bisschen Sonnenschein, ehe ich Lunch esse. Behüt dich Gott!

28-7-46 Engel, verzeih, wenn ich nicht mehr schreibe, ich bin so sehr einform! Und warum ich so bin, muss ich darum seinen Kürbis lernen, ehe ich wieder gesund kwank! Wenn ich schreibe oder nicht du bist immer mit mir!

29-7-46 Engel, ich habe deinen Geburtstag nicht vergessen! Wie könnte ich? Wenn ich immer bei dir bin, weisst du schon, dass diesen Freitag schon lange in meiner Erinnerung eingedrückt war! Leider habe ich keine Briefe von dir bekommen, aber ich erinnere über natürlich. Ich hoffe, dass du u. die Familie gesund sind, und dass die Pakete gut angekommen sind! Wenn ich zurück nach der kommen kann, dann werde ich schreiben, ob du noch hg. gehen sollst. Gott?

26.8.'46 Arthur to Anneliese,
Page 2 of letter written to her
crossing the Atlantic on his return to Germany

7.9.46.

Mein geliebtes Bubelin!

Wieder in Deutschland! Wie glücklich mich diese Nachricht macht! Unsagbar glücklich, nur zeigen kann ich Dir mein Glück, nur Dich spüren u. fühlen lassen meine grosse himmlische Glückseeligkeit!

Und wann wirst Du nun zu mir kommen? Muss Deine Anne mit ihrem ungeduldigen Herzen noch lange warten? Vor zwei Tagen warst Du in Frankfurt u. vielleicht gelingt es Dir in allernächster Zeit bei mir zu sein! Ach wie herrlich! Mir schwindelt fast bei dem Gedanken, dass ich Dich bald wieder bei mir haben werden. Dein liebes Gesicht u. Deine guten treuen Augen wieder sehen kann, Deine süsse Stimme hören, die immer so angenehm u. weich in meinen Ohren klingt!

Oh mein Lieb, wie unendlich dank-

7.9.'46 Anneliese to Arthur
on his return "again in Germany!"

bar bin ich Dir für Deine reiche grosse Liebe!
Mein Herz denkt Tag u. Nacht nur an Dich
u. will Dich beglücken u. Dir nur Freude
bringen!

Komme bald Bub, ich kann
kaum erwarten bis Du vor mir stehen
wirst! Morgen ist Sonntag, wie schön
wenn Du ihn mit mir verbringen könntest.
Darf ich hoffen? Oh ja, das kann u. darf ich
u. ich weiss auch dass all meine Geduld mein
sehnlichstes Warten mit dem höchsten
Preis belohnt wird, mit Deiner süssen
Gegenwart!
Bitte Bub, lasse mich nicht mehr
zu lange warten!
Immer Deine Anne.

7.9.'46 Anneliese to Arthur
Page 2, Wieder in Deutschland!
"Again in Germany!" letter

<u>1.</u>   9. Sept. 1946.

Mein Lieb!

Nur ein ganz kurzer aber sehr lieber Gruss zu Dir mein Herzchen! Ich bin so so müde, es ist 8 Uhr u. ich werde sofort zu Bette gehen. Ich hoffe, dass Du gut u. nicht all zu spät nach Frankfurt gekommen bist.

Gute Nacht Bubelein, träume süss von unseren herrlichen Stunden! Ich liebe Dich so sehr!

Deine Anne.

9. Sept. 1946 Anneliese to Arthur on their reunion

Guten Morgen mein Bub, bist Du
frisch u. munter? Ich habe bis 9 Uhr früh
geschlafen u. so tief u. fest, dass ich nicht
einmal geträumt habe. Aber beim Erwachen
bildete ich mir ein, du wärest noch bei mir
ich konnte Deine Nähe fühlen die letzten
Stunden mit Dir waren zu schön, wie im

10.Sept. 1946 Anneliese to Arthur
on their reunion, Page 1

576

Märchen u. Traumland.

Ich hoffe dass Du keine Schwierigkeiten
hattest, weil Du etwas später kamst.
Nun freue ich mich wieder für unser nächstes
Wiedersehen, wenn es am nächsten Wochen-
ende nicht ist, so hoffe ich am anderen.
Wenn es nur nicht so weit zu Dir wäre, oder
wenn ich wenigstens einen Pass bekommen
könnte. Bub, mein Herz ist jetzt so leicht,
so glücklich, habe ich Dich durch gesund wieder
gesehen, bin ich doch so reich durch Deine grosse
ehrliche Liebe! Habe ich wirklich so viel Glück verdient?

Bub ich werde jeden Tag zu Dir schreiben
wenn es auch nur ein paar Zeilen sind. Und bitte
mache Du dasselbe, Du weißt wie hungrig ich
für Deine Briefe bin!!
An Frau Feiner u. Ernst habe ich geschrieben
u. nachher will ich noch an Deine Eltern schreiben.
Ich denke sie werden sich freuen wenn sie von mir
hören! Bleib gesund Bub, komme bald wieder u.
träume von unseren herrlichen glücklichen Stunden.
Immer Deine Anne.

10. Sept. 1946, Page 2
Anneliese to Arthur on their Reunion

577

My darling,

I arrived home but half an hour ago. And I've had time just to wash my very dirty face. And though I have lots more yet to do— I'm letting everything hang in mid-air until this letter has been written.

I've just spent a pleasant weekend in my "old home town" ~ Heidenheim!

Mutter Zimer und Heiner und Vater waren natürlich, sehr begeistert mich so schnell zu sehen! Trotzdem waren sie sehr zufrieden. Und sie haben alles für mich sehr bequem und gemütlich gemacht!

Ich war auch einige Stunden mit Ernst und sein Mitarbeiter. Und ich war oben in seiner neuen Wohnung, seine Eltern und Schwester zu sehen. Und ich war bei Frau Voith, dass sie sehen könnte, dass Herr Katz ist wirklich zurückgekommen!!

15.9.'46 Arthur to Anneliese, Page 1

Sie war sehr nett zu mir und sagte, dass sie immer wüsste, dass ich zurückkommen würde! Und wenn ich schaute sie ein bisschen komisch an, sagte sie wieder und schnell: "Ja! Herr Katz, das ist wahr!" (?) Und sie fragte, ob du gesund warst, usw.

Perlow sah gut aus – und er war sehr freundlich und behilflich. Katte war wie immer "wortlos".

Alles war schön – nur die Reisen – diese gingen nicht ganz leicht. Die Verbindungen waren nicht zu gut. Und Heiner musste mich mit seinem Motorrad von Heidenheim nach Süssen fahren! Diese Reise war entzückend!

Aber ich bin endlich gut zu Hause angekommen. Und all meine Sorgen sind vorbei. Aber nicht meine Einsamkeit!

Morgen schickt Mutter alles weg über den Express. Und auch eine Postanweisung. Ich war sehr "zu Hause" bei ihr. Aber doch so sehr einsam! Ich schlief am Sofa. Und ich glaube du kannst vorstellen, die Gedanken ich hatte! Kannst Du?

15.9.'46 Arthur to Anneliese, Page 2

Ich werde wieder an H. Van Strinn schreiben
in Betreff einer neuen Stellung. Und morgen
fährt Arnold nach Stuttgart und er wird
auch mit ihm sprechen. Vielleicht! Ja, vielleicht!

(1300)
Samstag um 1 Uhr fahre ich wieder nach
Stuttgart – um zu treffen Wenn du einen
Pass bekommen hast – sende mich gleich/geschwind
ein Telegram – wenn nicht – auch – dass
ich wissen kann, ob es wertvoll ist nach
Stuttgart zu gehen – oder nicht. Verstanden?
Und wenn du solst, sag mir wenn dein
Zug in Stuttgart sein wird. Ich werde
Zivil Kleider tragen!

Dein „Gruss Brief" an mich war sehr
nett. Danke vielmals für ihn!

Nun, muss ich ins Bett – ich bin müde.
Behüt' dich Gott! Ich liebe dich!
dein Bub,
Arthur

Verzeih' wenn mein Schrift mehr komisch
wie oft ist. Ich bin bestimmt sehr müde!
doch! Doch!

15.9.'46 Arthur to Anneliese, Page 3

Episode Thirty Seven

In which I encounter delays in getting the U.S. State Dept. to issue a "War Brides Visa" to Anneliese allowing her to enter the United States for one month solely to marry me. If no timely marriage she is deported back to Germany. No worry on that score. A visa suddenly issues after "theatrics" on my part.

At approximately the same time that I began my rounds of the Four Occupying Powers (in the course of which I visited Düsseldorf, for the British, Berlin for the Soviets, Baden-Baden for the French and, of course, Frankfurt/Main for the USA), I filed with our State Department in Frankfurt Anneliese's Application for a Visa to enter the United States. Naturally, I was the Sponsor of her Application. I was informed by the State Department that the Visa, if issued, (no government agency ever gives a firm response to any request for action) would allow Anneliese to enter the United States solely for the purpose of marrying an American citizen resident in the States, and if the marriage did not occur within a thirty days period, measured from the time of Anneliese's arrival in the States, she would be deported back to Germany. The short time period caused neither Anneliese nor me any concern, *im Gegenteil*, on the contrary, since it was our greatest desire to consummate our union formally as quickly as feasible, so that we would be—forever and a day—Arthur Stanley Katz and Anneliese Baur Katz, Husband and Wife! *Mazal Tov*!!

I believe it was sometime in November 1946 that I hand delivered to the Consular Section of the State Department, in our Embassy in Frankfurt, Anneliese's Visa Application with supporting papers from me as her fiancé and sponsor. When I asked how long it might take for the Visa to issue—I was anticipating no problem in having the Visa issue—I was told it might take, at the most, a month once all the clearances from the Occupying Powers had been received, and the Department had completed its own examination procedures.

November 1946 ended with no word from the State Department having been received by Anneliese or me. Nor was any word received in December. I did not think to press the State Department as to the status of Anneliese's papers since I had not yet obtained the Clearances from the four Allied Occupying Powers. Absent these Clearances the issuance of any Visa to Anneliese would have no value as she would not be able to leave Occupied Germany. But now it was mid-January 1947. I had all the Clearances and this information had been forwarded to the State Dept. And so I turned my attention to the status of Anneliese's Visa Application. I had overcome road blocks in obtaining the Clearances; I was not anticipating running into any road block with regard to Anneliese's Visa. I did. Fortunately, I was able, in short order to remove it, but not without getting my dander up, and ruffling some feathers on our national symbol, the American Bald Eagle. Let me set the scene.

I was on my day off when I went to our Embassy to inquire as to the status of Anneliese's Visa Application. As I have related, when working "in house", in the office, I wore an Army Officers' uniform. When working "outside", I dressed in my fanciest civilian clothing which I have already described. The morning I went to the Embassy, it being my day off, I did not think to wear my Army Officer's uniform. Nor did I believe it appropriate to wear my fancy duds. I might "blow" whatever cover I had by so doing, particularly when seen entering our Embassy. And so I wore my regular civilian clothes, clean, but nondescript: a heavy sweater over an open necked shirt, trousers which had not seen an iron for a long time, a parka like jacket over the sweater—the weather being very cold, as usual—and thick soled, ankle high work shoes. And on my head, a knitted cap. Everything quite functional. Sitting there, on one of the benches outside the door to the Embassy, I was indistinguishable from the other nondescript people waiting for the Embassy to open for business. Based upon the polyglot snatches of conversation I overheard, my bench mates were a mixed lot of nationalities.

The sign on the wide, thick wooden Embassy door stated that the Embassy was open from 10 a.m. to 12 noon, and from 2 p.m. to 4 p.m. Not a lot of time for public visitation. I presumed that the balance of the day was taken up with other matters of concern to our government. I had arrived a bit past 9 a.m. to assure that I would be among the first to get in. Anneliese was at work in her warm office, no need for her to be sitting here with me in this cold antechamber. I had bought a copy of the *Frankfurter Allgemeine Zeitung*, the leading local paper on the way in, and read it to pass the time. Around 9:30 a.m. some pretty German girls, locals, according to their Hessen accents, knocked on the door, spoke to someone inside, and were let in. I guessed they were office personnel. 10 o'clock came and went. I tried the door. It was locked. Through it I heard the muffled chattering of voices, English mixed with German, and laughter. Those inside sounded like a jolly lot. I went back to my seat. Read a bit more. My wrist watch now read 10:15 a.m. The Embassy door remained shut. At 10:30 a.m. a tall, good looking guy, crew cut hair, sports coat, razor sharp creased slacks, black, highly polished tasseled loafers, walked past all of us, looking neither to his right nor left. He knocked on the door, said a few words, the portal opened wide enough to let him in, and then closed. I caught snatches of barely audible conversation in English. From what this guy was saying I gathered that he had managed to get in 9 holes of golf even though it was cold on the course! Before World War II had broken out The Ford Company had built an assembly plant in the Frankfurt area, and near it was a regulation 18 hole golf course. During the war the plant turned out vehicles for Hitler's *Wehrmacht*. For some reason I never could fathom, neither our precision bombers, nor those of the British, were ever able to hit the Ford plant, or the golf course. *C'est la guerre. C'est la vie.*

The sign on the Embassy door read: Open 10 a.m. to 12 noon. Here it was 10:30, and the Embassy was not open. I was growing impatient, and a tad hot under the collar. If those around me were impatient, they didn't show it. They sat there, impassive. Not me! I was an American citizen, a combat wounded veteran, and I deserved prompt service from my Government! You bet your ass I did! I got up, went to the Embassy door again. But this time I banged on it with both fists. Boom! Boom! Boom! I heard hurried footsteps approaching the door. One of the German girls I had seen when she had come in, opened the door slightly, and in an annoyed voice, said in German. *"Wir sind geschlossen! Mach' kein Lärm!"* "We're closed! Don't make any noise!" Based upon my attire she took me for one of those hapless foreigners patiently waiting for service, even late service. In a very loud voice I replied, in English, "Don't shush me! I'm an American citizen, and I want to see the officer handling visas! And I want to see him now!" She tried to push the door closed. I shoved my foot in to block it. Flustered, she said, in English, "You can't come in!" "Oh, yes I can!" I was shouting now. There was supposed to be a Marine guard about, but I saw none. Lucky for me! The tall guy I had seen coming in, the one talking of his golf game, came to the door. ""What's going on?" I told him I was an American, and that I was there to inquire about my fianceé's Visa. Aware that the commotion at the door was unseemly—the people waiting in the antechamber were now straining to hear what was going on—the tall guy told the girl to let me in. She did. I entered, and the door was slammed shut behind me

The tall guy signaled me to follow him. We entered his office. He sat down behind his desk and motioned me to sit down, I obliged. He wanted to know why I was making such a scene, that shouting wouldn't get me any where. (Well, it had, I was inside, talking to him). I told him I had been a GI in the war. He interrupted to ask whether I had seen any combat. I sure did, I replied. I then took up the opening he gave me by stating I had fought in the Cavalry, attached to Patton's Third Army, had been wounded twice and had received the Purple Heart, Bronze Star and 5 Battle Stars. After my recital his attitude towards me softened. He mentioned he had also been in the war, had been a Captain. He named no unit, nor did he refer to any combat experience.

What's this visa business all about, he wanted to know. I told him I had met a beautiful German girl, Anneliese Baur, during the war, that we had fallen in love, that I went home to get discharged and came back to Germany to work out her papers so that I could bring her back with me to the States and get married, that she had received clearances for exit from Germany from all four Occupying Powers, that the State Department had possessed her papers for almost two months, when would Anneliese's Visa be issued, why the delay, what's the hang-up? Then I engaged in a bit of trickery. I told him that I had informed my folks back home in Brooklyn that they should call our local Congressman and complain to him about the ineptness of our State Department in Frankfurt if I didn't get Anneliese's Visa by the middle of January.

The tall guy sat silent for a few seconds after I had finished my recital. He then stood up, said, "Stay here. I'll be right back." He was back in about five minutes. He said that his people had followed the book, had done everything they were required to do to process Anneliese's Visa Application, that their request for background information, a necessity under the law, had been sent to her home town, some place called Schwenningen in Bavaria, but no reply had ever been received, so that processing of the Application was stalled waiting for a response from Bavaria. "What?", I exclaimed, "You sent the request to the wrong Schwenningen! Fräulein Baur's hometown is Schwenningen am Neckar in Württemberg, in the French Zone." Württemberg abuts Bavaria on the latter's western flank. I pressed on. I couldn't recapture the lost time, but I could, possibly, shorten the time for submission of a new data request to Schwenningen/Neckar, and the review of such data by the State Department's ID, its Intelligence

Division. And so I told the tall guy (I can't recall his name or title) that Anneliese had already been cleared by the four Occupying Powers, that she had worked for our Military Government in Heidenheim and was working for us now in Offenbach, that to do such work meant she had been found OK, State Department clearance should be no problem—just get someone on it right away—and that I wanted her Application to be issued within the next 48 hours!! Boy, I was being brazen! But I had worn myself almost to a frazzle since returning to Germany in the first week of September 1946, running hither and yon with Anneliese's papers. I wanted out of Germany and back to the States, as quickly as possible, with my belóved Anneliese safe at my side.

The tall guy didn't say yes or no. All he said was, "We'll get right on it." He must have. Two days later Anneliese had her Visa. *Gott sei Dank!* Thank God!

Anneliese and I were now on Cloud Nine! Were it possible to climb aboard, and mount a propellor on it, we would have flown off immediately! Of such stuff are dreams made. After ten months of separation and longing, and five months of tension filled reunion in Germany, Arthur and Anneliese were finally able to travel together to Brooklyn, N.Y., to a wedding, and to a life together as Husband and Wife, never again to be separated. Anneliese and I thought only of creating a long, fruitful and glorious life together. We were going to face many unknowns, but we were not perturbed. We knew the certainty of our love, and that was all that mattered.

Episodes THIRTY EIGHT through FORTY

Der lang ersehnte Tag!

SIDEWALKS OF NEW YORK

East Side, West Side, all around the town
The kids sing "ring around the rosie",
"London Bridge is falling down"
Boys and girls together, me and Mamie O'Rourke
We tripped the light fantastic
On the sidewalks of New York!

James W. Blake, Charles E. Lawlor

TAKE ME OUT TO THE BALL GAME

Take me out to the ball game,
Take me out with the crowd.
Buy me some peanuts and Cracker Jack,
I don't care if I never get back,
Let me root, root, root for the home team,
If they don't win it's a shame.
For it's one, two, three strikes, you're out,
At the old ball game.

Jack Norworth, Albert Von Tilzer

Episode Thirty Eight

In which on the Thirty first of January, 1947, belóved Anneliese and I fly to the States.

With all the papers that Anneliese needed to leave Germany and enter the United States now in my possession, I informed my Supervisor in the latter part of January 1947 that I was quitting my job and returning to the States. I gave him no reason, made no reference to Anneliese. I did so in an excess of caution. Having gone through a roller coaster series of events, with matching emotions, I wanted to neither say, nor do anything which, in the last moment, might adversely affect our leaving Germany. At war's end our military had set a firm program against troops and civilians fraternizing with Germans. The instant I saw Anneliese I paid no regard to that policy, with some light negative reactions, as I have related in writing of my Military Government work in Heidenheim after hostilities had ended.

I understood the reason, at war's end, for the institution and maintenance of a non-fraternization policy. The Allies were still ferreting out the war criminals, the *Schwerbelastet*, and the *Minderbelastet*, from the followers, the *Mitläufer*, the German masses who were the duped asses. As a Jewish American youth, one year shy of completing college when I enlisted in the Cavalry, I was most mindful of the perils facing my country and my Jewish People, were Hitler's Nazi Germany to win its war against us—and as a combat veteran, whose wounds bled first into French soil, and then into that of Germany—I had personally experienced first hand the perils of Naziizm. Had all our troops the same informed, subjective approach to Germany and Naziism as I had, if they could have distinguished the Germany of Goethe, Schiller and Rilke from that of Göring, Göbbels and *Der Völkischer Beobachter*, and the music of Bach, Beethoven and Brahms from that of *Das Horst Wessel Lied*, then there might have been no immediate post war need for a Non-Fraternization Program—our troops from officers on down would have been able to separate wheat from chaff. But that was not the case. Hence a Non-Fraternization Program had to exist in conjunction with the Allies' search for Nazi war criminals through its Denazification Program. From that magical instant when first I gazed upon Anneliese I sensed her purity of body and soul. Would that I could have risen to her level! And so I did not see my intimate association with Anneliese as failing to keep faith with those of my fallen comrades in arms. On the contrary, I saw our loving relationship as being a small, unheralded step to an eventual reconciliation between my American Countrymen and my Jewish Brethren with the German People. And time has demonstrated that the union between Arthur and Anneliese has, in its own way played a tiny role in reuniting our respective peoples in peace. I've written all this by way of explaining why I told my Supervisor nothing of Anneliese. He was not pleased to see me leave. And I did not want him, in a moment of possible pique to seize upon my relationship with Anneliese to set up further obstacles to my departure with her from Germany. I was far from becoming an emotional basket case. But I had clearly lost a degree of that self assuredness which had stood me in such good stead in my active military days. I wanted out! I wanted home! *Tan pronto como posible! So schnell wie möglich!* As soon as possible!

Aside from reminding me that by not fulfilling the full term of my contract I was forfeiting my right to have the Government pay my passage home, my Supervisor did nothing to impede my leaving Germany. *Wunderbar!* Wonderful! When I gave up my job Anneliese gave up hers as well, saying only that she had matters to be attended to at home. Only two things now remained to be resolved before Anneliese and I could be on our way to *Das goldene medinah*, Yiddish for "The Golden Land: America". I had to arrange passage to the States for Anneliese and me, and then travel with Anneliese to Schwenningen where we would say good bye to her family and relatives. Both of us recognized that the latter event would be emotionally taxing for Anneliese.

I discussed the mode of travel with Anneliese. During the war I crossed the Atlantic in both directions by ship. The crossings were not fun and games. An ocean crossing this time would be wholly different. I would not be a GI. I would be an American civilian traveling with his bride to be on a modern ocean liner. Lots of luxury, lots of food, lots of dancing, lots of quality stateroom time. But time was the issue here. Depending upon the ship's ports of call, the crossing could take six to eight days. Too long at sea! The only way to go, then, was to fly. And fly we did. The name of the carrier was American Overseas Airlines (AOL). I believe it was later absorbed into the existing American Airlines. Before I describe our flight experiences—nothing ever seemed to go by the book—let me describe the farewells Anneliese and I made to her family and relatives, and our railway experiences upon returning from Schwenningen to Frankfurt.

When young people marry they cleave unto each other and separate from their familial surroundings, their parents, siblings, relatives and friends. It is a rite of passage: a time of happiness for the young people eager to start upon their joint journey through life, but also a time of happiness tinged with sadness. Leaving one's family behind is never easy, and it plumbs the depths of emotion when the leaving will mean a separation of thousands of miles, and for a length of time uncertain. Such a situation confronted Anneliese. Hers was a family close knit and loving. Saying *adieu* would be very difficult for her. She knew it might be years before she saw them again. She knew the grim economic environment in which her family was living—their situation much alleviated by the parcels of food, clothing and other necessities I had sent during my ten months away from her in the States—her concerns in this regard were lessened by her knowledge that such assistance would continue once we were in America, and for as long as necessary.

Anneliese was leaving her family, her country, at a time when her world was still in turmoil, and entering into a new phase in her life in a new world of which she knew little. She was doing so without reservation, without hesitation. She loved me with a love unbounded, and she knew my passion for her. Anneliese had absolute faith in me, and I intended never to let her faith in me flag. As she had declared to me in a letter written during our ten months' separation, and from which I have earlier quoted, it made no difference to Anneliese where she lived as long as I was with her, that my home was her home, and that she would follow me any where I went, even to the North Pole! I had told her of my conversation with my paternal grandfather, my Zaydeh, how he accepted her as part of our family, and that once the others knew of his approval, the issue of acceptance became a non-issue. I also told Anneliese that her acceptance by Americans, in general, would also pose no problems. She trusted me. She believed me. I was right. How could anyone not love my beautiful Anneliese once they got to know her! As I have earlier noted, Anneliese had corresponded with my Mom and Dad during our ten months of separation. From her letters my parents gained insight into her inner beauty. From her photos they knew her beauty of face and form. As noted within a week of the time she joined our family my Mom and Dad each came to me separately and said, "Arthur, she's too good for you!" They were right. She was!

Before we traveled down to Schwenningen I purchased our flight tickets. The flight would leave January 31, 1947. We then took the train from Frankfurt to Schwenningen, changing trains in Stuttgart. Anneliese had written to her folks telling them of our travel plans, that our visit would be for only two nights because of the flight schedule. *Mutter* and *Vater* Baur had told all the family of Anneliese's visit with me at her side. They all flocked in to greet us, to say their good byes and to bring little tokens for Anneliese to take along. Those who couldn't come to the Baur home, such as Anneliese's maternal grandmother and grandfather (her paternal grandparents were long deceased), Anneliese and I went to visit. The partings were a mixture of happiness and sadness. Happiness for the new life Anneliese was embarking upon with me, sadness for the realization it might be years, if ever, that they would see each other again.

Anneliese packed two suitcases with her personal things, and I made sure these included several of her dirndls. She was wearing a dirndl when I first saw her, and that image is seared into my brain. Anneliese wondered whether wearing a dirndl would be stylish in America. I told her not to worry. When the ladies saw her in a dirndl, and how it brought out the good points of one's figure, they would all want dirndls! She laughed and said I was being silly, but she packed several. I told Anneliese that once we were settled in at home I'd take her shopping for clothing made locally, but as far as I was concerned, she'd always be in style, and beautiful, to boot, wearing a dirndl.

Anneliese and I boarded the train in Schwenningen for the trip back to Frankfurt, late in the afternoon of the third day, so as to spend as much time with her family as our flight schedule allowed. *Mutter* and *Vater* were at the station, along with Hilde and Kurt. He had been fitted during my ten months in the States with a new, more comfortable prosthesis which allowed him to get around much better than the time I had first met him in the Fall of 1945. With hugs and tears exchanged, and wishes of a safe trip echoing in our ears, Anneliese and I waved good bye to a family she would not see again for a number of years.

Because of our late afternoon departure from Schwenningen it was nightfall when we arrived at the station in Stuttgart. On the 30th of January 1947. The times then were still quite bad. High unemployment, not enough foodstuffs, extremely cold, wet weather, made for a general feeling of malaise. Criminal activity was high, ranging from blackmarketeering, to robbery, to petty theft, to cases of murder. An unsavory time made so by an unhappy people. Thus, when Anneliese and I were in the rail road station in Stuttgart we were part of a large mix of people, most of whom were law abiding. But one could sense, if not see, the evil ones amongst us They would circle about, a blackmarketeer looking for another, a thief, like a leopard stalking a herd of grazing gazelles.

Moving slowly around and around, looking for an unwary target. Leave your bag unattended for an instance and it was gone! The connecting train to Frankfurt would not come for another hour. I had to go to the bathroom, as did Anneliese. She went first, and I sat on her suitcases, I had my briefcase with me. It contained copies of all of Anneliese's clearances, and her official Visa. Treasured documents! She returned, and like Rachel sitting on Laban's household teraphim (which she had taken) and concealed within Jacob's luggage, she sat gamely on her suitcases while I hurried off, briefcase in hand, to evacuate my bladder, then quickly back to Anneliese's side. The setting in which Anneliese and I found ourselves was made more grotesque by the fact that the roof over the station had been destroyed in the course of Allied bombings. Had the sky not been in its usual overcast mode, we could have seen the moon and stars shining through the twisted girders. The rail beds and the tracks had been repaired, but it would be several years before the railroad station would be fully rebuilt. Needless to say, we were quite relieved when the Frankfurt train arrived and we could get on board.

Having resigned my position I could no longer sleep in my usual government quarters. Mindful of this, Anneliese had retained her flat until the day we would leave Germany, the 31st of January. Earlier I had stowed my two suitcases in her flat, making sure that the new locks I had installed after the break-in, of which I have written, were fully operational. Both of us were so drained, emotionally and physically from our visit to Schwenningen and the trip back, that we both fell quickly asleep in each others arms, with our amorous dalliance limited to no more then several kisses.

Anneliese and I arrived at the Frankfurt/Main *Flughafen* Airport several hours before our flight was scheduled to leave. Boarding procedures then were simple. We could have arrived later. But we were both so keyed up to get going that we felt it best to be near the plane sooner than later. The plane was propellor driven. I do not know whether jet propulsion or turbo prop civilian aircraft existed in 1947. Ours was propellor driven and that was good enough for us. By the nature of the aircraft non-stop flights to New York from Frankfurt were not possible. Nor would there be food service on board. Accordingly, the flight would be made in stages. The first leg would be a short one, between Frankfurt and Amsterdam, where I presumed more overseas passengers would board, more fuel would be taken on, and where, I was told, we would disembark for a meal in the airport. Aware of this, I had with me only some chocolate I had bought some time earlier at our U.S. PX. Then the plane would fly on to Shannon Airport in Ireland, then over the Atlantic, landing in Gander, Newfoundland, then on to La Guardia Airport in New York City (John F. Kennedy Airport had not yet been built). I don't recall the plane being more than half full. Aside from Anneliese and me, the passengers were either military officers, or people who, by their dress could have been diplomats or businessmen. In addition to Anneliese there was another woman on board. I believe her name was Dorothy Thompson, or something like that. I recognized her. She was a famous journalist of that period.

The police/security controls through which Anneliese and I had to go to board the plane were not onerous, at least I don't recall having any difficulty being cleared to walk out onto the tarmac and then mount the steps, on those portable stairways wheeled to the side of the plane, in order to enter the plane. When we entered the plane and found our seats we were absolutely giddy. Ten months of separation and five months of running about—even though Anneliese and I were together again during those last five—were now behind us, as were the tensions connected with that period. As we sat side by side in the plane we tightly held hands. Neither of us had qualms about flying, although it was the first time for both of us. At that moment we were two bodies melded into one, two hearts entwined, two souls interlocked. We were the only couple on the craft, and clearly the youngest persons on board. Even the most blasé would have noticed that we were in love. When I gazed about before we took off I caught the eye of several passengers. They smiled. We know you're in love their smiles said.

A Stewardess came down the aisle (they were not called flight attendants then), to insure we were belted in. The engines sputtered, roared into action, we began to roll down the runway and were soon airborne, heading towards Amsterdam. Anneliese sat at the window and marveled at what she saw, and what she saw, and what I observed, peeking over her shoulder, were scenes of devastation, houses without roofs, bare walls where once factories stood, untilled fields. As we rose into the air the ground fell rapidly away from us, soon we were passing through a layer of gray, low hanging clouds, and then, suddenly, above them, into a clear blue sky. Both of us being neophyte fliers, our swift ascent into this bright, boundless, cerulean vastness impressed us mightily. We both had the same thought at the same time: we had risen from a world, too often drab, into a new and brighter life. We lifted the armrest between us and huddled closer together.

Sooner than we had imagined—what did we then know of flight speeds—we were descending back through the gray cloud cover and into the Amsterdam Airport. The countryside around the airport was unlike that we had observed in Germany. There were no signs of devastation, no roofless dwellings, whether, residential, commercial or industrial, no untilled fields. For the first time Anneliese was seeing the world outside Germany, and what she saw was different, and what she saw was good. She absorbed it all, but said nothing. We were on the ground, the plane rolled close to the terminal and stopped, the engines were stilled and a landing ladder was rolled to the side of the plane. A Stewardess opened the craft's door and passengers arose from their seats and made their way through it and onto the platform on top of the landing ladder. A man in a blue uniform, with a pistol in a holster on his belt, and a sheaf of papers in his hand, a Dutch official of some kind, I thought, smiled as each passenger approached him on the ladder's small platform, exchanged a few words, and the passenger descended the stairs and headed for the entrance to the terminal. We had been told there would be a buffet awaiting us in the Terminal. There were two or three passengers behind us when Anneliese and I stepped out of the plane and onto the ladder's platform. I had my American Passport in my hand, and the envelope containing Copies of Anneliese's Four Occupying Power Clearances, and her U.S. Visa. The official smiled at both of us, glanced at my Passport, looked at the papers in his hand, and, in English, said, "Welcome to the Netherlands". I took Anneliese's hand, and we began to descend the stairs. The official stepped in front of us, barring our way. "I am sorry", he said, "but Fräulein Baur cannot leave the aircraft." He knew Anneliese's name, apparently among his papers was the plane's passenger list, with the citizenship of each passenger noted. I was taken aback. "Why?" I asked. The official explained. The Netherlands did not allow German nationals to enter the country, even for transit purposes, unless permission had been sought and obtained. There was no record of permission being sought. Fräulein Baur had to stay on the plane. I was dumbfounded! I could see the distress on Anneliese's face, though she said not a word. I had touched all the bases in getting all the necessary paper work done. No one had told me that the Dutch might also require some clearance. I said so to the official, he asked me, politely, to step aside as he checked through the remaining passengers. One of them noted our dilemma and said he'd make sure that some food was brought back to us from the buffet. The Dutch official then informed me that the airline should have alerted me to the Dutch travel restrictions as they concerned German nationals. Had I known I could have worked things out. Mr. Katz, I was told, can leave the plane. But Frl. Baur is an enemy alien under Dutch law and is barred from entering the Netherlands! The official was courteous, but nothing could be done, he said. And he descended the stairs of the boarding ladder.

Anneliese and I went back into the empty plane. The joy which had welled up at the start of the flight, and suffused our two beings, was now gone. I took the chocolate from my carry on briefcase, and shared it with Anneliese. It didn't taste as sweet as it should have. We were two very disconsolate people. Outside our window we could see the crews adding fuel and placing bags in the hold for passengers boarding in Amsterdam. In about half an hour, passengers began to trickle back from the Terminal. They had heard about Anneliese's inability to leave the plane. They each brought something back for us. Rolls with little packets of butter and cheese, some apples, small containers of milk and a few pieces of Danish style pastry. We thanked everyone for their kindness and enjoyed every bit of the food brought us. They soon learned I was bringing Anneliese home with me to get married. They all wished us well. Anneliese and I started to feel better again. Soon all the passengers were settled, the original ones, and the three or four who came on in Amsterdam. The engines revved up, the propellers spun into action, the plane taxied onto a runway and we were off to Shannon, Ireland!

The reception accorded Anneliese in the Shannon airport was as dissimilar from that she had encountered in Amsterdam as is a stormy night from a sunlit day. *Welch ein Unterschied!* What a difference! She was treated with the same cordiality as were all the other passengers. She was just another passenger on an American plane flying on to the States. The meal we lost in Amsterdam was more than made up for in Shannon. What a spread! All kinds of meats, cheeses, dairy products, breads, rolls, butter, mixed green salads, coffee, tea and juices. And there was Irish whiskey and beers for sale, neatly packaged to take to the States. I bought none. I didn't want to lug about, and be concerned for breakable bottles of liquid, when my sole concern was to minister to the well being of Anneliese. She was entering a new world, and embarking upon a new life experience. Her demeanor, her public persona, was that of a beautiful woman, wholly comfortable with herself and her surroundings, with sparkling eyes and a smile frequently flashing across her high cheek boned face. Although I never did learn to fully plumb the depths of my Anneliese, I had learned by February 1947, from being with her, and from the letters she had written me during our separation of ten months in 1945/46, that she was as vulnerable, as any human being, to the vicissitudes of life, but that she had that inner serenity which enabled her to comport herself—whatever the situation or the surroundings—in a calm and dignified manner. This was the invisible aura which I sensed enveloped her beautiful face and form when first I beheld her in that wonderful week in mid-June, of 1945!

I have long sought to find that one word which could encompass within it that magical something, that special quality I had then sensed in Anneliese, and which she thereafter daily manifested throughout our lives together. I now believe I have found that word. It is the German word: *mutig*. *Mutig* is a multifaceted word. It translates into English as "courageous", "mettlesome", "stout hearted", "brave", "spirited". These English words are shadings, attributes of the German *"mutig"*. Anneliese possessed all the qualities of character expressed by them. Being *"mutig"* enabled Anneliese to adjust quickly, without injury to her own unique persona, to a new life, a new language, a new religion, and a new country.

Flying home I believe I felt more vulnerable than she may have. I was ending a fifteen months' phase where everything I had done turned upon maintaining Anneliese's welfare while I was away from her, returning to her, and then bringing her safely back with me to America. My single minded mission was on the verge of being accomplished. Now I had to contemplate making a life for both of us. I would soon have a wife, and in due course, children to support.

In her letter to me of February 25, 1946 (portions of which I have earlier translated herein) Anneliese wrote that I had bestowed upon her everything she wished for, everything she needed: Happiness, Love and Trust—everything that makes a life worth living! Her words brought me to tears when I first read them, and they bring me to tears now, as they are recalled. I was reborn when I met Anneliese, and since that moment I have always looked upon Anneliese as the Love of my life, and the cornerstone of my being. But I have never forgotten my duties to her—that she looked upon me as her Lover, Provider and Protector. Anneliese never once questioned my love or my ability, as her husband, to support and protect her. I remember telling her during those five idyllic Summer and Fall months in 1945 in Heidenheim, "Sweetheart, as long as I have a head on my shoulders you have nothing to worry about me once we are married!" Now the moment of truth for that boast was fast approaching.

To provide properly for my family I would have to earn a living. That's a given. But not any living. I wanted to make a living doing what I wanted to do—to make money, of course, but only by doing what I would love. The ideal situation for any family head. I had already determined, before I enlisted in the Army in November 1942, that after the war I would study law. (I have already related that throughout the war I carried two law books with me.) And so I knew I had to get into a top notch Law School—but how to pay the tuition and the costs of books? These questions were resolved, most favorably to me, within months of my return to Brooklyn. But I didn't know that as I snuggled up to my belóved as we flew across the Atlantic. These concerns were there, but seated next to my beautiful Anneliese her peacefulness enveloped me and my concerns melted away. As our plane flew westward across the Atlantic we both fell asleep, hands clasped, with Anneliese's head resting on my shoulder. We were both exhausted. Several hours later we awoke to learn that we would be landing in Gander, Newfoundland, Canada, within an hour. Anneliese would soon have the opportunity to look upon, and walk upon, the New World. She was excited! And, frankly, so was I!

Gander, as far as I recall, was a rudimentary airport. It had a control tower and a one story terminal. I noted at least one hangar, large enough to hold several planes of our craft's size. Gander was not important for what it was, but for where it was. It was a safe haven for pilots anxious to touch down, rest up and fuel up after a long flight across the cold North Atlantic. And it gave passengers and crew a chance to stretch one's legs and get some fresh food. The spread laid out for our flight was almost as good as that furnished by the airport in Shannon. Although Anneliese and I were beginning to feel the excitement of getting closer to New York City, we were not averse to sampling a broad array of the goodies laid out before us. In short, we probably ate too much, and too fast. Within less than an hour, the fueling being completed, we were back in the air, heading south for the last leg of our journey. Anneliese and I were now highly animated. We were looking forward to getting married speedily; that would stop the clock on Anneliese's visa restriction, and then we could live together, as Husband and Wife, forever and a day!! Our religious wedding, our Jewish wedding, would follow after Anneliese went through her conversion ceremonies. Getting married under the color of civil and religious law meant no change in our relationship to each other. We would have remained forever lovers, and each the best friend of the other, had we never celebrated our union formally.

We both began to feel the tension building within each of us. We were fast approaching the new homeland Anneliese would soon be sharing with me. The long awaited day—the phrase was Anneliese's—when she would really be in America with me was fast becoming a reality. Anneliese was as strong physically as she was emotionally. Speaking of tension, I had noted that I was beginning to feel a bit draggy. I put it down to the hectic schedule I had been keeping, and to the excitement of coming home with Anneliese at my side. My self diagnosis was in error, as the reader will soon learn.

Before leaving Frankfurt/Main I had sent a Western Union telegram to my folks giving them our flight number and arrival time at LaGuardia Airport. During the ten months that Anneliese and I were separated Anneliese corresponded with my folks (that meant, my Mom, my Dad was not a letter writer). The bond which ultimately grew between my Mother and Anneliese got its genesis in the letters the two exchanged during that trying period. I have quoted herein portions of these letters. They reveal the warmth my parents and Anneliese already felt for each other. Thus Anneliese and I anticipated that Anneliese would receive a warm welcome upon our arrival.

Our plane began its descent at what I assumed was the western portion of Connecticut, and it dropped out of the clouds over the Long Island Sound near the eastern reaches of Long Island. Brooklyn lay at the westernmost part of Long Island. Bordering Brooklyn on the east was Queens. These being two of the five boroughs/counties which made up the City of New York. Our plane was heading for LaGuardia Airport in northern Queens. The airport had been named for the "Little Flower", Fiorello LaGuardia, one of New York's most beloved mayors. During a newspaper strike I remember him reading the comics to us kids over the radio. I believe I was ten then. The counties to the east of Queens on Long Island were Nassau and Suffolk. They were not part of New York City. In 1947 they were sparsely populated, large estates, lots of greenery, lots of horses, lots of yachts, lots of snobbery. Anneliese was not aware of the snobbery, but as our plane skimmed low over Long Island she noted, wide eyed, the pristine areas speeding by beneath her. It was winter, but here and there was a patch of cultivated ground, a copse of evergreen trees, and easily seen, the southern flank of Long Island Sound, sparkling blue in the cold February morning sun. She was delighted by what she saw! What a contrast from the cold, gray, dank days of Frankfurt and Offenbach! We were now quite low, making our approach to LaGuardia. Anneliese noted with interest the density of structures below us, residential dwellings and commercial and industrial buildings. How different she remarked from the areas we had just flown over. I pointed out that we were now over the eastern edges of New York City, and the density of population would far exceed that of Nassau and Suffolk counties. With only a slight jar, our plane touched down, and roared down the runway, engines reversed to slow us down. A smooth landing, and as our plane taxied to its offloading spot I thought the smooth landing was a good sign that all would now be well with Anneliese and me, together at last in America!

Clearance through Passport Control and Customs was perfunctory. I presented my Passport and Anneliese's Visa. The official made a cursory examination of my Passport, handed it back after stamping in an entry stamp. He then examined Anneliese's Visa carefully. Apparently he had not seen many of the kind Anneliese now carried. While he checked it I said that my fiancée and I intended to be married very quickly. There was no need to say anything, but I felt I had to say something to bridge his silence. Anneliese stood silently next to me, her composure showing no concerns of any kind. The official, having perused the Visa, stamped an entry date on it, and handed it back to me after making some notation in his files. He then turned to Anneliese, and with a warm smile, said "Welcome to America, Fräulein Baur." His German pronunciation was pretty good. Anneliese smiled back and quietly said, "Thank you." We were safe and sound in America!! Thank you God! Now to start the next phase of our lives together. *Ach, wie wunderbar!* Oh, how wonderful!

Our suitcases unloaded and released to us we headed for the airport's public area where we expected my Mom and Dad to be waiting for us. They were not there. The plane had come in on time. So where were they? Had Anneliese not established such wonderful rapport with my Mom and Dad through their exchange of letters during the ten months we were separated, I might have considered their non-presence an ominous sign of last minute disapproval of my bringing Anneliese home with me. But I knew better than that. Yet where were they? I don't believe Anneliese read anything untoward into their absence. Outwardly she was her usual composed self. If anyone was upset, it was me. We waited a quarter hour, no Mom or Dad. I looked through my wallet. Found my Dad's business card. He was then operating his own oil burner installation and fuel oil delivery business, with a large fleet of vehicles, quite a big business for a man who came to America as a 12 year old, speaking no English, and placed in school to sink or swim. I called his office. His secretary answered. She was surprised. Where was I calling from? LaGuardia? I was supposed to let my folks know when I was flying in. I said, I had. I had sent a telegram yesterday, when Anneliese and I left Germany. No telegram had arrived. Well, could she track down my Dad and get him to the airport? She had his schedule, she'd find him and tell him Anneliese and I were at LaGuardia. Just stay there, don't go away. I had no intention to go anywhere.

Anneliese and I sat patiently waiting for my folks. I had, of course, recounted to Anneliese the reason why my folks had not been at the airport to greet us. Well, we had come this far, fifteen months of running hither and yon were behind us. We could wait another hour for the arrival of that special moment when my Mom and Dad would meet Anneliese and see for themselves why I was so crazy about her. About an hour after I had called my Dad's office he strode into the Airport's lobby, with my Mom at his side. Anneliese and I rose to meet them. My Mom and Dad had eyes only for Anneliese. My Mom immediately enveloped Anneliese in her arms and with great emotion said, "Oh, my dear, you are even more beautiful than your photos!" Whereupon she kissed Anneliese on her cheeks, and both were soon in tears! My Dad, who was never a demonstrative person, gave her a light hug after my Mom released Anneliese, and mumbled some words I did not hear. He did not kiss her. Nothing unusual. I don't recall that he ever kissed me, or my brother, Harold.

Once our suitcases were stowed in the car we drove home. I sat in front with my Dad, In the back, my Mom and Anneliese were soon happily chatting away. I had no qualms Anneliese would be well received. But it was wonderful to see how quickly the rapport which Anneliese had developed with my folks through their interchange of letters had instantly been translated into a relationship of a doting mother-in-law and a loving, respectful daughter-in-law. How thrilling! I knew my Anneliese would sweep them off their feet! And she had!

We were home not more than ten minutes in the family apartment on New Lots Avenue in Brooklyn when the doorbell rang. I went to the door, assuming well wishers were already calling. It was Western Union delivering the telegram with the arrival time of our flight from Germany!. Anneliese and I had beaten Western Union at its game! Everyone laughed. Anneliese and I were finally home together! That apartment would be our home until, almost a year later, after I had begun my law studies under the GI Bill at New York University School of Law, and the University then set up a housing development for married students.

Today, in the first decade of the 21st Century, it is hard to imagine a young, newly married couple living with the husband's parents, and his brother, in a compact but comfortable apartment. But we did. Anneliese was a homebody. She thrived in a warm, familial setting, and her cheerful nature contributed to its warmth. Living with my folks and brother immediately upon coming to the States was a wonderful way for Anneliese to make the transition from one world to another. I shall always be grateful for the gracious manner in which my family and our relatives immediately made Anneliese feel at one with them. We were part of the whole. But when Anneliese and I retired to our bedroom, and closed the door, we were secure within our private, passion filled world.

The kitchen was one place I tried to stay out of. Two is company, three is a crowd. The same for lovers as for cooks. I don't recall hearing of any discord between my Mom and Anneliese concerning their sharing of one kitchen. I, for one, was a winner by having two great chefs in the kitchen. I still got my Mom's thick beef-barley soup with lots of sauteed dried mushrooms and potatoes, rich matzo ball soup, potato and cheese blintzes—while also enjoying Anneliese's *Rindsrolladen, Kartoffelbrei, Spätzle* and *Pfannenkuchen*—with each learning to make the other's recipes. My Mother didn't keep a full kosher kitchen with its requirement for three sets of dishes, cutlery, pots and pans, and the segregation of milk and meat products in different parts of the refrigerator, and even in the kitchen sink! But *traif*, non-kosher foods, were not brought into the kitchen. Thus we never had any kind of pig meat, or scaleless sea food, such as lobster, shrimp and eel. I didn't miss them. And Anneliese came from the Black Forest where such things as *Hummer*, lobster, were not known. And like her local farmers, Anneliese didn't eat what she didn't know. As she told me, with her usual bright smile, speaking her Schwäbisch dialect to make her point: *"Wa' da' Booer nit kennt, frisst er nit."* "What the farmer doesn't know he doesn't eat."

I end this Episode concerning Anneliese and her entrance into a new phase in her life and mine—by noting she kept an album which contained photos taken of her and her family in Germany in the last days of January 1947, and then photos of her flight from Germany to the States, and of her new life with me, and her new family and relatives in Brooklyn. I had not seen the album for years, and I refrained from looking through it after losing Anneliese on March 20, 2002, for fear of its emotional impact upon me. And it was only after I began the final editing of this book did I steel myself to take it from its closet shelf and open it. I cried. Tears flowed down my cheeks one heart tearing moment, to be followed by smiles krinkling the corners of my wet eyes. Anneliese's wit and wisdom was evident on each album page!

The album consists of black pages, with Anneliese's text written in white crayon. In the upper left hand corner of the first page Anneliese wrote: *"Der lang ersehnte Tag"*. This can be translated as The long awaited day, or as The long sought for day. Yes, this day had been long in coming, from early November 1945 to February 1947. In the center of the page Anneliese wrote: *Flug ins neue Leben*, in English, Flight into a new life. Then she pasted in the oval logo of American Overseas Airlines, the kind of sticker people paste onto their steamer trunks. This was Anneliese's first flight. She expressed no qualms about flying. She and I were together, hand in hand. That was enough for her. Then, with her Teutonic efficiency, she notes the exact departure and arrival times:

Ab: Frankfurt 31. Jan. 47 11:15
An: New York 1. Feb. 47 10:00

Our flight into Anneliese's new life took 22 hours and 45 minutes, with stops in Amsterdam, Shannon Ireland and Gander Newfoundland before arriving at La Guardia Airport. One can see from this album page, and from several others reproduced herein—each of which contains her comments—that she was beautiful and witty, and ready for the adventures her new life would bring her. Her album comments reflect her keen sense of humor. She would need it to live with me.

Vater and Mutter Baur, sister Hilde, Anneliese and
Arthur, January 29, 1947, Schwenningen Germany

Vater and Mutter Baur, sister Hilde,
brother Kurt and Anneliese, January 29,
1947, Schwenningen, Germany

Anneliese and sister Hilde, Arthur and sister Hilde,
Schwenningen, Germany, January 29, 1947

Anneliese in snowball fight, relieving tension,
Schwenningen, Germany, January 29, 1947

Anneliese, Arthur and Mutter, pensive moment,
January 29, 1947, Schwenningen, Germany

Anneliese and Military Gov't co-worker,
saying *auf wiedersehen* at Frankfurt,
Germany airport, January 31, 1947

Anneliese and Military Gov't co-worker,
saying *auf wiedersehen* at Frankfurt,
Germany airport, January 31, 1947

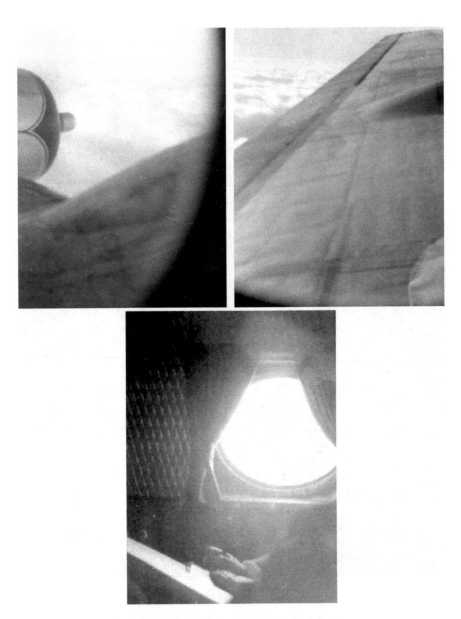

Photos by Anneliese: "Fly Arthur and me
to a new life together in America!
A dream fulfilled!" January 31, 1947

Anneliese contemplating her new life with
Arthur in America, on board American
Overseas Airlines, January 31, 1947

First page from Anneliese's photo Album with American
Overseas Airlines logo, and two heartfelt German
phrases: *Der lang ersehnte Tag*: The long awaited day,
and *Flug ins neue Leben*: Flight into a new life.

Episode Thirty Nine

In which Anneliese and I are married twice. Once, within days of Anneliese's arrival in America, in a civil ceremony at Brooklyn Borough Hall, the same place where I had enlisted four years earlier—it was *beschert* that the circle so close—and then having stopped the deportation clock, the Jewish religious wedding was held at our home, with Zaydeh and a half dozen rabbis officiating. Anneliese and I were finally Husband and Wife. *Mazal Tov!*

Anneliese and I arrived in the States on the first of February 1947. Anneliese's Visa was conditioned upon her marrying me within thirty days of her arrival in the United States. Let's not stand on ceremony. *Je schneller desto besser!* The sooner the better. We were not virgins breathlessly awaiting the Wedding Night! Every one of our nights together had been a Wedding Night reborn! What we wanted to do now was to stop the deportation clock, and that done, to get on with our lives together. And so, on February 7, 1947, with my Mother and Dad as witnesses, Anneliese and I were married in a civil ceremony in Brooklyn Borough Hall. This was the same Borough Hall where, in November 1942, I had waited on its steps for my left wing college buddies to join me in enlisting. None of them showed up—as I have related,—and I enlisted on my own. I never regretted that decision. And here I was marrying that wonderful creature, that Fairy Princess that God had meant for me to find as my special gift for my service in the war! Brooklyn Borough Hall was the place where my military adventures began, and Brooklyn Borough Hall—austere and gray though it be—was now the place where the gift the war had provided was now formally to become part of me, to have and to hold, to love and to cherish, forever and a day!! And I, in turn, was to become part of her being.

The day after Anneliese arrived in Brooklyn her first steps for conversion to Judaism were undertaken when she met with Zaydeh Katz. As with every person who ever sees her, and speaks with her, he immediately fell in love with her! The fact I had the ability to recognize immediately her inner beauty somehow enhanced my reputation for being a perceptive person. With my Mother and several female aunts and cousins from the Katz and Glicenstein sides of the family accompanying her, Anneliese was taken to a Mikva, where she was given a ceremonial bath. The Christian concept of baptism is derived from immersion in the waters of a Mikvah. Zaydeh Katz then spent several days with her outlining the principles of Judaism, and the duties of a wife and mother in fulfilling her role as a Jew. The study time was short, but Anneliese was an attentive student, and she already knew many of the major tenets of Judaism from my many conversations with her.

The date for the religious wedding ceremony was set for February 12. The wedding would be celebrated in my family's apartment in the evening of that day. Some days prior thereto my Aunt Rose, my Mother's youngest sister and about seven years my senior, went shopping with Anneliese for a dress to wear at the wedding. Anneliese selected a high collared, long sleeved, rose colored dress. Anneliese looked good in everything, but she looked particularly attractive in rose colored fabrics.

There was no need for Anneliese to be married dressed in white. We had lived and loved under trying circumstances, as if we were husband and wife, during our five months together in 1945 in Heidenheim before I returned to the States—where both of us suffered through ten months' of separation—and then when we were together again for another five months after I returned to Germany in September 1946. Further, on the 7th of February 1947 Anneliese and I had been lawfully married in a civil ceremony in Brooklyn Borough Hall. Anneliese had always made most of her clothes. She knew fabrics and what looked good on her. And she knew my tastes. Her choice of dress for our Jewish Wedding met these criteria. In her Letters Anneliese oft stated her desire to learn my mores and to adapt to them. As much as I, she wanted to formally consummate our union with a Jewish Ceremony. It was meant to be the culminating symbol of our relationship. Nothing else mattered. Writing of Anneliese's selection of a rose colored, high collared dress for the wedding, reminds me of a story concerning her choice of wearing apparel.

Should the reader look at the photos of Anneliese taken in late 1945 and early 1946, after I had returned to the States, it will be noted that in two of them she is wearing a hooded, camel hair coat. In sending me these photos she wrote on the back of one of them, *"Hier hast Du mich in meinem "Teddy—Bär" Mantel! Nun, wie gefällt er Dir?" "Here you have me in my "Teddy—Bear" coat! Well, how do you like it?"* I liked it a lot. She had it made from fabric I had provided. Anneliese was wearing that coat when we arrived in Brooklyn on the first of February 1947. My young aunts and female cousins had never seen a hooded winter coat, nor a coat with that kind of fabric. They all politely suggested to her that "Arthur should get you a more stylish coat, now that you are in America," Anneliese and I appreciated their kind suggestion, but declined to follow it. Imagine then the embarrassment they may have felt when the Fall advertising for winter clothes featured: "The newest thing from Europe" hooded winter coats in camel hair fabrics!

In writing of *Mishpacha*, family members, I note that Love at First Sight is apparently not an unknown phenomenon in my family. It happened, of course, to me. But it also happened to my maternal grandfather, Abraham Glicenstein. The story is told that as a young man he was drafted into the Russian Army, not known for treating its enlisted personnel well, especially if they were Jewish. After several years of enduring a worsening situation, Grandpa Glicenstein deserted, and disguised as a Turk, headed for Berlin which, in the 1890s had a large and thriving Jewish community. He finds lodging in a boarding house in the city's Jewish sector. A few days after moving in he is walking down the long corridor leading to his room. He passes a room in which the door is, by chance, partially ajar. My Grandma Fanny, then a girl of nineteen, was combing her long black hair before her mirror, and Grandpa Glicenstein spied her reflection in the mirror. Zap! Like his grandson, 50 years later he was instantly in love! My Grandma Fanny was a spunky girl. She had just fled her home in Austria after refusing to accept the man her parents had arranged for her to marry. My Glicenstein grandparents married in Berlin and then moved to England, where, while awaiting visas to the United States, my mother was born in 1901 and her sister Etta thereafter. In America my maternal grandparents had five more children, for a total of seven.

My Grandpa Glicenstein became a successful house painter, Within years of arriving in this country both my paternal and maternal grandparents had amassed enough money to buy their own homes. Neither had a formal education in English. Yet both learned it well enough to conduct business with a broad spectrum of customers. *America, das goldene medinah* was, indeed, a golden land if you worked hard to mine the gold!

I relate one story, oddly, the same story, which I learned from both grandparents. I'll tell the one concerning Grandpa Glicenstein. I attended Thomas Jefferson High School. It lay about a mile away from where we then lived, which was close to Zaydeh and Bubbeh Katz. I walked to school and back. Going home I passed 493 Vermont Street where Grandpa and Grandma Glicenstein lived. It would be around 3 p.m., or so when I came to their house. It was a two story brick house, one of many in what are now called brownstone row houses. There was a garden area in front, set off from the sidewalk by a black painted metal ornamental fence. The house had a stoop with five basalt steps. My brother Harold and I used to play ball off these steps with a hard rubber ball, Spaulding was its brand name, we mispronounced it as a spalldeen. The aim of the game was to throw the ball so that it hit the tip of the leading edge of a step and this, if done well, sent the ball flying. Your opponent had to catch it in order to get a chance to be "up". In front of the house was a wide sidewalk and then a broad planting area in which there was a row of Cottonwood Poplars, huge, leafy trees. The only problem with them was that as their root systems expanded they would buckle the sidewalks. When the weather was right Grandpa Glicenstein would be seen sitting at the upstairs open window overlooking the entrance to the house. He would be reading one of his Yiddish newspapers. If I wasn't going in to visit, I would call out—it was a game I played with him—because both of us knew the script. In Yiddish I would say, Grandpa, *zug mir, wuss steht geschrieben?* What is written? what does the newspaper say? And Grandpa Glicenstein would always respond. *"Es ist entwieder git fir die yidden, oynicht git fir die yidden"*. It's either good for the Jews, or not good for the Jews. "Grandpa, why do you always say that? Isn't there anything else that matters?" "Alter", my Yiddish name, "When you grow up, you'll understand". To the same query to Zaydeh Katz I got the same answer. I grew up, and now I understand.

I have digressed from describing our Jewish wedding, but before I do so, I believe it appropriate to set forth how quickly, and fully, Anneliese became comfortable in her role as a Daughter of Zion. At birth Jews are given Hebrew names in addition to their secular names. Mine is *Yeshoshua*, Joshua, in English. Male converts are generally given the name *Avraham*, Abraham. Female converts are called either *Sarah Leah*, after the wives of Abraham and Jacob, or *Rut*, Ruth, after the widowed daughter-in-law who followed her widowed mother-in-law from Moab back to Judea, saying (as did Anneliese in a letter to me), wither thou goest I go, thy land shall be my land, and thy God my God. At her conversion my Zaydeh Katz gave Anneliese the names of Sarah and Leah. (I would have preferred Ruth.) As is sometimes the case with converts, Anneliese had a deeper understanding of Judaism's Teachings, and a greater appreciation of its beauties, than many of those born into the Faith. It was she, after all, who, by her example, raised our five children to be Jews, who drove them to their religious study classes at the synagogue, in preparation for their Bar and Bat Mitzvahs, who lit and blessed the Sabbath candles, who observed the Holy Days, and whose beautiful Passover Seders were never lacking in appreciative guests. Yes, Anneliese was proud to be a Jew! An incident Anneliese related to me, after we left my folks' apartment and moved to the married students' housing project, illustrates how comfortable she was with her Jewishness. There were no stores on North Brother Island where we were housed. One shopped at a small market at 138th St. in The Bronx. Passover was approaching and included in Anneliese's purchases was a box of Matzoh. The check-out clerk knew Anneliese was German from her accent. He expressed surprise that she had bought Matzoh. "I thought you were German," he said. Anneliese replied, "I am. But didn't you ever hear of German Jews?" That's my Anneliese!

Anneliese and I were married under a makeshift *Chuppah*, a cloth canopy, this one made from a bed sheet supported on four bamboo poles. My Zaydeh Katz had invited every Rabbi in the neighborhood, including, of course, those who had assisted him with Anneliese's conversion. There must have been at least half a dozen, plus many of those who *davend*, prayed at the Shul he maintained in the basement of his house at 624 Ashford St. Quite a gathering of orthodox Jewish clergy and laity! All were clearly eager to see that beautiful German girl who had converted to Judaism in order to marry Reb Katz' grandson, the former soldier, *Yeshia Alter*. After the marital vows were exchanged I stamped on a glass, shattering it to cries of *Mazal Tov!* Good Luck! The shattering of the glass was to remind us of the destruction by the Romans of the Temple in Jerusalem in 70 CE. Jews are constantly reminded, even on the happiest of occasions, of their past communal sorrows. Thus have the Jewish People maintained their historicity for more than three millennia.

After the ceremony, photos were taken of the Bride and Groom. One shows Anneliese in her high collared dress I have earlier described, wearing a veil like headdress, and holding a bouquet of flowers. We are gazing at each other. I am wearing a dark suit, a white shirt and a bow tie (all law students, or those seeking to become law students, wore bow ties in the 40's and 50's, and I wore them as a lawyer for many years thereafter. Sitting atop my head was a large black *kipa* (*yarmulka* in Yiddish). We were in the dining room of my parents' apartment. On the wall one can see the water color painting of Schloss Hellenstein in Heidenheim, Germany. As I have earlier related, this is the painting I bought directly from the artist in 1945, and for which I paid *eine Stange Zigaretten*, a ten pack carton of cigarettes. This photographic juxtaposition of the Heidenheim water color with Anneliese and Arthur, Bride and Groom, demonstrates how everything was *beshert*—that Anneliese and I were destined to meet and fall in love in Heidenheim. The journey which began with my Cavalry enlistment in November 1942 in Brooklyn Borough Hall, had now, on the 12th day of February 1947, reached its predestined goal: Arthur had found and married his Fairy Princess and she her Prince Charming! *Und wenn sie nicht gestorben sind, so leben sie noch heute!*

About a day or two prior to our Jewish Wedding I began to feel physically weak, drained. I first attributed my condition to the frenetic pace I had been maintaining for months on end. Then my complexion began to take on a yellowish pallor. Clearly something was wrong with me. Anneliese noticed, my folks noticed. They were all concerned. Perhaps we should postpone the wedding. You and Anneliese are already legally married. The Government can't deport Anneliese. No! I said, let's have the wedding. And we did. After the ceremony, and as soon as social niceties permitted, I headed for the bedroom. Anxious to make love to my beautiful wife? Unfortunately, no. I just wanted to lie my aching self down, and with luck, fall rapidly to sleep. In a day or so I learned what was wrong with me. Somewhere in my last days in Germany, or perhaps on the flight home, I had contracted yellow jaundice. My ceaseless running around for almost six months in a stressful environment had finally taken its toll. In a few days I was no longer a Chinese prince, as Anneliese humorously referred to me. I was fully mended, just Art Katz again. Anneliese and I had no Honeymoon. Safely together in America as husband and wife was celebration enough for us—one we enjoyed every day and every night!

Anneliese getting ready for the Wedding Ceremony,
February 12, 1947, Brooklyn, NY

625

Anneliese getting ready for the Wedding Ceremony,
February 12, 1947, Brooklyn, NY

Mr. and Mrs. Louis Katz
Mr. and Mrs. Wilhelm Baur
announce the marriage of their children

Arthur
to
Anneliese
February 12th, 1947

Parental Announcement of Marriage of
Arthur and Anneliese, February 12, 1947

Jewish Wedding Scene: Arthur and Anneliese
being married under the *Chupah,* The Holy Canopy
enveloping them forever in a Happy Union.

Zaydeh, Anneliese and Arthur, and Rabbis,
enjoying Marriage Meal after Jewish Wedding
of Arthur and Anneliese, February 12, 1947, in
home of Arthur's parents, in Brooklyn, NY.

Anneliese and Arthur, and Rabbis, enjoying
Marriage Meal after Jewish Wedding of Arthur
and Anneliese, February 12, 1947, in home
of Arthur's parents, in Brooklyn, NY.

Arthur and Anneliese's Wedding
photograph, February 12, 1947.

On the wall, the water color painting of Schloss
Hellenstein in the rural town of Heidenheim,
Germany, where, on June 16, 1945, the two found
each other and fell in Love. In July 1945 Arthur
bought the painting from the artist for "*eine Stange
Zigaretten*" a carton of cigarette, which in 1945
occupied Germany had more worth than money.

Episode Forty

In which Anneliese adapts quickly to her new life in a new world and captures the hearts of all who meet her as easily as she had captured mine.

Anyone meeting Anneliese for the first time fell instantly in love with her. It was easy. I was the best example of that phenomenon. This had been my observation in Germany immediately at war's end. Would that same first reaction obtain when Anneliese began her new life in Brooklyn? In Germany Anneliese was in the midst of friendly GIs. None had been in combat to the extent I had been, nor had any been wounded. Further, the horrific story of the Holocaust was then beginning to unfold. In my Military Government Team little patent or latent hostility was shown to German civilians merely because they were Germans. We knew there were many Germans out there who were guilty, at various levels, of war crimes, as that term was defined in the Nuremberg Trials. One of our jobs was to ferret out these "bad Germans" from the general public. This was done through our Denazification Program. Her fine culinary skills aside, Anneliese was able to work for us because neither she, nor any member of her family, had been Nazi Party members. Thus, the reaction within my military circle to seeing Anneliese for the first time was not colored by the wide scope, then being revealed, of Nazi Germany's crimes against humanity.

But how would Anneliese fare when she came to America where she would face a civilian public who, in February 1947, generally deemed *all* Germans to be Nazis? How would she be viewed for the first time in a community consisting primarily of Jews, Italians, Russians and Poles, all of whose forebears had left countries now ravaged by Hitler and Mussolini, and whose relatives in Europe had suffered horribly, even unto death, under these two despots? How would they react when first they saw

Anneliese? *Not to worry!* They all fell in love with her as quickly as I had! How could they do otherwise? Like the Fairy Princess she was, her magical powers to captivate the hearts of all who fell under her sway were not affected by changes in latitudes and longitudes.

How did Anneliese manage this feat? Simply by being true to herself. Anneliese was mindful of the legacy of hatred left by the Nazis. She was no Pollyanna. She was a realist. She knew she was arriving in America at the early post-war phase in which Germans were all lumped together, and all tarred with the brush of Naziism. Did she have qualms? I'm sure she did. But Anneliese never revealed them to me. She knew I loved her and that I would protect her. She trusted me. And that was sufficient for her.

Trusting me was a tribute to me. Like Ruth, she said, without reservation, "Wither thou goest, I shall go. Thy land shall be my land, and thy God shall be my God." And it was so. But how did this come about?

In the Subtitle to this book, and throughout its pages I have used two adjectives to describe my Anneliese: *Courageous* and *Beautiful*, *Mutig* and *Schön* in German. Those who knew Anneliese when she was with us would remark that her beauty of face and form entranced not only the eye, but tugged at the heart. I have noted the same reaction in those who have "seen and known" Anneliese solely through her photographs. These feelings were akin to those I felt seeing Anneliese for the first time: the inner beauties of her heart and soul graced her physical being, unseen, yet palpable.

I need not dwell further on Anneliese's beauty. My words, bordering on the florid, can never fairly describe her beauty. So I move on. Courage—why that word? In whatever tongue it is rendered, Courage encompasses such attributes as bravery, self confidence, risk taking, even a dash of foolhardiness, independent thinking, and faith in oneself, and all coupled with the ability to learn which persons to trust, and the intelligence to meld all these disparate virtues into a force for action, namely *Courage/Mut*. And Anneliese possessed this force.

Anneliese possessed the courage to trust me, to leave her family and country, to travel almost half around the world to take up a new life in a land which only yesterday was her homeland's enemy, and which today was its occupier, to give up her religion to embrace an ancient one, yet one new to her, and to express herself daily, for the most part, in a language newly learned, and to do all these things precisely at that juncture of history when the open sores of Naziism were still festering and breeding hatred, and particularly in that part of America where she would take up her new life.

Anneliese trusted me, but how did I earn her trust? How did she determine she had sufficient confidence in herself, and in me, to take on challenges which would materially change our joint lives forever? The answer to these queries are found, I believe, in Anneliese's Letter No. 96 to me dated June 16, 1946. At that time we had been separated almost eight heart wrenching months. In eight pages, written wholly in German, in bed, late at night—sleep having escaped her—Anneliese describes her great longing for me as indescribably painful and bemoans our long separation. She reminds me that we had met on that date exactly one year earlier in 1945, on the day she began working for our Military Government Unit in Heidenheim, She reflects upon the hateful remarks of some of her neighbors concerning our relationship, She describes them as expressions of *Neid und Missgunst*, of jealousy and envy, and dismisses them. Anneliese then pens those insightful sentences which explain her confidence that together, she and I would face the unknown successfully. I translate from the German:

"And wouldn't this time of separation actually be a good thing, though a cruel testing of our love, of our belief in each other? Whatever life may bring, we two shall hold together, we shall not fail, and our life shall be a life of love, ready for anything."

Yes, Anneliese was mindful of all these perils when she, a Protestant *Schwarzwald Mädchen*, saw that my love was true, and returned it courageously, two fold, to me, a brash, big city Jewish American GI.

In her first letter to my parents, written on September 16, 1945, Anneliese noted how strange it must appear to them that I would want to marry a German girl in light of the horrendous crimes committed by the Nazis upon the Jewish People. She questioned when the hatred between peoples might end, asked that neither they, nor any religion, should stand in the way of our love, that the One God had created all of us, and given all his creatures the right to live, and that my parents should love her "a little", so that when she was with them it would make it easier for her to adapt to a new life.

The love, sincerity, warmth and wisdom expressed in Anneliese's letter stole the hearts of my Mom and Dad. From that letter on they loved her, not a little, but totally.

Jokes and stories abound about the friction between mothers-in-law and daughters-in-law. None can be recited concerning my Mother and Anneliese, for there was no friction. *Im Gegenteil*, on the contrary, they loved and respected each other. Hilda and Anneliese were Mother and Daughter-in Fact, not merely In-Law.

The numerous letters they exchanged during those dreadful ten months of separation, when I was home, and trying desperately to return to Occupied Germany to start to climb the mountain of paper work necessary to get Anneliese out of Germany and back with me to the States, are illustrative of this loving relationship.

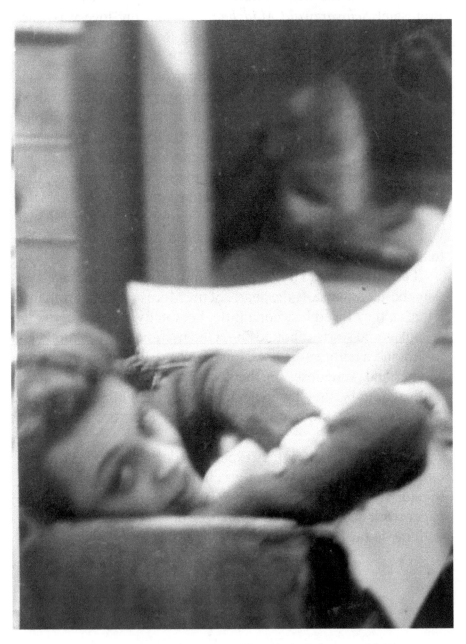

Unpacking Anneliese, Brooklyn, NY, February 1947

Sleeping Beauty, Anneliese,
Brooklyn, NY, February 1947

The sweet scent of togetherness
Cherry Blossoms, Prospect Park,
Brooklyn, NY, March 1947

A breezy day in Spring
Prospect Park, Brooklyn, NY, March 1947

Zaydeh Katz, Arthur's Mom, Hilda,
Anneliese and Arthur, Spring 1947

Anneliese with two aunts, Etta and Sally,
sisters of his Mom, and a niece, Spring 1947

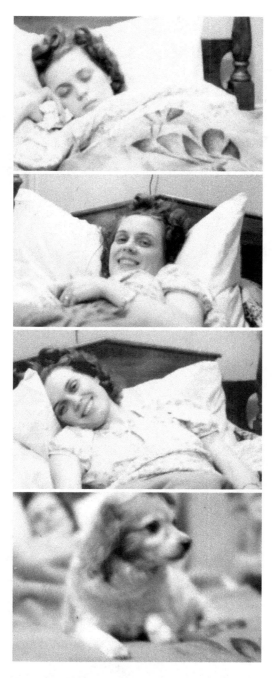

Anneliese is a tad tired, but still beautiful!
And Mickey is watching over her. March 1947

Arthur's Mom.   His Dad, and brother Harold.

His Mom, Dad and Mickey. Summer 1947

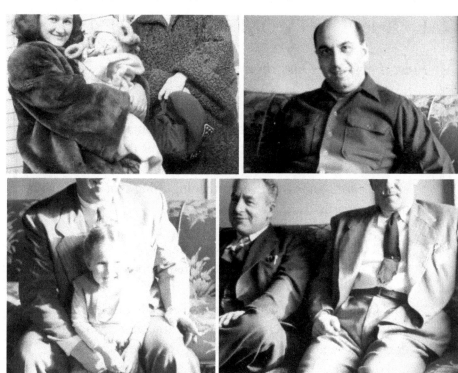

"Relatives, with and without heads"
Anneliese, with her humor, turns a
Negative into a Positive. April 1947
Anneliese's caption in her photo album

Episodes FORTY ONE through FORTY SIX

First there was One, then Two

And God said, Let us make man in our image, after our likeness: and let them have dominion over the fish of the sea, and over the fowl of the air, and over the cattle, and over all the earth, and over every creeping thing that creepeth upon the earth.

So God created man in his own image, in the image of God created He him; male and female created He them.

And God blessed them, and God said unto them, Be fruitful and multiply, and replenish the earth, and subdue it: and have dominion over the fish of the sea, and over the fowl of the air, and over every living thing that moveth upon the earth.

Genesis 1:26-28

וַיֹּאמֶר
אֱלֹהִים נַעֲשֶׂה אָדָם בְּצַלְמֵנוּ כִּדְמוּתֵנוּ
וְיִרְדּוּ בִדְנַת הַיָּם וּבְעוֹף הַשָּׁמַיִם
וּבַבְּהֵמָה וּבְכָל־הָאָרֶץ וּבְכָל־הָרֶמֶשׂ
הָרֹמֵשׂ עַל־הָאָרֶץ׃ וַיִּבְרָא אֱלֹהִים ׀
אֶת־הָאָדָם בְּצַלְמוֹ בְּצֶלֶם אֱלֹהִים
בָּרָא אֹתוֹ זָכָר וּנְקֵבָה בָּרָא אֹתָם׃
וַיְבָרֶךְ אֹתָם אֱלֹהִים וַיֹּאמֶר לָהֶם
אֱלֹהִים פְּרוּ וּרְבוּ וּמִלְאוּ אֶת־הָאָרֶץ
וְכִבְשֻׁהָ וּרְדוּ בִּדְנַת הַיָּם וּבְעוֹף הַשָּׁמַיִם
וּבְכָל־חַיָּה הָרֹמֶשֶׂת עַל־הָאָרֶץ׃

Episode Forty One

In which I introduce Anneliese to things especially American: baseball and root beer.

As I have earlier noted, in the letters Anneliese and I exchanged—each carefully numbered, to insure that we each were getting all, or most of them, and which were sent during the ten months we were separated, from the time I left Germany in November 1945 to receive my Honorable Discharge in the States, to my return to Germany in September 1946—we wrote about things each of us was doing to maintain our aplomb, while longing for that day when we would be together again, and so remain, forever and a day. Thus, in one letter I told Anneliese I had gone to a baseball game at Ebbets Field, the home of the Brooklyn Dodgers, and because I had not been there since the war, I had laid out the "large sum" of three dollars, and treated myself to a box seat! I mentioned that the Dodgers lost that day 7-3, but never noted the name of the winning team. When Anneliese was finally with me in Brooklyn, I took her to see the Dodgers play, at least once. She enjoyed the game. Being a quick study, she learned its basic principles very speedily. She enjoyed the game. As an athlete in her own right—being an excellent gymnast and a swimmer with mastery of several styles—she appreciated the fielding grace of the infielders, and the agility and catching skills of the outfielders. Television then was in its infancy and very expensive to own. We listened to the ball games on radio. I taught Anneliese how to keep the box score. She would listen to the Dodger games, amid her housekeeping chores, and keep a full record of runs, hits, errors, and strikeouts, and share them with me when I got home from Law School. *Welch eine Frau!* What a woman!

Back to our visit to Ebbets Field. During the game she enjoyed having a frankfurter with mustard and sauerkraut, and a beer.

However, she wanted to be assured that the latter item was *"ein echtes Bier"*, a "real beer"! Her query arose from an experience she had a weekend or two earlier. At that time I had taken her, for the first time, to Prospect Park, the Borough's largest park, and contiguous to Brooklyn Museum. It was the latter part of March, around the time we celebrated my 24th birthday. Anneliese had earlier told me she thought she was pregnant, which hugely pleased us both, but at that stage she showed nothing. Her figure was as trim as ever. Spring was on the cusp, and Prospect Park was already a beautiful, verdant area of undulating grasslands, and tree studded meadows, with moraine outcroppimgs of huge granite and basalt boulders carried by glaciers during the last ice age, from upstate New York and deposited in Brooklyn when the glaciers melted. And within the Park lay Brooklyn's rightly world famed Botanical Gardens. Both of us being gardeners, Anneliese and I paid several visits to the Gardens. The afternoon we were at the Park it was sunny and a "three bears day": not too hot, not too cold, just right, as Goldilocks said as she tasted, and ate, baby bear's porridge. Here and there were food vendors with their carts. We'd been strolling for a bit when I spied a vendor selling root beer. "Sweetheart, would you like a root beer?" "Yes, that would be nice." She reasoned that at the very beginning of her pregnancy, a little beer wouldn't hurt. I bought her a small root beer. It was ice cold, the foam on top ran down the sides of the waxed cup. It was a refreshing picture. Anneliese took a sip. Her face registered surprise! She was too polite to spit the drink out. She exclaimed, switching into German to make her point, *"Was für Bier ist das?"* "What kind of beer is this?" I then realized my mistake. Root beer is an American created soft drink. Anneliese was not aware of it when in Germany. When I had said, "root beer" Anneliese assumed it was a real beer with the brand name of "Root", or *"Würzel"* in German. We both laughed at the incident. Anneliese took a few more sips, and handed the drink to me. I finished hers and mine. No sense wasting anything, even root beer. Our not too distant pasts were still vibrant memories.

Thus, the root beer episode was fresh in Anneliese's mind when I took her to Ebbets Field to see her first baseball game after our outing in Prospect Park. To assure her that the beer being sold in the park was *"echt"*, genuine, real beer, I told her the brand was called Rheingold. The name was interesting to her, but the clincher was the taste, this was real German style beer! I don't recall whether the Dodgers won. But we had a good time. Were my belóved Anneliese still with me she would, most likely, have told me the name of the team the Dodgers played that day, the score and who won. She could really squirrel information away. But unlike the squirrels who buried acorns and nuts, and then forgot where, Anneliese could recall the data she stored away.

Writing of beer reminds me of an episode in which I became, the butt of some good natured humor. Many years later, when I would travel almost yearly to Europe in the course of my practice, I would, whenever feasible, take Anneliese, and one or more of the children with me. Anneliese was with me on one of these trips. We were visiting *Mutter* and *Vater*. Rather than have *Mutter* make a *Mitttagsessen*, the midday meal, I suggested we ride out to the countryside, find a nice restaurant and have a relaxing meal. Everyone liked my idea. We piled into my rented vehicle, drove down close to the Swiss border, found a nice inn. I remember ordering *Forelle Blau*, fresh killed trout, boiled, deboned, served in a white wine sauce, with lemon juice and *Petersilian*, parsley. Excellent! And since it was midday, and I was driving (although Anneliese could, if necessary, and sometimes it was), I thought I'd order a beer, a malty one, to complement the trout. In England, as a GI before the invasion, I had begun to enjoy the heavy malted British brews. The word for malt in German is *Malz*. And so, without much thought, I ordered a *"Malzbier"*. I noted that *Mutter* and *Vater*, and Anneliese, and even the *Kellner*, the waiter, gave me a quick stare when I said, in giving my order, *"und ein Malzbier bitte"* ". . . and a malt beer, please". The trout was swimming in the inn's tank, and had to be fished out to be killed and prepared for my meal. The *Malzbier* arrived well before the fish, as I had desired. It looked good, dark with a frothy head. I took a swallow. Boy, this beer was too sweet! "What's wrong with this beer?" Anneliese laughed, as did my in-laws, but not as openly. I even caught sight of the waiter, smiling in the background. "Dad", Anneliese said—she so addressed me now that we had children—"*Malzbier* is an alcohol free beer drunk mostly by pregnant women to give them the benefit of the malt without the alcohol. I thought your order was *seltsam* (odd) but I knew you liked to try different things." And everyone laughed again, and I joined in. I then ordered *"ein Bier vom Fass"*, a real draught beer, Beer from the keg. It was excellent. Wonderful memories, sadly recalled.

I made the same mistake in Spring 2005, in Israel. The night before I flew home, I stayed at a suites type hotel in Tel Aviv. These have nicely equipped kitchens. I shopped at a nearby market for my evening meal. In the liquor section I saw a bottle with the label, Malt Beer in English and Hebrew. I bought it. You're right! Approximately forty years after my mistake in Germany, I made the same one in Israel! Clearly, one cannot teach an old dog new tricks. Nor an old Art Katz either.

Episode Forty Two

In which Andrew Elliott, Avraham Eliyahu in Hebrew, our first of five, was born in Brooklyn Jewish Hospital, when I was a first year law student at New York University's School of Law.

Anneliese never demanded anything. But there was one thing Anneliese desired. She wanted a baby. We're married now, so lets have a baby—now. God has commanded us: be fruitful and multiply. Married life to Anneliese meant starting a family as soon as possible. I, too, wanted a family, and a large one. My brother and I had only each other, and sometimes both of us wished we had more siblings to share things with. But I was taken aback by the depth of Anneliese's desire for a baby—and to have one now! She would be carrying the child—a task I am glad God never assigned to a male. Becoming a mother did not faze Anneliese one jot or tittle. But I was concerned about providing for the financial needs of mother and child. I had just been accepted as a law student at New York University School of Law—an illustrious legal institution—and although all my tuition and books would be paid for under the GI Bill, I couldn't possibly generate much income while studying as a full time law student, particularly during that critical first year when law schools separated the wheat from the chaff. Furthermore, we'd now be a family of three, and still living with my parents! When I tallied up all these "realities" the time did not seem propitious for a baby. For a guy who, throughout his military career, had reveled in overcoming challenges, and had conducted himself with a self assuredness bordering sometimes on dumb ass cockiness, I was now showing signs of "morphing" into someone who had forgotten that challenges are merely obstacles to be overcome. In her own quite way Anneliese brought me to my senses.

649

Anneliese reminded me that from the moment we met in Heidenheim, on that glorious day in June 1945 the "realities" we thereafter jointly and singly encountered had not prevented us—in a world then in nightmarish disarray—from reaching our goal of becoming husband and wife. She was not fearful of the future, *Betreffs der Zukunft hatte Anneliese keine Angst.* Had I not assured her, that as long as I had a head upon my shoulders, she had nothing to worry about? Her faith in me was absolute. She knew I would never let her down. Her indomitable courage and her boundless trust in me, emboldened my spirits. I agreed with her that there was no need to postpone starting a family. On the 6th of November 1947 Anneliese and I had our baby: Andrew Elliott, in Hebrew *Avraham Eliyahu.* He would be the first of five. Andrew—we would call him Andy, and Zaydeh Katz called him *Avrumeleh*, Yiddish for little Abraham—weighed in at 6 lbs. 14 oz. Andrew was born in the Brooklyn Jewish Hospital, and therein lie two tales. One could have been a dire story—fortunately, it did not so end. The other was droll from the start. I relate them both in the order in which they unfolded.

At the time Andrew was born, and indeed, through the birth of Benjamin, our fifth child, fathers were not allowed in the delivery room. The delivery was performed, most often, in the obstetrics ward of a hospital, and by the family doctor who was a non-resident member of the hospital's staff. You knew him personally, or knew of him, from the other members of the family. He was particularly within the inner circle of the family if, as in the tale I relate, he was an uncle, married to one of my Mother's sisters. Thus, he was accorded the respect one gave to the purported all wise general practitioner, and reputed learned family member. I was attending classes at the Law School when my Mother thought it prudent, from the birthing signs she saw in Anneliese, that she should be promptly driven to the hospital by my Father, with my Mother in attendance. Before my folks drove off with Anneliese, the hospital being about a twenty minute drive, they called my uncle, the family physician to whom we had entrusted

Anneliese's care, to tell him to hurry to the hospital. My Mother assured him Anneliese was very close to delivering the baby. This being Anneliese's first child, the measurement of time was critical, but not certain. My folks could not reach me at the Law School, but I could have done nothing had I known. Under the medical mores of that time I was completely out of the loop. In less than twenty minutes Anneliese, game as ever, although obviously in pain, was wheeled into the delivery room of the Brooklyn Jewish Hospital. The attending staff physician examined Anneliese and he instructed the nurses to prep for her delivery. My uncle, the family physician, had not yet appeared on the hospital's premises. It soon became obvious to the staff physician that Anneliese was about to give birth. Still no sign of our friendly family physician. He should have been on the premises. His home and office was only a few miles removed from the hospital. Waiting any longer to deliver the baby would have endangered its life, and Anneliese's, as well. The staff physician delivered Andrew. He was a beautiful boy, a perfect baby! Clutching little Andy to her breast, the joys of Motherhood soon melted all of Anneliese's delivery pains away. So did Anneliese later recount her immediate post—partum feelings to me. Some time after Andy's birth, with mother and child in the recovery room, and Andy already nursing, my uncle, the family physician showed up, almost *an hour* later than he should have! Why hadn't he arrived on time? What took him so long to get to the hospital? His home and office were not more than five miles from the hospital. The answer to these queries turned on money. My uncle, the family doctor, was known to be a thrifty sort, tight fisted might be closer to the truth. He did not own a car. He could have called a cab for the short drive to the hospital. Instead, he walked to the streetcar stop, a few blocks from his home, and waited for the streetcar whose meandering route would take it closest to the hospital! His odyssey took him almost an hour to complete. I was angered that his penny pinching conduct could have placed my belóved Anneliese, and our newborn, into perilous jeopardy. Actually, I was more than angry. I was furious! Apparently he had forgotten his Hippocratic Oath which teaches all medical personnel this cardinal principle in the practice of medicine: "Do No Harm!" Although I thereafter saw my family doctor uncle at family gatherings, I never again spoke to him, acknowledged him, or shook his hand. Anneliese was more forgiving.

Now to the warm, humorous tale which relates to Andy's birth.

Episode Forty Three

In which I race to the hospital from school to see Anneliese and our first born, and a race it was!

On the day Anneliese gave birth to Andrew I came home late that afternoon from Law School and headed for our bedroom where I presumed Anneliese would be resting in her late stage of pregnancy. Upon entering the apartment I had breezed past my Mother, never giving her a chance to tell me anything. She followed me to bedroom, and before I could express concern that Anneliese wasn't there my Mom quickly related that hours earlier Anneliese had given birth to a healthy, beautiful boy, and that she was perfectly OK. My Mom put her arms about me, kissed me, and said, *"Mazal Tov!* You are now a father" I was happy to be a father, but more concerned about Anneliese's well being. I immediately called the hospital. There were no phones in the recovery room, she was being moved into the maternity ward—and there were no phones there—but I was assured, and re-assured, since my nervousness on the phone was obvious to the nurse I was speaking with, that mother and child were both doing well—, and ". . . yes, Mr. Katz, Mrs. Katz will be told you had called. Relax, Mr. Katz, your wife gave birth easily, no problems, and, yes, your son is also doing fine . . . . Of course, I'll tell her you called." The nurse had been very nice, but I'm sure she was pleased when our conversation was over.

My first opportunity to see Anneliese and our first born (Anneliese and I knew we would have more than one) would have to be late tomorrow afternoon after I finished my classes at the Law School. I could not afford to skip any classes in order to see Anneliese and the baby any sooner. This was the reason: To enable returning veterans to make up time spent serving their country, NYU School of Law had started a program whereby veterans accepted for admission to the School need not wait to enter until September of each year when new students ordinarily started. Instead, such veterans could enroll in February, then study non-stop through the Spring, Summer and Fall, and thus be even with the class which had regularly started its studies the previous September. A great help for me, and my veteran class mates, anxious to get out into the market place and start making a living. This non-stop pace of instruction was also a challenge intellectually and emotionally. Missing even one class could spell trouble. Thus, I determined that as soon as classes were over, at about 3 p.m., the next day, I would hurry off from Washington Square in Manhattan, where the Law School was located, and take the subway to the Jewish Hospital in Brooklyn. I must confess it was difficult that day to pay the degree of attention that the subjects studied deserved. Classes over I hurried to the subway. It would take about an hour's ride to get to the station in Brooklyn nearest the hospital. I had learned from my folks that visiting hours ended at 5 p.m. A lot different from today, when hospital visiting hours are almost around the clock. Close to 4 p.m. I exited the subway station nearest the hospital, and began a fast trot in its direction, my speed inhibited by the load of law books I was carrying.

A row of steps led to the hospital's entrance. I bounded up them, and into the hospital. A guard was sitting at a desk just inside the entrance. As I raced past him—my Mother had told me where the Maternity Ward was located, one flight up—he jumped from his chair and shouted after me, "Hey, sonny, we're you going?!" Apparently, an athletic young man of 24, running in full throttle, with a load of books under his arm, looked like a young kid. Over my shoulder, my pace not slackening as I ran down the corridor and climbing the nearest flight of stairs, I called out, "I'm going to see my wife!" "Like hell you are!" he shouted back, and began to race after me. I had a good lead, and I was younger. At the top of the stairs I saw a sign over a doorway marked Maternity Ward. I scooted to it, flung open the door, and there, in a bed at the far end of the room, I saw Anneliese! Calling out her name, mindless of the other ladies in their beds, I ran to her. Of course, she was elated to see me! I didn't have a chance to say a word to her when the guard, huffing and puffing, ran up to Anneliese, and pointing at me, asked, "Is he your husband?" Anneliese always had a wonderful sense of humor. She laughingly told me later that for an instant she was tempted to say "No!" She acknowledged I was, indeed, her husband. As the guard turned to leave he grumbled, "Visiting time ends at 5 p.m.!" Well, that left Anneliese and me a half hour to spend together. She looked radiant! As if nothing had happened just 24 hours earlier which would forever change our lives—or more likely, because she knew something glorious had happened: together we had made a baby, and she knew we could be fruitful and multiply! At Anneliese's request, a nurse brought Andrew to her, and I shared in Anneliese's joy as she nursed him!

Episode Forty Four

In which Anneliese, Andy, Zaydeh and *Kohenim*, all interrelate beautifully.

In accordance with Jewish Law Andrew was circumcised on the eighth day of his life, at his *Brith*, his Covenant Ceremony, conducted in my parents' apartment, the same apartment where Anneliese and I were married, and then living. This important ceremony was attended by members of the Katz and Glicenstein families, and friends, and overseen by Zaydeh Katz. It was a festive occasion! The actual *Beschneidung*, the removal of a portion of the foreskin, was done by a *Mohel*, one trained to perform this important religious ritual. Anneliese and I, standing arm in arm, were witnessing the continuation of a profound religious exercise which began almost four millennia ago, when Abraham, at the command of God, circumcised himself, and Ishmael, to seal the covenant which God had made with him and his progeny. Such pain as Andy may have felt in becoming a Member of the Covenant was dispelled the instant his lips were lightly bedaubed with a drop of sacramental wine. I believe I felt more pain than he did. Anneliese was a close observer of the proceedings. I do not recall that she said anything during or immediately after the circumcision. However, she smiled proudly when all shouted *Mazal Tov!* as Andy was placed in her arms.

Not only was *Avrumeleh* our first born, he was a male, and hence, a *Kohen*, a member of the hereditary Jewish Priesthood which God entrusted to Aaron, Moses' brother, and to all the males in Aaron's family, throughout their generations. Thus, in addition to Andrew, our other sons, Jonathan and Benjamin, are also *Kohenim*. With the second, and final destruction by the Romans of the Temple in Jerusalem in 70 CE, *Kohenim* could no longer perform their priestly duties, among them, offering animal sacrifices to God, as these could be performed only in the Temple. However, even before the first destruction of the Temple by Nebuchadnezzar, Jews had begun to develop localized places of worship. The Hebrew term is *Beit Knesset*, House of Assembly, in Greek, Synagogue. With the Temple destroyed the ritual offering role of the *Kohenim* ended. However, in many Jewish Congregations, whether Ashkenazic or Sephardic, of whatever degree of orthodoxy, *Kohenim* are honored by being the first person in the Congregation to be called up to the *Bimah*—the raised platform from which the Torah is read when taken from the Ark—to recite the prayers before the reading of the first portion of the Torah for that day. In some Congregations *Kohenim* are also called upon to bless the assembled with the Priestly Benediction:

> "May the Lord bless thee and protect thee,
> May the Lord shine His face upon thee,
> and be gracious unto thee.
> May the Lord lift up His face upon thee,
> and grant thee peace."
> (Numbers 6:24-26)

With the birth of Andrew continuation of the Priestly class in the family Anneliese and I would be raising was now assured. This was good news to the Katz and Glicenstein families. There were no *Kohenim* in the Glicenstein family. Incidentally, the name Katz is an acronym for *Kohen Tzedik*, Righteous Priest.

It would have been perfectly all right were our first born a girl. However, in light of Anneliese's conversion to Judaism, *Avrumeleh's* birth was looked upon as a further sign of Divine approbation of our Union. Anneliese was my Ruth: wither thou goest I will go, thy land shall be my land, and thy God my God. The beauty of Anneliese's being was such, that without in any wise changing any part of herself she instantly "fit in", and immediately became an integral part of our wide family circle. This was made most evident by the affection Zaydeh Katz showed her. Frankly, he was never as out going with me as he was with Anneliese. But then, even elderly, orthodox Jewish gentlemen, appreciate being in the presence of young, intelligent and beautiful women! Especially one who not only spoke English with him, but who could also understand his Yiddish, which had great similarity to the German dialect spoken in her Black Forest region of Germany.

Anneliese appreciated his attention to her and to *Avrumeleh*. Zaydeh learned when Anneliese would bathe Andy, and every day, at that time, except on *Shabbat*, he would climb the four flights of stairs to the apartment we shared with my folks and brother Harold. This was on the fourth floor of a building which had no elevator. Anneliese told me that Zaydeh would watch with delight as his *Avrumeleh* was being bathed. At that time I occasionally smoked a cigar or pipe. I did not smoke cigarettes. Anneliese had noted that Zaydeh smoked cigars, so she began the practice of offering him one before he left, after seeing Andy bathed, dried and swaddled. Zaydeh never asked for his cigar when he came to watch Anneliese bathe his new little *Kohen*, but neither did he refuse to accept one. Anneliese was pleased that Zaydeh would make his daily visits. Had she needed any signs of familial acceptance and affection, his visits would have been sufficient evidence of that. After recounting to me one of Zaydeh's visits, she joked that she wasn't sure whether Zaydeh climbed all those stairs to see his *Avrumeleh* being bathed, or to get his daily cigar! We both laughed at her "interpretation".

Episode Forty Five

In which I move my family of three from my parent's apartment in Brooklyn to NYU's married students' housing on North Brother Island in the East River off the east Coast of The Bronx.

As I have repeatedly noted, I have never kept a diary at any stage of my life. thus, the happenings I recount in these pages were either stored within the interstices of my brain—and kept fresh in my memory by frequent retellings over a period of more than six decades—or their dormant recollections were revived, and dated, by reference to written documents created during those 60 plus years. Letters sent and received, or government documents issued, such as my Honorable Discharge, are examples. And then there is the phenomenon where the present recollection of a past event will enable one to revive a date, a time certain, for the happening of an unrelated event. I have been a lawyer since my admission to my first State Bar, in New York, in 1950. After being a member, for more than half a century, of a profession I love, I respectfully ask my readers, the jury measuring the ultimate worth of my story, to give allowance to the fact that my writing style—to the extent my mode of committing words to paper can fit neatly under the rubric "style"—is colored by words and phrases, and methods of exposition, unique to the practice of Law. I write this by way of laying a foundation—aye, there's a choice legal phrase, dear reader—for establishing a time frame when Anneliese and I moved from my parents' apartment in Brooklyn, to housing provided to married NYU students on North Brother Island. For the first time we were going to live and love as husband and wife within our own four walls! Query, when did this auspicious event occur? Using the interrelated principles of evidence known as Past Recollection Recorded and Present Recollection Revived, I arrived at an approximate date. I recall our move to the Island—

which lies at the confluence of Long Island Sound and the East River—by remembering that Andy was a toddler when we moved. He was an early walker, between nine and ten months at that time. Andy was born on November 6, 1947. Thus, we must have moved sometime in the Fall of 1948. Remembering *Avrumeleh* taking his first steps helped me recall the approximate date of our move.! QED (*Quod erat demonstrandum)*!

Episode Forty Six

In which Heidi Faith, Freya in Hebrew, our second of five, and first daughter, is born in the charity ward of Columbia-Presbyterian Hospital in Manhattan.

Our first daughter, and second child, Heidi Faith, was born on April 12, 1950 in the Clinic Section of the Maternity Ward at the Columbia—Presbyterian Hospital in uptown Manhattan. Anneliese and I were charity users of the hospital's maternity facilities, although we may have paid a small fee. I was then a full time student at NYU School of Law, and Anneliese was a full time mother to Andy, and later to Heidi. My only income came from my monthly WWII disability compensation. I was rated initially at 20% disability, then increased to 30% (it did not go to the higher rating I now have until years later). In 1950 I believe my monthly disability check was $47, but our monthly rent for our small one bedroom apartment on North Brother Island was $46! This left us $1 a month to buy food, baby stuff and pay subway and ferry fares!. Fortunately, my Mother would make weekly visits laden with bags of foodstuffs. Anneliese was, of course, a professionally trained chef, and could magically turn almost nothing into something very appealing and nutritious. And I have a few dollars I had earlier laid away. I also worked a few hours on weekends, as a ferry toll collector. I don't recall whether I received monetary compensation, or the right to ride the ferry free. I would not allow Anneliese to be treated by my uncle, the family doctor—the one who never showed up for Andy's birth—even when my folks offered to pay his fees. And so Anneliese was a maternity clinic patient at the prestigious Columbia—Presbyterian Hospital. Its location was convenient to those of us living on North Brother Island. Anneliese's travel time was thus materially reduced.

I suggested names to Anneliese for our three boys. She accepted all of them. However, when she confirmed her second pregnancy Anneliese told me that if the child was a girl she would like to name her Heidi. Anneliese came from the Black Forest Region of Germany, *Der Schwarzwald*, bordering on Switzerland, and she knew the Heidi story and fancied the name for a female child. I readily agreed. To give the child a female Hebrew name we chose Freya, after my maternal Grandma Glicenstein. In English we gave Heidi the middle name of Faith. When it came to having children my approach was simple: I agreed with Anneliese that we should have a large family. Then, once Anneliese confirmed she was pregnant I would busy myself with selecting proposed male and female names, English and Hebrew. That done with her acquiescence, I turned the birthing process over to Anneliese. Her personality and constitution were such that she never had any problems in bringing five healthy and beautiful children into the world! I was, of course, a proud and dutiful husband, and always concerned about her well being. But Anneliese's attitude was that giving birth was a natural thing, and as long as she was under sound medical care, and lived her usual prudent life, everything would be all right. And five for five, it was. My Anneliese was as courageous, *mutig*, as she was beautiful!

Fortunately, I was home when she told me she thought it best that we go the the hospital. I put in a call to the Ferry Slip to tell them that my pregnant wife had to get to the mainland promptly for her hospital. The ferry management immediately altered their schedule and Anneliese and I were soon on our way to Columbia—Presbyterian Hospital. We left Andy, then two and a half, in the hands of a neighbor couple who had kids of their own. At the hospital I was told that Anneliese might take another four to six hours to deliver, and since I had a young son at home, even though in safe hands, it might be best I went home. From the maternity ward Anneliese waved, gave me a big smile and blew me a kiss. At that moment I was clearly more concerned for her well being than she was. I left for home. At that time of night the subway was not running at its peak scheduling, so that by the time the ferry arrived, and I crossed to the Island, more than an hour had gone by. I thought I'd call the hospital to make a last minute check on Anneliese's status. There was a public phone booth at the Island's ferry slip. I called the hospital, was transferred to the Maternity Ward. I inquired of the nurse how my wife, Anneliese Katz was doing. To my great surprise I was told that Anneliese had just delivered, and that she and the baby were doing fine!! "Wow!" I was relieved and elated. "Is the baby a boy or a girl?" "Sorry, sir", the nurse said, "We are not allowed to give out the sex over the telephone." I did not then understand the reason for this practice. Upon later reflection I realized that this was a sound policy for the hospital. Were the nurse accidentally to state the wrong sex the father arriving later might think he had the wrong baby—with all the consternation and possible litigation—which might then result. Suddenly I got a bright idea. I wasn't being trained to be a lawyer for nothing. I said to the nurse, "I have a son at home, does he have a brother or a sister?" Without hesitation she answered, "A sister". She immediately recognized her mistake, and laughed. "Thank you", I said, and hung up. How wonderful! Anneliese had her Heidi! And I was now the proud father of two kids, and I had yet to graduate from Law School and take—and pass—the Bar Examination! But so what? Anneliese was OK, the baby was OK. Life was good! Thank you, God!

As promptly as visiting hours allowed I was at Anneliese's side. She looked unruffled, and little Heidi was a doll! I recounted how I had learned that Anneliese had given birth to a girl. She admired my cleverness. I then mentioned that sometimes new born babies are mixed up, particularly in clinical facilities where the delivering physician, the one then on call, may be a total stranger to the mother. Anneliese saw my concern. "You have nothing to worry about, Dad. Our Heidi was the only white baby delivered last night!"

Episodes FORTY SEVEN through FIFTY

Onward and Upward

Gaudeamus Igitur

Nach C.W. Kindleben 1781 *Tr. J. Mark Sugars 1997* *J. F. Lentner, 1850*

1. |: Gaudeamus igitur,
Juvenes dum sumus; :|
Post jucundam
  juventutem,
Post molestam
  senectutem
|: Nos habebit humus!:|

2. |: Vita nostra brevis est,
Brevi finietur, :|
Venit mors velociter,
Rapist nos atrociter,
|: Nemini parcetur. :|

|: While we're young, let
  us rejoice,
Singing out in gleeful
  tones; :|
After youth's delightful
  frolic,
And old age (so
  melancholic!),
|: Earth will cover our
  bones. :|

|: Life is short and all too
  soon
We emit our final gasp; :|
Death ere long is on our
  back;
Terrible is his attack;
|: None escapes his dread
  grasp. :|

1. Lebt, so lang die
  Jugend schäumt,
Freudigen Gefühlen!
Nach der Jugend froher
  Hast,
Nach des Alters trüber
  Last,
Ruhen wir im Kühlen.

2. Kurz ist unser
  Lebenslauf,
Bündig ist's vorüber;
Kommt der Tod mit
  raschem Schritt,
Nimmt uns jähen Griffes
  mit,
Keinen schont sein
  Hieber!

3. |: Ubi sunt qui ante
Nos in mundo fuere? :|
Vadite ad superos,
|: Hos si vis videre. :|

|: Where are those who
    trod this globe
In the years before us? :|
They in hellish fires
    below,
Or in Heaven's kindly
    glow,
|: Swell th' eternal
    chorus. :|

3. Wo sind jene, die vor uns
    Diese Welt bebauet?
Schwinget Euch zum
    Götterzelt,
Steiget in die Unterwelt,
Wo ihr längst sie
    schauet!

4. |: Vivat academia,
Vivant professores, :|
Vivat membrum
    quodlibet,
Vivant membra
    quaelibet,
|: Semper sint in flore!:|

|: Long live our academy,
Teachers whom we
    cherish; :|
Long live all the
    graduates;
And the undergraduates;
|: Ever may they flourish.
    :|

4. Unsrer Schule nun ein
    Hoch!
Allen die da lehren!
Jedem Jünger ein Pokal!
Ihre Blüte allzumal,
Ewig soll sie währen!

5. |: Vivant omnes
    virgines
Faciles, formosae, :|
Vivant et mulieres,
Tenerae, amabiles,
|: Bonae, laboriosae! :|

|: Long live all the
    maidens fair,
Easy-going, pretty; :|
Long live all good ladies
    who
Are tender and so
    friendly to
|: Students in this city. :|

5. Alle Mädchen leben
    hoch,
Wohlgestalt und
    schmiegsam!
Auch den Frauen
    bringen's wir,
Freundlich und von
    holder Zier,
Häuslich, fromm und
    fügsam.

6. |: Vivat et respublica
Et qui illam regit, :|
Vivat nostra civitas,
Maecenatum caritas,
|: Quae nos hic
    protegit! :|

|: Long live our Republic
    and
The gentlefolk who lead
    us; :|
May the ones who hold
    the purse
Be always ready to
    disburse
|: Funds required to feed
    us. :|

6. Hoch auch das
    gemeine Wohl,
Jener die es leitet!
Trinkt auf unsre gute
    Stadt,
Auf der Gönner
    Freundestat,
Die uns Schutz bereitet!

7. |: Pereat tristitia,
Pereant osores, :|
Pereat diabolus,
Quivis antiburschius,
|: Atque irrisores! .|.

|: Down with sadness,
    down with gloom,
Down with all who hate
    us; :|
Down with those who
    criticize,
Look with envy in their
    eyes,
|: Scoff, mock and berate
    us. .|.

7. Nieder mti der
    Traurigkeit,
Mit den alten Drachen!
Nieder mit dem Teufel
    auch,
Nieder, die den
    Burschenbrauch
Schmähen und
    verlachen! . . .

666

Episode Forty Seven

In which the family enjoys an idyllic life on North Brother Island; I have a shaky start at NYU Law School, but quickly recover with aid of a group of bachelors, who happily come to the Island to study, once they have tasted Anneliese's cooking.

I have done no research to establish definitively when Anneliese and I moved with Andy to our NYU Married Students' Housing apartment on North Brother Island. Coupling the September start of the Law School's academic year with my remembrances of Andy as a toddler, suggests we most likely moved to the Island in September or October of 1948. The "catch-up" program set up by NYU in February of that year to accommodate returning WWII veterans had performed its function. Those who hadn't flunked out were now on an educational par with the Law School's second year students. All Spring and Summer of '48 my fellow veterans and I had been on a non-stop cycle of instruction, much like a hamster racing within his Ferris wheel cage—the difference being, fortunately, that we got somewhere with our unceasing effort. New York University School of Law was founded in 1835. From its outset it has always been ranked within the top five law schools in the United States. Thus our law professors pushed us very hard. They had the School's reputation to uphold. Unless you could meet their high standards you were soon out the door. Having survived that punishing accelerated First Year, I felt I would make it all the way through, and then pass the State Bar Examination.

My college academic status qualified me for admission to the School. But if the GI Bill had not existed, I could never have afforded NYU's tuition fees and book costs. I didn't enlist in the Cavalry in November 1942 to win medals, or to get a law degree, or to meet and marry a courageous and beautiful German girl. I enlisted to serve my country, to give Uncle Sam my full measure of devotion. That I spilled my blood in France and in Germany went with the territory. It was *beshert* that I give up my college student deferment and enlist. I did so of my own free will. God knew that I would, and that my enlistment would set off a train of events designed to bring Anneliese and me together! "Everything is foreseen, yet freedom of choice is given." So wrote Rabbi Akiba in Pirke Avot, 3:19. Thus, here in the Fall of 1948, three years after that magical day in June 1945 when God first brought Anneliese and me together in Heidenheim, Germany, we were now setting up our very own apartment as husband and wife!

We lived on North Brother Island for two years. They were idyllic years! The reader might question a description bordering on rapture after I have described our cramped living quarters, and the cold structure in which they were found. But once I leave the four walls of "our place", and describe the Island's locale and its terrain, and our neighbors, and the events which took place on our Island, then I believe the reader will agree that the words "idyllic years" are an apt description of that time.

Anneliese and I understood that the quarters we were moving into would have very little architectural relationship to what were then called rental/lease apartments or flats. We were told we were moving into bleak, concrete, industrial style structures— designed originally to be hospital wards for drug addicts in rehabilitation—or at least it was hoped there would be a modicum of rehabilitation—but now modified to turn the barren hallways, and hospital wards into compact "apartments". I have placed quotation marks about the term apartments because the living quarters we were given—although very private, for we had a front door we could lock—were simply one large room. On one side, was the wall which separated us from the long hallway, and in which the door, our sole means of ingress and egress, was placed. Directly opposite this wall was the building's outer wall. This wall contained a set of two windows. Their sills were about three feet above the floor. The windows were about six feet wide and rose to within three feet of the ceiling, which I guessed was at least a ten foot ceiling. The windows were the best part of our unit. They opened onto a vista which, if we were in The Hamptons, would have made our humble abode worth a cool million. We were on the second floor, and our view was of a broad swath of park like, tree studded greenery which must have measured one hundred feet from the walls of our building to the shoreline of the island. There, a low fence, which encircled the island's perimeter, in no way impaired our view of the outer reaches of the East River as its waters merged into those of Long Island Sound. The windows, with the fresh air, light and view they provided, made our all in one room quarters seem less confining. The layout of our apartment, had modest kitchen facilities along its left wall, this being the wall which separated us from our neighbor. An enclosed toilet, sink and shower were built into a corner of the right wall. And there was a least one clothing closet. The head of our bed was against the right wall. Any and Heidi slept some distance from us behind a fixed partition about six feet in height. We ate at the table which was the focal point of the apartment. Anneliese prepared her meals on it, we ate on it, the kids played on it, and I studied law on it. Had I known then Massenet's opera, Manon, I might have hummed the melody of Manon's aria, which she sings on moving from one lodging to another, "*Adieu, notre petite table*". We had some chairs, and, I believe, a couch and a floor lamp. I don't recall buying any furniture. Most likely my folks provided whatever we had. They were most helpful and generous to us. Neither Anneliese nor I complained about our living standards. Our memories of our lives and times in Germany were still so vivid that anything of a material nature which we had—or didn't have—in America was of no moment. What mattered was that we were no longer separated. We were together. We had each other. And that was enough!

Now let me tell you why Anneliese and I found the two years we lived on North Brother Island to be idyllic ones. Consistent with my narrative style, the reader will have to follow me as I wend my way back and forth in time, since the past is always the prologue to the future. If you have come this far then bear with me.

Studying Law successfully is a full time intellectual pursuit. At least it was if you were a returning WWII veteran, anxious to get started on your civilian career, and a student fortunate enough to get into NYU School of Law. I'd always considered myself a quick study. I had demonstrated this trait at Brooklyn College. My survival as a law student depended on it.

My first three years at Thomas Jefferson High School in the East New York section of Brooklyn—then one of the top schools in the New York City public education system—were mostly pissed away in fun and games activities, resulting in grade scores much lower than I should have earned. In fact, my Mother had to make several visits to the Principal's Office concerning my class behavior. If a class needed a class clown, it was my self appointed job to fill it. Reflecting back, that was a job I should have passed up. As I have noted, I was a quick study which put me out of synch with the pace of the class. Result: boredom and thus idle time to horse around. There were then, no "achievement classes" which could have fully exploited what ever academic potential I had. I recount two incidents at Thomas Jefferson which illustrate the nature of my first three years at the school. My Mother was the oldest of seven Glicenstein children. The youngest was her brother Bernard, only five years my senior. Bernie had just graduated from Thomas Jefferson when I began my freshman year. I was enrolled in a biology class taught by the same teacher who had instructed Bernie. I knew this because Bernie had given me an overview of the school and its faculty when I started out. Bernie had been something of a card himself, and within days, I was following his footsteps. A week into the biology class I remarked to my teacher, a very prim, maiden aunt type of pedagogue, that "My uncle Bernie was one of your students." Looking me up and down, she responded icily, "He was a bum, too!" I wasn't offended by her comment. I admired Bernie. And if I was following in his wake, that was good enough for me.

The second incident concerned my Spanish class. Language study, whether of our English tongue, or a foreign idiom, has always been of interest to me, undoubtedly because I have an affinity to this field of knowledge, as opposed to that of mathematics. In any case, in my first year Spanish class I was soon more proficient than most of the other students. My teacher, was a Latina, probably in her late thirties, and a tad high strung. To cover the extensive curriculum she worked very fast, covering the blackboards (today the slate is gone, replaced by white composition boards) with row after row of hastily written illustrations, *inter alia*, of the grammatical intricacies of the three classes of verbs, designated by their endings as ar, er and ir verbs, such as *hablar, vender, salir*. And she would then dash off *frases*, sentences, using these verbs in their various conjugations. Occasionally, in her haste to set things down before the bell rang, she would make an inadvertent spelling error. Instead of mentioning that fact to her privately after class, I would pipe up that the word at the end of the third chalked line was incorrect. That was terribly wrong of me! The kids would snicker, and she would be embarrassed. I was the class clown being smart ass. My Spanish teacher definitely did not like me. She didn't get mad. She got even. She flunked me! So I went to Summer School, took the same class again, kept my yap shut, passed, and when the Fall session opened, there I was in the front row of her Spanish 2 class. "What are you doing here?", she demanded, my presence clearly unsettling her. I told her I had gone to Summer School, retook Spanish 1, had passed, and was now in her Spanish 2 class. "Like hell you are!", she almost shouted, and ran out of the room. Within two minutes I was summoned to the Principal's Office. The Monitor began to tell me where the Office was. I cut him off. I already knew where the Principal's Office was. My Spanish teacher and the Principal told me I was a bright kid, but a trouble maker. If I promised to act civilly, and not embarrass her, or myself, I could stay in her class. I readily agreed. I kept my word. At least in her class.

By the end of my junior year my cumulative grade average hovered between B—and C. Had I been a C student at Yale or Harvard I could have ended up one day as President of the United States. But I was looking to enter Brooklyn College, a free New York State school where getting in was materially determined by your grades. And so, at the end of my junior year, I had an Epiphany! (I believe orthodox Jewish boys can have Epiphanies when suddenly, they recognize the error of their ways). I determined to improve my grade average by making my senior year an example of what I could do academically, if I exploited my intellectual skills properly—and kept my kisser sealed! I have been writing all this by way of laying a foundation—a neat, trial lawyer's phrase—for the admission of evidence relevant in describing my first month's experience as a law student—a scary experience, as you, dear reader will soon discern. I continue with my completion of this foundation.

How did I make my Senior High School year more representative of what I could do academically? I joined the school's creative writing club. The club's academic advisor had been my English teacher, and she had earlier remarked upon my writing skills. She was pleased to see me beginning to exploit my potential in that craft. The primary project for Seniors in the creative writing club was to work on producing that year's Senior Class Book. The Book was called Aurora. Each graduating class was given a theme which lent itself to an uplifting view of the future. This theme would become the subject of both a prose piece, and a poem. The theme for my June 1940 graduating class was "The Citadel". Seniors were encouraged to enter the competition to write an essay and poem on this theme for the Class Book, the prize being the publication in the Yearbook of the winning prose and poetry pieces. I entered both the prose and poetry competitions. And for the first time ever, one student won both competitions—and that student was me!. What a transition—from class clown to high school literary *maven*!

The faculty thought it "inappropriate" for one student to win both competitions. The solution? I was credited as the author of the prose piece, and one *Arturus Felinus* (a Latin misreading of Arthur Katz, Katz being read as "cats") was credited as the writer of the poem. These two writing honors were the only honors I won at Thomas Jefferson High School, plus a citation for perfect attendance. I may have horsed around at school, but I never missed a day to be on stage! In stark contrast to me was my younger brother, Harold. From each graduating class two persons, one a young man, the other a young woman, were selected as the two students with the highest level of academic achievement in their four years in school. Harold graduated two years after I did, and he won that honor. He had no trouble obtaining admission to the University of Chicago, a numero uno school. (He, like my daughter Heidi, is also a member of Phi Beta Kappa). In contrast, I applied for admission into the day school program of Brooklyn College, and was denied admission. My grade score was too low. I was only eligible to enter their part time evening program. As ye sow, so shall ye reap. I spoke with the Admissions Office personnel. They recognized the marked improvement in my Senior year. They made me a deal. Do A work across the board in your evening classes, and we'll let you transfer to full time day college. I accepted their challenge, met it, and in short order, became a full time day college student!

I have recited all of the foregoing as part of a lengthy laying of the foundation for the introduction of data relevant to my experiences in my critical first month in law school. I have already noted, in this meandering tale of war and love, that two of the books I carried with me, and studied, throughout WWII were *The Common Law* by Oliver Wendell Holmes, Jr. (later, Justice, U.S. Supreme Court) and *The Nature of the Judicial Process* by Benjamin Nathan Cardozo (later, Justice, U.S. Supreme Court). These two volumes fulfilled the purposes for which they were intended: they educated their readers, me included, on the philosophy of the law, and how this philosophy was applied by jurists in resolving cases before them. Thus, when I entered NYU's prestige School of Law I was thoroughly schooled, so I thought, in how the law works. I knew all the principles the way jurists would apply them in deciding cases before them. Getting through law school should, therefore, be a breeze! Yep! What a breeze! My first three months, especially that crucial first month, were more like a Category 5 hurricane which almost blew me out of law school!

Beginning law students start with courses such as contracts, torts, criminal law, and legal procedure. These were basic principles, but they had to be mastered early were one expecting to progress through the law school's maze of ever more complicated areas of jurisprudence, and survive to graduate with a *Juris Doctor* degree. I start with a humorous example concerning a deadly serious body of law: contracts. Samuel Goldwyn, the movie mogul, was correct when he said that an oral contract is not worth the paper it is written on! But there is a lot more to the law of contracts. Very quickly we February '48 WWII veterans were exposed to strange, new concepts such as bilateral and unilateral contracts, executed and executory contracts, void and voidable contracts, offers and acceptance, and, *inter alia*, the need for, and definitions of "consideration" in the law of contracts. In our accelerated program we veterans were being fed a lot of material which we were supposed to assimilate quickly—thus enabling us to start our second year in law school in September, in sync with the second year class before us which had enjoyed the luxury of having a full year to do what we were doing in almost half the time. Thus, we were given lots of exams early on. One month into our classes, my faculty advisor, a young professor not more than five or six years my senior, called me into his office to inform me that I had done so poorly in my exams, that unless I made marked improvement in the next month's series of exams I would be terminated as student! What a shock! I never recall feeling fear in combat. I felt concern, or apprehension, as when incoming shells seemed to be falling ever closer, and we were limited in our ability to move our vehicles quickly out of harm's way. But I never experienced the fear that freezes one into a state of despair or torpor.

I was stunned by my advisor's comments! For a moment I felt ill. Was I experiencing fear? Or was it despair? Even in my darkest days in my GI prison in England I had never experienced that kind of emotional upset. I had never come close to how I now felt. I had survived three years of military service, with its ups and downs as enumerated. I had survived fifteen heart wrenching, physically draining months in my ultimately successful quest to return to my belóved Anneliese in Germany, and then to bring her to the States. I was successfully coping with my rôle as husband and father of two youngsters. But suddenly, all seemed to be for naught! My certain expectation of becoming a lawyer appeared suddenly to be but an evanescent dream! What was I doing wrong, what was casting doubt upon my ability to become a lawyer?

My faculty advisor reviewed the subject test papers with me. He was also one of my professors, and he expressed his puzzlement that I was alert in class and responsive to his questions, but that I had written such poor examinations. My "problem" he said was the way I wrote my answers to the legal issues buried within the fact pattern set before me. First year law students were tested to determine how effectively they could see all the "issues", *i.e.*, the legal questions posed in the test's fact pattern recital, and then how to resolve the issues found by applying legal principles already learned. Thus the law student was supposed to dissect the problem, digging out every possible legal issue, the more the better, and then apply to their resolution the legal principles applicable, even pointing out which related legal principles would not be applicable because . . . . In short, a student would be deemed to have learned the law applicable to the problem stated if: (i) he/she tore the problem apart; (ii) dug out all the relevant facts; (iii) framed, *i.e.*, set forth issues, real or possible, based upon these facts; (iv) recited all the legal rules or principles which could address all these issues, real or perceived; and (v) then showed how the application of these legal principles could resolve these issues. That was the testing format. What was I doing wrong?

My advisor's response to my pained query was this: I was answering the problems in general terms. I was giving conclusions, generally correct, without demonstrating in detail how I had arrived at these conclusions. I was answering as if I were a judge writing an opinion based upon an *established* trial or appellate court record, or as a law professor writing a law review article on *specifically identified* issues. What I should be doing is to stop writing like a jurist or law professor, and, instead, to demonstrate my skill in dissecting a problem, down to the marrow in the bone, and then to give a detailed examination of the issues discovered. The law school wanted to learn, as rapidly as possible—student slots in law school being limited—which new students showed aptitude for the Law by demonstrating, early on, their ability to analyze a fact pattern quickly, to determine the controlling legal issues therein, and then to apply the applicable legal principles to a proper resolution of the legal issues found. NYU School of Law had always been a Top Five law school, and it was keen, and rightly so, to maintain its reputation by making sure that only the best and the brightest graduated under its banner. I understood the School's concerns, and it understood mine. I thanked my Advisor for his counsel and assured him he would see my rapid improvement. I had earlier remarked that I was a quick study. My next month's exams, and all subsequent ones through law school, demonstrated that I had learned how to write law school exams, and later, State Bar Examinations. Did I tell Anneliese about my "near death" law school experience? I did, but not until I had completed my second month of school and found I had gotten the knack of writing successful law examinations. Had I done so sooner, with my self confidence at a low ebb (something wholly unusual) I know Anneliese would have seen my concern, and feel unhappy that I was unhappy. And as *mutig*, as courageous as she was, she could well have had her own concerns as to the well being of our young family. After all, I had assured her that as long as I had a head on my shoulders she had nothing to fear about me supporting her and a family—and becoming a lawyer was the cornerstone of the economic life I was proposing to build for her and the kids. After I felt I was back on track, and knew I would make it through law school, I told Anneliese what had transpired. She immediately embraced me, kissed me and remarked that I must have been quite upset and uneasy until I resolved the problem. Anneliese also said I kept it a good secret, and then she came as close to reproving me as ever, when she quietly reminded me that husbands and wives shouldn't hold back their problems from each other, that's why lovers get married, because two persons together are stronger than one alone. *O, Anneliese, ich liebe dich so!*

Before I left my Advisor's office he advised me that law students should not study by themselves. His counsel was identical with that given by our Talmudic Sages more than two millennia earlier, see *e.g., Pirke Avot, I:16, VI:10.* The benefit of studying with one or more fellow students is that your fellows may see a question from a perspective different than yours, and their varying insights would contribute to each law student acquiring a greater grasp of the subject matter than each, studying alone, might have acquired. The beast of academic failure having rattled my cage of confidence, I looked about for study mates. I lighted upon three who, I had earlier discerned, were intellectually sharp, and about my age. I approached them and broached my idea of setting up a study group. They all liked the idea. But there was one major obstacle to setting up the group. All were single and lived in Greenwich Village near the Law School location in Washington Square in the lower reaches of Manhattan. I told them I was married, with two children, and living on North Brother Island. Thus, it would be impossible for me to be away from my family in the afternoons and evenings studying law with them in Greenwich

Village. Sorry, they said, no dice. You gave us a great idea Art, we'll start our own group down by the school. What to do? Then, as would happen a thousand plus times in my life with Anneliese, she came to the rescue. Without first consulting her (something I became prone to do too often) I volunteered to provide her culinary expertise as a key inducement for their traveling to North Brother Island. I told them that Anneliese was a professional chef, and that I was sure she would be happy to throw something together for them to eat in the course of our study sessions. I told them of the financial straits in which we were living. They also knew they would have to pay for their meals in some restaurant while studying. I asked for no cash contributions, but that if they brought foodstuffs along, however basic, Anneliese would turn them into a feast fit for a Three Star Michelin rating! It is said that the best way to get to a man's heart is through his stomach. How much more, then, it is true that there is no better way to lift the spirits of unmarried, often hungry law students, than to offer them top notch meals as a condition precedent for studying with me on North Brother Island? None of them had met Anneliese, or tasted her cooking, but I was a good salesman and they agreed to come to the Island for one afternoon and evening session.

A few days before my fellow students were scheduled to arrive for their "test" study session I informed Anneliese of what I had arranged, and why. She readily gave her approval. Studying on the Island, meant I would be home more often, something great for her and the children, further, cooking for more adults than two gave her greater opportunities to cook more elegantly. Cooking "fancy" for just two adults meant lots of leftovers. This would not be the case when cooking for five.

My three unmarried law school buddies arrived together for that first Saturday session. They brought along a couple pounds of raw hamburger, a couple pounds of potatoes, some onions, a baguette and a bottle of red wine. Anneliese was delighted to receive such bounty. She thanked them for helping her husband by coming to the Island to study. Her gracious reception, her smile, and her accent captivated them. They reacted the same way I had at that fateful moment in the late afternoon of that mid week in June 1945 in Heidenheim, Germany: they instantly fell in love with her! None of them ever made any passes, or inappropriate comments to me or to Anneliese. But from time to time, at school, they would say such things—in the Army lingo we often exchanged between us—as "What the fuck did you do to deserve such a bright, beautiful woman?" I never could properly answer such an incisive query. And I knew they envied me, young bachelors that they were, for being able to sack out at night with my beautiful Anneliese at my side.

These group study sessions continued through the balance of law school, and proved to be as valuable, as a learning device, as my Talmudic Sages, and my law school Advisor had noted. The friendships made during these study sessions continued after graduation from law school. Indeed, in an example of the *beshert* principle at work: *that which was meant to be came to pass*, I ran into one of my study buddies years later. He had moved to California, as Anneliese and I had done. As a youngster on North Brother Island, Andrew would overhear our group studies, now, many years later, as a graduate of UCLA—where he had earned a B.S. in Engineering and a J.D. Law Degree, and where he had also been Cadet Captain of the Air Force R.O.T.C, and President of his fraternity chapter, and having become a member of the California State Bar, Andy was looking to get started in the practice of law. For the bulk of my professional life—consistent with my proclivity to run mostly on solo pilot—and for the further reason that I wanted Andy to develop his own style of lawyering, free of any restraints, express or implied, I might impose upon him were he a junior in my firm,—I was looking about for a legal venue which would give him the unfettered opportunity to exploit, to the fullest, his warm, outward going personality, and his considerable intellectual attainments. My NYU Law School buddy and I met by chance at some Bar function. He was a senior partner in a small, but rapidly growing firm. I introduced

Andy to him. They hit it off immediately! Andy was hired. So began Andy's illustrious career which sees him today as a Senior Partner in an international law firm, one of the top 25 law firms in California and which has recently celebrated its one hundred years' birthday!

By design I have not mentioned the name of my law school buddy who gave Andy his start in the practice of law. Where persons are named herein (other than persons deceased and family members) the names I have given them are a figment of my fevered imagination. As I write this narrative, many are still alive. (Perhaps, when this book is published, is well received, and I am rich and famous, those who recognize themselves might wish to be identified in a footnote in subsequent editions. Oh, Arthur, you are a wishful thinker!)

These study sessions on North Brother Island with my three law school buddies were among the pleasant experiences which contributed to my memory of the Island as being an idyllic place. I now recount further episodes which evoke pleasant memories of the two years Anneliese and I shared there, initially with Andy, and then with Heidi as an infant. These memories are, however, tinged with sadness, as Anneliese figures prominently in all of them, and her loss is magnified as they are recalled.

This recollection concerns Andy. It occurred a few months before Heidi was born (on April 12, 1950). North Brother Island was teeming with babies, toddlers, and very active two and three year olds! The post WWII generation was intent on making up for lost time in the field of family building. We had almost as many kids on the Island as cockroaches (what a scourge!). Anneliese told me this story. (If it wasn't for the Mommas regaling their husbands with what went on with their kids, while the men were away studying, the Poppas would miss all the fun of their kids' growing up!) When Andy was in the two to three year age group, Roy Rogers was the leading radio/TV cowboy star, and the idol of every kid who thought being a cowboy was the best thing ever! Anneliese was like the Mommas of every first born male child: Andy got most everything he wanted, subject, of course, to the limitations of a very limited income. At that time my basic income was the $47 dollars monthly disability compensation I received from the Veterans Administration with reference to my WWII injuries, and the GI Bill student payment Our monthly rent for our apartment on the Island was $46! Were it not for the aid from my folks we would have had difficulty living on such income—Anneliese's culinary and homemaking skills notwithstanding. But back to Andy. He was a kid aged two and a half, and not aware of such things as money, or the lack thereof. If he wanted some toy or plaything, having seen another kid with whatever it was, he would point, say "please" and pout if his wish was not promptly fulfilled, which, frequently, it was not. But fortunately he had my Mother. On her frequent visits to the Island she watched Andy play, and saw what he liked, but didn't have. Even someone as disciplined in self sacrifice as my Mom was, could not resist the blandishments of a cute, smart, first born male grandchild. Anneliese related to me that Mom would then give Anneliese *"a pur groschen"*, Yiddish for a few dollars, to get *Avrumele* what he wanted.

Andy had fallen in love with Roy Rogers, actually, *in being* Roy Rogers. Thus, he was happiest when Anneliese dressed him up as Roy Rogers: cowboy shirt, bandana about his neck, jeans, 10 gallon hat and pistol belt with two holsters, in each of which was a "six shooter" which fired paper cap "cartridges". I believe Anneliese would have bought Andy spurs if they sold them! The crux of this Andy/Roy Rogers story is this: One morning, a young woman, about Anneliese's age, approached her. Anneliese recognized her as being one of the mothers of one of the myriad of children running around. This was the first time this woman had spoken to Anneliese. Smiling warmly, she said to Anneliese, "You have a very intelligent, good looking son, Mrs. Rogers", and the woman pointed to Andy, dressed as Roy Rogers, and milling about with the other kids. Anneliese told me she was confused at being addressed as Mrs. Rogers. She said to the woman, "My name is

Mrs. Katz". The woman, now as confused as Anneliese asked, "Isn't that child your son?" Anneliese readily acknowledged that he was, whereupon the woman laughed and said, "When I asked your son yesterday what his name was, he replied, "Roy Rogers!" so I presumed his family name was Rogers." For a brief period, a little boy's idea of who he *believed* he was had prevailed over reality. Of such fantasies are dreams made of—and why not?

Several other North Brother Island recollections spring from its rich, verdant soils. To assist its married families in coping with economic realities the Island's administration allotted small pots of land, to those who wanted them, to be tilled and turned into vegetable gardens. Anneliese immediately snapped up one of them. She and I laboriously turned the hard grassy turf and worked the soil free of weeds and stones and dug deeply enough to accommodate our expected root vegetables, such as carrots and radishes, and tomatoes with their long burrowing roots. In addition to the foregoing we planted onions, peppers, green beans, and lettuce. The soil, having lain dormant for so long, was extremely fertile. Our harvests, as they came due, were bountiful. Two memories concerning our little fertile garden come to the fore, one pleasant, the other, an example of how even in an idyllic place negative events can happen. I dispose quickly of the negative event. There is that saying that what goes around, comes around. Thus, in November 1942, when I gave up my student deferment and enlisted in the Army, I expected all my lefty friends—Commies some of them—would enlist with me, as they had promised, so that we, as students, could show support for an early opening by the Allies of a western front in an effort to save Mother Russia from facing Hitler all alone. I showed up at the induction center and enlisted, none of them did. They were long on talk but short on action. Well, on the Island, we had our share of left wingers. I caught a couple of guys pulling up some of our radishes and carrots. "Hey!", I shouted, "That's my garden!" These guys had planted nothing. One of them, I believe he was a political science student, says to me, real smart ass, "Haven't you heard of the social principle, "From each according to his ability, to each according to his need?" And then he added, "We didn't get around to growing anything, and you really have a lot of stuff." Well, Anneliese and I did have a "lot of stuff", but we had worked for it. With some effort I kept my cool and told the guy, waving the flag a bit, that what might work in Communist Russia didn't work in the USA. I then quoted him an old Chinese laundry proverb: "No tickee, no washee". He and his buddy, glared at me and walked off, but still holding the radishes and carrots they had pilfered from our garden.

A pleasant memory concerning our North Brother Island gardening concerned an engaging, newly married couple, so new, that if the wife, were pregnant, it did not show. Yes, Virginia, consistent with your name, there was a time that young couples waited to marry before having children. Both were native New Yorkers, and Jewish. This meant they were very sophisticated concerning many things, and very naive on others, gardening being one of the things where they were totally clueless. For that reason, they had not planted a garden. And so they admired ours. Anneliese's maiden name is Baur, which, in German can mean either farmer or builder. She grew up with maternal grandparents who had a small farm, and with relatives, living close by, each of whom had large fruit, nut and vegetable gardens. Anneliese knew how to make Mother Earth yield her bounty of fruits, vegetables, berries, nuts and flowers. I was not far behind. As a Boy Scout I collected perennial flower seeds and tree seeds, as from maples and ash, and the acorns of various oak varieties, and I planted them in the backyards of my grandparents, and they sprouted and, as far as I know, they can still be growing to this day. Our young couple came by our garden one Sunday afternoon as we were harvesting some of our crop. Anneliese had just pulled up a row of radishes, the small, red and white globe-like ones. She shook the loose moist earth off their long tap roots, fastened them together in bunches by tying a rubber band around the radishes where the radishes' leaves and its edible portion were joined. She then laid these neatly tied bunches of radishes in a row at the foot of our garden, waiting for me to pick them up, together with some earlier picked cherry tomatoes. Both of our newly married friends marveled at the bounty lying at their feet. The husband, pointing to the rubber band tied radish bunches, said, "I've seen radishes tied that way in the market, but I didn't know they grew that way!" Anneliese and I were amused by his naivety. Our joint first impression was to tell him, "yes", that's how they grew. But we relented and told them that the rubber band ties were the result of Anneliese's efforts. A great recollection!

Anneliese recounted to me a "woman to woman" conversation she had with the newly married wife. Let's call her Edith. Edith told Anneliese that she had been raised in an orthodox Jewish family, and such sex knowledge as she possessed was rudimentary. So much so, that when she saw her husband's erection for the first time she thought his penis had a bone in it which kept it rigid!

Anneliese and I were virgins when first we made love. Had the Army's ban on fraternization with Germans not barred our marriage in Germany, we would have begun to learn there, in wedlock, the glorious power and beauty of Love. This right of wedlock was denied us in Germany. But from the moment I saw Anneliese I was married to her, in spirit, if not in law and Anneliese, once assured my love was true, was equally married to me, in spirit, if not in law. Thus, the two marriage ceremonies we celebrated in Brooklyn, in February 1947, one a civil ceremony, one religious, were merely formal acknowledgments of the marriage of two bodies and souls which my belóved Anneliese and I had already consummated in the latter part of June 1945 in Heidenheim an der Brenz, Germany. And each time we walked, hand in hand, along the paths of North Brother Island, the salty scented breeze off Long Island Sound enveloping us, we were again, young lovers walking the meadows and woods of Heidenheim. Ah! Such sweet memories!

North Brother Island, when Anneliese and I first saw it, was a small sylvan setting perched, perhaps no more then three meters above flood stage—where the East River, which separates Manhattan Island, on its eastern flank, from the Boroughs of Brooklyn and Queens—merges with the western end of Long Island Sound. Accessible only by ferry at the foot of 138th St. in The Bronx, the Island was unknown to me, a native New Yorker, when married Students' housing on it was offered to us. Over a span of two years the Island was not only a home for our young family, it was also a retreat. The ferry ride was brief, and always exhilarating, the breezes cool, sea gulls wheeling overhead, and the sound of the water sloshing against the sides of the ferry made the home bound trip especially relaxing. Once on the Island the mighty Metropolis of New York ceased to exist. We were two miles, or less, off shore, and a million light years away. Tired as I was from a heavy day of schooling, and a long subway ride, *eo instanti* I set foot on the Island my life was transformed. When household/child care chores permitted, Anneliese was there to greet me as the ferry slid into its slip. Hands entwined, we would walk back to our apartment, two lovers locked into their private world. Our steps would rekindle sweet memories of the walks Anneliese and I took, hands similarly clasped, in the Summer of 1945, through the fields and dales of Heidenheim. And if Anneliese could not be there to greet me, my heart would leap when I opened our apartment door—and there she was—my radiant, beautiful, Anneliese! Could any man ask any more of life?

Weekends and holidays were especially wonderful, idyllic times. Anneliese and I then had so much more time to spend together—and I had a chance to play with Andy, and when Heidi joined our family, to watch Anneliese nurse her. Of course, I had concerns during this idyllic period: passing school exams, preparing for the State Bar exams, working part time as a toll collector at the Island's ferry slip, doing odd gardening jobs for one of my professors, and writing two law review articles, of which more below. But at the end of each day, I was home, safe and sound, basking in the recuperative powers of Anneliese's love. Some nights, I would wake, reach out and touch her sleeping form to reassure myself that she—the cornerstone of my life—was still at my side. Reassured, I would snuggle up against her, envelop her in my arms, and fall, peacefully to sleep.

At least once a month, Anneliese and I would leave the solitude of our Island to visit my parents, Zaydeh and Babba Katz, Grandma Glicenstein, and other family members in East New York, Brooklyn. The visit was made on a weekend when the subway was not as crowded as it would be during a work day. But it was a long trip: the ferry to The Bronx mainland, the subway ride from there through Manhattan, through Brooklyn, to the last stop of the IRT at New Lots Avenue. This was the same trip my sainted Mother would frequently make, bringing us sustenance in a shopping bag. Once back in Brooklyn, *Kol hamishpacha*, all the family, would ooh and aah at Andy, at how "grown up" he was, how "gorgeous" our newborn Heidi was, and "Anneliese, you are so beautiful and relaxed, how do you do it?" Anneliese would smile, and say nothing. I had always gotten the same response when I posed that question. So I ceased to ask, but I never ceased to ponder. God has blessed her with a special grace. I have never possessed it. But I have been the beneficiary of her's.

O meine geliebte Anneliese, mein Engel, du bist schwer vermisst!

Episode Forty Eight

In which I write an international constitutional law article, and a prize winning paper on international copyright and moral rights law, and both are published.

Writing has always been a vital part of my being. Army regulations against maintaining a diary, which I, an enlisted man, obeyed meticulously—and which no General did—kept me, for a three years' period, from recording on paper my views and feelings during a crucial portion of my life. My psyche compensated for this prohibition by recording, within the deepest interstices of my brain, the memory of those happenings which it felt should be preserved for future reference. Hence, this book, or a good part thereof.

I was the first person in my family circle to become a lawyer. In fact, my brother Harold, my cousin Marty from the Katz side, and I were the only first generation children who went to college and beyond. My blesséd Mother, oldest of seven, went to work at 14 after finishing grade school. It was only well after she married, had my brother and me, that, at the depths of the Depression she became a beautician, opened a beauty parlor in our home and helped my Dad feed our family. My Dad was in the parquet flooring business, and when new home construction took a dive, along with the stock market, that business was gone. My Mother was an avid reader, writer and amateur painter. She later got her high school equivalency diploma, and at age 40 learned to drive. She passed away, a few months shy of her one hundred and first birthday, as alert as ever. She said, "I'm tired, time to go home." And she did. What a woman! I have been doubly blessed with having the love and support of two women of valor: my Mom and my Anneliese! My Mom passed away on April 26, 2002, just a month after I had lost Anneliese. Within thirty days I lost the two underpinnings of my life!

Clearly, I was embedded within a warm family circle. But the reality was that I would be graduating from Law School with no relative having any legal profession nexus which might help lead me to a job after graduation. I would have to do it on my own. Writing for my high school yearbook had given me some fleeting fame, and the opportunity to enter Brooklyn College. So I turned to writing as the open sesame to employment after graduation from Law School. Good idea, Art! I determined to write at least two articles to demonstrate my ability to do complex research in fields of law not fully tilled, and to write, with literary flair, carefully constructed scholarly conclusions based on this research. Such articles would show prospective employers that I had mastered the research, analytical, and writing skills which would make me a good lawyer. Writing two articles, back to back, and in different areas of the law, would further indicate that I was capable of turning out a volume of excellent work in short order. Those were the goals I felt my articles would have to attain were they to be useful as door openers to employment. Now, in what fields of law should I work? Two fields were of particular interest to me: copyright and constitutional law. Two singular events occurred which enabled me to write, within one year, an article in each of these fields. And it came about in this wise:

In May 1948 the United Nations voted to terminate the British Mandate over Middle Eastern lands falling loosely under the rubric of Palestine, and to divide the territory between the indigenous Arabs and Jews. 2,000 years after the Romans had destroyed their Temple in Jerusalem, the Jews once again, had their own State of Israel and as a condition precedent to achieving statehood, the Jewish leaders covenanted to create a State which would grant equal religious and political rights to all its inhabitants. Consistent with this pledge the fledgling State of Israel created a draft constitution. Hey!, I thought, it would be interesting to see how Israel treated the issue of religious freedom in its proposed constitution in light of the horrendous mistreatment the Jews had received from their Christian and Muslim neighbors over the centuries—and how that proposed treatment compared to provisions on religious freedom in the constitutions of other countries. I set to work, and after many months of after hours research at NYU and at Columbia University's law library, I completed a work I entitled: *Provisions on Religious Freedom in the Draft Israeli Constitution—A Comparative Study.*

I thought the article was a good one. It said what I wanted to say, and in the manner I wanted to say it. That is the way I have measured all of my legal writings which have seen the light of day, whether these be law review articles, trial briefs or appellate arguments. Now to get my article published., and here I ran into a stonewall. The Law Quarterly refused to publish the work. Nothing to do with the quality of the writing, or its scholarship. Simply a matter of custom. The Law Quarterly had never published a law review level article written by an undergraduate. And tradition being what it is in an institution founded in 1835, the Law Review Board was not about to do so in my case. Not one to give up, and recalling the efforts I went through to get the clearances in Germany for Anneliese to come to America, and determined to demonstrate my skills as an advocate, I met with various Board members, and hammered out an arrangement whereby the Law Quarterly would publish my article *provided* I got a faculty member to read the article, and vouch for its scholarship by agreeing to put his name on the article as a co-author with me. Fair enough, I thought. Half a loaf is better than none—one of the many aphorisms my Mother taught me. So off I went to my constitutional law professor, feeling his area of expertise would make him admirably suited to review my article, see its merit and be happy to list himself as its co-author with me. And here, unexpectedly, I ran into an example of academic politics at play. My professor said he liked the article, would be happy to put his name on it, but solely as its author! I would be referred to in the first footnote as the undergraduate student whose efforts had assisted the professor in writing the article! He was stealing my intellectual work product, putting his name on it as its *sole*

author and relegating me to the rôle of a student who did some
pick and shovel work for him!

What a shock to me! I was learning again—as I had when
my college buddies failed, as promised, to enlist with me, and as
I had when, in England, my earned promotion was given to one
who did not deserve it, with related consequences—that life is
replete with negative surprises, that even in the exalted fields of
academe, a learned individual, a professor, ostensibly a person of
integrity, would not hesitate to aggrandize himself at the expense
of his student! How gross! Naturally, I rejected my professor's
dishonorable proposal. Instead, I turned to the professor who had
taught me real property law, and whose lawns I had mowed, and
whose hedges I had trimmed for pocket money (all of which was
turned over to Anneliese for household needs). I had established
intellectual rapport with him. He was a mid-westerner, but had
adjusted himself nicely to living in a "cosmopolitan society".
He read my article, liked it, suggested one or two phraseology
changes, and said he would consider it an honor to be listed with
me as co-author of the work. I was elated! And so my first law
review article was published in the October 1949 issue of the
New York University Law Quarterly. I had created the first of
two law articles as an undergraduate law student which I hoped
would be my door openers, my Open Sesame to employment
after graduation.

My second article was not written for publication in a law
review. It was written as an entry in a nationwide law schools
competition in which students were invited to write articles on
issues affecting copyright. The competition was sponsored by
the American Society of Composers, Authors and Publishers,
better known by its acronym ASCAP. ASCAP is a not for profit
organization founded in the early 1900's by a lawyer named
Nathan Burkan. The Society was created to monitor all entities
publishing, selling or performing copyrighted materials to insure
that the creators of such materials received appropriate royalties,
through the term of their copyrights, by setting up a worldwide

system to license and monitor the uses of such materials, and to collect appropriate user fees which were then distributed to the copyright owners who were ASCAP members. Attorney Burkan had a wonderful idea, and it has been realized in a remarkable manner for a century. Its royalty collection and distribution abilities have contributed mightily to the economic welfare of those whose gifts as creative artists in the fields of music, literature and drama have entertained, enlightened, and ennobled the world.

I chose to write on an issue which was, in American law, the "flip side" of copyright. In my younger days, when recordings were double sided, and, depending upon the turntable speed at which they played, were called 45s, 78s, or 33⅓s (a galaxy distant from the CDs and DVDs we now have), the two sides were designated A and B. The A side bore the composition the record company thought would be the "hit" side, and the B side, the flip side, would tag along as a filler. Sometimes the B side would sneak in and become a bigger hit than the A side. I was proposing to write an article which, if I were successful in my advocacy, would turn a B side concept in American intellectual property law—of which copyright was a major component—into an A side. Further, if I won the competition at NYU I would win a cash prize of $150, a sizeable sum at that time, and I might also have the chance to have my article reproduced, with that of selected winners, in a volume to be published by ASCAP and distributed nationally. Such an article could be another door opener for post graduation employment. I wrote an article entitled, "The Doctrine of Moral Right and American Copyright Law—A Proposal". I must have worked on the article for more than six months with all the research and writing being done after school hours. This meant I would often be coming home to North Brother Island late at night. But Anneliese was always there at the ferry slip to meet me, the kids being safely in bed. I would have called her earlier from the NYU or Columbia Law Libraries, that I was on my way. Fatigued as I was, physically and mentally, I was instantly revived *eo instanti* I saw my belóved's smiling face and graceful figure. And she had dinner ready for me. What was intended to be cold was cold; what was intended to be hot, was hot. How she managed to time everything so perfectly I never learned. I asked her once. Her reply was cryptic, "You have to know what you are doing." I never asked her again. Clearly, she knew what she was doing, however she did it.

I won the competition at NYU, and received the $150 prize. Hey!, I was making money in the Law, and I wasn't yet a lawyer! My article was also selected as one of the five best papers submitted throughout the country, and, as a consequence, published by ASCAP in a volume entitled Fourth Copyright Law Symposium. I thought the article was a good example of legal scholarship. It showed my ability to do historical research in English, American and foreign law, to translate German, French, Spanish and Latin materials into English, and to fashion viable arguments in support of my position. That position, simply put, was that the creator of an intellectual work, whatever the medium of expression, had a right of personality in it which existed separated from the creator's copyright in the work, and that this right of personality, in French, *Le droit moral*, this moral right, gave the creator the right, as a matter of law—even after the creator no longer owned the copyright—to protect the artistic integrity of the work, *e.g.*, by preventing its contents or appearance from being so altered as would result in a misrepresentation of the creator's intent in creating the work. My article contained 250 footnotes setting forth my sources, was 52 pages in length when published in the Southern California Law Review (of which more below), and 77 pages in the ASCAP book format. The article was lengthy, but in my opinion, not prolix.

Episode Forty Nine

In which I seek to become a law instructor at NYU, but am unsuccessful for non-academic reasons, and I pass the New York State Bar Examination.

Once I had learned how to write, *i.e.*, to answer law school examinations, my first month's debacle was never repeated. My self confidence, again at its usual ebullient level, I found exploring ever new avenues of the Law to be intellectually exciting, how our American jurisprudence was heavily indebted to the English common law of our forebears, and how our legal system, and that of Great Britain, differed from that of countries such as Germany, France and Spain. Throughout my half century plus as a lawyer I have never lost that sense of excitement which comes with discovering something new in fields once thought to have been thoroughly plowed. The Law is not perfect, but what human institution is? Those not versed in the Law may often find its operations odd, if not stupid. Such was the sentiment of Mr. Bumble in Charles Dickens' Oliver Twist, when he said, "If the law supposes that . . . the law is a ass—a idiot". New York University's School of Law, since its founding in 1835, rightly prides itself on teachings its students to understand, the deep underpinnings of the Law. Once the cardinal principles upon which the Law is bedded are fully understood, only then can a law student learn to appreciate how the Law exercises its majesty and how, rather than ossifying in a world always in flux, it adapts itself to new conditions, economic, social and political, yet all the while remaining true to its bedrock fundamentals. How many law schools today teach the history of, and the difference between, substantive and procedural law, and their necessary interrelationship? And if they do, is the text they use the 1909 seminal work of F. W. Maitland, *The Forms of Action At Common Law*? I still have my much handled paperback copy, replete with my underlinings and marginal notes. My copy notes it was specially reprinted in 1947 for the Law School. I received a fine legal education at NYU. I am grateful for that, and for the wisdom of the United States Government in creating the GI Bill which gave me, and countless other returning veterans of World War II, the opportunity to further advance the general welfare of our country in peace time by affording us the means to make further contributions to our beloved Country. Love, in all of its ramifications, is the subject of this portion of my story, so, dear reader, having come this far, let's explore this concept together.

Anneliese has been the cornerstone of my being, her courage, grace and beauty have enthralled me and shaped me for the better. "I am my beloved's, and my beloved is mine", אני לדודי ודודי לי The Song of Songs 6:3. Anneliese was, and remains, the Love of my life. But she knew I had another love. She knew, yet it troubled her not. She knew I was in love with the Law. She saw me come home, all too frequently, from a long day in court and office, stay up until 2 a.m., preparing for the next day's tasks, leaving at 7 a.m. for the office and then to court, to begin the cycle again. Anneliese readily perceived that I loved the Law. She knew she shared me with the Law, and that the Law was a jealous mistress, always demanding more. Yet so secure was she in the certainty of my love that the inordinate time I spent with my mistress caused her no concern for her own well being. True to her selflessness, her concern was solely for me. Only once did she raise the issue of the time I was spending with my jealous mistress—missing out on seeing our children grow up, just being home and spending joyful, golden, idle hours with her. After one particularly grueling week, in a federal court matter where I, a sole practitioner, was up against a top line law firm with a deep bench of lawyers and para-legals, Anneliese saw the physical toll the matter was taking on me, and she asked, in her quiet way, "Dad, how long will you keep this up?" No recriminations, just a simple question. "Until it stops being fun." My answer was glib. It was an answer, I'm sure, that Anneliese was not wanting to hear. "Fun" for me then, was the satisfaction of winning substantially more often than losing, of making good law while making good money. Many decades later, when it ceased being fun (the loss of family time becoming a greater factor than winning cases, making law and money), I climbed down from my merry-go-round's shining steed, and jumped off. Catching the brass ring was no longer a prize worth the effort. However, I still remain a Member of The State Bar of California, Member No. 23624, and I do Counsel work in Intellectual Property Matters.

I've gotten ahead of myself again. So I go back to what will be laying the foundation for my professional future. Follow me back to the simple classrooms of what was then New York University's School of Law circa 1948-1950, before a new building was specially erected for the School. As memory serves, the School shared a drab, brick, multi-storied structure with the School of Accounting, or the Business School, or perhaps, with both. The only thing that suggested we law students might be better than the other groups was that we were housed above them!

After my shaky first month, the rest of my law school career was upward and onward towards the stars. I was a good student, but I never made Law Review. In common with other law schools of stature, NYU maintained a Law Review, a scholarly magazine, which appeared quarterly, and published articles on various aspects of the law written by law professors, and by others prominent in their areas of expertise. The Law Review also carried shorter pieces, or Notes, written by students. The School's top academic students were invited to join the Editorial Board of the Review, and the Numero Uno academic student in the School would be named its Editor-in Chief. Being a Law Review Editor, or on its Board, gave one a boost up to getting a good job once one graduated and passed the State Bar Examination. As noted, after my sloppy first month, I did well in school, but I never made "making Law Review" a goal. I was a family man, married to a beautiful woman, with two wonderful kids! I wasn't about to put in that extra effort—at the expense of having more time at home—which would raise me to Law Review status. No thanks! However, I did have intellectual ideas I wanted to pursue, but on my own schedule. If being a member of Law Review was a calling card for finding a good job after graduation and admission to the Bar, why not, Art Katz, write some scholarly articles, within your own time frame, get them known, and hopefully, published, and use these articles as your calling card.? Why not, indeed? And that's what I did. As Frank Sinatra sang, "I did it my way."

But before I go on to delineate what I did to turn my love of writing into a medium to help me establish and maintain a mentor-less nascent career as a lawyer, let me tell you about law school politics and unrequited love. These two facially unrelated concepts have created an ambivalence in my feelings for my law school which exists to this day. As I have made clear, I love NYU School of Law for the fine legal education it afforded me (with the considerable help of Uncle Sam's GI Bill). Sadly, this love has not been returned. Politics got in the way. I do not use the term "politics" in the lofty sense as defined by Aristotle in his *Nichomachean Ethics* as being the master art which aims at attaining the highest common good. I employ it in its much degraded sense, as exemplified by the phrase" playing politics". Getting things done, or undone, through intrigue, nefarious design, or the exercise of bias is what "playing politics" is all about. I was not a stranger to the game of "playing politics" when I encountered it at the Law School. I had already learned, in the U.S. Cavalry in the Spring of 1944, in England, that military organizations are as astute as civilian bodies in the black art of "playing politics". As my schooling progressed I began to toy with the idea of becoming a teacher of law, in lieu of becoming a lawyer in the business world, or in the government. By the middle of my Senior Year (the Third Year in Law School), I had already written two law articles, one concerning international constitutional law, the other international intellectual property law, with the latter wining a competition at NYU and later, national honors. I felt these two articles demonstrated my ability to do extensive legal research in several languages, and to be an effective advocate of my views in "first impression matters", the latter phrase referring to areas of law in flux. Staying on at the Law School as a an Instructor after graduating, passing the State Bar Examination and being admitted to practice Law in New York State was, to my mind, a great way to start my career in the Law. I could see myself in time earning tenure as a full professor. What a wonderful, scholarly way to make a living in the Law without the hassle of seeking, obtaining and maintaining clients in the outside world! And so I approached several professors who had taken my measure, and I told them of my desire to remain on at NYU as a law instructor in lieu of seeking employment after graduation in the world outside the halls of academia. Each professor told me I had the intellectual skills and requisite love of the law to make a great law teacher. I was also happily informed that a position was opening—the Law School was expanding its faculty—and an additional instructor for first year students was being added to the faculty. What luck!

After comparing with Anneliese the career opportunities which academic life might afford me with those private practice or government service might provide, Anneliese observed that I should do whatever would make me happiest, adding that she was certain I would be successful at whatever course I chose. She voiced, as she had many times before, that she had no qualms about me making a living for her and the children. Emboldened by her unequivocal support for which ever choice I made (such support was the only kind she ever gave me, I wish now she had taken me more to task when I proposed doing something different), I sought and obtained an appointment with the Dean of the Law School. I had heard him speak at various assemblies, but I had never had any one on one sessions with him. The Dean already knew the purpose of our meeting. He began our meeting, which was a brief one, by stating that I was well qualified for the new Instructor's position I was seeking. Everything went downhill from that juncture. He stated that NYU School of Law was a venerable institution which, for more than a century, had turned out lawyers who had distinguished themselves in academia, business and government, and that the Law School enjoyed a reputation of being one of the finest in the country, indeed, in the world. The self laudatory accolades attended to, the Dean leaned towards me and observed that within the last decade the School had become "Quite cosmopolitan, perhaps, overly so." Hence, he, and the Board of Trustees, felt that any new staff should reflect a broader national image of the School. As a consequence, the new instructor would be coming from North Dakota, which, by coincidence, happened to be the Dean's home state! I immediately recognized that this new appointment had nothing to do with my academic stature. It had everything to do with my being a New York Jew. If one would look at the Law Review roster in the October 1949 issue of the *New York University Law Quarterly*, at page 845 (Volume XXIV, No, 4), the issue in which one of my law articles appears, one will quickly recognize that the bulk of the Review's Staff bear names with a decidedly Jewish cast. "Cosmopolitan" was the code word for "Too many Jews". The School had "played politics" with my request for employment, and in that kind of a game I was a sure loser—struck out before I ever got to bat!

Now, how does one cope with a situation such as I had experienced? I saw three alternatives. One, I could forget it. I wouldn't do that. I wouldn't let this act of prejudice to my People and to me fade into oblivion. I would remember. Two, I could get angry. I wouldn't do that. Righteous anger can sometimes be a cathartic for the spirit. But I neither wanted, nor needed any of that. Instead, I chose alternative three. I remembered that old phrase: "Don't get mad, get even!" And that's what I have been doing to NYU School of Law since my graduation in June 1948. I am very proud of being a graduate of the Law School. Nevertheless, despite annual fund raising appeals I have never given the Law School one cent in cash or kind. When the School's fund raisers call I tell them why. I haven't forgotten. I haven't gotten mad. I've just gotten even! And yet, out of this negative event, a positive one soon appeared. It was *beschert*, it was meant to be, as the reader shall soon learn.

While all this was happening I was studying for the New York State Bar Examination, and then took it. I had taken many exams. Yet this one was different. It would shape my life. I felt prepared for it. Still, it was a nervous time—but I had been in tighter places as a GI. Then there is a second nervous period: waiting for the results. I passed! Anneliese and I were ecstatic! We were on our way. Where? We didn't know. But we were sure something good would soon turn up. The year was Nineteen Fifty. Eight years had passed since I had enlisted in the Cavalry, and five years since that wonderful day in June 1945 in Heidenheim, Germany, when Providence led me to my beautiful, belóved Anneliese. With Anneliese there to keep my backbone straight, and my head up, things would work out—and they did.

Episode Fifty

In which it is *beshert* that I get my first job as a lawyer in California, where Anneliese, Andy and Heidi join me in December 1950, and where, with Anneliese's love, courage and guidance our family grows and prospers.

At the time I graduated from Law School I had not yet begun to look for employment in a serious way. I was a tad tired from writing the two articles I have noted, from preparing for final exams, and taking bar review courses to prepare for the New York State Bar Examination. Anneliese saw how beat I was and suggested I try to catch up on my sleep, and spend some more time with her and the kids. When I pointed out that when I was formally through with school we'd soon have to move from North Brother Island, she reminded me that the the two of us had come through a lot of trying times, and that what we were facing now was a lot better than what both of us had experienced in Germany. And then she said to me in German, a language she now used infrequently, unless she wished to emphasize a personal point, *"Dad, ich bin nicht ängstlich, du bist mein Mann, was soll ich fürchten?"* "Dad, I'm not uneasy, you are my husband, what should I fear?" Oh God! Her *Mut*, her courage, restored mine! *O Anneliese du warst wirklich den Eckstein meines Lebens!* Oh, Anneliese you were truly the cornerstone of my life! Emboldened by her words, warmed by her love, and spending a little more time with Andy and Heidi, soon put me back on track, comfortable with myself and my future possibilities. One of these was right in the city. ASCAP was administered by lawyers, and its headquarters were in Manhattan. After I won the competition at NYU and learned I was one of the top five winners nationally, I went to ASCAP to see about a job. The top lawyer there, the man who could hire me, told me he was very impressed with me. In fact, so much so, that although they had only hired graduates from

Yale and Harvard Law Schools, (he was a Yale man himself), he was prepared to give me a job! Wow! What was the starting salary? Forty Five Dollars a week! We were then living off of $46 a month from my GI Disability and GI Bill compensation, plus money made doing odd jobs, and food help and gifts to the children (mostly in cash) from my folks. But Anneliese and I had made it because we were living on North Brother Island. Rent for an apartment in a decent neighborhood in Brooklyn would make living on $45 a week a close call. I discussed the offer with Anneliese. The fact that an offer was made was a sign that I was "marketable". We both agreed I could do better money wise once I really started looking. So I said thanks to ASCAP, but no thanks. But before I could start worrying whether I had made a mistake I got a phone call from my Dad. It was one which would lead to a momentous change for the better for the welfare of my young family. The story I am about to relate has its humorous aspects, but its conclusion is yet another demonstration that my finding Anneliese, and the unfolding of our lives together was *beshert*, and that what would now transpire would be another example of divine providence at work.

At the time I was in Law School my Dad was in the process of keeping up with changing times by adapting his business from the sale of coal for domestic and industrial heating, to the sale and installation of oil burners and fuel oil. Heating by oil was cleaner than burning coal. The latter fuel had to be delivered in bulk, down chutes into large cellar areas reserved for it. It was a dusty, space consuming product. Fuel oil was delivered cleanly, pumped through a hose from the oil delivery truck into a compact oil storage tank which took substantially less space than did coal, and was a much cleaner, and less laborious way of supplying heating to a building than coal. Some coal burning facilities could be modified to burn oil. My Dad would do these modifications, install the oil burner and then sell and deliver the oil through his fleet of trucks. Where modifications were not possible, my Dad would design and install an oil burning unit.

In the course of his business, and as a self taught engineer he invented, and patented, several pieces of technical equipment, including an oil burner. But he never had enough financing to exploit these inventions effectively. In this regard his experiences with partners was very poor. My desire to practice law as a sole practitioner was probably shaped by his experiences. The one time I became a member of a law partnership (for a short period) turned out badly for me. I found myself doing the work, while the other partners took off for long weekends, ski trips or camping expeditions, depending upon the season. Since I was doing most of the work, and bringing in a goodly number of clients, I thought it best to return to a solo practice—which I maintained throughout my active legal career, except for those early years when I was counsel at various motion picture studios and at a major television station.

As I have noted, my Father, age 12, came to this country in the first decade of the 20th century, speaking no English. He was placed in an English only class, sink or swim was the approach then, and one I agree with. He swam and completed grade school. He never went to high school. My Father's engineering skills exceeded those in English. Yet this did not prevent him from becoming a very successful salesman. He was a handsome, carefully groomed, clean shaven man, with a muscular build. He carried himself well, so that he appeared taller than his 5'6" in height. He related well with women, many of whom were among his clientele. Because of the sections in the City where he had developed his business, many were Jewish or Italian.

The telephone call my Dad made to me, and which ultimately raised employment possibilities resulted from a business visit he made to one of his Jewish lady customers to discuss converting her house from coal to oil heating. My Dad had been using a form contract bought at a stationer's, to sign up his customers. I had seen the contract. I thought it was a terrible selling tool. It was long, by several pages, and filled with what we lawyers call "boilerplate language": clauses, indeed, whole paragraphs, written in an obtuse manner, and designed to protect the vendor from just about any liability imaginable. Definitely a one sided legal document. My Dad acknowledged that some prospects declined to sign it, hence no deal. I told my Dad I would write him one which would be even handed, protecting his interests, while according the customer properly conditioned warranties which my Dad said he could live with. I drew up such a contract. It was a one page, double sided contract, in two colors, white for my Dad, the carbon copy, in yellow for the customer. At the time I drafted the contract I believe I had just graduated, or was about to, and had taken the New York State Bar Examination, and was anxiously awaiting word whether I had passed. My Dad liked the contract. On reading it through he said, "Very nice, Arthur." As I have also noted, perhaps on more than one occasion, my Father was not an effusive, openly affectionate man when it came to expressing love or appreciation to my brother, Harold, or to me.

The contract I had drafted for my Dad came into play when he visited this elderly Jewish lady. Before dealing with my Father, she had bought her coal from his Father, my Zaydeh. So they had a long business relationship. She liked, and trusted my Dad, but what did she know about oil burners? What was she buying? What would it cost her every month? What would my Father do if something didn't work? Legitimate questions. *"Di hust nichts zu sorgen"*, "You have nothing to worry about", my Dad assured her in Yiddish. "Here, read this contract", proffering her the contract I had just drafted. *"Alles wus du fraygst steht darin geschriben"* "Everything you ask is in this contract." He further assured her, "It's a fair contract. My son, the lawyer, drafted it." I had not yet learned whether I had passed the Bar, but that did not prevent my Dad from assuming a fact not in evidence. The elderly Jewish lady was not persuaded. "What do I know from contracts? Your son, the lawyer wrote the contract. *Git* Good. But I have a son who is also a lawyer." Touché. "When he gets here from California, I'll have him look at the contract. Then we'll see." Having her lawyer son look at the contract didn't faze my Dad. "So, when your lawyer son comes in, please call me, and I'll come right over to discuss everything with him. Is that OK? It was.

About a week later my Dad is back at the lady's house. Her son, the lawyer from California, is there. Ever the salesman, my Dad chats most engagingly with him. He told me later they got on fine. He described the California lawyer as being distinguished looking and in his forties. The lawyer reads the contract. He queries his mother on the costs of installation, and on the fuel prices. She says she understands them. The lawyer is very solicitous for his mother's well being. She is a widow, and none of her children live close by. How long has she been dealing with Mr. Katz he asks her. *"Oi, a lange zite"*, a long time. "Well", the California lawyer says to his mother, "If you are comfortable with Mr. Katz, sign the contract, it's a fair one." The deal is made. My Dad is pleased, of course. Ever the salesman he says to the California lawyer, "My son, the lawyer, wrote this contract for me. He just passed the Bar, (my Dad had learned that Bar phrase from me, what it meant to him was that I was a lawyer) and he is looking for a good job. Do you have a business card?"

I'm sure the California lawyer was not expecting to hear Mr. Louis Katz make a job pitch for his son. But, according to my Dad, he responded politely by asking what law school I had attended. Fortunately, my father remembered, and told him it was NYU. Then, according to my Dad the lawyer said, "Well, if your son is ever in California, let him give me a call. I'll be happy to talk to him." These were polite throw away lines. No offer of employment was made, or suggested. My Dad, the super salesman, believed that every lead can become a closed deal. He called me that evening. There was a pay phone in the hallway of our building on North Brother Island. If it rang long enough, someone would answer and then shout out the name of the person being called. Art Katz was paged and I went to the phone. With more emotion than I ordinarily heard in his conversations with me, my Dad related his meeting with this California lawyer, that he was returning to California in about a week, that my Dad had his business card, that the guy was a vice president of some big corporation in the oil business (actually the company did seismic exploration work for oil companies, and my Dad assumed the company had to be a big one for that reason), and that if I went to California my Dad was sure I'd get a job. My Dad was the eternal optimist, a trait, unrealistic though it be, that I inherited from him. As far as my Dad was concerned, this was a done deal. I copied down the information my Dad read me from the California lawyer's card and I promised to call the lawyer the following week.

During the week, plus, that I waited for the lawyer to return to California, I discussed with Anneliese, the realities the family might face were I to get a job in California, and were we to move to Los Angeles, where the lawyer's company was located. I would have to study for, take and pass the California Bar, and then we'd have to have the money to fly to California, find an apartment, furnish it, etc., etc. I remembered California faintly, but fondly for the most part, having spent the early part of 1943 with the 4th Cavalry in desert warfare training in its southern reaches. I recalled the one time I had been given a 12 hour pass and had visited Los Angeles and had appreciated its beauty, temperate climate and sunshine, and had mused that maybe I'd come back to live there. An idle thought. But after that phone call from my Dad the remote possibility of living in Los Angeles might yet become a reality. Whatever my employment prospects in California, they wouldn't be worse than those in New York City, with Los Angeles having the advantage of affording the Katz Family a climate more hospitable year 'round than that of New York City.

I called the telephone number my Dad had given me from the California lawyer's business card. It was about eight days after my Dad had met the lawyer. I assumed he was now back in California. He was. A receptionist answered my call. I asked to speak to the lawyer. She asked my name. After a long pause,—I presumed she was talking with the lawyer—I was connected to him. He was polite, but puzzled, why was I calling? I told him who I was, Arthur Stanley Katz, the son of Louis Katz of Armstrong

Engineering, the oil burner gentleman he had met some days back at his mother's house in Brooklyn. There was dead air at his end. I quickly added that he had given his business card to my Dad, that I had just graduated from NYU Law School and that he had told my Dad, on learning this fact, that if I were ever in Los Angeles to look him up, perhaps we could talk about some employment opportunities. The last part was my embellishment. His recollection refreshed, the lawyer (consistent with my style, I'm giving no names) asked me a few questions, my age, marital and family status and whether I was a member of any State Bar. I answered the last query in the affirmative and the others, as well, and added I was a combat wounded veteran (flag waving never hurts). There was a short spell of silence at his end as he digested my data. Well, he said, if you care to come out to California for an interview, and if everything worked out, there was a possibility of employment. No promises. No money offered to pay my airfare or my expenses in Los Angeles while being interviewed. Simply, if you come out, we'll see. I was elated! I sensed that if I showed up in his office, at my own expense (borrowed from my folks), and was my best, out going self at the interview, that I would be offered a job. I told him I was prepared to fly out and meet with him. He gave me his business address and told me to call with the date I was coming out to make sure it was a date he'd be in town. I thanked him for his courtesies, and hung up.

I raced to our apartment and related everything to Anneliese. Wow! A good chance of getting a job in Los Angeles! Anneliese was so pleased and happy for me. She knew that getting a job was preying on my mind. We hugged and kissed, and danced around our apartment, no music, just what was in our hearts! Anneliese had already crossed Europe and an ocean, and if I got the job, she would now be crossing a continent. My *Schwarzwald Mädel* would have moved, within three years, from the *Ursprung des Neckars*, deep in the southernmost part of Germany, half across the world to Los Angeles, California! Traveling such a distance didn't bother Anneliese one jot or tittle. My belóved Anneliese was everything a man would want in his wife and helpmate. She had beauty, wit, grace and above all, courage. *Mutig war sie!*

The next day I made my way to Times Square, in midtown Manhattan to find a newsstand which carried state maps. I found a map of California which showed a detailed portion of downtown Los Angeles. According to the address the lawyers's business office was located on the corner of Fifth and Grand, in a building I later learned was called the Pacific National Bldg. I than checked out the bus lines on the map, noted which of them ran close to Fifth and Grand, and plotted out a radius of ten miles from the building in which I proposed to search for an apartment. I wanted to be able to get to the office by public transit, but I didn't want Anneliese and the kids to be living too close to the business center. My folks offered to buy my round trip air ticket NYC/LA/NYC. I said no, I'd rather treat it as a loan. A week after my phone conversation with the California lawyer I was in his office. He spent about half an hour with me. The interview covered a broad area of interests in addition to the Law. Apparently satisfied with what he saw and heard, he walked with me to another part of the office complex where he introduced me to the President and owner of the business. I shook hands with the President, exchanged a few pleasantries with him and was asked to wait outside the President's office while the President and his counsel discussed the possibility of my employment. After a five minutes' wait—which seemed much longer to me, as my tension rose with each passing minute—the lawyer came out, smiled, and said, "You have a job as my assistant, if you want it." The starting salary would be $150 a week, and the job would start as soon as I moved my family to Los Angeles. Did I want the job? You betcha! $150 a week was *mucho mas mejor* than ASCAP's $45 a week.

I was on cloud nine as the plane flew me back to NYC. My career as a lawyer had begun! I hadn't been formally sworn in as a member of the State Bar of New York. That ceremony wouldn't take place until January 1951. I wanted to be sworn in before I moved to California, and I wanted to move to California as quickly as possible. Admission to the Bar was administered then by the Appellate Division of the New York Supreme Court. I visited with the Clerk of that Court, explained the situation to him and respectfully asked whether I could be sworn in as soon as possible so that I could move as promptly as possible to California to start earning a living for my wife and our two kids. The Court was very accommodating, and I was sworn in separately on 14 November 1950. On the 16th of November 1942 I enlisted in the Cavalry. On the 18th of November 1945 I was Honorably Discharged from the Service. Almost five years to the day I completed my military duties I was now a member of my first State Bar! *Mazal Tov Yihoshuah!* A week later I was back in California. We had cousins on my Mother's side living in Tujunga, a northern suburb of Los Angeles. I visited with them during Thanksgiving. A few days earlier I had found an apartment in a new development within walking distance to a bus line I had noted on the map I had bought in Times Square. I had to buy all the household furnishings, from beds, towels, linens, to pots and pans. Anneliese and the children would arrive only with the clothes they wore on the flight, and several suitcases filled with other items of wearing apparel, and personal memorabilia, such as our photographs and the love letters Anneliese and I had exchanged in 1945-1946. I went to the May Co. to do my shopping. I knew no other stores. I chose the May Co. because I recalled that Mary Livingston, on the Jack Benny Show "worked" at the May Co. Thus did fantasy become reality.

I played tennis with my cousins during my Thanksgiving visit. The weather was dry and sunny with a light breeze. Three Bears weather: not too hot, not too cold, just right. I called North Brother Island to boast to Anneliese that I had been playing tennis on a warm, balmy day. No one answered the phone. Unusual, hence alarming. I then called my folks. Anneliese and the kids were there. Why were they with my folks? Anneliese explained. While I was enjoying dry sunny weather in California New York City was being savaged by a severe Nor'easter storm, high velocity winds and cold sheets of rain. The waters at the confluence of the East River with the Long Island Sound, roiled by the turbulent weather, rose to unprecedented flood levels. North Brother Island was swamped, with wave after wave crashing onto the Island and flooding the basements of the buildings. My Mother, God Bless her!, recognizing early on the dangers the storm might pose to Anneliese and the children, made her way by subway and ferry onto the Island just before the rough seas halted further ferry operations. The Coast Guard then arrived and safely evacuated all the Island's inhabitants to The Bronx. Once assured that she and the children were OK I asked, stupidly, whether she had taken my Army uniform with her. No, was her reply. Why not? I'm sure my queries annoyed her. Her voice revealing just a touch of exasperation, she answered, "Your uniform was stored in the basement, the basement was flooded, and the Coast Guard wouldn't let me go down there to get it." Yep, in light of the circumstances I had asked a stupid question. Fortunately, before the Island was flooded, in preparation for her flight with the children to Los Angeles, Anneliese had begun to pack our several suitcases with those items I have described above. She and my Mother lugged them and the two kids all the way back to Brooklyn, a bit wet, but happy to be safe on dry ground.

It was the first week of December 1950 when Anneliese, Andy and Heidi joined me in our new apartment at 4105 West Boulevard in the Baldwin Hills section of Los Angeles. Anneliese and I remembered the pangs of longing, *die Qualen der Sehnsucht* we each had suffered when separated in the past. This last separation, perhaps only ten days at most, rekindled memories of those times, and when Anneliese crossed the threshold of our new home I drew her to me. We embraced and kissed and laughed and cried tears of joy. Anneliese and I were again at peace in each other's arms. We were beginning a new phase of our lives in a city I had first glimpsed on a 12 hour pass in the Summer of 1943, and, on seeing it—even so briefly—thought it might be a nice place to live. And it was—for a very long time.

Final Words:
Der Eckstein / The Cornerstone

אֲנִי חֲבַצֶּלֶת הַשָּׁרוֹן שׁוֹשַׁנַּת
הָעֲמָקִים:

I am a rose of Sharon,
A lily of the valleys.

*   *   *

עוּרִי צָפוֹן וּבוֹאִי תֵימָן הָפִיחִי
גַּנִּי יִזְּלוּ בְשָׂמָיו יָבֹא דוֹדִי לְגַנּוֹ
וְיֹאכַל פְּרִי מְגָדָיו:

Awake, O north wind;
And come, thou south;
Blow upon my garden,
That the spices thereof may flow out.
Let my beloved come into his garden,
And eat his precious fruits.

שיר השירים
THE SONG OF SONGS
(2:1, 4:16)

Final Words

I have come to the end of my story. It is not a memoir. It covers but one decade in my life, measured from December 7, 1941, through the first weeks of December 1950. Yet the impress of these years has left an indelible mark on my heart, and on my soul. From the moment I first gazed entranced upon Anneliese Baur, on that magical June afternoon in 1945, in Heidenheim, Germany, until God called her Home to Him on the first day of Spring in March 2002, my Anneliese was the *Eckstein meines Lebens*, the cornerstone of my life! Her beauty enraptured me! Her love, which passed all understanding, her courage, wit and wise counsel, emboldened me to reach for the stars, sometimes, to touch them.

I am now in my ninth decade, hale, suffering—in the anguished words of King David—the pangs of a broken and contrite heart. Everything that Anneliese and I built together had its genesis in that decade. Those ten years were the bedrock upon which Anneliese's wisdom and courage helped us build a wonderful life for ourselves and our five children: Andrew Elliott and Heidi Faith, born in New York, and Pamela Diane, Jonathan David and Benjamin Wilhelm, born in California. Were this tome a memoir, it would have been brimming with prideful accounts of how each of our five children, and their children, have enriched Anneliese's life and mine, and how they have made this world a better place for all God's creatures.

Anneliese wished to be cremated. I was surprised. Each of us was so full of life, that we made only passing references to such distant things as "final arrangements." I learned of Anneliese's wishes only after she had left us. All the children knew. Not I. Why? Heidi explained. Mother knew that Jews did not ordinarily cremate their dead. In common with Muslims, the deceased are quickly buried in simple ceremonies. Mother knew too, Heidi said, that the Nazis had cremated the remains of most of the victims of their genocide. Discussing cremation might upset me. Hence Anneliese's silence. But all of her forebears, including her mother and father, had been cremated. And that was Anneliese's wish. She would be gone. But I would have her ashes. In that form she would be with me always. I see now the wisdom of her choice. I have her ashes in the house we built in Deerfield Township in Ohio. Anneliese never had the opportunity, with her grace, and her beautiful, physical presence, to turn this house into a home. But with her ashes encircled by the high school graduation photographs of our five children (with each photograph accompanied by a photo, selected by Anneliese, of each graduate when a wee youngster) and flanked by vases of lowers—Anneliese is always present, and has made this house a home for me

Ashes of Anneliese which Arthur keeps
at home encircled by High School
graduation photos of their five children.

Andrew Elliot
Palisades High School
Pacific Palisades, CA
June 1965

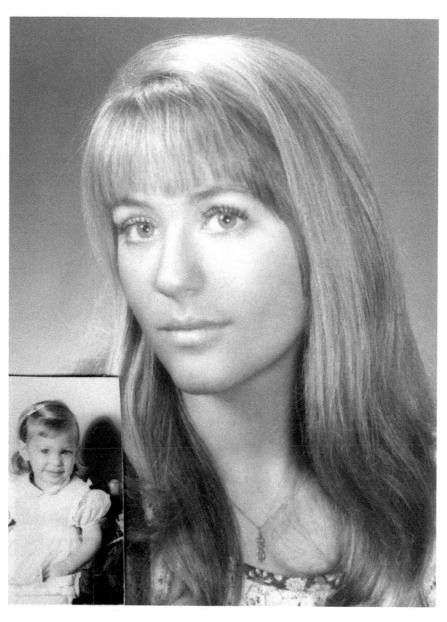

Heidi Faith
Palisades High School
Pacific Palisades, CA
June 1967

Pamela Diane
Palisades High School
Pacific Palisades, CA
June 1972

Jonathan David
Palisades High School
Pacific Palisades, CA
June 1979

Benjamin Wilhelm
Palisades High School
Pacific Palisades, CA
June 1982

In the *Zohar: The Book of Splendor*, in the Portion *Male and Female* in the tractate *Genesis—Bereshith [50a]* it is written:

> "When a man is at home, the wife is the foundation of a man's house, for it is by virtue of her being there that the *Shechinah*, the Divine Presence, does not leave the house."

So it is with our house. Anneliese's spiritual presence has made our house our home. I speak to her during the day, in English, in German, read her things I have written, tell her my experiences, seek her counsel. And each Friday night, standing before her, I kindle the *Shabbat* candles, and recite the Prayer for Sabbath Peace which Anneliese had chanted as הבעלת הבית *HaBaalat HaBayit*: The Mistress of the House *she* had made *our* Home. Before I lie down, I say good night to her, and ask her blessings and protection. When I rise up I thank her for carrying me through the night free of evil dreams.

Even where a marriage is made in Heaven, as was ours, the playing out of events after the Holy Union are left wholly within the control of the two beings joined in matrimony. Thus there would be times, happily not many, when Anneliese and I would have differences of opinion on matters of import. But whatever the tensions of the day by bedtime they were resolved. All rancor was erased by tearful apologies offered and tearfully accepted, and, there being neither a winner nor a loser, we both would fall asleep warmed and sheltered in the embrace of the other.

The God who created my beautiful Anneliese, and then cruelly took her physical being from me, has not been able to keep the sweetness of her eternal soul from enveloping me within its comforting warmth—as oft she did when, safe within her arms, my tired head between her scented breasts, she soothed my path to sleep. *O meine Geliebte Anneliese, du bist schwer vermisst!*

My narrative fits neatly under no rubric. It is a *sui generis* work, blurred by my tears in the telling. It is a story of war, a story of history in the making, but above all, it is a unique Love Story, a story of how God, in his wond'rous ways, led me, episode upon episode, to find my beautiful, courageous Anneliese Baur, who, from the instant I saw her, became the cornerstone of my new life!

I end this book, this rambling recital of two lives from the embers rising, with the observation that there would have been no story, indeed, there would have been no need for one, were it not that I had to tell the world of my Anneliese Baur, that remarkable woman of beauty, strength, grace and courage, God's Gift to our children, to me, and to all who were fortunate to know her.

Anneliese Baur, Fall, 1940
Schwenningen, Germany

Anneliese Baur Katz
Pacific Palisades, CA 1954

Anneliese Baur Katz
Pacific Palisades, CA 1954
With Heidi and Pamela

Anneliese Baur Katz, Oma Christine Baur, and Benjamin Wilhelm, Pacific Palisades, CA 1946

Anneliese Baur Katz
Maui, Hawaii 1975

First Fruits from her vineyard, Anneliese Baur Katz, Running Deer Ranch, Paso Robles, California 1983.

Arthur and Anneliese, Running Deer Ranch, Paso Robles,
California, 1983.

Anneliese Baur Katz
Paso Robles, CA 1999

Anneliese Baur Katz,
Mason, Ohio 2001

An Anneliese Baur

O, meine Geliebte,
du bist wie eine Blume,
so hold, so schön und rein,
ich denk' an dich, und Sehnsucht
schleicht mir ins Herz hinein!

Geliebtes Herz!
du bist wie eine Blume
die ewig blüht,
wohlriechend, leuchtend,
immer hold und schön und rein!
aber leider,
so weit von mir entfernt!

To Anneliese Baur

Oh, my Belóved,
thou art like a flower,
so fair, so beautiful, so pure,
I think of thee, and longing
softly steals into my heart!

Belóved Heart!
thou art like a flower
which blooms eternally,
sweet scented,
brightly hued,
forever fair and beautiful and pure!
but sadly,
so very far from me!

(With thanks to Heinrich Heine for some lines culled from his poem,
Du bist wie eine Blume.)

אֵשֶׁת חַיִל מִי יִמְצָא
וְרָחֹק מִפְּנִינִים מִכְרָהּ׃

Who can find a woman of valor?
For her worth is far above rubies.
Proverbs 31:10
Du bist die Ruh'

[First stanza of poem by Friederich Rückert, set to music
by Schubert, D776]
(English translation by Arthur Stanley Katz)

Du bist die Ruh'   Thou art Tranquility
der Friede mild,   untroubled Peace,
die Sehnsucht du   thou art Longing
und was sie stillt.   and all it soothes.

Dove sei, amato bene?

[Bertarido's aria, Act 1, *Rodelinda*, opera by George Frideric Händel,
1725] (English translation from the Italian by Arthur Stanley Katz)

Dove sei, amato bene?   Where art thou, dearly beloved?
Vieni, l'alma a consolar!   Come, and console my heart!

Sono oppresso da' tormenti   I am oppressed by torments,
ed i crudi miei lamenti   and only with thee beside me
sol con te posso bear.   can my cruel sorrows be soothed.

Dost Thou Not Remember?

Dost thou not remember
those sylvan slopes
and silver streams
about us?

Those walks we took
'neath the boughs
of evergreens, and oaks
of birch and beech
and willow.
Dost thou not remember?

And the birds
that flew about us,
singing merry songs,
darting hither and yon,
their wings a 'whirring—
Dost thou not remember?

And how, hand in hand
we stepped, with care
along some narrow path
of damp, sweet scented earth
of fallen leaves,
of pine cones and pebbles
which crunched
'neath our feet
as we trod upon them.
Dost thou not remember?

And the gentle breezes,
heard their murmurs,
felt their strokes
upon our cheeks,
their touch
as soft
as a lover's sigh,
saw them set
tree tops a'swaying
amid the rustling
of a million leaves.
Dost thou not remember?

And how we reveled
in the wonders
about us,
knew they were there—
but our eyes and ears
were those of lovers
who saw and heard
only the other.
Dost thou not remember?

And how we'd find
a sheltered nook
of forest growth,
and stop,
and within its verdant
folds
hold each other tightly,
kiss, caress and fondle,
softly laugh and whisper
words of endearment
that lovers

where e'er they be,
what e'er the age,
have confided
to each other.
Oh! How blissful
we were!
Dost thou not remember?

And then,
warmed with love
given and received,
we went our way
across the sunlit dappled
forest floor
and wondered
why life could never
forever be
as it was
then.
Dost thou not remember?

And those glorious days
deep within the bosom
of the woods,
when we would search
for wild strawberries,
red currants, black berries,
and those translucent
green globes
of gooseberries,
and finding them—
ate as fast
as we picked,
our stained fingers
wet lips

and smudged faces
attesting to
the ferocity
of our feasting—
with our laughter
sending a deer
and her fawn,
who earlier
paid us no heed
now quickly went
a'bounding—
with the raven above
sounding
his raucous call
as he swooped
o'er our heads,
denouncing our noisy
intrusion
into the silence
of his glen.
Dost thou not remember?

And how our berry sweetened
lips
made our kisses
even sweeter,
and how we scampered
childlike,
about the boulders
and trunks
of fallen trees,
in a mindless game
of "catch me!"
And when caught,
quite easily, indeed,

gleefully accepted
the "punishment"
of more kisses!
Oh! How love enthralled
were we!
Dost thou not remember?

And once,
standing in a field,
the sun glinting off
its golden heads
of grain,
impulsively I swept you up
held you aloft
close to my chest—
your arms tightened
about me,
I asked whether
you were holding so tight
because you loved me so much,
or were fearful of falling.
You laughed and answered
that it was
a little bit of both!
Dost thou not remember?
Dost thou not remember?

*   *   *

O! Mein ferner Geliebtes Herz!
My distant, Belóved Heart!
I have seen your beautiful
blue eyes
glisten with tears,

and watched
as thy tears
ran down thy cheeks
and into the corners
of thy sweet mouth—
and I cried with you
as you tasted
their bitterness.

Do I not remember?
Do I not remember?

Oh! My Bubelein, my darling!
How could I not remember
those glorious, fleeting
Heidenheim
days and nights
we spent together!

Art not thy heart
and soul
eternally entwined
with mine?
Do I not hear
thy words to me
during thy day?
Do I not hear
thy sobs
and see thy tears
at night?
And seeing them—
I weep for thee.

I know the depths
of thy longing
for me—
how sorely
I am missed!

And how oft thou
hold out thy arms
to me.

Dearest Bubelein,
I cannot come to thee
in the fullness
that thou seek.

Oh! How would I love
again
to cling to thee,
to feel
our hearts
race
within our embrace!

Do I not remember?

Oh, Bub!,
I remember
all that thou
hast related,
vielleicht mehr,
perhaps more
than thou.

The paths that felt
our tread,
the brooks from which
we drank,
the flowers we picked
in the meadows—
all were mine
long before
you found me, and them.

Oh! Belóved Heart,
thou art crying!

I see thy tears
spatter upon thy pages
of memories recalled,
of glorious times shared
discovering a new world—
as we discovered
each other:

Thou, my handsome, fair haired,
blue eyed American GI,
and I, *dein schönes
Schwarzwaldmädchen*,
whose beauties
I shall let you describe—
as oft you have
to all about you.

And so, dearest Arthur,
dearest Dad,
Be patient,
hab' Geduld.

Enjoy thy life,
as once I enjoyed
mine with thee.

That time will come
when, forever,
thou shall be
with me.

Dearest one,
do naught
to hasten
that time.

True, we are
in different spheres.

But *art* we not together
every night and day?
Art not our hearts and souls
entwined?

Yes, my belóved,
wir sind immer zusammen
through our thoughts
exchanged—
our hearts and souls
entwined—
and through thy poetry.

Yes, write to me, my belóved,
then recite your words
in a voice as vibrant
as when you first said,
Anneliese, ich liebe dich sehr!

And, if you must,
cry to me,
cry out for me,
then wipe
those blue eyes
I've loved
so much,
and smile
knowing I have
heard thee.

Yes, call to me,
and I shall comfort thee,
as in life I sought
to do.

Nun, geh' jetzt ins Bett,
es ist spät,
träume süsse Träume,
und wie immer,
werde ich dich behüten.

And when thy time
has come,
I shall be there
happily waiting
to greet thee!

Then, arm in arm,
heads high,
shoulders back,
steps firm,
with a song
on our lips,

we shall walk,
as in our
Heidenheim days—
Arthur and Anneliese
Together
through eternity!

POET'S NOTE: *This poem could stand as a universal ode to Love and the Remembrances of Love. It was written as my way to recall that all too brief period of five month's enchantment shared with my Anneliese, of bléssed memory, from June to November 1945 in Occupied Germany. We later had a marriage truly made in Heaven for fifty seven years until death did us part—at least for the time being.*

ASK

11 May 2008

Anneliese Baur Katz
Pacific Palisades, California 1956
23 August 1921-20 March 2002
"Welch' eine Ehre für mich dass du meine Frau warst."

About the Author and Anneliese

ARTHUR STANLEY KATZ
21 March 1923-
BORN: Brooklyn, NY; gave up College Student Draft Deferment to enlist U.S. Cavalry, November 16, 1942, Honorably Discharged November 18, 1945; served under General Patton; awarded Purple Heart, Bronze Star, Five Campaign Stars. He is an Intellectual Property Law attorney.

ANNELIESE BAUR KATZ
23 August 1921-20 March 2002
BORN: Schwenningen am Neckar, in the Black Forest Region of Southern Germany, oldest of three in a Protestant family; trained as a hotel chef; fluent in High German, South German dialects

744

and English; aside from her culinary skills, gifted in clothing design and knitting, drawing and gardening; established two acclaimed specialty foods businesses.

Lynn Donoghue, Dust Jacket and Soft Cover Design

Heidi Faith Katz, Photographs of Anneliese and Arthur pp 732,733

Index

im Gegensatz zu der vollendeten
Schöpfung der "Natur". Leider laufen
so viele Menschen an all dieser
Schönheit vorbei, haben keinen
Sinn u. kein Auge dafür,
kennen nur ihr eigenes Ich,
ihre persönlichen Intressen u. werden
dabei doch nie glücklich, bleiben
unzufriedene gleichgültige Menschen! Ach Bub, ich bin so
glücklich, dass Du auch diese
Freude, die ich an solchen Dingen
empfinde, teilst! Weiss ich doch,
wie lieb auch Du all das Schöne
liebst was uns Gott durch
seine Schöpfung gegeben hat!
Ach Bubelein, geliebtes
teures Herzchen, ich lieb dich

so viel, so unsagbar viel!!

Wie sehne ich mich nach
Dir, nach Deiner Liebe, die Du
mir in so überreichem Masse
zuteil werden lässt!

O, ich freue mich auf
Deinen nächsten Brief, ich
hoffe, ich brauche nicht mehr
all zu lange warten! Und ich
hoffe, er klingt dann glücklich
u. zufrieden, nicht so traurig
wie der letzte!

Leb wohl mein Lieb,
Gott behüt Dich u. Deine liebe
Familie!

Deine Anne

Heute geht auch ein Brief durch den
zivilen Briefverkehr weg! Bin neu-
gierig, wie lange er unterwegs ist!

Lightning Source UK Ltd.
Milton Keynes UK
UKHW020627031222
413194UK00016B/825